# ASSESSMENT OF
# ADDICTIVE BEHAVIORS

# ASSESSMENT OF ADDICTIVE BEHAVIORS

Edited by

## DENNIS M. DONOVAN

*Veterans Administration Medical Center, Seattle*
*University of Washington School of Medicine*

and

## G. ALAN MARLATT

*University of Washington*

THE GUILFORD PRESS
New York   London

© 1988 The Guilford Press
A Division of Guilford Publications, Inc.
72 Spring Street, New York, NY 10012

Printed in the United States of America

Last digit is print number: 9  8  7  6  5  4  3  2


**Library of Congress Cataloging-in-Publication Data**

Assessment of addictive behaviors.

(The Guilford behavioral assessment series)
Includes bibliographies and index.
1. Substance abuse—Psychological aspects.
2. Substance abuse—Treatment. I. Donovan, Dennis M.
(Dennis Michael) II. Marlatt, G. Alan. III. Series.
[DNLM: 1. Behavior—drug effects. 2. Cognition—
drug effects. 3. Substance Dependence. WM 270 A8458]
RC564.A87    1988          616.86          87-19674
ISBN 0-89862-144-5

# CONTRIBUTORS

Helen M. Annis, PhD, Clinical Institute, Addiction Research Foundation, Toronto, Ontario, Canada.

John S. Baer, PhD, Department of Psychology, University of Oregon, Eugene, Oregon. (Present affiliation: Department of Psychology, University of Washington, Seattle, Washington.)

Deborah J. Brief, PhD, Department of Psychology, University of Washington, Seattle, Washington.

Edward J. Callahan, PhD, Department of Family Practice, University of California at Davis Medical Center, Sacramento, California.

Gerard J. Connors, PhD, Research Institute on Alcoholism, Buffalo, New York.

Susan Curry, PhD, Group Health Cooperative of Puget Sound, Center for Health Studies, Seattle, Washington.

Christine S. Davis, MA, Clinical Institute, Addiction Research Foundation, Toronto, Ontario, Canada.

Brenda Dawson, PhD, Department of Psychology, University of Southern Mississippi, Hattiesburg, Mississippi.

Dennis M. Donovan, PhD, Veterans Administration Medical Center, Seattle, Washington; Department of Psychiatry and Behavioral Sciences, University of Washington School of Medicine, Seattle, Washington.

David M. Garner, PhD, Department of Psychiatry, University of Toronto, Toronto, Ontario, Canada.

William H. George, PhD, Department of Psychology, State University of New York at Buffalo, Buffalo, New York.

Lynn M. Harllee, BA, Department of Psychiatry and Center for Alcohol Research, University of Florida, Gainesville, Florida. (Present affiliation: University of Miami, Miami, Florida.)

Edward C. Hendrickson, PhD, Addiction Recovery Center, Yorktown Heights, New York.

Seymore Herling, PhD, Smoking Research Program, Addiction Research Foundation, Toronto, Ontario, Canada.

C. Peter Herman, PhD, Department of Psychology, University of Toronto, Toronto, Ontario, Canada.

D. Balfour Jeffrey, PhD, Department of Psychology, University of Montana, Missoula, Montana.

Lynn T. Kozlowski, PhD, Smoking Research Program, Addiction Research Foundation, Toronto, Ontario, Canada; Department of Psychology, University of Toronto, Toronto, Ontario, Canada.

Gillian Leigh, PhD, Clinical Institute, Addiction Research Foundation, Toronto, Ontario, Canada. (Presently at the Braemore Home, Sydney, Nova Scotia.)

Edward Lichtenstein, PhD, Department of Psychology, University of Oregon, Eugene, Oregon; Oregon Research Institute, Eugene, Oregon.

Jon Lutton, BS, Consultant, Department of Psychology, University of Washington, Seattle, Washington.

Stephen A. Maisto, PhD, Brown University Medical School, Providence, Rhode Island; Butler Hospital, Providence, Rhode Island.

G. Alan Marlatt, PhD, Department of Psychology and Addictive Behaviors Research Center, University of Washington, Seattle, Washington.

Ella H. Pecsok, MA, MEd, Department of Psychology, West Virginia University, Morgantown, West Virginia.

Arthur V. Peterson, Jr., PhD, Fred Hutchinson Cancer Research Center, Public Health Sciences Division, Seattle, Washington.

Janet Polivy, PhD, Departments of Psychology and Psychiatry, University of Toronto, Toronto, Ontario, Canada.

Roger A. Roffman, DSW, School of Social Work, University of Washington, Seattle, Washington.

Saul Shiffman, PhD, Department of Psychology, University of Pittsburgh, Pittsburgh, Pennsylvania.

Harvey A. Skinner, PhD, Clinical Institute, Addiction Research Foundation, Toronto, Ontario, Canada.

Nannette S. Stone, MS, Creative Solutions and Associates, New York, New York.

Jalie A. Tucker, PhD, Department of Psychiatry and Center for Alcohol Research, University of Florida, Gainesville, Florida. (Present affiliation: Department of Psychology, Wayne State University, Detroit, Michigan.)

Rudy E. Vuchinich, PhD, Department of Psychiatry and Center for Alcohol Research, University of Florida, Gainesville, Florida. (Present affiliation: Department of Psychology, Wayne State University, Detroit, Michigan.)

Arnold M. Washton, PhD, The Washton Institute, New York, New York.

Gregory L. Wilson, PhD, Department of Psychology, Washington State University, Pullman, Washington.

Stephen C. Woods, PhD, Department of Psychology, University of Washington, Seattle, Washington.

# PREFACE

The past decade has seen an increased focus on what have been described as the "addictive behaviors." In the mid-1970s there was a restricted view of addictions: Such a label was given primarily if not exclusively to dependence on alcohol and opiates, because of the ability of these substances to generate both tolerance and withdrawal distress. Research was fragmentary. Each drug assumed to be addictive was investigated in isolation; a wide variety of professional and scientific disciplines also worked in relative isolation. Physiological, psychological, behavioral, and social factors were each seen as important in the etiology of addictions, yet little effort was expended in integrating these domains into a unified model of addiction.

Much has changed over the past decade. A more "generic" view has emerged concerning the addictions. That is, there appear to be a number of processes that are common across a wide range of behaviors, such as drinking, smoking, eating, drug use, and gambling. Although the objects of addiction may vary both within and across individuals, the process of addiction appears comparable. This broadened view of what constitutes an addiction has resulted from a shift in research away from the evaluation of treatment interventions to more process-oriented studies of those factors contributing to the development and maintenance of, as well as relapse to, the addictive behaviors. There has also been an increased integration of research across disciplines. It has become increasingly clear that we must incorporate factors from each of the previously noted domains if we are to fully understand and modify addictive behaviors. A guiding principle in this regard has been derived from the early work of Lindesmith. Addiction appears to be an interactive product of learning in a situation and setting involving physiological events as they are interpreted, labeled, and given meaning by the individual. Physiological, psychological, cognitive, and social elements are indispensable features of the total experience and process of addiction. This proposition is also consistent with the emerging biopsychosocial model of addiction, which implies multiple causality, involvement of multiple systems, and multiple levels of analyses.

Although there has been an increased focus on the multiple systems involved in addictive behaviors, there has been less emphasis on clinically relevant methods of assessing such factors. Our primary goal, and the motivation behind the current book, is to provide an update and expansion of previously available information on the assessment of addictive behaviors. The intended audience for this book includes students, clinicians (therapists and counselors), and researchers who are working in the field of the addictive behaviors. It is our belief that assessment represents an important step in the therapeutic process. The clinician, through his or her interaction with the client, the actual assessment process, and the provision of feedback, may facilitate the individual's move from a somewhat tenuous commitment to change to a stage in which active steps are taken to modify the addictive behavior. A thorough assessment also holds the promise of more closely matching the individual's needs to the most appropriate form of treatment.

The book is divided into six parts. Part I provides a general overview of the process of assessment within the addictive behaviors. Donovan, in Chapter 1, focuses on the commonalities across addictive behaviors, the emergent biopsychosocial model of addictions, and the implications of this model for the process of assessment. Parts II, III, and IV focus on drinking behavior, smoking behavior, and eating behaviors and disorders, respectively. We have attempted to provide a common structure within each of these sections. Each section includes three chapters dealing with the assessment of behavioral, psychological/cognitive-expectational, and physiological components of the particular addictive behavior. The separate coverage of each of these domains is intentional. However, as we have noted above, we feel that the addictive process involves complex interactions among these factors. A second organizational structure is found at the chapter level. We have asked the contributors, to the extent possible, to incorporate the notion of a "behavioral assessment funnel" within their chapters. This concept, derived from the work of Cone and Hawkins, involves the use of general screening techniques to identify problems; more specific assessment procedures to provide a more detailed picture of the disorder, as well as a diagnostic label; continued assessment during the course of treatment; and posttreatment monitoring across time to determine generalization and outcome. Each of the chapters has attempted to address these issues.

Part II includes chapters by Vuchinich, Tucker, and Harllee on the behavioral assessment of alcohol dependence (Chapter 2); by Annis and Davis on the assessment of expectations related to drinking and alcohol dependence (Chapter 3); and by Leigh and Skinner on the assessment of physiological factors associated with alcohol dependence (Chapter 4). Part III focuses on smoking behavior. In Chapter 5, Shiffman discusses behavioral assessment for smoking cessation. Baer and Lichtenstein focus on cognitive-expectational factors involved in smoking behavior (Chapter 6). Objective physiological measures that may be useful for the treatment of smoking are presented by Kozlowski and Herling in Chapter 7. Part IV has three chapters addressing eating behaviors and disorders. In Chapter 8, Jeffrey,

Dawson, and Wilson discuss behavioral components involved in adult and childhood obesity, anorexia nervosa, and bulimia. Polivy, Herman, and Garner focus on the cognitive and attitudinal features associated with these disorders (Chapter 9). Woods and Brief, in Chapter 10, present an overview of physiological and endocrinological changes involved in eating disorders; they also provide a theoretical integration in which the relationship between eating disorders and other addictive behaviors is presented.

Part V also contains three chapters, with a focus on the assessment of other drugs of abuse. Although there has been an increase in the availability of information concerning drugs, such information appears to be accruing at a relatively slower pace than for alcohol, smoking, and eating disorders. As such, we felt that there was not yet enough information within the literature on the assessment of drug abuse to support separate chapters on behavioral, cognitive-expectational, and physiological factors. Thus, the authors of the three chapters in Part V were asked to try to provide an overview of these three primary assessment domains within each of their chapters. Roffman and George (Chapter 11) discuss the assessment of cannabis abuse. Chapter 12, by Washton, Stone, and Hendrickson, focuses on the clinical evaluation of the cocaine abuser. The assessment of heroin addiction is presented by Callahan and Pecsok in Chapter 13.

The final section of the book, Part VI, focuses on the relevance of the assessment process to the selection and evaluation of treatment interventions for an addictive behavior. Maisto and Connors (Chapter 14) discuss both general and specific aspects of the assessment process related to the evaluation of treatment outcome across the addictive behaviors. Curry, Marlatt, Peterson, and Lutton (Chapter 15) present an overview of a statistical procedure, survival analysis, that is particularly helpful in determining the relative risk of relapse at differing points in time following treatment. Finally, in Chapter 16, Marlatt discusses practical and heuristic issues involved in the selection of appropriate treatment strategies based on the outcome of the assessment process.

It is the standard protocol to include expressions of appreciation at the close of a preface; we have a number that we would like to include. The first is to Julia's 14 Carrot Cafe in the University district of Seattle. Julia's was the site of many early-morning planning and progress meetings during the course of this project; we gained much food for thought (as well as for breakfast) through these meetings. Many individuals have contributed to the material presented in this book. First and foremost, we would like to thank the authors and their colleagues for the chapters they have contributed. Without their research and their ability to integrate the work of others, we would be unable to present such a comprehensive view of assessment in the addictive behaviors. We also express gratitude to our own present and former students and clinical trainees, who have continued to stimulate our interest in the addictions and have challenged us to expand our understanding and conceptualization of such behaviors. In this regard, special thanks go to Daniel Kivlahan and Carla Bradshaw, who have become valued colleagues at the Addictions Treatment Center of the Veterans Administration Medical Center in Seattle. A special note must be given to our spouses, Anne and Judith, who initially questioned our taking on this project but who provided us with support and encouragement once the decision had been made. We also wish to express our heartfelt appreciation to Donald Wood for the extensive work that went into the preparation and editing of the manuscripts; his efforts have enhanced the quality of the final product.

A final word of thanks goes to those clients and patients with whom we have worked over the years. By letting us get to know them better, they have given us important insight into the phenomenology of addictions and the addictive process. They have shown us the value of clinical assessment and the important role of the client–therapist relationship in the assessment process.

Dennis M. Donovan
G. Alan Marlatt
*Seattle, Washington*

# CONTENTS

# III. SMOKING BEHAVIOR

# IV. EATING BEHAVIORS AND DISORDERS

# I

# INTRODUCTORY OVERVIEW

# 1

## ASSESSMENT OF ADDICTIVE BEHAVIORS
### Implications of an Emerging Biopsychosocial Model

**DENNIS M. DONOVAN**
*Veterans Administration Medical Center, Seattle*
*University of Washington School of Medicine*

### Introduction

It has been over a decade since Sobell and Sobell (1976) published a chapter focusing on the assessment of addictive behaviors. Their review was a milestone, for it was one of the first to categorize more than one specific class of drugs together within the broader context of addictive behavior. Alcohol, opiates, and barbiturates were mentioned as falling into this category. These substances were grouped together because of their ability to induce tolerance, physical dependence, and withdrawal distress when used habitually in sufficient quantities over a prolonged period of time. These features are the ones that have traditionally defined addiction (Einstein, 1975; Sobell & Sobell, 1976). Although the Sobells presented a conceptually broadened view of addictions, their actual review of the literature focused almost exclusively on alcoholism. There had previously been too little clinical research on the assessment of opiate and barbiturate use to be included in the review.

The state of the art in the addictions left much to be desired at that point. As P. M. Miller (1979) and Shaffer and colleagues (Burglass & Shaffer, 1984; Shaffer & Milkman, 1985) have noted, the tendency during this era was for each drug of addiction to be investigated independently and in relative isolation. A variety of professional disciplines, including pharmacology, biochemistry, psychology, psychiatry, and sociology, engaged in research focusing on that component of the addictive process most consistent with the discipline's unique professional contributions. Unfortunately, there was little sharing of information across these disciplinary lines, promoting a fragmentary view of what leads to, constitutes, and maintains addiction to a given drug. The result was a series of independent theories with little overlap or integration (e.g., Lettieri, Sayers, & Pearson, 1980; Orford, 1985; Peele & Alexander, 1985). There was even controversy concerning the extent to which addictive behaviors reflected unidimensional or multidimensional phenomena (Shaffer & Milkman, 1985).

Many things have changed in the years since the publication of the review by Sobell and Sobell (1976); some have not. With regard to the latter, a substantial number of individuals, often beginning at a relatively young age, have experimented with alcohol, tobacco, and/or drugs such as marijuana, cocaine, or opiates (Clayton, 1986). The popular media have focused on the death of talented young athletes and celebrities from drug overdoses, arrests of well-known entertainers and politicians for driving while intoxicated, the attempts of family and friends to understand a starving death through anorexia nervosa, the continued health hazards of smoking, and the multibillion-dollar treatment industry that has emerged to deal with alcohol, drug, and eating disorders. The accompanying impression is that the incidence and prevalence of addictive behaviors are increasing and that these problems are affecting a broad spectrum of individuals in our society.

Another feature that has remained unchanged is the high rate of morbidity and mortality associated with those behaviors involved with the addictions. Brownell (1982), in reviewing issues related to obesity, alcoholism, and smoking, noted the direct and indirect health risks accompanying these behaviors. Alcoholism was described as the nation's number one health problem. Smoking was characterized as the largest preventable cause of death in the nation, primarily through its contribution to cancer and heart disease. Obesity, similarly contributing to the risk of coronary heart disease, was characterized as unmatched by other medical or psychological problems in its seriousness, prevalence, and resistance to treatment.

The popular focus on addictive behaviors, while accentuating the magnitude of the problem, also reflects a number of more positive changes over the past decade. First, there has been an increased focus on the addictions within the research and clinical communities. The nature of this attention has shifted as well: An increased emphasis has been placed on process-oriented studies of the social, behavioral, and physiological determinants of addictive behaviors, with the primary aim of understanding them better (Brownell, 1982). Such an approach has led to a much broader and more inclusive view of what constitutes an addictive behavior (e.g., Orford, 1985; Peele, 1985). There has also been an increased appreciation of common processes that appear to underlie a broad range of such behaviors (P. M. Miller, 1980; W. R. Miller, 1980; Orford, 1985).

A second and related change is an increase in the interdisciplinary approach to investigating the addictions. There has been a growing awareness that addictions are behaviors developed and maintained by multiple sources; they are multiply determined and multidimensional in nature. As such, a multifaceted approach is needed to understand them. Clinicians and researchers from a variety of areas are working more closely together. More integrative work is being done at both the theoretical and practical levels. Each professional discipline is able to provide necessary but not sufficient information for understanding the addictions. It is becoming more clear that models failing to take into account biological, psychological, or social components will be incomplete in their explanatory power (Wallace, 1985). It is a situation in which the whole is greater than the sum of its parts. The fragmentation of the past decade is being reduced, with an increased effort toward the development of general theories of addiction. A cornerstone in this effort is the emergence of a biopsychosocial model in the areas of health psychology and behavioral medicine (Engel, 1977; Matarazzo & Carmody, 1983; Pomerleau, 1982; Schneiderman & Tapp, 1985; Schwartz, 1982). At a general level, this model is seen as providing a framework within which biological, psychological, and sociocultural approaches to health and illness can be integrated (Schwartz, 1982). As it relates more specifically to the area of addiction, an interactive biopsychosocial model provides a bridge across the varying perspectives of different disciplines, ideologies, and paradigms (Galizio & Maisto, 1985; Kissin & Hanson, 1982; Meyer, 1986; Shaffer & Milkman, 1985; Wallace, 1985; Zucker & Gomberg, 1986).

The purpose of this chapter is to present a brief overview of the commonalities across addictions and of the biopsychosocial model as it applies to the addictions. The main function, however, is to discuss the implications of this model for the clinical tasks of assessment and treatment planning with individuals engaging in addictive behaviors.

## Commonalities across Addictive Behaviors

As I have noted above, the past decade has been characterized by a move toward a more broadly based view of what constitutes addictive behavior (Hodgson & Miller, 1982; P. M. Miller, 1980; W. R. Miller, 1980; W. R. Miller & Heather, 1986; Nathan, 1980; Orford, 1985; Peele, 1985). This view is based in part on what appear to be a number of common processes across behaviors considered to be addictive. Also, individuals who have problems with excessive behaviors such as eating, drinking, drug use, gambling, smoking, and sexuality present very similar descriptions of the phenomenology of their disorders (Cummings, Gordon, & Marlatt, 1980; Orford, 1985; Stall & Biernacki, 1986; Wallace, 1977).

Because of this expanded view, a more inclusive definition of "addiction" is also needed. For the purposes of the present chapter, a working definition has been derived from those presented by Peele (1985), Burglass and Shaffer (1983), and Shaffer and Milkman (1985). Within this framework, an "addiction" is seen as a complex, progressive behavior pattern having biological, psychological, sociological, and behavioral components. What sets this behavior pattern apart from others is the individual's overwhelmingly pathological involvement in or attachment to it, subjective compulsion to continue it, and reduced ability to exert personal control over it. Peele (1985) indicates that the object of addiction is the addicted person's experience of the combined physical, emotional, and environmental elements that make up the involvement for that person. The behavior pattern continues despite its negative impact on the physical, psychological, and social function of the individual. The individual chooses to maintain the addictive involvement even when other, more gratifying sources of reinforcement are present. There appears to be a dependence upon the behavior or experience, either on a physiological or a psychological level, that may lead to withdrawal distress when the individual is prevented from engaging in the behavior. There may be an increasingly high need for a given experience or behavior, representing a form of tolerance. "Craving," having both physiological and cognitive underpinnings, may be experienced as the powerfully strong desire and perceived need for the experience. The strength of the craving may be gauged by how willing the person is to sacrifice other sources of reward or well-being in life to continue engaging in the addictive behavior. Finally, the power of the addictive experience promotes a tendency for rapid reinstatement of the behavior pattern following a period of noninvolvement in it.

This definition, at first glance, does not appear much different from that used by Sobell and Sobell (1976). However, there are a number of important distinctions. First, a distinction is made between the "object of addiction" and the "addictive process" (Peele, 1985). The compulsive involvement in a behavior pattern represents the addictive process. It is this process, along with its multidimensional determinants, that is comparable across different objects of addiction. Second, the ability to induce dependence, tolerance, craving, and withdrawal is not inherent only in those drugs defined as addictive by the Sobells. It appears difficult for an individual to discontinue any behavior associated with repeated physiological changes or arousal, whether this change is induced by psychoactive drugs or not (Solomon, 1977; Wray & Dickerson, 1981); if the individual does discontinue the behavior, it typically results in disturbances of mood and behavior. Finally, the experience representing the object of addiction is multiply determined. In addition to the physiological changes involved, the experience to which one becomes addicted is also determined by the psychological set of the individual and the setting in which the behavior occurs (Peele, 1985; Wallace, 1985; Zinberg, 1984). The person's set includes aspects of personality function, attitudes, mood states, and expectations about the addictive behavior's effect on feelings, thinking, and behavior. The setting reflects both the specific physical and social stimulus matrix of the environment in which the addictive behavior occurs, as well as the much broader sociocultural context involving formal and informal rules, explicit and implicit rewards and punishments, and attitudes related to the behavior. Lindesmith (1968) has argued that neither physiological nor social, cognitive, or psychological factors alone are sufficient to explain addiction. Rather, addiction appears to be an interactive product of social learning in a situation involving physiological events as they are interpreted, labeled, and given meaning by the individual. Both the social and psychological factors and the physiological elements are indispensable features of the total experience and process of addiction. This proposition is consistent with a biopsychosocial view of addiction, which implies multiple causality, involvement of multiple systems, and multiple levels of analyses (Donovan & Chaney, 1985; Galizio & Maisto, 1985; Marlatt & Donovan, 1981).

The present working definition suggests a number of the common features across addictive behaviors. First, the addictive experience provides a potent and rapid means of changing one's mood and sensations because of both direct physiological effects and learned expectations (Falk, Dews, & Schuster, 1983; Orford, 1985; Peele, 1985). The individual engages in a form of self-indulgence for short-term pleasure or satisfaction, despite an awareness of the long-term negative consequences (W. R. Miller, 1980). The immediacy of the more gratifying effects appears to outweigh these more adverse and distant effects (Solomon, 1977). A second, and related, feature is the extent to which various physical and psychological states such as general arousal, stress, pain, or negative moods tend to be associated with and to influence the likelihood of engaging in the addictive behavior (Donegan, Rodin, O'Brien, & Solomon, 1983). Peele (1985) has suggested that having such states relieved is a primary component of the addictive experience. However, this does not represent the traditional hypothesis of tension reduction. For the addicted individual, changes in arousal levels from the accustomed baseline may be interpreted as craving and may lead him or her to engage in the addictive behavior, with a goal of reinstating a more optimal level of arousal (P. M. Miller, 1980). Within this framework, the addictive behavior may function either to overcome a reduced level of stimulation (e.g., boredom, depression) or to minimize an increased level of stimulation (e.g., stress, withdrawal distress).

A third feature that the present definition suggests is the role of both classical and instrumental conditioning in the addictive process (Donegan et al., 1983). The changes that are induced when the individual engages in the addictive behavior serve as an unconditioned stimulus. Through repeated association with these changes, a wide variety of other stimuli acquire the power of conditioned stimuli. The latter may include mood states, cognitive expectations, and levels of physiological arousal, as well as more specific features of the social or physical environment in which the behavior typically occurs. The presence of such conditioned stimuli may elicit changes that the individual may interpret as a strong desire or craving for the addictive experience, and may also contribute to the set and setting events that predict engaging in the behavior (Ludwig & Wikler, 1974; P. M. Miller, 1980; Zinberg, 1984). Similarly, the changes induced by the addictive experience also serve to reinforce those behaviors associated with it; those behaviors instrumental in the individual's engaging in the addictive experience become more frequent, vigorous, and persistent (Donegan *et al.*, 1983). These reinforcement processes, in conjunction with physiological factors, contribute to the development of acquired tolerance, psychological dependence, and/or physical dependence on the addictive experience (Donegan *et al.*, 1983; Marlatt & Donovan, 1981; Siegal, 1979; Tiffany & Baker, 1986, Wikler, 1965). The individual may experience withdrawal distress when unable to engage in the addictive behavior. This appears to be the case when any habitually sought-after event or experience is unavailable (Donegan *et al.*, 1983; Wray & Dickerson, 1981). The effects of withdrawal that appear consistent across addictive behaviors include craving, emotional distress, and disruption of behavior. Also, the level of withdrawal distress appears related to the extent of dependence (e.g., Hodgson, Rankin, & Stockwell, 1979; Rankin, Hodgson, & Stockwell, 1980; Skinner & Goldberg, 1986; Stockwell, Hodgson, Rankin, & Taylor, 1982; Sutherland *et al.*, 1986). Finally, the experience of this distress generates a state of disequilibrium that may motivate continued involvement in the addictive behavior.

Another feature that appears consistent across addictions is what has been described as the "paradox of control" (Marlatt & Gordon, 1985). On the one hand, the addictive behavior is one that the individual can engage in to produce prompt effects on the immediate physical, psychological, or social environment (Falk *et al.*, 1983). As Peele (1985) notes, there is both an immediacy and predictability of effects. The addictive experience is valued because it appears to make the individual's life more manageable. Wills and Shiffman (1985) suggest that addictive behaviors may represent the individual's attempt to cope by trying to manage his or her mood state (reducing negative affect or increasing positive affect), to keep an optimal balance in biochemical and physiological states (including those involved in the processes of tolerance and physical dependence), to maintain a positive sense of self, and/or to solve practical problems. The addicted person is attempting to exert control over areas of physical, emotional, or behavioral function that are felt to be otherwise uncontrollable (Donovan & O'Leary, 1983; Peele, 1985). On the other hand, the addictive behavior is often described as being excessive, out of control, and beyond the individual's control. The behavior pattern is said to be under stimulus control and under the control of the reinforcing properties of the addictive experience (Donegan *et al.*, 1983). The individual is unable to use either the cues in the environment and the larger sociocultural setting, or those self-generated cues representing the psychological set to exert self-control over the addictive behavior (Falk *et al.*, 1983; Rodin, Maloff, & Becker, 1984; Zinberg, 1984). This paradox—the apparent lack of self-control over a behavior that is used by the addicted person to exert control over and cope with other aspects of life—appears to cut across the objects of addiction.

Because of the reinforcing properties of the addictive experience, the perceived control it provides the individual, and its function as an alternate form of coping behavior, it is not surprising to find treatment to be relatively ineffective (W. R. Miller, 1980). Another commonality across addictions, then, is the high rate of relapse following a period of abstinence or not engaging in the behavior (Abrams, Niaura, Cary, Monti, & Binkoff, 1986; Brownell, Marlatt, Lichtenstein, & Wilson, 1986; Chaney, Roszell, & Cummings, 1982; Cummings *et al.*, 1980; Hunt, Barnett, & Branch, 1971; Marlatt & Gordon, 1985; Tucker, Vuchinich, & Harris, 1985). It appears that a number of cognitive-expectational, emotional, and behavioral factors make comparable contributions to the relapse process in eating disorders, drinking, drug use, gambling, and smoking. Three general situational categories have been found to account for the greatest proportion of relapses across these addictive behaviors. These "high-risk" situations include negative emotional states such as anxiety, depression, boredom, and loneliness; interpersonal conflicts typically resulting in feelings of frustration, anger, and resentment; and social pressure associated with being in a physical, social, or emotional context in which the addictive behavior has occurred in the past and is being directly or indirectly encouraged by peers (Cummings *et al.*, 1980; Marlatt & Gordon, 1985). More recent conceptualizations of the relapse process (e.g., Abrams *et al.*, 1986; Brownell *et al.*, 1986; Donovan & Chaney, 1985) have also suggested the need to incorporate the influence of physiological variables when attempting to understand relapse. Consistent with a biopsychosocial perspective, Brownell *et al.* (1986) have asserted that the risk of relapse across addictive behaviors is determined by an interaction of individual, situational, and physiological factors.

An additional risk of relapse is the possibility of "triggering" a return to the target addictive behavior by engaging in an alternative behavior having a strong association with the target behavior (P. M. Miller, 1980). This risk appears to be particularly high among multiple-substance abusers. Clayton (1986) has noted these primary reasons for multiple-drug use: (1) to enhance the effects of another drug, (2) to counteract the effect of another drug, (3) to substitute for preferred but unavailable drugs, and (4) to conform to the normative ways of using drugs within one's peer group. Because of the close association of drugs used in this fashion, the use of one substance probably elicits a conditioned response motivating the use of the target drug within an environmental and social setting conducive to its use. For instance, a clinical observation of increasing frequency is an individual's returning to cocaine use through drinking behavior (Smith, 1986).

The alternative behavior in which the addicted individual engages, besides increasing the risk of relapse as noted above, may have the potential to become an object of addiction in its own right. As P. M. Miller (1980) has indicated, there seems to be a strong overlap across unhealthy habits (e.g., Istvan & Matarazzo, 1984; Mintz, Boyd, Rose, Charuvasta, & Jarvik, 1985; O'Farrell, Connors, & Upper, 1983; Zeiner, Stantis, Spurgeon, & Nichols, 1985). It appears that the interrelationship among potentially addictive behaviors is inverse in nature, with a decrease in the target behavior being associated with a subsequent increase in a different behavior. Three detrimental outcomes may result from this relationship. First, a new and independent addictive pattern may develop with the alternate behavior. Second, relapse back to the primary addictive behavior may be precipitated. Third, if the individual relapses and also continues to engage in the alternate behavior, two independent yet related addictions—with their compounded health risks (P. M. Miller, 1980)—may be maintained. This pattern of interrelationships among addictive behaviors is consistent with Peele's (1985) contention that addiction is not inherently related to a given object or involvement. Rather, it is the person who becomes addicted to an experience, and addiction for an individual may take on a number of different objects.

Although the rate of relapse across addictive behaviors is high, a number of individuals are able to overcome their addictions without formal help (Schacter, 1982; Stall & Biernacki, 1986). It appears that the stages through which individuals move in the process of this "spontaneous remission" are comparable across alcohol use, opiate use, smoking, obesity, and general psychological distress (DiClemente & Prochaska, 1985; Ludwig, 1985; Perri, 1985; Prochaska & DiClemente, 1985, 1986; Stall & Biernacki, 1986; Tuchfeld, 1981). In reviewing different models of spontaneous remission, Brownell et al. (1986) indicate that most investigators consistently find three stages. The first involves recognition of a problem, contemplating change, becoming motivated, and making a commitment to change. The second stage involves actively modifying the addictive behavior, often following a public announcement of one's intent to change (Stall & Biernacki, 1986). The latter factor is important in starting a process of renegotiating the user's social identity. The individual must also initiate a form of self-control to deal with withdrawal and craving. The final stage involves the maintenance of the behavior change. This requires the continued use of coping strategies to deal with specific risks of relapse as well as with general life stress; the maintenance of a new identity as a nonaddicted individual; an integration into a nonaddictive lifestyle; the development of alternative sources of reinforcement; and the reliance on the support of significant others (Donovan & Chaney, 1985; Marlatt & Gordon, 1985;

Stall & Biernacki, 1986). Not only are the stages of change similar across addictive behaviors; so also are the general strategies that individuals employ to overcome their addictions (Perri, 1985; Prochaska & DiClemente, 1985, 1986). Those individuals found to have successfully overcome their problems tend to use a wider array of self-control strategies and to be more persistent in their coping attempts than those individuals who are unsuccessful (Perri, 1985).

This section has pointed out the many commonalities across addictive behaviors. A view in terms of commonalities leads to a "generic" concept of addictions (Carroll, 1986), which suggests that all addictions are part of a similar problematic process, even though the object of addiction varies from person to person and the manifestations and consequences of the addiction vary across different objects of addiction. However, it is important to avoid a "uniformity myth" that all addictions are equivalent. There are special characteristics of various addictions that make them distinguishable from one another (Carroll, 1986). For instance, there may be differences in the relative importance and/or timing of the physiological and psychological factors involved in the development and maintenance of different disorders (Donegan et al., 1983). Differences are found across addictions in the relative risk of relapse associated with a variety of possible precipitants. For example, whereas negative emotional states were found in one study to be a primary precipitant of relapse across addictive behaviors, this category accounted for over twice the percentage of relapses among alcoholics, smokers, and gamblers as it did among heroin addicts (Cummings et al., 1980). The rates at which and degree to which tolerance and withdrawal states develop, if at all, differ across addictions (Carroll, 1986; Donegan et al., 1983; Tiffany & Baker, 1986). Also, it has been found that certain types of coping and self-control strategies are used more frequently and successfully for certain problems than for others (Litman, Eiser, Rawson, & Oppenheim, 1979; Perri, 1985; Prochaska & DiClemente, 1985). Thus, it is important to consider both the commonalities involved in the addictive process and the unique features associated with specific objects of addiction when attempting to understand, assess, and treat an individual with an addictive behavior problem.


## An Emergent Model of Addictive Behaviors

A second major change in the field of the addictions over the past decade has been a move toward the development of more integrative models or theories. Shaffer and colleagues (Burglass & Shaffer, 1984; Shaffer & Kauffman, 1985; Shaffer & Milkman, 1985) have suggested that until recently the field of addictions has been in a preparadigm stage of scientific development. Without the conceptual framework, unitary set of rules, or standards of practice provided by a paradigm, it has been difficult to agree on the important parameters of addictive behaviors (Shaffer & Milkman, 1985). This situation led to a number of "reductionistic" and "mechanistic" approaches to the addictions (Peele & Alexander, 1985; Schwartz, 1982; Shaffer & Milkman, 1985). That is, there was a tendency to reduce the focus on an addiction to a single, unidimensional causative factor. It assumed a process involving a single cause and a single effect. Peele and Alexander (1985) reviewed genetic theories involving inherited mechanisms that cause or predispose people to be addicted; metabolic theories that focus on biological, cellular adaptation to different objects of addiction; conditioning theories that focus on the reinforcing properties of the addictive object; and adaptation theories involving the social and psychological functions served by the addictive behavior. Each of these models, as well as a variety of additional ones (e.g., Lettieri *et al.,* 1980), has merit and support. However, the apparent independence of such models may be less reflective of addictive behaviors than it is of the nature of addictionologists. Such reductionistic theories are overly narrow and restrictive and fail to account adequately for the total addictive experience.

There has recently been a move away from such reductionistic thinking. Addiction is seen as being determined by the interaction of psychological, environmental, and physiological factors. Both biological and nonbiological factors are seen as essential ingredients of addiction (Peele, 1985). This formulation is consistent with a biopsychosocial approach to health and illness (Schwartz, 1982). Such a model provides a metatheoretical framework in which biological, psychological, and social factors are seen as interacting to determine a given health status. This approach assumes that the individual's status emerges as a result of the interaction of multiple causes. More specifically, Schwartz (1982) has described the thinking style associated with the biopsychosocial model as follows:

> The essence of systems thinking is that the functioning of a system as a whole emerges out of the dynamic interactions of its parts (subsystems) and the system's interaction with its environment (the supra system of which the system is a part).
>
> In terms of medicine, examples of organistic thinking include the belief that specific diseases (constellations of symptoms) represent the complex *interaction* of specific environment stresses (including germs) *and* the organism in question (including its genetic and experiential history) and that biological and behavioral stresses always interact with each other to produce particular constellations of signs and symptoms in particular individuals. (p. 1042)

Consistent with this perspective, addiction is seen as a total experience involving physiological changes in individuals (many of whom may be genetically and/or psychologically predisposed) as these are interpreted and given meaning by the individual within the sociocultural context in which the addictive behavior occurs (Lindesmith, 1968; Peele, 1985; Zinberg, 1984).

## Implications of a Biopsychosocial Model of Addiction for Assessment

The biopsychosocial model represents an emergent paradigm within the field of the addictions. To a large extent, the nature and focus of clinical assessment are guided by the assumptions of the theoretical system from which the clinician operates (Shaffer & Kauffman, 1985). The theoretical orientations and paradigms help to determine the focus of the assessment conducted by the clinician; the nature and sources of information considered either important and relevant or irrelevant and to be ignored; and the ways in which such information will be organized to try to provide an understanding of the client and the presenting problem (Shaffer & Kauffman, 1985; Shaffer & Neuhaus, 1985). As such, there are a number of implications from the emergent biopsychosocial model that bear on the assessment of addictive behaviors.

An important feature of the biopsychosocial model is a move away from a reductionistic view of illness. It is insufficient to say that a person is either well or ill. Such binary, "either–or" views have been replaced by a broader, wholistic view. This conceptual change would appear to have an impact on the process of diagnosis within the addictions. As Shaffer and Neuhaus (1985) have noted, the concept of addiction is not categorical, and, as such, addictive behaviors are not easily defined by a set of consensually agreed-upon criteria. This point is most evident in the area of alcoholism. At least three major sets of clinical criteria have been published over the past 15 years to help clinicians diagnose individuals with alcohol-related problems. These include the criteria of the National Council on Alcoholism (1972); the third edition of the *Diagnostic and Statistical Manual of Mental Disorders* (DSM-III) of the American Psychiatric Association (1980); and the World Health Organization (Edwards & Gross, 1976). However, each of these systems places differential emphases on different aspects of behavioral and physiological functioning in their definitions (Caetano, 1985). It is not surprising, then, to find concerns expressed about the reliability of diagnostic classifications derived from such systems (e.g., Jolly, Fleece, Galanos, Milby, & Ritter, 1983; Pattison, 1981). Similarly, it is not surprising to find that the incidence of alcoholism diagnosed depends on the definitional system used (Boyd, Weissman, Thompson, & Myers, 1983; Leonard, Bromet, Parkinson, & Day, 1984). Boyd *et al.* (1983), using seven prominent clinical and research diagnostic systems, found that between 47% and 100% of the subjects diagnosed by one set of criteria as alcoholic were similarly diagosed by another diagnostic criteria set. The clinical utility of such diagnostic categories also has been questioned recently (Schuckit, Zisook, & Mortola, 1985). Using DSM–III criteria, Schuckit *et al.* (1985) found that individuals differentially diagnosed with Alcohol Dependence or Alcohol Abuse were comparable on a number of pretreatment and posttreatment outcome measures on which one would expect them to differ if the diagnostic classification had prognostic value.

The criteria for the Substance Use Disorders within DSM–III are currently being revised, based upon a number of concerns expressed by both researchers and clinicians (Rounsaville, Spitzer, & Williams, 1986). One of the proposed changes in this diagnostic system is to eliminate the previously noted distinction between substance abuse and dependence. This change has a number of potential advantages. One is that it will eliminate the problems associated with such an arbitrary distinction within the area of alcohol-related problems. Another advantage is that it will allow cocaine to be considered an object of addiction/dependence rather than an object of abuse. As the area of alcoholism exemplifies, the process of diagnosis in the addictions is as complex as are the behaviors under consideration (Burglass & Shaffer, 1984; Donovan & Marlatt, 1980). Whereas improvements in formalized diagnostic systems are needed and are promising, a simple binary classification scheme will remain insufficient to provide an adequate understanding of the addicted individual.

A second implication of the biopsychosocial model flows from the assumption that variables interact and that one can gain an understanding of a clinical condition by considering the interaction of variables that cut across multiple levels (Schwartz, 1982). This situation highlights the distinction made by a number of authors (e.g., Kanfer & Saslow, 1969; Shaffer & Kauffman, 1985) between diagnosis and clinical assessment. The former is a process of classification; the latter is a process of information gathering for the purpose of understanding. Thus, in addition to the process of classification inherent in providing a diagnosis, the clinician must also engage in a clinical assessment of the multiplicity of interacting variables that contribute to the individual's uniqueness and general level of function, as well as to the person's attraction toward and susceptibility to an addictive behavior (Peele, 1985). This makes the task of assessment more difficult, because it suggests that multiple measures of biological, psychological, and social systems be collected, integrated, and interpreted. This undertaking requires the clinician to be systematic, thorough, and yet flexible in the assessment process (P. M. Miller, 1980; Shaffer & Neuhaus, 1985). Failure to attend to the multiplicity of such variable domains and to their interaction may lead to a reduced effectiveness of treatment (Donovan, Kivlahan, & Walker, 1986; Shaffer & Neuhaus, 1985).

Another assumption of the biopsychosocial model is that treatments will interact with each other as well as with the person and his or her environment (Schwartz, 1982). A resultant implication is that the assessment process is not static; rather, it is a dynamic process. Both the clinician and the process of assessment represent important initial components in a larger system of treatment. Assessment introduces the individual to formalized aspects of treatment and may be therapeutic in its own right (W. R. Miller, 1983, 1985). This is discussed further in a subsequent section. Also, because of the anticipated impact of treatment, it is important to consider the interaction among individual, environmental, and physiological factors at each stage of the change process (Brownell et al., 1986).

## Issues in the Assessment Process: Systems, Levels, Phases, and Stages

The practical implication of the biopsychosocial approach to the addictions is that the assessment process assumes a more expanded and more prominent role than it may have had in previous approaches. The focus on multiple factors that may be addictive or interactive in nature suggests the need for a broad-spectrum assessment (Haynes, 1983). Such an approach involves the use of multiple assessment procedures and a focus on multiple target behaviors. The general methods of assessment in the addictions are similar to those used in the broader context of psychological assessment. These include self-reports of the client and reports from significant others (gained through self-monitoring, clinical interview, and/or structured reporting forms); direct observation of the client's behavior in laboratory, quasi-naturalistic, or naturalistic settings; physiological measures; and psychometric testing (P. M. Miller, 1980; Shaffer & Kauffman, 1985). The procedures involved in the assessment of eating, smoking, drinking, and drug use are quite similar (P. M. Miller, 1980). As noted previously, the clinician's general theoretical orientation will determine the assessment protocols used, the relative salience of the information collected, and the manner in which it is organized and interpreted (Shaffer & Kauffman, 1985; Shaffer & Neuhaus, 1985). However, the acquisition of clinical information is also guided by the primary goals of the assessment process (Cone & Hawkins, 1977; Donovan & Marlatt, 1980; Mash & Terdal, 1974; Shaffer & Kauffman, 1985; Stuart, 1970). These include describing the presenting problem (symptom pattern) clearly enough to provide both a clinical understanding and a diagnosis of it; identifying those conditions (on behavioral, psychological, and physiological levels) associated with the problem's occurrence and maintenance; selecting an appropriate, prescriptive intervention plan for therapeutically removing the problem (differential treatment planning); and predicting and evaluating the treatment process and outcome.

The choice of the more specific procedures to be employed in the assessment of addictive behaviors depends on a number of factors. In addition to the clinician's theoretical perspective and the general goals of the assessment, the procedures used will be determined by the level of precision desired, the phase of progression of the target behavior, the stage in the treatment process, and the system(s) (behavioral, psychological, or physiological) assumed to be primarily involved in the disorder. Each of these factors is discussed in turn, expanding on conceptual models presented by Skinner (1981) and Cone and Hawkins (1977).

## Systems of Functioning

A major emphasis of the biopsychosocial model is on multiple systems and the ways in which they interact. Within this context, a given disorder, including an addiction, is viewed as being determined by physiological, social, behavioral, and environmental factors. The concept of multiple-systems involvement is not new. Its incorporation into the biopsychosocial perspective represents a renewal, expansion, and reaffirmation of the relevance and importance of multiple systems in a variety of behavioral disorders (Kratochwill & Mace, 1983). The foundation of this approach can be attributed to the work of Lang (1977), who determined that anxiety, fear, and other emotions could be understood best as a function of (1) self-report or cognitive, (2) motoric or behavioral, and (3) physiological systems. The resultant approach has been described as a "triple-response mode" and as "multiple response components" (Kratochwill & Mace, 1983). Within the realm of addictions, the interaction among these multiple systems contributes to the set and setting that may influence the development and maintenance of an addictive behavior (Wallace, 1985; Zinberg, 1984).

A number of general issues related to the multiple-component approach are important to consider in the assessment of addictive behaviors. First, the involvement of multiple systems (and the resultant need to assess them) reflects the complexity of various behavioral and personality disorders (Kratochwill & Mace, 1983). It also increases the complexity of the assessment process. The lack of consistency that frequently is seen across the different response modes further increases the difficulty of the assessment, as well as of the integration and interpretation of information derived from it. Such discrepancies might be interpreted by clinicians as examples of the lack of reliability or validity of the self-reports of addicted individuals, often attributed to the influence of denial, defensiveness, or purposeful misrepresentation. However, it has recently been suggested that certain addictive behaviors, such as alcoholism and eating disorders, are characterized by a notable lack of awareness of internal cues associated with physiological activities related to the particular disorder (e.g., blood alcohol concentrations, gastric motility) (Gannon, 1984; Tarter, Alterman, & Edwards, 1984). The apparent deficits in the perception of such internal cues and in the appraisal of the significance of environmental events may contribute to the lack of correspondence across the systems assessed. Furthermore, there may be differences both within and across individuals with respect to the system(s) most responsive within a given situation (Epstein, 1976). Both response stereotypy and specificity need to be taken into account. "Response stereotypy" refers to an individual's idiosyncratic pattern of responding to a wide range of situations; "response specificity" refers to the fact that an individual will respond maximally and most reliably to various stimuli in one particular system (Epstein, 1976). Thus, for one client a physiological response may be the most prominent and sensitive, whereas for another a cognitive response may be the most sensitive and likely to occur. The task of the clinician, then, is to determine the unique contributions made to the addictive behavior by each system, the way in which the different systems interact, and the system making the greatest contribution to the behavioral disorder. The variability across individuals in the relative involvement of a given system in a disorder necessitates accurate assessment in all systems to identify the most appropriate target for intervention (Epstein, 1976).

The particular system under consideration will influence the specific methods of assessment to be employed. The emergent biopsychosocial model of addictive behaviors stresses the importance of physiological, cognitive-expectational, and behavioral systems. The remaining chapters of this volume provide a detailed and thorough review of the assessment process within these three systems of functioning in alcohol dependence; smoking; eating disorders; and the abuse of or dependence on cocaine, heroin, and marijuana. A brief overview of some general issues related to assessment of addictive behaviors within these systems is presented here.

*Physiological Factors*

The role of physiologically based variables in the addictions involves a number of possible influences. The first level is predispositional. There is increasing evidence that certain disorders, including eating disorders, alcoholism, and drug dependence, may be genetically predisposed. The results of adoption and family studies (e.g., Goodwin, 1984, 1986) have found that sons of alcoholics, for instance, are particularly vulnerable to alcoholism, with approximately 20%–25% of sons of alcoholics ultimately becoming alcoholics themselves. Thus, individuals from families in which one or more other members have an identified addiction are at increased risk for subsequent problems. These predispositions in sons of alcoholics are often manifested in subtle cognitive and attentional deficits as well as in problematic behavior patterns that, if not addressed by preventive interventions, may contribute to the development of alcoholism (Tarter, Alterman, & Edwards, 1985; Tarter & Edwards, 1986; Tarter, Hegedus, Goldstein, Shelly, & Alterman, 1984).

A second level of involvement consists of the physiological effects of the object of addiction (Kauffman, Shaffer, & Burglass, 1985). Substances such as alcohol, nicotine, cocaine, heroin, and marijuana all have direct pharmacological effects on the individual; the presence, as well as the prolonged absence, of food induces a wide range of biochemical and endocrinological changes. If consistently associated with internal and/or external stimuli, these physiological changes may become conditioned and subsequently elicited when these stimuli are presented (Kaplan *et al.,* 1985; Kaplan, Meyer, & Virgilio, 1984; Siegel, 1979). It should be noted that those factors increasing one's risk of developing an addictive behavior may mediate the subjective experience of the substance-specific physiological response. For example, it has been found that, in comparison to appropriate controls, individuals at risk due to a family history of alcoholism experienced less intense feelings of subjective intoxication, even though all subjects in the study reached comparable blood alcohol levels (Pollock, Teasdale, Gabrielli, & Knop, 1986; Schuckit, 1984).

A broad class of physiological factors to consider consists of those most commonly associated with addictions. These include the development of tolerance, dependence, and withdrawal. As Sobell and Sobell (1976) noted in their early review of assessment, the presence of such phenomena is critical in the definition of an addiction. Both direct effects of substances and conditioned physiological responses appear to contribute to the changes associated with tolerance and dependence (Jaffe, 1985; Tiffany & Baker, 1986). It is important to recall, however, that these features may be experienced in addictive behaviors such as gambling, in which no substances are ingested but repeated and marked changes in arousal levels occur. Similarly, withdrawal distress may be experienced when one is unable to engage in any habitually sought-after experience (Donegan *et al.,* 1983; Wray & Dickerson, 1981). Brownell *et al.* (1986) have suggested that physiological factors associated with withdrawal, often experienced and interpreted by the individual as craving, may be a central determinant in relapse.

A final variable to be assessed in this broad class of physiological factors is that of the organic sequelae that result from the addiction. A wide range of negative physical consequences may develop from continued involvement in the addictive behavior (e.g., Holt, Skinner, & Israel, 1981; Krieg, Backmund, & Pirke, 1986). Although health crises are often insufficient to halt the addictive process, many individuals have reported that such crises have contributed to their decisions to discontinue their addictive behaviors (Stall & Biernacki, 1986; Tuchfeld, 1981).

*Cognitive-Expectational Factors*

There has been an increased emphasis on the role that cognitive-expectational factors play in the area of addictive behaviors (Adesso, 1985; Donovan & Marlatt, 1980; Marlatt & Donovan, 1981; Marlatt & Gordon, 1985; Robertson, 1986). Within general psychological assessment, cognitive variables have been investigated to determine the relationship of covert processes to patterns of behavior, the expression of emotions, and the development of distinct psychopathologies (Kendall, 1982). Cognitive variables are conceptualized as functioning as causal precipitating events that may evoke or elicit certain physiological and/or behavioral responses; positive or negative contingencies that serve to increase or decrease a given behavior; independent forms of responses to be considered as primary target behaviors for intervention; and variables mediating treatment and its outcome (Haynes, 1983).

A number of cognitive variables are relevant to the addictions. One involves the positive outcome expectancies the individual holds concerning the addictive behavior (Brown, Goldman, Inn, & Anderson, 1980; Connors, O'Farrell, Cutter, & Thompson, 1986; Donovan & Marlatt, 1980). Through past experiences, direct and indirect, the individual has come to believe that drinking, smoking, eating/not eating, or using drugs has some functional utility. That is, the individual believes that engaging in these addictive behaviors may serve to produce positive outcomes that have a high level of perceived reinforcement value for him or her. The anticipated effects may include enhanced positive moods and reduced negative emotional states; physical or social pleasures; increased social interaction, interpersonal intimacy, and sexual arousal; heightened cognitive function and creativity; reduced levels of tension and increased relaxation; and increased feelings of arousal and aggression (Brown *et al.,* 1980; Connors *et al.,* 1986). It appears that the longer the individual has engaged in the addictive behavior, the stronger the associated expectancies and the greater their influence on continued involvement in the behavior (Adesso, 1985).

Some individuals may have other predispositions toward addiction besides genetic ones. Peele (1985) has suggested that increased susceptibility to and choice of addiction are based on a variety of sociocultural, situational, individual, and developmental factors. Certain cognitive-expectational factors, in addition to the positive outcome expectancies, may also contribute to this susceptibility. Addictive behaviors may be particularly attractive to individuals deficient in coping skills (Wills & Shiffman, 1985). A number of methods available to cope with stress or interpersonal or intrapersonal problems are cognitive in nature. Such coping skills may either deter or promote the addictive behavior (Wills &

Shiffman, 1985). Those cognitive processes that may contribute to the addiction include distortions in thinking; cognitive errors; maladaptive assumptions, unrealistic expectations of the self and others; and defensive strategies such as rationalization, intellectualization, and minimization (Marlatt & Gordon, 1985). Among those cognitive coping strategies that may help deter involvement in addictions are cognitive competencies such as interpersonal and emotional problem-solving skills; an awareness of and ability to recognize, accurately label, experience, and appropriately express emotions; an ability to generate, maintain, and modulate appropriate levels of arousal; an adequate level of self-esteem and realistic expectations for oneself; an ability to sustain goal-directed effort; and an ability to experience healthy pleasure and satisfaction (DeNelsky & Boat, 1986).

An important cognitive variable related to coping is the individual's appraisal of potentially stressful situations (Lazarus, 1966; Marlatt & Gordon, 1985; Sanchez-Craig, 1976). This formulation suggests that it is mainly the way in which situations are perceived, appraised, and interpreted, rather than the situations in and of themselves, that determines an individual's behavior. In addition to the influence of real or imagined features of the situation, the individual's repertoire of available coping strategies is thought to affect appraisals. When faced with potentially threatening situations, individuals who are deficient in those skills necessary to cope with the situational demands will experience increased stress and negative emotions. This increased arousal may be misinterpreted as a craving for the addictive experience. Another important consequence of the appraisal process and the absence of coping skills is the challenge to one's perception of control (Donovan & O'Leary, 1983). Similarly, such deficits may have a negative impact on the individual's perceived "self-efficacy" (Bandura, 1977), or the belief that one is capable of successfully executing those behaviors required in a given situation to produce a desired outcome. Negative self-efficacy expectancies, particularly if attributed to internal and stable personal characteristics or deficiencies, contribute to a further sense of lack of control, depression, and helplessness (Abramson, Seligman, & Teasdale, 1978; Donovan & O'Leary, 1983). The role of self-efficacy is seen as important in a variety of addictive behaviors and in the relapse process (e.g., Baer, Holt, & Lichtenstein, 1986; Donovan & Chaney, 1985; Glynn & Ruderman, 1986; Marlatt & Gordon, 1985; Rollnick & Heather, 1982; Yates & Thain, 1985). The belief that one is unable to cope effectively may prevent the individual from attempting to overcome a problem. Rather, he or she may passively give in to the situational demands, with their related negative emotions. In the absence of more adaptive cognitive or behavioral coping strategies, the individual may see involvement in the addictive behavior as one of the few means available to help him or her try to exert control and to cope.

*Behavioral Factors*

Other contributors to be considered in the development and maintenance of addictions are what have been described as "behavioral construction competencies" (Donovan & Chaney, 1985; Mischel, 1981). These consist of the individual's level of social competence or repertoire of behaviors necessary to cope adequately with a variety of situational demands. Such behaviors complement the cognitive coping strategies (DeNelsky & Boat, 1986; Wills & Shiffman, 1985). Included in this category are general social and interpersonal communication skills; assertiveness; decision making and the ability to take direct action; active avoidance of or withdrawal from problematic situations; the ability to seek out help and social support; the ability to relax; and the ability to gain positive experiences through entertainment or social and leisure activities. Deficits in these behavioral coping skills will have negative effects on the individual's appraisal of problematic situations, perception of control, and self-efficacy similar to those resulting from deficits in cognitive coping strategies. Again, a likely consequence is that the salience of the addictive behavior as a possible and available alternative, and of the related expectancies concerning the antici-pated positive effects, is enhanced; the likelihood of actually engaging in the addictive behavior is thus increased.

As described previously, physiological, cognitive, and behavioral com-ponents contribute interactively to the addiction process. Most often, how-ever, the presence of an addiction is manifested behaviorally and inferred from aspects of one's drinking, smoking, drug-taking, or eating behaviors. Thus, an important focus in the assessment is on the parameters of the actual behavior. A detailed functional analysis of the behavior can provide a wide range of information useful in treatment planning (Marlatt & Donovan, 1982; Sobell, Sobell, & Sheahan, 1976). Such an assessment would include a focus on the social, physical, and emotional environments in which the behavior occurs; the pattern and topography of the behavior (e.g., time, duration, frequency, level or intensity, quantity); and both the immediate and delayed positive and negative consequences that serve as contingen-cies to shape and maintain the behavior. Although no longer considered necessary features of a dependence syndrome (Edwards, 1986; Rounsaville *et al.,* 1986; Skinner & Goldberg, 1986), the effects of the addictive behavior on other areas of psychosocial functioning, such as marital, familial, social, vocational, financial, and legal, is important. An evaluation of these areas provides a sense of the severity or spreading effects of the addiction, possible contingencies governing the behavior, and an index of those social supports and resources important to the recovery process.

A multiple-systems approach to the addictions is based on an assump-tion of multiple causality of behavior. That is, any behavior can, and usually does, result from multiple and interacting causes. The expanded scope of the assessment process derived from this model requires the application of multiple-domain and multiple-method strategies (Kendall, 1982). While providing the prospect of more comprehensive knowledge about the individual and his or her addiction, the multiple-systems approach will probably add a great deal of complexity to the assessment and therapy processes for both the client and clinician (Kratochwill & Mace, 1983).

*Levels of Assessment*

A tenet of the biopsychosocial model (Schwartz, 1982) is that the clinician should *always* consider the interaction of biological, psychological, and social factors in assessing the person's condition and in making appropriate recommendations for treatment. The underlying assumption is that "more is better." However, such a comprehensive approach may not be feasible because of the constraints often experienced within many clinical settings. Furthermore, Morganstern (1976) has suggested that such an approach may not be appropriate, and presents somewhat more limited perspective: "The answer to the question 'What do I need to know about the client?' should be: 'Everything that is relevant to the development of effective, efficient, and durable treatment interventions.' And from an ethical (and economical) consideration, one could add, 'And no more' " (p. 52). Thus, although the acquisition of a wide range of information is necessary, the assessment process should be directed toward the primary goals outlined previously. Moreover, the focus should be on assessing what are assumed to be the most critical variables, measuring them with the most efficient yet reliable and valid procedures, and using the information in the most effective manner in making decisions relevant to the treatment process (Skinner, 1981).

Two different yet related approaches have been presented as ways of trying to strike a balance between the need for information and the cost-efficiency of the assessment process. The first represents a form of clinical hypothesis testing (Shaffer & Kauffman, 1985; Shaffer & Neuhaus, 1985), in which the clinician generates a number of hypotheses or partial formulations from biological, sociological, psychological, and behavioral perspectives concerning the addictive behavior under consideration. Information relevant to the hypotheses within each domain will be gathered by means of assessment methods that will allow the clinician to test the validity of each hypothesis. At each stage, the information collected will be (1) insufficient to determine the validity of the hypothesis and will then necessitate the acquisition of more detailed, similar data; (2) sufficient either to confirm or to disconfirm the clinician's hypothesis; or (3) suggestive of alternative or additional hypotheses requiring a redirection in one's approach or the use of different assessment strategies. Such a general approach to assessment requires a sound fundamental knowledge of the specific addictive behavior under consideration, in order to allow the generation of relevant hypotheses. It also requires a considerable degree of flexibility to allow the shifting of cognitive sets within the assessment process. Shaffer and Neuhaus (1985) have noted that the testing of hypotheses derived from these four domains makes the assessment task much more manageable and time-efficient, reduces the likelihood of premature closure in the collection of information, encourages the exploration of a broader range of clinically relevant questions, and facilitates the collection and organization of clinical information.

The second general approach to assessment in the addictions involves a sequential process with different levels of measurement (Cone & Hawkins, 1977; Skinner, 1981). Cone and Hawkins (1977) describe these levels as forming a "behavioral assessment funnel." At the top of the funnel is a very broad assessment that serves as a brief screening. The purpose of this rather gross screening is to determine general problem areas. The relative brevity of testing time and the breadth of coverage are often gained at the expense of the precision of measurement; however, the former factors contribute to the low cost of such screening tests (Skinner, 1981). The results from such initial measures are used to determine the nature of the more precise procedures to be used at the next level in the assessment funnel. Skinner (1981) describes this next level as "basic assessment." Two functions are involved at this level (Cone & Hawkins, 1977). The first is a general measurement function; this includes defining the extent and nature of the addictive behavior, in descriptive, functional, and diagnostic terms, in an individual previously determined in the brief screening to have a problem. Tentative decisions are made concerning the need for treatment, the general type of intervention (e.g., inpatient vs. outpatient, group vs. individual), and the treatment program to which this individual might be referred. The second function involves hypothesis formation concerning the more specific factors across a number of dimensions that help to maintain the behavior, as well as those that may be instrumental in overcoming the problem. The next, and most precise, level of the assessment funnel involves what Skinner (1981) describes as "specialized assessment." A more thorough, specific, and detailed set of information is gathered, often pursuing hypotheses generated at the preceding level. Specific aspects of the addictive behavior across the behavioral, social, psychological, and physiological dimensions are pinpointed as the targets of intervention. More specific decisions are made about the exact nature of these interventions.

The increased breadth of assessment associated with the biopsychosocial model of addictions seems overwhelming at first glance. However, as is noted above, the use of clinical hypothesis testing and sequential assessment strategies makes this process more focused, manageable, and cost-efficient.

### Phases of the Addictive Behavior

A second general factor that will have an impact on the assessment process is the phase of the addictive behavior at the time of the clinician's contact with the individual. Previous views of the addictions, best exemplified by Jellinek's (1960) early work in the area of alcoholism, suggested a Guttman scaling continuum to define the progression of the disorder (Donovan & Marlatt, 1980; Wanberg, Horn, & Foster, 1977). That is, it was assumed that an individual progresses inexorably through a fixed set of increasingly serious symptoms. A corollary of this assumption was that if an individual experiences a symptom presumed to characterize a more advanced phase of the disorder, then this inevitably has been preceded by symptoms of earlier phases.

The lockstep progression of such symptom manifestation has been challenged by clinical observations as well as by research findings (e.g., Wanberg & Horn, 1983). For alcoholism, a multiple-syndrome perspective is a more viable alternative view of the disorder (Wanberg & Horn, 1983). This latter view is consistent with that of Edwards (1986) and Skinner and Goldberg (1986) concerning the syndromes of alcohol and drug dependence. These syndromes are described as a clustering of certain key elements (e.g., a narrowing of one's drinking or drug-using repertoire, salience of alcohol- or drug-seeking behavior, increased tolerance, repeated withdrawal symptoms, relief or avoidance of withdrawal symptoms by further drinking or drug use, subjective awareness of a compulsion to drink or use drugs, a tendency to relapse following abstinence).

Unlike the earlier unitary view of symptom progression, the perspective of alcohol and drug dependence as syndromes assumes that not all elements need always be present, or be present to the same degree. The syndromes are viewed as being continuous in nature, falling along a dimension of increasing intensity. As the intensity of the dependence syndrome increases, there is assumed to be an increased presence of and coherence among the cluster of key features defining the syndrome. This perspective has exerted an influence on the planned revisions of the diagnostic criteria for Substance Use Disorders in DSM–III (Rounsaville *et al.,* 1986). These revisions involve removal of the distinction between abuse and dependence; broadening of the definition of "dependence" to a syndrome of clinically significant behaviors indicating a serious degree of involvement with psychoactive substances; the use of an identical set of symptoms and behaviors to determine dependence across different classes of substances; and the provision of a system for rating the severity of dependence. The view of dependence as a syndrome also implies that multidimensional criteria are necessary for its assessment (Burglass & Shaffer, 1984).

It would appear that the conceptual framework of the alcohol and drug dependence syndromes can be generalized to a wide variety of addictive behaviors. Analogously, one would be able to determine the relative phase of the addictive behavior according to the intensity, occurrence, and coherence of those cognitive, behavioral, and physiological features associated with the specific object of addiction. Skinner (1981) has noted that assessment measures appropriate to one phase of a disorder may or may not be suitable for other phases. As an example, extensive neuropsychological assessment may be inappropriate for a young, moderate drinker, but may be indicated in dealing with an older individual who has a long history of heavy drinking and alcohol dependence (e.g., Donovan, Kivlahan, Walker, & Umlauf, 1985). The level of assessment (brief screening, basic assessment, or specialized assessment, as outlined previously) may interact with the phase of the disorder in shaping the nature of both the assessment protocol and the subsequent intervention. As the phase of the disorder manifests greater severity and/or intensity of dependence, the likelihood that a more thorough, comprehensive, and specialized assessment will be needed increases.

Skinner (1981) indicates that at early phases, the focus is on identifying those individuals who are at risk for developing more serious problems if no intervention is implemented. Brief screening measures are appropriate to this task. The objective of such assessment is to target individuals or groups of individuals for primary prevention interventions. At the next phase, evidence of the addictive behavior and its related problems is apparent. Skinner (1981) describes this as the "early diagnosis and treatment phase"—the point at which basic assessment procedures are employed to evaluate the extent of the addiction-related disabilities. Such an assessment has as its therapeutic goal secondary prevention, with early case finding and prompt treatment. At the final phase along the dependence continuum is what Skinner (1981) describes as the "rehabilitation phase." The individual has experienced a wide variety of chronic functional disabilities as a result of continued involvement in the addictive behavior. More extensive and specialized assessments are often required at this point. The goal is one of tertiary prevention, in which an attempt is made to rehabilitate the individual to an effective level of functioning and to minimize further disabilities.

### Stages of Treatment

A third factor that influences the nature and focus of the assessment process is the point at which it occurs within treatment. As Brownell *et al.*

(1986) have indicated, it is important to consider the interaction of individual, environmental, and physiological factors at each stage of the change process.


*Preintervention: Motivation and Commitment*

Assessment is typically viewed as the initial step in the process of treatment. As noted earlier, a primary goal is to gain a sufficient understanding of the individual and the addictive behavior to determine the most appropriate treatment. In addition to this component of information acquisition, the initial interaction of client and clinician during the course of the assessment may also serve important therapeutic functions. In particular, the process of assessment may contribute significantly to the individual's motivation for and commitment to change.

Choosing to give up an addictive behavior is not a decision that is arrived at easily. There is often a history of prior unsuccessful attempts at change (Schacter, 1982), as well as a "selective recollection" of the aspects of the addictive experience that remain appealing. Many addicted individuals have gone many years without thinking about their behavior as problematic; many others have contemplated the need for changing their behavior for quite some time without taking action (Prochaska & DiClemente, 1986). Thus, when an individual seeks treatment, either on his or her own volition or because of extrinsic pressures (e.g., from family, friends, employers, courts), there appears to be a high degree of ambivalence. On the one hand is an awareness of a problem requiring change; on the other is a set of reservations about and obstacles to change (Kanfer, 1986; W. R. Miller, 1983). Kanfer (1986) has suggested that an individual's initial commitment when seeking treatment is usually not based upon a genuine desire to give up the addictive behavior. Instead, the individual usually desires to change only the consequences of the addiction rather than the behavior itself. The clinician's task, even while engaged in the assessment process, is to "hook" the side of the client's ambivalence that is positively inclined toward change. It is necessary to tip the balance by strengthening the commitment and motivation for change, by increasing the attractiveness of a new behavior pattern and lifestyle associated with the cessation of the addictive behavior, and by helping reduce the fears and concerns about change (Kanfer, 1986; W. R. Miller, 1983).

Addicted individuals have often been viewed clinically as unmotivated to change their behaviors. This apparent lack of motivation has typically been attributed to generalized personality characteristics or inherent traits of the individual, which are manifested as defensiveness, denial, and resistance. W. R. Miller (1983, 1985) has pointed out a number of limitations associated with this view and has suggested an alternative approach. A potential outcome of the trait view of motivation is an expectancy of poor prognosis that may lead to a self-fulfilling prophecy. That is, the client may perceive a sense of frustration and futility about changing, based upon past unsuccessful attempts and/or clinical feedback, and may subtly undermine treatment. From the clinician's standpoint, viewing the addicted client as inherently unmotivated may contribute to reduced empathy and increased suspiciousness, hostility, moralizing, and power struggles, which compromise any attempt at intervention. The alternative presented by W. R. Miller (1983, 1985) is to view motivation as the result of the interaction between the clinician and the client. Within this framework, the way in which the clinician affectively, cognitively, and behaviorally approaches and deals with the client, his or her addiction, and the ambivalence concerning change will elicit responses that will be interpreted as evidencing either "motivation" or "resistance." W. R. Miller (1983, 1985) suggests a number of general principles involved in increasing the motivation of the addicted individual. An initial one involves a de-emphasis on labeling. Attempts to persuade an individual to accept a label (e.g., "alcoholic," "drug addict") may represent a potential obstacle to the individual's entering the role of client and to the development of a therapeutic relationship. An understanding of what problems the individual is having in relation to the addiction and what needs to be done about them may be more crucial than the individual's accepting a self-label. Second, there is a focus on the individual's responsibility for both a thorough self-evaluation of the problem and tentative decisions about the appropriate course of action. The clinician serves as a knowledgeable consultant who provides information and perspectives and suggests alternative courses as needed. Third, and related to the previous principle, the individual must accept the responsibility for positive changes, attributing them to his or her efforts. Fourth, there needs to be a sufficient level of cognitive dissonance to lead to change. That is, the individual needs to recognize that the addictive behavior is significantly discrepant with his or her personal beliefs, attitudes, values, and feelings. The acknowledged inconsistency produces a state of internal conflict serving as a motivator to change, bringing about a greater degree of consistency. The clinician's task is both to increase the level of dissonance and to direct the resultant motivational state so that it leads to changed behavior, rather than to a shift in cognitive and affective sets in a manner consistent with continuing in the addictive behavior.

Increasing dissonance involves a form of awareness raising or consciousness building (W. R. Miller, 1983). One method that may be helpful in the assessment process is to elicit self-motivational statements from the client. These statements are ones that reflect a cognitive awareness of problems associated with the addiction, express affective concern about the problem, and recognize the need to make behavioral changes (W. R. Miller, 1983). As Kanfer (1986) has noted, the client's commitment must be verbalized, felt, experienced, and acted on to effect a lasting change.

The clinician can also influence the client after this initial phase of the assessment process has been completed. W. R. Miller (1985) has described a number of "motivational interventions," defined as operations "that [increase] the probability of entering, continuing, and complying with an active change strategy" (p. 88). A number of these interventions involve the integration of information gained through the assessment process (W. R. Miller, 1983, 1985). For instance, providing objective feedback concerning the extent of an addictive behavior, the severity of the accompanying dependence syndrome, and other aspects of physical and psychosocial functioning appears to be effective in increasing the dissonance between the individual's current state and the ideal state of health. When accompanied by advice concerning the need for the person to make a change in his or her behavior, such a brief motivational intervention appears effective in eliminating the addictive behavior of a large number of individuals in the absence of any further treatment (e.g., Edwards *et al.,* 1977; Miller & Taylor, 1980; Ritson, 1986). It appears that the provision of feedback and advice can be enhanced further when combined with setting goals or standards of behavior (W. R. Miller, 1985). The more realistic, specific, challenging, and yet attainable the goals are, the greater the apparent motivational impact will be. W. R. Miller (1985) also notes that providing the individual with an active involvement in and sense of choice of the goals for treatment and the therapeutic measures used to achieve them may increase motivation and compliance.

The goals of the clinician during this initial phase of the assessment process extend well beyond what has been seen traditionally as the primary task—namely, information gathering. It also involves increasing the client's motivation for treatment. Within Prochaska and DiClemente's (1986) model of change, the therapist is instrumental in moving the client from the "contemplation phase" (in which the person has an awareness of needing to change) through the "determination phase" (in which the person has decided that changing is essential and is willing to pursue avenues of change). W. R. Miller (1983) has indicated that the client is at a crucial point once he or she is in the determination phase, with a relatively limited time to move on to the point of taking action. It may represent a moment at which the clinician has an opportunity to make a profound impact. Using the techniques described by W. R. Miller (1983, 1985), Kanfer (1986), and Appel (1986), which appear to increase both the person's awareness of the problem and the level of dissonance, may be particularly helpful. Prochaska and DiClemente (1986) have found that certain processes of change are emphasized during and are relatively more effective in particular stages of change. Those individuals in the contemplation phase have been found to be most open to consciousness-raising interventions such as observations, confrontations, and interpretations, as well as others that lead them to re-evaluate themselves both cognitively and affectively. By effectively motivating the client during the course of the pretreatment assessment, the clinician may increase the likelihood that the individual will engage positively in the subsequent therapeutic process.

## Intervention: Action and Initial Behavior Change

Assessment is conducted with a purpose (Mash & Terdal, 1974): to determine the nature of the clinical problem, the need for treatment, and the form of treatment that appears most appropriate for the given problem. Whereas the clinical decision making involved in the negotiation of the treatment goals and specific therapeutic interventions is based on the results of the initial assessment, the process of assessment is still incomplete. There are at least four areas that require continued monitoring: the match between the client and treatment, the assessment of the target behavior to be modified, the evaluation of change in other related areas, and a determination of possible risks of relapse.

Schwartz (1982) has suggested that one of the theoretical implications of the biopsychosocial model is that a thorough assessment consistent with this approach should lead to a more effective match between the individual and the therapy to which he or she is assigned. Shaffer and Neuhaus (1985) have made similar suggestions concerning the assignment of addicted individuals to different forms of treatment based upon the outcome of clinical assessment. Although there has been an increased focus on client--treatment matching on a theoretical and heuristic level (e.g., Finney & Moos, 1986; Glaser, 1980; McCrady & Sher, 1983; McLellan, O'Brien, Kron, Altermann, & Druley, 1980; W. R. Miller & Hester, 1986b), there has been considerably less empirical work evaluating the viability of such an approach (e.g., McLellan, Woody, Luborsky, O'Brien, & Druley, 1983; Walker, Donovan, Kivlahan, & O'Leary, 1983; Woody, McLellan, Luborsky, & O'Brien, 1985).

It is apparent that individual differences across clients have an influence on the process and outcome of treatment of alcoholism (e.g., Caddy & Block, 1985; Gibbs & Flanagan, 1977; McCrady & Sher, 1983). However, such individual differences appear to account for a limited amount of the variance in subsequent drinking and related behaviors (Cronkite & Moos, 1978, 1980; Moos & Finney, 1983). It has been assumed that a closer match between the patient and the specific treatment would enhance treatment outcome and be more cost-effective. Glaser (1980) has suggested that matching might be considered between characteristics of clients and therapists, between client attributes and the goals of treatment, or between the nature of the client's problems and the specific focus of treatment.

McCrady and Sher (1983) have indicated that the ideal approach would be to identify active elements in treatment and match these to certain patient characteristics or presenting problems. The clinician, based on the assessment findings, would identify specific problem areas to target for intervention and then select those interventions having the best proven effectiveness for these specified problems. Although heuristically appealing, such an approach is considerably more complex than it appears on the surface (Finney & Moos, 1986). It assumes the availability of a wide array of effective treatments from which to choose, the selection of appropriate client characteristics, and the derivation of strategies (either clinical or statistical) to maximize the outcome of treatment through matching (Finney & Moos, 1986).

Finney and Moos (1986) suggest two broad dimensions of client variables, from among the vast array available, to consider in the process of matching clients to treatments. The first represents a dimension of individual deficits-resources. Toward the deficits end are those problems related to the person's addictive behavior and to other spheres of psychosocial function that are involved in his or her seeking treatment. In this regard, it should be noted that psychiatric problems are frequently associated with addictive behaviors (e.g., Allen & Frances, 1986), and that the severity of psychiatric symptomatology has been found to be an important factor in determining the effectiveness of differential treatments among substance abusers (McLellan, 1986; McLellan, Luborsky, Woody, O'Brien, & Druley, 1983). Thus, it is important to include measures of psychopathology in the assessment of such deficits. The resources represent relatively stable strengths, including social skills and coping abilities (e.g., DeNelsky & Boat, 1986; O'Leary, O'Leary, & Donovan, 1976; Van Hasselt, Hersen, & Milliones, 1978; Wills & Shiffman, 1985); these can be reinforced and built upon during the course of treatment, and, it is hoped, can facilitate the recovery process and minimize relapse. The second broad dimension of client variables discussed by Finney and Moos (1986) consists of the client's neuropsychological abilities, such as general information processing, abstract reasoning, and problem-solving skills. The individual's level of functioning needs to be taken into account in determining the level of complexity of the intervention; more impaired individuals may not be able to adequately assimilate, organize, or use information presented in cognitively mediated therapies (e.g., Donovan, Walker, & Kivlahan, 1987; Walker et al., 1983). Tarter et al. (1984) have suggested further that such neuropsychological deficits among alcoholics, particularly deficits in accurately perceiving internal cues of physiological arousal and emotion and in appraising the significance of environmental events, may underlie what has been described as "alcoholic denial."

Although there is increasing evidence concerning the differential effectiveness of certain forms of treatment in the addictions, particularly alcoholism (Miller & Hester, 1986a), it is still necessary to determine the active ingredients to facilitate matching (Finney & Moos, 1986; Moos & Finney, 1983, 1986). Finney and Moos (1986) have again suggested two broad areas to be considered. The first includes those therapeutic components aimed at reducing those deficits associated with the addictive behavior and other psychosocial problems, at strengthening those resources the client has, and at producing positive posttreatment functioning. Aspects of the actual delivery of the treatments comprise the second area to be considered. This category includes variables such as the cognitive complexity, clarity, and organization of the intervention, as well as the manner in which it is implemented, its sequencing, its intensity, its duration, and its quality (Finney & Moos, 1986; Moos & Finney, 1983, 1986).

This overview indicates that the process of treatment matching is a complex one; however, it is a goal toward which future clinical and research work should progress. Finney and Moos (1986) have also noted a number of limitations that clinicians should consider. First, the incremental benefits of matching on the basis of client characteristics to different forms of treatment may not be as great as one would expect. Second, within the realm of clinical practice, such an approach, which requires new assessments and the provision of multiple treatments, may prove to be administratively complex, staff-intensive, and possibly not particularly cost-effective. Future research must evaluate these administrative aspects of the matching process as well as its clinical efficacy.

Once the client has begun treatment, there is a need for continued monitoring. The point at which the decision is made concerning the appropriate type of treatment to provide represents the base of the behavioral assessment funnel in Cone and Hawkins's (1977) model. The focus of assessment during the course of treatment is on changes in the specified target behaviors associated with the client's addiction, progress toward the specified goals of the intervention, and changes in other areas of general life functioning. A number of issues should be kept in mind during this part of the assessment. First, whereas the focus of the intervention is geared toward removal of the addictive behavior, the focus of assessment cannot be restricted to this area alone. This would appear self-evident; however, previous reviews (e.g., Maisto & McCollam, 1980) have suggested that other areas of functioning are frequently neglected in such evaluations. Second, measures of the addiction will probably be collected repeatedly, thus requiring an economical scale. However, because the clinician hopes to gain a better sense of the nature of the addictive behavior, it is important not to reduce the measure to a dichotomous one (e.g., smoking or not smoking, binge-eating or not binge-eating, etc.). Rather, it is important to retain measures of factors such as craving and temptation, as well as a gradation of the actual addictive behavior if the client has engaged in it (McCrady & Sher, 1983).

Third, although it is important to assess other areas of general life functioning, as noted previously, this does not imply the use of general measures. As McCrady and Sher (1983) noted, measures of occupational functioning, physical health, interpersonal relationships, and subjective life satisfaction may be applied equally to all clients. However, there often is no specific attention paid to those areas in which the individual initially presented problems or to changes in these specific problem areas. The use of an ideographic assessment approach, focusing on individualized measures of behavior change and goal attainment ratings, should be considered (Mintz & Kiesler, 1982). This seems particularly important because positive changes in an addictive behavior are not always associated with comparable positive changes in other areas (Pattison, Sobell, & Sobell, 1977); the initial process of giving up an addiction may tax the individual's coping abilities and lead to increased psychological distress. A second reason for attention to the assessment of these other areas of functioning is based upon the findings reported by Tucker *et al.* (1985). At the time of entering treatment, alcoholics were assessed concerning the extent to which alcohol had disrupted their functioning in six life areas (social, family, and intimate relationships; vocational functioning; financial status; physical health). At a 6-month follow-up, it was found that the occurrence of negative events in those life areas disrupted by past alcohol use was more likely both to precipitate relapse and to result in more severe drinking episodes than were negative events outside of these areas. Finally, it is important to assess other factors during the course of treatment that may represent particular risks for relapse (Cummings *et al.,* 1980; Marlatt & Gordon, 1985). These may represent changes in the individual's set or setting in relation to the addictive behavior that may increase the likelihood of return to the addiction.

During this phase of treatment, there continues to be a dynamic interplay between the assessment and therapy processes. Information from such assessments provides feedback to both client and therapist about the progress being made, the adequacy of the treatment implementation, the level of client motivation and compliance with the intervention, the appropriateness of new therapy objectives, and/or the need for modifications in the treatment (Finney & Moos, 1986; Moos & Finney, 1983). The process is meant to facilitate the client's move from the stage of motivation, commitment, and determination associated with the pretreatment assessment to the action stage of change, in which the client's efforts are meant to bring about modifications in the addictive behavior (Prochaska & DiClemente, 1986). This phase of assessment corresponds to the initial portion of the "neck" of the behavioral assessment funnel, involving repeated monitoring of a relatively narrow, specified range of behaviors and environmental events (Cone & Hawkins, 1977).

*Postintervention: Maintenance*

Cone and Hawkins (1977) note that it is appropriate that the remaining portion of the "neck" of the assessment funnel is extended, because responsible assessment typically involves some form of follow-up after the intervention is terminated. The primary focus of the assessments conducted during this stage is on the short-term impact of the intervention, on generalization, and on the maintenance of behavior change over time. Brownell *et al.* (1986) and Jeffrey (1975) have indicated that the client should be involved in some form of continued self-evaluation or contact with professionals following treatment. Not only does such continued monitoring serve to assess the impact of the intervention; it also helps maintain the client's long-term vigilance in regard to the problem (Brownell *et al.,* 1986). Such cognitive vigilance has been found to be an important factor in minimizing the probability of relapse (e.g., Litman, Stapleton, Oppenheim, Peleg, & Jackson, 1983).

Jeffrey (1975) has indicated that the generalization of treatment effects can occur across situations, time, and behaviors; addiction treatment research until recently has been concerned primarily with the first two of these. Generalization across situations involves the transfer of the desired response from therapy to the patient's life situation. In addition to this form of behavioral generalization beyond the treatment setting, the extent to which the situation-specific coping and self-management skills generalize to other potential relapse situations is important. An assumption of relapse prevention models is that, as the client successfully copes with high-risk situations without reverting back to the addictive behavior, his or her perceived control, self-efficacy, and confidence increase (Donovan & Chaney, 1985; Marlatt & George, 1984; Marlatt & Gordon, 1985). The predicted outcome is not only a decreased likelihood of relapse in similar situations in the future, but also a greater likelihood of attempting appropriate coping strategies in other possible relapse situations. The assessment of such factors following the completion of treatment also involves an examination of generalization across time (Jeffrey, 1975). The majority of relapses in addictive behaviors occur within the first 3 months following treatment (Hunt *et al.,* 1971). This suggests the need for more frequent assessment or self-monitoring during this time period. However, it has been suggested that adequate follow-up assessment should extend well beyond this period, with a 12- to 24-month follow-up being recommended (Nathan & Lansky, 1978).

Jeffrey (1975) noted that at the time of his writing there was relatively less focus on generalization across behaviors within the addictions; however, this appears to be changing. Schwartz (1982) indicates that assessment within the biopsychosocial framework considers disorders in interaction rather than in isolation; thus recommended treatment may apply to two or more problems simultaneously (e.g., Zeiner *et al.,* 1985). Given the interrelatedness of unhealthy behaviors among addicted individuals, the likelihood of a shift among such behaviors may be predicted (Clayton, 1986; Istvan & Matarrazo, 1984; P. M. Miller, 1980; Mintz *et al.,* 1985). The probability of relapse in the addictive behavior for which treatment has been sought is frequently increased when these alternatives are engaged in (Smith, 1986). Schwartz (1982) has also posited that the biopsychosocial model anticipates treatment interactions across modalities with potentially additive and/or synergistic effects. Consistent with this position, the risk of relapse is seen as being determined by an interaction of individual, environmental, and physiological factors. Brownell *et al.* (1986) suggest that variables within each of these categories may have different effects at different stages in the recovery process. It is postulated that physiological factors, potentially related to the level of dependence and experienced as craving, may promote an initial return to the addictive behavior. A variety of cognitive, psychological, behavioral, and environmental variables, both predating the lapse and in response to it, interact to determine whether a full-blown relapse will occur. This suggests that the clinician needs to be sensitive to the systems of functioning in which the client most frequently experiences potential relapse precipitants (physiological, cognitive, or behavioral), their interrelationship, and the likely sequence of their occurrence for the individual. Marlatt and Gordon (1985) have suggested a number of more specific assessment techniques that are helpful in this regard.

Another form of generalization across behavior involves the extent to which changes in the addiction affect other areas of life functioning. Issues related to this process have been discussed briefly in the preceding section. However, the other side of this relationship deserves further attention—that is, the influence that the individual's level of functioning in these other life areas exerts on the recovery process. Clinicians, for a variety of practical reasons, have focused considerable attention on the characteristics of both clients and treatments in predicting and evaluating treatment outcome. However, Cronkite and Moos (1980) and Billings and Moos (1983) have suggested that such variables, even in combination, account for a relatively limited amount of variance in the outcome of treatment for addictive behavior. Conversely, they suggest that a considerable amount of the outcome variance, up to double that attributable to client and treatment factors, can be accounted for by extratreatment factors involved in the recovery process.

Billings and Moos (1983) recommend that extratreatment factors, such as the occurrence of chronic or acute life stressors, family environment, work environment, and social support, should be included in the clinical assessment process because of their implications for identifying clients with a high risk of relapse and for formulating more effective treatment and aftercare plans. Although such factors are likely to be included in an initial assessment, there is some evidence that baseline assessment of social support, for instance, may be of limited value in predicting subsequent measures of support (Bruhn & Phillips, 1984). This may be particularly true in the treatment of addictions in which the nature of the client's support networks may be modified indirectly (e.g., giving up peers who encourage continued engagement in the addictive behavior) or directly through the therapy process (e.g., Azrin, Sisson, Meyers, & Godley, 1982). Furthermore, although there are exceptions to the rule (Pattison, Sobell, & Sobell, 1977), there generally appears to be a positive and bidirectional relationship between extratreatment factors and recovery (Billings & Moos, 1983). That is, increased abstinence from the addictive behavior tends both to result from and to make contributions to more adaptive functioning in these other life areas. Thus, it is important to note these extratreatment variables, both independently and in relation to changes in the addictive behavior, across the follow-up assessment process.

Billings and Moos (1983) consider the relevance of extratreatment factors within the context of a stress and coping framework. This framework views the client's status at follow-up as a function of variables related to the addictive behavior prior to treatment (e.g., level of dependence or symptom severity), variables related to the intervention process (e.g., the type and amount of treatment received), and a variety of factors associated with the posttreatment environment. Three domains are included in the last category: life stressors, coping processes, and social resources. It is important to consider three different forms of stressors in the individual's life (Wills & Shiffman, 1985). The first category consists of major negative life events, which typically occur suddenly, require major lifestyle changes, and usually involve an initial period of shock followed by a period of gradual readjustment (e.g., major physical illness or death of a family member). The second form of stressor involves relatively persistent and enduring life strains (e.g., dissatisfaction in a marital relationship or with one's job circumstances) that are neither easily nor quickly resolved. The final form of stressor consists of relatively minor problems that occur in everyday life and are resolved relatively rapidly and easily, but are soon replaced by other demands. Each of these forms of stress may contribute to the negative emotional states, the interpersonal conflict situations, and the lifestyle imbalance that may precipitate the relapse process (Cummings *et al.,* 1980; Marlatt & Gordon, 1985). Wills and Shiffman (1985) have suggested that the second category of stressors, enduring life strains, may be the most problematic for habitual substance abusers.

The extent and nature of the individual's coping skills must also be taken into consideration. These include behavioral and cognitive coping strategies that will mediate the person's appraisal of and response to either the stresses produced by negative life events or persistent strains or the temptation to engage in an addictive behavior within particular situations (Wills & Shiffman, 1985). Craving and the temptations to engage in the behavior appear to be higher within those situations having physical, emotional, and/or social similarities to those in which the addictive behavior previously occurred (e.g., Donovan & Chaney, 1985; Ludwig & Wikler, 1974). It appears that different types of coping may be more or less effective in minimizing relapse across a variety of addictive behaviors (Billings & Moos, 1983; Chaney & Roszell, 1985; DiClemente & Prochaska, 1985; Donovan & Chaney, 1985; Litman, 1986; Litman, Stapleton, Oppenheim, Peleg, & Jackson, 1984; Perri, 1985; Prochaska & DiClemente, 1985). It also appears that the relative effectiveness of coping strategies will vary as a function of the individual's position in the process of recovery (Litman, 1980).

Not only do the individual's coping skills influence the impact of stress; so also do the social resources available to the person. It is assumed that a supportive and cohesive support system, such as family, friends, employers, and coworkers, contributes to a positive outcome (Billings & Moos, 1983). A similar assumption is made concerning clients' involvement in self-help organizations such as Alcoholics Anonymous, Cocaine Anonymous, Narcotics Anonymous, and Overeaters Anonymous, or in other more formalized aftercare services following the completion of treatment (Ito & Donovan, 1986; Thoits, 1986). Again, it is important to assess the extent and nature of the client's support system across time, because it is likely to change (Bruhn & Phillips, 1984).

A number of variables need to be considered in this assessment. These include the availability of some source of support, the quantity of support (i.e., the number of individuals in one's social network), the quality of the support provided, the accessibility of members of the network to the individual, the likelihood that the individual will seek out support in times of need, and the functions served by the support provided (Bruhn & Phillips, 1984; Thoits, 1986). Not all social systems are necessarily supportive (e.g., Bruhn & Phillips, 1984; Coyne & DeLongis, 1986; Mermelstein, Cohen, Lichtenstein, Baer, & Kamarck, 1986; Vannicelli, Gingerich, & Ryback, 1983). The presence of problems or conflicts within a marriage, within the family system, and/or within the work setting may mean that these settings serve as stressors rather than as stress buffers. In addition, the presence of individuals within one's peer group who exert either direct or indirect pressure to resume an addictive behavior has been associated with relapse (Cummings et al., 1980; Mermelstein et al., 1986).

In the more frequent instances in which social support facilitates positive outcome, it appears to do so by providing a sense of belonging, modifying the effects of negative stress, restoring or strengthening hope, and enhancing the person's ability to learn new skills and both see their use modeled and attempt to use them within new situations (Bruhn & Phillips,

1984). Thoits (1986) has suggested that social support might usefully be reconceptualized as coping assistance. Within this framework, the active participation of significant others contributes to the client's efforts at stress management. The client is assisted in changing a situation that causes stress, the meaning or appraisal of the situation, and/or the emotional reaction to the situation. The result of both individual coping and social support is to change or eliminate the primary source of threat to the individual. Assessment of the client's support system should thus include measures of such functions.

It must also be kept in mind that the relative importance of social support, or of its subcomponents, varies as a function of the individual's cultural background, age, and life situation (Bruhn & Phillips, 1984); thus, it should not be assumed that the availability, accessibility, intensity, and meaning of social supports remain constant across time. Finally, it is important to keep in mind that different components of social support will exert their influence at different points in the recovery process (Mermelstein *et al.,* 1986).

As noted earlier, the probability of relapse is high across the addictive behaviors (Cummings *et al.,* 1980; Hunt *et al.,* 1971). Although it is important to identify those variables that may predict relapse, it is equally important to assess the impact of relapse on the individual. Marlatt and Gordon (1985) have suggested that a number of cognitive and emotional reactions typically result when one has violated a commitment to abstain from an addictive behavior. The impact of this violation through an initial slip will vary as a function of the strength of one's commitment to abstinence, the length of time the individual has maintained abstinence, and the way in which the person attributes responsibility for the slip. The "abstinence violation effect" (Marlatt & Gordon, 1985) will be heightened if the individual attributes the initial return to the addiction to internal personal characteristics thought to be relatively global, stable, and beyond personal control (e.g., lack of willpower or an underlying disease state). In such instances, the slip is accompanied by a sense of anger, self-blame, guilt, and depression, with a resultant decrease in perceived control and self-efficacy. The risk is that the individual will view himself or herself as an addict who is helpless to exert control over the addiction. The eventual result is an increased probability that the initial slip will lead to a more extensive and serious relapse. The processes underlying the abstinence violation effect suggest the importance of assessing the client's general attributional style, the relapse-specific attributions, the resultant emotional reactions to the slip, and the impact on the person's perceived self-efficacy and ability to cope effectively in similar situations in the future. It is also necessary to determine the impact of the client's relapse on his or her social support systems. A return to addictive behavior, even if only a relatively circumscribed slip, engenders frustration, anger, anxiety, a sense of futility and hopelessness, and loss of trust in the individual (e.g., Moos, Finney, & Gamble, 1982). The negative emotions and attitudes among members of the client's support system may impede their attempting to provide assistance at the point when it may be most needed.

The goal of assessment during the follow-up period is to determine the extent to which those behaviors acquired or modified during the active stage of treatment have generalized and are maintained over time. The model of behavior change presented by Prochaska and DiClemente (1986) is cyclical in nature. That is, an individual involved in treatment for an addictive behavior is assumed to move in and out of different stages of change across time. It also recognizes relapse as one stage in the process of recovery in the addictions. A potential benefit of such a perspective is that it may minimize the negative stigma often associated with relapse. As Prochaska and DiClemente (1986) note, a large number of individuals who have relapsed find themselves once again at the stage of contemplating change. Thus, an important added task of the clinician is not only to assess variables involved with a return to the addictive behavior, but also to facilitate the individual's movement back through the stages of motivation, commitment, and active behavior change.

## Summary and Conclusion

It is clear that a number of positive changes in the assessment of the addictive behaviors have taken place over the past decade. Addictions are seen as complex behavioral patterns having multiple causes. The addictive experience is determined by equally complex interactions among biological, psychological, and social variables. It appears that a biopsychosocial model, which is emerging within the areas of behavioral medicine, provides a heuristic framework within which to understand and assess addictive behaviors. As Schwartz (1982) has noted, "Implicit in the biopsychosocial approach to behavioral medicine is the view that variables interact and that health and illness can best be understood by considering interactions of variables that cut across multiple levels. This view makes the task of research and practice much more difficult because it requires that multiple variables be assessed and then integrated and interpreted" (p. 1043). As the present chapter has described, a number of factors will influence the variables to be included in such an assessment. These include factors common to addictive behaviors, those specific to a given addictive experience, the particular response system under consideration, the degree of thoroughness required, the phase of the addictive disorder, and the stage of the change process. Within this context, assessment is seen as the initial step in a longer-range therapeutic process. The hope is that the clinician, both through motivating the client's commitment to change and through reaching clinical decisions based on assessment, will facilitate the individual's move-ment into an active stage of change. It is also the clinician's task both to assess and to help maintain the desired behavior change.

## Acknowledgments

General institutional support for the preparation of this chapter was provided in part by the Veterans Administration Medical Center, Seattle, and the Addictive Behaviors Research Center, Department of Psychology, University of Washington. I would particularly like to thank Ingrid Meyer for assisting in the word processing of the manuscript.

## References

Abrams, D. B., Niaura, R. S., Carey, K. B., Monti, P. M., & Binkoff, J. A. (1986). Understand-ing relapse and recovery in alcohol abuse. *Annals of Behavioral Medicine, 8,* 27-32.

Abramson, L. Y., Seligman, M. E. P., & Teasdale, J. (1978). Learned helplessness in humans: Critique and reformulation. *Journal of Abnormal Psychology, 87,* 49-74.

Adesso, V. J. (1985). Cognitive factors in alcohol and drug use. In M. Galizio & S. A. Maisto (Eds.), *Determinants of substance abuse: Biological, psychological, and environmental factors* (pp. 179-208). New York: Plenum Press.

Allen, M. H., & Frances, R. J. (1986). Varieties of psychopathology found in patients with addictive disorders: A review. In R. E. Meyer (Ed.), *Psychopathology and addictive disorders* (pp. 17-38). New York: Guilford Press.

American Psychiatric Association. (1980). *Diagnostic and statistical manual of mental disor-ders* (3rd ed.). Washington, DC: Author.

Appel, C.-P. (1986). From contemplation to determination: Contributions from cognitive psychology. In W. R. Miller & N. Heather (Eds.), *Treating addictive behaviors: Processes of change* (pp. 59-89). New York: Plenum Press.

Azrin, N. H., Sisson, R. W., Meyers, R., & Godley, M. (1982). Alcoholism treatment by disulfiram and community reinforcement therapy. *Journal of Behavior Therapy and Experimental Psychiatry, 13,* 105-112.

Baer, J. S., Holt, C. S., & Lichtenstein, E. (1986). Self-efficacy and smoking reexamined: Construct validity and clinical utility. *Journal of Consulting and Clinical Psychology, 54,* 846-852.

Bandura, A. (1977). Self-efficacy: Toward a unifying theory of behavioral change. *Psychological Review, 84,* 191-215.

Billings, A. G., & Moos, R. H. (1983). Psychosocial processes of recovery among alcoholics and their families: Implications for clinicians and program evaluators. *Addictive Behaviors, 8,* 205-218.

Boyd, J. H., Weissman, M. M., Thompson, W. D., & Myers, J. K. (1983). Different definitions of alcoholism: I. Impact of seven definitions on prevalence rates in a community survey. *American Journal of Psychiatry, 140,* 1309-1313.

Brown, S. A., Goldman, M. S., Inn, A., & Anderson, L. R. (1980). Expectations of reinforce-ment from alcohol: Their domain and relation to drinking patterns. *Journal of Consult-ing and Clinical Psychology, 48,* 419-426.

Brownell, K. D. (1982). The addictive disorders. In C. M. Franks, G. T. Wilson, P. C. Kendall, & K. D. Brownell, *Annual review of behavior therapy: Theory and practice* (Vol. 8, pp. 208-272). New York: Guilford Press.

Brownell, K. D., Marlatt, G. A., Lichtenstein, E., & Wilson, G. T. (1986). Understanding and preventing relapse. *American Psychologist, 41,* 765-782.

Bruhn, J. G., & Phillips, B. V. (1984). Measuring social support: A synthesis of current approaches. *Journal of Behavioral Medicine, 7,* 151-169.

Burglass, M. E., & Shaffer, H. (1984). Diagnosis in the addictions: I. Conceptual problems. *Advances in Alcohol and Substance Abuse, 3,* 19-34.

Caddy, G. R., & Block, T. (1985). Individual differences in response to treatment. In M. Galizio & S. A. Maisto (Eds.), *Determinants of substance abuse: Biological, psychological, and environmental factors* (pp. 317-362). New York: Plenum Press.

Caetano, R. (1985). Two versions of dependence: DSM-III and the alcohol dependence syndrome. *Drug and Alcohol Dependence, 15,* 81-103.

Carroll, J. F. X. (1986). Treating multiple substance abuse clients. In M. Galanter (Ed.), *Recent developments in alcoholism* (Vol. 4, pp. 85-103). New York: Plenum Press.

Chaney, E. F., & Roszell, D. K. (1985). Coping in opiate addicts maintained on methadone. In S. Shiffman & T. A. Wills (Eds.), *Coping and substance use* (pp. 267-293). New York: Academic Press.

Chaney, E. F., Roszell, D. K., & Cummings, C. (1982). Relapse in opiate addicts: A behavioral analysis. *Addictive Behaviors, 7,* 291-297.

Clayton, R. P. (1986). Multiple drug use: Epidemiology, correlates, and consequences. In M. Galanter (Ed.), *Recent developments in alcoholism* (Vol. 4, pp. 7-38). New York: Plenum Press.

Cone, J. D., & Hawkins, R. P. (1977). Introduction. In J. D. Cone & R. P. Hawkins (Eds.), *Behavioral assessment: New directions in clinical psychology* (pp. xiii-xxiv). New York: Brunner/Mazel.

Connors, G. J., O'Farrell, T. J., Cutter, H. S. G., & Thompson, D. G. (1986). Alcohol expectancies among male alcoholics, problem drinkers, and nonproblem drinkers. *Alcoholism: Clinical and Experimental Research, 10,* 667-671.

Coyne, J. C., & DeLongis, A. (1986). Going beyond social support: The role of social relationships in adaptation. *Journal of Consulting and Clinical Psychology, 54,* 454-460.

Cronkite, R. C., & Moos, R. H. (1978). Evaluating alcoholism treatment programs: An integrated approach. *Journal of Consulting and Clinical Psychology, 46,* 1105-1119.

Cronkite, R. C., & Moos, R. H. (1980). Determinants of the posttreatment functioning of alcoholic patients: A conceptual framework. *Journal of Consulting and Clinical Psychology, 48,* 305-316.

Cummings, C., Gordon, J. R., & Marlatt, G. A. (1980). Relapse: Prevention and prediction. In W. R. Miller (Ed.), *The addictive behaviors: Treatment of alcoholism, drug abuse, smoking, and obesity* (pp. 291-321). New York: Pergamon Press.

DeNelsky, G. Y., & Boat, B. W. (1986). A coping skills model of psychological diagnosis and treatment. *Professional Psychology: Research and Practice, 17,* 322-330.

DiClemente, C. C., & Prochaska, J. O. (1985). Processes and stages of self-change: Coping and competence in smoking behavior change. In S. Shiffman & T. A. Wills (Eds.), *Coping and substance use* (pp. 319-343). New York: Academic Press.

Donegan, D. H., Rodin, J., O'Brien, C. P., & Solomon, R. L. (1983). A learning-theory approach to commonalities. In P. K. Levison, D. R. Gerstein, & D. R. Maloff (Eds.), *Commonalities in substance abuse and habitual behavior* (pp. 111-156). Lexington, MA: Lexington Books.

Donovan, D. M., & Chaney, E. F. (1985). Alcoholic relapse prevention and intervention: Models and methods. In G. A. Marlatt & J. R. Gordon (Eds.), *Relapse prevention: Maintenance strategies in the treatment of addictive behaviors* (pp. 351-416). New York: Guilford Press.

Donovan, D. M., Kivlahan, D. R., & Walker, R. D. (1986). Alcoholic subtypes based on multiple assessment domains: Validation against treatment outcome. In M. Galanter

(Ed.), *Recent developments in alcoholism* (Vol. 4, pp. 207-222). New York: Plenum Press.

Donovan, D. M., Kivlahan, D. R., Walker, R. D., & Umlauf, R. (1985). Derivation and validation of neuropsychological clusters among male alcoholics. *Journal of Studies on Alcohol, 46,* 205-211.

Donovan, D. M., & Marlatt, G. A. (1980). Assessment of expectancies and behaviors associated with alcohol consumption: A cognitive-behavioral approach. *Journal of Studies on Alcohol, 41,* 1153-1185.

Donovan, D. M., & O'Leary, M. R. (1983). Control orientation, drinking behavior and alcoholism. In H. M. Lefcourt (Ed.), *Research with the locus of control construct: Vol. 2. Development and social problems* (pp. 107-153). New York: Academic Press.

Donovan, D. M., Walker, R. D., & Kivlahan, D. R. (1987). Recovery and remediation of neuropsychological functions: Implications for alcoholism rehabilitation process and outcome. In O. A. Parsons, N. Butters, & P. E. Nathan (Eds.), *Neuropsychology of alcoholism: Implications for diagnosis and treatment* (pp. 339-360). New York: Guilford Press.

Edwards, G. (1986). The alcohol dependence syndrome: A concept as stimulus to inquiry. *British Journal of Addiction, 81,* 171-183.

Edwards, G., & Gross, M. M. (1976). Alcohol dependence: Provisional description of a clinical syndrome. *British Medical Journal, i,* 1058-1061.

Edwards, G., Orford, J., Egert, S., Guthrie, S., Hawker, A., Hensmen, C., Mitcheson, M., Oppenheimer, E., & Taylor, C. (1977). Alcoholism: A controlled trial of "treatment" and "advice." *Journal of Studies on Alcohol, 38,* 1004-1031.

Einstein, S. (1975). *Beyond drugs.* New York: Pergamon Press.

Engel, G. L. (1977). The need for a new medical model: A challenge for biomedicine. *Science, 196,* 129-136.

Epstein, L. H. (1976). Psychophysiological measurement in assessment. In M. Hersen & A. S. Bellack (Eds.), *Behavioral assessment: A practical handbook* (pp. 207-232). New York: Pergamon Press.

Falk, J. L., Dews, P. B., & Schuster, C. R. (1983). Commonalities in the environmental control of behavior. In P. K. Levison, D. R. Gerstein, & D. R. Maloff (Eds.), *Commonalities in substance abuse and habitual behavior* (pp. 47-110). Lexington, MA: Lexington Books.

Finney, J. W., & Moos, R. H. (1986). Matching patients with treatments: Conceptual and methodological issues. *Journal of Studies on Alcohol, 47,* 122-134.

Galizio, M., & Maisto, S. A. (1985). Toward a biopsychosocial theory of substance abuse. In M. Galizio & S. A. Maisto (Eds.), *Determinants of substance abuse: Biological, psychological, and environmental* (pp. 425-429). New York: Plenum Press.

Gannon, L. (1984). Awareness of internal cues and concordance among verbal, behavioral, and physiological systems in dysfunction. *Psychological Reports, 54,* 631-650.

Gibbs, L., & Flanagan, J. (1977). Prognostic indicators of alcoholism treatment outcome. *International Journal of the Addictions, 12,* 1097-1141.

Glaser, F. B. (1980). Anybody got a match? Treatment research and the matching hypothesis. In G. Edwards & M. Grant (Eds.), *Alcoholism treatment in transition* (pp. 178-196). Baltimore: University Park Press.

Glynn, S. M., & Ruderman, A. J. (1986). The development and validation of an eating self-efficacy scale. *Cognitive Therapy and Research, 10,* 403-420.

Goodwin, D. W. (1984). Studies of familial alcoholism: A review. *Journal of Clinical Psychiatry, 45* (12, Sec. 2), 14-17.

Goodwin, D. W. (1986). Heredity and alcoholism. *Annals of Behavioral Medicine, 8,* 3-6.

Haynes, S. N. (1983). Behavioral assessment. In M. Hersen, A. E. Kazdin, & A. S. Bellack (Eds.), *The clinical psychology handbook* (pp. 397-425). New York: Pergamon Press.

Hodgson, R., & Miller, P. (1982). *Self-watching. Addictions, habits, compulsions: What to do about them.* New York: Facts on File.

Hodgson, R. J., Rankin, H. J., & Stockwell, T. (1979). Alcohol dependence and the priming effect. *Behaviour Research and Therapy, 17,* 379–387.

Holt, S., Skinner, H. A., & Israel, Y. (1981). Early identification of alcohol abuse: 2. Clinical and laboratory indicators. *Canadian Medical Association Journal, 124,* 1279–1295.

Hunt, W. A., Barnett, L. W., & Branch, L. G. (1971). Relapse rates in addiction programs. *Journal of Clinical Psychology, 27,* 455–456.

Istvan, J., & Matarazzo, J. D. (1984). Tobacco, alcohol, and caffeine use: A review of their interrelationships. *Psychological Bulletin, 95,* 301–326.

Ito, J. R., & Donovan, D. M. (1986). Aftercare in alcoholism treatment: A review. In W. R. Miller & N. Heather (Eds.), *Treating addictive behaviors: Processes of change* (pp. 435–456). New York: Plenum Press.

Jaffe, J. H. (1985). Drug addiction and drug abuse. In L. Goodman & L. Gilman (Eds.), *The pharmacological basis of therapeutics* (pp. 532–581). New York: Macmillan.

Jeffrey, D. B. (1975). Treatment evaluation issues in research on addictive behaviors. *Addictive Behaviors, 1,* 23–36.

Jellinek, E. M. (1960). *The disease concept of alcoholism.* New Brunswick, NJ: Hillhouse Press.

Jolly, P. A., Fleece, E. L., Galanos, A. N., Milby, J. B., & Ritter, S. C. (1983). DSM-III: Alcohol abuse and alcohol dependence; Inter-rater diagnostic reliability. *Addictive Behaviors, 8,* 201–204.

Kanfer, F. H. (1986). Implications of a self-regulation model of therapy for treatment of addictive behaviors. In W. R. Miller & N. Heather (Eds.), *Treating addictive behaviors: Processes of change* (pp. 29–47). New York: Plenum Press.

Kanfer, F. H., & Saslow, G. (1969). Behavioral diagnosis. In C. M. Franks (Ed.), *Behavior therapy: Appraisal and status* (pp. 417–444). New York: McGraw-Hill.

Kaplan, R. F., Cooney, N. L., Baker, L. H., Gillespie, R. A., Meyer, R. E., & Pomerleau, O. F. (1985). Reactivity to alcohol-related cues: Physiological and subjective responses in alcoholics and nonproblem drinkers. *Journal of Studies on Alcohol, 46,* 267–272.

Kaplan, R. F., Meyer, R. E., & Virgilio, L. M. (1984). Physiological reactivity to alcohol cues and the awareness of an alcohol effect in a double-blind placebo design. *British Journal of Addictions, 79,* 439–442.

Kauffman, J. F., Shaffer, H., & Burglass, M. E. (1985). The biological basics: Drugs and their effects. In T. E. Bratter & G. G. Forrest (Eds.), *Alcoholism and substance abuse: Strategies for clinical intervention* (pp. 107–136). New York: Free Press.

Kendall, P. C. (1982). Behavioral assessment and methodology. In C. M. Franks, G. T. Wilson, P. C. Kendall, & K. D. Brownell, *Annual review of behavior therapy: Theory and practice* (Vol. 8, pp. 39–81). New York: Guilford Press.

Kissin, B., & Hanson, M. (1982). The bio-psycho-social perspective in alcoholism. In J. Solomon (Ed.), *Alcoholism and clinical psychiatry* (pp. 1–19). New York: Plenum Press.

Kratochwill, T. R., & Mace, F. C. (1983). Experimental research in clinical psychology. In M. Hersen, A. E. Kazdin, & A. S. Bellack (Eds.), *The clinical psychology handbook* (pp. 197–221). New York: Pergamon Press.

Krieg, J-C., Backmund, H., & Pirke, K.-M. (1986). Endocrine, metabolic, and brain morphological abnormalities in patients with eating disorders. *International Journal of Eating Disorders, 5,* 999–1006.

Lang, P. J. (1977). Physiological assessment of anxiety and fear. In J. D. Cone & R. P. Hawkins (Eds.), *Behavioral assessment: New directions in clinical psychology* (pp. 178–195). New York: Brunner/Mazel.

Lazarus, R. S. (1966). *Psychological stress and the coping process.* New York: McGraw-Hill.

Leonard, K. E., Bromet, E. J., Parkinson, D. K., & Day, N. (1984). Agreement among Feighner, RDC, and DSM-III criteria for alcoholism. *Addictive Behaviors, 9,* 319-322.

Lettieri, D. J., Sayers, M., & Pearson, H. W. (Eds.). (1980). *Theories on drug abuse: Selected contemporary perspectives* (NIDA Research Monograph No. 30). Washington, DC: U.S. Government Printing Office.

Lindesmith, A. R. (1968). *Addiction and opiates.* Chicago: Aldine.

Litman, G. K. (1980). Relapse in alcoholism: Traditional and current approaches. In G. Edwards & M. Grant (Eds.), *Alcoholism treatment in transition* (pp. 294-303). Baltimore: University Park Press.

Litman, G. K. (1986). Alcoholism survival: The prevention of relapse. In W. R. Miller & N. Heather (Eds.), *Treating addictive behaviors: Processes of change* (pp. 391-405). New York: Plenum Press.

Litman, G. K., Eiser, J. R., Rawson, N. S. B., & Oppenheim, A. N. (1979). Towards a typology of relapse: Differences in relapse and coping behaviours between alcoholic relapsers and survivors. *Behaviour Research and Therapy, 17,* 89-94.

Litman, G. K., Stapleton, J., Oppenheim, A. N., Peleg, M., & Jackson, P. (1983). Situations related to alcoholism relapse. *British Journal of Addiction, 78,* 381-389.

Litman, G. K., Stapleton, J., Oppenheim, A. N., Peleg, M., & Jackson, P. (1984). The relationship between coping behaviours, their effectiveness and alcoholism relapse and survival. *British Journal of Addiction, 79,* 283-291.

Ludwig, A. M. (1985). Cognitive processes associated with "spontaneous" recovery from alcoholism. *Journal of Studies on Alcohol, 46,* 53-58.

Ludwig, A. M., & Wikler, A. (1974). "Craving" and relapse to drink. *Quarterly Journal of Studies on Alcohol, 35,* 108-130.

Maisto, S. A., & McCollam, J. B. (1980). The use of multiple measures of life health to assess alcohol treatment outcome: A review and critique. In L. C. Sobell, M. B. Sobell, & E. Ward (Eds), *Evaluating alcohol and drug abuse treatment effectiveness: Recent advances* (pp. 15-76). New York: Pergamon Press.

Marlatt, G. A., & Donovan, D. M. (1981). Alcoholism and drug dependence: Cognitive social-learning factors in addictive behaviors. In W. E. Craighead, A. E. Kazdin, & M. J. Mahoney (Eds.), *Behavior modification: Principles, issues, and applications* (2nd ed., pp. 264-285). Boston: Houghton Mifflin.

Marlatt, G. A., & Donovan, D. M. (1982). Behavioral psychology approaches to alcoholism. In E. M. Pattison & E. Kaufman (Eds.), *Encyclopedic handbook of alcoholism* (pp. 560-576). New York: Gardner Press.

Marlatt, G. A., & George, W. H. (1984). Relapse prevention: Introduction and overview of the model. *British Journal of Addiction, 79,* 261-273.

Marlatt, G. A., & Gordon, J. R. (Eds.). (1985). *Relapse prevention: Maintenance strategies in the treatment of addictive behaviors.* New York: Guilford Press.

Mash, E. J., & Terdal, L. G. (1974). Behavior therapy assessment: Diagnosis, design and evaluation. *Psychological Reports, 35,* 587-601.

Matarazzo, J. D., & Carmody, T. P. (1983). Health psychology. In M. Hersen, A. E. Kazdin, & A. S. Bellack (Eds.), *The clinical psychology handbook* (pp. 657-682). New York: Pergamon Press.

McCrady, B. S., & Sher, K. J. (1983). Alcoholism treatment approaches: Patient variables, treatment variables. In B. Tabakoff, P. B. Sutker, & C. L. Randall (Eds.), *Medical and social aspects of alcohol abuse* (pp. 309-373). New York: Plenum Press.

McLellan, A. T. (1986). "Psychiatric severity" as a predictor of outcome from substance abuse treatment. In R. E. Meyer (Ed.), *Psychopathology and addictive disorders* (pp. 97-139). New York: Guilford Press.

McLellan, A. T., Luborsky, L., Woody, G. E., O'Brien, C. P., & Druley, K. A. (1983). Predicting response to alcohol and drug abuse treatments: Role of psychiatric severity. *Archives of General Psychiatry, 40,* 620–625.

McLellan, A. T., O'Brien, C. P., Kron, R., Alterman, A. I., & Druley, K. A. (1980). Matching substance abuse patients to appropriate treatment: A conceptual and methodological approach. *Drug and Alcohol Dependence, 5,* 189–195.

McLellan, A. T., Woody, G. E., Luborsky, L., O'Brien, C. P., & Druley, K. A. (1983). Increased effectiveness of substance abuse treatment: A prospective study of patient–treatment "matching." *Journal of Nervous and Mental Disease, 171,* 597–605.

Mermelstein, R., Cohen, S., Lichtenstein, E., Baer, J. S., Kamarck, T. (1986). Social support and smoking cessation and maintenance. *Journal of Consulting and Clinical Psychology, 54,* 447–453.

Meyer, R. E. (1986). Psychobiology and the treatment of drug dependence: The biobehavioral interface. *American Journal of Drug and Alcohol Abuse, 12,* 223–234.

Miller, P. M. (1979). Interactions among addictive behaviors. *British Journal of Addiction, 74,* 211–212.

Miller, P. M. (1980). Theoretical and practical issues in substance abuse assessment and treatment. In W. R. Miller (Ed.), *The addictive behaviors: Treatment of alcoholism, drug abuse, smoking, and obesity* (pp. 265–290). New York: Pergamon Press.

Miller, W. R. (1980). The addictive behaviors. In W. R. Miller (Ed.), *The addictive behaviors: Treatment of alcoholism, drug abuse, smoking, and obesity* (pp. 3–7). New York: Pergamon Press.

Miller, W. R. (1983). Motivational interviewing with problem drinkers. *Behavioural Psychotherapy, 11,* 147–172.

Miller, W. R. (1985). Motivation for treatment: A review with special emphasis on alcoholism. *Psychological Bulletin, 98,* 84–107.

Miller, W. R., & Heather, N. (Eds.). (1986). *Treating addictive behaviors: Processes of change.* New York: Plenum Press.

Miller, W. R., & Hester, R. K. (1986a). The effectiveness of alcoholism treatment: What research reveals. In W. R. Miller & N. Heather (Eds.), *Treating addictive behaviors: Processes of change* (pp. 121–174). New York: Plenum Press.

Miller, W. R., & Hester, R. K. (1986b). Matching problem drinkers with optimal treatments. In W. R. Miller & N. Heather (Eds), *Treating addictive behaviors: Processes of change* (pp. 175–203). New York: Plenum Press.

Miller, W. R., & Taylor, C. A. (1980). Relative effectiveness of bibliotherapy, individual, and group self-control training in the treatment of problem drinkers. *Addictive Behaviors, 15,* 13–24.

Mintz, J., Boyd, G., Rose, J. E., Charuvasta, V. C., & Jarvik, M. D. (1985). Alcohol increases cigarette smoking: A laboratory demonstration. *Addictive Behaviors, 10,* 203–208.

Mintz, J., & Kiesler, D. J. (1982). Individualized measures of psychotherapy outcome. In P. C. Kendall & J. N. Butcher (Eds.), *Handbook of research methods in clinical psychology* (pp. 491–534). New York: Wiley.

Mischel, W. A. (1981). A cognitive–social learning approach to assessment. In T. V. Merluzzi, C. R. Glass, & M. Genest (Eds.), *Cognitive assessment* (pp. 479–502). New York: Guilford Press.

Moos, R. H., & Finney, J. W. (1983). The expanding scope of alcoholism treatment evaluation. *American Psychologist, 38,* 1036–1044.

Moos, R. H., & Finney, J. W. (1986). The treatment setting in alcoholism program evaluations. *Annals of Behavioral Medicine, 8,* 33–39.

Moos, R. H., Finney, J. W., & Gamble, W. (1982). The process of recovery from alcoholism: II. Comparing spouses of alcoholic patients and matched community controls. *Journal of Studies on Alcohol, 43,* 888–909.

Morganstern, K. P. (1976). Behavioral interviewing: The initial stages of assessment. In M.

Hersen & A. S. Bellack (Eds.), *Behavioral assessment: A practical handbook* (pp. 51-76). New York: Pergamon Press.

Nathan, P. E. (1980). Etiology and process in the addictive behaviors. In W. R. Miller (Ed.), *The addictive behaviors: Treatment of alcoholism, drug abuse, smoking, and obesity* (pp. 241-263). New York: Pergamon Press.

Nathan, P. E., & Lansky, D. (1978). Common methodological problems in research on the addictions. *Journal of Consulting and Clinical Psychology, 46,* 713-726.

National Council on Alcoholism (Criteria Committee). (1972). Criteria for the diagnosis of alcoholism. *American Journal of Psychiatry, 129,* 127-135.

O'Farrell, T. J., Connors, G. J., & Upper, D. (1983). Addictive behaviors among hospitalized psychiatric patients. *Addictive Behaviors, 8,* 329-333.

O'Leary, D. E., O'Leary, M. R., & Donovan, D. M. (1976). Social skill acquisition and psychosocial development of alcoholics: A review. *Addictive Behaviors, 1,* 111-120.

Orford, J. (1985). *Excessive appetites: A psychological view of addictions.* New York: Wiley.

Pattison, E. M. (1981). The NCA diagnostic criteria: 10 years later. In R. E. Meyer, T. F. Babor, B. C. Glueck, J. H. Jaffe, J. E. O'Brien, & J. R. Stabenau (Eds.), *Evaluation of the alcoholic: Implications for research, theory, and treatment* (NIAAA Research Monograph No. 5, pp. 3-24). Washington, DC: U.S. Government Printing Office.

Pattison, E. M., Sobell, M. B., & Sobell, L. C. (1977). Toward an emergent model. In E. M. Pattison, M. B. Sobell, & L. C. Sobell (Eds.), *Emerging concepts of alcohol dependence* (pp. 189-211). New York: Springer.

Peele, S. (Ed.). (1985). *The meaning of addiction: A compulsive experience and its interpretation.* Lexington, MA: Lexington Books.

Peele, S., & Alexander, B. K. (1985). Theories of addiction. In S. Peele (Ed.), *The meaning of addiction: Compulsive meaning and its interpretation* (pp. 47-72). Lexington, MA: Lexington Books.

Perri, M. G. (1985). Self-change strategies for the control of smoking, obesity, and problem drinking. In S. Shiffman & T. A. Wills (Eds.), *Coping and substance use* (pp. 295-317). New York: Academic Press.

Pollock, V. E., Teasdale, T. W., Gabrielli, W. F., & Knop, J. (1986). Subjective and objective measures of response to alcohol among young men at risk for alcoholism. *Journal of Studies on Alcohol, 47,* 297-304.

Pomerleau, O. F. (1982). A discourse on behavioral medicine: Currrent status and future trends. *Journal of Consulting and Clinical Psychology, 50,* 1030-1039.

Prochaska, J. O., & DiClemente, C. C. (1985). Common processes of self-change in smoking, weight control, and psychological distress. In S. Shiffman & T. A. Wills (1985). *Coping and substance use* (pp. 345-363). New York: Academic Press.

Prochaska, J. O., & DiClemente, C. C. (1986). Toward a comprehensive model of change. In W. R. Miller & N. Heather (Eds.), *Treating addictive behaviors: Processes of change* (pp. 3-27). New York: Plenum Press.

Rankin, H., Hodgson, R., & Stockwell, T. (1980). The behavioral measurement of alcohol dependence. *British Journal of Addiction, 75,* 43-47.

Ritson, B. (1986). Merits of simple intervention. In W. R. Miller & N. Heather (Eds.), *Treating addictive behaviors: Processes of change* (pp. 375-387). New York: Plenum Press.

Robertson, I. (1986). Cognitive processes in addictive behavior change. In W. R. Miller & N. Heather (Eds.). *Treating addictive behaviors: Processes of change* (pp. 319-329). New York: Plenum Press.

Rodin, J., Maloff, D., & Becker, H. S. (1984). Self-control: The role of environmental and self-generated cues. In P. K. Levison (Ed.), *Substance abuse, habitual behavior, and self-control* (pp. 9-47). Boulder, CO: Westview Press.

Rollnick, S., & Heather, N. (1982). The application of Bandura's self-efficacy theory to abstinence oriented alcoholism treatment. *Addictive Behaviors, 7,* 243-250.

Rounsaville, B. J., Spitzer, R. L., & Williams, J. B. W. (1986). Proposed changes in DSM-III Substance Use Disorders: Description and rationale. *American Journal of Psychiatry, 143,* 463–468.

Sanchez-Craig, M. (1976). Cognitive and behavioral coping strategies in the reappraisal of stressful social situations. *Journal of Counseling Psychology, 23,* 7–12.

Schacter, S. (1982). Recidivism and self-cure of smoking and obesity. *American Psychologist, 37,* 436–444.

Schneiderman, N., & Tapp, J. T. (Eds.). (1985). *Behavioral medicine: The biopsychosocial approach.* Hillsdale, NJ: Erlbaum.

Schuckit, M. A. (1984). Subjective responses to alcohol in sons of alcoholics and controls. *Archives of General Psychiatry, 41,* 879–884.

Schuckit, M. A., Zisook, S., & Mortola, J. (1985). Clinical implications of DSM-III diagnosis of alcohol abuse and alcohol dependence. *American Journal of Psychiatry, 142,* 1403–1408.

Schwartz, G. E. (1982). Testing the biopsychosocial model: The ultimate challenge facing behavioral medicine. *Journal of Consulting and Clinical Psychology, 50,* 1040–1053.

Shaffer, H., & Kauffman, J. (1985). The clinical assessment and diagnosis of addiction: Hypothesis testing. In T. E. Bratter & G. G. Forrest (Eds.), *Alcoholism and substance abuse: Strategies for clinical intervention* (pp. 225–258). New York: Free Press.

Shaffer, H. J., & Milkman, H. B. (1985). Introduction: Crisis and conflict in the addictions. In H. B. Milkman & H. J. Shaffer (Eds.), *The addictions: Multidisciplinary perspectives and treatments* (pp. ix–xviii). Lexington, MA: Lexington Books.

Shaffer, H. J., & Neuhaus, Jr., C. (1985). Testing hypotheses: An approach for the assessment of addictive behaviors. In H. B. Milkman & H. J. Shaffer (Eds.), *The addictions: Multidisciplinary perspectives and treatments* (pp. 87–103). Lexington, MA: Lexington Books.

Siegel, S. (1979). The role of conditioning in drug tolerance and addiction. In J. D. Keehen (Ed.), *Psychopathology in animals: Research and treatment implications* (pp. 143–168). New York: Academic Press.

Skinner, H. A. (1981). Assessment of alcohol problems: Basic principles, critical issues, and future trends. In Y. Israel, F. B. Glaser, H. Kalant, R. E. Popham, W. Schmidt, & R. G. Smart (Eds.), *Research advances in alcohol and drug problems* (Vol. 6, pp. 319–369). New York: Plenum Press.

Skinner, H. A., & Goldberg, A. E. (1986). Evidence for a drug dependence syndrome among narcotic users. *British Journal of Addiction, 81,* 479–484.

Smith, D. E. (1986). Cocaine–alcohol abuse: Epidemiological, diagnostic, and treatment considerations. *Journal of Psychoactive Drugs, 18,* 117–130.

Sobell, M. B., & Sobell, L. C. (1976). Assessment of addictive behavior. In M. Hersen & A. S. Bellack (Eds.), *Behavioral assessment: A practical handbook* (pp. 305–336). New York: Pergamon Press.

Sobell, M. B., Sobell, L. C., & Sheahan, D. B. (1976). Functional analysis of drinking problems as an aid in developing individual treatment strategies. *Addictive Behaviors, 1,* 127–132.

Solomon, R. L. (1977). An opponent-process theory of acquired motivation: The affective dynamics of addictions. In J. R. Maser & M. E. P. Seligman (Eds.), *Psychopathology: Experimental models* (pp. 66–103). San Francisco: W. H. Freeman.

Stall, R., & Biernacki, P. (1986). Spontaneous remission from the problematic use of substances: An inductive model derived from a comparative analysis of the alcohol, opiate, tobacco, and food/obesity literatures. *International Journal of the Addictions, 21,* 1–23.

Stockwell, T., Hodgson, R., Rankin, H., & Taylor, C. (1982). Alcohol dependence, beliefs, and the priming effect. *Behaviour Research and Therapy, 20,* 513–522.

Stuart, R. B. (1970). *Trick or treatment: How and when psychotherapy fails.* Champaign, IL: Research Press.

Sutherland, G., Edwards, G., Taylor, C., Phillips, G., Gossop, M., & Brady, R. (1986). The measurement of opiate dependence. *British Journal of Addiction, 81,* 485–494.

Tarter, R. E., Alterman, A. I., & Edwards, K. L. (1984). Alcoholic denial: A biopsychological interpretation. *Journal of Studies on Alcohol, 45,* 214–218.

Tarter, R. E., Alterman, A. I., & Edwards, K. L. (1985). Vulnerability to alcoholism in men: A behavior–genetic perspective. *Journal of Studies on Alcohol, 46,* 329–356.

Tarter, R. E., & Edwards, K. L. (1986). Antecedents to alcoholism: Implications for prevention and treatment. *Behavior Therapy, 17,* 346–361.

Tarter, R. E., Hegedus, A. M., Goldstein, G., Shelly, C., & Alterman, A. I. (1984). Adolescent sons of alcoholics: Neuropsychological and personality characteristics. *Alcoholism: Clinical and Experimental Research, 8,* 216–222.

Thoits, P. A. (1986). Social support as coping assistance. *Journal of Consulting and Clinical Psychology, 54,* 416–423.

Tiffany, S. T., & Baker, T. B. (1986). Tolerance to alcohol: Psychological models and their application to alcoholism. *Annals of Behavioral Medicine, 8,* 7–12.

Tuchfeld, B. S. (1981). Spontaneous remission in alcoholics: Empirical observations and theoretical implications. *Journal of Studies on Alcohol, 42,* 626–641.

Tucker, J. A., Vuchinich, R. E., & Harris, C. V. (1985). Determinants of substance abuse relapse. In M. Galizio & S. A. Maisto (Eds.), *Determinants of substance abuse: Biological, psychological, and environmental factors* (pp. 383–421). New York: Plenum Press.

Van Hasselt, V. B., Hersen, M., & Milliones, J. (1978). Social skills training for alcoholics and drug addicts: A review. *Addictive Behaviors, 3,* 221–233.

Vannicelli, M., Gingerich, S., & Ryback, R. (1983). Family problems related to treatment and outcome of alcoholic patients. *British Journal of Addiction, 78,* 193–204.

Walker, R. D., Donovan, D. M., Kivlahan, D. R., & O'Leary, M. R. (1983). Length of stay, neuropsychological performance, and aftercare: Influences on alcohol treatment outcome. *Journal of Consulting and Clinical Psychology, 51,* 900–911.

Wallace, J. (1977). Alcoholism from the inside out: A phenomenological analysis. In N. J. Estes & M. Heinemann (Eds.), *Alcoholism: Development, consequences and interventions* (pp. 3–14). St. Louis: C. V. Mosby.

Wallace, J. (1985). Predicting the onset of compulsive drinking in alcoholics: A biopsychosocial model. *Alcohol, 2,* 589–595.

Wanberg, K. W., & Horn, J. L. (1983). Assessment of alcohol use with multidimensional concepts and measures. *American Psychologist, 38,* 1055–1069.

Wanberg, K. W., Horn, J. L., & Foster, F. M. (1977). A differential assessment model for alcoholism: The scales of the Alcohol Use Inventory. *Journal of Studies on Alcohol, 38,* 512–543.

Wikler, A. (1965). Conditioning factors in opiate addiction and relapse. In D. I. Wilner & G. G. Kassebaum (Eds.), *Narcotics* (pp. 85–100). New York: McGraw-Hill.

Wills, T. A., & Shiffman, S. (1985). Coping and substance use: A conceptual framework. In S. Shiffman & T. A. Wills (Eds.), *Coping and substance use* (pp. 3–24). New York: Academic Press.

Woody, G. E., McLellan, A. T., Luborsky, L., & O'Brien, C. P. (1985). Sociopathy and psychotherapy outcome. *Archives of General Psychiatry, 42,* 1081–1086.

Wray, I., & Dickerson, M. G. (1981). Cessation of high frequency gambling and "withdrawal" symptoms. *British Journal of Addiction, 76,* 401–405.

Yates, A. J., & Thain, J. (1985). Self-efficacy as a predictor of relapse following voluntary cessation of smoking. *Addictive Behaviors, 10,* 291–298.

Zeiner, A. R., Stantis, T., Spurgeon, M., & Nichols, N. (1985). Treatment of alcoholism and concurrent drugs of abuse. *Alcohol, 2,* 555–559.

Zinberg, N. E. (1984). *Drug, set, setting: The basis for controlled intoxicant use.* New Haven, CT: Yale University Press.

Zucker, R. A., & Gomberg, E. S. L. (1986). Etiology of alcoholism reconsidered: The case for a biopsychosocial process. *American Psychologist, 41,* 783–793.

# II

# DRINKING BEHAVIOR AND ALCOHOL DEPENDENCE

# 2

# BEHAVIORAL ASSESSMENT

RUDY E. VUCHINICH
JALIE A. TUCKER
LYNN M. HARLLEE
*University of Florida*

## Introduction

This chapter is about the behavioral assessment of alcohol dependence. The general orienting assumptions and strategies of behavioral assessment are discussed in Chapter 1 of this volume and in, for example, Barlow (1981) and Hersen and Bellack (1981). As with other orientations, the behavioral assessment of alcohol dependence must address two general questions: (1) What aspects of the client's behavior and environment do we select to measure, given current knowledge of the determinants of the problem behavior (i.e., drinking)? (2) What procedures do we use to measure these selected characteristics, bearing in mind issues of reliability and accuracy and their practicality in clinical settings?

An adequate answer to the first question depends on an adequate theory of alcohol abuse. Unfortunately, a generally accepted characterization of the variables that produce and maintain alcohol abuse remains elusive. Thus, as is often the case, clinicians must contend with managing the treatment of difficult problems while lacking complete guidance from the scientific community. However, significant advances have occurred in our understanding of the determinants of alcohol problems (e.g., Nathan, Marlatt, & Loberg, 1978; Pattison, Sobell, & Sobell, 1977; Marlatt & Gordon, 1985), and much of this increased knowledge has been due to an application of the principles of behavioral psychology to an analysis of alcohol abuse. Although the approach contains some differing viewpoints, it generally maintains that abusive drinking is best viewed as emerging out of the individual's commerce with his or her environment, rather than as emerging out of intrapsychic dynamisms, stable personality traits, or somatic disease states. This conceptual orientation toward the determinants of alcohol abuse, coupled with the methodological preferences of behavioral psychology, exerts considerable influence on addressing the question of what is important to measure.

51

Under this view, alcohol consumption is seen as discriminated operant behavior that is, in many cases, emitted in a circumscribed set of environmental contexts and controlled by its consequences. Drinking is amenable to description via a functional analysis aimed at identifying (1) the environments in which the behavior occurs; (2) the amount of consumption and the topography of the drinking response; (3) the consequences of consumption, both positive and negative and immediate and delayed; and (4) contingencies between consumption and access to rewards in major life–health areas such as vocational or marital functioning. This type of analysis is the core method of organization of behavioral assessment data for alcohol problems (M. B. Sobell, Sobell, & Sheahan, 1976) and requires data that represent how a client's drinking changes over time and how it fits into the general scheme of his or her activities, resources, and relationships. Such data are made available through use of the behavioral assessment procedures described in this chapter.

Individual clients differ greatly in each of the four classes of variables relevant to a functional analysis. With respect to the environmental contexts of drinking and amounts consumed, the goal is to identify the conditions surrounding both appropriate and inappropriate drinking. For example, M. B. Sobell *et al.* (1976) mentioned a client who became intoxicated each time he drank except when his wife was present in a well-lit room while he was eating. As another example, a married professional woman treated by one of us often consumed only one or two drinks while preparing dinner at home with her family on weeknights. When away from home at conventions, however, she often became intoxicated at cocktail parties, usually with negative professional consequences. Similar variability exists with respect to the consequences of consumption and the relationships between drinking and functioning in major life–health areas. Like alcohol consumption patterns, the latter two classes of variables are likely to covary with specific environmental circumstances or to be imbedded within complex but stable patterns of behavior.

Identifying the relevant environmental circumstances and describing the behavioral dynamics of a client's drinking problem along these four dimensions allow the clinician to define and prioritize specific problem areas for treatment interventions. For instance, in the second case described above, the client's drinking problem was more closely tied to work- than to family-related events, and disentangling the contingencies between her drinking and professional activities proved essential to treatment progress. For other clients, their vocational functioning may be little affected by drinking, but they may experience disruptions in their marriage or family life. The functional analysis permits these critical distinctions for individual clients and yields an empirical base for devising individualized treatment goals and programs. Moreover, the organization of assessment data in this fashion generates a baseline of behavioral observations relevant to specific problem areas and can be used throughout treatment to evaluate a client's progress.

Answering the second general question (What procedures do we use to assess these selected characteristics?) is more constrained by the practicalities of the clinical situation. The methodological ideal would be direct observation of the variables chosen for assessment. This is impractical as a routine, however; the variables selected to define the problem necessarily occur in the client's natural environment and often require measurement over a long period of time. Because we cannot directly observe the "problem," we must deal with a representation of it, and this representation usually must be generated by the person who has directly observed it—namely, the client. Thus, most behavior assessment procedures for alcohol dependence have relied on self-reports by clients of the variables of interest; as shown in this chapter, a number of procedures of adequate reliability and accuracy have been developed to collect data on important alcohol-related variables. These procedures represent important advances in the assessment of alcohol problems.

## Clinical Applications

### Screening and General Disposition

Most treatment facilities are appropriate only for certain clients (e.g., inpatients, outpatients, residential communities) or treatment phases (e.g., detoxification, outpatient behavior therapy). The clinician usually must first decide whether the client is appropriate for treatment at the clinician's facility. This requires a rapid determination of the client's overall condition, including physical condition and level of alcohol intoxication (Pattison, 1985). A nonphysician mental health professional often makes this determination and refers clients to a medical facility for supervised detoxification, after which he or she may follow them for assessment and treatment of their alcohol problems.

To make this preliminary determination, all clients should immediately (1) be given a test to estimate blood alcohol level (BAL); (2) queried about symptoms of alcohol withdrawal; and (3) asked about the time and duration of, and quantity of alcohol consumed during, their most recent drinking episode. Whenever possible, a physical examination by a physician is advisable even for clients who appear not to be physically dependent, and thus appropriate for immediate entry into outpatient treatment. Administering a BAL test is especially important for two reasons. First, alcoholics can reach very high BALs without exhibiting significant motor impairment (Mello & Mendelson, 1970), and clinicians cannot always determine whether clients have been drinking by observing their behavior (e.g., M. B. Sobell, Sobell, & Vanderspek, 1979). Second, clients' reports of recent drinking behavior are questionable if they have a positive BAL at the time of the interview (Polich, 1982; M. B. Sobell *et al.,* 1979). Such evidence highlights the utility of breath testing in clinical settings.

The most common withdrawal symptoms experienced by alcohol-dependent clients are discussed by Mendelson and Mello (1985); the more serious of these include seizures, hallucinations, and delerium tremens. Information regarding a client's past or current withdrawal symptoms is important, because substantial individual differences exist in the amount, duration, and pattern of alcohol consumption that produce physical dependence. However, the accuracy of clients' reports on past withdrawal symptoms is often ambiguous, as the symptoms usually are not observed by other individuals (Midanik, 1982). Measures have been developed, none-theless, to assess physical dependence and withdrawal symptoms. These include the Alcohol Dependence Scale developed by Skinner and Allen (1982) and the Severity of Alcohol Dependence Questionnaire developed by Stockwell, Hodgson, Edwards, Taylor, and Rankin (1979). These scales may help assess the likelihood of a client's experiencing a withdrawal syndrome upon cessation of alcohol consumption, which is critical information for assessing the need for medical attention.

If hospital detoxification is not required, the next decision is whether the client should be placed in a residential program. This decision depends on the extent of recent drinking and associated physical complications, as well as on the client's social–familial–economic situation. Individuals who are transient, unemployed, or in quite debilitated condition are probably appropriate for a residential program; otherwise, they are probably more appropriate for an inpatient or outpatient treatment program. The decision to hospitalize a client may depend on whether he or she has adequate health insurance or financial resources. Aside from this consideration, hospitalization may be indicated if the client is in severely stressful circum-stances or if his or her support systems have collapsed. Otherwise, an outpatient program probably is most suitable. When combined with the preliminary procedures described earlier, intake interviews that explicitly address these basic issues are usually sufficient to determine the most appropriate entry point for a client in the alcohol treatment system (cf. Pattison, 1985).

## Creating a Context for Effective Assessment

After a client has entered a treatment program, assessment procedures aimed at problem definition that will serve the design of an appropriate treatment plan are implemented. Because many behavioral assessment procedures rely on clients' self-reports, client cooperation is critical for their success. Alcohol clients, however, have negative reputations regarding their willingness and/or ability to discuss their drinking problems candidly. Distorted or incomplete reports are usually viewed as deriving from (1) normal forgetting that may be worsened by chronic alcohol consumption, or (2) intentional efforts to deny or minimize the extent of the problem. Although concerns about the inaccuracy of alcoholics' self-reports are probably more negative than is warranted, it is important for the clinician to create a context in which clients will cooperate to the best of their ability, or, at least, for the clinician to be aware of forces that may produce inaccurate reports.

There are several things the clinician can do toward this end. Because some alcohol-induced cognitive deficits abate after a period of abstinence (e.g., Goldman, 1983), distortions related to memory may be reduced somewhat by delaying assessment procedures after the preliminary screening until the client has been detoxified and, if possible, for another 2 or 3 weeks. A neuropsychological evaluation may be appropriate in cases in which memory problems appear to be present. Their continued presence may complicate the assessment and treatment process, and clients with memory problems may require additional treatment interventions (Goldman, 1983).

In order to evaluate client motives for inaccurate reporting, clinicians should have a clear idea of the circumstances surrounding their clients' referral and current living arrangements. Many alcohol clients enter treatment under coercion (e.g., court or employer referrals, the sometimes forceful suggestions of loved ones) and have usually suffered serious negative consequences of drinking. Further negative consequences may be highly probable unless the other interested parties are unaware of future drinking. This obviously creates a context in which clients may distort self-reports of drinking, and is a difficult problem for the clinician. The clinician can first make very clear, and reiterate several times, the extent of confidentiality of the information provided by the client. Second, with permission of the client, the clinician can talk with other interested parties to explain the importance of client confidentiality for treatment success, to the extent that such confidentiality exists, and to gain their support in the treatment process. This can be presented to the client as wanting to obtain the other persons' perspective on the situation, rather than as wanting to "check up" on the client. Third, if appropriate for the clinical situation, the clinician can make it very clear that he or she is an agent of the client and not an agent of other interested parties.

Another consideration that may encourage distorted reporting is that many clients, especially those in treatment for the first time, are quite reluctant to be labeled "alcoholic" and thus may minimize the severity of their alcohol problem. To counteract this situation, the clinician can explain that he or she is not interested in labeling the client, but instead is interested in learning whether the client has a problem and, if so, its specific nature and extent. This can be coupled with an understandable explanation of the behavioral view of drinking problems as learned patterns of behavior that can be changed.

It is unlikely that in all cases the clinician will be able to create a context without some incentives for the client to distort reports of some information. Even when conditions are conducive to accurate reporting, the clinician may still introduce unreliability and inaccuracies into the assessment data by failing to implement behavioral assessment methods in an optimal fashion. The assessment techniques and research summarized next indicate how to create conditions, in addition to the considerations described here, in which the reports of most alcohol clients are sufficiently reliable and accurate for most clinical purposes.

## Problem Definition

This section summarizes assessment procedures and research pertinent to evaluating two major areas involved in most clients' alcohol problems: (1) the level, pattern, and duration of alcohol consumption and events directly related to consumption (e.g., alcohol treatments, arrests); and (2) problems related to drinking in other areas of life–health functioning (e.g., job, marriage, finances). This information is critical for setting initial treatment goals for drinking behavior and for targeting other areas that may benefit from treatment interventions. It is at this point that the various behavioral assessment procedures have their greatest clinical utility.

### *Assessment of Alcohol-Related Events*

It is important to collect information regarding drinking history, such as past alcohol-related arrests and alcohol treatments. Not only are such data informative regarding the direct negative consequences of drinking, but they may also clarify more general behavior patterns of the client, as well as possible motivators for behavior change. In addition to alcohol-related arrests, it is obviously necessary to assess the client's participation in past treatments for alcohol problems, including the circumstances surrounding program admission, type of treatment provided, length of treatment, and the outcome. Such data are often informative with respect to the client's receptiveness to the current treatment program and may be of prognostic value.

Most alcohol treatment programs have standard intake forms or interview protocols that contain questions regarding arrests and prior hospitalizations. Because the client is the primary source of these data, several studies (e.g., Cooper, Sobell, Maisto, & Sobell, 1980; Cooper, Sobell, Sobell, & Maisto, 1981; M. B. Sobell, Sobell, & Samuels, 1974; L. C. Sobell, & Sobell, 1975) have evaluated the reliability and accuracy of client reports of this information by interviewing clients twice using the same protocol and by comparing their reports with official records. For example, in two interviews conducted 3 weeks apart, L. C. Sobell and Sobell (1975) found an overall agreement of 91.98% between client reports of the frequency of alcohol-related events (e.g., arrests, incarcerations). Checks of the clients' reports against law and other state agency records showed only a 14.01% discrepancy. The other studies found similar agreements between client reports and official records, although lower agreements were found by Cooper *et al.* (1980) for client reports of arrests. These studies suggest that clinicians can be moderately confident that clients will report such information with sufficient reliability and accuracy.

## Assessment of Alcohol Consumption

Measurement of the client's past drinking and the occurrence of any drinking after entry into treatment is essential to a behavioral assessment of alcohol problems. Although there are a number of questionnaires available for this purpose (reviewed by W. R. Miller, 1976), the summary information they typically yield (e.g., a total score) is inadequate for representing a client's alcohol consumption pattern over time with the detail required for a functional analysis of alcohol problems. As summarized earlier, the goal is to describe how a client's problem and nonproblem alcohol use is imbedded within his or her ongoing commerce with the environment—that is, the antecedent conditions and consequences of consumption (both positive and negative and immediate and delayed), and the topographical characteristics of the drinking response that are associated with problem drinking (e.g., rapid consumption of unmixed drinks; cf. M. B. Sobell, Schaeffer, & Mills, 1972). Only with this kind of information can primary problem areas be identified for specific treatment interventions. Their identification requires measurement of a client's alcohol consumption in ways that do not overly simplify or obscure important relationships between consumption and the surrounding environmental circumstances.

Commonly used behavioral methods for assessing alcohol consumption include retrospective interview and questionnaire procedures, the most extensive of which are the Comprehensive Drinking Profile (CDP; Marlatt & Miller, 1984) and the Time-Line Follow-Back (TLFB) interview (M. B. Sobell *et al.,* 1980), and prospective self-monitoring procedures, which are most useful for assessing alcohol consumption after treatment initiation and during follow-up. Discussion of observation methods (e.g., laboratory or simulated-bar studies of alcohol consumption) is omitted here because of the practical and ethical obstacles to their implementation in most treatment settings; the interested reader is referred to a review by M. B. Sobell and Sobell (1976).

## Retrospective Procedures

Marlatt and Miller's (1984) CDP, which is a revised version of Marlatt's (1976) Drinking Profile, is an interview procedure for collecting drinking information for a period of time prior to treatment. The protocol categorizes a client as a periodic, a steady, or a combination drinker and allows calculation of typical amounts consumed per day or per drinking episode. The CDP also includes open- and closed-ended questions related to demographics; employment; family and familial alcoholism; development of the drinking problem; medical history and health problems due to drinking; and typical circumstances surrounding drinking. The CDP manual contains rules that allow reliable coding of the open-ended questions. The protocol also includes the questions from the Michigan Alcoholism Screening Test (Selzer, 1971), which is a useful screening device for alcohol problems. Much of the information gathered via the CDP is relevant for conducting a functional analysis of the client's drinking behavior.

We are aware of only one study (W. R. Miller, Crawford, & Taylor, 1979) that evaluated the accuracy of the drinking behavior questions included in this interview protocol. Correlations between client and collateral reports of client drinking at intake, treatment termination, and a 3-month follow-up were .48, .66, and .79, respectively, for 145 participants in four different outcome studies. W. R. Miller et al. (1979) discuss several possible reasons unrelated to the CDP why these correlations were lower than those typically found in such studies.

A second procedure for assessing past alcohol consumption, the TLFB interview, was developed by Mark and Linda Sobell and their colleagues (M. B. Sobell et al., 1980). This technique gathers detailed information on daily alcohol consumption for up to 12 months prior to the interview. Because this procedure is an invaluable tool in the behavioral assessment of alcohol clients and is readily implemented in most clinical settings, we describe it in some detail here.

The TLFB interview is initiated with instructions that orient the client to approach the procedure with the appropriate set. Clients are instructed that the purpose of the interview is to reconstruct their drinking behavior in great detail, on a daily basis if possible, for the past 12 months. We typically say that this can indeed be difficult, but that it actually is easier than it may sound; most persons are surprised at how well they can recall their behavior. It is essential that clients feel that the TLFB interview is a worthwhile part of assessment, since their full cooperation is important for its successful completion. The clinician can facilitate client participation by explaining the need to obtain a thorough understanding of the extent of the client's drinking behavior and how it has varied over the previous year. Upon completion, it is not uncommon for clients to comment on the helpful nature of the interview; many are unaware of the extent of their drinking or of patterns that are apparent in their behavior.

Following these instructions, the client is presented with a calendar that contains the preceding 12 months on a single sheet of paper. This is an invaluable interviewing aid, and an example from our work with the TLFB procedure is shown in Figure 2-1. The drinking information is then gathered with a number of techniques. M. B. Sobell *et al.* (1980) describe the procedures as follows:

> One of the most effective methods for filling in the time line is to identify anchor points, generally defined as distinctive, time-bound events. Some anchor points are shared by respondents, such as holidays, weekends, birthdays, and major news or sporting events. Other anchor points are more idiosyncratic, such as days marked by arrests, hospitalizations, illnesses, starts or terminations of employment, entry into treatment, court appearances, marital separations or reconciliations and children's birthdays. These days are considered "anchor points" because as they are recorded on the calendar, the subject is asked to recall his drinking on the days of those events as well as the days immediately preceding and following those events.
>
> Another method of filling in the calendar is to search for extended periods of relatively invariant drinking behavior. Usually, this can be accomplished by asking the subject to recall the longest series of consecutive days during the interval under investigation when he consumed absolutely no alcoholic beverages, as well as the longest series of days when he drank daily. In many cases, individuals are able to cite extended intervals for each of these criteria. Similar data can then be gathered for the second longest episodes of abstinence and heavy drinking and so on, until distinct episodes can no longer be identified. In other cases, subjects may be able to report extended periods when they engaged in a distinct, almost ritualistic drinking pattern, such as not drinking during the week until Friday evening, and then drinking heavily until early Sunday evening. Over the course of several studies, we have found that it is atypical for subjects to report totally unpatterned drinking, and that time line data are more difficult to gather from subjects who have less serious drinking problems (and often highly variable patterns of alcohol use). (p. 135)

M. B. Sobell *et al.* also stress the importance of the interviewer's minimizing his or her influence on the clients' reports by avoiding any form of evaluative feedback (comments or gestures). On the other hand, clients should be encouraged to report amounts of alcohol consumption as specifi-

FIGURE 2-1. A 13-month calendar with holidays used as a visual aid to assist subject recall during the TLFB interview procedure.

60

cally as possible; that is, "the subject is not asked to report days when he was 'drunk' or 'sober,' but rather is asked to report days when he consumed 'any alcohol at all,' and the 'amount consumed on each day' " (1980, p. 135).

The goal of the TLFB procedure is to measure a client's quantity of ethanol consumption on each day of the period covered by the interview. As typically practiced, each day is classified into one of four disposition categories: (1) abstinent, (2) light drinking (3 ounces of ethanol consumed or less), (3) heavy drinking (more than 3 ounces of ethanol consumed), or (4) hospitalized or incarcerated. In our work using the TLFB, we found it possible in most cases to obtain reports of quantities consumed each day that can be expressed in milliliters of ethanol consumption. When clients cannot remember the exact amount consumed on a particular day, we ask them to establish a range within which they are certain their quantity of consumption fell and then use the midpoint as an estimate. These data can be represented graphically and are quite useful for identifying patterns of abusive consumption and for relating them to environmental circumstances as part of a functional analysis.

To illustrate the information yielded by the procedure, Figure 2-2 shows graphs of TLFB data that we collected for the pretreatment year from three alcohol-dependent inpatients who were research subjects (Subjects 38, 46, and 48). Day 364 was the day before admission, and alcohol consumption is expressed in milliliters of ethanol per day. Even though all three inpatients reported high mean levels of alcohol consumption aggregated over the pretreatment year, the temporal patterning of their consumption was quite different and suggests the need for individualized treatment strategies. Subject 38 drank the same amount almost daily, and Subjects 46 and 48 showed intermittent but different patterns of consumption. Whereas Subject 46 alternated regularly between abstinence and very heavy drinking, Subject 48 showed a more variable but near-monthly pattern of negatively accelerating alcohol intake, with his highest intake occurring immediately after receipt of his monthly Veterans Administration (VA) disability check.

Several studies have evaluated the reliability and accuracy of the TLFB procedures. L. C. Sobell, Maisto, Sobell, and Cooper (1979) interviewed 12 outpatients 6 weeks apart. Summed over the pretreatment year, the correlations for the number of abstinent, light-drinking, heavy-drinking, and incarcerated days reported in the two interviews were .93, .94, .94, and .98, respectively. In a similar study with 26 inpatients, we (Vuchinich, Tucker, Harllee, Hoffman, & Schwartz, 1985) replicated these high correlations for drinking category assignments summed over all days in the pretreatment year, and also analyzed the data at the individual subject level to evaluate the reliability of reports of the temporal patterning of alcohol consumption. The mean percentage of agreement across subjects for reports of any drinking on each individual day during the pretreatment year was

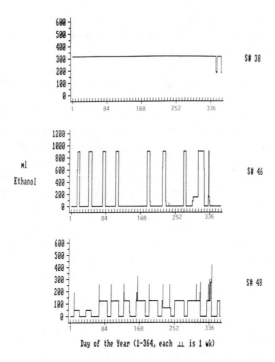

FIGURE 2-2. Reports of daily alcohol consumption (in milliliters of ethanol) for the pretreatment year collected during TLFB interviews with three inpatient alcohol clients (Subjects 38, 46, and 48). Day 364 is the day before admission.

84.98% (range = 55.49% to 99.45%). These data further support the reliability of the TLFB procedures at the level of the group of subjects, but also indicate the importance of investigating variables that may predict individual differences in clients' ability to give consistent reports, particularly of quantities of alcohol consumption. Finally, O'Farrell, Cutler, Bayog, Deutch, and Fortgang (1984) evaluated the accuracy of inpatient male alcoholics' TLFB reports of drinking during the pretreatment year by comparing their reports with those of their spouse. Patient–wife correlations for the number of abstinent, light-drinking, heavy-drinking, hospital, jail, and total drinking days were .88, .38, .59, .98, .99, and .91, respectively. These studies suggest that the TLFB procedure provides detailed information on past drinking behavior that is of sufficient reliability and accuracy for clinical purposes.

In addition to the TLFB and CDP, other structured interview and questionnaire measures of drinking behavior have been evaluated with respect to their reliability (e.g., Davidson & Stein, 1982; Maisto, Sobell,

Cooper, & Sobell, 1982; Summers, 1970) and/or accuracy (e.g., Freedberg & Johnston, 1980; Guze, Tuason, Steward, & Picken, 1963; Leonard, Dunn, & Jacob, 1983; McCrady, Paolino, & Longabaugh, 1978; Polich, 1982; Verinis, 1983; Watson, Tilleskjor, Hoodecheck-Schow, Pucel, & Jacobs, 1984). With the exception of Summers (1970) and Watson et al. (1984), these studies found moderate to excellent agreement for their indices of reliability or accuracy (cf. Midanik, 1982), and the Watson et al. data, which have renewed debate about the validity of alcoholics' self-reports (Maisto & O'Farrell, 1985; Watson, 1985), are open to a more favorable interpretation than that given by the authors. Nevertheless, whereas most studies support the reliability and accuracy of alcoholics' self-reports, the less-than-optimal agreements found in some studies have implications for clinical assessment and for future research on these issues. Notably, the studies that obtained lower agreements (Summers, 1970; Watson et al., 1984) did not ask specific questions about behavioral events, but instead required clients or collaterals to make subjective evaluations or inferences about clients' drinking behavior. Thus, it seems that the reliability and accuracy of clients' reports increase when the clients are asked about specific events that minimize interpretation of meaning.

It also is clear from these studies and our research (Vuchinich et al., 1985) that individual differences exist in clients' ability to give reliable and accurate retrospective reports of their drinking, even though indices of reliability or accuracy aggregated across a group of individuals may be quite high. Whereas this is adequate for research concerned with group data, the clinician interested in individual clients must contend with identifying clients who give less-than-optimal reports. As discussed earlier, a number of factors can influence client cooperation, and clinical skills must be brought to bear to counteract forces that facilitate distorted reports and to create a context in which clients view the assessment procedures as worthwhile. Research aimed at identifying variables that predict individual differences in client reports may eventually provide more guidance in clinical settings. At present, the clinician must carefully assess motives for distorted reports (e.g., referrals involving coercion) and must proceed with assessment procedures in ways that are known to facilitate accurate reporting (e.g., conducting assessments only while clients are sober, asking for specific information that requires minimal inferences).

*Prospective Self-Monitoring Procedures*

Assessment may also include having the client self-monitor relevant events. As typically practiced (e.g., Hay & Nathan, 1982), self-monitoring entails (1) selecting variables of interest based on the client's presenting problem, which will probably include alcohol consumption and events associated with problem drinking (e.g., marital arguments); (2) developing definitions and rules of observation that the client understands and can use to guide his or her self-observation; (3) training the client to record self-observations accurately in units of measurement that reflect important properties of the events (e.g., amount and type of any alcoholic beverage consumption); and (4) explaining the rationale and value of self-monitoring to the client and implementing the record-keeping task in a manner that minimizes intentional or unintentional inaccuracies (e.g., asking clients to record events daily to lessen forgetting; assuring clients that the self-monitoring records are as confidential as any other aspect of treatment).

Self-monitoring is usually most informative when conducted with outpatient clients who encounter circumstances similar to those that were associated with past alcohol consumption. When relapses occur, which is likely (e.g., Marlatt, 1978; Tucker, Vuchinich, & Harris, 1985), information on the surrounding circumstances collected via self-monitoring can be invaluable for treatment purposes. Even if a client is committed to an abstinence goal, subjective urges to drink or thoughts about alcohol can be recorded and may aid in identifying situations or events that place the client at risk for relapse. Moreover, the self-monitoring data can suggest new problem areas that were unidentified or incompletely assessed initially, perhaps because the client forgot them, did not appreciate their significance, or did not feel comfortable revealing them earlier in treatment. As new information emerges, the target behaviors in the self-monitoring task can be changed accordingly.

Like retrospective methods, the self-monitoring procedure may be undermined by several client problems, including lack of motivation, illiteracy, personal disorganization, very heavy drinking, or distortions in the recorded information due to the perceived social (un)desirability of the target behaviors or the consequences of reporting them. Clinician oversights can also contribute to ineffective self-monitoring. These include, among others, (1) inadequate specification of the events to be observed and recorded, (2) poorly devised recording forms, (3) requests for information that require an inordinate amount of client inference, (4) premature requests without adequate client training for records of complex behavioral events, and (5) failure to reinforce the client's record keeping by making use of the information in treatment. When the client fails to self-monitor effectively after a reasonable training period, exploration of the causes of failure may lead to important revisions in goals and interventions, which may include simplification of the self-monitoring task itself.

Other, more general problems with self-monitoring include concerns about measurement reactivity and the accuracy of the data (e.g., Fremouw & Brown, 1980; Hayes & Cavior, 1977, 1980; Stephens, Norris-Baker, & Willems, 1984). Although much discussed, measurement reactivity does not appear to be a major, ongoing source of invalidity (e.g., Stephens *et al.,*

1984), and such effects are minimal when more than one behavior is recorded (e.g., Hayes & Cavior, 1977, 1980). Moreover, if reactivity acts to reduce a client's drinking behavior, this can be viewed as a positive therapeutic effect even if it may seem to interfere with the assessment process.

Compared to retrospective methods, the reliability and accuracy of self-monitored alcohol consumption data have not been well investigated. Several case studies have reported the effective use of self-monitoring with alcoholics (e.g., Brigham *et al.*, 1981; P. M. Miller, 1972; M. B. Sobell & Sobell, 1973b), but only a handful of studies have evaluated the reliability or accuracy of self-monitoring reports (e.g., Gerstel, Harford, & Paulter, 1980; Goldstein, Stein, Smolen, & Perlini, 1976; Strickler, Bradlyn, & Maxwell, 1980; Uchalik, 1979), and several used nonalcoholics as subjects. Although more research is needed on these issues, the few studies that included partial reliability or validity checks (e.g., Goldstein *et al.*, 1976; Strickler *et al.*, 1980) tentatively support the integrity of self-monitored reports of drinking behavior. As in retrospective methods, obtaining verification of client self-monitoring reports (e.g., through collaterals) is highly desirable.

These caveats notwithstanding, appropriate self-monitoring affords a number of advantages and is an indispensable assessment tool that is widely used in clinical practice. First, self-monitoring does not rely on client memory as much as do retrospective procedures, and this should increase accuracy. Second, retrospective interviews cannot yield complete information on the often subtle character of the relationship between a client's drinking and the events of the client's day-to-day life. Important patterns regarding drinking and environmental events may become apparent only when contemporaneously monitored by the client. Such monitoring not only yields important assessment information for the clinician; it also often makes the client aware of patterns that heretofore have gone unnoticed. The latter can be a powerful reinforcer for the client's involvement. Third, because self-monitoring requires clients to be active participants on a continuous basis and not just during office visits, their degree of cooperation is often informative about their motivation for change, while allowing them to acquire observational skills that may facilitate and maintain therapeutic changes. Fourth, self-monitoring information gives both the clinician and client a relatively objective and continuous behavioral record with which to evaluate progress and setbacks throughout treatment.

To our knowledge, there are currently no widely available and standardized self-monitoring forms and training manuals for clinical use in assessing alcohol consumption and related events. To illustrate how clinicians might devise forms for this purpose, Figure 2-3 shows a 6-hour portion of an 84-day self-monitoring record (12:00–6:00 P.M. on day 67) obtained from a 62-year-old male subject who was a heavy normal drinker. The portion of the record shown here has duration columns with time expressed in 10-minute intervals for recording the start and stop times of alcohol consumption episodes, environmental locations, being with other people, and being with the subject's identified collateral. Write-in spaces are included for subjects to record the quantity and type of alcoholic beverage consumption and their environmental locations, which are coded elsewhere on the form (not shown) by the investigators. Although the records are printed as "bubble sheets" to allow them to be entered directly into a computer file by an optical-mark reader, this same information can be collected with hand-designed forms that ask for the information in a similar format.

Self-monitoring forms such as this allow a fine-grained inspection of the temporal patterning of drinking over the course of the day and as a function of environmental locations and the presence or absence of other people. These data are quite germane to a functional analysis of drinking, and they highlight the specificity of information that self-monitoring can yield compared to even the best retrospective methods such as the TLFB procedure. For example, as this 6-hour record shows, the subject reported three drinking episodes between 12:00 and 6:00 P.M. involving a total intake of three 12-ounce beers and a double martini. Twenty minutes of the first drinking episode occurred while the subject was in his car, and he drove again later in the day after having consumed a total of three beers. If this were an alcohol client's record, driving while drinking and drinking during weekday afternoons would probably be identified as problem parameters of the client's drinking. Note also that only the second drinking episode occurred in the collateral's presence, which would be the portion of subject data compared with the collateral's report for the same period to assess accuracy.

Although this degree of detail may not be required clinically in all cases, it is invaluable for outpatient clients who are still engaging in some alcohol consumption. With self-monitoring, as in retrospective procedures, it is important to ask for specific information about observable behavioral events and to verify the information whenever possible. The relative complexity of self-monitoring may necessitate more client training, but the wealth of data obtained usually justifies the extra effort.

### Assessment of Alcohol-Related Dysfunction in Other Areas of Life–Health

Any definition of alcohol problems includes a component stating that drinking has led to or exacerbated disrupted functioning in important areas of the client's life, such as work, physical health, marital, family, or social relationships. Often these problems associated with drinking, rather than the drinking itself, provide the impetus for entering treatment and the motivation to alter the behavior. For three reasons, assessment of a client's alcohol problem requires evaluation of possible disruption in these areas.

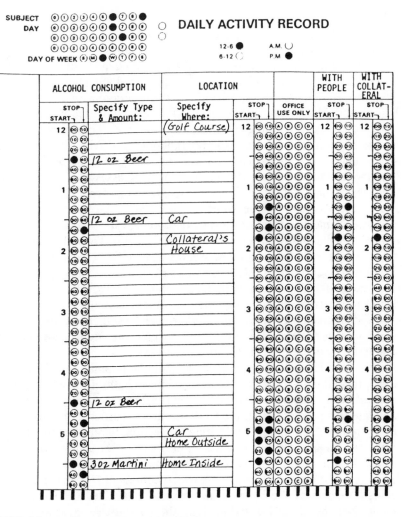

FIGURE 2-3. A 6-hour portion (12:00–6:00 P.M.) on day 67 of an 84-day self-monitoring record, showing subject reports of alcohol consumption, environmental locations, and the presence of other people, including the subject's identified collateral. Time is expressed in 10-minute intervals.

First, an understanding of how drinking fits into the general organization of the client's activities, resources, and relationships is essential for designing appropriate and successful interventions. Second, a reduction or cessation of alcohol consumption may not ameliorate these other problems (Pattison *et al.,* 1977). Alcohol-related dysfunctions may require a direct intervention that is in addition to any intervention aimed specifically at drinking behavior. Third, evaluation of treatment outcome should include consideration of changes in the major life–health areas, and an initial assessment of these areas is necessary to conduct this evaluation.

Despite the clinical importance of functioning in the life–health areas, surprisingly little research has been aimed at developing behavioral assessment procedures specifically to evaluate the functioning of alcohol clients. Maisto and McCollam (1980) reviewed 103 alcohol treatment outcome studies that used multiple measures of outcome. The most commonly measured variables were vocational functioning (77.7% of the studies); social functioning, including marriage and family (61.2%); and emotional functioning (40.8%). Even though a number of assessment devices were used, Maisto and McCollam were critical of the lack of specificity, variability, and ad hoc nature of the measurement practices employed, noting that the rationale for measurement of a given nondrinking variable usually "appeared to be that a standardized test was available" (p. 45). Thus, this literature is noteworthy for (1) the paucity of studies of specific behavioral manifestations of alcohol-related dysfunctions in individuals with alcohol problems; (2) a lack of comparisons with nonalcoholics to ascertain whether the degree of such dysfunctions is actually greater in alcoholics; and (3) considerable discrepancy concerning whether such dysfunctions are causes or consequences of heavy drinking, when most relevant studies have not been longitudinal and cannot address this issue.

Despite this lack of research with alcoholic populations, the clinician must proceed with some type of assessment, in light of the clinical importance of life–health dysfunctions. Several instruments are available that will facilitate this process. First, the CDP (discussed earlier) contains a checklist of "other life problems," including depression, family, health, and work problems; the client indicates whether or not he or she is now experiencing each item and ranks them in order of importance. Second, the Alcohol Use Inventory (Wanberg & Horn, 1983), which contains 147 items on 22 scales, yields measures of the behavioral, physical, cognitive, and social consequences of the client's drinking. Like the CDP, these measures provide leads to important areas of dysfunction in need of further assessment and possible intervention. Third, we have used a modified version of the Drinking Problem Scales (DPS) developed by Cahalan (1970). This structured interview asks the client five questions about specific events in each of six areas of life–health functioning (Intimate Relations, Family Relations, Social Relations, Vocational Functioning, Financial Status, and Physical Health). For example, the five questions for Vocational Functioning are as follows: (1) Have you ever gotten intoxicated while on the job? (2) Have you ever missed work because you were drinking or had a hangover? (3) Have your superiors at work ever suggested that you cut down on your drinking without threatening to fire you? (4) Have your superiors at work ever threatened to fire you because of your drinking without really doing so? (5)

Have you ever been fired from a job because of your drinking? In each of the other life–health areas, the five questions are similar to these in that they ask about increasing negative consequences. Each question is scored 0 if the answer is no and 1 if the answer is yes, so that the client receives a score from 0 to 5 in each life–health area. In an evaluation of the accuracy of alcohol clients' reports of these consequences (Vuchinich & Tucker, 1987), 84% of the clients' responses were rated as accurate or probably accurate: Either the clients agreed with the collaterals' responses, or the clients reported that a consequence had occurred but the collaterals did not, thus indicating the probable validity of the clients' responses.

These instruments will provide leads about client functioning in other life–health areas, but, by themselves, none provide the kind of information necessary for sound treatment decisions. For specific assessment procedures for problems in the major life–health areas, techniques developed for use with nonalcoholic populations must typically be employed, because few available procedures are specific to alcohol-related dysfunctions. Such behavioral assessment strategies for a variety of disorders are discussed by Barlow (1981) and Hersen and Bellack (1981). The relevant alcohol literature suggests three areas most likely to need clinical attention with alcohol clients: social skills deficits (e.g., Chaney, O'Leary, & Marlatt, 1978), marital problems (e.g., Paolino & McCrady, 1977), and vocational functioning (e.g., Whitehead & Simpkins, 1983).

## Relevance of Assessment to Treatment Goal Setting and Treatment Interventions

The preceding discussion highlights the major behavioral assessment techniques and areas of client functioning that require evaluation. Assessment data, usually collected during the early phases of the treatment process, are organized using the functional-analytic approach described earlier. These assessment data establish specific treatment goals regarding a client's drinking behavior and drinking-related dysfunctions, and they guide the choice of appropriate treatments for individual clients. This section outlines general considerations involved in this process. The reader interested in specific alcohol treatments is referred to W. R. Miller and Hester (1980).

Three fundamental issues characterize the clinical literature on alcohol treatment goals and interventions. First, considerably more attention has been paid to changing a client's alcohol consumption than to dealing directly with alcohol-related dysfunctions. In many cases, and especially early in treatment, this emphasis is wholly appropriate. When a client is consuming large quantities of ethanol, curtailing consumption is of paramount importance; neither the assessment nor treatment of related problems can proceed effectively until the client's drinking is reduced or eliminated. This does not, however, obviate the need for addressing alcohol-related dysfunctions at an appropriate point in treatment.

A second issue is the growing recognition of a need to tailor treatment goals and interventions to the needs of individual clients. The functional-analytic approach facilitates such individualization, but many treatment programs make less-than-maximal use of this information and offer fairly standardized treatment. Individualizing alcohol treatments and establishing criteria for matching clients to available treatments will probably remain priorities for clinical research in the coming decade. The full benefits of behavioral assessment of individual clients' drinking problems will probably not be realized until the information obtained via such assessment is used to devise individualized treatment programs.

The third focal issue concerns goal setting regarding a client's alcohol consumption—that is, abstinence or moderation of consumption. This contentious issue has generated much discussion (e.g., Heather & Robertson, 1981; Marlatt, 1983; Pendery, Maltzman, & West, 1982; M. B. Sobell & Sobell, 1973a, 1984), and while treatment outcome studies indicate that some alcohol clients can engage in moderate drinking after treatment, well-controlled, predictive studies concerning which clients may be better suited for which treatment goal are lacking. Certain "rules of thumb" have been articulated, nevertheless, based on contraindications to one goal or the other (e.g., W. R. Miller, 1983; W. R. Miller & Caddy, 1976). As summarized by W. R. Miller and Caddy (1976, pp. 995–996), contraindications to a goal of reduced consumption include the following: (1) presence of liver disease or other physical or psychiatric problems that would be adversely affected by alcohol consumption; (2) use of medications that would produce negative side effects if combined with alcohol; (3) history of pathological intoxication, wherein moderate alcohol intake is associated with violent or bizarre behavior; (4) history or presence of physiological addiction to alcohol, since dependence may be re-established more readily in such persons; (5) client request for, and commitment to, an abstinence goal; (6) lack of environmental support for a reduced-consumption goal and/or strong environmental support or mandate for an abstinence goal; and (7) past failure to maintain moderate drinking over time under similar environmental conditions and/or past success in maintaining abstinence, both inside or outside the context of any prior treatment. Subsequent treatment outcome studies (e.g., Polich, Armor, & Braiker, 1981) further suggest that the relative severity of alcohol dependence may be important in the choice of treatment goals, with an abstinence goal being more appropriate for individuals with severe alcohol problems. Conversely, contraindications to an abstinence goal include (1) patient's refusal of the goal; (2) ongoing environmental demands to drink and lack of environmental supports for abstinence; (3) younger age and absence of severe alcohol dependence; and (4) past failure to benefit from reputable abstinence-oriented treatment.

Although these two goals may be reasonable alternatives for most clients under the circumstances outlined above, initial goals do not need to be viewed as permanent (Heather & Robertson, 1983). For some clients, a lengthy initial period of abstinence may be desirable (due to health or interpersonal reasons), followed by an experimental therapeutic effort to train the clients to resume moderate alcohol consumption. Other clients may initially refuse an abstinence goal, attempt to drink in a nonproblem manner and fail, and then accept an abstinence goal.

Regardless of a client's goal regarding alcohol consumption, it is important to emphasize that some clients may reduce alcohol-related problems by changing the environments in which they drink or the temporal patterning or topography of drinking, without greatly reducing the quantities consumed. Conversely, abstinence does not guarantee improved functioning in other life–health areas (Pattison et al., 1977). Thus, the current tendency to dichotomize treatment goals for alcohol clients into abstinence versus reduced-consumption categories should not blind the therapist to other possible drinking goals or to the need to deal directly with alcohol-related dysfunctions in the main life–health areas.

## Monitoring Progress, Including Follow-Up

An optimal relationship between behavioral assessment and treatment is one in which the two procedures are reciprocally intertwined throughout the course of contact with an alcohol client. Initial assessment data will suggest initial treatment goals and interventions, but the latter will likely be modified as continued assessments during treatment suggest new problem areas or the ineffectiveness of preliminary interventions. As ongoing assessments reveal new problems, or indicate the successful resolution of initial problems, the focus of assessment may change from one set of behaviors to another. For example, curtailing a client's consumption of a pint of gin each evening may be the initial focus of treatment; once consumption is reduced, however, problems with marital interactions may become apparent, and these become the new focus of treatment. Even after formal treatment is terminated, periodic follow-up assessments for 12 months or more allow for an evaluation of treatment effectiveness and can expedite identification of the need for renewed treatment efforts.

Self-monitoring procedures conducted continuously or intermittently throughout treatment allow ongoing evaluation of patient progress and are recommended. Periodic structured interviews during treatment and follow-up that pertain to specific drinking and drinking-related events, like the interviews used in the initial assessment phase, are also effective monitoring procedures. Whenever possible, these data should be corroborated.

Because the individualization of behavioral treatments for alcohol problems based on assessment data obtained from individual clients is fundamental to this approach, it is difficult to be more specific than this about the course of assessment and treatment with any one client. However, regardless of treatment goals, it is likely that most clients will have a period of relapse to abusive consumption (e.g., Marlatt, 1978; Tucker et al., 1985). Assessment of such episodes is crucial to allow them to serve as informative events about the variables maintaining a client's alcohol problems, rather than as failure experiences for client and therapist alike. Discussions early in treatment should explore the client's views on relapse (e.g., does the client hold the view that one drink may precipitate a serious bout of intoxication?). Early intervention points in the relapse event should be identified that would minimize the severity and duration of the drinking episode (see Marlatt & Gordon, 1985). Value judgments should be avoided whenever possible by the client and therapist. The information provided by such events, coupled with a comparison of the context in which the client can maintain abstinence or moderation, allow the therapist to refine the functional analysis of the variables controlling the client's alcohol consumption, and thus to intervene more effectively.

## Future Issues and Illustrative Cases

The preceding material indicates that alcohol consumption and alcohol-related events (e.g., arrests, hospitalizations) can be assessed in most instances in an accurate, reliable, and relatively convenient fashion. The same cannot be said for the measurement of alcohol-related dysfunctions in the life–health areas or the assessment of how alcohol consumption varies with changes of circumstance or events in important areas of the client's life. The relative lack of the latter assessment procedures is a significant gap in what would approach an optimal representation of a client's problems for use by clinicians. In the remainder of this chapter, we summarize some of our work on this problem. Two case examples illustrate the issues involved and the use of several assessment procedures described earlier.

Elaboration of the conceptual framework used in this work (cf. Tucker et al., 1985; Vuchinich, 1982; Vuchinich & Tucker, 1983) is beyond the scope of this chapter. Very generally, it maintains that alcohol consumption will vary with changes in constraints on access to other valuable activities in the client's life; this notion is consistent with clinical (e.g., Polich et al., 1981) and naturalistic (e.g., Tuchfield, 1981) studies showing that significant changes in alcoholics' drinking patterns often correlate with major changes in life circumstances (e.g., marriage). From this perspective, a key issue for assessment is to find ways of representing and measuring relationships over time between clients' alcohol consumption and access to other important activities or reinforcers (e.g., job, marriage). Although this is clearly a complex task because of the diverse behaviors and environments involved (which may be why less progress has been made in this area), this type of analysis perhaps will allow a more complete functional analysis of drinking behavior. Thus, development of a systematic measurement approach to represent how an alcohol client's drinking problem is enmeshed over time with the client's functioning in other areas would greatly facilitate both clinical assessment and research on the determinants of drinking.

In an initial effort to relate clients' alcohol consumption to the surrounding circumstances in the major life–health areas, we focused on the measurement of relationships between the occurrence of life events and drinking episodes during a 6-month period after inpatient treatment. Our perspective suggested that the critical property of events with respect to changes in the probability of drinking behavior was what an event signaled regarding an individual's future access to other valued activities. This general view led to two hypotheses: (1) Relapses associated with events should be more severe than those unrelated to events, and (2) events in the life–health area(s) that had been most disrupted by past alcohol consumption would be most likely to be related to drinking episodes.

We evaluated these hypotheses in a study with inpatients from the Alcohol Dependence Treatment Program at the Veterans Administration Medical Center (VAMC) in Gainesville, Florida. We employed several interview-based assessment procedures while the patients were hospitalized, and they self-monitored any drinking behavior and the occurrence of life events for 6 months after discharge. This study is described more fully in Tucker *et al.* (1985), and data from one individual are presented here.

This patient (Subject 6) was a 43-year-old divorced white male who was a disabled construction worker. He reported a 10-year drinking problem, one arrest for drunk driving, no prior alcohol treatments, and gastrointestinal upset due to heavy drinking.

We conducted a TLFB interview regarding the 6 months prior to admission. The client reported 127 abstinent days, 41 heavy-drinking days, no light-drinking days, and no days hospitalized or incarcerated. We also conducted an interview using the DPS, discussed earlier. This individual's scores representing alcohol-related disruptions were as follows: Intimate Relations, 2; Family Relations, 3; Social Relations, 2; Vocational Functioning, 0; Financial Status, 3; and Physical Health, 3.

Figure 2-4 presents the client's self-monitoring reports of daily alcohol consumption in standard drinks for 6 months after discharge. The consecutive numbers above the graph indicate when life events occurred (17 events total). The specific events that occurred in each life–health area were as follows: Intimate Relations, two events (1, 14); Family Relations, five events (4, 5, 12, 13, 16); Financial Status, two events (2, 3); and Physical Health, eight events (6, 7, 8, 9, 10, 11, 15, 17). No events were reported for social relations or vocational functioning. The client reported five drinking episodes after discharge and a mean consumption of 12 drinks per day during each episode. Each drinking episode seemed to be associated temporally with an event occurrence, and only events in the areas of Family Relations (5, 12, 13, 16) and Physical Health (6, 9, 15) seemed to show this relationship. Because the patient obtained two of his three highest DPS scores in these two areas, this is consistent with our hypotheses, which also received some support from the data analysis of the entire sample ($n$ = 26). Collaterals generally verified the subject's reports of alcohol consumption.

This example illustrates several points of clinical relevance. First, the procedures used to assess this client's pre- and posttreatment alcohol consumption and alcohol-related dysfunctions are readily usable in most clinical settings. Second, the example shows that episodes of alcohol consumption can be meaningfully related to other events in the client's life. Identifying such relationships is quite important for conducting the functional analysis of a client's alcohol problem, which, in turn, guides the development and implementation of treatment interventions. Third, the example illustrates the importance of assessing the degree of alcohol-related dysfunction in the life–health areas, since such dysfunction was related to drinking episodes during the follow-up period.

The results of this study are promising, but the measurement procedures were not wholly adequate for representing ongoing relationships between engaging in alcohol consumption and other valued activities.

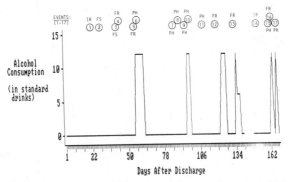

FIGURE 2-4.   Event occurrences and alcohol consumption in standard drinks for Subject 6 during the 6 months following discharge from inpatient treatment. IR, Intimate Relations; FR, Family Relations; PH, Physical Health; FS, Financial Status.

Although events were related to relapses, their measurement was discrete and categorical; we had no means of representing any lasting consequences of events with respect to clients' access over time to important activities or resources. It is presumably this aspect of event occurrences that will bear contingent relationships with drinking behavior, and measures that could relate alcohol consumption directly to variables reflecting clients' access to important activities and resources are essential for this type of analysis.

The identification of such relationships would be greatly facilitated if the variables of interest (i.e., alcohol consumption, access to alternative reinforcers) could be measured over time using the same dimensional properties. This would permit meaningful comparisons between topographically dissimilar behaviors using common units of measurement. We are currently approaching this problem by focusing on two properties common to individuals' engagement in most naturalistic activities—namely, their allocation of time and money to different activities, including but not limited to alcohol consumption. The idea is that these properties indicate an individual's allocation of resources to activities, and that the proportional allocation of resources among available activities reflects the relative reinforcement value of a given activity (cf. Rachlin, Battalio, Kagel, & Green, 1981). Thus, as applied to alcohol consumption, the relative severity of a client's alcohol problem may be usefully represented by the proportion of time or income allocated to drinking behavior. Eventually, episodes of abusive drinking may be predictable from shifts in the individual's overall distribution of time or monetary resources among the different commodity classes.

To illustrate the kinds of relationships sought with this approach, a case example is presented here from our work on monetary allocation (see Tucker, Vuchinich, Rudd, & Harris, 1984, and Figure 2-3 regarding our similar work on time allocation). This work, which is in the preliminary stages, is concerned with developing retrospective interview and prospective self-monitoring procedures to assess clients' income and commodity expenditures for extended periods before and after treatment. The interviews include an elaborated version of the TLFB procedure to collect information for the year prior to admission about clients' alcohol consumption, income, expenditures, and life event occurrences. Information on the same four variables are collected prospectively after treatment using a daily self-monitoring procedure. These data are supplemented and verified whenever possible with clients' financial records. When available, collaterals are used to verify client reports of alcohol consumption and life events. The overall goal is to devise a verifiable procedure that allows the development of profiles for each client showing income acquisition; sources of income (e.g., job or pension); and the absolute and proportional amounts of income allocated to different commodity classes, including alcohol consumption.

The client (Subject 66) whose data are presented here was a 44-year-old divorced white male who had been hospitalized for the second time for alcohol problems. His usual occupation was as a blue-collar worker in manufacturing. He reported a 17-year history of alcohol problems, multiple physical symptoms due to heavy drinking, and two alcohol-related arrests. His DPS scores reflecting negative consequences due to drinking during the pretreatment year were as follows: Intimate Relations, 0; Family Relations, 3; Social Relations, 4; Vocational Functioning, 4; Financial Status, 4; and Physical Health, 2.

The many job- and income-related consequences of drinking for this client, as summarized on the DPS, were borne out in detail by his TLFB interview and self-monitoring data. Figure 2-5 displays portions of these data over the entire study interval; weeks 1-52 are the pretreatment year, weeks 53-56 are his inpatient stay, and weeks 57-74 follow discharge. Panels A and B show the client's reported weekly alcohol consumption in milliliters of ethanol and his income in dollars, respectively. Panel C shows the proportion of his biweekly income expended for ethanol versus all nondrinking commodities, including housing, durable goods, and non-durable goods; biweekly intervals were used because the client typically was paid every 2 weeks. The client's periods of employment are indicated on the top of Figure 2-5. In addition, he reported 41 events during the study interval, 19 (46.37%) of which were job- or income-related. The client verified 48.6% of his reports of income with financial records (including 76.1% of his work income), and a collateral available during a portion of the posttreatment interval verified the client's reports of drinking days during this period.

As Figure 2-5 indicates, this client showed (1) quite heavy but variable pretreatment levels of alcohol consumption; (2) a sharp decrease in consumption shortly before and after treatment; and (3) a steady increase in consumption across the posttreatment interval. In addition to the effects of treatment, a portion of the variability in his alcohol consumption was temporally associated with job-related events. During the pretreatment interval, his ethanol consumption attained its maximum levels in weeks 11-14 when he was anticipating but did not receive a pay raise. Consumption then decreased sharply starting in week 15 when he quit his job, and then increased again starting in week 20 when he obtained a new job. Consumption remained high until shortly before inpatient treatment, when he entered a 4-day detoxification program in week 48. After inpatient treatment, his consumption started increasing upon discharge when he returned to his former job. He changed jobs in week 61, was fired in week 69, and secured a new job in week 74; there was a relative decrease in his alcohol consumption during this period of unemployment, even though his

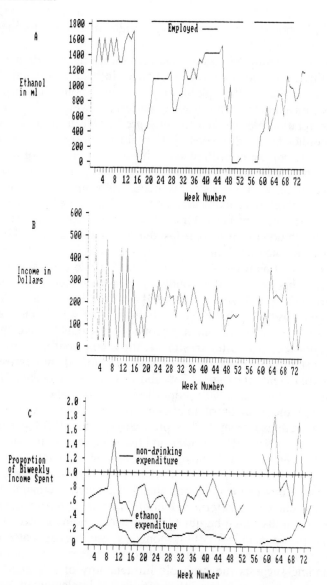

FIGURE 2-5. Weekly alcohol consumption and income and proportion of biweekly income spent for alcohol versus all nondrinking commodities for Subject 66 for the 12 months before and 4.5 months after inpatient treatment.

level of alcohol consumption was generally increasing throughout the posttreatment period.

Although treatment was associated with a brief but dramatic reduction in this client's alcohol intake, changes in his environmental circumstances as manifested through his employment, income, and expenditures were also associated with his drinking pattern. However, this environment-behavior relationship was not directly predictable from absolute income levels; neither his alcohol consumption nor his absolute expenditures for ethanol were correlated with income. Instead, description of this relationship requires consideration of the client's ongoing "personal economy" as measured by the proportions of his income allocated to alcohol consumption versus other nondrinking commodities. Panel C and the data summary reveal several relevant facts: First, engaging in treatment cost this client money. In addition to any income lost due to not working while hospitalized, which was not measured, the client's weekly mean income decreased from pre- to posttreatment by 14.34% (i.e., from $186.96 per week to $163.51). Conversely, his mean total expenditures per week increased from pre- to posttreatment by 8.15% (from $149.91 to $162.13). Thus, although the client had a positive cash flow before treatment, he was expending virtually all of his income after treatment. Second, even though his income fell and his expenditures rose after treatment, the client continued to expend a fairly constant percentage of his total income on ethanol across the pre- and posttreatment intervals (14.75% and 12.10%, respectively). Thus, treatment did not alter the client's proportional resource allocation to alcohol, even though the mean absolute amount in dollars he spent on alcohol per week was reduced from $27.58 pretreatment to $19.78 posttreatment. Third, the client's biweekly income and the proportion of income expended on ethanol were negatively correlated across the study interval ($r = -.42$, $df = 35, p = .01$); in other words, when his income decreased, the client increased the proportion of income that he allocated to ethanol. Therefore, despite the client's short-term reduction in drinking during the treatment interval, upon discharge he quickly returned to homeostasis with respect to the proportional amount of his monetary resources allocated to alcohol consumption, even though his income fell and expenses rose after treatment. This finding suggests the probable intractability of this client's alcohol problem to treatment unless interventions are implemented that directly address and ameliorate the seemingly important relationships existing between his drinking and monetary resource allocation.

These data are only descriptive, and causal inferences cannot be made, but they generally demonstrate how an individual's abusive pattern of alcohol consumption covaries with changes in income and expenditures and can be measured accordingly. If successfully developed, this assessment approach may eventually yield predictive relationships between changes in economic variables and/or time allocation patterns and changes in alcohol consumption. Although drinking problems are widely acknowledged to be preceded by changes in individuals' life circumstances and to adversely affect their functioning, a coherent measurement scheme that allows the systematic assessment of environment–behavior relationships involved in individual drinking problems is currently lacking. The approach we are taking may partially redress this need by allowing comparisons between drinking behavior and functioning in other life–health areas using common metric units that facilitate quantification of such relationships. The interview and self-monitoring procedures employed are readily usable in clinical practice.

The literature reviewed in this chapter shows that behavioral approaches to alcohol abuse have contributed greatly to the assessment methods available to clinicians who work with alcohol clients. Alcohol consumption, the variable of primary interest, usually can be measured accurately and reliably. Much work needs to be done, however, in developing measures of functioning in the major life–health areas and in developing a characterization of, and measures of, the variables that maintain alcohol abuse. We view the development of such measurement schemes for nondrinking behaviors and their relationship to alcohol consumption as a challenge for the coming years in the behavioral assessment of alcohol abuse.

## Acknowledgments

Preparation of this chapter was supported in part by Grant Nos. 1-P50-AA05793 and 1-R01-AA06122 from the National Institute on Alcohol Abuse and Alcoholism. Rudy E. Vuchinich and Jalie A. Tucker are currently at Wayne State University, and Lynn M. Harllee is at the University of Miami, Florida.

## References

Barlow, D. H. (Ed.). (1981). *Behavioral assessment of adult disorders.* New York: Guilford Press.

Brigham, S. L., Rekers, G. A., Rosen, A. C., Swihart, J. J., Pfrimmer, G., & Ferguson, L. N. (1981). Contingency management in the treatment of adolescent alcohol drinking problems. *Journal of Psychology, 109,* 73–85.

Cahalan, D. (1970). *Problem drinkers: A national survey.* San Francisco: Jossey-Bass.

Chaney, E. F., O'Leary, M. R., & Marlatt, G. A. (1978). Skill training with alcoholics. *Journal of Consulting and Clinical Psychology, 46,* 1092–1104.

Cooper, A. M., Sobell, M. B., Maisto, S. A., & Sobell, L. C. (1980). Criterion intervals for pretreatment drinking measures in treatment evaluation. *Journal of Studies on Alcohol, 41,* 1186–1195.

Cooper, A. M., Sobell, M. B., Sobell, L. C., & Maisto, S. A. (1981). Validity of alcoholics' self-reports: Duration data. *International Journal of the Addictions, 16,* 401–406.

Davidson, R. S., & Stein, S. (1982). Reliability of self-report of alcoholics. *Behavior Modification, 6,* 107–119.

Freedberg, E., & Johnston, W. (1980). Validity and reliability of alcoholics' self-reports of use of alcohol submitted before and after treatment. *Psychological Reports, 46,* 999–1005.

Fremouw, W. J., & Brown, J. P., Jr. (1980). The reactivity of addictive behaviors to self-monitoring: A functional analysis. *Addictive Behaviors, 5,* 209–217.

Gerstel, E. K., Harford, T. C., & Pautler, C. (1980). The reliability of drinking estimates obtained with two data collection methods. *Journal of Studies on Alcohol, 41,* 89–93.

Goldman, M. S. (1983). Cognitive impairment in chronic alcoholics: Some cause for optimism. *American Psychologist, 38,* 1045–1054.

Goldstein, M. K., Stein, G. H., Smolen, D. M., & Perlini, W. S. (1976). Bio-behavioral monitoring: A method for remote health measurement. *Archives of Physical Medicine and Rehabilitation, 57,* 253–258.

Guze, S. B., Tuason, V. A., Steward, M. A., & Picken, B. (1963). The drinking history: A comparison of reports by subjects and their relatives. *Quarterly Journal of Studies on Alcohol, 24,* 249–260.

Hay, W. M., & Nathan, P. E. (Eds.). (1982). *Clinical case studies in the behavioral treatment of alcoholism.* New York: Plenum.

Hayes, S. C., & Cavior, N. (1977). Multiple tracking and the reactivity of self-monitoring: Negative behaviors. *Behavior Therapy, 8,* 819–831.

Hayes, S. C., & Cavior, N. (1980). Multiple tracking and the reactivity of self-monitoring: II. Positive behaviors. *Behavior Therapy, 11,* 283–296.

Heather, N., & Robertson, I. (1981). *Controlled drinking.* London: Methuen.

Heather, N., & Robertson, I. (1983). Why is abstinence necessary for the recovery of some problem drinkers? *British Journal of Addiction, 78,* 139–144.

Hersen, M., & Bellack, A. S. (Eds.). (1981). *Behavioral assessment: A practical handbook* (2nd ed.). New York: Pergamon Press.

Leonard, K., Dunn, N. J., & Jacob, T. (1983). Drinking problems of alcoholics: Correspondence between self and spouse reports. *Addictive Behaviors, 8,* 369–373.

Maisto, S. A., & McCollam, J. B. (1980). The use of multiple measures of life health to assess alcohol treatment outcome: A review and critique. In L. C. Sobell, M. B. Sobell, & E. Ward (Eds.), *Evaluating alcohol and drug abuse treatment effectiveness: Recent advances* (pp. 15–76). New York: Pergamon Press.

Maisto, S. A., & O'Farrell, T. J. (1985). Comment on the validity of Watson *et al.*'s "Do alcoholics give valid self-reports?" *Journal of Studies on Alcohol, 46,* 447–450.

Maisto, S. A., Sobell, L. C., Cooper, A. M., & Sobell, M. B. (1982). Comparison of two techniques to obtain retrospective reports of drinking behavior from alcohol abusers. *Addictive Behaviors, 7,* 33–38.

Marlatt, G. A. (1976). The Drinking Profile: A questionnaire for the behavioral assessment of alcoholism. In E. J. Mash & L. G. Terdal (Eds.), *Behavior therapy assessment: Diagnosis, design, & evaluation* (pp. 121–137). New York: Springer.

Marlatt, G. A. (1978). Craving for alcohol, loss of control, and relapse: A cognitive–behavioral analysis. In P. E. Nathan, G. A. Marlatt, & T. Loberg (Eds.), *Alcoholism: New directions in behavioral research and treatment* (pp. 271–314). New York: Plenum.

Marlatt, G. A. (1983). The controlled-drinking controversy: A commentary. *American Psychologist, 38,* 1097–1110.

Marlatt, G. A., & Gordon, J. R. (Eds.). (1985). *Relapse prevention: Maintenance strategies in the treatment of addictive behaviors.* New York: Guilford Press.

Marlatt, G. A., & Miller, W. R. (1984). *Comprehensive Drinking Profile.* Odessa, FL: Psychological Assessment Resources.

McCrady, B. S., Paolino, T., Jr., & Longabaugh, R. (1978). Correspondence between reports of problem drinkers and spouses on drinking behaviour and impairment. *Journal of Studies on Alcohol, 39,* 1252–1257.

Mello, N. K., & Mendelson, J. H. (1970). Experimentally induced intoxication in alcoholics: A comparison between programmed and spontaneous drinking. *Journal of Pharmacology and Experimental Therapeutics, 173,* 101–116.

Mendelson, J. H., & Mello, N. K. (1985). Diagnostic criteria for alcoholism and alcohol abuse. In J. H. Mendelson & N. K. Mello (Eds.), *The diagnosis and treatment of alcoholism* (2nd ed., pp. 1–20). New York: McGraw-Hill.

Midanik, L. (1982). The validity of self-reported alcohol consumption and related problems: A literature review. *British Journal of Addiction, 77,* 357–382.

Miller, P. M. (1972). The use of behavioral contracting in the treatment of alcoholism: A case report. *Behavior Therapy, 3,* 593–596.

Miller, W. R. (1976). Alcoholism scales and objective assessment methods: A review. *Psychological Bulletin, 83,* 649–674.

Miller, W. R. (1983). Controlled drinking: A history and a critical review. *Journal of Studies on Alcohol, 44,* 68–83.

Miller, W. R., & Caddy, G. R. (1977). Abstinence and controlled drinking in the treatment of problem drinkers. *Journal of Studies on Alcohol, 38,* 986–1003.

Miller, W. R., Crawford, V. L., & Taylor, C. A. (1979). Significant others as corroborative sources for problem drinkers. *Addictive Behaviors, 4,* 67–70.

Miller, W. R., & Hester, R. K. (1980). Treating the problem drinker: Modern approaches. In W. R. Miller (Ed.), *The addictive behaviors: Treatment of alcoholism, drug abuse, smoking, and obesity* (pp. 11–141). New York: Pergamon Press.

Nathan, P. E., Marlatt, G. A., & Loberg, T. (1978). *Alcoholism: New directions in behavioral research and treatment.* New York: Plenum Press.

O'Farrell, T. J., Cutter, H., Bayog, R. D., Deutch, G., & Fortgang, J. (1984). Correspondence between one-year retrospective reports of pre-treatment drinking by alcoholics and their wives. *Behavioral Assessment, 6,* 263–274.

Paolino, T. J., Jr., & McCrady, B. S. (1977). *The alcoholic marriage: Alternative perspectives.* New York: Grune & Stratton.

Pattison, E. M. (1985). The selection of treatment modalities for the alcoholic patient. In J. H. Mendelson & N. K. Mello (Eds.), *The diagnosis and treatment of alcoholism* (2nd ed., pp. 189–294). New York: McGraw-Hill.

Pattison, E. M., Sobell, M. B., & Sobell, L. C. (1977). *Emerging concepts of alcohol dependence.* New York: Springer.

Pendery, M. L., Maltzman, I. M., & West, L. J. (1982). Controlled drinking by alcoholics? New findings and a reevaluation of a major affirmative study. *Science, 217,* 169–175.

Polich, J. M. (1982). The validity of self-reports in alcoholism research. *Addictive Behaviors, 7,* 123–132.

Polich, J. M., Armor, D. J., & Braiker, H. B. (1981). *The course of alcoholism: Four years after treatment.* New York: Wiley-Interscience.

Rachlin, H., Battalio, R., Kagel, J., & Green, L. (1981). Maximization theory in behavioral psychology. *Behavioral and Brain Sciences, 4,* 371–417.

Selzer, M. L. (1971). The Michigan Alcoholism Screening Test: The quest for a new diagnostic instrument. *American Journal of Psychiatry, 127,* 1653–1658.

Skinner, H. A., & Allen, B. A. (1982). Alcohol dependence syndrome: Measurement and validation. *Journal of Abnormal Psychology, 91,* 199–209.

Sobell, L. C., Maisto, S. A., Sobell, M. B., & Cooper, A. M. (1979). Reliability of alcohol abusers' self-reports of drinking behaviour. *Behaviour Research and Therapy, 17,* 157–160.

Sobell, L. C., & Sobell, M. B. (1975). Outpatient alcoholics give valid self-reports. *Journal of Nervous and Mental Disease, 161,* 32–42.

Sobell, M. B., Maisto, S. A., Sobell, L. C., Cooper, A. M., Cooper, T. C., & Sanders, B. (1980). Developing a prototype for evaluating alcohol treatment effectiveness. In L. C. Sobell,

M. B. Sobell, & E. Ward (Eds.), *Evaluating alcohol and drug abuse treatment effectiveness: Recent advances* (pp. 129-150). New York: Pergamon Press.

Sobell, M. B., Schaefer, H. H., & Mills, K. E. (1972). Differences in baseline drinking behavior between alcoholics and normal drinkers. *Behaviour Research and Therapy, 10,* 257-267.

Sobell, M. B., & Sobell, L. C. (1973a). Individualized behavior therapy for alcoholics. *Behavior Therapy, 4,* 49-72.

Sobell, M. B., & Sobell, L. C. (1973b). A self-feedback technique to monitor drinking behaviour in alcoholics. *Behaviour Research and Therapy, 11,* 237-238.

Sobell, M. B., & Sobell, L. C. (1976). Assessment of addictive behavior. In M. Hersen & A. S. Bellack (Eds.), *Behavioral assessment: A practical handbook* (2nd ed., pp. 305-336). New York: Pergamon Press.

Sobell, M. B., & Sobell, L. C. (1984). The aftermath of heresy: A response to Pendery *et al.*'s (1982) critique of "Individualized behavior therapy for alcoholics." *Behaviour Research and Therapy, 22,* 413-440.

Sobell, M. B., Sobell, L. C., & Samuels, F. (1974). Validity of self-reports of alcohol-related arrests by alcoholics. *Quarterly Journal of Studies on Alcohol, 35,* 276-280.

Sobell, M. B., Sobell, L. C., & Sheahan, D. B. (1976). Functional analysis of drinking problems as an aid in developing individual treatment strategies. *Addictive Behaviors, 1,* 127-132.

Sobell, M. B., Sobell, L. C., & Vanderspek, R. (1979). Relationships among clinical judgment, self-report, and breath analysis measures of intoxication in alcoholics. *Journal of Consulting and Clinical Psychology, 47,* 204-206.

Stephens, M. A. P., Norris-Baker, C. N., & Willems, E. P. (1984). Data quality in self-observation and report of behavior. *Behavioral Assessment, 6,* 237-252.

Stockwell, T., Hodgson, R., Edwards, G., Taylor, C., & Rankin, H. (1979). The development of a questionnaire to measure severity of alcohol dependence. *British Journal of Addiction, 74,* 79-87.

Strickler, D. P., Bradlyn, A. S., & Maxwell, W. A. (1980). Teaching moderate drinking behaviors to young adult heavy drinkers: The effects of three training procedures. *Addictive Behaviors, 6,* 355-364.

Summers, T. (1970). Validity of alcoholics' self-reported drinking history. *Quarterly Journal of Studies on Alcohol, 31,* 972-974.

Tuchfield, B. S. (1981). Spontaneous remission in alcoholics: Empirical observations and theoretical implications. *Journal of Studies on Alcohol, 42,* 626-641.

Tucker, J. A., Vuchinich, R. E., & Harris, C. V. (1985). Determinants of substance abuse relapse. In M. Galizio & S. A. Maisto (Eds.), *Determinants of substance abuse: Biological, psychological, and environmental factors* (pp. 383-421). New York: Plenum.

Tucker, J. A., Vuchinich, R. E., Rudd, E. J., & Harris, C. V. (1984). Changes in drinking behavior after retirement: Preliminary assessment procedures. *Bulletin of the Society of Psychologists in Addictive Behaviors, 3,* 77-84.

Uchalik, D. C. (1979). A comparison of questionnaire and self-monitored reports of alcohol intake in a nonalcoholic population. *Addictive Behaviors, 4,* 409-413.

Verinis, J. S. (1983). Agreement between alcoholics and relatives when reporting follow-up status. *International Journal of the Addictions, 18,* 891-894.

Vuchinich, R. E. (1982). Have behavioral theories of alcohol abuse focused too much on alcohol consumption? *Bulletin of the Society of Psychologists in Substance Abuse, 1,* 151-154.

Vuchinich, R. E., & Tucker, J. A. (1983). Behavioral theories of choice as a framework for studying drinking behavior. *Journal of Abnormal Psychology, 92,* 408-416.

Vuchinich, R. E., & Tucker, J. A. (1987). *Identifying the determinants of alcoholic relapse: The role of life-event occurrences.* Manuscript submitted for publication.

Vuchinich, R. E., Tucker, J. A., Harllee, L. M., Hoffman, S., & Schwartz, J. (1985, November). *Reliability of reports of temporal patterning of drinking behavior by alcoholics.* Poster presented at the annual meeting of the Association for Advancement of Behavior Therapy, Houston, TX.

Wanberg, K. W., & Horn, J. L. (1983). Assessment of alcohol use with multidimensional concepts and measures. *American Psychologist, 38,* 1055–1069.

Watson, C. G. (1985). More reasons for a moratorium: A reply to Maisto and O'Farrell. *Journal of Studies on Alcohol, 46,* 450–453.

Watson, C. G., Tilleskjor, C., Hoodecheck-Schow, E. A., Pucel, J., & Jacobs, L. (1984). Do alcoholics give valid self-reports? *Journal of Studies on Alcohol, 45,* 344–348.

Whitehead, P. C., & Simpkins, J. (1983). Occupational factors in alcoholism. In B. Kissin & H. Begleiter (Eds.), *The biology of alcoholism* (Vol. 6, pp. 405–553). New York: Plenum.

# 3

# ASSESSMENT OF EXPECTANCIES

**HELEN M. ANNIS**
*Addiction Research Foundation*
*University of Toronto*

**CHRISTINE S. DAVIS**
*Addiction Research Foundation*

## Introduction

One of the most influential social learning theories in the alcoholism treatment field today is self-efficacy theory (Bandura, 1977, 1978, 1981). Bandura's theory addresses specifically the role played by clients' cognitive expectations in treatment and their effect on subsequent behavior. According to self-efficacy theory, behavioral changes produced by different types of treatment are mediated by a common cognitive mechanism—efficacy expectations. An "efficacy expectation" is defined as a judgment that one has the ability to execute a certain behavior pattern. The theory proposes that any treatment procedure is effective only to the extent that it increases a client's expectations of personal efficacy. The strength of a client's efficacy expectations determines the nature of coping behavior and how long such behavior will be maintained in the face of obstacles and adverse consequences.

### Self-Efficacy Theory, Cognitive Appraisal, and Alcoholic Relapse

According to self-efficacy theory, when a client enters a high-risk situation for alcoholic relapse, a cognitive process is set up that involves an appraisal on the part of the client of his or her past performances in that situation. The process of cognitive appraisal culminates in the formation of an efficacy judgment, which in turn mediates actual drinking behavior (see the top half of Figure 3-1). Self-efficacy theory suggests that it is not the consumption of alcohol per se that is responsible for a full-blown relapse. Rather, it is the meaning that the act of drinking has for the client, the coping strategies that he or she has available, and the persistence with

THEORETICAL PROCESS

Microanalysis of Drinking Behavior within a High-Risk Situation

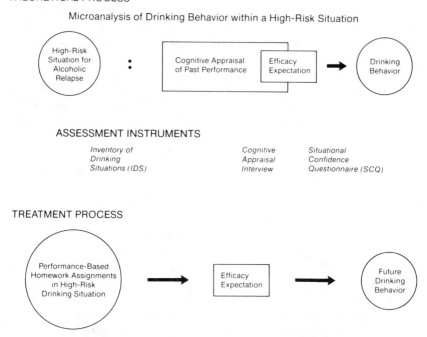

FIGURE 3-1.   Top: A microanalysis, in terms of self-efficacy theory, of drinking behavior within a high-risk situation; the emphasis is on the client's cognitive mechanisms. Bottom: The treatment process, with emphasis on performance-based situations.

which he or she engages in coping behavior, which in turn is dependent on perceived self-efficacy.

Although efficacy expectations are considered the central factor in all behavior change, other cognitive mediators, as expressed in the process of cognitive appraisal, have important implications for the individual's expectations about his or her ability to cope. At each stage in the relapse process, efficacy expectations are subject to the direct or indirect influence of other assumptions, attributions, expectancies, and defensive distortions. As such, these other cognitive factors should not be overlooked in the areas of assessment and treatment design.

In cognitive appraisal, an individual's judgment of the relative stressfulness of high-risk situations is a primary issue of concern. This is consistent with the strong emphasis on a situation-specific approach proposed by self-efficacy theory. Marlatt (1985c), using Lazarus's (1966) model of primary and secondary appraisal in the coping process, has related self-efficacy to the perceived stressfulness of high-risk situations. Drawing on the similarity between judgments of self-efficacy and secondary appraisal, Marlatt argues that "when that which is at stake is meaningful (primary appraisal) and coping responses are judged less than adequate for managing the situation (secondary appraisal), psychological stress is experienced" (Marlatt, 1985c, p. 120). Under these circumstances, the individual is increasingly likely to resort to drinking because it is the response that was previously dominant in the coping hierarchy (Marlatt, 1985b). Thus, the assessment process has a twofold function: first, to determine which situations have previously been dealt with by excessive drinking, and, second, to assess current expectations about the adequacy of coping resources. Litman, Stapleton, Oppenheim, Peleg, and Jackson (1984), in their research on the assessment of coping behaviors, have suggested that "not only may a flexible coping repertoire be associated with survival, but . . . the experience of the effectiveness of these behaviors is also important" (p. 290). This experience is likened to those that are instrumental in the development of increasing self-efficacy. From this perspective, treatment aimed at preventing relapse would focus on the strengthening of alternative cognitive and behavioral coping strategies in these high-risk, stressful situations.

Marlatt (1985b) identifies another feature of these stressful situations that can have a critical influence both on efficacy expectations and on the initiation of drinking after a period of abstinence. He points out that the way in which an individual "labels" the emotional arousal accompanying a high-risk situation may lead to a false assumption about outcome. The person experiencing a state of emotional arousal "may misinterpret this reaction as craving for the drug rather than attributing it to the stress of the situation itself" (Marlatt, 1985b, pp. 141–142). If the person further assumes that craving has a set course and its intensity will of necessity increase rather than decrease, and thus that craving is a precursor of certain relapse, then efficacy expectations drop and a self-fulfilling prophecy is set in motion. Thus, misinterpretation and mistaken assumptions lead to a slip, which can then escalate into a full-blown relapse. Donovan and Chaney (1985) argue that these kinds of misinterpretations are consistent with the clinical observation that alcoholics are "deficient in their ability to recognize, differentiate, and label mood states" (p. 388). The therapist must be alert in detecting and correcting such clients' assumptions that craving and urges are a sign of imminent relapse, and should assess whether individual clients require help in accurately identifying and labeling their emotional reactions.

The resumption of drinking, as a way of coping, is also associated with another sort of expectancy: outcome expectancy. Marlatt (1985b) has postulated that the initially reinforcing properties of alcohol consumption are responsible for the formation of strong expectancies that the use of alcohol will have positive and desirable outcomes—for example, the alleviation of negative mood states. Sanchez-Craig (1979), following Lazarus's

(1966) theory of appraisal, has stated that unless alcohol is reappraised as a negative stimulus, the initial positive appraisal will be most salient and the risk of relapse will remain high. Some theorists (e.g., Eastman & Marzillier, 1984; Kazdin, 1978) have suggested that outcome and efficacy expectations are either reciprocal or at least not conceptually distinct. Bandura (1977), on the other hand, has argued that they are distinct and that efficacy expectancies are the more critical predictors of behavior. Clearly, outcome expectancies play a significant role in cognitive appraisal, and they also have important motivational implications within the treatment relationship. In this light, Marlatt and Parks (1982) have devised a "decision matrix" that probes the client's positive and negative outcome expectancies about returning to previous drinking patterns or maintaining the treatment goal. More specifically, Marlatt (1985a) has suggested that in planning treatment interventions, the therapist not only should explore self-efficacy in high-risk situations, but should also determine situation-specific outcome expectancies, focusing on situations in which urges occur.

Outcome expectancies are particularly relevant to the belief system promoted by treatment programs. Most traditional alcoholism treatment programs, including Alcoholics Anonymous, inculcate the belief that the alcoholic has an irreversible disease that can only be brought under control by lifelong abstinence. Alcoholics in these treatment programs are taught that they are qualitatively different from nonalcoholics because they will never be able to exert control over consumption once drinking has been initiated. Wilson (1978a, 1978b, 1979, 1980) and Marlatt and his colleagues (Marlatt & George, 1984; Marlatt & Gordon, 1980) have commented that such a belief system can vitally affect relapse by deliberately minimizing the alcoholic's efficacy expectations about his or her ability to cope with alcohol once he or she takes a drink. Given the low efficacy expectations about handling a drinking episode that such a therapeutic philosophy promotes, it would be expected that an alcoholic's attempts at coping behavior will be quickly extinguished once a slip from sobriety occurs. Marlatt has referred to the alcoholic's reaction to a transgression of an absolute abstinence rule as the "abstinence violation effect" (AVE; Marlatt, 1978; Marlatt & George, 1984; Marlatt & Gordon, 1980). In the presence of low self-efficacy about one's ability to exert control once drinking has been initiated, the intensity of the AVE would be expected to be high, thereby contributing to a full-blown relapse. Because it is known that the great majority of clients engage in some posttreatment drinking, it is of critical importance that clients develop in treatment a sense of personal capability (i.e., high efficacy expectations) in dealing with drinking incidents.

Finally, at each point in the relapse process, cognitive appraisals can be affected by the distortions in thinking and defensive tactics that characterize the more general coping patterns of the individual client. Efficacy expectations, based on these appraisals, are similarly open to the possibility of distortion and inaccuracy. Beck and his colleagues (Beck, Rush, Shaw, & Emery, 1979) and Ellis (1970) have provided two of the dominant directions for conceptualizing these thought processes from the perspective of cognitive therapy. Attribution theory (Weiner, 1979, 1980) has been another model for understanding the ways in which alcoholics can systematically make sense of their experiences, and consequently increase or decrease their feelings of self-efficacy.

Beck *et al.* (1979) differentiate between primitive and mature modes of organizing reality, whereas Ellis (1970) focuses on the difference between irrational and rational thinking. Both approaches have generated a series of cognitive errors and maladaptive assumptions that have relevance when viewed as facilitators in the relapse process. Marlatt (1985b) and McCrady, Dean, Dubreuil, and Swanson (1985) have argued that alcoholics with, for example, a tendency to overgeneralize and catastrophize, or with unrealistic expectations of self and others, are making errors that can precipitate or exacerbate a drinking episode and contribute to lessened self-efficacy. Similarly, individuals with acute self-doubts (i.e., low efficacy expectations) about their ability to handle drinking are likely to catastrophize the consequences and to feel that all will be lost following a single drink. Typically, traditional alcoholism treatment programs have failed to offer their clients any cognitive preparation for the drinking "slips" that are likely to occur, and have also failed to provide instruction in coping strategies that could help to deal with the consequences associated with relapse. Such instruction in treatment would be expected to help minimize the destructive effects of relapse episodes.

Donovan and Chaney (1985), from a slightly different perspective, cite a number of studies suggesting that intellectualization, rationalization, and denial, often in conjunction with lessened cognitive vigilance, are components in a pattern of defenses allowing the individual to covertly "set up" a relapse. Here, the result can be an inflated judgment of self-efficacy—an outcome that may be responsible for the ceiling effect sometimes observed in self-efficacy ratings (Chaney, O'Leary, & Marlatt, 1978).

The attributional approach, as developed by Weiner (1979, 1980), is particularly useful because it characterizes the appraisal process along a number of bipolar dimensions. Moreover, this approach allows any attribution to be either adaptive or maladaptive, depending on the specific circumstances being appraised. Marlatt (1985b), in adapting this model to addictive behaviors, has claimed that the form of attribution made in a specific high-risk situation will either decrease or increase the probability of relapse. There are clear implications for self-efficacy in the individual's attributional style. For example, the client who attributes his or her actions to coping skills (an internal, controllable factor) is more open to an increasing sense of self-efficacy than the client who, in a similar situation, attributes those actions to luck (an external, uncontrollable factor).

In summary, self-efficacy theory proposes that efficacy expectations act as a common cognitive mediator for all behavior change in treatment. In a high-risk situation, the strength of the client's efficacy expectations will be most predictive of perseverance in coping behavior. Judgments of self-efficacy are based on a process of cognitive appraisal, which includes the assumptions, attributions, expectations, and defensive distortions each client brings to a specific high-risk situation.

## Self-Efficacy and the Treatment Process

Recent trends in the cognitive–behavioral field suggest a divergence between the hypothesized theoretical process of behavior change and the treatment process. On the one hand, cognitive mechanisms (e.g., efficacy expectations) are proposed as mediating or explaining behavior change. On the other hand, performance-based treatment procedures (e.g., mastery experiences in high-risk situations) are proposed as the most powerful procedures for producing and maintaining behavior change. This distinction between theoretical process and treatment process as it relates to self-efficacy theory is shown in Figure 3-1.

If one extrapolates the principles of self-efficacy theory into the alcoholism field, what is needed in treatment planning is a highly individualized microanalysis of the drinking behavior of the client within high-risk situations for relapse. Although cognitive mechanisms mediate behavior, self-efficacy theory proposes that the most powerful methods of changing cognitions of self-efficacy, and thereby of changing drinking behavior, are performance-based. Thus the preferred treatment strategy focuses on having the client engage in homework assignments tailored to his or her particular high-risk situations for relapse. Under appropriate conditions, mastery experiences in these high-risk drinking situations have a powerful impact on the client's cognitive appraisal of his or her coping abilities, resulting in an increase in efficacy expectations and a change in future drinking behavior.

Recent empirical findings provide support for the principles of self-efficacy theory. Self-efficacy ratings have been found to be valid predictors of posttreatment eating behavior (Chambliss & Murray, 1979), smoking behavior (Condiotte & Lichtenstein, 1981; Cooney, Kopel, & McKeon, 1982; Prochaska, Crimi, Lapsanski, Martel, & Reid, 1982), and drinking behavior (Chaney et al., 1978; Condra, 1982). Moreover, there is some evidence that a client's ratings of perceived self-efficacy in specific situations may be predictive of the actual situations in which relapse will occur (Condiotte & Lichtenstein, 1981). Performance assignments successfully executed by clients within high-risk situations for relapse have been demonstrated to have a powerful effect in changing efficacy expectations and subsequent behavior in relation to phobic conditions (Bandura, Adams, Hardy, & Howells, 1980; Blanchard, 1970), obsessive–compulsive disorders (Rachman & Hodgson, 1979) and sexual dysfunctions (Kockott, Dittmar, & Nusselt, 1975; Mathews *et al.*, 1976). No reports have yet appeared demonstrating the superiority of performance tasks in changing drinking behavior, although two clinical trials addressing this issue are currently under way at the Addiction Research Foundation in Ontario (Annis, 1986).

## Clinical Applications

Self-efficacy theory has direct implications for the design of treatment strategies for alcoholic clients. Treatment planning begins with a highly individualized microanalysis of the drinking behavior of the client. Three central elements are assessed: high-risk situations for relapse; cognitions associated with past performance in these high-risk situations; and efficacy expectations. On the basis of this assessment, performance tasks are designed in the form of homework assignments to be undertaken by the client. Throughout treatment, assessment and treatment planning remain highly interrelated; monitoring by the therapist of the client's efficacy expectations and cognitions associated with drinking situations serves to guide the development and ordering of further homework assignments.

What follows below is a description of the assessment instruments and procedures that Annis has developed to tap the central elements of the model. The relevance of the assessment process to the tailoring of treatment plans to the needs of the individual alcoholic client is examined.

### Screening and General Disposition

Following a medical examination and the taking of a psychosocial and alcohol and drug use history, a situational assessment is made of the client's drinking problem through administration of the Inventory of Drinking Situations (IDS; Annis, 1982a). The IDS is a self-report questionnaire designed to assess situations in which the client drank heavily over the past year. Based on the work of Marlatt and associates (Marlatt, 1978, 1979a, 1979b; Marlatt & Gordon, 1980) in analyzing the nature of alcoholic relapse episodes, the questionnaire is designed to assess eight categories of drinking situations divided into two major classes: (1) Intrapersonal Determinants, in which drinking involves a response to an event that is primarily psychological or physical in nature; and (2) Interpersonal Determinants, in which a significant influence of another individual is involved. Intrapersonal Determinants are subdivided into five categories: Negative Emotional States, Negative Physical States, Positive Emotional

States, Testing Personal Control, and Urges and Temptations. Interpersonal Determinants are divided into three categories: Interpersonal Conflict, Social Pressure to Drink, and Positive Emotional States. Details of the development and scoring of the IDS are given in Annis (1986). Subscale reliabilities and normative data for the 100-item IDS, and a description of the derivation and factor structure of the 42-item IDS short form, are given in Annis and Kelly (1984). The IDS short form (Annis, 1984a) is presented in Table 3-1.

In Marlatt and Gordon's (1980) original work, which formed the conceptual basis for the development of the IDS, chronic male alcoholics were interviewed concerning the circumstances surrounding their first relapse episode following discharge from treatment. Over two-thirds of the relapse episodes described by the clients fell into just three categories: Negative Emotional States, Interpersonal Conflict, and Social Pressure to Drink. The percentage of clients reporting relapses in each area in Marlatt's study is shown in Table 3-2. Also shown in Table 3-2 are the results of a study (Annis & Davis, 1984) in which therapists rank-ordered clients' high-risk drinking situations, using the information in the IDS completed by the clients on admission. The results agreed well with the frequency of relapses within categories reported by Marlatt and Gordon. Over two-thirds of the clients had their highest-ranked risk situation for drinking in response to Negative Emotional States, Interpersonal Conflict, or Social Pressure to Drink.

It has been found that the types of high-risk situations for drinking reported on the IDS vary across age and sex (Annis & Kelly, 1984). Younger clients report drinking heavily across a wider range of situations than older clients, and are more likely to drink in response to both Positive and Negative Emotional States, Interpersonal Conflict, and Social Pressure to Drink. In terms of sex differences, male clients are more likely than female clients to report drinking heavily in response to Positive Emotional States or Social Pressure to Drink. These age and sex differences in risk situations for drinking can be instructive in designing general program components suited to the needs of the younger drinker versus the elderly alcoholic, and the male versus the female alcoholic.

## Defining the Problem

Following the principles of self-efficacy theory, clinical work with a client begins with a situational diagnosis of the drinking problem—that is, a microanalysis of the client's drinking behavior within high-risk situations for relapse (see Figure 3-1). Central to this analysis is an assessment of the efficacy expectations of the client in relation to each high-risk drinking situation.

TABLE 3-1. Inventory of Drinking Situations, Short Form

Listed below are a number of situations or events in which some people drink heavily.
Read each item carefully, and answer in terms of your own drinking **over the past year.**

If you "NEVER" drank heavily in that situation, circle "1"
If you "RARELY" drank heavily in that situation, circle "2"
If you "FREQUENTLY" drank heavily in that situation, circle "3"
If you "ALMOST ALWAYS" drank heavily in that situation, circle "4"

I DRANK HEAVILY

| | Never | Rarely | Frequently | Almost always |
|---|---|---|---|---|
| 1. When I had an argument with a friend. | 1 | 2 | 3 | 4 |
| 2. When I felt uneasy in the presence of someone. | 1 | 2 | 3 | 4 |
| 3. When someone criticized me. | 1 | 2 | 3 | 4 |
| 4. When I would have trouble sleeping. | 1 | 2 | 3 | 4 |
| 5. When I wanted to heighten my sexual enjoyment. | 1 | 2 | 3 | 4 |
| 6. When other people around me made me tense. | 1 | 2 | 3 | 4 |
| 7. When I would be out with friends and they would stop by a bar for a drink. | 1 | 2 | 3 | 4 |
| 8. When I wanted to feel closer to someone I liked. | 1 | 2 | 3 | 4 |
| 9. When I felt that I had let myself down. | 1 | 2 | 3 | 4 |
| 10. When other people treated me unfairly. | 1 | 2 | 3 | 4 |
| 11. When I would remember how good it tasted. | 1 | 2 | 3 | 4 |
| 12. When I felt confident and relaxed. | 1 | 2 | 3 | 4 |
| 13. When I would convince myself that I was a new person now and could take a few drinks. | 1 | 2 | 3 | 4 |
| 14. When I would pass by a liquor store. | 1 | 2 | 3 | 4 |
| 15. When I felt drowsy and wanted to stay alert. | 1 | 2 | 3 | 4 |
| 16. When I would be out with friends "on the town" and wanted to increase my enjoyment. | 1 | 2 | 3 | 4 |
| 17. When I would unexpectedly find a bottle of my favorite booze. | 1 | 2 | 3 | 4 |
| 18. When other people didn't seem to like me. | 1 | 2 | 3 | 4 |
| 19. When I felt nauseous. | 1 | 2 | 3 | 4 |
| 20. When I would wonder about my self-control over alcohol and would feel like having a drink to try it out. | 1 | 2 | 3 | 4 |

*(continued)*

TABLE 3-1 (Continued).

| | I DRANK HEAVILY | | | |
| --- | --- | --- | --- | --- |
| | Never | Rarely | Frequently | Almost always |
| 21. When other people interfered with my plans. | 1 | 2 | 3 | 4 |
| 22. When everything was going well. | 1 | 2 | 3 | 4 |
| 23. When I would be at a party and other people would be drinking. | 1 | 2 | 3 | 4 |
| 24. When pressure would build up at work because of the demands of my supervisor. | 1 | 2 | 3 | 4 |
| 25. When I was afraid that things weren't going to work out. | 1 | 2 | 3 | 4 |
| 26. When I felt satisfied with something I had done. | 1 | 2 | 3 | 4 |
| 27. When I would be in a restaurant and the people with me would order drinks. | 1 | 2 | 3 | 4 |
| 28. When I wanted to celebrate with a friend. | 1 | 2 | 3 | 4 |
| 29. When I was angry at the way things had turned out. | 1 | 2 | 3 | 4 |
| 30. When I would feel under a lot of pressure from family members at home. | 1 | 2 | 3 | 4 |
| 31. When something good would happen and I would feel like celebrating. | 1 | 2 | 3 | 4 |
| 32. When I would start to think that just one drink could cause no harm. | 1 | 2 | 3 | 4 |
| 33. When I felt confused about what I should do. | 1 | 2 | 3 | 4 |
| 34. When I would meet a friend and he/she would suggest that we have a drink together. | 1 | 2 | 3 | 4 |
| 35. When I was not getting along well with others at work. | 1 | 2 | 3 | 4 |
| 36. When I would be enjoying myself at a party and wanted to feel even better. | 1 | 2 | 3 | 4 |
| 37. When I would suddenly have an urge to drink. | 1 | 2 | 3 | 4 |
| 38. When I wanted to prove to myself that I could take a few drinks without becoming drunk. | 1 | 2 | 3 | 4 |
| 39. When there were fights at home. | 1 | 2 | 3 | 4 |
| 40. When there were problems with people at work. | 1 | 2 | 3 | 4 |

*(continued)*

TABLE 3-1 (Continued).

|  | I DRANK HEAVILY | | | |
| --- | :---: | :---: | :---: | :---: |
|  | Never | Rarely | Frequently | Almost always |
| 41. When I would be relaxed with a good friend and wanted to have a good time. | 1 | 2 | 3 | 4 |
| 42. When my stomach felt like it was tied in knots. | 1 | 2 | 3 | 4 |

*Note.* From *Inventory of Drinking Situations, Short Form* by H. M. Annis, 1984, Toronto: Addiction Research Foundation. Copyright 1984 by the Addiction Research Foundation. Reprinted by permission. The categorization of the 42 items into the eight categories of drinking situations is as follows:

I. Intrapersonal Determinants
  1. Negative Emotional States—items 9, 25, 29, 33
  2. Negative Physical States—items 4, 15, 19, 42
  3. Positive Emotional States—items 12, 22, 26, 31
  4. Testing Personal Control—items 13, 20, 32, 38
  5. Urges and Temptations—items 11, 14, 17, 37
II. Interpersonal Determinants
  1. Interpersonal Conflict
    a. Social Rejection—items 10, 18, 21
    b. Work Problems—items 24, 35, 40
    c. Tension—items 2, 3, 6
    d. Family/Friend Problems—items 1, 30, 39
  2. Social Pressure to Drink—items 7, 23, 27, 34
  3. Positive Emotional States
    a. Social Drinking—items 16, 28, 36, 41
    b. Intimacy—items 5, 8

The Situational Confidence Questionnaire (SCQ; Annis, 1982b) is a self-report instrument designed as a measure of Bandura's concept of self-efficacy for alcohol-related situations. An original 100-item form and a 42-item short form of the SCQ parallel the drinking situations of the two forms of the IDS (see Annis, 1986). The abbreviated version of the SCQ (Annis, 1984b) is presented in Table 3-3. As with the IDS, the eight-category classification system derived from the work of Marlatt and Gordon (1980) is used to categorize high-risk drinking areas. Clients are asked to imagine themselves in each situation and indicate on a 6-point scale (0, "not at all confident"; 20, "20% confident"; 40, "40% confident"; 60, "60% confident"; 80, "80% confident"; and 100, "very confident") how confident they are that they will be able to resist the urge to drink heavily in that situation. The items within each of the eight drinking categories are shown in Table 3-4. A client's scores on the SCQ at intake to treatment provide a diagnostic profile of the relative confidence levels of the client in being able to cope with different types of drinking situations.

### Relevance to Intervention

The aim of treatment is to effect a rise in self-efficacy across all areas of perceived drinking risk. On the basis of the client's profile of efficacy

TABLE 3-2. Comparison of Relapse Episodes (Marlatt & Gordon, 1980) and Therapists' Ranking (on the Basis of IDS Scores) of Clients' Highest-Risk Situations for Drinking (Annis & Davis, 1984)

| Category | % Reported relapses (Marlatt & Gordon, 1980) | % Clients with highest ranking of risk (IDS) (Annis & Davis, 1984) |
|---|---|---|
| *Intrapersonal Determinants* | | |
| Negative Emotional States | 38% | 39% |
| Testing Personal Control | 9% | 12% |
| Urges and Temptations | 11% | 7% |
| Positive Emotional States | 0% | 2% |
| Negative Physical States | 3% | 0% |
| *Interpersonal Determinants* | | |
| Interpersonal Conflict | 18% | 17% |
| Social Pressure to Drink | 18% | 12% |
| Positive Emotional States | 3% | 10% |

expectations on the SCQ, a hierarchy of situations involving drinking risk is constructed, and this guides the development of an individualized treatment plan. Beginning with drinking situations representing areas of moderate confidence for the client, therapy proceeds to focus on areas of progressively higher risk (i.e., lower confidence ratings). Consistent with the treatment implications of self-efficacy theory, the focus of therapy is on the design and execution of performance-based homework assignments with regard to specific high-risk drinking situations as a means of changing the client's underlying cognitions of self-efficacy.

In structuring homework assignments during treatment, it is important that conditions be arranged so that the client can perform successfully and thereby experience "mastery" in formerly problematic drinking situations. In addition to the use of a hierarchy of graduated tasks, this may be facilitated by the use of a variety of response induction aids. These may include the use of modeling or rehearsal of activities during therapy sessions (Chaney *et al.,* 1978; Marlatt & Gordon, 1985), joint performance of the task with the therapist or a responsible collateral (Bandura *et al.,* 1980), programmed relapse (Marlatt & Gordon, 1985), alternative coping strategies (Beck, 1976; Sanchez-Craig, 1975; Sobell & Sobell, 1973), and the use of protective aids such as antialcohol drugs (Peachey & Annis, 1984, 1985). However, external aids to which the client may attribute his or her success should be gradually withdrawn toward the end of treatment to insure that the client's cognitive appraisals or self-inferences from mastery experiences are consistent with those known to facilitate strong maintenance of behavior change. Monitoring of the client's cognitions following successful homework assignments can alert the therapist to the presence of

TABLE 3-3.   Situational Confidence Questionnaire, Short Form

Listed below are a number of situations or events in which some people experience a drinking problem.

Imagine yourself as you are right now in each of these situations. Indicate on the scale provided how confident you are that you would be able to resist the urge to drink heavily in that situation.

Circle 100 if you are 100% confident right now that you could resist the urge to drink heavily; 80 if you are 80% confident; 60 if you are 60% confident. If you are more unconfident than confident, circle 40 to indicate that you are only 40% confident that you could resist the urge to drink heavily; 20 for 20% confident; 0 if you have no confidence at all about that situation.

|  | | I would be able to resist the urge to drink heavily | | | | | |
|---|---|---|---|---|---|---|---|
|  | | Not at all confident | | | | | Very confident |
| 1. | If I had an argument with a friend. | 0 | 20 | 40 | 60 | 80 | 100 |
| 2. | If I felt uneasy in the presence of someone. | 0 | 20 | 40 | 60 | 80 | 100 |
| 3. | If someone criticized me. | 0 | 20 | 40 | 60 | 80 | 100 |
| 4. | If I would have trouble sleeping. | 0 | 20 | 40 | 60 | 80 | 100 |
| 5. | If I wanted to heighten my sexual enjoyment. | 0 | 20 | 40 | 60 | 80 | 100 |
| 6. | If other people around me made me tense. | 0 | 20 | 40 | 60 | 80 | 100 |
| 7. | If I would be out with friends and they would stop by a bar for a drink. | 0 | 20 | 40 | 60 | 80 | 100 |
| 8. | If I wanted to feel closer to someone I liked. | 0 | 20 | 40 | 60 | 80 | 100 |
| 9. | If I felt that I had let myself down. | 0 | 20 | 40 | 60 | 80 | 100 |
| 10. | If other people treated me unfairly. | 0 | 20 | 40 | 60 | 80 | 100 |
| 11. | If I would remember how good it tasted. | 0 | 20 | 40 | 60 | 80 | 100 |
| 12. | If I felt confident and relaxed. | 0 | 20 | 40 | 60 | 80 | 100 |
| 13. | If I would convince myself that I was a new person now and could take a few drinks. | 0 | 20 | 40 | 60 | 80 | 100 |
| 14. | If I would pass by a liquor store. | 0 | 20 | 40 | 60 | 80 | 100 |
| 15. | If I felt drowsy and wanted to stay alert. | 0 | 20 | 40 | 60 | 80 | 100 |
| 16. | If I would be out with friends "on the town" and wanted to increase my enjoyment. | 0 | 20 | 40 | 60 | 80 | 100 |
| 17. | If I would unexpectedly find a bottle of my favorite booze. | 0 | 20 | 40 | 60 | 80 | 100 |

*(continued)*

TABLE 3-3 (Continued).

| | I would be able to resist the urge to drink heavily | | | | | |
|---|---|---|---|---|---|---|
| | Not at all confident | | | | | Very confident |
| 18. If other people didn't seem to like me. | 0 | 20 | 40 | 60 | 80 | 100 |
| 19. If I felt nauseous. | 0 | 20 | 40 | 60 | 80 | 100 |
| 20. If I would wonder about my self-control over alcohol and would feel like having a drink to try it out. | 0 | 20 | 40 | 60 | 80 | 100 |
| 21. If other people interfered with my plans. | 0 | 20 | 40 | 60 | 80 | 100 |
| 22. If everything were going well. | 0 | 20 | 40 | 60 | 80 | 100 |
| 23. If I would be at a party and other people would be drinking. | 0 | 20 | 40 | 60 | 80 | 100 |
| 24. If pressure would build up at work because of the demands of my supervisor. | 0 | 20 | 40 | 60 | 80 | 100 |
| 25. If I were afraid that things weren't going to work out. | 0 | 20 | 40 | 60 | 80 | 100 |
| 26. If I felt satisfied with something I had done. | 0 | 20 | 40 | 60 | 80 | 100 |
| 27. If I would be in a restaurant and the people with me would order drinks. | 0 | 20 | 40 | 60 | 80 | 100 |
| 28. If I wanted to celebrate with a friend. | 0 | 20 | 40 | 60 | 80 | 100 |
| 29. If I were angry at the way things had turned out. | 0 | 20 | 40 | 60 | 80 | 100 |
| 30. If I would feel under a lot of pressure from family members at home. | 0 | 20 | 40 | 60 | 80 | 100 |
| 31. If something good would happen and I would feel like celebrating. | 0 | 20 | 40 | 60 | 80 | 100 |
| 32. If I would start to think that just one drink could cause no harm. | 0 | 20 | 40 | 60 | 80 | 100 |
| 33. If I felt confused about what I should do. | 0 | 20 | 40 | 60 | 80 | 100 |
| 34. If I would meet a friend and he/she would suggest that we have a drink together. | 0 | 20 | 40 | 60 | 80 | 100 |
| 35. If I were not getting along well with others at work. | 0 | 20 | 40 | 60 | 80 | 100 |
| 36. If I would be enjoying myself at a party and wanted to feel even better. | 0 | 20 | 40 | 60 | 80 | 100 |
| 37. If I would suddenly have an urge to drink. | 0 | 20 | 40 | 60 | 80 | 100 |

*(continued)*

TABLE 3-3 (Continued).

| | I would be able to resist the urge to drink heavily | | | | | |
|---|---|---|---|---|---|---|
| | Not at all confident | | | | | Very confident |
| 38. If I wanted to prove to myself that I could take a few drinks without becoming drunk. | 0 | 20 | 40 | 60 | 80 | 100 |
| 39. If there were fights at home. | 0 | 20 | 40 | 60 | 80 | 100 |
| 40. If there were problems with people at work. | 0 | 20 | 40 | 60 | 80 | 100 |
| 41. If I would be relaxed with a good friend and wanted to have a good time. | 0 | 20 | 40 | 60 | 80 | 100 |
| 42. If my stomach felt like it was tied in knots. | 0 | 20 | 40 | 60 | 80 | 100 |

*Note.* From *Situational Confidence Questionnaire, Short Form* by H. M. Annis, 1984, Toronto: Addiction Research Foundation. Copyright 1984 by the Addiction Research Foundation. Reprinted by permission.

self-defeating ideation that may undermine the development of self-efficacy and the maintenance of gains following discharge from treatment.

### Monitoring Progress

Successful experiences in controlling drinking behavior do not always result in improvement in the client's efficacy expectations in relation to future drinking situations—improvement that is necessary for treatment effects to be maintained over time. Therefore, it is important for the therapist to monitor the client's cognitions throughout the course of treatment following the successful completion of homework tasks. Bandura (1978) has commented on four cognitive appraisals on the part of the client that promote maintenance of behavior change by engendering strong efficacy expectations following a successful experience in a high-risk situation: (1) The situation is challenging (i.e., in the past, the situation was one that had been risky); (2) only a moderate degree of effort is needed to experience success in the situation (i.e., the effort expended is not aversive); (3) little external aid is involved in the success (i.e., the success is attributable to the client, not to the therapist, a significant other, a drug, etc.); and (4) the success is part of an overall pattern of improved performance (i.e., the client perceives that he or she is making steady improvement). Two additional factors derived from the literature on self-perception and attribution theory have been found to enhance positive self-inferences: (5) a perception on the part of the client that an increase in personal control has been

TABLE 3-4.   Subscales of the SCQ Short Form (42 Items)

| SCQ subscale | Test items (SCQ short form item numbers) |
|---|---|
| *Intrapersonal Determinants* | |
| Negative Emotional States | 9. If I felt that I had let myself down.<br>25. If I were afraid that things weren't going to work out.<br>29. If I were angry at the way things had turned out.<br>33. If I felt confused about what I should do. |
| Negative Physical States | 4. If I would have trouble sleeping.<br>15. If I felt drowsy and wanted to stay alert.<br>19. If I felt nauseous.<br>42. If my stomach felt like it was tied in knots. |
| Positive Emotional States | 12. If I felt confident and relaxed.<br>22. If everything were going well.<br>26. If I felt satisfied with something I had done.<br>31. If something good would happen and I would feel like celebrating. |
| Testing Personal Control | 13. If I would convince myself that I was a new person now and could take a few drinks.<br>20. If I would wonder about my self-control over alcohol and would feel like having a drink to try it out.<br>32. If I would start to think that just one drink could cause no harm.<br>38. If I wanted to prove to myself that I could take a few drinks without becoming drunk. |
| Urges and Temptations | 11. If I would remember how good it tasted.<br>14. If I would pass by a liquor store.<br>17. If I would unexpectedly find a bottle of my favorite booze.<br>37. If I would suddenly have an urge to drink. |
| *Interpersonal Determinants* | |
| Interpersonal Conflict<br>  a. Social Rejection | 10. If other people treated me unfairly.<br>18. If other people didn't seem to like me.<br>21. If other people interfered with my plans. |
| b. Work Problems | 24. If pressure would build up at work because of the demands of my supervisor.<br>35. If I were not getting along well with others at work.<br>40. If there were problems with people at work. |
| c. Tension | 2. If I felt uneasy in the presence of someone.<br>3. If someone criticized me.<br>6. If other people around me made me tense. |
| d. Family/Friend Problems | 1. If I had an argument with a friend.<br>30. If I would feel under a lot of pressure from family members at home.<br>39. If there were fights at home. |

*(continued)*

TABLE 3-4 (Continued).

| SCQ subscale | Test items (SCQ short form item numbers) |
|---|---|
| Social Pressure to Drink | 7. If I would be out with friends and they would stop by a bar for a drink. |
| | 23. If I would be at a party and other people would be drinking. |
| | 27. If I would be in a restaurant and the people with me would order drinks. |
| | 34. If I would meet a friend and he/she would suggest that we have a drink together. |
| Positive Emotional States | |
| a. Social Drinking | 16. If I would be out with friends "on the town" and wanted to increase my enjoyment. |
| | 28. If I wanted to celebrate with a friend. |
| | 36. If I would be enjoying myself at a party and wanted to feel even better. |
| | 41. If I would be relaxed with a good friend and wanted to have a good time. |
| b. Intimacy | 5. If I wanted to heighten my sexual enjoyment. |
| | 8. If I wanted to feel closer to someone I liked. |

*Note.* From *Situational Confidence Questionnaire, Short Form* by H. M. Annis, 1984, Toronto: Addiction Research Foundation. Copyright 1984 by the Addiction Research Foundation. Reprinted by permission.

demonstrated, and (6) the client's perception that the successful performance is highly relevant to problematic situations frequently encountered. These six cognitive-appraisal factors determine whether self-efficacy will be enhanced following a successful behavioral performance.

Monitoring of the client's judgments of self-efficacy with regard to drinking situations provides the therapist with an excellent tool for assessing progress in treatment. Following the successful completion of a homework assignment, a report by the client of high efficacy expectations for coping with the risk situation is a good indication that future drinking behavior in that situation may have been brought under control. However, if a client's efficacy expectations fail to improve following the successful execution of a homework assignment, probing by the therapist of the six factors outlined above should reveal the cause of the failure and suggest how future homework assignments can be modified to effect increases in self-efficacy. The need for an assessment instrument that would aid the therapist in probing these factors has led to the development of the Cognitive Appraisal Interview. This semistructured interview was designed to explore, in depth, cognitions associated with the client's previous experiences in high-risk situations. It is currently in the preliminary stages of development; efforts are being made to incorporate assessment of the six cognitive-appraisal factors mentioned above, and to supplement this with an investigation of other related aspects of the appraisal process (as discussed earlier in the chapter). Examples in each of the six areas are given below.

A task that is not judged as challenging may indicate that the client is ready to make faster progress through the hierarchy to assignments involving higher-risk drinking situations. On the other hand, if a client has had to exert a highly aversive level of effort to succeed with the homework assignment, slower progress through the hierarchy may be needed for the client to gain confidence in his or her ability to handle drinking situations. For instances in which a client attributes his or her behavioral improvement to an external source (e.g., the therapist; a collateral such as a spouse, concerned friend, or employer; or the use of an antialcohol drug), the involvement of such sources in the design and execution of future homework assignments should be phased out. The client can be encouraged to become his or her own therapist and held responsible for the planning of future homework assignments. The involvement of a spouse or a boss in accompanying and supporting the client on homework assignments can be decreased. The use of an antialcohol drug can be terminated; or, with shorter-acting alcohol-sensitizing agents, frequency of use can be restricted to progressively fewer risk situations (see Peachey & Annis, 1985), so that attribution for improvement becomes instated in the client. For a client who discounts the significance of a mastery experience by failing to perceive it as part of an overall pattern of improvement, the therapist may have the client (1) list all the changes that have occurred in his or her drinking behavior and adjustment since entering treatment; and (2) design a performance task that, if successfully accomplished, would be seen as indicative of significant improvement. This latter assignment can also be of value when clients fail to perceive an increase in their personal control or feel that they have not yet experienced mastery in their most problematic drinking areas.

In summary, monitoring of a client's efficacy expectations following performance assignments can provide a valid indicator of the progress being made in treatment. When self-efficacy is not enhanced despite successful experiences in controlling drinking behavior, monitoring of cognitive factors known to influence the formation of efficacy judgments can reveal the nature of the self-defeating ideation and suggest modification in performance tasks to facilitate the development of self-efficacy.

## Clinical Examples

Brief accounts are presented in this section of eight alcoholics who received therapy involving cognitive assessment and self-efficacy counseling. These clinical examples are chosen to illustrate the design of treatment strategies in relation to the diagnosis of a drinking problem within each of the eight categories of drinking risk on the IDS and SCQ. In reading the case material, it should be kept in mind that only a single problem category within each client's hierarchy of risk situations is being discussed for illustrative purposes. Each client's hierarchy typically contained three to five areas of drinking risk that were addressed over the course of eight treatment sessions through a median of 35 homework assignments (see Annis & Davis, 1984).

The first clinical example below is presented in somewhat greater detail than the others, to provide an understanding of the context of treatment planning in which the particular category of drinking risk was addressed.

### Case 1: Interpersonal Conflict

K. H. was a 35-year-old laborer who had worked for the same company for the previous 9 years. On intake he reported a long-standing daily drinking style that had risen over the previous 18 months from an average of 20 ounces of liquor a day to 40 ounces a day. K. H. was single and lived in a building where all the tenants were heavy drinkers. A situational assessment of his drinking problem on the IDS showed that his heavy drinking over the previous year had tended to take place in positive social contexts with drinking friends where he felt under some pressure from others to drink.

K. H.'s SCQ profile of efficacy expectations at intake to treatment in relation to the eight categories of drinking situations is shown in Figure 3-2. Following feedback and discussion of the profile with K. H., the therapist developed a three-level hierarchy of drinking risk to serve as a guide for treatment planning and the design of homework assignments; the hierarchy is presented here from highest- to lowest-risk areas.

1. Social Pressure to Drink/Positive Emotional States (Social Drinking). Over time, K. H. had developed a social network composed almost exclusively of heavy drinkers, with the result that all of his social activities now involved some drinking. The problems raised by living in a building in which all the tenants were heavy drinkers, and by associating with coworkers who drank, were seen as major areas to be addressed in treatment.

2. Negative Emotional States/Interpersonal Conflict. K. H. often drank excessively when feelings of stress, anger, or depression would build up to intolerable levels. Current sources of stress included difficulties he was having with his foreman at work and financial problems. In the past, drinking in response to stress had resulted in episodes of physical violence on several occasions.

3. Urges and Temptations/Testing Personal Control. K. H. frequently

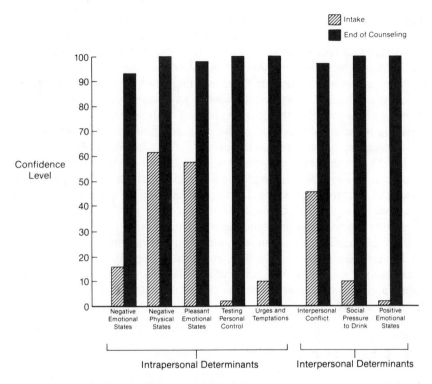

FIGURE 3-2.   SCQ profile for Case 1 (K. H.) at intake and the end of counseling.

experienced strong urges to drink when he was exposed to cues that had been associated with habitual drinking in the past. He was tempted, in such circumstances, to test his control over alcohol, but expressed great apprehension about what might happen if he took a single drink. K. H. had very little confidence in his ability to prevent a full-scale relapse if he drank in response to such urges.

In the initial treatment sessions, K. H. was asked to monitor his urges to drink in terms of the situational context in which they arose; their intensity; and his thoughts, feelings, and behavior when urges were experienced. The aim here was to increase K. H.'s awareness of the types of cues that were triggering his urges and temptations and how he was reacting to them, so that alternative coping responses could be discussed. Other assignments included his taking steps to bring his payments to his finance company up to date, putting a deposit on a new apartment, avoiding a weekly poker game at which heavy drinking took place, developing new social contacts by joining a local baseball team, and going to Bingo games and other social activities with a new woman friend who was supportive of K. H.'s abstinence goal and the changes he was trying to make in his life.

In the fourth counseling session, K. H. complained of mounting stresses in the workplace. He felt that his foreman did not trust him and was attempting to smell his breath in the morning and note with whom he went to lunch. Although he was continuing to have lunch with coworkers who drank, he was proud of the progress he had made and the fact that he was ordering nonalcoholic drinks. In the past, conflicts with the foreman had occasioned angry outbursts on the part of K. H., often followed by drinking bouts. The emergence of Interpersonal Conflict at work presented an opportunity during treatment to deal directly with this area through the design of performance tasks. During the counseling session, K. H. was encouraged to plan and rehearse what he could say to his foreman to deal constructively with the problem. Subsequently, in the workplace K. H. was able to approach his foreman in a nonemotional manner and was pleased by his foreman's explanation and concerned response. K. H.'s efficacy expectations with regard to being able to handle such situations without drinking rose substantially over the course of treatment (see Interpersonal Conflict, Figure 3-2).

## Case 2: Social Pressure to Drink

K. D. was a single man in his mid-30s living at home with his mother. At the time of his seeking treatment, his drinking had not caused any difficulties in the workplace, but had resulted in several driving-while-impaired (DWI) charges and an assault charge that was pending. Although he described himself as a binge drinker, these binges were relatively infrequent events within a pattern of heavy daily drinking. He usually drank with other people, described himself as shy, and used alcohol as a social facilitator.

At the outset of treatment, K. D. expressed his intention to continue to visit a local bar where he used to drink because he valued the social interaction. The therapist attempted to explore alternatives and expressed concern that K. D. might find himself under more Social Pressure to Drink in the bar setting than he could handle in the early stages of treatment. Although K. D. acknowledged the risks involved, he remained adamant about socializing in bars. The following plan was adopted: Initially, he would take an antialcohol drug as a safeguard for exposure to this setting; in time, when he felt more confident about his ability to cope without this external aid, the drug would be withdrawn. K. D. continued to visit the local bar, using the antialcohol drug and drinking soft drinks or coffee. He found that the setting was easier to deal with if he did not socialize with some of his former drinking buddies. In later weeks, K. D. increased his involvement in other activities, decreased his use of the antialcohol drug, and found the bar neither as attractive nor as troublesome as it had been initially.

## Case 3: Positive Interpersonal Emotional States

O. N. was a 46-year-old married man who was drinking 12–16 beers daily at the time of entering treatment. For the past 3 years, his drinking had been causing serious problems in his marriage and with the company in which he was employed as a store manager. O. N. complained of having become "paranoid" in social drinking situations because of an increasing tendency to ruminate over what others were thinking about him. He considered himself a compulsive drinker and was interested in receiving help in gaining long-term abstinence.

Soon after O. N. entered treatment and began abstaining from alcohol, it became clear that he was no longer experiencing the "paranoid" thoughts in social situations that had been so troublesome to him. However, the temptation to drink in social settings remained very high. He was particularly concerned about how he would cope with business and other parties. In the first weeks of treatment, O. N. planned to avoid social functions in which he anticipated that the temptation to drink would be too high. Since he felt somewhat more confident about abstaining at family parties, it was decided to begin assignments in this area. Fortunately, because the Christmas holiday season was approaching, there were several family parties at which new strategies could be tested. O. N. and his wife worked out a signal whereby O. N. could alert his wife when he felt tempted to drink, so that she could leave the room with him and offer some support until he regained his confidence. The mere availability of this plan proved to be sufficient. To his surprise, O. N. experienced little need to implement the strategy and reported feeling comfortable acting as bartender at the family parties.

## Case 4: Negative Emotional States

J. A. was a 53-year-old woman who had been living alone for 3 years since the breakdown of her marriage. She was a binge drinker, consuming about 8 ounces of liquor on drinking days. She reported that her drinking had been problematic for many years, but that things had worsened over the past couple of years to the point that she was now experiencing hangovers on weekdays and missing time from her job as a grocery store clerk. Almost all of her drinking took place when she was home alone, feeling bored and depressed, and ruminating over past disappointments.

J. A. recognized that her social isolation and inactivity led to feelings of loneliness and depression, which frequently resulted in heavy drinking.

Because J. A. had been very active in earlier years, the plan was adopted that she would work on renewing social activities that had been rewarding in the past, and look into a new idea she had of working as a volunteer at a center for emotionally disturbed children. J. A. found this assignment more difficult than originally anticipated. In the first few weeks, she reported a number of "legitimate" excuses for not initiating several of the activities she had planned. In later sessions, she claimed to be exploring other options that had arisen during treatment. It was only after repeated attempts over many weeks that J. A. was able to resume a few of her interests. At discharge from treatment, she reported improved self-efficacy in dealing with loneliness and depression without the use of alcohol.

## Case 5: Negative Physical States

G. D. was a 63-year-old divorced woman who lived alone and worked as a physiotherapist with chronic care patients. Her drinking had been problematic for many years and had resulted in her admission to an inpatient treatment program 10 years earlier. She was concerned that her current alcohol use was causing her problems with her supervisor and jeopardizing her job and her pension. Examination of her SCQ scores on intake revealed a fairly flat profile with low confidence ratings across risk situations within each category. G. D. was resistant to the idea of total abstinence, but did agree to abstain at least in the early phases of treatment.

G. D. attributed a recent drinking episode to the stress of having some of her teeth extracted. She reported a habitual pattern of reacting to stress by self-medicating with alcohol or Valium. G. D. complained of arthritis, which now prevented her from knitting and sewing, and of physical and emotional stress related to her work as a physiotherapist, which often resulted in difficulty falling asleep. G. D. had already tried getting up and having some warm milk as a relaxant, but had not found this beneficial. Because she had tried relaxation techniques in the past and was open to trying this alternative, it was agreed that she would obtain a copy of a relaxation tape and start using it at bedtime. However, G. D. did not follow through on this plan. Her health deteriorated rapidly over the next few weeks, and she resumed the use of sleeping pills. Although no excessive drinking was reported during the course of treatment, on a couple of occasions G. D. did engage in some unplanned drinking.

## Case 6: Positive Emotional States

B. F. was a 51-year-old salesman who had lived alone since his divorce over 10 years ago. He had engaged in a steady drinking style for many years, consisting of about 7 drinks per day after work and 13 drinks on days off. B. F. had no serious physical, legal, or financial problems, but was concerned about keeping his job. He had been referred to treatment by his company because of deteriorated performance. B. F. agreed that his work performance had deteriorated, and he did not want to lose his job. However, he enjoyed relaxing with a drink, and, apart from the work situation, he did not feel that his drinking was a problem.

B. F. had for many years spent his Christmas vacation gambling in Las Vegas. Because he lived alone and had no family, he was unwilling to cancel this trip, despite the obvious risk that he might resume drinking. Several months before his vacation, B. F. began planning with his therapist a number of specific coping strategies. B. F. developed a timetable for his activities, decided to rent a car so that he could spend more time sightseeing, and practiced ordering ginger ale because he felt that this soft drink would look like a mixed drink when he was playing at the tables and would not attract notice. Some time was spent on imagined "slip" rehearsal (i.e., how he might stop if any drinking occurred); however, he failed to gain confidence in being able to stop after one or two drinks. On a weekend "dry-run" trip out of town to test the strategies, B. F. reported that the temptations to drink had been great, but that no drinking had taken place. At the end of treatment, B. F. remained convinced that "the test was worth it" and that he would go to Las Vegas. He did not report back to the therapist on the outcome of the trip.

## Case 7: Testing Personal Control

L. M. was a young man in his early 20s who was referred to counseling by his company when his chronic absenteeism was found to be alcohol-related. Drinking for L. M. had become an adjunct to almost all social activities. Most of his friends drank, as did his coworkers, especially when they were on jobs that took them out of town for extended periods of time. He felt that he never really drank much more than his friends but that he had been irresponsible in letting his drinking interfere with his work. On entering treatment, L. M. expressed the desire to learn to drink socially and confine his drinking to the weekends. He did agree to remain entirely abstinent in the early weeks of treatment.

In his fourth counseling session, L. M. raised the issue of having a few drinks before the next session. He would be spending the weekend at home with his parents and felt confident that he could test his control over alcohol safely in that situation and limit his consumption to two beers. L. M. was successful in meeting this goal. For several subsequent drinking assignments, his girlfriend was enlisted to support his attempts to (1) drink only when planned on weekends, (2) maintain a preset drinking limit, and

(3) pace his drinks. Although experience in keeping his drinking within the planned limits proved more difficult when his girlfriend was not present, L. M. was largely successful in meeting his drinking goals.

## Case 8: Urges and Temptations

K. E. was a married man in his late 20s whose drinking had resulted in excessive absenteeism from the workplace. Shortly before entering treatment, he had received his third DWI charge within 4 years. He was a steady, daily drinker who consumed about 10 beers a day, usually at a local social club.

K. E. expressed greatest concern about learning to handle urges to drink. It was decided that he would monitor such urges for a month, noting their intensity and antecedents, as well as his own cognitive, affective, and behavioral responses to them. K. E. and his therapist worked on the premise that the time between an urge and behavior could be lengthened by having available prearranged coping strategies that could take the place of drinking. K. E. felt that initially he would like to try removing himself from the situation and "waiting out the urge." This strategy proved to work well for him. As he had anticipated, he experienced an urge to drink some time later while attending his social club. However, he was able to leave and wait it out as he had planned. With this strategy in hand, his confidence in his ability to handle future urges and temptations was strengthened.

## Summary and Conclusion

The relevance of Bandura's theory of self-efficacy to the assessment and treatment of alcoholic clients is examined in this chapter. According to this theory, when a client enters a high-risk situation for alcoholic relapse, a process of cognitive appraisal is set up, culminating in the formation of an efficacy judgment that in turn mediates drinking behavior. It is proposed that the most powerful methods for producing lasting changes in efficacy expectations and related drinking behavior will involve performance-based homework assignments conducted in the client's natural environment. Treatment planning begins with a highly individualized microanalysis of the drinking behavior of the client. Two assessment instruments are described that assist in this analysis. The IDS assesses situations in which the client drank heavily over the past year; the SCQ provides a profile of the client's efficacy expectations in each of these high-risk situations, which can be of value in planning homework assignments and monitoring progress in treatment. Six cognitive-appraisal factors influential in the formation of efficacy judgments are discussed; it is recommended that these factors be monitored in treatment to insure that the successful completion of homework assignments is leading to the formation of strong efficacy expectations, which is required for the maintenance of behavior change. Eight clinical cases are presented to illustrate the design of performance tasks within the eight categories of drinking risk on the IDS and SCQ.

Two randomized clinical trials are presently under way at the Addiction Research Foundation in Ontario to test the value of this relapse prevention model in improving alcoholism treatment outcome.

## Acknowledgment

The views expressed in this chapter are our own and do not necessarily reflect those of the Addiction Research Foundation.

## References

Annis, H. M. (1982a). *Inventory of Drinking Situations.* Toronto: Addiction Research Foundation. (Available in paper-and-pencil and software versions from the Marketing Department, Addiction Research Foundation, 33 Russell Street, Toronto, Ontario M5S 2S1, Canada. Telephone 416-595-6056.)

Annis, H. M. (1982b). *Situational Confidence Questionnaire.* Toronto: Addiction Research Foundation. (Available in paper-and-pencil and software versions from the Marketing Department, Addiction Research Foundation, 33 Russell Street, Toronto, Ontario M5S 2S1, Canada. Telephone 416-595-6056.)

Annis, H. M. (1984a). *Inventory of Drinking Situations, short form.* Toronto: Addiction Research Foundation.

Annis, H. M. (1984b). *Situational Confidence Questionnaire, short form.* Toronto: Addiction Research Foundation.

Annis, H. M. (1986). A relapse prevention model for treatment of alcoholics. In W. R. Miller & N. Heather (Eds.), *Treating addictive behaviors* (pp. 407–433). New York: Plenum Press.

Annis, H. M., & Davis, C. (1984, November). *Relapse prevention treatment for alcoholics: Initial findings.* Paper presented at the Third International Conference on the Treatment of Addictive Behaviours, North Berwick, Scotland.

Annis, H. M., & Kelly, P. (1984, August). *Analysis of the Inventory of Drinking Situations.* Paper presented at the convention of the American Psychological Association, Toronto.

Bandura, A. (1977). Self-efficacy: Toward a unifying theory of behavioral change. *Psychological Review, 84,* 191–215.

Bandura, A. (1978). Reflections on self-efficacy. *Advances in Behaviour Research and Therapy, 1,* 237–269.

Bandura, A. (1981). Self-referent thought: A developmental analysis of self-efficacy. In J. H. Flavell & L. Ross (Eds.), *Social cognitive development: Frontiers and possible futures* (pp. 200–239). New York: Cambridge University Press.

Bandura, A., Adams, N. E., Hardy, A. B., & Howells, G. N. (1980). Tests of the generality of self-efficacy theory. *Cognitive Therapy and Research, 4,* 39–66.

Beck, A. T. (1976). *Cognitive therapy and the emotional disorders.* New York: International Universities Press.

Beck, A. T., Rush, A. J., Shaw, B. F., & Emery, G. (1979). *Cognitive therapy of depression.* New York: Guilford Press.

Blanchard, E. B. (1970). Relative contributions of modeling, informational influences, and physical contact in extinction of phobic behavior. *Journal of Abnormal Psychology, 76,* 55-61.

Chambliss, C., & Murray, E. J. (1979). Cognitive procedures for smoking reduction: Symptom attribution versus efficacy attribution. *Cognitive Therapy and Research, 3,* 91-95.

Chaney, E. F., O'Leary, M. R., & Marlatt, G. A. (1978). Skill training with alcoholics. *Journal of Consulting and Clinical Psychology, 46,* 1092-1104.

Condiotte, M. M., & Lichtenstein, E. (1981). Self-efficacy and relapse in smoking cessation programs. *Journal of Consulting and Clinical Psychology, 49,* 648-658.

Condra, M. S. (1982). *The effectiveness of relapse-prevention training in the treatment of alcohol problems.* Unpublished doctoral dissertation, Queen's University, Kingston, Ontario, Canada.

Cooney, N. L., Kopel, S. A., & McKeon, P. (1982, August). *Controlled relapse training and self-efficacy in ex-smokers.* Paper presented at the convention of the American Psychological Association, Washington, DC.

Donovan, D. M., & Chaney, E. F. (1985). Alcoholic relapse prevention and intervention: Models and methods. In G. A. Marlatt & J. R. Gordon (Eds.), *Relapse prevention: Maintenance strategies in the treatment of addictive behaviors* (pp. 351-416). New York: Guilford Press.

Eastman, C., & Marzillier, J. S. (1984). Theoretical and methodological difficulties in Bandura's self-efficacy theory. *Cognitive Therapy and Research, 8,* 213-229.

Ellis, A. (1970). *The essence of rational psychotherapy: A comprehensive approach to treatment.* New York: Institute for Rational Living.

Kazdin, A. E. (1978). Conceptual and assessment issues raised by self-efficacy theory. *Advances in Behaviour Research and Therapy, 1,* 177-185.

Kockott, G., Dittmar, F., & Nusselt, L. (1975). Systematic desensitization of erectile impotence: A controlled study. *Archives of Sexual Behavior, 4,* 493-500.

Lazarus, R. S. (1966). *Psychological stress and the coping process.* New York: McGraw-Hill.

Litman, G. K., Stapleton, J., Oppenheim, A. N., Peleg, M., & Jackson, P. (1984). The relationship between coping behaviours, their effectiveness and alcoholism relapse and survival. *British Journal of Addiction, 79,* 283-291.

Marlatt, G. A. (1978). Craving for alcohol, loss of control, and relapse: A cognitive-behavioral analysis. In P. E. Nathan, G. A. Marlatt, & T. Løberg (Eds.), *Alcoholism: New directions in behavioral research and treatment* (pp. 271-314). New York: Plenum Press.

Marlatt, G. A. (1979a). Alcohol use and problem drinking: A cognitive-behavioral analysis. In P. C. Kendall & S. D. Hollon (Eds.), *Cognitive-behavioral interventions: Theory, research and procedures* (pp. 319-355). New York: Academic Press.

Marlatt, G. A. (1979b). A cognitive-behavioral model of the relapse process. In N. A. Krasnegor (Ed.), *Behavioral analysis and treatment of substance abuse* (NIDA Research Monograph No. 25, pp. 191-200). Washington, DC: U.S. Government Printing Office.

Marlatt, G. A. (1985a). Cognitive assessment and intervention procedures for relapse prevention. In G. A. Marlatt & J. R. Gordon (Eds.), *Relapse prevention: Maintenance strategies in the treatment of addictive behaviors* (pp. 201-279). New York: Guilford Press.

Marlatt, G. A. (1985b). Cognitive factors in the relapse process. In G. A. Marlatt & J. R. Gordon (Eds.), *Relapse prevention: Maintenance strategies in the treatment of addictive behaviors* (pp. 128-200). New York: Guilford Press.

Marlatt, G. A. (1985c). Situational determinants of relapse and skill-training interventions. In G. A. Marlatt & J. R. Gordon (Eds.). *Relapse prevention: Maintenance strategies in the treatment of addictive behaviors* (pp. 71-127). New York: Guilford Press.

Marlatt, G. A., & George, W. H. (1984). Relapse prevention: Introduction and overview of the model. *British Journal of Addiction, 79,* 261–275.

Marlatt, G. A., & Gordon, J. R. (1980). Determinants of relapse: Implications for the maintenance of behavior change. In P. O. Davidson & S. M. Davidson (Eds.). *Behavioral medicine: Changing health lifestyles* (pp. 410–452). New York: Brunner/Mazel.

Marlatt, G. A., & Gordon, J. R. (Eds.). (1985). *Relapse prevention: Maintenance strategies in the treatment of addictive behaviors.* New York: Guilford Press.

Marlatt, G. A., & Parks, G. A. (1982). Self-management of addictive disorders. In P. Karoly & F. H. Kanfer (Eds.), *Self-management and behavior change* (pp. 243–288). New York: Pergamon Press.

Mathews, A., Bancroft, J., Whitehead, A., Hackman, A., Julier, D., Bancroft, J., Garth, D., & Shaw, P. (1976). The behavioural treatment of sexual inadequacy: A comparative study. *Behaviour Research and Therapy, 14,* 427–436.

McCrady, B. S., Dean, L., Dubreuil, E., & Swanson, S. (1985). The problem drinkers project: A programmatic application of social-learning-based treatment. In G. A. Marlatt & J. R. Gordon (Eds.), *Relapse prevention: Maintenance strategies in the treatment of addictive behaviors* (pp. 417–471). New York: Guilford Press.

Peachey, J. E., & Annis, H. M. (1984). Pharmacologic treatment of chronic alcoholism. *Psychiatric Clinics of North America, 7,* 745–755.

Peachey, J. E., & Annis, H. M. (1985). New strategies for using the alcohol-sensitizing drugs. In C. A. Naranjo & E. M. Sellers (Eds.), *Research advances in new psychopharmacological treatments for alcoholism.* Amsterdam: Elsevier.

Prochaska, J. O., Crimi, P., Lapsanski, D., Martel, L., & Reid, P. (1982). Self-change processes, self-efficacy and self-concept in relapse and maintenance of cessation of smoking. *Psychological Reports, 51,* 983–990.

Rachman, S., & Hodgson, R. (1979). *Obsessions and compulsions.* Englewood Cliffs, NJ: Prentice-Hall.

Sanchez-Craig, M. (1975). A self-control strategy for drinking tendencies. *The Ontario Psychologist, 7,* 25–29.

Sanchez-Craig, M. (1979, February). *Reappraisal therapy: A self-control strategy for abstinence and controlled drinking.* Paper presented at the Taos International Conference on Treatment of Addictive Behaviors, Taos, NM. (Available as ARF Substudy 1057 from the Library, Addiction Research Foundation, Toronto.)

Sobell, M. B., & Sobell, L. C. (1973). Individualized behavior therapy for alcoholics. *Behavior Therapy, 4,* 49–72.

Weiner, B. (1979). A theory of motivation for some classroom experiences. *Journal of Educational Psychology, 71,* 3–25.

Weiner, B. (1980). *Human motivation.* New York: Holt, Rinehart & Winston.

Wilson, G. T. (1978a). Booze, beliefs and behavior: Cognitive processes in alcohol use and abuse. In P. E. Nathan, G. A. Marlatt, & T. Løberg (Eds.). *Alcoholism: New directions in behavioral research and treatment* (pp. 315–339). New York: Plenum Press.

Wilson, G. T. (1978b). The importance of being theoretical: A commentary on Bandura's "Self-efficacy: Towards a unifying theory of behavioral change." *Advances in Behavior Research and Therapy, 1,* 217–230.

Wilson, G. T. (1979). Perceived control and the theory and practice of behavior therapy. In L. C. Perlmuter & R. A. Monty (Eds.), *Choice and perceived control* (pp. 175–189). Hillsdale, NJ: Erlbaum.

Wilson, G. T. (1980). Cognitive factors in lifestyle changes: A social learning perspective. In P. O. Davidson & S. M. Davidson (Eds.), *Behavioral medicine: Changing health lifestyles* (pp. 3–37). New York: Brunner/Mazel.

# 4

# PHYSIOLOGICAL ASSESSMENT

**GILLIAN LEIGH**
**HARVEY A. SKINNER**
*Addiction Research Foundation*

## Introduction

Excessive alcohol consumption may lead to a wide range of effects on the life and health of an individual. For this reason, no single method of assessment has been found to give a complete picture of the nature and severity of alcohol problems. There is a general consensus that individuals should be assessed using a variety of methods, including self-report, behavioral observation, collateral reports, official records, and physiological procedures such as laboratory tests (Skinner, 1981, 1984). Convergence of information across several assessment methods can be used to validate the level of alcohol consumption and alcohol-related problems. However, such a multimodal assessment is costly to implement, and thus may not be feasible in many treatment settings. The need to develop corroborative indices has arisen partly in response to a general skepticism about the validity of self-reported drinking. Considerable efforts have been directed toward the development of "objective markers" of alcohol consumption (Holt, Skinner, & Israel, 1981; Salaspuro, 1986; Skinner, Holt & Israel, 1981; Watson, Mohs, Eskelson, Sampliner, & Hartmann, 1986).

The purpose of this chapter is to outline progress that has been made in the development of laboratory indices. The chapter is divided into four sections. First, attention is given to what would constitute ideal markers of alcohol consumption. Then, a brief review is given of alternative methods for assessing alcohol use. The third section focuses upon clinical applications of laboratory tests for assessing alcohol use in the past 24 hours and over longer time intervals. Emphasis is placed upon (1) the use of composite indices that increase diagnostic accuracy by combining information from several tests, and (2) the establishment of a within-subject baseline on a given laboratory test. Finally, case studies are presented regarding use of laboratory tests with a patient manifesting major symptoms of alcohol dependence, and with early-stage problem drinkers.

## Ideal Markers of Alcohol Consumption

Imagine some point in the future when the "perfect marker" of alcohol use has been established. What would this test actually assess? A few moments of reflection suggest that one would need several markers to serve different purposes. For instance, one would want to be able to differentiate among different patterns of alcohol use over varying time intervals. The only true indicator of alcohol consumption is the detection of alcohol in an individual's body fluids. However, these compounds have a relatively short half-life, which limits their applications to drinking in the previous 24 hours. With a longer time window (say, 4–8 weeks), one would probably need different tests that could provide information on such parameters as the total amount of ethanol consumed during this period, the maximum blood alcohol concentration (BAC) achieved, and the variability in drinking style (e.g., frequent vs. binge drinking). The situation becomes even more complicated when one attempts to develop markers for drinking histories over much longer periods, such as the previous 12 months. From this discussion, it should be clear that we are actually seeking several "ideal" tests that serve different purposes in assessing an individual's drinking history.

Another reason underlying the need for several tests is the growing recognition of the multidimensional nature of alcohol abuse. Skinner (1984, 1985) has described a three-dimensional framework (Table 4-1), which is based in part upon recent classifications by the World Health Organization (Edwards, Gross, Keller, Moser, & Room, 1977) and the American Psychiatric Association (1980). The first dimension concerns the individual's drinking behavior. Key variables include the frequency of drinking, quantity consumed per drinking occasion, variability in consumption, types of beverages consumed, time of day when alcohol was consumed, and situations where drinking occurred. With these data, one may calculate various indices for a given time period, such as the number of abstinent days, light- or moderate-drinking days (less than 60 g ethanol), and heavy-drinking days (more than 60 g ethanol). Most of the research to date on laboratory indices has focused on the measurement of total alcohol consumption.

The second dimension concerns the alcohol dependence syndrome, which is marked by an impaired control over alcohol intake, increased tolerance to alcohol, severe withdrawal symptoms following cessation of drinking, and a compulsive drinking style (Edwards & Gross, 1976). It is estimated that approximately 5%–7% of men in North America exhibit major symptoms of alcohol dependence (Polich, 1982). Although little research has been done to date on physiological indices of the alcohol dependence syndrome, some important work has been conducted on quantifying the severity of alcohol withdrawal symptoms (Naranjo & Sellers, 1986).

The third dimension concerns the various biomedical and psychosocial

TABLE 4-1 .   Multiaxial Classification ofA lcohol Problems

| Axis | Status (ratings given for each variable) |
|---|---|
| I.   Drinking history | |
| Frequency of drinking | 0 = abstinent/light drinking |
| Quantity consumed | (0-1 drinks/day) |
| Drinking style (continuous vs. binge) | 1 = medium drinking |
| Drinking situation/antecedents | (2-3 drinks/day) |
| Duration of hazardous/harmful drinking | 2 = hazardous drinking |
| | (4-6 drinks/day) |
| | 3 = harmful drinking |
| | (7 or more drinks/day) |
| II.  Dependence syndrome | |
| Impaired control over drinking | 0 = no symptoms |
| Increased tolerance | 1 = mild/moderate |
| Withdrawal symptoms | 2 = substantial symptoms |
| Compulsive drinking style | 3 = severe symptoms |
| III. Problems related to drinking | |
| Biomedical (e.g., traumatic injury, liver disease, hypertension, gastritis) | 0 = no problems |
| | 1 = mild/moderate |
| | 2 = substantial problems |
| | 3 = severe problems |
| Psychosocial (e.g., absenteeism at work, family problems, anxiety/depression, intellectual impairment, legal problems) | |

*Note.* Adapted from "Assessing Alcohol Use at Patients in Treatment" by H. A. Skinner, 1984, in Y. Israel, F. B. Glaser, H. Kalant, R. E. Popham, W. Schmidt, and R. G. Smart (Eds.), *Research Advances in Alcohol and Drug Problems* (Vol. 8, pp. 183-207), New York: Plenum Press. Copyright 1984 by Plenum Publishing Corporation. Adapted by permission.

problems that are associated with excessive drinking. The prevalence of nondependent alcohol abuse has been estimated at between 15% and 35% of the adult male population (Polich, 1982). This type of problem drinking tends to be more prevalent among young males, in whom alcohol-related disabilities (e.g., accidental injuries) are often linked to acute episodes of intoxication. There is an extensive body of literature on the use of laboratory tests for the assessment of physical disorders that may be related to alcohol abuse. An example is the combined clinical and laboratory index developed by Orrego, Israel, Blake, and Medline (1983) for the assessment of alcoholic liver disease.

The multiaxial classification of Table 4-1 provides a conceptual framework for intake assessment, differential treatment planning, and outcome evaluations. Although the present chapter focuses primarily on the use of laboratory tests for the assessment of alcohol consumption (Dimension I), one must not lose sight of the need to carefully assess an individual's status with respect to dependence symptoms (Dimension II) and problems related to drinking (Dimension III).

## Different Approaches for Assessing Alcohol Use

Self-reports of recent alcohol consumption have in fact been found to be fairly accurate, especially if the patient is sober at the time of assessment. Studies to validate self-reports by collaterals have generally shown a high degree of agreement between patients and collaterals, with no consistent direction of error (Skinner, 1984). Underestimation is more likely to occur if the patient records a positive BAC at the time of assessment (M. B. Sobell, Sobell, & Vanderspek, 1979), and the longer the patient remains in treatment, the greater the accuracy of self-reported consumption appears to become (McCrady, Paolino, & Longabaugh, 1978). The accuracy of self-reports also depends upon the patient's memory and ability to comprehend instructions, both of which may be impaired in heavy alcohol consumers (Carlen, Wilkinson, Wortzman, & Holgate, 1984), as well as upon the effects of withdrawal from alcohol, such as heightened anxiety and poor concentration.

Structured interviews and carefully developed drinking questionnaires may help in the collection of self-report data (Skinner & Allen, 1983; L. C. Sobell & Sobell, 1981). Rohan (1976) designed a lifetime drinking history using an interview format, and found a test–retest reliability above .97 for information on a patient's duration of regular drinking. Skinner and Sheu (1982) also found highly reliable coefficients for lifetime duration of drinking (.94) and lifetime total volume consumed (.80), and a slightly lower reliability score for lifetime daily average (.68). These studies agree with that of Armor, Polich, and Stambul (1978), in which reports of *frequency* of consumption were more consistent than actual *quantity* consumed on a given day.

Behavioral observation studies have shown that a person can recall recent drinking episodes fairly accurately. A controlled study found that approximately half of the individuals (54%) could recall the exact number and type of drinks they had consumed 3–7 days previously, whereas 21% underreported and 9% overreported (Hartford, Dorman, & Feinhandler, 1976). In this study, the more individuals drank, the less accurately they remembered the exact amount. The accuracy of self-report can be increased if patients are asked to monitor their consumption by keeping daily diaries (Sanchez-Craig & Annis, 1982).

Using BAC in breath samples as a measure to corroborate self-reports, two studies have found patients to underreport the amount of alcohol recently consumed. Armor, Polich, and Stambul (1978) found self-reported alcohol consumption to fall about 25% below that which was recorded by

BAC; Polich (1982), conducting a further follow-up study on the same population, found that 35% of those cases reporting drinking in the past 24 hours underreported their consumption, and only 7% overreported.

In summary, research suggests that patients may be expected to report more accurately on consequences related to alcohol abuse and the frequency of drinking than on the actual quantity consumed (Skinner, 1984). There may be various reasons why a patient should wish to underreport the amount of alcohol consumed, or it may simply be difficult to keep track of the total quantity. Whatever the patient's reason for doing this, the clinician needs to have accurate information on consumption at assessment before treatment so that the best type of treatment may be planned. It is also important to have accurate information on consumption during the treatment period itself to make sure that patients are complying with program requirements.

### Clinical Applications

*Indicators of Drinking in the Past 24 Hours*

Detection of the presence of alcohol by breath or urine analysis is fairly sensitive for alcohol use within the past 24 hours. In estimating BACs, an accurate recording can be made, provided that the breathalyzer is correctly calibrated, a sample of alveolar air is obtained, and the patient has not ingested other chemicals or smoked a cigarette immediately before giving the breath sample. The advantages of using a breathalyzer are the noninvasive character of the test, rapid determination of consumption, and the possibility of making multiple determinations.

The urine alcohol concentration (UAC) parallels the BAC when serial collections are obtained (Kalant, 1971), indicating that the two measures are subject to similar metabolic factors. Alcohol absorption is affected by the quantity and speed of alcohol consumption, gastric content, other drug use, body type, individual differences in alcohol metabolism by the liver, and the presence of certain disease states (Sellers & Kalant, 1976). Screening by use of urine samples can establish the presence not only of alcohol, but also of other drugs. Urine samples may be used routinely in clinics to insure both that drug regimens are being adhered to and that alcohol is not being used when abstinence is required (Orrego, Blendis, Blake, Kapur, & Israel, 1979).

A new method of assessing for the presence of alcohol in body fluids is the use of a dipstick (Kapur & Israel, 1983). This is a solid support system method in which strips of a filter paper, impregnated with a specific buffered enzyme–cofactor–inhibitor system, change color in response to contact with alcohol. The dipstick is based on the alcohol dehydrogenase-nicotinamide ademine dinucleotide (ADH–NAD) system, which has been found to be specific for alcohol. The acceptable range of alcohol concentration is 5–160 mg/dl (1–35 mmol/liter), resulting in changes of color from a light pink to deep red, the gradations being observable by the human eye. The dipstick reacts to alcohol in solutions of saliva, urine, and blood, and is reported to have an analytic sensitivity of 97.5% and a specificity of 98.8%. When compared against spectrophotometric and gas-chromatographic methods, correlation coefficients were found to be on the order of $r = .90$ (Kapur & Israel, 1985).

The advantages of the dipstick are its portability, ease of administration by untrained personnel, and rapid estimation of recent alcohol consumption. When dipped into a blood or urine sample, or when soaked in saliva from a cotton swab color changes are observed after 1 minute. The color can then be compared against a color-coded chart. Because this technique is relatively new, its full value has not yet been documented; however, it promises to be a very useful device for determining the presence of alcohol in body fluids.

The sweat-patch technique was introduced by M. Phillips and McAloon in 1980. It is intended to provide a noninvasive technique of estimating alcohol consumption for periods of up to 10 days. It consists of self-impregnated absorbent pads protected by a plastic chamber and a plastic water-tight adhesive. Original claims were that the patch could collect transepidermal fluid at a steady rate over the period in which the patch was in place. The assay technique is highly specific for ethanol, and M. Phillips and McAloon (1980) reported a sensitivity and specificity of 100% for distinguishing nondrinkers from drinkers of over 0.5 g/kg alcohol per day in a hospital sample. However, an actual quantitative estimation of alcohol consumption has not yet been reliably demonstrated. In testing 22 volunteer social drinkers, only 9 (40.9%) fell within the category of accurate reporting when self-reports were compared with the sweat-patch analysis (M. Phillips, 1984). Two volunteers (9.1%) were categorized as overreporters, and 11 (50.%) as underreporters. Further field tests by E. L. R. Phillips, Little, Hillman, Labbe, and Campbell (1984) have found variations in fluid volume collected among individuals, as well as variations at different body placement sites. Activity levels of the volunteers also influenced fluid collection levels, as did variations in ambient temperature. Again, the test detected the presence of alcohol above 0.5 g/kg, but not the actual amount of alcohol ingested within the previous 24 hours with any degree of certainty.

Although the test shows promise for future clinical use, there are some important problems to be solved. For example, how does one control for inter- and intraindividual alterations in skin permeability from wearing the patch, individual differences in sweat produced in response to changing temperatures and activity level, and the overall maximum saturation level of the patch? Some female volunteers also found the patch to be unsightly if visible, and some complained of skin irritation caused either by the adhesive material or by the saline-impregnated cotton pledget inside the patch.

## Indicators of Alcohol Use over Longer Periods

The laboratory tests described above have been devised to detect the amount of alcohol present in sweat, urine, or blood; however, they record only transient volumes. To get a measure of longer-term alcohol consumption, other laboratory tests have been sought. Holt *et al.* (1981) provide a detailed review of these laboratory tests and biochemical markers. The most promising indicators at present are serum gamma-glutamyl transferase (GGT) and mean corpuscular volume (MCV). Two other tests that have attracted interest are high-density lipoproteins (HDLs) and glutamate dehydrogenase (GDH).

### Gamma-Glutamyl Transferase

The association between excessive alcohol consumption and a raised level of GGT was first reported in 1972 (Rollason, Pincherle, & Robinson, 1972; Rosalki & Rau, 1972), although the enzyme had been identified as a potential diagnostic aid in liver dysfunction in 1960 (Szewczuk & Orlowski, 1960). The enzyme, which is a membrane-bound glycoprotein, is found in high concentrations in the kidney and pancreas, with low concentrations but large total quantity in the liver. It is a sensitive but nonspecific indicator of primary liver disease, and altered GGT activity may be the only biochemical abnormality in cirrhosis, with values being on average five times the upper reference limit (Penn & Worthington, 1983). However, GGT has also been found to decrease to normal values in alcoholics whose alcohol use is of long standing (Skude & Wadstein, 1977).

The reference range for GGT is higher for men than for women, and it increases with age and body weight (Chick, Kreitman, & Plant, 1981; Schiele, Guilmin, Detienne, & Siest, 1977). Chick *et al.* (1981) found that the relationship of GGT to frequency of drinking in two groups of employees disappeared when amount of drinking, weight, and age were controlled. As an indicator of excessive alcohol use, the test appears most effective in the absence of other abnormal biochemical tests of liver function. However, in some cases GGT is not raised in excessive drinkers (Bernadt, Mumford, Taylor, Smith, & Murray, 1982; Rosalki & Rau, 1972), and Robinson, Monk, and Bailey (1979) found GGT to have little relationship with reported consumption above 80 g of alcohol per week in 260 men attending a routine health examination. Trell, Kristenson, and Fex (1984) found GGT to increase linearly with *frequency* of use, but not with actual *quantity* consumed. Their large screening study comprised a group of healthy middle-aged men ($n$ = 317) scoring in the top 10% for GGT on a general medical screening investigation, as well as a comparable control group ($n$ = 213). An evaluation of the elevated levels of GGT in the former group indicated that alcohol was the predominant cause in 59.6% of the group and the probable cause in another 16.4%. However, GGT was also raised in 19% of abstainers or individuals with very limited alcohol use. Other studies have also found that GGT can be elevated in healthy individuals who cannot be said to drink excessively (Penn, Worthington, Clarke, & Whitfield, 1981; Whitehead, Clarke, & Whitfield, 1978).

In brief, multiple variables influence the activity of GGT, and the measure lacks sufficient sensitivity. Because it appears to have no direct relationship with quantity of alcohol use, especially in chronic drinkers with liver problems, it is questionable whether it should be used on its own. Some studies, however, have shown that it may have greater discriminative power when combined with other markers, and this question is discussed in a later section.

### Mean Corpuscular Volume

Several studies using hematological tests have found an increased mean corpuscular volume (MCV) to be associated with heavy alcohol consumption. MCV has been proposed as a useful means of detecting alcohol abuse (Atchinson, Hunt, & Morse, 1981; Chick *et al.,* 1981; Myrhed, Berglund, & Bottinger, 1977; Unger & Johnson, 1974; Whitehead *et al.,* 1978; Wu, Chanarin, & Levi, 1974). Atchinson *et al.* (1981) found MCV to be elevated in 20% of patients in routine laboratory testing of 143 alcoholics. Unger and Johnson (1974) found that 3% of 8,000 employees had high MCV values (more than 96 fl for men and more than 100 fl for women). A large proportion of those with high MCV values were considered to be consuming excessive amounts of alcohol. Wu *et al.* (1974) found that 89% of 63 alcoholic inpatients had high MCVs; the macrocytosis resolved with alcohol withdrawal, but persisted if alcohol intake continued.

Like GGT, MCV appears to lack sufficient sensitivity as a single measure. Bernadt *et al.* (1982) found MCV to have almost no sensitivity in the detection of "excessive drinking" (defined as more than 16 drinks per day). MCV also bears some relationship to age and smoking (Eschwege, Papoz, & Lellouch, 1978; Unger & Johnson, 1974). After controlling for frequency of drinking, age, and smoking, however, Chick *et al.* (1981) found modest partial correlations with amount of alcohol consumed ($r$'s = .29 and .14 in two groups of employed men). Although MCV was also found to have low sensitivity in this study, few false positives were detected when 98 fl was used as a cutoff point.


*High-Density Lipoproteins*

The relationship between alcohol consumption and changes in HDLs appears a complex one. An increase in HDL levels in response to alcohol consumption in rats was demonstrated by Baraona and Lieber in 1970. In 1974, two Scandinavian studies reported elevated HDL-cholesterol (HDL-C) levels in alcoholic men who had been drinking before admission to a hospital (Danielsson *et al.,* 1978; Johansson & Medhus, 1974). Levels tended to return to normal within 2 weeks of abstinence. In both studies, no relationship was observed between HDL-C and other tests of liver function.

The relationship between HDL-C levels and alcohol consumption in patients with liver disease was examined by Kapur, Holt, Blake, and Orrego (1980). These authors measured UAC and HDL-C in a group of alcoholic patients with liver disease and a control group of hospital employees with no known history of hazardous alcohol consumption. In the patient group, HDL-C was significantly higher in patients who were still drinking (identified by positive UAC), and an inverse correlation was found between HDL-C and severity of liver disease. A further study confirmed that HDL-C was raised only in patients with intact liver functioning. Devenyi, Kapur, and Roy (1984) tested 36 alcoholic men who were admitted to a hospital when intoxicated (mean BAC 61 mmol/liter). HDL-C levels were raised (1.5 mmol/liter or greater) with alcohol consumption and reduced (0.2 mmol/liter or more) after 1 or 2 weeks of abstinence. These changes were not seen in patients with severe liver disease. The authors concluded that recent alcohol intake had the greatest impact on HDL-C levels in alcoholics without liver disease. An HDL level of less than 1.5 mmol/liter after excessive drinking was an indication of severe liver damage.

A controlled study with 24 male moderate drinkers found changes in one subfraction of HDL-C, but no change in the other subfraction (Haskell *et al.,* 1984). HDL-C is carried in roughly equivalent amounts on two types of HDL: a less dense $HDL_2$ and a more dense $HDL_3$. Haskell *et al.* (1984) found $HDL_3$ to decrease after a 6-week abstinence period and to increase when drinking was resumed. There were no changes in the $HDL_2$ subfraction. Although the mechanism whereby $HDL_3$ is increased by alcohol consumption is unknown, it may be derived from "nascent" HDL released from the liver (Lieber, 1984). On the other hand, $HDL_2$ is thought to be increased after consuming large amounts of alcohol because of enhanced catabolism of very-low-density lipoproteins, which carry most of the serum triglycerides (Lieber, 1984). These triglycerides have been found to increase after large quantities of alcohol are consumed—an increase that is no longer apparent after long-term alcohol abuse. The decrease in triglycerides parallels a decrease in HDL, both measures indicating liver dysfunction (Devenyi, Robinson, & Roncari, 1980). However, both $HDL_2$ and serum triglyceride are sensitive to many other factors, especially body weight (Whitehead *et al.*, 1978). Perhaps the two subfractions of HDL–C reflect two stages of alcohol use, with moderate alcohol consumption affecting the $HDL_3$ subfraction, and excessive alcohol use in alcoholics without liver disease affecting $HDL_2$. This hypothesis needs further examination.

### *Glutamate Dehydrogenase*

In comparing the ability of different laboratory tests to screen for the presence of excessive drinking in large populations, Bernadt, Mumford, and Murray (1984) found the best laboratory test to be GDH. However, even this test did not discriminate as well as brief interview screening tests, such as the Michigan Alcoholism Screening Test (MAST; Selzer, 1971) or the Reich interview (Reich *et al.*, 1975).

GDH was found to be a reliable marker of liver cell necrosis in a study of 100 alcoholic patients, distinguishing between those patients with hepatic necrosis and those without (Van Waes & Lieber, 1977). However, these findings were not replicated by Jenkins, Rosalki, Foo, Sheuer, and Sherlock (1980), and GDH was not markedly raised in nonalcoholics consuming 2 g/kg ethanol every day for 4 weeks (Worner & Lieber, 1980). The enzyme GDH appears to have low sensitivity on its own (Bernadt *et al.*, 1982).

### Problems in Using a Single Laboratory Test

There are two major problems that severely constrain the use of any single laboratory test as a marker of alcohol consumption. First, no laboratory test possesses both high sensitivity and high specificity for detecting heavy alcohol use outside of the past 24 hours. For screening purposes, a test should have high *sensitivity* (proportion of excessive drinkers with an abnormal test result) in detecting genuine cases of alcohol abuse. On the other hand, *specificity* (proportion of nonexcessive drinkers with normal results) is important in diagnosis to rule out individuals who are not drinking excessively. The various laboratory tests that have been studied to date are not highly specific to alcohol use. For example, GGT may be elevated as the result of ingestion of a hepatic-enzyme-inducing medication, such as barbiturates; MCV may be elevated because of cigarette smoking; and HDL may be depressed because of liver disease (Holt *et al.*, 1981). For instance, an abstainer from alcohol who smokes cigarettes and is taking barbiturates may have elevated GGT and MCV tests. Thus, clinicians who are considering laboratory tests as markers of alcohol use must make a careful appraisal of factors other than drinking that are known to cause abnormal laboratory results.

With respect to sensitivity, several studies have shown that the laboratory tests have only moderate value (approximately 30%–40% sensitivity) in ambulatory populations with known alcohol problems (Bernadt et al., 1982; Chick et al., 1981; Skinner, Holt, Schuller, Roy & Israel, 1984). For example, a recent study by Cushman, Jacobson, Barboriak, and Anderson (1984) examined various laboratory tests in 543 relatively healthy alcoholics entering ambulatory rehabilitation treatment. The diagnostic sensitivities were as follows: 49% for GGT, 45% for MCV, 25% for HDL, 28% for serum glutamic–oxaloacetic transaminase (SGOT), and 21% for BAC. A more detailed analysis revealed that sensitivities were even lower with individuals who were intermittent users of alcohol or who were recently abstinent. These results indicate that with an ambulatory population—that is, relatively healthy individuals who are drinking excessively—one cannot rely solely on laboratory tests, because the majority of these individuals will have normal test results.

A second problem is that the various laboratory tests tend to have fairly complex relationships with different patterns of alcohol use. To illustrate this point, data are presented for a sample of 335 outpatients who voluntarily presented for help for a broad range of alcohol- and/or drug-related problems at the Addiction Research Foundation in Ontario. The mean age was 32 years ($SD$ = 11), 79% were male, and the mean daily alcohol consumption was 95 g of ethanol ($SD$ = 103). Various relationships were explored between GGT, MCV, and HDL values and alcohol use patterns during the past 6 months (see Skinner, Holt, Schuller, Roy, & Israel, 1985, for further details).

Although the three laboratory tests showed a linear increase in abnormal results with the *frequency* of drinking (Figure 4-1), more complex relationships were evident with respect to the actual *quantity* of alcohol consumed per drinking day (Figure 4-2). MCV tended to become abnormally elevated around a threshold of 60 g of ethanol and declined somewhat at very large consumption levels. HDL also showed a decrease at the level of 160 g ethanol/day. A curvilinear relationship between HDL and alcohol consumption level has been noted previously by Sanchez-Craig and Annis (1981). In contrast, GGT demonstrated a linear increase with drinking quantity (Figure 4-2). Whereas MCV would appear to be useful for discriminating individuals near a threshold of "health risk" from drinking (60 g ethanol), GGT would appear to be more useful for discriminating at much higher alcohol consumption levels (160 g ethanol) and may be useful as an indicator of drinking to intoxication. The accuracy of all three laboratory tests decreased progressively with respect to the time interval since the last drink (Figure 4-3). This decline was most evident over the first 14 days.

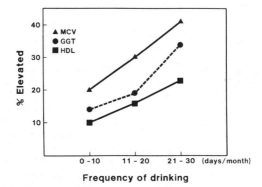

**Frequency of drinking**

FIGURE 4-1.   Relationship between three laboratory tests (MCV, GGT, HDL) and frequency of drinking during the past 6 months. Adapted from "Identification of Alcohol Abuse: Trauma and Laboratory Indicators" by H. A. Skinner, S. Holt, R. Schuller, J. Roy, and Y. Israel, 1985, in N. C. Chang and H. M. Chao (Eds.), *Early Identification of Alcohol Abuse* (NIAAA Research Monograph No. 17, pp. 285–302), Washington, DC: U.S. Government Printing Office.

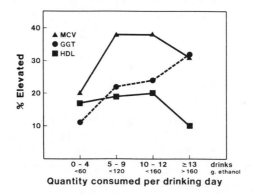

**Quantity consumed per drinking day**

FIGURE 4-2.   Relationship between three laboratory tests (MCV, GGT, HDL) and quantity of alcohol consumed per drinking day during the past 6 months. Adapted from "Identification of Alcohol Abuse: Trauma and Laboratory Indicators" by H. A. Skinner, S. Holt, R. Schuller, J. Roy, and Y. Israel, 1985, in N. C. Chang and H. M. Chao (Eds.), *Early Identification of Alcohol Abuse* (NIAAA Research Monograph No. 17, pp. 285–302), Washington, DC: U.S. Government Printing Office.

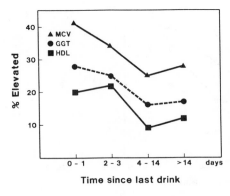

FIGURE 4-3. Relationship between three laboratory tests (MCV, GGT, HDL) and time since last taking a drink of alcohol. Adapted from "Identification of Alcohol Abuse: Trauma and Laboratory Indicators" by H. A. Skinner, S. Holt, R. Schuller, J. Roy, and Y. Israel, 1985, in N. C. Chang and H. M. Chao (Eds.), *Early Identification of Alcohol Abuse* (NIAAA Research Monograph No. 17, pp. 285–302), Washington, DC: U.S. Government Printing Office.

Thus, the time interval since the last drink is an important variable influencing the potential diagnostic value of these laboratory tests.

It must be emphasized that the trends depicted in Figures 4-1, 4-2, and 4-3 are based on group data. Relationships between drinking parameters and laboratory tests at the individual level tend to show considerable variability (e.g., Morgan, Colman, & Sherlock, 1981). Thus, caution must be exercised in clinical practice when interpreting laboratory results for a given patient.

*Use of Composite Indices*

Given the problems in the use of a single laboratory test, various attempts have been made to improve diagnostic accuracy by combining laboratory tests and clinical history information into composite indices. For example, Ryback, Echardt, and colleagues have conducted an extensive series of studies in which various laboratory tests are combined into an overall index using the multivariate statistical procedure of quadratic discriminant analysis (Echardt, Ryback, Rawlings, & Graubard, 1981; Ryback, Echardt, Felsher, & Rawlings, 1982; Ryback, Echardt, & Paulter, 1980). They have demonstrated that a composite index based on commonly ordered laboratory tests can substantially increase diagnostic accuracy. Similarly, Chalmers, Rinsler, MacDermott, Spicer, and Levi (1981) used a linear discriminant analysis to determine an optimal combination of laboratory tests that discriminated between hospital patients with low and high alcohol intake. They found that the best discrimination was provided by a combination of MCV, GGT, and serum alkaline phosphatase (AP).

Other investigators have developed composite indices by examining abnormal results from two or more laboratory tests. For example, Sanchez-Craig and Annis (1981) found that a combined index of GGT and HDL improved discrimination between abstinent/light and heavy drinkers over either measure alone. Chick *et al.* (1981) found the probability of being a heavy drinker to increase with raised GGT and MCV, but found both tests to lack sufficient sensitivity to be used on their own. When GGT was set at 50 I.U./liter or over and MCV at 98 fl or over, few false positives were detected, although sensitivity remained at about 20%. Whitehead *et al.* (1978) found raised levels of GGT in 14.9% of 2,034 healthy men, and raised serum aspartate transaminase (AT) levels in 8%. In 4.2%, both enzymes were raised. Other measures—serum urate, serum triglycerides, and MCV—also showed raised levels in relation to reported alcohol intake. Although many other factors appeared to contribute to these elevated levels, raised serum AT and urate in combination with GGT made it probable that a subject was consuming four or more drinks per day.

Bernadt *et al.* (1984) compared the efficacy of brief questionnaire administration with laboratory tests in screening 385 psychiatric admissions for excessive alcohol use. On a discriminant analysis, the brief MAST (Selzer, 1971) was the best discriminator of the presence of alcoholism and of excessive drinking, followed by the CAGE (Mayfield, McLeod, & Hall, 1974) and the Reich interview (Reich *et al.*, 1975). In contrast, most of the laboratory tests were poor discriminators, the best being GDH. When GDH was combined with each of the three questionnaires, there was considerably more sensitivity than each of the three questionnaires obtained alone. The GDH–Reich combination produced a sensitivity of 100%. In this study, both GGT and HDL-C were very poor discriminators on their own.

When screening for alcohol problems, a physical examination for signs and symptoms of excessive alcohol use combined with brief questionnaires and laboratory tests may also improve assessment (Holt *et al.,* 1981; Skinner & Holt, 1983). Early signs include a general appearance of excitability; nervousness and hand tremor; gastrointestinal problems; palpitations; hypertension; insomnia; poor memory; and signs of trauma. Skinner *et al.* (1984) evaluated the identification of alcohol abuse using three laboratory tests (GGT, MCV, HDL) and a history of trauma (five brief questions). In a sample of 68 ambulatory patients with known alcohol problems and 68 social drinkers matched for age and sex, a brief trauma scale identified 7 out of 10 subjects with drinking problems. In contrast, the laboratory tests had only moderate sensitivity for identifying alcohol problems, but excellent specificity for ruling out cases. Diagnostic accuracy was improved by combining test results using logistic regression analysis. Diagnostic sensitivity using the composite index exceeded 80%, while maintaining excellent specificity (90%).

TABLE 4-2.   Examples of the Logistic Regression Indices in Diagnosis

| | Trauma scale | MCV (fl) | GGT (I.U./liter) | HDL (mg/dl) | Probability of excessive drinking |
|---|---|---|---|---|---|
| Patient I | 0 (low) | 82 (normal) | 35 (normal) | 50 (normal) | .01 |
| Patient II | 3 (medium) | 100 (abnormal) | 45 (normal) | 60 (normal) | .85 |
| Patient III | 5 (high) | 107 (abnormal) | 100 (abnormal) | 92 (abnormal) | .99 |

*Note.* Adapted from "Identification of Alcohol Abuse Using Laboratory Tests and a History of Trauma" by H. A. Skinner, S. Holt, R. Schuller, J. Roy, and Y. Israel, 1984, *Annals of Internal Medicine, 101,* 847–851. Copyright 1984 by the American College of Physicians. Adapted by permission.

Table 4-2 illustrates the potential value of composite indices for diagnosis, using three hypothetical patients (adapted from Skinner *et al.,* 1984). The first patient, with normal results on the laboratory tests and a score of 0 on the trauma scale, would have a very low probability of excessive drinking. In contrast, the second patient, who has an abnormal result on one laboratory test (MCV) and three positive responses to the trauma questionnaire, would have a fairly high probability of excessive drinking. The third patient, with abnormal results on all three laboratory tests and a maximum score on the trauma scale, would have an extremely high likelihood of excessive drinking.

### Establishing a Within-Subject Baseline

One of the most important uses of laboratory tests is to corroborate patients' self-reports of alcohol consumption during treatment and follow-up. Estimates of BAC or UAC can be used to check whether a patient is complying with a drinking goal of total abstinence. An accurate method of monitoring drinking during treatment is to measure BAC or UAC when the patient comes for a treatment appointment, or by asking the patient to mail in urine samples. However, this procedure will only detect drinking during the previous 24 hours and, if not performed daily, will not reveal drinking that has occurred during days previous to the treatment appointment. Orrego *et al.* (1979) measured urine samples on a daily basis for a 6-month period in 37 chronic alcoholics attending a liver clinic. Patients were told that their urine was being monitored for compliance with taking medication, but they were not told that UAC would be assessed. Patients with positive

UACs denied drinking alcohol 52% of the time. UACs were usually lower when drinking was denied than when it was admitted. In contrast to this finding, Iber and Miller (1981) found only 7% denial of drinking when positive UACs were found. However, this second study took samples *only* at each outpatient visit. Thus, there would appear to be considerable merit in obtaining daily urine samples, or random samples thereof, while a patient is in treatment and aftercare.

It had been hoped that laboratory tests that are sensitive to alcohol use over longer time intervals would provide useful corroboration with self-reported alcohol consumption during treatment. When using group or aggregate data, studies have shown that the laboratory tests are useful for discriminating among subjects at various consumption levels. For example, GGT and HDL discriminated among patients who had been grouped according to (1) abstinent/light, (2) moderate, and (3) heavy drinking at several points during a 2-year follow-up from treatment (Sanchez-Craig & Annis, 1981; Sanchez-Craig, Annis, Bornet, & Mac-Donald, 1984).

Although the laboratory tests appear to have value when different *groups* are compared at treatment outcome, serious questions remain about their value for monitoring alcohol use at the *individual* level. Morgan *et al.* (1981) have reported one of the few studies on the use of laboratory indices for monitoring alcohol consumption with patients. They assessed GGT, MCV, and AT biweekly for 3 months in 20 alcoholics who had precirrhotic, alcohol-related liver disease. After 3 months, the laboratory tests did not differentiate patients who abstained, decreased, or continued their alcohol abuse. However, at the individual-patient level, Morgan *et al.* (1981) found that one or more biochemical markers tended to mirror changes in alcohol intake. These authors concluded that response to alcohol was reflected differently between patients for different markers. Moreover, individual differences were noted in the threshold of alcohol intake, below which the laboratory measures remained normal. This study underscores the need to establish a baseline level of laboratory indices for each individual. Subsequent measures relative to this baseline will more closely mirror individual patterns of alcohol consumption. This within-subject relationship may be masked or washed out in analyses that consider only group data.

In a recent study, Orrego, Blake, and Israel (1985) also reported individual variations in GGT with respect to alcohol consumption. In a sample of 42 patients with alcoholic liver disease, they found that GGT correlated .69 with UAC. They cautioned that this individual variability in GGT level precludes the use of this test as an indicator of the *exact amount* of ethanol consumed. They also found in this chronic alcoholic sample that individuals who had been abstinent from ethanol for 1 month or more could still show elevated GGT levels. The half-life of GGT decay in 32 patients remaining abstinent for an 8-week period was estimated to be 26 days. Orrego *et al.* (1985) concluded that a baseline level of GGT activity should be established for the individual patient as a prerequisite for monitoring continued alcohol consumption.

## Case Studies

The following case studies are helpful for illustrating advantages and limitations of the use of laboratory tests as corroborators of alcohol consumption. The first case represents an individual with a chronic history of alcohol abuse. This case is typical of an individual who has accrued fairly severe physical and psychosocial consequences related to excessive drinking. The other two cases represent problem drinkers who had been carefully selected for a randomized trial of controlled drinking versus abstinence (Sanchez-Craig *et al.*, 1984).

### *A Case of Chronic Alcoholism*

Mr. F was first admitted to the Clinical Institute, Addiction Research Foundation, Ontario, in December 1980 for bleeding gastric ulcers. He was then 50 years old. Mr. F reported drinking problems for the past 10 years. He had been married for about 30 years, and there was considerable marital discord. Mr. F experienced hallucinations during withdrawal from alcohol, and a medical assessment revealed evidence of liver damage. Mr. F remained abstinent for 6 months, but then resumed drinking about 120 g ethanol per day (nine standard drinks).

In March 1982, Mr. F was readmitted after a year without employment and with deteriorating physical health. The results of neuropsychological assessment indicated that Mr. F had short-term memory impairment and poor concentration. A computerized axial tomography (CAT) scan revealed moderate to severe cortical atrophy and some atrophy in posterior fossa, indicating chronic effects of alcohol in the central nervous system. On the Wechsler Adult Intelligence Scale (WAIS) Full Scale IQ, Mr. F was functioning within the bright–normal range, but was showing at least a moderate degree of organic impairment. Following the assessment, Mr. F attended a liver clinic and also received outpatient sessions of conjoint therapy. Six months after this outpatient treatment began, Mr. F was seen in the emergency department with retroperitoneal hematoma and was admitted to the medical unit.

Figure 4-4 gives the results for three laboratory tests (MCV, GGT, HDL) that were recorded for Mr. F during his 61-day stay on the medical

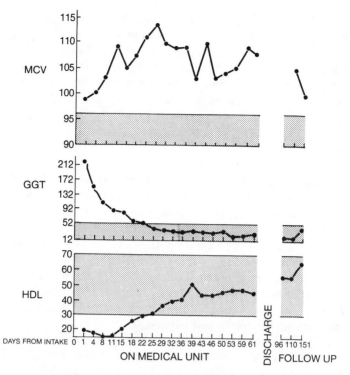

FIGURE 4-4. Sequential laboratory tests (MCV, GGT, HDL) for a patient in treatment with a chronic history of alcohol dependence. The shaded area depicts the normal reference range.

unit. Before admission he was drinking large quantities of alcohol (150 g ethanol/day). Although his initial GGT value was substantially elevated, results for GGT dropped fairly dramatically over the next 3 weeks. By the 25th day, his GGT values were within the normal reference range. In contrast, results for MCV remained abnormally elevated throughout his stay on the medical unit. A number of factors may underlie this finding, one of which is that Mr. F continued his habit of smoking cigarettes. Because liver disease may exert a major effect on HDL (Holt *et al.,* 1981), one would not expect this laboratory test to be a useful marker of alcohol consumption for a patient such as Mr. F. The initial values on HDL were abnormally low, and his HDL results entered the normal reference range on day 25 (similar to GGT). Following his 61 days as an inpatient on the medical unit, Mr. F was discharged. He returned for three outpatient counseling sessions at days 96, 110, and 151 following intake. Although Mr. F did not drink during his stay on the medical unit, it was recorded at the third outpatient visit (day 151) that he was drinking two or three standard drinks of liquor daily (40 g ethanol). One can see in Figure 4-4 that both GGT and HDL appeared to be rising at this third follow-up contact. Unfortunately, Mr. F did not comply with further follow-up appointments. His wife reported that he was seriously bingeing on alcohol and refusing to go to the hospital. Approximately 6 months later, Mr. F died in a fire that he accidentally started through smoking cigarettes in bed.

### Problem Drinkers

The following cases are drawn from a sample of problem drinkers who had attended an outpatient treatment program designed to evaluate goals of controlled drinking versus abstinence (Sanchez-Craig et al., 1984). At intake, the severity of alcohol dependence was assessed using the Alcohol Dependence Scale (ADS; Skinner & Horn, 1984), and problems related to drinking were measured using the MAST (Selzer, 1971). GGT values were assessed at intake to treatment, 3 weeks later, and at four intervals throughout a 2-year follow-up (6, 12, 18, and 24 months). These results, displayed in Figure 4-5, appeared to show little relationship to reported weekly consumption during treatment and follow-up.

The first subject (Subject I) owned his own furniture store and was a volunteer at the local YMCA as a physical education instructor. He was 46 years of age and married. He reported that he had started drinking at the age of 35 and had gradually increased consumption of liquor to the rate of 17 standard drinks per day. He drank to get to sleep, and also drank in the mornings. Subject I exhibited a substantial level of alcohol dependence (ADS = 25), as well as considerable problems related to drinking (MAST = 18). Although in good health, he reported having had a heart attack at the age of 39. He functioned successfully through the treatment program and follow-up. Four years later, he was seen in the emergency department and

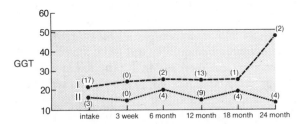

FIGURE 4-5.  Sequential GGT measurements for two early-stage problem drinkers. The number in brackets is the number of daily average standard drinks (13.6 g ethanol) at the time of the laboratory test. The shaded area depicts the normal reference range.

was transferred to a detoxification unit. Except for an increase at the 24-month follow-up, his GGT values remained relatively stable, even though he reported some variations in the quantity of alcohol consumed.

The second subject (Subject II) was a 56-year-old widowed male with no children. At the time of the study, he was recently retired due to a large inheritance. However, he did some volunteer work and consulting. During the past 12 years he had had intermittent periods of moderate to heavy drinking, but these had only become problematic in the past 3 years after the death of his wife. His poststudy drinking averaged five standard drinks a day, with a maximum consumption of two 26-ounce bottles of rum per week. Subject II reported an intermediate level of alcohol dependence (ADS = 14), and a fairly broad range of drinking problems (MAST = 24). His GGT values also remained quite stable throughout the follow-up period.

## Conclusion

The establishment of a "gold standard" objective measure of alcohol use remains elusive. Breath and urine screenings for alcohol are excellent for confirming self-reported abstinence; however, these tests are relevant only to drinking in the past 24 hours. The availability of fairly inexpensive breathalyzers, and the recent development of a dipstick technology, make breath and urine screenings feasible in most treatment settings. Moreover, if patients are told that their self-reports of alcohol consumption will be checked against routine or random blood or urine screenings, then this "awareness" factor in itself may be quite instrumental for enhancing the validity of self-reports (Skinner, 1984). Urine samples may also be analyzed for traces of drugs other than alcohol. However, some questions must be raised regarding patients' compliance with this procedure, especially that of less motivated individuals and patients who are under some form of coercion to undergo treatment (e.g., driving-while-intoxicated offenders).

The search for laboratory tests that would detect alcohol use over longer periods (e.g., 4–8 weeks) has yet to produce a procedure that possesses both high sensitivity and specificity. Although biochemical markers such as GGT and MCV can be useful for detecting alcohol abuse, their diagnostic sensitivities tend to be fairly low (20%–30%) in relatively healthy, ambulatory populations in which one would find their use most helpful. More promising results have been achieved with the use of composite indices, especially when laboratory tests are combined with pertinent medical history and psychosocial data. For monitoring patients' alcohol use in treatment follow-up, several studies have underscored the need to establish a within-subject baseline on a given laboratory test. Subsequent measurements relative to this baseline will tend to mirror patterns of alcohol consumption. However, there is an urgent need for further research on individual variations in the threshold of alcohol intake at which the laboratory tests respond abnormally, as well as on individual variations in dose-response curves.

In conclusion, laboratory tests can add important information in the assessment of alcohol use and alcohol dependence. Given the considerable amount of research activity on this topic, we are fairly optimistic that laboratory tests (or composite indices) will be developed that possess much better diagnostic sensitivity and specificity. In the meantime, laboratory tests should *always* be considered in combination with data from other assessment methods. Confidence in the validity of assessments of alcohol use and dependence is established by convergence among these alternative measurement techniques. This basic mechanism of science also makes good clinical sense.

## Acknowledgment

Gillian Leigh is presently at the Braemore Home, Sydney, Nova Scotia.

## References

American Psychiatric Association. (1980). *Diagnostic and statistical manual of mental disorders* (3rd ed.). Washington, DC: Author.

Armor, D. J., Polich, J. M., & Stambul, H. B. (1978). *Alcoholism and treatment.* New York: Wiley.

Atchinson, S. R., Hunt, R. D., & Morse, R. M. (1981). The value of the mean corpuscular hemoglobin and mean corpuscular volume in screening for alcoholism. *Alcoholism: Clinical and Experimental Research, 5,* 143. (Abstract)

Baraona, E., & Lieber, C. S. (1970). Effects of chronic ethanol feeding on serum lipoprotein metabolism in the rat. *Journal of Clinical Investigation, 49,* 289–300.

Bernadt, M. W. Mumford, J., & Murray, R. M. (1984). A discriminant function analysis of screening tests for excessive drinking and alcoholism. *Journal of Studies on Alcohol, 45,* 81–86.

Bernadt, M. W., Mumford, J., Taylor, C., Smith, B., & Murray, R. M. (1982). Comparison of questionnaire and laboratory tests in the detection of excessive drinking and alcoholism. *Lancet, i,* 325–328.

Carlen, P. L., Wilkinson, D. A., Wortzman, G., & Holgate, R. (1984). Partially reversible cerebral atrophy and functional improvement in recently abstinent alcoholics. *Canadian Journal of Neurological Science, 11,* 441–446.

Chalmers, DM., Rinsler, M. G., MacDermott, S., Spicer, C. C., & Levi, A. J. (1981). Biochemical and hematological indicators of excessive alcohol consumption. *Gut, 22,* 992–996.

Chick, J., Kreitman, N., & Plant, M. (1981). Mean cell volume and gamma-glutamyl-transpeptidase as markers of drinking working men. *Lancet, i,* 1249–1251.

Cushman, P., Jacobson, G., Barboriak, J. J., & Anderson, A. J. (1984). Biochemical markers for alcoholism: Sensitivity problems. *Alcoholism: Clinical and Experimental Research, 8,* 253–257.

Danielsson, B., Ekman, R., Fex, G., Johansson, B. G., Kristensson, H., Nilsson-Ehle, P., & Wadstein, J. (1978). Changes in plasma high density lipoproteins in chronic male alcoholics during and after alcohol abuse. *Scandinavian Journal of Clinical Laboratory Investigation, 38,* 113-119.

Devenyi, P., Kapur, B. M., & Roy, J. H. J. (1984). High-density lipoprotein response to alcohol consumption and abstinence as an indicator of liver function in alcoholic patients. *Canadian Medical Association Journal, 130,* 1445-1447.

Devenyi, P., Robinson, G. M., & Roncari, D. A. K. (1980). Alcohol and high density lipoproteins. *Canadian Medical Association Journal, 123,* 981-984.

Echardt, M. J., Ryback, R. S., Rawlings, R. R., & Graubard, B. I. (1981). Biochemical diagnosis of alcoholism. *Journal of the American Medical Association, 246,* 2707-2710.

Edwards, G., & Gross, M. M. (1976). Alcohol dependence: Provisional description of a clinical syndrome. *British Medical Journal, i,* 1058-1061.

Edwards, G., Gross, M. M., Keller, J., Moser, J., & Room, R. (1977). *Alcohol related disabilities* (WHO Offset Publication No. 32). Geneva: World Health Organization.

Eschwege, E., Papoz, L., & Lellouch, J. (1978). Blood cells and alcohol consumption with special reference to smoking habits. *Journal of Clinical Pathology, 31,* 654-658.

Harford, T. C., Dorman, N., & Feinhandler, S. J. (1976). Alcohol consumption in bars: Validation of self-reports against observed behavior. *Drinking and Drug Practices Survey, 11,* 13-15.

Haskell, W. L., Camargo, C., Williams, P. T., Vranizan, K. M., Krauss, R. M., Lindgren, F. T., & Wood, P. D. (1984). The effect of cessation and resumption of moderate alcohol intake on serum high-density-lipoprotein subfractions. *New England Journal of Medicine, 310,* 805-810.

Holt, S., Skinner, H. A., & Israel, Y. (1981). Early identification of alcohol abuse: 2. Clinical and laboratory indicators. *Canadian Medical Association Journal, 124,* 1279-1295.

Iber, F. L., & Miller, P. A. (1981). Alcohol among stable cirrhotic patients in a liver clinic. *Hepatology, 2,* 692.

Jenkins, W. J., Rosalki, S., Foo, Y., Sheuer, P. J., & Sherlock, S. (1980). Is serum glutamate dehydrogenase a reliable marker of liver cell necrosis in the alcoholic? The effect of recent alcohol excess. *Drug and Alcohol Dependence, 6,* 16-17. (Abstract)

Johansson, B. G., & Medhus, A. (1974). Increase in plasma alpha-lipoproteins in chronic alcoholics after acute abuse. *Acta Medica Scandinavica, 195,* 273-277.

Kalant, H. Absorption, diffusion, distribution, and elimination of ethanol: Effects on biological membranes. In B. Kissin & H. Begleiter (Eds.), *The biology of alcoholism* (pp. 1-63). New York: Plenum Press.

Kapur, B. M., Holt, S., Blake, J., & Orrego, H. (1980). HDL-cholesterol in alcoholics with liver disease. *Clinical Chemistry, 26,* 966. (Abstract)

Kapur, B. M., & Israel, Y. (1983). A dipstick methodology for rapid determination of alcohol in body fluids. *Clinical Chemistry, 29,* 1178. (Abstract)

Kapur, B. M., & Israel, Y. (1985). Alcohol dipstick—a rapid method for analysis of ethanol in body fluids. In N. C. Chang & H. M. Chao (Eds.), *Early identification of alcohol abuse* (NIAAA Research Monograph No. 17, pp. 310-320). Washington, DC: U.S. Government Printing Office.

Lieber, C. S. (1984). To drink (moderately) or not to drink? *New England Journal of Medicine, 310,* 846-848.

Mayfield, D., McLeod, G., & Hall, P. (1974). The CAGE questionnaire: Validation of a new alcoholism screening instrument. *American Journal of Psychiatry, 131,* 1121-1123.

McCrady, B. S., Paolino, T. J., & Longabaugh, R. (1978). Correspondence between reports of problem drinkers and spouses on drinking behavior and impairment. *Journal of Studies on Alcohol, 39,* 1252-1257.

Morgan, M. Y., Colman, J. C., & Sherlock, S. (1981). The use of a combination of peripheral markers for diagnosing alcoholism and monitoring for continued abuse. *British Journal of Alcohol and Alcoholism, 16,* 167–177.

Myrhed, M. Berglund, L., & Bottinger, L. E. (1977). Alcohol consumption and hematology. *Acta Medica Scandinavica, 202,* 11–15.

Naranjo, C. A., & Sellers, E. M. (1986). Clinical assessment and pharmacotherapy of the alcohol withdrawal syndrome. In M. Galanter (Ed.), *Recent developments in alcoholism* (pp. 265–281). New York: Plenum.

Orrego, H., Blake, J. E., & Israel, Y. (1985). Relationship between gamma-glutamyl-transpeptidase and mean urinary alcohol levels in alcoholics while drinking and after alcohol withdrawal. *Alcoholism: Clinical and Experimental Research, 9,* 10–13.

Orrego, H., Blendis, L. M., Blake, J. E., Kapur, B. M., & Israel, Y. (1979). Reliability of assessment of alcohol intake based on personal interviews in a liver clinic. *Lancet, ii,* 1354–1356.

Orrego, H., Israel, Y., Blake, J. E., & Medline, A. (1983). Assessment of prognostic factors in alcoholic liver disease: Toward a global quantitative expression of severity. *Hepatology, 3,* 896–905.

Penn, R., & Worthington, D. J. (1983). Is serum gamma-glutamyl transferase a misleading test? *British Medical Journal, 286,* 531–535.

Penn, R., Worthington, D. J., Clarke, C. A., & Whitfield, A. G. W. (1981). Gamma-glutamyl-transpeptidase and alcohol intake. *Lancet, i,* 894.

Phillips, E. L. R., Little, R. E., Hillman, R. S., Labbe, R. F., & Campbell, C. (1984). A field test of the sweat patch. *Alcoholism: Clinical and Experimental Research, 8,* 233–237.

Phillips, M. (1984). Sweat-patch testing detects inaccurate self-reports of alcohol consumption. *Alcoholism: Clinical and Experimental Research, 8,* 51–53.

Phillips, M., & McAloon, M. H. (1980). A sweat-patch test for alcohol consumption: Evaluation in continuous and episodic drinkers. *Alcoholism: Clinical and Experimental Research, 4,* 391–395.

Polich, J. M. (1982). The validity of self-reports in alcoholism research. *Addictive Behaviors, 7,* 123–132.

Reich, T., Robins, L. N., Woodruff, R. A., Taibleson, M., Rich, C., & Cunningham, L. (1975). Computer-assisted derivation of a screening interview for alcoholism. *Archives of General Psychiatry, 32,* 847–852.

Robinson, D., Monk, C., & Bailey, A. (1979). The relationship between serum gamma-glutamyl-transpeptidase level and reported alcohol consumption in healthy men. *Journal of Studies on Alcohol, 40,* 896–901.

Rohan, W. P. (1976). Quantitative dimensions of alcohol use for hospitalized problem drinkers. *Diseases of the Nervous System, 37,* 154–159.

Rollason, J. G., Pincherle, G., & Robinson, D. (1972). Serum gamma-glutamyl transpeptidase in relation to alcohol consumption. *Clinica Chimica Acta, 39,* 75–80.

Rosalki, S. B., & Rau, D. (1972). Serum-gamma-glutamyl transpeptidase activity in alcoholism. *Clinica Chimica Acta, 39,* 41–47.

Ryback, R. S., Echardt, M. J., Felsher, B., & Rawlings, R. R. (1982). Biochemical and hematologic correlates of alcoholism and liver disease. *Journal of the American Medical Association, 248,* 2261–2265.

Ryback, R. S., Echardt, M. J., & Paulter, C. P. (1980). Biochemical and hematological correlates of alcoholism. *Research Communications in Chemical Pathology and Pharmacology, 27,* 533–550.

Salaspuro, M. (1986). Conventional and coming laboratory markers of alcoholism and heavy drinking. *Alcoholism: Clinical and Experimental Research, 10* (6, Suppl.), 55–125.

Sanchez-Craig, M., & Annis, H. M. (1981). Gamma-glutamyl transpeptidase and high-density lipoproteins cholesterol in male problem drinkers: Advantages of a composite index for predicting alcohol consumption. *Alcoholism: Clinical and Experimental Research, 5,* 540–544.

Sanchez-Craig, M., & Annis, H. M. (1982). Self-monitoring and recall measures of alcohol consumption: Convergent validity with biochemical indices of liver function. *British Journal of Alcohol and Alcoholism, 17,* 117-121.

Sanchez-Craig, M., Annis, H. M., Bornet, A. R., & MacDonald, K. R. (1984). Random assignment to abstinence and controlled drinking: Evaluation of a cognitive behavioral program for problem drinkers. *Journal of Consulting and Clinical Psychology, 52,* 390-403.

Schiele, F., Guilmin, A. M., Detienne, H., & Siest, G. (1977). Gamma-glutamyl transferase activity in plasma: Statistical distributions, individual variations and reference intervals. *Clinical Chemistry, 23,* 1023-1028.

Sellers, E. M., & Kalant, H. (1976). Alcohol intoxication and withdrawal. *New England Journal of Medicine, 294,* 757-762.

Selzer, M. L. (1971). The Michigan Alcoholism Screening Test: The quest for a new diagnostic instrument. *American Journal of Psychiatry, 127,* 1653-1658.

Skinner, H. A. (1981). Assessment of alcohol problems: Basic principles, critical issues and future trends. In Y. Israel, F. B. Glaser, H. Kalant, R. E. Popham, W. Schmidt, & R. G. Smart (Eds.), *Research advances in alcohol and drug problems* (Vol. 6, pp. 319-369). New York: Plenum Press.

Skinner, H. A. (1984). Assessing alcohol use by patients in treatment. In Y. Israel, F. B. Glaser, H. Kalant, R. E. Popham, W. Schmidt, & R. G. Smart (Eds.), *Research advances in alcohol and drug problems* (Vol. 8, pp. 183-207). New York: Plenum Press.

Skinner, H. A. (1985). Clinical spectrum of alcoholism: Implications for new drug therapies. In C. A. Naranjo & E. M. Sellers (Eds.), *Research advances in new psychopharmacological treatments for alcoholism* (pp. 123-135). Amsterdam: Elsevier.

Skinner, H. A., & Allen, B. A. (1983). Does the computer make a difference? Computerized versus face-to-face versus self-report assessment of alcohol, drug and tobacco use. *Journal of Consulting and Clinical Psychology, 51,* 267-275.

Skinner, H. A., & Holt, S. (1983). Early intervention for alcohol problems. *Journal of the Royal College of General Practitioners, 33,* 787-791.

Skinner, H. A., Holt, S. & Israel, Y. (1981). Early identification of alcohol abuse: 1. Critical issues and psychosocial indicators for a composite index. *Canadian Medical Association Journal, 124,* 1141-1152.

Skinner, H. A., Holt, S., Schuller, R., Roy, J., & Israel, Y. (1984). Identification of alcohol abuse using laboratory tests and a history of trauma. *Annals of Internal Medicine, 101,* 847-851.

Skinner, H. A., Holt, S., Schuller, R., Roy, J., & Israel, Y. (1985). Identification of alcohol abuse: Trauma and laboratory indicators. In N. C. Chang & H. M. Chao (Eds.), *Early identification of alcohol abuse* (NIAAA Research Monograph No. 17, pp. 285-302). Washington, DC: U.S. Government Printing Office.

Skinner, H. A., & Horn, J. L. (1984). *Guidelines for using the Alcohol Dependence Scale (ADS).* Toronto: Addiction Research Foundation.

Skinner, H. A., & Sheu, W. J. (1982). Reliability of alcohol use indices: Lifetime drinking history and MAST. *Journal of Studies on Alcohol, 42,* 1157-1170.

Skude, G., & Wadstein, J. (1977). Amylase hepatic enzymes and bilirubin in serum of chronic alcoholics. *Acta Medica Scandinavica, 201,* 53-58.

Sobell, L. C., & Sobell, M. B. (1981). Effects of three interview factors on the validity of alcohol abusers' self-reports. *American Journal of Drug and Alcohol Abuse, 8,* 225-237.

Sobell, M. B., Sobell, L. C., & Vanderspek, R. (1979). Relationships among clinical judgment, self-report, and breath analysis measures of intoxication in alcoholics. *Journal of Consulting and Clinical Psychology, 47,* 204-206.

Szewezuk, A., & Orlowski, M. (1960). The use of alpha-(*N*-gamma-DL-glutamyl)-aminonitriles for the colorimetic determination of a specific peptidase in blood serum. *Clinica Chimica Acta, 5,* 680-688.

Trell, E., Kristenson, H., & Fex, G. (1984). Alcohol-related problems in middle-aged men with elevated serum gamma-glutamyltransferase: A preventive medical investigation. *Journal of Studies on Alcohol, 45,* 302–309.

Unger, K. W., & Johnson, D. (1974). Red blood cell mean corpuscular volume: A potential indicator of alcohol usage in a working population. *American Journal of Medical Science, 267,* 281–289.

Van Waes, L., & Lieber, C. S. (1977). Glutamate dehydrogenase: A reliable marker of liver cell necrosis in the alcoholic. *British Medical Journal, ii,* 1508–1510.

Watson, R. R., Mohs, M. E., Eskelson, C., Sampliner, R. E., & Hartmann, B. (1986). Identification of alcohol abuse and alcoholism with biological parameters. *Alcoholism: Clinical and Experimental Research, 10,* 364–385.

Whitehead, T. P., Clarke, C. A., & Whitfield, A. G. W. (1978). Biochemical and haematological markers of alcohol intake. *Lancet, i,* 978–981.

Worner, T. M., & Lieber, C. S. (1980). Plasma glutamate dehydrogenase (GDH) as a marker of alcoholic liver injury. *Drug and Alcohol Dependence, 6,* 36–37. (Abstract)

Wu, A., Chanarin, I., & Levi, A. J. (1974). Macrocytosis of chronic alcoholism. *Lancet, i,* 829–830.

# III

# SMOKING BEHAVIOR

# 5

# BEHAVIORAL ASSESSMENT

SAUL SHIFFMAN

*University of Pittsburgh*


## Introduction

Cigarette smoking is the greatest single cause of preventable death and disease in the Western world (U.S. Surgeon General, 1979), contributing to 1,000 deaths per day in the United States alone. Most smokers want to stop, and, indeed, have tried unsuccessfully to do so (U.S. Surgeon General, 1982). Treatment of cigarette smoking thus has the potential to make substantial contributions to the public health.

Though behavioral treatments for smoking cessation have recently proliferated, little attention has been given to assessment in smoking treatment. This chapter reviews behavioral assessment procedures that may be useful in smoking cessation programs. Because relapse appears to be the greatest problem in smoking cessation—the vast majority of those who quit relapse within months (Hunt & Matarazzo, 1973)—much of the discussion focuses on assessment for relapse prevention.

Assessment is an ongoing process intimately tied to the course of treatment. Some assessments occur prior to or early in treatment, whereas others are only possible once the smoker has achieved abstinence, and still others are most relevant in long-term follow-up. Finally, some assessments cannot be scheduled, but are cued by events that occur in treatment.

Generally, assessment begins with a smoking history leading up to the current cessation attempt. Self-reports of smoking patterns and motives are also best obtained early in treatment, because responses change as treatment proceeds. Assessment then progresses to more detailed evaluation of the client's current smoking behavior. Self-reports and self-monitoring are used to measure the amount and distribution of smoking. As the "quit date" approaches, difficulties in abstinence may be anticipated by assessments of the client's vulnerabilities and resources.

Immediately after cessation is achieved, assessment focuses on the withdrawal syndrome. Assessment then enters a prolonged phase of problem solving to identify factors that promote relapse and to assess the client's resources for coping with them. This process is iterative and open-ended. Assessment is thus initiated at the very outset of treatment and ends only when abstinence is well established. A more specific discussion of the timing and sequence of assessment activities follows the description of the assessment procedures themselves.

Assessment procedures vary in their clinical utility. Many valid assessments yield information that is primarily of prognostic value, predicting the client's probability of success. Although such prognostic information is intellectually interesting, it is of little clinical utility because it has few implications for action. Knowing that a particular person is a poor risk in treatment for smoking cessation is of little use unless this information leads to action that improves the outcome. To be clinically useful, an assessment should have immediate implications for the conduct of treatment. Assessment is most valuable when linked to a set of clinical procedures that are differentially applied, depending on the results of the assessment. The failure of most assessment procedures to meet this criterion is a consistent theme throughout this chapter.

## Initial Assessments

Demographic and smoking data are typically obtained at intake. Self-report questionnaires are most efficient.

### Demographics and Smoking History

Demographic data may be prognostically useful. Smokers are more likely to succeed in quitting, for example, if they are male (Gritz, 1979; Tongas, Patterson, & Goodkind, 1976) and older (Eisinger, 1971; Gottleib, Friedman, Cooney, Gordon, & Marlatt, 1981; Murphy, 1983; though see Garvey, Bosse, Glynn, & Rosner, 1983, and Hjalmarson, 1984, for contradictory findings).

Smokers' previous smoking and quitting histories may also be prognostically useful. Those who have been smoking for a shorter period of time are generally more successful (Graham & Gibson, 1971; Pomerleau, Adkins, & Pertschuk, 1978). Smokers making their first cessation attempt also seem to be most successful (Eisinger, 1972; Gottleib et al., 1981; Graham & Gibson, 1971; Ockene, Benfari, Nuttall, Hurwitz, & Ockene, 1982), probably because those who are able to quit easily do so on the first attempt, whereas the "tougher cases" must try again. In practice, one rarely sees smokers making their first attempt to quit in treatment; smokers typically accumulate several failures before resorting to formal treatment.

Still, a history of past attempts does not doom one to failure. More than half of those who succeed in quitting did so after three or more attempts (U.S. Surgeon General, 1983), and multiple attempts typify the natural history of cessation (Schachter, 1982). Among smokers who have made previous attempts, those with more attempts seem to have a poorer prognosis (Gottleib *et al.,* 1981). More recent findings suggest that only the number of *nonserious* attempts predicts failure (Murphy, 1983), and that the number of *serious* past attempts is of little predictive value. "Serious" and "nonserious" are loosely defined according to subjects' definitions in these studies, but most smokers are able to classify their quitting efforts accordingly.

The *duration* of past cessation attempts also has prognostic value. Smokers who held out longer in their most recent and in their best cessation attempts are more likely to succeed (Murphy, 1983). One might think of these prior attempts as successive approximations to permanent abstinence — the characteristics of smokers with longer recent abstinence generally resemble those of ex-smokers (Murphy, 1983). Assessments of smoking history should therefore include accounts of past attempts and their seriousness.

## Amount of Smoking

### Self-Report

How much a client smokes can be assessed adequately from self-report, though smokers tend to report their smoking rounded to decimal figures. More accurate data may be obtained through self-monitoring, described below. The amount of smoking is a surprisingly poor predictor of response to cessation. Whereas some studies find that heavy smokers suffer more severe withdrawal (Burns, 1969; Wynder, Kaufman, & Lesser, 1967), many others do not (J. S. Mausner, 1970; Myrsten, Elgerot, & Edgren, 1977; Shiffman & Jarvik, 1976). Similarly, some studies find lighter smokers more successful in cessation (e.g., Ockene, Hymowitz, Sexton, & Broste, 1982; Thompson & Wilson, 1966), but many others find no such effect (Eisinger, 1971; Garvey *et al.,* 1983; Graham & Gibson, 1971; Hjalmarson, 1984; Murphy, 1983).[1]

The relationship between amount of smoking and the effects of cessation may be nonlinear. D. G. Williams (1979), for example, found that smokers of less than 15 cigarettes per day suffered less mood disturbance in

---

1. Smoking dose has been assessed much more precisely with measures of smoking topography, which quantify the exact number, duration, and volume of puffs on each cigarette. Although useful in basic research on smoking behavior, these currently have no role in smoking cessation treatment. Biochemical measures of exposure are also accurate, but have no apparent relation to outcome (Killen, Taylor, Maccoby, Fong, & Bachman, 1984; Zeidenberg *et al.,* 1977).

withdrawal, but there were no differences between "medium" (16–25 cigarettes per day) and "heavy" (more than 25 cigarettes per day) smokers. In a review of the cessation literature (Shiffman, 1980), I concluded that the advantage of light smokers in cessation is limited to the very lightest smokers and may not apply to treatment populations. Thus, the amount of smoking is an inconsistent prognostic sign, and heavier smokers should not be considered poor risks.

## Self-Monitoring

Self-monitoring is another method often used to estimate the amount of clients' smoking. Self-monitoring of smoking is fairly accurate, though not perfectly so (McFall, 1970; Ober, 1968). Its accuracy is enhanced if each cigarette is monitored at the time it is smoked (Frederiksen, Epstein, & Kosevsky, 1975). The validity of self-monitoring data is impaired by reactivity. Among subjects motivated to reduce or stop smoking, self-monitoring results in smoking reductions (Lipinski, Black, Nelson, & Ciminero, 1975; McFall, 1970). Reactivity is minimized if subjects are instructed to maintain normal smoking (Epstein & Collins, 1977).

Whereas reactivity is a liability for assessment purposes, it may be an asset in treatment. Indeed, self-monitoring can be considered an active component of treatment (McFall & Hammen, 1971). Reactivity is enhanced if self-monitoring is arranged to influence, as well as record, smoking behavior. Thus reactivity is greatest if cigarettes are recorded *before* they are smoked (cf. Bellack, Rozensky, & Schwartz, 1974) or if smoking *urges* are monitored (Rozensky, 1974). Focusing on a salient aspect of smoking also enhances reactivity. It should be emphasized that the assessment and treatment applications of self-monitoring are inevitably at war with each other; one must choose between accuracy and clinical impact. Most clinicians choose the latter.

Self-monitoring plays a more central role in gradual reduction regimens, where it aids in selecting cigarettes for elimination and in monitoring treatment progress. In such cases, the monitoring must be suited to the reduction strategy. A strategy of eliminating cigarettes in one context after another—for example, first those smoked while feeling bored, then those smoked after meals, and so on—requires careful monitoring of smoking in each situation, using a form such as that in Figure 5-1. Other strategies involve eliminating cigarettes according to the time of day or according to how desirable they are, and each requires a different self-monitoring focus.

Noncompliance with instructions to self-monitor is a common difficulty. Clients who are noncompliant have a poorer prognosis (Pomerleau *et al.,* 1978, though see Falk, Tryon, & Davis, 1984). Whether noncompliance indicates lesser motivation, undermines the therapeutic effects of self-

Name _____

Day of week _____

Date _____

Page _____

| Time | Food and/or alcohol | Relaxation | Work | Social, Recreational | Other | Activity | Angry | Anxious | Bored | Depressed | Frustrated | Happy | Relaxed | Tired | Need rating Most — Least |
|---|---|---|---|---|---|---|---|---|---|---|---|---|---|---|---|
| 1 | | | | | | | | | | | | | | | 1 2 3 4 5 |
| 2 | | | | | | | | | | | | | | | 1 2 3 4 5 |
| 3 | | | | | | | | | | | | | | | 1 2 3 4 5 |
| 4 | | | | | | | | | | | | | | | 1 2 3 4 5 |
| 5 | | | | | | | | | | | | | | | 1 2 3 4 5 |
| 6 | | | | | | | | | | | | | | | 1 2 3 4 5 |
| 7 | | | | | | | | | | | | | | | 1 2 3 4 5 |
| 8 | | | | | | | | | | | | | | | 1 2 3 4 5 |
| 9 | | | | | | | | | | | | | | | 1 2 3 4 5 |
| 10 | | | | | | | | | | | | | | | 1 2 3 4 5 |

Wrap this Daily Cigarette Count around your pack of cigarettes and hold it fast with a rubber band. When you are about to take a cigarette, but *before* you actually put it in your mouth and light up, (1) check the activity you are doing; (2) check the word or words that best describes your feeling at the time; and (3) indicate how important that particular cigarette is to you at the time:

1. most important
2. above average
3. average
4. below average
5. least important

FIGURE 5-1. Daily cigarette count. From "Preventing Relapse in Ex-Smokers: A Self-Management Approach" by S. Shiffman, L. Read, J. Maltese, D. Rapkin, and M. E. Jarvik, 1985, in G. A. Marlatt and J. R. Gordon (Eds.), *Relapse Prevention: Maintenance Strategies in the Treatment of Addictive Behaviors* (pp. 472–520), New York: Guilford Press. Copyright 1985 by Guilford Publications, Inc. Reprinted by permission.

monitoring, or is related to other factors is unknown. In any case, interventions designed to improve compliance, such as making sessions contingent on compliance, may be helpful.

## Assessing Dependence

Cigarette smoking is increasingly recognized as an expression of dependence on nicotine. Indeed, Tobacco Dependence is now a recognized psychiatric diagnosis in the third edition of the *Diagnostic and Statistical Manual of Mental Disorders* (DSM-III; American Psychiatric Association, 1980, p. 178). To be considered dependent, a smoker must (1) continue to smoke despite awareness that it exacerbates a medical condition, (2) experience withdrawal symptoms upon cessation, *OR* (3) have a history of unsuccessful attempts to stop. By these criteria, 90% of smokers, and probably nearly all who seek formal treatment, are dependent (Gust, Hughes, & Pechacek, 1986). This definition is therefore of little use in treatment.

A useful instrument for measuring individual differences in degree of dependence is the Tolerance Questionnaire developed by Fagerstrom (1978; see Table 5-1). Tolerance Questionnaire scores consistently predict the severity of craving (Gunn, 1983; Killen, *et al.,* 1984) and physical withdrawal symptoms (cf. Fagerstrom, 1978; Hughes & Hatsukami, 1986) on cessation. The scale is also a powerful predictor of relapse, accounting for as much as 44% of the outcome variance in some studies (Killen *et al.,* 1984; see also Gunn, 1984; Kozlowski, Director, & Harford, 1981; Murphy, 1983). Among the most consistent findings, discussed below, is that highly dependent smokers are more likely to benefit from the use of nicotine supplements in cessation (Christen, McDonald, Olson, Drook, & Stookey, 1984; Fagerstrom, 1982; Hughes, 1985; Jarvik & Schneider, 1984).

The Tolerance Questionnaire assesses three content areas: smoking dosage, the importance of smoking in the morning, and the person's ability to restrain smoking. The Morning Smoking factor appears to be the most powerful in predicting both withdrawal (Fagerstrom, 1978) and outcome (Kozlowski *et al.,* 1981; Murphy, 1983). This reflects the dynamics of nicotine dependence and nicotine regulation. Nicotine has a short half-life in the body of about 120 minutes (Benowitz, Jacob, Jones, & Rosenberg, 1982). As nicotine levels drop, the dependent smoker is thought to experience a subliminal withdrawal syndrome that cues smoking to replenish nicotine. During sleep, the body is depleted of nicotine. A smoker who craves cigarettes immediately upon waking, therefore, is likely to be particularly sensitive to internal nicotine levels—that is, highly dependent.

Despite its validity, the Tolerance Questionnaire may have limited clinical utility in nonpharmacological treatment. Whereas scores on this

TABLE 5-1.   The Tolerance Questionnaire

---

*Dose*

How many cigarettes a day do you smoke? (greater number)

What brand do you smoke? (higher nicotine delivery)

Do you inhale? (greater frequency)

*Morning Smoking*

Do you smoke more during the morning than during the rest of the day? (affirmative)

How soon after you wake up do you smoke your first cigarette? (sooner)

Which cigarette would you hate to give up? (citation of morning cigarette)

*Restraint*

Do you find it difficult to refrain from smoking in places where it is forbidden—for example, in a church, at the library, cinema, and so on? (greater frequency)

Do you smoke if you are so ill that you are in bed most of the day? (affirmative)

---

*Note.* Adapted from "Measuring Degree of Physical Dependence to Tobacco with Reference to Individualization of Treatment" by K.-O. Fagerstrom, 1978, *Addictive Behaviors, 3*, 235–241. Copyright 1978 by Pergamon Journals, Ltd. Adapted by permission. Parenthetical notes indicate direction of scoring.

instrument are prognostic, they have few specific treatment implications: There are currently no differential behavioral treatments for dependent and nondependent smokers. Thus, the scores serve only to warn the clinician of cases in which prognosis is poor and in which extra effort might therefore be required. Smokers who are highly dependent should be prepared for an especially severe or prolonged withdrawal syndrome marked by craving, psychological discomfort, and physical symptoms.

## Screening for Pharmacotherapy

Scores on the Tolerance Questionnaire *do* have implications for pharmacological treatment, however. The idea that cigarette smoking is driven by dependence on nicotine naturally suggests that providing nicotine from another source would facilitate smoking cessation. A corollary of this idea is that nicotine supplements should be most valuable to those who are most dependent. Research has borne this out. Studies consistently show that subjects who are highly dependent, as assessed by the Tolerance Questionnaire, are more likely to benefit from treatment with nicotine supplements (Christen *et al.,* 1984; Fagerstrom, 1982; Jarvik & Schneider, 1984).

The superiority of nicotine therapy with dependent smokers is relative, however: Christen *et al.* (1984) report significant benefit even for nondependent smokers (though see Fagerstrom, 1982). Moreover, because proper use of Nicorette® (a prescription product delivering nicotine; see below) carries few serious risks, there seems little rationale for excluding nondependent smokers from pharmacotherapy. Many clinical researchers now advocate nicotine supplementation as a part of smoking cessation treatment for *any* smoker for whom it is not medically contraindicated (Hughes, 1985; N. G. Schneider, personal communication, January 2, 1985). In most cases, therefore, the Tolerance Questionnaire will not serve a screening function. Where there is reason to select the most suitable candidates for nicotine therapy, however, the Tolerance Questionnaire provides a valid basis for making this discrimination. The use of Nicorette® in conjunction with behavioral treatment raises a host of special assessment challenges, which are discussed in a separate section below.

## Assessing the Withdrawal Syndrome

One of the apparent obstacles to successful smoking cessation is the emergence of a withdrawal syndrome. Withdrawal symptoms often appear upon reduction of smoking, even before cessation is achieved (Perlick, 1977; Raw, Jarvis, Feyerabend, & Russell, 1980; Shiffman, 1979), and may thus serve as a barrier to cessation as well as maintenance.

Several scales may be used to assess withdrawal symptoms. The Shiffman–Jarvik Withdrawal Scale (Table 5-2), developed through factor analyses of ex-smokers' symptom reports, yields scores for *groups* of symptoms: Craving, Psychological Symptoms, Physical Symptoms, Arousal Disturbance, and Appetite Disturbance (Shiffman, 1979; Shiffman & Jarvik, 1976). Hughes and Hatsukami (1986) have developed a shorter rating scale (Table 5-3) and identified a subset of symptoms amenable to relief by nicotine administration. They and others (e.g., Hall, Rugg, Runstall, & Jones, 1984) have also found the Profile of Mood States (McNair, Lorr, & Droppleman, 1971) useful as a measure of withdrawal-induced mood disturbance. Standard measures of sleep disturbance (Carskadon *et al.,* 1976) may also be useful.[2]

Although these scales are useful for measuring typical symptoms or symptom groups, they cannot cover the withdrawal syndrome's remarkable variability, especially in regard to physical complaints. Clinically, one observes reports of constipation and diarrhea, headaches, muscle aches, intestinal aches, dizziness, and other symptoms. These range in severity from minor annoyances to major dysfunctions. From a practical standpoint, there is little point in determining whether these can truly be attributed to tobacco withdrawal. The symptoms should be evaluated and, if appropriate, treated

---

2. The time of day is an often-ignored factor in assessing withdrawal. Withdrawal symptoms show considerable circadian variability with a consistent peak in the early evening (Shiffman, 1979). It is best, therefore, to fix the time of assessment.

TABLE 5-2.   Shiffman–Jarvik Withdrawal Scale

*Craving*

If you could smoke freely, would you like a cigarette this minute?
If you had just eaten, would you want a cigarette?
Are you thinking of cigarettes more than usual?
If you were permitted to smoke, would you refuse a cigarette right now?[a]
Do you miss a cigarette?
Do you have an urge to smoke a cigarette right now?
Would you find a cigarette unpleasant right now?[a]

*Psychological Symptoms*

Do you feel more calm than usual?[a]
Are you feeling very frustrated?
Do you feel more restless than usual?
Do you feel more tense than usual?
Do you feel anxious?
Are you feeling irritable?
Are you less nervous than usual?
Do you feel content?
Are you able to concentrate as well as usual?

*Physical Symptoms*

Are your hands shaky?
Is your heart beating faster than usual?
Do you have fluttery feelings in your chest right now?

*Arousal Disturbance*

Do you feel wide awake?[a]
Are you unusually sleepy for this time of day?
Do you feel alert?[a]
Do you feel unusually tired?

*Appetite Disturbance*

Do you feel hungrier than usual for this time of day?
Is your appetite smaller than normal?[a]

*Note.* See Shiffman and Jarvik (1976). Note that the Arousal Disturbance items are bipolar, with deviations from normal in either direction.

[a]Indicates reverse-scored item.

by a physician. Nicotine supplementation should be tried if not contra-indicated.

The clinical significance of withdrawal symptoms in smoking cessation is unclear. Theoretically, withdrawal symptoms are hypothesized to be major factors in relapse, which is thought to be motivated by the negative reinforcement of relief from withdrawal (see Shiffman, 1979). This position is supported by retrospective studies showing that recidivists report more

TABLE 5-3.   Hughes Withdrawal Scale

| Rate each of the following symptoms as: None, Mild, Moderate, or Severe | |
| --- | --- |
| Craving for a cigarette | Increased eating |
| Irritable/angry | Insomnia |
| Anxious/tense | Drowsiness |
| Impatient | Headaches |
| Restless | Bowel or stomach problems |
| Difficulty concentrating | Any of the following: Tremor, heart racing, sweating or |
| Excessive hunger | dizziness, stomach or bowel problems |

*Note.* Adapted from "Signs and Symptoms of Tobacco Withdrawal" by J. R. Hughes and D. K. Hatsukami, 1986, *Archives of General Psychiatry, 43,* 289–294. Copyright 1986 by the American Medical Association. Reprinted by permission.

severe withdrawal symptoms (e.g., Burns, 1969; Murphy, 1983), but this may reflect retrospective self-justification. A few prospective studies also relate withdrawal severity and outcome (mood disturbance in Hall *et al.,* 1984; craving in Killen *et al.,* 1984). Many other studies show no relationship between relapse and withdrawal symptom frequency or severity (Goldstein, 1981; Gunn, 1983; Hughes & Hatsukami, 1986; Killen *et al.,* 1984; Lawrence, Amodei, & Murray, 1982) on symptoms other than craving, suggesting that a severe withdrawal syndrome does not necessarily doom an ex-smoker to relapse.

There is also limited support concerning the immediate role withdrawal symptoms play in precipitating relapse episodes. In a study of specific relapse episodes (Shiffman, 1982), only half of the ex-smokers reported experiencing withdrawal symptoms at the time of the relapse crisis. Perhaps withdrawal symptoms play a role in relapse only when their persistence results in fatigue and surrender. In any case, the major clinical utility of assessing withdrawal may be to indicate when pharmacotherapy, which is highly effective in reducing withdrawal, is indicated.

## Background Factors Amenable to Intervention

We have seen that many factors associated with outcome in smoking cessation are of limited clinical utility because of their limited potential for intervention. Stress, social contagion, and social support are recently identified factors that do lend themselves to intervention. In each case, assessment may help to identify those at greatest risk and therefore in greatest need of intervention. The interventions are without risk, however, and need not be limited to those at risk unless the costs are excessive.

*Stress*

Stress has long been associated with relapse in anecdote, and this association has recently been corroborated by research. Several studies have found that relapse episodes are often directly precipitated by stress (Lichtenstein, Antonuccio, & Rainwater, 1983; Marlatt & Gordon, 1980; Shiffman, 1982, 1987). These studies imply that relapse is more likely under stress, but not necessarily that ex-smokers under more stress are more likely to relapse. Studies on the latter issue vary as a function of how stress is measured.

Studies using life events measures have been the least consistent, with some finding an effect (Gunn, 1983; Ockene, Benfari, *et al.,* 1982) and others finding no effect (Mermelstein, Cohen, & Lichtenstein, 1983; Shiffman, Read, & Jarvik, 1983). Traditional life events measures are unsuited by nature to predicting relapse; they focus on relatively rare events that are unlikely to account for the many relapses observed in the first few months of abstinence. Measures of small-scale, everyday stressors or of perceived stress are more promising. Cohen, Kamarck, and Mermelstein (1983) found that perceived stress predicted success in smoking cessation. A form of their Perceived Stress Scale as short as four items significantly predicted relapse months later. The full scale is shown in Table 5-4, with these four key items marked. Preliminary findings from an ongoing study by the author also indicate that the Hassles Scale, a measure of everyday stressors (Kanner, Coyne, Schaefer, & Lazarus, 1981), prospectively predicts relapse.

Because relapse can be predicted prospectively from posttreatment Perceived Stress Scale scores, stress should be assessed regularly throughout treatment so that stress-reducing interventions can be implemented with clients who need them. Relaxation training, cognitive approaches, and meditation may all reduce stress. However, evidence that stress reduction helps prevent relapse is scant (see, e.g., Pechacek, 1976).

*Social Contagion*

The smoker is not the only target for assessment or intervention. Assessing "social contagion"—exposure to other smokers as a stimulus for temptation or relapse—is important. Social contagion appears to be a major factor in relapse (Shiffman, 1982). One-third of smoking relapses are attributed to social influence (Cummings, Gordon, & Marlatt, 1980). Many studies show that people whose friends and coworkers smoke are more likely to relapse (Eisinger, 1972; Goldstein, 1981; Gottleib *et al.,* 1981; Mermelstein, Cohen, Lichtenstein, Baer, & Kamarck, 1986; Ockene, Benfari, *et al.,* 1982; Tongas *et al.,* 1976).

Clients' exposure to smoking in various social environments (home,

TABLE 5-4.    Perceived Stress Scale

---

In the last month, how often have you . . .

Been upset because of something that happened unexpectedly?

Felt that you were unable to control important things in your life?†

Felt nervous and stressed?

Dealt successfully with irritating life hassles?[a]

Felt you were effectively coping with important changes occurring in your life?[a]

Felt confident about your ability to handle personal problems?†[a]

Felt that things were going your way?†[a]

Found that you could cope with all of the things you had to do?[a]

Been able to control irritations in your life?[a]

Felt you were on top of things?[a]

Been angered because of things that happened that were outside your control?

Found yourself thinking about things you have to accomplish?

Been abler to control the way you spend your time?[a]

Felt difficulties were piling up so high you couldn't overcome them?†

---

*Note.* From "A Global Measure of Perceived Stress" by S. Cohen, T. Kamarck, and R. Mermelstein, 1983, *Journal of Health and Social Behavior, 24,* 385–396. Copyright 1983 by the American Sociological Association. Reprinted by permission. The items marked with daggers constitute a four-item short version.

[a]Reverse scoring.

work, social circles, etc.) should be assessed. Intervention is called for if any of these environments offer substantial exposure. If the environment cannot be avoided, clients may need to master the assertive behaviors necessary to influence others not to smoke around them. Horwitz, Hindi-Alexander, and Wagner (1982) found that smokers who asked others not to smoke were more likely to succeed in smoking cessation. There is insufficient space here to review the assessment of assertion, but it should be emphasized that most smokers find this task difficult and do not approach it skillfully. A simple role play will quickly reveal most problems.

The smoking status of the smoker's spouse appears particularly important. Tongas *et al.* (1976) and McIntyre-Kingsolver, Lichtenstein, and Mermelstein (1986) report near-universal failure among those with smoking spouses, *even when both spouses are treated* (McIntyre-Kingsolver *et al.,* 1986). On the optimistic side, Graham and Gibson (1971) report that those whose spouses are already ex-smokers are especially likely to succeed in cessation and maintenance.

## Social Support

Others can help as well as hinder the smoker in giving up the habit. Social support may play a role in successful cessation; the details of its role are unclear, however. Coppotelli and Orleans (1985) and Mermelstein *et al.* (1986) found that perceived availability of support (especially appraisal and self-esteem support) predicted initial cessation and short-term, but not long-term, maintenance. In contrast, Horwitz *et al.* (1982) and Ockene, Benfari, *et al.* (1982) report that support predicts maintenance, but not initial cessation.

Social support is best assessed through measures of *perceived* support (Cohen & Wills, 1985) such as the Interpersonal Support Evaluation List (ISEL; Cohen & Hoberman, 1983). The treatment implications following from observed support deficiencies are unclear, as studies do not yet support the efficacy of support-boosting interventions in general or in smoking cessation (e.g., Klesges, Glasgow, & Fleeker, 1985).

Although global social support represents a resource that may aid in successful cessation, specific social support in the process of cessation may be more relevant. Ockene, Benfari, *et al.* (1982), for example, found that clients whose spouses were willing to accompany them to clinic sessions were more successful in maintenance (there was no effect on cessation). Actively including the partner in treatment has been effective in weight control programs (Brownell, Heckerman, Westlake, Hayes, & Monti, 1978).

A series of studies by a group at the University of Oregon has established more precisely how the behavior of others affects cessation and maintenance. Smokers' partners' relative degree of involvement was unrelated to outcome; simply being more involved was not necessarily helpful. Rather, the *type* of involvement was critical. Mermelstein and colleagues (Mermelstein *et al.,* 1986; Mermelstein, Lichtenstein, & McIntyre, 1983) obtained reports of specific partner behaviors, which they divided into two major types (Table 5-5): Encouragement, consisting of positive and encouraging responses to the smoker's efforts, and Nagging or Policing, consisting of punitive or controlling efforts focused on detecting or punishing negative behaviors.

The two were found to have opposite effects. In one study, Encouragement had positive effects, whereas the negative effects of Nagging were not significant. A subsequent study found significantly deleterious effects for Nagging, but nonsignificant effects for reinforcement (Mermelstein *et al.,* 1986). Most of the effects were limited to the first 3 months of abstinence. Although the detailed findings are mixed, the clinical implications seem

TABLE 5-5.   Partner Interaction Questionnaire

---

How often has (a partner, friend, etc.) done the following: (Never, Almost Never, Sometimes, Fairly Often, Very Often)

*Encouragement*

Complimented my not smoking

Talked me out of smoking a cigarette

Congratulated me for my decision to quit smoking

Helped me think of substitutes for smoking

Celebrated my quitting with me

Helped to calm me down when I was feeling stressed or irritable

Told me to stick with it

Expressed confidence in my ability to quit/remain quit

Helped me to use substitutes for cigarettes

Expressed pleasure at my efforts to quit

Participated in an activity with me that keeps me from smoking (e.g., going for a walk instead of smoking)

*"Nagging" or Policing*

Commented that smoking is a dirty habit

Commented on my lack of willpower

Commented that the house smells of smoke

Refused to let me smoke in the house

Mentioned being bothered by smoke

Criticized my smoking

Expressed doubt about my ability to quit/stay quit

Refused to clean up my cigarette butts

Asked me to quit smoking

---

*Note.* See Mermelstein, Lichtenstein, and McIntyre (1983).

clear: Partner reinforcement should be promoted and partner nagging inhibited.[3]

The questionnaire developed by Mermelstein, Lichtenstein, and McIntyre (1983; Table 5-5) may be used to assess the nature of the partner's involvement in the smoking cessation effort; the items can also be used as a list of suggested dos and don'ts. The client's assertiveness in requesting aid from

---

3. It is worth noting that partners who were smokers were *not* less supportive than ex-smokers. Partners who had never smoked were less supportive than either group, perhaps because they lacked empathy for the experience of quitting (Mermelstein, Lichtenstein, & McIntyre, 1983).

the partner is an apt target for assessment and intervention. As usual, there are no data directly assessing the efficacy of support-enhancing interventions, but the process data suggest that such interventions may be worthwhile.

## An Assessment Model for Relapse Prevention

The assessments discussed thus far have focused on background factors that may affect a person's success in quitting smoking, but are not necessarily active at the moment of relapse. Because most behavioral smoking cessation programs are oriented toward relapse prevention, and because relapse always begins with a first "slip," factors contributing to initial lapses deserve attention. A lapse is likely to occur when the smoker experiences temptation and does not adequately master it. Coping with temptation is a key process in maintaining abstinence (see Shiffman, 1984b, 1987).

This formulation suggests two foci for assessment: the smoker's vulnerability to temptation, and his or her resources for preventing or resisting temptation. Assessment of relapse vulnerability focuses on situational stimuli, whereas assessment of resources focuses on coping. This model may provide a context for individually tailored treatment, as it suggests the potential for assessing and addressing individual differences in vulnerability to temptation and in coping resources.

### Assessment of Relapse Vulnerability

A major goal of assessment for relapse prevention is to predict when the ex-smoker will be most vulnerable (most tempted) to relapse, so that interventions can be targeted to these situations. Two closely related assumptions underlie the idea that temptation is predictable. The first is that smoking is stimulus-bound and that smoking and craving become classically conditioned to specific stimuli that, upon cessation, elicit further craving and/or smoking. The implication is that if the relevant conditioned stimuli can be identified (by studying when the person smokes), temptation can be predicted.

A second common assumption is that smoking can, under some circumstances, serve an instrumental function for the smoker. Most commonly, smoking is thought to serve a function of stress reduction. There is ample evidence that smokers smoke more when under stress, and also some evidence that smoking reduces stress (Gilbert, 1979; Rose, Anada, & Jarvik, 1983). In this model, temptation is related to underlying needs, rather than merely conditioned to neutral stimuli. (However, such stimuli might signal the availability of reinforcement through smoking.)

The two models, although not contradictory, differ in their assessment and treatment implications. The first model implies that one must determine the conditioned stimuli for craving and either extinguish them or teach the smoker to avoid them. The second implies that one must identify the needs served by smoking and develop alternative ways to meet those needs (e.g., by teaching relaxation to someone who smokes to relieve stress).[4] This model implies that assessment must extend beyond smoking behavior to encompass whatever other needs and skills are relevant to the person's smoking. What both models share is an emphasis on examining when the person smokes as a means of determining when he or she will be tempted to smoke and therefore vulnerable to relapse.

### Assessing Smoking Patterns and Motives

In the models described above, patterns of smoking are relevant to prediction of relapse vulnerabilities. Self-monitoring may be used to assess when a person smokes in terms of time of day, situation, affect, self-reported motive, or any other antecedent of interest. A sample self-monitoring form used for this purpose has been presented in Figure 5-1. Although reactivity may cause a drop in the amount smoked, self-monitoring one's reasons for smoking apparently does not much affect smoking patterns (Joffe, Lowe, & Fisher, 1981; Leventhal & Avis, 1976).

Several self-report scales have also been devised to measure differences in smoking patterns. Some purport to measure motives, and are thus more consistent with the "functional" model of smoking, whereas others direct their attention to situational cueing of smoking. This distinction is not clearly implemented in the items themselves; the two types of scales are not distinguished here.

The Horn–Waingrow Reasons for Smoking (RFS) Scale (Table 5-6), based on Tomkins's (1966) theoretical work, is the prototype of these scales (Ikard, Green, & Horn, 1969). The items consistently fall into six factors: (1) Automatic Smoking, (2) Addictive Smoking, (3) Negative Affect Reduction Smoking, (4) Indulgent Smoking, (5) Stimulation Smoking, and (6) Sensorimotor Smoking. Russell, Peto, and Patel (1974) failed to find a Negative Affect Reduction factor in an extension of the RFS Scale, but most investigators extract such a factor and find it among the most clinically useful subscales of this measure. It should thus be retained. Russell *et al.* (1974) also extracted higher-order factors, which they labeled Pharmacological Smoking and Nonpharmacological Smoking. The first measures pharmacological motives for smoking, as embodied in

---

4. Identifying such needs or deficits can involve a wide range of assessment procedures not directly related to smoking. There is insufficient space in this chapter for a thorough discussion of the full spectrum of assessment.

TABLE 5-6.   The Reasons for Smoking Scale

How much is each of the following characteristic of you?

### Negative Affect Reduction Smoking

When I feel uncomfortable or upset about something, I light up a cigarette.

When I feel "blue" or want to take my mind off cares and worries, I smoke cigarettes.

I light up a cigarette when I feel angry about something.

### Automatic Smoking

I smoke automatically without even being aware of it.

I light up a cigarette without realizing I still have one burning in the ashtray.

I find myself smoking without remembering lighting up.

### Addictive Smoking

I get a real gnawing hunger to smoke when I haven't smoked for a while.

When I have run out of cigarettes, I find it almost unbearable until I can get them.

Without a cigarette, I don't know what to do with my hands.

### Sensorimotor Smoking

I smoke because I like the smell so much.

Part of the enjoyment of smoking is watching the smoke as I blow it out.

Part of the enjoyment of smoking comes from the steps I take to light up.

### Stimulation Smoking

Smoking helps me think and concentrate.

I smoke more when I am rushed and have lots to do.

Smoking helps to keep me going when I'm tired.

I get a definite lift and feel more alert when smoking.

### Indulgent Smoking

After meals is one of the times I most enjoy smoking.

I like a cigarette best when I am having a quiet rest.

I want to smoke most when I am comfortable and relaxed.

I usually only smoke when I can really sit back and enjoy it.

### Psychosocial Smoking

It is easier to talk and get on with other people when smoking.

I smoke much more when I am with other people.

While smoking I feel more confident with other people.

*Note.* Adapted from "The Classification of Smoking by Factorial Structure of Motives" by M. A. H. Russell, J. Peto, and U. A. Patel, 1974, *Journal of the Royal Statistical Society, 137,* 313-346.

the Stimulation Smoking, Automatic Smoking, and Addictive Smoking factors, whereas the latter measures an aggregate of the Sensorimotor Smoking and Psychosocial Smoking factors.

A similar distinction has been made by McKennel (1970) on the basis of the more situationally focused Smoking Situations Questionnaire. The McKennel scale is composed of seven factors: (1) Nervous Irritation Smoking, (2) Relaxation Smoking, (3) Solitary Smoking (smoking when alone or *feeling* alone), (4) Activity Accompaniment Smoking (smoking as an adjunct to other activities), (5) Food Substitution Smoking (smoking instead of eating), (6) Social Smoking (smoking in the company of others), and (7) Social Confidence Smoking (smoking in order to bolster one's social confidence). McKennel groups the first five into an Inner Need factor and the remainder into a Social Smoking factor. Similar instruments have been published by Best and Hakstian (1978), Frith (1971), and B. Mausner and Platt (1971).

It should be emphasized that these instruments yield continuous and independent scores on each scale for each smoker. Many factor-analytic studies have confirmed that the scales are orthogonal (J. Williams, Crumpacker, & Krier, 1980). The scales do not identify discrete groups of smokers; one can be both a Negative Affect Reduction smoker *and* a Psychosocial smoker.

Assessment of smoking patterns has potential as a basis for directing and individualizing treatment. Both stimulus control and "coping" strategies are common. A smoker who frequently smokes when drinking alcohol might be advised to avoid drinking for a few months. A smoker who smokes when under stress might learn relaxation techniques to relieve stress without smoking. Because smokers may have high scores on several dimensions, a single client may need to anticipate difficulty in several situations and to combine several techniques.

### Validity of Smoking Typologies

Despite their widespread use, there is meager support for the validity of self-report smoking typologies. I address three aspects of their validity: their criterion validity in relation to *ad libitum* smoking, their predictive validity, and their clinical utility.

#### Criterion Validity

The validity of most self-report smoking questionnaires rests on their relation to *ad lib.* smoking: Subjects who are, say, Negative Affect smokers should indeed smoke more in response to negative affect. Several studies have used analogues or experimental manipulations to test the scales' validity. Leventhal and Avis (1976) found that subjects scoring high on the Automatic Smoking factor of the RFS Scale were, as hypothesized, more reactive to self-monitoring. The study yielded no support for the Addictive Smoking factor, however, and only mixed support for the Indulgent factor. Ikard and Tomkins (1973) reported mixed support for the RFS Scale. Adesso and Glad (1978) found little relation between scores on the B. Mausner and Platt (1971) scales and actual smoking in an analogue study. Joffe *et al.* (1981) criticize analogue studies because their demand characteristics tend to elicit from subjects behavior consistent with their responses to the questionnaires.

Naturalistic studies of *ad lib.* smoking yield a bleaker view of the scales' validity. Mark Prange and I (Shiffman & Prange, 1984) recently compared RFS and McKennel scores to data from situational self-monitoring; the latter were obtained using the form shown in Figure 5-1. Very few of the hypothesized correlations were significant. Overall, the RFS Negative Affect Reduction Smoking factor proved to be the most valid. In an earlier study, Joffe *et al.* (1981) also found poor support for the RFS Scale; the Negative Affect Reduction Smoking and Automatic Smoking factors fared best. On the assumption that self-monitoring data are more accurate, these studies suggest that the scales only measure subjects' *beliefs* about their smoking.


*Predictive Validity*


Smoking typologies have a mixed track record in predicting response to smoking cessation. Ikard and Tomkins (1973) found that Addictive smokers on the RFS Scale missed cigarettes more when abstinent; however, this finding is rather tautological; since the scale asks how much one misses cigarettes when not smoking. In an experimental study, D. G. Williams (1979) showed that "high-arousal" smokers (see Frith, 1971) developed more mood disturbance on cessation. In a study by Hughes and Hatsukami (1986), however, neither Addictive Smoking nor Negative Affect Reduction Smoking scores predicted the severity of withdrawal symptoms. Though there are contrary data (Eisinger, 1972; Joffe *et al.,* 1981), a frequent finding is that Psychosocial or Sensorimotor smokers (McKennel's Social smokers) are more likely to succeed in quitting than are Negative Affect Reduction smokers (Murphy, 1983; Pomerleau *et al.,* 1978).

It should be noted, however, that the clinical use of these scales goes beyond such prognostics. Their clinical use does not depend on their ability to predict *who* will relapse, but *when* (in what circumstances) an individual will relapse. The association between smoking "type" and relapse situation has never been empirically tested. Despite its intuitive appeal, the hypothesis that smoking patterns are related to relapse patterns currently has no empirical basis.

*Clinical Utility*

The clinical appeal of these scales rests on the vision of differential treatment. It is appealing to imagine different protocols and prescriptions to suit the special needs of each type of smoker. The findings to date do not support this application. Flaxman (1979) found that different types of smokers do not, of their own accord, use different techniques in smoking cessation. The strategy of specifically assigning smokers to different treatments based on their smoking type has, unfortunately, seldom been evaluated.

In one of the few exceptions, Pechacek (1976) devised a specialized treatment package for people who were especially anxious (not necessarily those who *smoked* when anxious). Though the pattern of data looked promising, there was no significant interaction of treatment with subject characteristics in this small sample. Stress management training seemed to help everyone. Although the RFS Scale is widely used, there have been no reports of strong interactions between RFS smoker types and particular treatments. Contributing to these poor outcomes is the fact that smokers who seek treatment are a relatively homogeneous lot, especially as regards Negative Affect Reduction Smoking, which is nearly universal among heavy or dependent smokers. At present, the hope of individualized treatment is an unproven hypothesis.

In summary, smoking typology measures have great intuitive appeal, reasonable psychometric credentials, and substantial educational value; however, their clinical utility is unproved.

### Assessment of Relapse Crises

Another method of identifying a smoker's relapse vulnerability is to assess the smoker's historical or current temptations. On the principle that past behavior is the best predictor of future behavior, situations that have prompted relapse in the past may be expected to elicit temptation in the future. The smoking history should include questions about the situations that elicited strong temptation or relapse in previous quitting efforts. Once the smoker has achieved abstinence, attention should focus on situations that currently produce strong temptations to smoke. Contemporaneous assessment of temptations is the most direct method of assessing relapse vulnerability, for it requires the least inference.

Table 5-7 presents a questionnaire useful in obtaining information about relapse crises. See Shiffman, Read, Maltese, Rapkin, & Jarvik, 1985, for an interview method.) A simple way to summarize such relapse descriptions is provided by a cluster-analytic typology of four relapse types: (1) Social Situations, in which the person is usually drinking and in the presence of others who are smoking (positive affect generally predominates, though the person may feel some social anxiety); (2) Relaxing Situations, often following a meal, in which the relaxation itself is the cue for smoking; (3) Tense Work Situations, in which the person feels anxious and may be under extreme performance demands; (4) Emotionally Upsetting Situations, involving either boredom/depression during a period of inactivity or anger/anxiety resulting from interpersonal conflict (see Shiffman, 1986; Shiffman, Read, & Jarvik, 1985).

In assessing relapse crises, the single most important factor to consider is the affective tone of the situation. The other major factor is the role of smoking stimuli (both primary ones, such as seeing a pack of cigarettes, and secondary ones, such as drinking alcohol or coffee) in precipitating the crisis. The role of the former implies a need for affect management strategies, whereas the latter suggests a need for stimulus control strategies.

Although the intuitive appeal of this relatively direct assessment is great, its validity for predicting subsequent temptations remains to be established. Its utility depends on the stability of individuals' vulnerabilities to relapse. Knowing about past relapse episodes is most useful if they inform the clinician about the client's stable vulnerabilities and thereby predict subsequent episodes. If there is no consistent "theme" in a client's relapse episodes, however, past episodes are much less useful.

I recently examined the consistency of ex-smokers' relapse vulnerabilities by assessing the similarity of two relapse episodes reported by the same person. Data were from 52 ex-smokers who reported two crises to a relapse prevention hotline (Shiffman, 1984c). There was at best a weak resemblance between the two situations. The two relapse crises tended to have similar ratings on the Social Smoking factor of McKennel's (1970) Smoking Situations Questionnaire. The affective tones of the two situations were not systematically related.

Overall, the situations seemed independent. The situations did not systematically fall into the same clusters, for example. In effect, a smoker who suffered an episode triggered by emotional upset on Monday might have one triggered by alcohol on Tuesday, one triggered by relaxation on Wednesday, and so on. These data imply that the predictive power of information about a past relapse episode may be limited. The usefulness of such assessments may lie primarily in their ability to highlight coping deficits. Assessment of relapse crises, when coupled with assessment of coping, remains one of the most promising areas in behavioral assessment of smoking cessation.

## Assessment of Coping

The assessments discussed thus far have focused on predicting temptation to smoke, either globally or in particular circumstances. Yet prediction of

TABLE 5-7.    Relapse Debriefing Form

The following questions deal with the circumstances in which you were recently tempted to smoke or did smoke. Please answer each one.

Where were you?
__ Home        __ Work        __ Someone else's home
__ A restaurant or bar        __ A vehicle    __ Other

What were you doing?
__ Working    __ Eating or drinking        __ Socializing
__ Relaxing    __ Other

Had you been consuming coffee? __ Yes   __ No

Had you been consuming alcohol? __ Yes   __ No

Were other people with you? __ Yes   __ No

How many of them were smoking? __

Were cigarettes available? __ Yes   __ No

From what source? _____

If you smoked, how did you get the cigarette?
__ I asked someone for it
__ It was offered to me
__ I bought it
__ I found it (Where? _____)
__ Other

How were you feeling?
__ Happy        __ Relaxed        __ Neutral
__ Angry        __ Anxious        __ Depressed

What single thing contributed most to your being tempted to smoke?
__ How you were feeling
__ Seeing cigarettes or people smoking
__ Habit of smoking along with food, coffee, or relaxation
__ Symptoms you were having
__ Other

How did you feel after the episode was over? (check all that apply)
__ Relieved                    __ Hopeful
__ Successful                  __ Worried
__ Disappointed                __ Guilty
__ Like a failure              __ Other
__ Hopeless

Did you anticipate that this situation would tempt you to smoke?
__ Yes   __ No

How often do you encounter situations like this one?
__ More than once per day
__ About once per day
__ A few times per week
__ About once per week
__ A few times per month
__ Less than twice a month

*(continued)*

TABLE 5-7 (Continued).

| |
|---|
| When you're in situations like this, are you always very tempted to smoke? |
| __ Always |
| __ Usually |
| __ Rarely |
| __ Never |

temptation is of little use unless it helps mobilize or direct action to prevent or resist temptation. Indeed, data on relapse crises (situations in which strong temptation is experienced) suggest that the person's coping efforts are a key to preventing relapse (Curry & Marlatt, 1985; Shiffman, 1982). The importance of coping is supported in many studies covering several stages of the smoking cessation process. In discussing—or assessing—coping, it is useful to consider several different types of coping, which differ in their aim and in the stage of cessation in which they are most prominent.

## Stages of Coping

As they begin to embark on a smoking cessation effort, smokers engage in "preparatory coping"—"gearing up" for the cessation attempt by mustering commitment and resources. One typical activity is self-education in the dangers of smoking as a means of enhancing commitment. Public statements of commitment and explicit contracting are other commitment enhancers. Seeking professional help is itself a form of preparatory coping. Preparatory activities are concentrated in the early phases of cessation (DiClemente & Prochaska, 1985) and should be assessed at intake.

"Anticipatory coping" takes on a prominent role once the cessation effort has begun. Anticipatory coping consists of ongoing activities to prevent or minimize temptation to smoke. Stimulus control strategies such as removing smoking cues (e.g., ashtrays) or avoiding smoking-related activities (e.g., drinking coffee) are common examples. Several studies highlight the importance of anticipatory coping (Evans & Lane, 1981; Horwitz et al., 1982; Perri & Richards, 1977). Although often initiated early, anticipatory coping should continue through most of a cessation effort and thus should be assessed on an ongoing basis.

"Immediate coping" consists of attempts to resist smoking when one is faced with actual temptation to smoke. Substitution strategies (e.g., eating a carrot stick instead of smoking when one craves a cigarette) are common responses. Several strategies represented in other phases are repeated at this stage. Hurriedly escaping the tempting situation (e.g., leaving a cocktail party) is a stimulus control strategy, for example, but differs from an avoidance strategy in its immediacy and urgency. Performance of immediate coping has emerged as the single best predictor of success in relapse crises (Curry & Marlatt, 1985; Shiffman, 1982). Most ex-smokers who perform coping in relapse crises weather the crises without smoking (82%); in contrast, most of those who do not cope go on to relapse (79%) (Shiffman, 1982). Immediate coping begins as soon as the person tries to limit smoking and must continue as long as temptations are experienced.

Finally, "restorative coping" involves attempts to recover from breaches of abstinence or from relapse crises. Marlatt (1978) has suggested that lapses lead to relapse because of their psychological effects, which he has labeled the "abstinence violation effect" (AVE). A lapse often leaves ex-smokers feeling demoralized, blaming themselves for the lapse, and feeling pessimistic about their ability to persevere in their nonsmoking efforts (e.g., Colletti, Supnick, & Rizzo, 1981; Mermelstein & Lichtenstein, 1983). Many of these effects are experienced by ex-smokers following *any* severe temptation, even if they do not actually smoke (Shiffman, 1984a). To the extent that they are overcome by these effects and define themselves as having failed, ex-smokers are left highly vulnerable to relapse.

Restorative coping tries to combat the AVE and to restore the ex-smoker to the path of abstinence. It includes efforts to overcome the AVE directly (e.g., telling oneself that one can do better next time), as well as efforts to reaffirm commitment and restore lapsed anticipatory coping (e.g., swearing off situations similar to that in which the lapse occurred). There is little data on restorative coping, but investigations have shown that subjects who are more positive following a slip are more likely to recover from it (Goldstein, 1981; Mermelstein & Lichtenstein, 1983). Mermelstein and Lichtenstein (1983) also found that ex-smokers who used restorative coping (especially its cognitive forms) were more likely to recover following a slip. Although only relevant following relapse crises, the client's potential for restorative coping must be assessed early in anticipation of such crises. Each form of coping is amenable to assessment by self-report. Immediate and restorative coping, being responsive to particular situations, may also be assessed through analogue methods.

### Assessing Coping by Self-Report

Coping is easily assessed by self-report. Clients may be asked with open-ended questions what they have been doing or saying to themselves to prevent, resist, or recover from temptation. Clients should regularly be queried about ongoing coping activities. Accounts of how clients responded to specific recent crises are invaluable as a means of directly assessing coping deficits. Queries about coping should always be included in debriefing of relapse crises (see "Assessment of Relapse Crises," above).

More structured accounts of coping can be obtained by presenting clients with a list of relevant coping responses and asking them to indicate how frequently each has been used. Table 5-8 shows the Coping With Temptation Inventory (CWTI) for use in structured assessment of anticipatory,

TABLE 5-8.    The Coping With Temptation Inventory

BEHAVIORAL COPING RESPONSES

ALTERNATIVES
*Alternative consumption*
  Food and drink
    Allow yourself to eat more to avoid smoking
    Chew gum
    Drink a lot of water
    Eat more fruit
  Nicotine
    Chew nicotine gum
    Use snuff
*Alternative activities*
  Exercise
    Exercise
    Lift weights
    Take walks
  Distraction
    Keep busy
    Distract yourself
    Crochet
    Doodle when on phone to avoid smoking
  Relaxation
    Do deep-breathing exercises
    Engage in more relaxing activities
    Listen to tape on relaxation
    Take hot showers in order to relax

SELF-CARE—activities to promote well-being
*Stress reduction*
  Isolate yourself for a weekend of peace and quiet
  Keep out of stressful situations
  Remove yourself from stressful situation
  Scream to relieve frustration
*Other self-care activities*
  Eat better
  Go shopping to feel better
  Set aside time for yourself
  Spent more of your free time doing things for yourself

STIMULUS CONTROL
*Cigarettes and paraphernalia*
  Buy cigarettes by pack rather than by carton
  Do not keep cigarettes in house
  Leave cigarettes in a part of the house that is away from you
  Get rid of ashtrays
*Other substances*
  Avoid alcohol
  Avoid coffee
  Drink juice instead of coffee so as not to smoke

*(continued)*

TABLE 5-8 (Continued).

---

STIMULUS CONTROL (Continued)

*People*

 Avoid friends who smoke

 Do not visit any smokers

*Situations*

 Avoid situations where you used to smoke

 Change places of relaxation at home (favorite chair, etc.)

 Leave tempting situations

 Sit in nonsmoking section of restaurants

HELP FROM OTHERS

*Social support*

 Ask kids to throw away your cigarettes if you are smoking

 Call a "buddy" from the clinic

 Get support from someone else who quit

*Wagers, dares*

 Arrange a wager with a friend as a motivator

 Arrange a dare with a friend as a motivator

*Treatment*

 Attend the clinic

 Enroll in clinic

 Sign up for four-session course with hypnotist

DIRECT CONTROL OF SMOKING

*Cut down* — includes rules restricting smoking, reduction of tar and nicotine

 Buy low-tar cigarettes

 Cut down from 20 to 10 cigarettes a day

 Eliminate your least important cigarettes

 Do not smoke in car or socially

*Satiation*

 Smoke cigar to make you sick

 Smoke until sick prior to quitting

OTHER TECHNIQUES

*Self-reward*

 Put $1 in jar for each day quit

 Reward yourself for 3-hour abstinence periods

*Focus on techniques* — behaviors "one step removed" from coping

 Keep clinic material handy

 Reread manual given you at a clinic

 Take literature with you

*Cognitive cueing* — behaviors meant primarily to cue cognitions

 Get out and read list of reasons for quitting

 Look at jar of cigarette butts when tempted

 Make list of reasons, hang it on a mirror

OTHER RESPONSES

*(continued)*

TABLE 5-8 (Continued).

## COGNITIVE COPING RESPONSES

CONSEQUENCES
*Health consequences*
  Your own health
    Positive consequences
      Future—large-scale, abstract, future consequences
        Think about wanting a longer life
        Think about being here for a grandchild
        Think that by quitting you will improve your health
      Immediate—small-scale, concrete, immediate consequences
        Think how much better you will feel if you quit
        Think how nice it will be to be able to breathe deeply
        Notice that you feel better physically
        Think about no longer waking up coughing
    Negative consequences
      Future—large-scale, abstract, future consequences
        Think about getting cancer, dying, and leaving kids alone
        Think of someone who died of lung disease
        Think, "I don't want emphysema"
        Think about the possibility of lung cancer
      Immediate—small-scale, concrete, immediate consequences
        Think, "I don't feel well when smoking"
        Think about not being able to breathe deeply
        Think, "I get colds because of smoking"
        Think, "My lungs hurt from smoking"
  Others' health—smoking's effects on others
    Think, "It would be nice for kids to have fresh air"
    Think, "My son's health problems are due to my smoking"
*Social consequences* —including modeling and social reactions
  Positive
    Try to set example to daughter who is pregnant
    Think, "Quitting would make my spouse happy"
    Think that your family will be proud
  Negative
    Think about getting grief from friends about not being able to quit
    Think, "A relapse would disappoint my doctor"
    Think, "My daughter will know if I smoke and be disgusted"
*Financial consequences*
  Think, "I can use the money for something else"
  Remember that smoking is an expensive habit
  Think about the money you are saving
*Other consequences* —sensory, sanitary, etc.
  Positive
    Think, "Food tastes better"
    Think, "The house smells cleaner"
    Think, "I want my complexion to look better"
    Notice that you're not as nervous now

*(continued)*

TABLE 5-8 (Continued).

CONSEQUENCES (Continued)
  Negative
    Notice you don't like the smell of smoke in the house
    Think, "The smell is offensive"
    Think about yellow teeth from smoking
    Think, "My mouth tastes like a garbage can"

DEVALUATION OF SMOKING—downplaying value of smoking
  *General devaluation* ("not worth it")
    Tell yourself it's not worth it to have a cigarette
    Think, "Smoking is disgusting"
    Think, "I'm sick of cigarettes"
  *Disappointment of expectations of smoking*
    Remind yourself that cigarettes are not a solution to problems
    Think, "Smoking didn't make me feel better"
    Think, "Smoking won't improve anything"
  *Sensory devaluation*
    Think, "Smoking tasted bad"
    Remember that cigarettes didn't really taste good

SELF-TALK
  *Self-motivation*
    Denying want or need—restatements of motivation
      Keep telling yourself that you don't really want to smoke
      Think, "I don't need them"
      Think, "I must quit"
    Reviewing reasons for quitting
      Remind yourself that you wanted to quit in order to breathe better
      Remind yourself of why you quit
  *Willpower*—solely expression of mental effort
    Give yourself orders not to smoke
    Resolve to quit
    Tell yourself "no" when tempted
    Using willpower
  *Self-redefinition*
    Tell yourself, "I'm a nonsmoker"
    Think of yourself as a nonsmoker
    Visualize yourself as a nonsmoker
  *Positive thoughts*
    Self-confidence, efficacy
      Think, "I can do it"
      Think, "I can be in smoking situations—no problem"
      Think, "If others can do it, so can I"
    Accomplishment
      Feel good because you've done this
      Think about your enjoyment of quitting
      Pat yourself on back for abstinence
    Hopeful prospects—expectation of improvement
      Think, "It will get better"
      Tell yourself that after 4–6 weeks the urges won't be so severe
      Think, "It will get easier"

*(continued)*

TABLE 5-8 (Continued).

---

SELF–TALK (Continued)
   General positive attitudes
      Encourage yourself
      Keep a positive attitude
      Take a positive attitude toward the quitting attempt
ORIENTING THOUGHTS
   *Planning* — higher-order cognitive activities
      Methods, plans — including plans for other responses
         Plan on substituting exercise when you feel tempted
         Think, "I'll use nicotine gum"
         Think about getting rid of cues for smoking
         Think, "I can get antianxiety pills from my doctor"
      Setting a quit date
         Decide to quit on the National Smoke-Out Day
         Set a new quit date
         Think, "I can quit if I set a date 2 weeks hence"
      Self-monitoring, awareness, analysis
         Feel aware every time you light a cigarette
         Be aware of tension and anxiety
         Think about particular situations responsible for temptation
         Understand situations under which you smoke
   *Temporal orientation*
      Hour at a time
         Think about not smoking an hour at a time
         Think, "One day at a time"
         Think that you only have to make it through the day
      Stages
         Think, "If this quit doesn't work, the next one will"
         Think, "I will encounter strong temptations for some time"
         Think that it has been easier these last 2 weeks
         Think, "I'm not safe from relapse yet"
ALTERNATIVE COGNITIONS
   *Distraction*
      Actively push thoughts about smoking out of your head
      Keep the urge out of your mind
      Keep your mind busy
      Think about other things when there is an urge to smoke
   *Relaxation*
      Fantasize about a cabin
      Try to stay calm
      Try to relax
OTHER COGNITIONS
   *Remorse*
      Self-punitive — has an insulting, punitive aspect
         Accuse yourself of being weak-minded, lacking willpower
         Say to yourself, "You fool, you've started again!"
         Think, "I'm an idiot"

*(continued)*

TABLE 5-8 (Continued).

---

OTHER COGNITIONS (Continued)
    Guilt, remorse—may include reasonable reconsideration
        Feel guilty about relapsing
        Think, "I wasted the last 2 weeks of work by relapsing"
        Think, "I haven't really tried hard enough"
    *Consequences of lapses*
    Lead to relapse
        Say to yourself, "Don't start, you'll go right back"
        Think, "If I have one cigarette, I will relapse"
        Think, "It must be all or nothing"
    Undo progress
        Think, "I do not want to go through withdrawal again"
        Think, "I've been off 4 weeks—it would be a shame to start again"
        Think, "I got to this point, it's not worth blowing it"
    Promote feeling of failure
        Concentrate on how guilty you will feel if you smoke
        Think, "I don't want to relapse because it would be a defeat"
        Think how sorry you will be if you she relapse
    *Minimizing of lapses*
        Remember prior relapse—it wasn't as major as you thought
        Think, "One cigarette does not mean complete relapse"
        Think, "Holding it down to 20 per day is keeping it in hand"
        Think, "Just one is not the end of the world"

---

*Note.* The items were developed from open-ended reports of coping by many ex-smokers. The categories were derived by having many independent judges sort the responses and then using cluster analysis of their ratings to construct categories. This produced a hierarchical category system reflected in the higher-order headings for categories.

immediate, and restorative coping. Rather than attempting an exhaustive listing of all possible responses, the CWTI is organized around *categories* of responses, which are in turn defined by example. The categories were derived from open-ended reports of coping collected from hundreds of people quitting smoking. These open-ended reports were judged and sorted by both naive and expert judges to arrive at the category structure shown in Table 5-8.

An advantage of the inventory method is that it leads readily to intervention; the CWTI can be treated as a menu of suggestions for expanding the coping repertoire. A disadvantage is that it is easy for clients to "fake good" by endorsing many coping responses they don't actually use. Another limitation is that the CWTI does not assess the client's *skill* in performing coping. Two subjects may both report that they have asked others for support; one may have assertively suggested some specific behaviors, whereas the other may have aggressively made global demands. Analogue methods, discussed below, allow further assessment of coping skill.

## Assessing Coping by Analogue Methods

Analogue assessments are useful for assessing immediate and restorative coping responses to relapse crises. A typical analogue assessment presents the client with a selection of hypothetical situations demanding coping; the client is asked to produce appropriate responses. The situations and responses may be written, spoken, or enacted; the more realistic, the better. Analogues have the advantage of allowing assessment of coping skill and of being harder to fake: Clients must produce coping responses, rather than choosing from a list provided to them. Perhaps their most important advantage is that they allow the clinician to assess clients' reactions to situations they may not yet have encountered. Thus, for example, restorative coping can be assessed (and, one hopes, improved) *before* a relapse crisis occurs. The disadvantage of analogues is that they are not always accurate representations of real-life situations. The demand characteristics of the situation call for subjects to "be on their best behavior"—to respond as they *should* respond, rather than as they *would* respond or *have* responded. Nevertheless, analogues can be useful and often valid assessment tools.[5]

The construction of analogue stimuli is critical to an analogue's validity. Care must be taken in initial assessments to sample a broad range of stimulus situations so that situation-specific coping deficits may be identified. Once a specific area of difficulty has been identified, assessments may narrow to focus on specific problematic situations. Table 5-9 presents a representative set of stimulus situations chosen on the basis of our experience with callers to our relapse prevention hotline (Shiffman, Read, Maltese, *et al.*, 1985). The medium in which subjects respond to the situations is also critical. Role playing is best, as it allows one to evaluate how the client actually implements coping. Purely verbal media are less desirable but more efficient.

5. In a recent study of coping skill, my colleagues and I were able to evaluate the validity of ex-smokers' responses to an analogue coping task (Shiffman, Maltese, Read, & Jarvik, 1982). We presented 88 subjects who had participated in a smoking cessation program with the 10 situations in Table 5-9. Each response was categorized by a trained judge. Although the categories were not identical to those used to classify coping data from callers to our relapse prevention hotline (Shiffman, 1984b), there was enough overlap so that the frequency with which six behavioral responses were recorded under the two methods could be compared. There was a correlation of .61 between a response's frequency in the hotline data and its frequency in the analogue data. That is, the responses cited most frequently by hotline callers were also listed most frequently in responses to the analogue, suggesting that the analogue data accurately mirror actual coping performance.

TABLE 5-9.    Situational Narratives for Smoking Situation Competency Test

*Negative Affect*

You've just picked up your car from the mechanic and the bill is twice as much as you expected it to be. As you drive home you find that the very thing you took the car in for is still not fixed. The car stalls in rush-hour traffic. You feel angry and frustrated; you crave a cigarette.

You're at work and you've been pressured all day, the phone has been ringing and you haven't been able to handle all the calls and still get your work done. Finally you get home and you want to relax but you are still tense from work—a cigarette would help.

A traffic jam on the freeway kept you in stop-and-go traffic for half an hour. Now you're late for your appointment and you're still not exactly sure of the directions. You start to feel very anxious, and you imagine a cigarette could relax you.

Your boss has been pressuring you to finish a project you've been working on. You know you'll be pressured all day. A cigarette might ease the pressure so that you could work better.

*Positive Affect*

You're sitting on the back patio with a few friends on a warm evening. You are relaxing and enjoying the company. One of your friends lights a cigarette. It looks so refreshing.

You're at a party with friends. People are smoking and drinking. You're having a glass of wine and intense conversation. You always used to have a cigarette with your drink. It looks good.

You've just finished dinner and you're feeling relaxed. You push back your chair and suddenly, you really crave a cigarette.

*Neutral Affect*

While waiting at the market checkout stand, you find yourself next to the cigarette stand and you notice that the market carries your own brand of cigarettes. Boy, do those cigarettes look good—you can almost taste one!

You are home, alone. You feel bored. There isn't anything you have to do, and nothing you think of seems particularly appealing—except maybe a cigarette.

You are at a restaurant waiting for your friend who promised to meet you for lunch. Your friend is already 30 minutes late. You've have a drink and a few breadsticks. You think a cigarette would help pass the time.

*Note.* From "Preventing Relapse in Ex-Smokers: A Self-Management Approach" by S. Shiffman, L. Read, J. Maltese, D. Rapkin, and M. E. Jarvik, 1985, in G. A. Marlatt and J. R. Gordon (Eds.), *Relapse Prevention: Maintenance Strategies in the Treatment of Addictive Behaviors* (pp. 472–520), New York: Guilford Press. Copyright 1985 by Guilford Publications, Inc. Reprinted by permission.

## *Issues and Targets for Assessment of Coping*

What aspects of coping are most clinically relevant? Potential targets of assessment and intervention include coping skill, the use of specific coping strategies, the balance of cognitive and behavioral coping, and the volume and breadth of coping.

*Coping Skill*

An obvious candidate for assessment and intervention is clients' coping skill (i.e., the quality of the clients' coping responses). The relevance of analogue assessments of coping skill to outcome is not established. In a recent study, we presented the situations in Table 5-9 to 44 recidivists and compared their written responses to those of 44 successful ex-smokers (Shiffman *et al.*, 1982; see also Shiffman, Read, Maltese, *et al.*, 1985). Although trained judges were able to reliably rate the diversity and skill of the responses, their ratings were unrelated to outcome.

More recently, Davis and Glaros (1980) carefully developed an analogue task for skills assessment, starting with an item pool of situations ex-smokers thought difficult to resist and developing a scoring system based on successful ex-smokers' responses to them. Although a coping skill intervention improved performance in the analogue, analogue performance was unrelated to abstinence status at follow-up. The one encouraging finding was that ex-smokers who scored higher maintained abstinence an average of 3 weeks longer before relapsing. Either coping skill is not a major determinant of success, or analogue methods are inadequate to assess it.

*Specific Coping Strategies*

At this stage in research on coping, it has been very difficult to identify specific coping strategies that are consistently associated with success. Evaluations of anticipatory strategies involving stimulus control, for example, have yielded mixed results, in part because of methodological variations. Thus, some studies find that recidivists and successful ex-smokers are equally likely to use stimulus control strategies (DiClemente & Prochaska, 1985; Gottlieb *et al.*, 1981; Perri & Richards, 1977; Perri, Richards, & Schultheis, 1977), whereas others find that they are associated with success (Horwitz *et al.*, 1982). A key may be that the positive studies defined "stimulus control" more narrowly as avoidance of specific smoking stimuli (e.g., smoking friends, smoking sections in public places), whereas the negative ones defined "stimulus control" as an aggregate. Perhaps narrower definition of categories will yield more specific findings and recommendations. For now, the results are ambiguous.

Data on specific, immediate coping responses also do not pinpoint especially successful strategies. Most immediate coping responses seem to be about equally effective (Shiffman, 1984b). Two exceptions are self-punitive cognitions or vague reliance on "willpower," which have proved to be less effective. Assessment should identify clients who rely on these responses so that alternatives may be taught. Overall, however, there seem to be few effects related to the use of particular coping strategies. Assessment should not focus on which specific coping responses the person is using, but rather on broader properties of the coping repertoire as a whole.

### Cognitive–Behavioral Balance

Although the specific strategies used may not matter, the relative mix of cognitive and behavioral strategies may be important. In studies of immediate coping, cognitive and behavioral responses were equally effective, but those who combined both strategies were most likely to succeed in resisting temptation (Shiffman, 1982, 1984b; Curry & Marlatt, 1985). Another finding is that behavioral coping is more readily inhibited by situational influences (Shiffman, 1982; Shiffman & Jarvik, 1987), suggesting that sole reliance on behavioral coping may be a weak strategy.

This conclusion is reinforced by findings from a retrospective assessment of immediate coping over an entire cessation effort. Using a coping inventory, we found that successful ex-smokers relied more heavily on cognitive than on behavioral coping, whereas the reverse was true of recidivists (Shiffman et al., 1982). Finally, Mermelstein and Lichtenstein (1983) found that ex-smokers who used cognitive forms of restorative coping were more likely to recover from lapses in abstinence. It thus seems important to insure that ex-smokers have an adequate complement of cognitive strategies in their repertoire.

### Volume and Variety of Coping

Whether "more is better" when it comes to coping is unclear. Data on immediate coping derived from hotline interviews suggest that volume does not guarantee success: Those who reported only one coping response were as successful as those who reported several (when the effects of combining cognitive and behavioral responses were removed; Shiffman, 1984b). Retrospective self-reports of coping using a coping inventory yielded similar results: Successful exsmokers reported the same average frequency of coping as recidivists (Shiffman et al., 1982).

Other studies have yielded more positive results. In studies by Perri and his colleagues (Perri & Richards, 1977; Perri et al., 1977), smokers who were successful in quitting reported using more anticipatory strategies. Hall et al. (1984) and Sjoberg and Samsonowitz (1978) report similar findings for a mix of anticipatory and immediate strategies. Although the data are not yet in, there seems to be a good basis for promoting diversity in ex-smokers' coping repertoires. Diversity is readily assessed in the coping inventories by counting the number of strategies employed with some minimum frequency. A more diverse coping repertoire has the advantage of flexibility and is less likely to be disrupted by changing conditions.

*Qualitative Factors in Coping*

In evaluating a client's coping repertoire, the clinician should also assess other, more subjective factors. An important one is the "readiness" of often-used coping strategies—that is, the ease with which the response can be produced or enacted. Responses requiring specific conditions may fail when the conditions are absent: Social support requires access to others, for example, and exercise requires freedom of movement, which may be absent when one is driving. This again highlights the importance of a diverse repertoire to insure that coping is not disrupted by environmental conditions.

The response cost of coping must also be considered. Coping strategies that are effective but costly—consider the social "cost" of leaving a business meeting, for example—are unlikely to be maintained. Avoidance of many threatening stimuli (drinking alcohol, socializing with smoking friends, etc.) is another example. It is preferable to have ways of coping with these situations, rather than relying on avoiding them entirely.

Finally, one should consider the speed with which responses are likely to be produced. Although there are no parallel studies in ex-smokers, Chaney, O'Leary, and Marlatt (1978) showed that how quickly alcoholic patients produced a response when presented with hypothetical tempting situations significantly predicted outcome 1 year later. Very complex responses may slow coping, as may decision rules that are overly complex.

**Problem Solving and Metacoping Skill**

Coping is a dynamic process. Coping strategies must change with experience and in response to changing circumstances. Coping responses which were effective early in abstinence may need to be displaced by new ones in later stages (DiClemente & Prochaska, 1985). "Metacoping skill" refers to the problem-solving skill necessary to make appropriate adjustments in one's coping repertoire. In our retrospective study of coping (using a coping inventory) in recidivists and ex-smokers, we asked subjects how often they used each response and how helpful they thought it was. One factor that distinguished the successful ex-smokers was a closer correspondence between how helpful they thought a response was and how often they used it (Shiffman et al., 1982; Shiffman, Read, Maltese, et al., 1985). This suggests that they were more responsive to their experience with coping strategies, discarding the ones that were not helpful and persisting in those that were. Such fine-tuning can be assessed by periodically readministering the coping inventories and correlating response frequency with response effectiveness, thus highlighting responses that are frequent but ineffective or effective but rarely used.

Because coping may be taught, assessment of coping, although still in its infancy, has the potential to be among the more promising assessment devices. It must be emphasized that its usefulness depends on coupling it with effective and specific interventions. It should also be emphasized that assessment of coping—and, indeed, most assessment—is an ongoing process that must continue throughout treatment and follow-up. A subsequent section suggests a time line for assessment.

## Assessment in Nicotine Pharmacotherapy

The use of nicotine supplements in smoking cessation has been mentioned earlier. This section deals with the specialized assessment tasks associated with cessation programs relying on pharmacotherapy with nicotine supplements. The idea that cigarette smoking is driven by dependence on nicotine naturally suggests that providing nicotine from another source should facilitate smoking cessation. This nicotine replacement strategy is embodied in Nicorette®, a nicotine chewing gum that has been in use in Europe for years and was recently introduced in the United States. Although Nicorette® must be prescribed by a physician, it is best used as a supplement to behavioral cessation programs (or vice versa),[6] and involves several specialized assessment procedures. I address in turn three specialized assessments that arise with the use of Nicorette®: assessment of side effects, assessment of proper use of the gum, and assessment of suitability for pharmacotherapy.

### *Assessing Nicotine Side Effects*

It is widely thought that experience of uncontrolled side effects is a major cause of treatment dropout in Nicorette®-enhanced smoking cessation. This is particularly unfortunate, because many side effects can be controlled through proper use of the gum (see below). The following side

6. Although the data are clear that Nicorette® is effective in promoting smoking cessation, many professionals suggest that it should be used in conjunction with behavioral treatment. In most studies of the efficacy of Nicorette®, it was administered as part of a behavioral cessation program. Only Schneider *et al.* (1983) specifically evaluated the interaction of nicotine gum and clinic intervention, and the results were striking. When Nicorette® was dispensed without any supporting program, it was not significantly superior to a placebo preparation. Only when combined with a psychological intervention was the gum a significant aid in smoking cessation.

effects are most commonly encountered: (Jarvis, Raw, Russell, & Feyerabend, 1982): "feeling sick" (31%), hiccups (24%), intestinal discomfort (41%), and dizziness (17%). These side effects must be closely monitored early in treatment. Frequent or severe side effects may indicate improper use of the gum and should stimulate careful assessment and instruction (see below). Of course, some side effects may reflect physical difficulties and should be brought to the attention of a physician.

### Assessing Proper Use of Nicorette®

Improper use of Nicorette® is a major source of treatment failure. One problem arises because the dynamics of nicotine delivery by Nicorette® are quite different from those of cigarette smoking. By delivering volatized nicotine to the lungs, smoking provides for very rapid nicotine absorption—a bolus of nicotine-rich blood reaches the brain in 7 seconds (Russell & Feyerabend, 1978). This provides the smoker with immediate feedback that can be used to regulate blood nicotine levels. In contrast, Nicorette® is absorbed through the membranes in the mouth, where it diffuses slowly into the bloodstream. The result is that the gum user gets only delayed feedback about the amount of nicotine absorbed, making it easy to overdose.

Nicorette® is formulated so that the rate of nicotine release is controlled by the user's chewing action. Learning to chew Nicorette® properly is thus a key element in nicotine supplementation therapy. A user's first impulse is to chew Nicorette® like any chewing gum; this inevitably results in overdosing and side effects, which in turn lead to treatment dropout and subsequent failure. Proper use involves chewing slowly and pausing to self-monitor one's dose through proprioceptive cues such as autonomic stimulation and tingling sensations in the mouth. Clients' compliance with these directions must be assessed by observation early in treatment. There is no substitute for direct observation of a client's chewing procedure.

Another frequent cause of treatment failure with Nicorette® is failure to use a sufficient dose of the drug for a sufficient period of time. Studies show that clients who use Nicorette® for longer periods are more successful (Raw et al., 1980; Jarvis et al., 1982); 3 months appears to be the key cutoff point. Despite some negative findings (Hjalmarson, 1984), most clinical investigators also feel that the number of Nicorette® units used is critical and should not drop below four per day during treatment (N. G. Schneider, personal communication, January 2, 1985). Even when not actively used, the ready availability of the product "in case of emergency" may be critical. Difficulty arises in part because clients resist continuing to use the drug after they feel they have successfully mastered their smoking.

An indirect means of monitoring the adequacy of nicotine dosing is to monitor withdrawal symptoms, which are discussed above. Nicorette®

significantly reduces most withdrawal symptoms (Hughes *et al.,* 1984; Schneider, Jarvik, & Forsythe, 1984; West, 1984); an ideal dose would suppress withdrawal without eliciting severe side effects. Nicorette® apparently has little effect on craving for cigarettes, however (Hughes *et al.,* 1984; Ohlin & Westling, 1975; West, Jarvis, Russell, Caruthers, & Feyerabend, 1984; though see Schneider & Jarvik, 1985).

To enhance treatment success, Nicorette® use and availability should be continually assessed through self-monitoring and self-report. Self-monitoring of Nicorette® use in follow-up will also allow the clinician to detect development of dependence on the product, which is thought to occur in 7%–10% of treated clients (Russell, Raw, & Jarvis, 1980; Jarvis *et al.,* 1982). Six months is generally considered the maximum desirable duration of treatment, though some recommend a longer course.

### Timing and Sequence of Assessments

Grouping assessment procedures by purpose may have obscured the temporal organization of assessments in smoking cessation. In this section, I briefly outline the sequence in which these assessments might be implemented. For convenience, I divide the assessments into five intervals: intake, precessation, postcessation, early maintenance, and long-term follow-up. Table 5-10 outlines the distribution of assessment procedures across these intervals.

Much assessment should be completed at intake—not only for convenience, but to insure that the data are not affected by early interventions. The decision to use Nicorette® would typically be made at this time, based on information obtained at intake.

The next phase of assessment stretches from intake until cessation is achieved. Self-monitoring may be initiated immediately and may continue until cessation is achieved, so long as the burden is not so great as to promote noncompliance. This is also a good time at which to assess stress and global and smoking-specific social support, so that interventions can be initiated early. As the "quit date" approaches, focus shifts toward anticipating the effects of cessation and preparing for them. Information from smoking typology measures, self-monitoring, and history should be integrated to anticipate cravings and withdrawal symptoms. Initial assessment of anticipatory and immediate coping should occur prior to cessation. Nicorette® may be introduced at the point of cessation and its proper use assessed.

The first 7–10 days after cessation constitute a critical period for assessment and intervention. This is usually the most difficult period subjectively, and many relapses occur this early. It is also the first opportunity to directly observe the client's behavior in abstinence. Monitoring of

TABLE 5-10.   Suggested Assessment Plan

| Intake | Precessation | Postcessation | Early maintenance | Long-term maintenance |
|---|---|---|---|---|
| Smoking history | | | | |
| Smoking typology | | | | |
| Dependence | | | | |
| Smoking dose | | | | |
| | Self-monitoring smoking | | | |
| | | Self-monitoring urges | | |
| | Global social support | | | |
| | | Specific social support ─────────→ | | |
| | Stress ─────────────────→ | | | |
| | Withdrawal symptoms ───────→ | | | |
| Preparatory coping ──→ | | | | |
| | Anticipatory coping ───────────→ | | | |
| | | Immediate coping ───────────→ | | |
| | | | Restorative coping ───────────→ | |
| | | | Relapse crisis debriefing ─── ───→ | |

urges is useful. Early in this period, monitoring "relapse crises" may be difficult because ex-smokers subjectively experience temptation as nearly continuous and have difficulty isolating situational determinants. Preventive and immediate coping are at their peaks in this period and should be carefully assessed. This is also the first opportunity to observe restorative coping. Specific social support should also be reassessed during this period, because in this key phase the ex-smoker begins to draw on it. If Nicorette® is used, side effects must be assessed. If side effects are present or withdrawal symptoms are uncontrolled, chewing behavior should be carefully assessed *in vivo* and regulated so that the best compromise between effectiveness and toxicity is achieved.

One to two weeks after cessation, most withdrawal symptoms will have subsided, and temptations are more clearly experienced as episodic "crises." Assessment then focuses on relapse crises and on immediate and restorative coping. Debriefing of lapses is especially important. Particularly if crises are frequent, anticipatory coping should be re-evaluated. Coping patterns should also be reassessed to insure that responses that have lost their usefulness are not retained in the repertoire. Most Nicorette® side effects will have been resolved at this time, and attention shifts to monitoring use to insure that it does not drop off too quickly.

Although none of these phases are clearly demarcated, the transition into long-term follow-up is especially subtle. The transition is marked by a shift of the client's attention *away* from smoking cessation. Abstinence is taken for granted, and vigilance atrophies. This may be cued by the end of formal treatment or simply by the person's judgment that he or she is "in the clear." Monitoring of relapse crises, which become increasingly infrequent, and monitoring of preventive and immediate coping serve to promote awareness of continuing risk as well as maintenance of coping behavior. Intermittent evaluation should continue for about 6 months or until relapse risk is low.

## Case History

Michael T was referred by his physician for individual smoking cessation treatment. Michael's father had recently died of heart disease. Although Michael himself was currently asymptomatic, his doctor had told him that he was at risk for heart disease if he continued to smoke. Michael reported being highly motivated to stop smoking.

Michael was a 41-year-old accountant. He had been smoking since age 15 and currently smoked one and a half packs per day of unfiltered cigarettes. Self-report and direct observation revealed that he inhaled each puff deeply. Michael had tried to quit smoking twice before, but both times he had experienced substantial withdrawal discomfort and relapsed after less than 1 month. The initial assessment yielded other evidence of extreme dependence. Michael always smoked immediately upon awakening and experienced a gnawing hunger when he was even temporarily unable to smoke.

These initial data suggested that Michael was a highly dependent smoker with a relatively poor prognosis. On the basis of the initial evaluation, a decision was made to treat Michael with pharmacological as well as behavioral techniques, and he was referred back to his physician for evaluation and prescription.

Further precessation assessment was undertaken. Michael was asked to complete a battery of self-report measures and to initiate self-monitoring. The smoking typology and self-monitoring data painted a relatively consistent picture of his smoking pattern. Michael's highest scores on the RFS Scale were on the Negative Affect Reduction Smoking and Stimulation Smoking factors. His self-monitoring data revealed that Michael smoked heavily at work, particularly when he was working under time pressure, which occurred frequently. Although Michael also smoked steadily in the evenings, his "need" ratings for evening cigarettes were much lower than for cigarettes smoked under stress at work. He described his work as intense but not stressful, except when he was under time pressure. His Perceived Stress Scale score was moderate. Michael was unable to recall much about his past relapses except that they had occurred at work and against a background of rising work pressure. In both cases, he had obtained cigarettes from coworkers.

These data pinpointed Michael's work as a high-risk situation. With some reluctance, he agreed to take steps to reduce his workload by delegating and postponing tasks. He was also instructed to deal with stress by taking periodic breaks at work, especially when things were hectic.

Analysis of social contagion again targeted the workplace as a source of high risk. About half of the workers in Michael's office smoked. More importantly, his secretary, with whom he worked closely, also smoked. She agreed to Michael's request not to smoke in his office. Michael also agreed to make his quitting effort public and to ask that people not offer him cigarettes.

Michael's social environment was supportive of smoking cessation. The ISEL scale suggested that he had adequate and broad social support. No one in his household smoked, and his wife, an ex-smoker, had expressed a willingness to help him quit. Michael was also able to identify a potential supporter in the workplace, and both he and Michael's wife were provided with materials suggesting how best to help Michael quit smoking. Brief role plays and Michael's reports of assertion in other domains suggested that his social skills were equal to the task of eliciting support.

As an agreed-upon quit date approached, Michael was introduced to Nicorette®. He was instructed on its proper use, and his self-administration was observed directly. He was asked to track gum use and to record side effects. Self-monitoring of urges and withdrawal symptoms was also instituted. His progress was followed closely by daily meetings in the first few days, and several problems were identified. Michael reported that the gum made him "jittery." His records showed that he sometimes chewed several gums in succession. He was instructed to wait at least 30 minutes between doses, and the jitteriness lessened.

A review of Michael's coping repertoire revealed few problems. Under instruction, he had instituted a variety of anticipatory coping responses, including removing ashtrays when he could; avoiding alcohol; getting more sleep; carrying the Nicorette® everywhere; and keeping supplies of the gum at home, at work, and in his car. His immediate coping with temptations relied heavily on cognitive coping, especially thoughts about his father's death and the threat to his own health. He also tried to control urges by eating or by changing activity or location when tempted. He reported feeling no need for restorative coping, as he felt successful and confident. Overall, his pattern of coping appeared adequate, except for a slight overemphasis on cognitive coping and some unpreparedness for dealing with "failure."

Michael reported that his wife was being very supportive, taking an active interest in his quitting effort, but not nagging him. People at work were also generally positive. Michael had identified one difficulty with his support partner at work, who Michael felt was monitoring him too closely; the situation had been improved through discussion with the coworker.

Michael's self-monitoring of urges also provided an impetus for problem solving. The records suggested that early mornings were a particularly difficult time, marked by severe withdrawal symptoms, including irritability, "spaciness," and craving. Discussion and examination of his gum use records revealed that Michael never used nicotine gum until after breakfast, about 2 hours after waking, because he found the idea of chewing the gum before breakfast repulsive. He agreed, however, to chew one gum immediately upon arising and to change his routine to eat breakfast earlier. These changes largely dispelled the morning difficulty.

Analyses of Michael's urges also revealed peaks during certain work periods. These proved to be times when Michael was concentrating intensely on a work problem. Nicotine gum seemed ineffective in increasing his concentration or quelling his urge in this context. Other solutions, such as short exercise breaks, were tried with little effect on his craving.

Eight days after quitting smoking, Michael smoked half a cigarette during a period of intense work. He had been feeling increasingly frustrated by his difficulty in concentrating. On this particular day, his frustration built to the point where he impulsively asked a visitor to his office for a cigarette. He reported trying to cope with the urge by thinking about his health, but reported that these thoughts seemed remote and feeble in the face of his frustration. Halfway through the cigarette, however, he stopped smoking by reminding himself how much effort he had put into quitting and thinking about how disappointed his wife would be if he relapsed. He put out the cigarette and chewed a nicotine gum. When he called the therapist to report his slip (as he had been instructed to do), it was with a tone of apology and failure. He reported feeling ashamed and disgusted with himself. Debriefing emphasized the positive aspects of Michael's performance and encouraged him to build up his coping repertoire against future crises.

This slip occasioned a reassessment of Michael's coping. Michael's coping repertoire seemed adequate overall. He was engaged in a variety of anticipatory activities, including "prophylactic" use of the gum when he anticipated being tempted. He continued to avoid social drinking and to be vigilant about being around smokers. He had increased the diversity of his immediate coping to include walks, but still relied heavily on cognitive coping, especially thoughts about health. Michael generally felt that the responses he used most heavily were effective; he had dropped several coping alternatives (e.g., eating) that he found unhelpful. The greatest residual problem seemed to be his difficulty dealing with situations at work in which he had to concentrate under pressure. He had had some success in reducing pressure at work by more careful scheduling and by the addition of rest periods, but these were evidently insufficient. Use of relaxation techniques was ineffective, as anxiety was not the key problem. Rearrangement of Michael's work schedule so that he worked on projects for shorter blocks of time produced some benefit. Fortunately, his concentration returned to normal about 2 weeks after cessation.

Assessment of Michael's response to his slip also highlighted deficiencies in his restorative coping. His ability to limit a slip had reflected good restorative coping, but his later reaction suggested that he needed more skill in dealing with the AVE. Practice and assessment were implemented by having Michael rebut AVE-type thoughts (e.g., "You've blown it now") with alternative thoughts presented by the therapist. Subsequent assessment (following crises not presented in detail here) suggested that this helped bolster Michael's restorative coping skills.

As time progressed, ongoing assessment revealed a pattern of decreasing difficulties. By the third week of abstinence, Michael was reporting few withdrawal symptoms. His urges to smoke became increasingly weaker. As they also grew less frequent, Michael was increasingly able to identify specific situations associated with temptations to smoke. Among these were situations that had not been anticipated by the earlier assessments (e.g., after dinner when eating out). Working with his wife, Michael formulated specific coping plans for each. Michael continued to receive appropriate support from his wife. An assessment 1 month after cessation showed some drop in her positive support, but no increase in negative behaviors.

The 1-month follow-up assessment also uncovered a problem related to use of the nicotine gum. Michael had reduced his consumption to two or three per day and was considering dropping the gum altogether. He was urged (and agreed) to double his consumption and continue chewing for another 2 months. At the 2-month follow-up, however, Michael insisted on terminating regular gum use, although he agreed to taper use off over a week's time and to carry an "emergency" supply. At 3 months, Michael was reporting an occasional temptation to smoke, but few strong urges, which he was able to handle with cognitive coping alone. He had not used any nicotine gum since tapering off a month earlier. Some anticipatory coping activities were still in place: Michael only frequented restaurants that had a nonsmoking section and avoided going out for a drink "with the boys," for example. At 6 months, Michael reported no urges or difficulties, and follow-up was discontinued.

## Conclusion

Assessment has a great potential role in behavioral treatment for smoking cessation. Techniques are available for assessing every aspect of the client's behavior, from the amount and reasons for smoking to the circumstances of relapse. Despite much effort, however, many of these techniques have not lived up to their promise, and are subject to some of the very criticisms leveled against traditional approaches to assessment. Several of these criticisms are discussed below.

1. *Procedures are seldom empirically validated against relevant criteria.* Instead, many assessment practices rely on face validity or on hypothesized intervening variables. Smoking or relapse history is often used to predict in which situations a smoker is most likely to experience difficulty abstaining. Smoking typologies and self-monitoring data are commonly used in this way. Yet, though it seems intuitively plausible that people will most crave cigarettes when they would otherwise have smoked them, there is not a single empirical study relating these measures to relapse vulnerability. Empirical validation of these clinically appealing procedures is sorely needed.

2. *Assessment outcomes are seldom associated with specific treatment decisions.* This is not so much a problem of assessment as it is of intervention technology. Even when assessment techniques have been validated, they are largely prognostic. They have little bearing on treatment decisions because treatments are applied homogeneously and few specialized treatment programs exist. If one *could* reliably type smokers and predict when they were at greatest risk for relapse, on what basis would one choose the best treatment for each group? Subject × treatment interactions need more attention.

3. *Considerations of marginal utility are needed to justify screening.* The decision to screen subjects for differential treatments depends not only on the availability of valid measures and tailored treatments, but also on the marginal utility of assessment. The use of the Fagerstrom Tolerance Questionnaire (see Table 5-1) to select clients for pharmacotherapy is a classic example. The scale reliably predicts who will respond best to nicotine supplementation. Yet the absence of a more effective treatment for *nondependent* smokers and the low risk and cost of nicotine supplementation make screening illogical.

It is not that the behavioral assessment techniques described herein are invalid; it is only that their validity remains to be firmly established. Until these issues are resolved, behavioral assessment in smoking cessation programs will remain intuitively appealing rather than empirically proven. As always, clinical practice must operate on ground not fully charted by empirical research. In the interim, a wide variety of promising assessment techniques are available to the clinician engaged in smoking cessation treatment.

# References

Adesso, V. J., & Glad, W. R. (1978). A behavioral test of a smoking typology. *Addictive Behaviors, 3,* 35–38.

American Psychiatric Association. (1980). *Diagnostic and statistical manual of mental disorders* (3rd ed.). Washington, DC: Author.

Bellack, A. S., Rozensky, R., & Schwartz, J. (1974). A comparison of two forms of self-monitoring in a behavioral weight reduction program. *Behavior Therapy, 5,* 523–530.

Benowitz, N. L., Jacob, P., Jones, R. T., & Rosenberg, J. (1982). Interindividual variability in the metabolism and cardiovascular effects of nicotine in man. *Journal of Pharmacology and Experimental Therapeutics, 221,* 368–372.

Best, J. A., & Hakstian, A. R. (1978). A situation-specific model of smoking behavior. *Addictive Behaviors, 3,* 79–92.

Brownell, K. D., Heckerman, C. L., Westlake, R. J., Hayes, S. C., & Monti, P. M. (1978). The effect of couples training and partner cooperativeness in the behavioural treatment of obesity. *Behaviour Research and Therapy, 16,* 323–333.

Burns, B. H. (1969). Chronic chest disease, personality, and success in stopping cigarette smoking. *British Journal of Preventive and Social Medicine, 23,* 23–37.

Carskadon, M. A., Dement, W. C., Mitler, M. M., Guilleminault, M. D., Zarcone, V. D., & Spiegel, R. (1976). Self-report versus sleep lab findings in 122 drug free subjects with complaints of chronic insomnia. *American Journal of Psychiatry, 133,* 82–88.

Chaney, E. F., O'Leary, M. R., & Marlatt, G. A. (1978). Skill training with alcoholics. *Journal of Consulting and Clinical Psychology, 46,* 1092–1104.

Christen, A., McDonald, J. L., Olson, B. L., Drook, C. A., & Stookey, G. K. (1984). Efficacy of nicotine chewing gum in facilitating smoking cessation. *Journal of the American Medical Association, 108,* 594–597.

Cohen, S., & Hoberman, H. (1983). Positive events and social supports as buffers of life change stress. *Journal of Applied Social Psychology, 13,* 99–125.

Cohen, S., Kamarck, T., & Mermelstein, R. (1983). A global measure of perceived stress. *Journal of Health and Social Behavior, 24,* 385–396.

Cohen, S., & Wills, T. A. (1985). Stress, social support, and the buffering hypothesis. *Psychological Bulletin, 98,* 310–357.

Colletti, G., Supnick, J. A., & Rizzo, A. A. (1981, August). *An analysis of relapse determinants for treated smokers.* Paper presented at the annual convention of the American Psychological Association, Los Angeles.

Coppotelli, H., & Orleans, C. T. (1985). Partner support and other determinants of smoking cessation among women. *Journal of Consulting and Clinical Psychology, 53,* 455–460.

Cummings, C., Gordon, J. R., & Marlatt, G. A. (1980). Relapse: Strategies of prevention and prediction. In W. R. Miller (Ed.), *The addictive behaviors* (pp. 291–321). New York: Pergamon Press.

Curry, S., & Marlatt, G. A. (1985). Unaided quitters' strategies for coping with temptations to smoke. In S. Shiffman & T. A. Wills (Eds.), *Coping and substance use* (pp. 243–265). New York: Academic Press.

Davis, J. R., & Glaros, A. G. (1980, August). *Relapse prevention and smoking cessation.* Paper presented at the annual convention of the American Psychological Association, Anaheim, CA.

DiClemente, C. C., & Prochaska, J. O. (1985). Processes and stages of self-change: Coping and competence in smoking behavior change. In S. Shiffman & T. A. Wills (Eds.), *Coping and substance use* (pp. 319–343). New York: Academic Press.

Eisinger, R. A. (1971). Psychosocial predictors of smoking recidivism. *Journal of Health and Social Behavior, 12,* 355–362.

Eisinger, R. A. (1972). Psychosocial predictors of smoking behavior change. *Social Science and Medicine, 6,* 137–144.

Epstein, L. H., & Collins, F. L. (1977). The measurement of situational influences of smoking. *Addictive Behaviors, 2,* 47–53.

Evans, D., & Lane, D. S. (1981). Smoking cessation follow-up: A look at post-workshop behavior. *Addictive Behaviors, 6,* 325–329.

Fagerstrom, K.-O. (1978). Measuring degree of physical dependence to tobacco with reference to individualization of treatment. *Addictive Behaviors, 3,* 235–241.

Fagerstrom, K.-O. (1982). A comparison of psychological and pharmacological treatment in smoking cessation. *Journal of Behavioral Medicine, 5,* 343–351.

Falk, J. R., Tryon, W. W., & Davis, K. K. (1984, August). *Smoking rates as a function of treatment and mechanical compliance in a behaviorally based smoking program.* Paper presented at the annual convention of the American Psychological Association, Toronto.

Flaxman, J. (1979). Affect-management and habit mechanisms in the modification of smoking behavior. *Addictive Behaviors, 4,* 39–46.

Frederiksen, L. W., Epstein, L. H., & Kosevsky, B. P. (1975). Reliability and controlling effects of three procedures for self-monitoring smoking. *Psychological Record, 25,* 255–264.

Frith, C. D. (1971). Smoking behavior and its relation to the smoker's immediate experience. *British Journal of Social and Clinical Psychology, 10,* 73–78.

Garvey, A. J., Bosse, R., Glynn, R. J., & Rosner, B. (1983). Smoking cessation in a prospective study of healthy adult males: Effects of age, time period, and amount smoked. *American Journal of Public Health, 73,* 446–450.

Gilbert, G. (1979). Paradoxical tranquilizing and emotion-reducing effects of nicotine. *Psychological Bulletin, 86,* 643–661.

Goldstein, S. J. (1981). Maintenance of nonsmoking following self-initiated cessation. *Dissertation Abstracts International, 42,* 542B. (University Microfilms No. 82-12, 783)

Gottlieb, A., Freidman, L. F., Cooney, N., Gordon, J., & Marlatt, G. A. (1981, November). *Quitting smoking in self-help: Relapse and survival in unaided quitters.* Paper presented at the annual convention of the Association for Advancement of Behavior Therapy, Toronto.

Graham, R., & Gibson, R. W. (1971). Cessation of patterned behavior: Withdrawal from smoking. *Social Science and Medicine, 5,* 319–337.

Gritz, E. (1979). Women and smoking: A realistic appraisal. In J. L. Schwartz (Ed.), *Progress in smoking cessation: Proceedings of the International Conference on Smoking Cessation* (pp. 119–141). New York: American Cancer Society.

Gunn, R. C. (1983). Smoking clinic failures and recent life stress. *Addictive Behaviors, 8,* 83–87.

Gust, S., Hughes, J. R., & Pechacek, T. (1986). Prevalence of tobacco dependence and withdrawal. In L. Harris (Ed.), *Problems of drug dependence 1985: Proceedings of the 47th annual scientific meeting of the Committee on Problems of Drug Dependence* (NIDA Research Monograph No. 67). Washington, DC: U.S. Government Printing Office.

Hall, S. M., Rugg, D., Runstall, C., & Jones, R. T. (1984). Preventing relapse to cigarette smoking by behavioral skill training. *Journal of Consulting and Clinical Psychology, 52,* 372–382.

Hjalmarson, A. I. (1984). Effect of nicotine chewing gum in smoking cessation. *Journal of the American Medical Association, 252,* 2835–2838.

Horwitz, M. B., Hindi-Alexander, M., & Wagner, T. J. (1982, August). *Psychosocial mediators of long-term abstinence following smoking cessation.* Paper presented at the annual convention of the American Psychological Association, Washington, DC.

Hughes, J. R. (1985). Defining the dependent smoker: Validity and clinical utility. *Behavioral Medicine Abstracts, 5,* 202–204.

Hughes, J. R., & Hatsukami, D. K. (1986). Signs and symptoms of tobacco withdrawal. *Archives of General Psychiatry, 43,* 289–294.

Hughes, J. R., Hatsukami, D. K., Pickens, R. W., Krahn, D., Malin, S., & Luknic, A. (1984). Effect of nicotine on the tobacco withdrawal syndrome. *Psychopharmacology, 83,* 82–87.

Hunt, W. A., & Matarazzo, J. E. (1973). Three years later: Recent developments in the experimental modification of smoking behavior. *Journal of Abnormal Psychology, 81,* 107–114.

Ikard, F. F., Green, D., & Horn, D. (1969). A scale to differentiate between types of smoking as related to the management of affect. *International Journal of the Addictions, 4,* 649–659.

Ikard, F. F., & Tomkins, S. (1973). The experience of affect as a determinant of smoking behavior: A series of validity studies. *Journal of Abnormal Psychology, 85,* 478–488.

Jarvik, M. E., & Schneider, N. G. (1984). Degree of addiction and effectiveness of nicotine gum therapy for smoking. *American Journal of Psychiatry, 141,* 790–791.

Jarvis, M. J., Raw, M., Russell, M. A. H., & Feyerabend, C. (1982). Randomized controlled trial of nicotine chewing gum. *British Medical Journal, 285,* 537–540.

Joffe, R., Lowe, M. R., & Fisher, E. B. (1981). A validity test of the Reasons for Smoking test. *Addictive Behaviors, 6,* 41–45.

Kanner, A. D., Coyne, J. C., Schaefer, C., & Lazarus, R. S. (1981). Comparison of two modes of stress measurement: Daily hassles and uplifts versus major life events. *Journal of Behavioral Medicine, 4,* 1–39.

Killen, J., Taylor, C., Maccoby, N., Fong, T., & Bachman, J. (1984). *Investigating predictors of smoking relapse: An analysis of biochemical and self-report measures of tobacco dependence.* Unpublished manuscript.

Klesges, R. C., Glasgow, R. E., & Fleeker, J. (1985, November). *Programmed social support and smoking cessation: A controlled investigation in the worksite.* Paper presented at the annual convention of the Association for Advancement of Behavior Therapy, Houston.

Kozlowski, L. T., Director, J., & Harford, M. A. (1981). Tobacco dependence, restraint and time to the first cigarette of the day. *Addictive Behaviors, 6,* 307–312.

Lawrence, P. S., Amodei, N., & Murray, A. L. (1982). *Withdrawal symptoms associated with smoking cessation.* Paper presented at the annual convention of the Association for Advancement of Behavior Therapy, Los Angeles.

Leventhal, H., & Avis, N. (1976). Pleasure, addiction, and habit: Factors in verbal report of factors in smoking behavior? *Journal of Abnormal Psychology, 5,* 478–488.

Lichtenstein, E., Antonuccio, D. O., & Rainwater, G. (1983). *The resumption of cigarette smoking: A situational analysis of retrospective reports.* Unpublished manuscript, University of Oregon.

Lipinski, D. P., Black, J. L., Nelson, R. O., & Ciminero, A. R. (1975). Influence of motivational variables on the reactivity and reliability of self-recording. *Journal of Consulting and Clinical Psychology, 5,* 637–646.

Marlatt, G. A. (1978). Craving for alcohol, loss of control, and relapse: A cognitive–behavioral analysis. In P. E. Nathan, G. A. Marlatt, & T. Løberg (Eds.), *Alcoholism: New directions in behavioral research and treatment* (pp. 271–314). New York: Plenum.

Marlatt, G. A., & Gordon, J. R. (1980). Determinants of relapse: Implications for the maintenance of behavior change. In P. O. Davidson & S. M. Davidson (Eds.), *Behavioral medicine: Changing health lifestyles* (pp. 410–452). New York: Brunner/ Mazel.

Mausner, B., & Platt, E. S. (1971). *Smoking: A behavioral analysis.* New York: Pergamon Press.

Mausner, J. S. (1970). Cigarette smoking among patients with respiratory disease. *American Review of Respiratory Disease, 102,* 704–713.

McFall, R. M. (1970). Effects of self-monitoring on normal smoking behavior. *Journal of Consulting and Clinical Psychology, 35,* 135–142.

McFall, R. M., & Hammen, C. (1971). Motivation, structure, and self-monitoring: Role of nonspecific factors in smoking reduction. *Journal of Consulting and Clinical Psychology, 37,* 80–86.

McIntyre-Kingsolver, K., Lichtenstein, E., & Mermelstein, R. (1986). Spouse training in a multi-component smoking-cessation program. *Behavior Therapy, 17,* 67–74.

McKennel, A. C. (1970). Smoking motivation factors. *British Journal of Social and Clinical Psychology, 9,* 8–22.

McNair, D. M., Lorr, M., & Droppleman, L. F. (1971). *Profile of Mood States.* San Diego: Educational and Industrial Testing Service.

Mermelstein, R., Cohen, S., & Lichtenstein, E. (1983, August). Perceived and objective stress, social support, and smoking cessation. In S. Shiffman (Chair), *Stress and smoking: Effects on initiation, maintenance, and relapse.* Symposium conducted at the annual convention of the American Psychological Association, Anaheim, CA.

Mermelstein, R., Cohen, S., Lichtenstein, E., Baer, J., & Kamarck, T. (1986). Social support and smoking cessation and maintenance. *Journal of Consulting and Clinical Psychology, 54,* 445–453.

Mermelstein, R., & Lichtenstein, E. (1983, April). *Slips versus relapses in smoking cessation: A situational analysis.* Paper presented at the meeting of the Western Psychological Association, San Francisco.

Mermelstein, R., Lichtenstein, E., & McIntyre, K. (1983). Partner support and relapse in smoking-cessation programs. *Journal of Consulting and Clinical Psychology, 51,* 465–466.

Murphy, M. (1983, February). *The self-help process in smoking cessation.* Paper presented at a meeting on The Role of Self-Help in Smoking Prevention and Cessation, National Cancer Institute, Bethesda, MD.

Myrsten, A. L., Elgerot, A., & Edgren, B. (1977). Effects of abstinence from tobacco smoking on physiological and psychological arousal levels in habitual smokers. *Psychopharmacologia, 27,* 305–312.

Ober, D. C. (1968). Modification of smoking behavior. *Journal of Consulting and Clinical Psychology, 32,* 543–549.

Ockene, J. K., Benfari, R. C., Nuttall, R. L., Hurwitz, I., & Ockene, I. S. (1982). Relationship of psychosocial factors to smoking behavior change in an intervention program. *Preventive Medicine, 11,* 13–28.

Ockene, J. K., Hymowitz, N., Sexton, M., & Broste, S. K. (1982). Comparison of patterns of smoking behavior change among smokers in the Multiple Risk Factor Intervention Trial (MRFIT). *Preventive Medicine, 11,* 621–638.

Ohlin, P., & Westling, H. (1975). Nicotine containing chewing gum as a substitute for smoking. In R. G. Richardson (Ed.), *The Second World Conference on Smoking and Health* (pp. 171–174). London: Pitman.

Pechacek, T. F. (1976, August). *Anxiety and smoking cessation: The search for specialized treatment packages.* Paper presented at the meeting of the Western Psychological Association, Los Angeles.

Perlick, D. (1977). *The withdrawal syndrome: Nicotine addiction and the effects of stopping smoking in heavy and light smokers.* Unpublished doctoral dissertation, Columbia University.

Perri, M. G., & Richards, C. S. (1977). An investigation of naturally occurring episodes of self-controlled behaviors. *Journal of Counseling Psychology, 24,* 178–183.

Perri, M. G., Richards, C. S., & Schultheis, K. R. (1977). Behavioral self-control and smoking reduction: A study of self-initiated attempts to reduce smoking. *Behavior Therapy, 8,* 360–365.

Pomerleau, O., Adkins, D., & Pertschuk, M. (1978). Predictors of outcome and recidivism in smoking cessation treatment. *Addictive Behaviors, 3,* 65–70.

Prochaska, J. O., & DiClemente, C. C. (1985). Common processes of change in smoking, weight control, and psychological distress. In S. Shiffman & T. A. Wills (Eds.), *Coping and substance use* (pp. 345–363). New York: Academic Press.

Raw, M., Jarvis, M. J., Feyerabend, C., & Russell, M. A. H. (1980). Comparison of nicotine chewing-gum and psychological treatments for dependnet smokers. *British Medical Journal, 281,* 481–482.

Rose, J., Anada, R., & Jarvik, M. E. (1983). Cigarette smoking during anxiety-provoking and monotonous tasks. *Addictive Behaviors, 8,* 353–359.

Rozensky, R. H. (1974). The effect of timing of self-monitoring behavior on reducing cigarette consumption. *Journal of Behavioral Research and Experimental Psychiatry, 5,* 301–303.

Russell, M. A. H., & Feyerabend, C. (1978). Cigarette smoking: A dependence on high-nicotine boli. *Drug Metabolism Reviews, 8,* 29–57.

Russell, M. A. H., Peto, J., & Patel, U. A. (1974). The classification of smoking by factorial structure of motives. *Journal of the Royal Statistical Society, 137,* 313–346.

Russell, M. A. H., Raw, M., & Jarvis, M. (1980). Clinical use of nicotine chewing gum. *British Medical Journal, 280,* 1599–1602.

Schachter, S. (1982). Recidivism and self-cure of smoking and obesity. *American Psychologist, 37,* 436–444.

Schneider, N. G., & Jarvik, M. E. (1985). Nicotine gum vs. placebo gum: Comparisons of withdrawal symptoms and success rates. In J. Grabowski & S. M. Hall (Eds.), *Pharmacological adjuncts in smoking cessation* (NIDA Monograph No. 53, pp. 83–10). Washington, DC: U.S. Government Printing Office.

Schneider, N. G., Jarvik, M. E., & Forsythe, A. B. (1984). Micotine versus placebo gum in the alleviation of withdrawal during smoking cessation. *Addictive Behaviors, 9,* 149–156.

Schneider, N. G., Jarvik, M. E., Forsythe, A. B., Read, L. L., Elliott, M. L., & Schweiger, A. (1983). Nicotine gum in smoking cessation: A placebo-controlled, double-blind trial. *Addictive Behaviors, 8,* 253–261.

Shiffman, S. (1979). The tobacco withdrawal syndrome. In N. M. Krasnegor (Ed.), *Cigarette smoking as a dependence process* (NIDA Research Monograph No. 23, pp. 158–184). Washington, DC: U.S. Government Printing Office.

Shiffman, S. (1980). Diminished smoking withdrawal symptoms, and cessation: A cautionary note. In G. B. Gory & F. G. Bock (Eds.), *A safe cigarette?* (pp. 283–297). Cold Springs Harbor, NY: Cold Springs Harbor Laboratory.

Shiffman, S. (1982). Relapse following smoking cessation: A situational analysis. *Journal of Consulting and Clinical Psychology, 50,* 71–86.

Shiffman, S. (1984a). Cognitive antecedents and sequelae of smoking relapse crises. *Journal of Applied Social Psychology, 14,* 296–309.

Shiffman, S. (1984b). Coping with temptations to smoke. *Journal of Consulting and Clinical Psychology, 52,* 261–267.

Shiffman, S. (1984c, August). *Trans-situational consistency in smoking relapse.* Paper presented at the annual convention of the American Psychological Association, Toronto.

Shiffman, S. (1986). A cluster-analytic typology of smoking relapse episodes. *Addictive Behaviors, 11,* 295–307.

Shiffman, S. (1987). Maintenance and relapse: Coping with temptation. In T. D. Nirenberg (Ed.), *Advances in the treatment of addictive behaviors* (pp. 353–385). Norwood, NJ: Ablex.

Shiffman, S., & Jarvik, M. E. (1976). Trends in withdrawal symptoms in abstinence from cigarette smoking. *Psychopharmacologia, 50,* 35–39.

Shiffman, S., & Jarvik, M. E. (1987). Situational determinants of coping in smoking relapse crises. *Journal of Applied Social Psychology, 17,* 3–15.

Shiffman, S., Maltese, J., Read, L., & Jarvik, M. E. (1982, August). Coping skill and coping style in the maintenance of nonsmoking. In S. Shiffman (Chair), *Coping strategies in the maintenance of nonsmoking.* Symposium conducted at the annual convention of the American Psychological Association, Washington, DC.

Shiffman, S., & Prange, M. (1984). Self-reported and self-monitored smoking patterns. *Pharmacology, Biochemistry and Behavior, 20,* 983–996.

Shiffman, S., Read, L., & Jarvik, M. E. (1983, August). The effect of stressful events on relapse in exsmokers. In S. Shiffman (Chair), *Stress and smoking: Effects on initiation, maintenance, and relapse.* Symposium conducted at the annual convention of the American Psychological Association, Anaheim, CA.

Shiffman, S., Read, L., & Jarvik, M. E. (1985). Smoking relapse episodes: A preliminary typology. *International Journal of the Addictions, 29,* 315–322.

Shiffman, S., Read, L., Maltese, J., Rapkin, D., & Jarvik, M. E. (1985). Preventing relapse in exsmokers: A self-management approach. In G. A. Marlatt & J. R. Gordon (Eds.), *Relapse prevention: Maintenance strategies in the treatment of addictive behaviors* (pp. 472–520). New York: Guilford Press.

Sjoberg, L., & Samsonowitz, V. (1978). Volitional problems in trying to quit smoking. *Scandinavian Journal of Psychology, 19,* 205–212.

Thompson, D. S., & Wilson, T. R. (1966). Discontinuance of cigarette smoking: "Natural" and with "therapy." *Journal of the American Medical Association, 96,* 1048.

Tomkins, S. (1966). Psychological model for smoking behavior. *American Journal of Public Health, 56,* 17–20.

Tongas, P. N., Patterson, J., & Goodkind, S. (1976, December). *Cessation of smoking through behavior modification: Treatment and maintenance.* Presented at the annual convention of the Association for Advancement of Behavior Therapy, New York.

U.S. Surgeon General. (1979). *The health consequences of smoking.* Rockville, MD: U.S. Department of Health and Human Services.

U.S. Surgeon General. (1982). *The health consequences of smoking.* Rockville, MD: U.S. Department of Health and Human Services.

U.S. Surgeon General. (1983). *The health consequences of smoking.* Rockville, MD: U.S. Department of Health and Human Services.

West, R. J. (1984). Psychology and pharmacology in cigarette withdrawal. *Journal of Psychosomatic Research, 28,* 379–386.

West, R. J., Jarvis, M. J., Russell, M. A. H., Caruthers, M. E., & Feyerabend, C. (1984). Effect of nicotine replacement on the cigarette withdrawal syndrome. *British Journal of the Addictions, 79,* 215–219.

Williams, D. G. (1979). Different cigarette-smoker classification factors and subjective state in acute abstinence. *Psychopharmacology, 64,* 231–235.

Williams, J., Crumpacker, D., & Krier, M. (1980). Stability of a factor-analytic description of smoking behavior. *Drug and Alcohol Dependence, 5,* 467–478.

Wynder, E. L., Kaufman, P. L., & Lesser, R. L. (1967). A short-term follow up study on ex-cigarette smokers, with special emphasis on persistent cough and weight gain. *American Review of Respiratory Disease, 96,* 645–655.

Zeidenberg, P., Jaffe, J. H., Kanzler, M., Levitt, M. D., Langone, J. J., & Van Vunakis, H. (1977). Nicotine: Cotinine levels in blood during cessation of smoking. *Comprehensive Psychiatry, 18,* 93–101.

# 6

# COGNITIVE ASSESSMENT

## JOHN S. BAER
*University of Oregon*

## EDWARD LICHTENSTEIN
*University of Oregon*
*Oregon Research Institute*

## Introduction

Cognitions such as knowledge, beliefs, attitudes, and expectations have been of central concern in the study of smoking for many years. Professionals in education and health education, public health, and social psychology have emphasized the role of specific knowledge about the health consequences of smoking, beliefs about personal susceptibility, attitudes toward smoking, and expectations of the benefits of quitting as decisive both for the initiation of cessation efforts and for their long-term success or failure.

Interest in cognitive variables in smoking has also emerged as a concern with cognitive variables has developed in the behavioral therapy literature. This trend is evident both in theoretical models of smoking cessation and in the use of cognitive variables in multicomponent behavioral treatment programs. Cognitive–behavioral models of smoking cessation and maintenance emphasize the individual's interpretation of health risks and perceived ability to quit (Pechacek & Danaher, 1979), as well as attributions about addiction and lapses during maintenance (Marlatt & Gordon, 1985). Similarly, most intervention programs focus on participants' attitudes and beliefs, as well as on their behavior during the quitting process. For example, a review of the health consequences of smoking is often used as a motivational boost for quitting. Programs may also emphasize clients' self-defeating thoughts or covert verbalizations and attributions, particularly at the point of focusing on maintenance of treatment gains or relapse prevention.

One particular set of cognitions has recently been given a good deal of attention in the smoking literature, as well as elsewhere in behavior therapy.

These cognitions reflect perceived ability to refrain from smoking in various situations or for designated periods of time. These "self-efficacy" beliefs (Bandura, 1977) can serve clinicians as indicators of subjects' progress at the end of treatment and may also be useful predictors of risk for relapse posttreatment.

Our review and analysis indicates that, with the exception of self-efficacy, little systematic research has been devoted to the assessment of cognitive variables in the treatment of smoking. Our review, therefore, emphasizes theories and clinical approaches rather than validated clinical instruments. This chapter also suggests that social-psychological formulations of perceived risk and decision making can be integrated with behavioral treatment strategies. We do not present social-psychological approaches solely because of their theoretical value, but rather because of their potential utility for application by treatment planners and providers.

Throughout this chapter, we emphasize the conceptualization of smoking cessation as a process. There are at least three stages or phases in the process of quitting: preparing to quit, quitting itself, and maintaining cessation (Danaher & Lichtenstein, 1978; Lichtenstein & Brown, 1980). These stages have direct implications for treatment planning because different psychosocial factors seem to be predictive of success at different stages of the quitting process. For example, Pomerleau, Adkins, and Pertschuk (1978), in a prospective study of clients in a stop-smoking program, found that treatment compliance was predictive of initial cessation, and that smoking during periods of negative affect was predictive of relapse. In a similar manner, Rosen and Shipley (1983) reported that a measure of self-esteem predicted cessation, but that health locus of control and motivation predicted successful maintenance.

Prochaska and DiClemente (1983) have extended this line of research by demonstrating that individuals who are quitting smoking tend to use different types of coping strategies at different stages of the quitting process. These investigators have also elaborated the preparation stage of quitting by describing "contemplation" and "precontemplation" phases. In light of the importance of the process of quitting, we attempt to describe appropriate points of application for each construct reviewed.

This review focuses on cognitive variables associated with the stages of preparation, quitting, and maintenance. We begin with a discussion of expectancy value models of smoking and smoking cessation. We briefly describe their application to the decision to attempt to quit smoking and propose how they can be used in clinical treatment programs. We then discuss locus of control, rationalizations, and attributions as they relate to the cessation and maintenance processes. The second half of this chapter is devoted to the construct of self-efficacy as applied to the treatment of smoking.

## Expectancy Value Models

### Theoretical Applications to Smoking Cessation

Expectancy value models have guided social-psychological approaches to smoking behavior and smoking cessation. Expectations have included the positive (e.g., enjoyment) and negative (e.g., disease) consequences of smoking, and the positive (e.g., enhanced lung capacity) and negative consequences (e.g., loss of enjoyment, withdrawal) of quitting. Such expectations have been termed "outcome expectations" because they refer to the consequences that are expected to occur if one continues smoking or quits smoking (Bandura, 1977). The concept of "value" is typically attached to outcome expectations and refers to the personal importance or weight given to the various possible outcomes. The value concept can also be extended to concerns about what significant others are perceived to wish one to do, as in Fishbein's (1982) theory of reasoned behavior.

Expectancy value models tend to assume that human behavior is rationally guided by logical or at least internally consistent thought processes (Henderson, Hall, & Linton, 1979). Decision-making models represent one variant of this approach. Individuals are assumed to "assess the personal, social, and psychological costs and benefits of their actions and the resulting cost–benefit ratio determines behaviors" (Henderson et al., 1979, p. 149). If a decision is not successfully acted upon, there is assumed to be interference from cognitive defenses. Cognitive intervention procedures should then be employed to counteract rationalizations (Reed & Janis, 1974).

The health belief model (Rosenstock, 1974) is another scheme for incorporating expectancy value concepts that has been applied to smoking cessation. According to this model, attempting to quit smoking is a function of three factors: (1) beliefs about the health consequences of smoking and perceived susceptibility to the disease consequences; (2) perceptions of available actions that can reduce one's risk; and (3) perceptions of the costs and benefits of accomplishing these actions (Kirscht & Rosenstock, 1979). More recent elaborations of health belief models have incorporated individuals' belief in their ability to change behaviors or self-efficacy (Bandura, 1977; Eiser, 1983; Eiser & Sutton, 1977; Sutton & Eiser, 1984). That is, individuals can vary in how confident they are about their ability to quit smoking, and these expectations can affect decisions about whether to try to quit (Eiser, 1983; Sutton & Eiser, 1984).

Expectancy value models have been used as a frame for the effects of fear-arousing communications (Leventhal, 1968; Sutton & Eiser, 1984) and other health-related information (Kirscht, 1983) on the individual's attempts to quit smoking. We suggest that outcome expectations (perceived consequences of smoking or quitting) are more closely related to the decision to quit smoking or the initiation of quit attempts than to success in the quitting process. Kirscht and Rosenstock (1979) suggest that "at present, the model seems least applicable to behaviors that are strongly habitual" (p. 204), and note that the factors predicting initiation of some action may not be predictive of success in carrying out that action. Two recent studies provide some indirect empirical support for this conclusion. Klesges, Vasey, and Glasgow (1984) found that introducing a competition into a worksite smoking intervention induced more subjects in the competition group to try to quit than in the noncompetition group. However, the actual rates of quitting among participants in the two conditions were the same. Similarly, in a study by Russell, Wilson, Taylor, and Baker (1979), brief advice from a physician served to motivate more subjects to try to quit relative to control subjects. Again, the actual rates of quitting among those who did try were not different. These two rather different interventions can both be seen as having served to enhance the positive consequences of quitting smoking (Klesges *et al.,* 1984) or the negative consequences of continuing (Russell *et al.,* 1979), and thus the decision to attempt to quit.

From this perspective, cognitions concerning the health risks of smoking and the positive benefits of quitting remain very important, but primarily from a public health or health education perspective.

### Expectancy Value in the Clinical Context

Formulations of expectancy value, however, have been given little attention in the literature on behavioral treatment—perhaps because investigators studying treatment seldom convince clients to attempt quitting, but rather deal primarily with clients or patients who have already made the decision to try to quit smoking. Yet clinicians who work with smokers have long recognized individual differences in knowledge and motivation. Intervention programs routinely but informally assess clients' knowledge and beliefs concerning the health consequences of smoking, the health benefits of quitting, and their own personal reasons for wanting to quit. Information about health consequences is usually provided. For example, although most smokers are generally aware of the relationship between smoking and lung cancer, many are not so aware of the relationship of smoking to cardiovascular disease and emphysema.

We have found it clinically useful, and relatively inexpensive in terms of program time, to ask subjects to list their reasons for wanting to quit on 3 × 5 cards. It is helpful if clients list their reasons as concretely as possible. Participants can then be asked to carry these cards with them and to refer to them periodically, sometimes using them as a way of coping with urges or difficult situations.

It is also possible, but somewhat more time-consuming, to have subjects draw up a decision balance sheet specifying the costs and benefits of both smoking and quitting. Procedures for so doing have been described both by Janis (1983) and by Velicer, DiClemente, Prochaska, and Brandenburg (1985). Although these assessment techniques have been used with persons who are considering a quit attempt, we believe that the procedures can be helpful in treatment as well. Assessment and review of these cost–benefit issues can serve to strengthen the clients' motivation or commitment to the intervention program, especially during the preparation phase.

Although we are suggesting that such procedures be used at the beginning or early in treatment as a means of enhancing motivation and commitment, they have another possible use as well. After participants have reached initial abstinence, a cost–benefit review may be useful in strengthening their commitment to remain abstinent. There is at least some theoretical reason to believe that subjects may be more receptive to processing such information about the negative consequences of smoking and the benefits of quitting after they have changed their behavior rather than before (Best, 1975).

During each treatment phase, emphasis in both assessment and treatment utilization should be on more temporally immediate or salient consequences. It is axiomatic that immediate, more likely consequences will have greater impact on behavior than will more distal, low-probability consequences. Getting lung cancer or heart disease will occur, if it occurs at all, long into the future; coughing, shortness of breath, stained teeth, bad breath, and foul-smelling clothes and rooms are all much more immediate consequences of smoking that can be emphasized.

It should also be noted that we are not implying that only positive results of quitting be emphasized. We recommend that the benefits of smoking and the costs of quitting also be explicitly acknowledged in order to retain program credibility and to provide an opportunity for countering or rebutting these concerns.

We conclude this section with a brief comment on the direct assessment of motivation for quitting. Manipulations of expectancies and values can be thought of as increasing motivation to quit. Although most persons entering treatment are relatively well motivated, it is possible that individual differences on this dimension may relate to treatment outcome. It is appealingly simple to ask clients directly about their motivation via questionnaire items. Often a one-item (10-point) scale of motivation to quit is employed. We found such an item to be predictive in one of our own programs, but not in a second study. Marlatt, Curry, and Gordon (1987) did find small but significant differences in motivation between those who were and were not successful quitting without program support at a 2-year follow-up.

## Locus of Control

One cognitive construct that has received a great deal of attention in smoking (as well as in virtually all areas of clinical and social psychology) is Rotter's (1966) formulation of perceived locus of control of reinforcement, or internal versus external locus of control. The sheer amount of this research is perhaps due to the relative ease of assessment using the standard 20-item Rotter Internal–External (I–E) Control of Reinforcement Scale. Unfortunately, the balance of research with the I–E instrument does not support its general use. Some research has suggested that persons who smoke are more likely to exhibit external locus of control (Foss, 1973; James, Woodruff, & Werner, 1965; Straits & Sechrest, 1963). Even this concurrent relationship has not been found consistently, however (Best & Steffy, 1971; Lichtenstein & Keutzer, 1967). From a cognitive–behavioral model of behavior change, it seems reasonable that those persons with more internal locus of control would be more likely to access coping strategies and thus to be able to quit smoking. Yet prospective studies with clients in treatment more often find no significant relationships (Benfari, Eaker, Ockene, & McIntyre, 1983; Danaher, 1977; Johnson & Chamberlain, 1978; Kilmann, Wagner, & Sotile, 1977) than they find positive relationships (Best & Steffy, 1975; Rosenbaum, 1980). Furthermore, efforts at tailoring treatment on the basis of perceived locus of control are generally unsuccessful (Best, 1978; Best & Steffy, 1971; Chambliss & Murray, 1979).

The failure of the Rotter I–E measure to relate to success in quitting smoking does not come as a surprise to those working with personality variables in smoking research. In fact, no general personality differences have been found to consistently predict treatment impact (Best, 1978). This may be due to the inaccuracies of personality measurement or to the tremendous heterogeneity in personality of those who smoke and attempt to quit. In either case, more specific individual differences directly related to smoking behavior may prove to be more closely linked to the quitting process (cf. Mischel, 1973). In the area of locus of control, the Multidimensional Health Locus of Control (MHLC) scales (Wallston, Wallston, & DeVellis, 1978) are more specifically related to quitting smoking, and appear to have more potential for clinical use.

Three recent studies (Kaplan & Cowles, 1978; Rosen & Shipley, 1983; Shipley, 1981) have reported significant prospective relationships between subscales of the MHLC instrument and maintenance of abstinence. In a study of 43 persons in a multicomponent treatment program, Shipley (1981) reported that for both the Internal and Chance subscales at a 3-month follow-up, 47% of persons with high scores on the subscales were abstinent, whereas only 17% of persons with low scores were abstinent. This relationship was replicated with a sample of unaided quitters in a study by Rosen and Shipley (1983). They report that the Internal subscale was a significant predictor of maintenence of reductions in smoking. At this point it is still unclear how best to use the MHLC scales in clinical settings; however, these preliminary results suggest that the Internal subscale may be useful during the maintenance phase of the quitting process. In particular, low-scoring clients could be considered either poor risks for treatment success or candidates for more preliminary or follow-up training procedures.

## Rationalizations and Thought Management

We have commented earlier on the use of cost–benefit assessment and decision balance sheet procedures in dealing with clients' ambivalence about quitting or making a commitment to a treatment program. During the course of a cessation program, especially after initial quitting, ambivalence about staying quit or rationalizations for resuming smoking may become critical concerns. As clients strive to maintain their newly achieved nonsmoking status, they are often beset with cognitions that can undermine their efforts. We have found that the measurement of such thoughts or rationalizations can be a useful stimulus for treatment planning and coping. Danaher and Lichtenstein (1978) have outlined a number of such potentially self-defeating thoughts or rationalizations. We have found that it is quite feasible to elicit many of these by means of an open-ended group discussion. Alternatively, a list with examples may be presented to subjects for their possible endorsement. Below we present a short list of the rationalizations that subjects in our programs have most commonly identified and that have also been noted by Danaher and Lichtenstein (1978).

1. Nostalgia: "I sure did like to smoke with coffee after dinner. I wonder how one would taste now."
2. Testing: "I wonder if I could smoke just one cigarette and then not have any more."
3. Crisis: "I could handle this situation much better if I only had a cigarette"; or, alternatively, "I've been under such pressure that I deserve a cigarette."
4. Avoiding unwanted side effects: "Quitting smoking is causing me to become overweight."
5. Self-doubts: "I'm still getting strong urges to smoke. I must be one of those addicted people."

Labeling such rationalizations for smoking helps the client to recognize how they can undermine their efforts. Clients can then be trained and encouraged to combat or rebut these self-defeating thoughts.

## Attributions

Multicomponent treatment programs aim to help clients avoid any further smoking. But clients do have lapses or slips. Recent theoretical models of relapse suggest that the cognitive and emotional reaction to a lapse in abstinent behavior is central to understanding the process of resuming smoking (or other addictive behavior). Marlatt and associates (Marlatt & Gordon, 1980, 1985) have postulated an "abstinence violation effect" as causal in the process of relapse. Marlatt suggests that, once abstinent behavior is compromised, a series of cognitive changes undermine future coping. Clients are believed to attribute the lapse as a personal failure. This attribution leads to an emotional response and a decline in self-efficacy. In short, persons who violate abstinent behavior feel that they have "blown it" and that they are hopeless addicts. Data from studies by Shiffman (1984) and Glasgow, Klesges, Mizes, and Pechacek (1985) are consistent with this formulation. Although retrospective, both studies associate lapses with subsequent relapse.

Clients are often warned of such reactions to lapses in relapse prevention training (Lichtenstein & Brown, 1980; Marlatt & Gordon, 1985); they are encouraged to make more external and specific attributions about lapses, such as "It was a difficult situation, and I made a mistake." Clients are encouraged to "get back on their feet" and to continue to feel capable of refraining from addictive behavior.

The typical informal assessment procedure is similar to that used to identify self-defeating thoughts. That is, a group discussion can be used to elicit self-reports or endorsement of material presented by group leaders. A more systematic method of assessing attributions surrounding abstinence violations is suggested by the recent work of Curry, Marlatt, and Gordon (1987). Curry *et al.* adapted methodology originating from attributional research (Weiner, 1974) and subsequently applied to cognitive formulations of depression by Abramson and others (Abramson, Garber, & Seligman, 1980; Abramson, Seligman, & Teasdale, 1978). Within this framework, attributions were measured on three dimensions: "locus of causality" (external vs. internal), "stability" (unchanging vs. changeable), and "specificity" (global vs. specific). Clients were asked to read descriptions of smoking incidents or lapses and to rate their own attributional response to each situation. Based on Marlatt and Gordon's model (1980, 1985), Curry *et al.* (1987) expected that those with more internal, global, and enduring attributions would be more likely to relapse during follow-up. Their results were just the opposite: Those who rated failure as external and specific during treatment were significantly more likely to resume smoking after treatment ended. Although these results are difficult to interpret, this research represents a first step toward better understanding how attributional style might be related to smoking. This assessment methodology seems particularly sound. Curry *et al.* (1984) used this method to assess attributions after clients actually lapsed during the follow-up period, and found that external, specific, and unstable attributions were highly related to success in resuming abstinence.

## Self-Efficacy in Smoking Treatment Programs

Self-efficacy has been the most extensively used cognitive variable in the treatment of smoking behavior. Bandura (1977, 1982) defines "self-efficacy" as an individual's belief in his or her ability to perform a given behavior. As noted above, the belief in one's ability to quit has been implicated in the health belief model and in Eiser's (1983) analysis of decision making about quitting. Bandura's formulation is considerably more precise. Self-efficacy is defined as confidence in specific behavioral attainments, rather than more global beliefs. For example, in the realm of phobias, self-efficacy is assessed with respect to specific approach behaviors to the feared stimulus (e.g., touching a snake). Bandura argues that self-efficacy beliefs represent a final common pathway mediating behavior change. Information from past behavior, modeling, affective states, and instruction all combine to produce a performance expectation, which then predicts future behavior. This behavior would, in turn, influence subsequent self-efficacy; behavior and self-efficacy are reciprocally related (Bandura, 1982). Self-efficacy expectations are proposed to be better predictors of behavior than are previous behaviors alone (Bandura, 1977).

Our analysis of self-efficacy in smoking treatment addresses measurement issues first, followed by the evidence for predictive validity. Throughout this review, we are particularly concerned with the potential clinical application of self-efficacy scales in treatment programs.

It is important to emphasize initially that all significant results with self-efficacy pertain to client ratings *after* they quit smoking, and thus predict smoking during follow-up periods. We know of no research that has demonstrated prediction of initial cessation through *pretreatment* ratings of self-efficacy; in fact, our own data indicate that pretreatment self-efficacy ratings are routinely unrelated to treatment success. These findings are consistent with one limitation of the expectancy value models noted earlier: Expectations about success do not relate to success once a decision has been made to try to quit.

Posttreatment self-efficacy assessment, however, can provide a measure of risk for smoking during a maintenance phase after treatment. Clients with relatively low posttreatment self-efficacy scores are at high risk for smoking, and are thus candidates for additional treatment or possibly booster sessions. Self-efficacy measures may even suggest problematic high-risk situations that need to be addressed.

*Measurement Issues*

In work with phobic clients, Bandura (1977) has developed a specific assessment procedure. Clients are asked to rate their confidence in their ability to perform a set of specific behaviors that are arranged as graded accomplishments on a Guttman scale (e.g., stand near a snake, touch a snake, hold a snake). There are three dimensions to assessed self-efficacy: "Level" is defined as the number of behaviors clients judge they can perform; "efficacy strength" is defined as the average rating across behaviors; "generality" is defined as differences between self-efficacy ratings for behavior in a given specific situation relative to other situations (i.e., touching a green snake vs. touching a brown snake). To assess predictive utility of self-efficacy, Bandura (1980) uses "congruence microanalyses," comparing the number of tasks behaviorally accomplished with a client's efficacy expectations about his or her capability of accomplishing each of these tasks.

It is not obvious how to apply Bandura's conceptual framework directly to smoking behavior. In the area of addictions, self-efficacy is most often defined as judgments about one's ability to *refrain* from engaging in a behavior, rather than one's ability to perform a task. In the area of smoking cessation treatment, assessment usually involves clients' making a series of judgments about confidence in their ability to "resist the urge to smoke." Judgments are typically made relative to a variety of situations (e.g., "How confident are you that you can resist smoking when you feel angry? . . . when you are drinking alcohol?"). Efficacy strength is taken as the average rating across situations, and generality is measured as the variability between items that describe different smoking situations. Because there is no graded Guttman scale that is applicable in this realm, an index of level is not obtained. Furthermore, a congruence analysis similar to those computed by Bandura in other applications of self-efficacy is not possible here. Relationships with other variables tend to be assessed with standard correlational techniques, using strength as the measure of efficacy.

Efficacy scales can be derived for any number of specific criteria. For example, Erickson, Tiffany, Martin, and Baker (1983) used a single question regarding confidence in one's ability to remain abstinent for 1 year. This measure was highly related to successful maintenance. Godding and Glasgow (1985) developed self-efficacy scales for the target behaviors of nicotine content (brand smoked), percentage of cigarette smoked (butt length), and rate reduction in the context of a controlled-smoking program. Scores on these scales were highly related to their respective target behaviors. Our evaluation of the construct of self-efficacy is based on its use in abstinence-based smoking treatment programs. The Confidence Questionnaire (Condiotte & Lichtenstein, 1981) is representative of self-efficacy scales typically used for smoking cessation. This 46-item scale asks for confidence judgments about refraining from smoking in specific situations. Responses for each item range from 0 ("no confidence, will smoke") to 100 ("absolutely confident, will not smoke"). Items were based on Best and Hakstian's (1978) model of situation-specific smoking. The majority of studies reviewed here use this instrument. Several other self-efficacy scales related to smoking cessation (Colletti, Supnick, & Rizzo, 1981; DiClemente, 1981; Shiffman, Read, & Jarvik, 1981) are quite similar, varying only in the wording, number, and nature of situation-specific items.

*Psychometric Properties*

We have examined the psychometric properties of the Confidence Questionnaire, using a sample of 226 clients from the Oregon Smoking Control Program. Clients completed the scale at the end of a cessation program, 2 weeks after an assigned quit date. The scale proved to be highly reliable and primarily unidimensional (Baer, Holt, & Lichtenstein, 1986). Internal consistency was extremely high (coefficient alpha = .99). Principal-components analysis revealed that the first factor removed accounted for 60% of scale variance, and subsequent factors each accounted for less than 5% of scale variance. This finding is at odds with a cluster analysis reported earlier (Condiotte & Lichtenstein, 1981), but is consistant with the factor results of other self-efficacy questionnaires (DiClemente, Prochaska, & Gibertini, 1985; S. Shiffman, personal communication, 1983). This discrepancy may be due to the type of factoring procedure used (principal-components analysis instead of ICLUST), or to the fact that we factored posttreatment confidence scales, whereas Condiotte and Lichtenstein (1981) clustered pretreatment scales. Posttreatment scales were used because of their demonstrated predictive power. This principal-components analysis suggests that the use of the Confidence Questionnaire is limited to generalized self-efficacy beliefs. Specific situational ratings account for limited variance in the scale, and thus should not be differentially predictive for specific behaviors.

Situation-specific self-efficacy ratings may still be useful for clinical discussions with newly abstinent clients, however. To better guide these interactions, we developed a five-factor representation of the scale from principal-components analysis after each subject's responses were standardized. The standardization procedure adjusted for individual differences in average response (all subjects were given a mean response of 50), as well as extremity bias (standard deviation of all responses was set at 10). These two operations removed approximately 60% of the scale variance (roughly equivalent to the first unrotated principal component). The remaining variance can be represented by subscales we have termed Social Image (e.g., "When you want to feel more mature and sophisticated"), Diet (e.g., "When you want to avoid eating sweets"), Social Influence (e.g., "When someone offers you a cigarette," "When you are drinking an alcoholic beverage"), Pleasure (e.g., "When you have finished a meal or snack"), and Negative Affect (e.g., "When you feel tense").

The 46-item Confidence Questionnaire is also rather cumbersome to administer. Thus, for brevity, we have developed a much shorter assessment form. The Confidence Questionnaire Form S, shown in Table 6-1, is composed of 14 items from the original 46-item scale. Items were chosen to represent the five factors described above, and are labeled in the table. Internal consistency of the short form remained high (coefficient alpha = .92). The predictive validity of Form S was tested, using a sample of 63 clients. Mean scores from Form S correlated .98 with the full scale and appeared equally predictive of smoking status and smoking rates up to 1 year after treatment. This relationship held both for the full sample ($n = 63$) and for those abstinent at the end of treatment ($n = 40$). Factor analysis of Form S ($n = 226$) revealed that the items maintain the original five-factor solution, with the exception of item 9, which refers to the use of alcohol.

In summary, the Confidence Questionnaire is internally consistent, but is much more unidimensional than the underlying theory would imply. That is, the Confidence Questionnaire measures a generalized self-efficacy expectation, rather than self-efficacy for specific situations. We now turn to the predictive and construct validity of the self-efficacy construct, with emphasis on the Confidence Questionnaire.

### Predictive Validity

An analysis of the potential use of self-efficacy ratings in smoking treatment programs must demonstrate that these ratings are predictive of future behavior. When all clients in treatment are considered, results with posttreatment self-efficacy ratings tend to be quite encouraging. Mean confidence ratings from the Confidence Questionnaire correlated .59 with abstinence and .68 with time to relapse during a 3-month follow-up period (Condiotte & Lichtenstein, 1981). Results of similar magnitude have been reported by Coelho (1984), Erickson *et al.* (1983), McIntyre, Lichtenstein, and Mermelstein (1983), and Tiffany, Martin, and Baker (1986). For the most part, efficacy scores seem to correlate with outcome most highly when the follow-up interval is shorter, and to diminish over time (Coelho, 1984; McIntyre *et al.,* 1983). This should be expected, for self-efficacy is hypothesized to be a state measure. We have been able to replicate these relationships on three additional samples of clients.

For self-efficacy to be clinically useful, self-efficacy ratings should be better predictors of behavior than is past behavior, and not a simple

TABLE 6-1.  Confidence Questionnaire, Form S

Below is a list of 14 situations in which people frequently smoke. Please read each one carefully. Then circle the number underneath that best describes THE PROBABILITY THAT YOU WILL BE ABLE TO *RESIST* THE URGE TO SMOKE IN THAT SITUATION IN THE FUTURE IF THE SITUATION ARISES. If you are *absolutely certain* that you will *not* smoke in that situation, circle 100%. If you have *no confidence* in your ability to *resist* a cigarette in that situation, circle 0%. More likely, your confidence will vary. For example, if you are pretty sure that you will be able to *resist* the urge to smoke if and when you want to relax, but not absolutely certain, you might circle 80%. If you are pretty sure you would *not* be able to *resist* a cigarette if that situation arises, but not absolutely sure you couldn't, you might circle 20%.

0% — 10% — 20% — 30% — 40% — 50% — 60% — 70% — 80% — 90% — 100%

| Item no. | Factor | Item |
|---|---|---|
| 1 | Negative Affect | When you feel anxious |
| 4 | Negative Affect | When you are nervous |
| 8 | Negative Affect | When you feel tense |
| 2 | Pleasure | When you want to sit back and enjoy a cigarette |
| 3 | Pleasure | When you have finished a meal or snack |
| 6 | Pleasure | When you want to relax |
| 5 | Social Image | When you want to feel more attractive |
| 7 | Social Image | When you feel smoking is part of your self-image |
| 13 | Social Image | When you want to feel more mature and sophisticated |
| 9 | Social Influence | When you are drinking an alcoholic beverage |
| 10 | Social Influence | When you see others smoking |
| 11 | Social Influence | When someone offers you a cigarette |
| 12 | Diet | When you want to avoid eating sweets |
| 14 | Diet | When you want to keep slim |

reflection of other psychosocial predictor variables. In a sample of 65 clients seen through the Oregon Smoking Control Program, we related self-efficacy to other commonly used predictor measures. Baseline or pretreatment measures were completed 1 week prior to the beginning of a 6-week stop-smoking program. Other psychosocial ratings were administered together with the Confidence Questionnaire at the last meeting of the group.

As seen in Table 6-2, self-efficacy scores were only moderately related to a number of variables that have been associated with treatment success, such as baseline smoking rate and stress. Self-efficacy is therefore not simply a reflection of motivation, previous confidence, physical symptoms, or a measure of self-control (Rosenbaum, 1980). Current smoking behavior appeared to be by far the strongest correlate (see also Erickson *et al.,* 1983). Thus, correlations between self-efficacy and follow-up status may

TABLE 6-2.  Correlations between End-of-Treatment Confidence Questionnaire Scores and Antecedent Variables

| Predictor variables | $r$ | $n$ |
|---|---|---|
| Baseline smoking rate | $-.25^{*}$ | 65 |
| Pretreatment motivation | .02 | 63 |
| Pretreatment confidence | .20 | 63 |
| Perceived stress (Cohen, Kamarck, & Mermelstein, 1983) | $-.18$ | 63 |
| Perceived Social Support (Cohen, Mermelstein, Kamarck, & Hoberman, 1985) | $.32^{**}$ | 62 |
| Physical symptoms (Cohen & Hoberman, 1983) | .02 | 65 |
| Self-Control Schedule (Rosenbaum, 1980) | .17 | 21 |
| Number of cigarettes smoked previous week | $-.64^{***}$ | 65 |

$^{*}p < .05.$
$^{**}p < .01.$
$^{***}p < .001.$

strongly reflect the consistency of behavior (smoking or not) from the end of treatment to follow-up assessments. Relationships between self-efficacy ratings and follow-up smoking status, then, do not necessarily indicate an improved clinical prediction from one based on current behavior. To be truly useful, self-efficacy must demonstrate significant incremental predictive power above that accounted for by current behavior.

### Self-Efficacy versus Performance in the Prediction of Maintenance

One approach to this question of incremental utility is to statistically control for current behavior by the use of partial correlation techniques. We have completed this analysis on a sample of 140 subjects seen through the Oregon Smoking Control Program. The resulting relationships are presented in Table 6-3. These results suggest that self-efficacy scores do lend information above and beyond that of current behavior.

Unfortunately, partial correlations are not easily applied to clinical prediction. A more applied approach to this problem is to consider only a subset of clients—those for whom the prediction is used. In the case of predicting relapse after treatment, one can correlate self-efficacy and follow-up status only for those clients who initially quit. Those clients who are smoking at the end of treatment are already known to be at risk for future smoking.

These relationships have been reported in two published studies. McIntyre et al. (1983) reported the correlation between end-of-treatment confidence scores and smoking status at a 3-month follow-up to be .37 ($n =$

TABLE 6-3. Correlations between Mean End-of-Treatment Confidence and Subsequent Smoking Status, Partialing-out Smoking at Time of Confidence Assessment

|  | Partial correlation |
| --- | --- |
| Status at 1 month | .28* |
| Status at 2 months | .27* |
| Status at 3 months | .32* |
| Status at 6 months | .18 |

*Note. n* = 136–141.
*p < .001.

41, $p < .01$). The relationship to 6-month posttreatment status was in the correct direction, but did not reach statistical significance ($r = .18$). Coelho (1984, using a scale developed by DiClemente, 1981) reported similar findings ($r = .43, n = 42, p < .01$) at a 3-month follow-up when only quitters were analyzed.

In the last few years, however, we have been unable to consistently replicate the findings for end-of-treatment abstainers. One cohort of clients ($n = 63$) yielded lower correlations at both a 3-month follow-up ($r = .26, p < .11$) and a 6-month follow-up ($r = .27, p < .10$). In a second sample of clients ($n = 41$), end-of-treatment self-efficacy was unrelated to follow-up status for treatment quitters. Our most recent data suggest a relationship of borderline significance at a 3-month follow-up ($r = .35, n = 24, p < .09$).

In view of the low order of these relationships (as well as the partial correlations presented earlier), the clinical utility of end-of-treatment self-efficacy ratings appears to be limited. Although these relationships may be statistically significant, very little variance is accounted for in prospective prediction when only successful clients are considered.

## Follow-Up Self-Efficacy Assessment

Self-efficacy assessed at the end of treatment may still be part of the cessation phase of the quitting process, and thus is based on treatment experience and initial coping attempts. Self-efficacy can also be assessed after treatment has ended, during the maintenance phase of quitting, to reflect the clients' experiences in coping with urges and incorporating nonsmoking into their regular lifestyles. One study has examined these relationships. DiClemente (1981) interviewed recent quitters 2 months after they had quit smoking and found self-efficacy ratings to be predictive of smoking status 3 months later. The magnitude of the mean differences reported by DiClemente (1981) of 73.9 for abstainers and 66.7 for recidivists is impressive, considering that all subjects had quit for 2 months when self-efficacy was assessed.

We have tested the utility of follow-up assessment of self-efficacy with a sample of 72 initially successful quitters (Baer *et al.,* 1986). Clients were contacted by telephone at 1-, 2-, and 3-month follow-ups. At each phone call, clients were asked to rate their confidence in each of four situations selected from the original 46-item scale: "When you feel tense," "When you are drinking an alcoholic beverage," "When you see others smoking," and "When you are feeling bored or restless." The average across the four ratings was taken as generalized self-efficacy. For each analysis, only those not regularly smoking (not more than one cigarette a day) received the self-efficacy probes. These ratings were then related to subsequent status (no smoking in the week prior to a subsequent call), thus predicting the resumption of smoking.

Results from these analyses suggest that self-efficacy ratings were a significant predictor of relapse after the 1-month follow-up point. A series of prospective point-biserial correlations is shown in Table 6-4. As can be seen, the prediction from 1-month self-efficacy to subsequent status was statistically significant, yet of the same magnitude as that reported for end-of-treatment scores, described earlier. However, predictions from the 2-month and 3-month confidence ratings were considerably higher. On a scale from 1 to 10 (the average of the four self-efficacy questions), those clients who had not resumed smoking at 3 months had average self-efficacy scores at 2 months of 9.01. Those who were smoking at 3 months had average 2-month efficacy scores of 7.48. Means associated with the prediction to 6-month status were of a similar magnitude: Nonsmokers at 6 months had average 3-month self-efficacy scores of 9.25, whereas those who were smoking at 6 months had average 3-month self-efficacy scores of 8.06.

Further examination of the distributions of confidence scores relative to subsequent status suggested that a cutoff score could be developed to identify those at risk for relapse. If the purpose of assessment is to minimize false-positive predictions, a fairly high cutoff score would provide

TABLE 6-4.   Point-Biserial Correlations of Confidence and Subsequent Smoking Status

| Confidence | Smoking status assessment | | |
|---|---|---|---|
| assessment | 2 months | 3 months | 6 months |
| 1 month ($n$ = 66) | $-.23$ | $-.26*$ | $-.25*$ |
| 2 months ($n$ = 61) | — | $-.55**$ | $-.56**$ |
| 3 months ($n$ = 55) | — | — | $-.54**$ |

$*p < .05.$

$**p < .001.$

conservative assignment. For example, only 3 out of 36 (8%) clients with 2-month average self-efficacy scores over 8.5 subsequently smoked at the 3-month point. Confidence ratings of 10 were obtained 28 times across the three assessment points. In all but 2 of these cases, clients remained abstinent at the subsequent follow-up. Thus, clients with particularly high scores (i.e., 10) could be considered relatively risk-free. Low self-efficacy scores tended to be less accurate in predicting those who would smoke; thus false-negative predictions were more likely. For example, 15 of 32 (47%) of clients with self-efficacy scores below 8.5 at 2 months smoked at 3 months, and 16 of 23 (70%) of clients with scores below 8.5 at 3 months smoked by the 6-month follow-up. Yet false-negative predictions are conservative, and serve to identify those at *risk* for relapse. Potentially, follow-up self-efficacy scores could provide a screening for individuals who may benefit from some form of booster intervention.

### *Self-Efficacy Beliefs about Behavior in Specific Situations*

Self-efficacy beliefs about behavior in specific situations may also be useful for those working in smoking cessation. Bandura (1977, 1982) argues that beliefs in self-efficacy begin as quite situation-specific expectations about behavioral capabilities. Beliefs that are initially specific gradually become more general as mastery is attained. If self-efficacy has the same properties in the smoking realm, then perhaps self-efficacy beliefs could be related to specific situational difficulties. This notion has been addressed in one study (Condiotte & Lichtenstein, 1981), which reported strong congruence between the kinds of situations given lower posttreatment self-efficacy ratings and the nature of the actual relapse situations. However, a reanalysis of these data revealed that out of seven possible clusters, 80% of clients relapsed in one of their three lowest (least confident) self-efficacy cluster categories: 35% in their lowest self-efficacy cluster, 20% in their second lowest cluster, and 24% in their third lowest cluster (Baer *et al.,* 1986). Hence, when near-misses were given partial credit for agreement (as in weighted kappa), measured correspondence between self-efficacy clusters and relapse situations appeared quite high. Although this relationship provides evidence for the construct validity of the Confidence Questionnaire, it overstates the specificity with which self-efficacy ratings can be used to predict situational characteristics of relapses. In fact, we have been unable to replicate statistical relationships between specific self-efficacy items and relapse characteristics (Baer, 1985; Baer & Lichtenstein, in press).

This conclusion is consistent with the unidimensional nature of the Confidence Questionnaire, described earlier. From our analyses of the Confidence Questionnaire, we must conclude that it is highly unlikely that any normalized factor score from the scale will be of situationally specific predictive value. This is not to say, however, that self-efficacy *beliefs* are always general—only that our assessment of them is. It is possible that other assessment techniques may better measure these qualities.

It is possible that situation-specific self-efficacy beliefs could prove useful in an idiographic prediction procedure. A casual examination of a set of completed Confidence Questionnaires suggests that some individuals rank all items at 10, whereas others use considerable variability in their situational judgments. Even though no general factors exist, particular items could be predictive of behavior for given clients. How to operationalize an idiographic prediction procedure is a question for further research.

## *Summary*

In summary, the use of end-of-treatment self-efficacy ratings in smoking cessation programs can give the clinician a measure of risk for future smoking. Self-efficacy beliefs are prospectively related to behavior during the maintenance phase of treatment. Efficacy assessed 2 weeks after the quit date in a cessation program is largely reflective of treatment success, but maintains some unique predictive power. The incremental prediction is marginal, however, and is difficult to use in a clinical context. Assessment of self-efficacy during the maintenance process has the greatest potential for clinical use. Abstinent clients with low self-efficacy as long as 2 months after quitting are at high risk for the resumption of smoking. The magnitude of these relationships indicates that self-efficacy phone probes can be used as a screening device for those at risk for relapse. That clients who have been abstinent for 2 months may still rate their self-efficacy at 8 (rather than 10) suggests that they have not incorporated nonsmoking comfortably into their lifestyles. These persons may well benefit from booster interventions. The use of the Confidence Questionnaire as a measure of self-efficacy expectations about specific situations appears limited.

## Clinical Example

The following case exemplifies the use of cognitive assessment in the treatment of smoking. This example does not exhaust the possibilities for the clinical use of cognitive variables, but rather demonstrates how we have used these constructs in the Oregon Smoking Control Program.

Barbara was a 38-year-old divorced woman who lived with her 16-year-old daughter. She had been smoking regularly for over 20 years and was smoking 25 cigarettes a day prior to treatment. She had made one prior attempt to quit 5 years earlier and was able to quit for a brief period; however, she became quite uncomfortable and frustrated with withdrawal symptoms (inability to concentrate, craving for cigarettes), and resumed smoking after 5 days.

Within the initial assessment prior to treatment, Barbara was asked for her reasons for wanting to quit. She stated that she knew cigarettes were bad for her and she was afraid of getting cancer. Furthermore, cigarettes were becoming more expensive, and her 16-year-old daughter kept telling her to stop. Barbara's concerns about health apparently had been present for many years, but had become more salient in the past 2 years as her daughter had begun to learn of the health consequences of smoking and to question her mother's behavior.

Barbara was also asked why she smoked, or might want to continue smoking in the future. She noted that she had always enjoyed smoking and that cigarettes had long been a "good friend," helping her through stressful and difficult times.

In the course of the 6-week quitting program, Barbara participated with a group of seven others in a program of nicotine fading, self-monitoring, self-management techniques, and, after quitting, relapse prevention training. One week before the quit date, group members were asked to list on 3 × 5 cards their concrete, specific reasons for quitting smoking that were of immediate concern. Another member of the group said that he did not like the way cigarettes interfered with his breathing. Barbara agreed and listed the more specific health concern, "trouble breathing," along with her fear of cancer. Barbara also listed "saving money" and "pleasing my daughter" as her reasons for quitting. Barbara, along with the other group members, was instructed to carry these cards and to read them as a boost of motivation to avoid smoking.

On the night of the quit date (as well as at the next group meeting 1 week later), Barbara was asked to describe her rationalizing thoughts about returning to smoking. Barbara noted several common rationalizations she had experienced that day: "One cigarette won't hurt," "I really can't do this," "I'm just going to gain weight," "I miss my old friend," "Something is missing from my life." Barbara and the other group members practiced refuting these thoughts in a group discussion and added their refutations to their cards. One week after quitting, Barbara's rationalizations for resuming smoking had been reduced to one: She continued to feel that she had lost a friend. This thought persisted in spite of her efforts to argue with herself that cigarettes were "an old enemy."

At the end of treatment, 2 weeks after quitting, Barbara completed the Confidence Questionnaire. Her confidence, or self-efficacy, regarding her ability to refrain from smoking in all situations averaged 80 on a 100-point scale. This level of self-efficacy was somewhat low for a person who had been abstinent for 2 weeks, but could not be considered predictive of future difficulties.

In a final discussion of her quitting efforts, Barbara admitted that she still felt as though she were fighting to stay quit and that she was tempted to smoke almost every day. At this point, Barbara was asked to describe how she might attribute an "accidental" slip or lapse in her abstinence. Barbara noted that she would be quite upset, and certainly would feel as though she had "blown it" and "failed." Barbara was encouraged not to give up if she had difficulty during the first several weeks of abstinence, even if she had a setback. The counselor also reviewed how she might construe a slip or lapse in a more constructive way.

During the follow-up period after the program, Barbara was phoned once a month. One month after the end of treatment (6 weeks after the quit date) Barbara's confidence in her ability to resist smoking averaged 8.2 on a 10-point scale. Her level of confidence was low relative to that of others at this time, and had not improved despite continued abstinence. Barbara was thus still at risk for relapse.

Barbara reported an isolated incident of smoking when she was called two months after the end of the program. Approximately 1 week earlier, she had been at home alone and feeling blue. She missed cigarettes and thought she would feel better if she smoked. After fighting the urge for over an hour, Barbara went to the store, bought a pack, and smoked one. She reported that it tasted "awful" and didn't help her feel better. She threw the pack away. When asked about her attributions at the time of the lapse, Barbara said that she felt pretty bad but still tried to "get back in control." She admitted that she still felt as though she had "failed" because she smoked. Her self-efficacy remained relatively low at this time, at 8.1 of a possible 10.

When called 3 months after the end of the program, Barbara reported that she had resumed smoking. Barbara stated that she had never fully recovered from her lapse, and had continued to have intermittent strong urges for a cigarette. She had had two more lapses in the week following the earlier phone call, each time throwing the pack away after smoking one cigarette. Finally, 2 weeks prior to the current call, she had kept a pack, thinking that she was wasting money. With the cigarettes available, her smoking gradually reached her old rate of a pack a day.

Due to the research nature of our program, no intervention was offered to Barbara during follow-up when she was at risk for relapse. It is unclear whether further intervention could or would have been helpful. Many clients do not want further assistance, and the research on booster sessions is equivocal at best. It is possible, however, that with more help Barbara could have avoided relapse. Only further research can begin to answer these important questions.

## Conclusion

We have reviewed the assessment methodology and potential application of several cognitive variables as they relate to three stages in the process of quitting smoking: preparation, quitting, and maintenance. Consistent with previous research, different constructs appear to be associated with success in different stages of the quitting process. Outcome expectations—the perceived positive and negative consequences of smoking or quitting—appear to influence primarily the decision to try to quit, rather than success in doing so. We have offered some suggestions for the more informal clinical assessment and exploration of these expectations and values. The MHLC scales are potentially useful as an index of risk during maintenance; however, more research is needed to confirm the relationships reported thus far.

Rationalizations about smoking and attributions concerning slips or lapses have become important issues in cognitive–behavioral cessation programs, but virtually no systematic assessment research has been completed. We consider these constructs particularly interesting, and, in an effort to promote research and application in this area, we have described some procedures for clinical assessment and use of these constructs.

Self-efficacy expectations have become a key construct in cognitive accounts of smoking cessation and maintenance. We conclude that the assessment of self-efficacy beliefs at particular stages of the quitting process can be quite useful for the clinician. The evidence thus far suggests that self-efficacy beliefs may influence the decision to quit but have little effect on the initial quitting process. Self-efficacy beliefs are most useful when assessed during the maintenance phase, as long as 3 months after initial quitting.

It has been our experience that few variables, cognitive or otherwise, successfully predict who will quit smoking once a decision has been made to try to quit. Perhaps the support and instruction within a treatment program are strong enough to promote initial quitting, regardless of other psychosocial factors. Indeed, most treatment programs achieve impressive end-of-treatment quit rates. It is only after treatment has concluded and participants must cope with urges to smoke on their own that variables such as self-efficacy, locus of control, and attributions seem to affect successful abstinence. Perhaps research efforts should focus on this final stage of the process—maintenance and/or relapse—as a means of improving smoking cessation technology.

In general, research on the assessment of cognitive processes related to smoking cessation has lagged far behind theoretical and clinical concerns. Unfortunately, research in this area is inherently difficult: Cognitive constructs are difficult to define and measure consistently. We believe that better assessment of cognitive processes will lead to improved understanding and successful treatment of smoking. In this spirit, this chapter can be considered a description of potential areas of investigation rather than a formal review of research findings.

## Acknowledgments

Preparation of this chapter was supported by U.S. Public Health Service Grant No. CA38243, awarded by the National Cancer Institute. We wish to thank Russell E. Glasgow and Thomas W. Kamarck for their helpful comments on an earlier version of this chapter, and Charles C. Ransom, Jr., for his assistance in preparation of the manuscript. John S. Baer is presently at the University of Washington.

## References

Abramson, L. Y., Garber, J., & Seligman, M. E. P. (1980). Learned helplessness in humans: An attributional analysis. In J. Garber & M. E. P. Seligman (Eds.), *Human helplessness: Theory and application* (pp. 3–34). New York: Academic Press.

Abramson, L. Y., Seligman, M. E. P., & Teasdale, J. (1978). Learned helplessness in humans: Critique and reformulation. *Journal of Abnormal Psychology, 87,* 49–74.

Baer, J. S. (1985). *Patterns of relapse after cessation of smoking: Cluster analysis and prospective prediction.* Unpublished doctoral dissertation, University of Oregon.

Baer, J. S., Holt, C. S., & Lichtenstein, E. (1986). Self-efficacy and smoking reexamined: Construct validity and clinical utility. *Journal of Consulting and Clinical Psychology, 54,* 846–852.

Baer, J. S., & Lichtenstein, E. (in press). Classification and prediction of smoking relapse episodes: An exploration of individual differences. *Journal of Consulting and Clinical Psychology.*

Bandura, A. (1977). Self-efficacy: Toward a unifying theory of behavioral change. *Psychological Review, 84,* 191–215.

Bandura, A. (1980). Gauging the relationship between self-efficacy judgement and action. *Cognitive Therapy and Research, 4,* 263–268.

Bandura, A. (1982). Self-efficacy mechanism in human agency. *American Psychologist, 37,* 122–147.

Benfari, R. C., Eaker, E. D., Ockene, J., & McIntyre, K. M. (1983). Hyperstress and outcomes in a long-term smoking intervention program. *Psychosomatic Medicine, 44,* 227–235.

Best, J. A. (1975). Tailoring smoking withdrawal procedures to personality and motivational differences. *Journal of Consulting and Clinical Psychology, 43,* 1–8.

Best, J. A. (1978). Targeting and self-selection of smoking modification methods. In J. L. Schwartz (Ed.), *Progress in smoking cessation: Proceedings of the International Conference on Smoking Cessation* (pp. 105–118). New York: American Cancer Society and World Health Organization.

Best, J. A., & Hakstian, A. R. (1978). A situation-specific model for smoking behavior. *Addictive Behaviors, 3,* 79–92.

Best, J. A., & Steffy, R. A. (1971). Smoking modification procedures tailored to subject characteristics. *Behavior Therapy, 2,* 177–191.

Best, J. A., & Steffy, R. A. (1975). Smoking modification procedures for internal and external locus of control clients. *Canadian Journal of Behavioural Science, 7,* 155–165.

Chambliss, C., & Murray, E. J. (1979). Cognitive procedures for smoking reduction: Symptom attribution versus efficacy attribution. *Cognitive Therapy and Research, 3,* 91-95.

Coelho, R. J. (1984). Self-efficacy and cessation of smoking. *Psychological Reports, 54,* 309-310.

Cohen, S., & Hoberman, H. M. (1983). Positive events and social supports as buffers of life change stress. *Journal of Applied Social Psychology, 13,* 99-125.

Cohen, S., Kamarck, T., & Mermelstein, R. (1983). A global measure of perceived stress. *Journal of Health and Social Behavior, 24,* 385-396.

Cohen, S., Mermelstein, R., Kamarck, T., & Hoberman, H. (1985). Measuring the functional components of social support. In I. Sarason & C. Spielberger (Eds.), *Social support: Theory, research and applications* (pp. 73-94). Dordrecht, The Netherlands: Martinus Nijhoff.

Colletti, G., Supnick, J. A., & Rizzo, A. A. (1981, August). *An analysis of relapse determinants for treated smokers.* Paper presented at the 89th annual convention of the American Psychological Association, Los Angeles.

Condiotte, M. M., & Lichtenstein, E. (1981). Self-efficacy and relapse in smoking cessation programs. *Journal of Consulting and Clinical Psychology, 49,* 648-658.

Curry, S., Marlatt, G. A., & Gordon, J. R. (1987). Abstinence violation effect: Validation of an attributional construct with smoking cessation. *Journal of Consulting and Clinical Psychology, 55,* 145-149.

Danaher, B. (1977). Rapid smoking and self-control in the modification of smoking behavior. *Journal of Consulting and Clinical Psychology, 45,* 1068-1075.

Danaher, B. G., & Lichtenstein, E. (1978). *Become an ex-smoker: A comprehensive program for permanent smoking control.* Englewood Cliffs, NJ: Prentice-Hall.

DiClemente, C. C. (1981). Self-efficacy and smoking cessation maintenance. *Cognitive Therapy and Research, 5,* 175-187.

DiClemente, C. C., Prochaska, J. O., & Gilbertini, M. (1985). Self-efficacy and the stages of self-change of smoking. *Cognitive Therapy and Research, 9,* 181-200.

Eiser, J. R. (1983). Smoking, addiction and decision-making. *International Review of Applied Psychology, 32,* 11-28.

Eiser, J. R., & Sutton, S. R. (1977). Smoking as a subjectively rational choice. *Addictive Behaviors, 2,* 129-134.

Erickson, L. M., Tiffany, S. T., Martin, E. M., & Baker, T. B. (1983). Aversive smoking therapies: A conditioning analysis of therapeutic effectiveness. *Behaviour Research and Therapy, 21,* 595-611.

Fishbein, M. (1982). Social psychological analysis of smoking behavior. In J. R. Eiser (Ed.), *Social psychology and behavioral medicine* (pp. 179-197). New York: Wiley.

Foss, R. (1973). Personality, social influence and cigarette smoking. *Journal of Health and Social Behavior, 14,* 279-286.

Glasgow, R. E., Klesges, R. C., Mizes, J. S., & Pechacek, T. F. (1985). Quitting smoking: Strategies and variables associated with success in a stop-smoking contest. *Journal of Consulting and Clinical Psychology, 53,* 905-912.

Godding, P. R., & Glasgow, R. E. (1985). Self-efficacy and outcome expectancy as predictors of controlled smoking status. *Cognitive Therapy and Research, 9,* 583-590.

Henderson, J. B., Hall, S. M., & Linton, H. L. (1979). Changing self-destructive behaviors. In G. C. Stone, F. Cohen, N. E. Adler, & Associates (Eds.), *Health psychology: A handbook* (pp. 141-160). San Francisco: Jossey-Bass.

James, W. H., Woodruff, A. B., & Werner, W. (1965). Effect of internal and external control upon changes in smoking behavior. *Journal of Consulting Psychology, 29,* 184-186.

Janis, I. L. (1983). *Short-term counseling.* New Haven, CT: Yale University Press.

Johnson, E. K., & Chamberlain, J. M. (1978). The treatment of smoking as a self-defeating behavior. *Journal of Psychology, 98,* 34-43.

Kaplan, G. D., & Cowles, A. (1978). Health locus of control and health value in the prediction of smoking reduction. *Health Education Monographs, 6,* 129–137.

Kilmann, P. R., Wagner, M. K., & Sotile, W. M. (1977). The differential impact of self-monitoring on smoking behavior: An exploratory study. *Journal of Clinical Psychology, 33,* 912–214.

Kirscht, J. P. (1983). Preventive health behavior: A review of research and issues. *Health Psychology, 2,* 277–301.

Kirscht, J. P., & Rosenstock, I. M. (1979). Patients' problems in following recommendations of health experts. In G. C. Stone, F. Cohen, N. E. Adler, & Associates (Eds.), *Health psychology: A handbook* (pp. 189–215). San Francisco: Jossey-Bass.

Klesges, R. C., Vasey, M. W., & Glasgow, R. E. (1984). *Evaluation of a worksite smoking competition program.* Unpublished manuscript, North Dakota State University.

Leventhal, H. (1968). Experimental studies of anti-smoking communications. In E. F. Borgatta & R. R. Evans (Eds.), *Smoking, health, and behavior* (pp. 95–121). Chicago: Aldine.

Lichtenstein, E., & Brown, R. A. (1980). Smoking cessation methods: Review and recommendations. In W. R. Miller (Ed.), *The addictive behaviours: Treatment of alcoholism, drug abuse, smoking, and obesity* (pp. 169–206). Oxford: Pergamon Press.

Lichtenstein, E., & Keutzer, C. S. (1967). Further normative and correlational data on the Internal–External (I-E) Control of Reinforcement Scale. *Psychological Reports, 21,* 1014–1016.

Marlatt, G. A., Curry, S., & Gordon, J. R. (1987). *Unaided smoking cessation: A prospective analysis.* Unpublished manuscript, University of Washington.

Marlatt, G. A., & Gordon, J. R. (1980). Determinants of relapse: Implications for the maintenance of behavior change. In P. O. Davidson & S. M. Davidson (Eds.), *Behavioral medicine: Changing health lifestyles* (pp. 410–452). New York: Brunner/Mazel.

Marlatt, G. A., & Gordon, J. R. (Eds.). (1985). *Relapse prevention: Maintenance strategies in the treatment of addictive behaviors.* New York: Guilford Press.

McIntyre, K., Lichtenstein, E., & Mermelstein, R. (1983). Self-efficacy and relapse in smoking cessation: A replication and extension. *Journal of Consulting and Clinical Psychology, 51,* 632–633.

Mischel, W. (1973). Toward a cognitive social learning reconceptualization of personality. *Psychological Review, 80,* 252–283.

Pechacek, T. F., & Danaher, B. G. (1979). How and why people quit smoking: A cognitive--behavioral analysis. In P. C. Kendall & S. D. Hollon (Eds.), *Cognitive behavioral intervention: Theory, research and procedures* (pp. 389–422). New York: Academic Press.

Pomerleau, O. F., Adkins, D., & Pertschuk, M. (1978). Predictors of outcome and recidivism in smoking cessation treatment. *Addictive Behaviors, 3,* 65–70.

Prochaska, J. O., & DiClemente, C. C. (1983). Stages and processes of self-change of smoking: Toward an integrative model of change. *Journal of Consulting and Clinical Psychology, 51,* 390–395.

Reed, H. B., & Janis, I. L. (1974). Effects of a new type of psychological treatment on smokers' resistance to warnings about health hazards. *Journal of Consulting and Clinical Psychology, 42,* 748.

Rosen, T. J., & Shipley, R. H. (1983). A stage analysis of self-initiated smoking reductions. *Addictive Behaviors, 8,* 268–272.

Rosenbaum, M. (1980). A schedule for assessing self-control behaviors: Preliminary findings. *Behavior Therapy, 11,* 109–121.

Rosenstock, I. M. (1974). The health belief model and preventive health behavior. *Health Education Monographs, 2,* 354–386.

Rotter, J. B. (1966). Generalized expectancies for internal versus external control of reinforcement. *Psychological Monographs, 80*(Whole No. 609).

Russell, M. A. H., Wilson, C., Taylor, C., & Baker, C. D. (1979). Effect of general practitioners' advice against smoking. *British Medical Journal, ii,* 231-235.

Shiffman, S. (1984). Coping with temptations to smoke. *Journal of Consulting and Clinical Psychology, 52,* 261-267.

Shiffman, S., Read, I., & Jarvik, M. E. (1981, August). *Self-efficacy changes following relapse crises.* Paper presented at the 89th annual convention of the American Psychological Association, Los Angeles.

Shipley, R. H. (1981). Maintenance of smoking cessation: Effect of follow-up letters, smoking motivation, muscle tension, and health locus of control. *Journal of Consulting and Clinical Psychology, 49,* 982-984.

Straits, B., & Sechrest, L. (1963). Further support of some findings about the characteristics of smokers and nonsmokers. *Journal of Consulting Psychology, 27,* 282.

Sutton, S. R., & Eiser, J. R. (1984). The effect of fear-arousing communications on cigarette smoking: An expectancy-value approach. *Journal of Behavioral Medicine, 7,* 13-33.

Tiffany, S. T., Martin, E. M., & Baker, T. B. (1986). Treatments for cigarette smoking: An evaluation of the contributions of aversion and counseling procedures. *Behaviour Research and Therapy, 24,* 437-452.

Velicer, W. F., DiClemente, C. C., Prochaska, J. O., & Brandenburg, N. (1985). Decisional balance measure for assessing and predicting smoking status. *Journal of Personality and Social Psychology, 48,* 1279-1289.

Wallston, K. A., Wallston, B. S., & DeVellis, R. (1978). Development of the Multidimensional Health Locus of Control (MHLC) scales. *Health Education Monographs, 6,* 160-170.

Weiner, B. (1974). *Achievement motivation and attribution theory.* Morristown, NJ: General Learning Press.

# 7

# OBJECTIVE MEASURES

**LYNN T. KOZLOWSKI**
*Addiction Research Foundation*
*University of Toronto*

**SEYMORE HERLING**
*Addiction Research Foundation*

## Introduction

This chapter deals with objective assessment procedures used in the treatment of smoking behavior. These procedures do not depend on what smokers tell us about their smoking; rather, they depend on either the biochemical or physical consequences of smoking behavior. Because up to 35% of those who claim to have stopped smoking after attending a smoking clinic have not actually done so (Delarue, 1973; Ohlin, Lundh, & Westling, 1976; Sillett, Wilson, Malcolm, & Ball, 1978; Wilcox, Hughes, & Roland, 1979), biochemical validation of posttreatment smoking status can be an important adjunct in any smoking treatment assessment.

The biochemical measures of smoking that we describe here are mainly the observed levels of constituents of tobacco smoke that are found in bodily fluids or expired air. The physical measures of smoking, on the other hand, are the objective signs of smoking behavior that are found in the tar stains of cigarette filters (Kozlowski, 1981, 1983b). Traditionally, analyses of cigarette filters have used the residue of nicotine in the spent filter to estimate so-called "mouth-level delivery" of smoke products to the smoker (e.g., Forbes, Robinson, Hanley, & Colburn, 1976). A more recent technique is based on identical principles, but uses ratings of the *appearance* of the tar stains in the filter to estimate mouth-level deliveries (Kozlowski, Rickert, Pope, & Robinson, 1982).

As for the debilitating and deadly biological consequences of smoking (U.S. Public Health Service, 1979), we think that all long-term, daily smokers should be encouraged to undergo thorough medical examinations whenever they enroll in smoking treatment programs. (This encouragement should be especially strong for those who smoke at least 20 cigarettes per day.) The examining physician should evaluate the client for indications of any smoking-related diseases. Early detection of smoking-related diseases is always advisable, and, in some instances, early evidence of the biological costs of smoking may make a smoker more willing to give up cigarettes.

Objective assessment procedures try to answer two questions as precisely and accurately as possible: (1) Do you smoke cigarettes? and (2) How much do you smoke? These procedures can be applied to treatments involving either smoking cessation or smoking reduction (Kozlowski, 1984). The other chapters on smoking in this volume have focused on assessment techniques for smoking cessation. We agree that cessation is the ideal goal of all smoking treatment, but biochemical and physical assessments are especially important in smoking reduction programs; without them, one can be seriously misled by reported changes in smoking rate.

For many purposes, no blood samples need be taken, no urine need be bottled, and no cigarette butts need be analyzed to classify human beings as smokers or nonsmokers. Resorting to a standard subjective assessment procedure will often suffice; if clients are asked about smoking as part of a general screening procedure, they will usually confess to their smoking status (Pettiti, Friedman, & Kahn, 1981). Because this chapter is directed to treatment professionals, it is reasonable to note that a smoker who is unwilling to admit to smoking cigarettes is also unlikely to be ready to receive smoking treatment. Also, from the clients' point of view, biochemical measures of their pretreatment smoking status (smoker vs. nonsmoker) offer little. Only clients with deep-set perceptual or psychological problems could fail to notice whether they are smokers. Biochemical measures of the presence or absence of smoking may be of more importance to the evaluator of smoking treatment programs than to the clients of these programs.

Objective assessment procedures should be crucial components of any smoking reduction or "controlled-smoking" program, because both clients and therapists can easily and unknowingly be misled about the success of a reduction therapy (Kozlowski, 1981, 1983a). With other drug problems, the obvious unit of consumption is also the unit of dose. When one drinks a bottle of beer, one can be confident about the dose of alcohol ingested. When a smoker is puffing on a cigarette, he or she is essentially in a race with the burning coal for the consumption of the tobacco column. Whenever the smoker takes a break between puffs, the burning coal is creating so-called "sidestream smoke." The smoke that issues from the smoker end of a cigarette as a result of the smoker's puffing is the "mainstream smoke." Smokers can differ dramatically in the kind and amount of puffing they do on cigarettes of even the same brand—both from individual smoker to individual smoker, and from cigarette to cigarette in the same smoker (e.g., Moody, 1980). Thus, the amount of smoke constituents ingested by an individual smoking a single cigarette can vary drastically.

The standard tar and nicotine ratings of cigarettes are derived from a highly regimented smoking of these cigarettes by a machine (one 35-ml puff per minute until a certain butt length is reached). The actual amount of tar, nicotine, and carbon monoxide (CO) delivered to a smoker can be determined more by a smoker's exact manner of smoking than by the standard tar and nicotine yields, and hence these values for machine smoking are not very good predictors of actual yields to smokers (Kozlowski, 1983a; Kozlowski, Rickert, Pope, Robinson, & Frecker, 1982). The lowest-yield cigarettes (1 mg tar) can be turned into medium- to high-yield cigarettes by simple adjustments in smoking behavior (Kozlowski, Rickert, Pope, Robinson, & Frecker, 1982).

Smoking reduction treatments should only be considered as a last resort; only after failing to give up cigarettes entirely should a client be offered a reduction program. We think that one of the key roles for biochemical techniques in smoking reduction programs is to demonstrate when they are obviously not successful. If a smoker tries to reduce intake of tar, nicotine, and CO by smoking fewer cigarettes per day and by smoking "low-yield" cigarettes, biochemical indicators can show when this effort is a success or failure (Kozlowski, 1984). Even so, it is often not appreciated that measurable reductions in exposure to smoke products may not produce equivalent reductions in disease risk. Benowitz, Kuyt, and Jacob (1982) have shown that despite substantial reduction in plasma nicotine levels (as the result of a switch to an experimental low-nicotine cigarette), the acute cardiovascular consequences of smoking are essentially unchanged. This study may give insight into why low-yield cigarettes have had little impact on cardiovascular consequences of smoking, despite their modest success in decreasing lung cancer risks (U.S. Public Health Service, 1981).

## Review of Biochemical Indicators

Four main biochemical correlates of smoking behavior are used to verify changes in smoking status: (1) CO in blood or expired air; (2) thiocyanate (SCN) in blood, urine, and saliva; (3) nicotine, primarily in blood or urine; and (4) cotinine in blood, urine, and saliva. The reader is referred to other recent reviews of biochemical indicators of smoking behavior (Benowitz, 1983; Orleans & Shipley, 1982a; Pechacek, Fox, Murray, & Luepker, 1984).

### Carbon Monoxide

CO is a combustion by-product present in tobacco smoke. During smoke inhalation, CO is rapidly absorbed across pulmonary alveoli into the bloodstream. Little or no CO is absorbed across the buccal mucosa (Guyatt,

Holmes, & Cumming, 1981; Stewart, 1975). In the blood, CO competes with oxygen for binding sites on hemoglobin to form carboxyhemoglobin (COHb). The half-life of CO in the body is approximately 3–5 hours, but it can be considerably less in physically active individuals (Hawkins, 1976; Stewart, 1975).

COHb levels can be measured directly from blood samples or estimated using noninvasive expired-air samples. Expired-air CO and COHb are highly correlated (e.g., $r = .97$: Wald, Idle, Boreham, & Bailey, 1981). The major advantages of expired-air CO as a indicator of smoking behavior are the strong relationship between expired-air CO and cigarette smoke exposure, the ease and speed of assessment, and the relatively low cost of sampling and equipment (see below).

Although low-level exposure to CO from sources other than tobacco smoke (e.g., industrial and auto exhaust, open fires, etc.) can produce CO levels in nonsmokers that are similar to those observed in light smokers (e.g., Stewart, 1975), nonsmokers in general have COHb levels that average only about 1%. In contrast, regular smokers have COHb levels above 4% (Table 7-1). If 2% COHb is used as a cutoff point, anywhere from 81% to 96% of smokers are classified correctly (sensitivity), whereas nonsmokers are almost always identified correctly (specificity—see Table 7-1). Similarly, if a concentration of 8 parts per million (ppm) CO in expired air is used as a cutoff point, 66% to 97% of smokers and 96% to 99% of nonsmokers are classified appropriately. The sensitivity of CO as an indicator of smoking status is enhanced if so-called "atypical" smokers (e.g., those who smoke less than half a pack per day, pipe and cigar smokers, noninhalers, etc.) are excluded from the calculations (Table 7-1).

The primary disadvantage of CO as a biochemical marker of smoking is its relatively short half-life. Thus, the time of day when samples are taken and time since the last cigarette was smoked become important considerations. Consequently, CO is less likely to distinguish nonsmokers from light smokers (e.g., those who smoke less than half a pack per day; e.g., Petitti *et al.*, 1981; Vogt, Selvin, Widdowson, & Hulley, 1977). In addition, because CO is absorbed into the bloodstream primarily across pulmonary alveoli, it will not identify smokers who do not inhale. Horan, Hackett, and Linberg (1978) suggest taking CO readings late in the day, because the lowest CO levels occur in the morning following overnight abstinence (see also Henningfield, Stitzer, & Griffiths, 1980). In fact, morning expired-air CO levels in smokers can approximate those of nonsmokers (Henningfield *et al.*, 1980), although in heavy smokers (e.g., 30 cigarettes/day), smoker-range levels of CO ($>4$%) can be detected even before the first cigarette of the day is smoked (Benowitz, Kuyt, & Jacob, 1982).

Despite CO's short half-life, positive correlations ($r$'s $= .27$–$.81$) have been shown between CO levels and self-reported daily smoking rates (e.g.,

TABLE 7-1.   Carbon Monoxide in Blood or Expired Air as an Indicator of Smoking Status

| Reference | Mean Nonsmokers[a] | Smokers[a] | Sensitivity | Specificity |
|---|---|---|---|---|
| *Carboxyhemoglobin (%)[b]* | | | | |
| Cohen & Bartsch (1980) | 1.1 | 4.5 | 83 | 81 |
| | (191) | (426) | | |
| Wald, Idle, Boreham, & Bailey (1981) | Means not given | | 81 | 99 |
| | (6,641) | (2,613) | | |
| Saloojee, Vesey, Cole, & Russell (1982) | 0.7 | 7.1 | 96 | 99 |
| | (79) | (360) | | |
| Pojer *et al.* (1984) | 0.9 | 4.4 | 88 | 98 |
| | (181) | (187) | | |
| *Expired-air CO concentration (ppm)[c]* | | | | |
| Vogt, Selvin, Widdowson, & Hulley | 4.9 | 17.5 | 88 | 96 |
| (1977); Vogt, Selvin, & Hulley (1979) | (44) | (98) | (99)[d] | |
| Petitti *et al.* (1981) | Means not given | | 66 | 99 |
| | (181) | (86) | (87)[d] | |
| Fortmann *et al.* (1984) | 4.6 | 27.3 | 97 | 96 |
| | (742) | (400) | | |

[a]Numbers in parentheses indicate number of nonsmokers or smokers studied.

[b]Cutoff point = 2%.

[c]Cutoff point = 8 ppm.

[d]Sensitivity values if "atypical" smokers are excluded (i.e., those who smoke less than half a pack per day, noninhalers, pipe or cigar smokers, etc.).

Cohen & Bartsch, 1980; Hawkins, Cole, & Harris, 1976; Hill, Haley, & Wynder, 1983; Jaffe, Kanzler, Friedman, Stunkard, & Verebey, 1981; Rickert & Robinson, 1981). Table 7-2 shows that both COHb and expired-air CO are positively related to the number of self-reported cigarettes smoked per day. Similarly, throughout the smoking day, the CO levels of individual smokers increase with the number of cigarettes smoked (Henningfield *et al.,* 1980), although after about 9 hours of smoking, CO levels tend to reach a plateau (Benowitz, Kuyt, & Jacob, 1982). In contrast to cigarettes smoked per day, neither cigarette brand nor CO yield (based on machine-smoked values) significantly predicts COHb levels (Jaffe *et al.,* 1981; Rickert & Robinson, 1981). Because CO levels are sensitive to recent changes in smoking rate (as a result of CO's short half-life) and to changes in smoking style (e.g., inhalation depth, etc.; Frederiksen & Martin, 1979), CO may be useful in providing immediate feedback on the results of changes in smoking habits (e.g., Martin & Frederiksen, 1980; Orleans and Shipley, 1982b; Stitzer & Bigelow, 1983).

TABLE 7-2.   Biochemical Indices of Smoking Behavior as a Function of Cigarettes Smoked per Day

| Biochemical marker | Reference | Cigarettes/day | | | | |
|---|---|---|---|---|---|---|
| | | 0 | 1-9 | 10-19 | 20-29 | >30 |
| COHb (%) | Cohen & Bartsch (1980) | 1.1 | 1.8 | 3.0 | 4.0 | 5.0 |
| | | (191) | (10) | (22) | (106) | (288) |
| | Hill, Haley, & Wynder (1983)[a] | – | 3.5 | 4.7 | 6.1 | 7.6 |
| | | | (88) | (224) | (115) | (70) |
| CO (ppm) | Vogt, Selvin, & Hulley (1979) | 4.9 | 8.4 | 12.0 | 15.1 | 21.2 |
| | | (44) | (13) | (8) | (21) | (56) |
| | Fortmann et al. (1984)[b] | 4.6 | 11.1 | – | 27.3 | – |
| | | (742) | (98) | | (400) | |
| SCN ($\mu$mol/liter) | Cohen & Bartsch (1980) | 73.5 | 123.5 | 141.9 | 169.6 | 189.0 |
| | | (191) | (10) | (22) | (106) | (228) |
| | Hill et al. (1983)[a] | – | 96.0 | 137.6 | 156.6 | 165.0 |
| | | | (81) | (207) | (100) | (44) |
| | Vogt et al. (1979) | 55.4 | 77.9 | 127.1 | 165.6 | 181.9 |
| | | (44) | (13) | (8) | (21) | (56) |
| | Fortmann et al. (1984)[b] | 53.1 | 89.4 | – | 163.7 | – |
| | | (970) | (121) | | (543) | |
| Cotinine (ng/ml) | Hill et al. (1983)[a] | – | 132.1 | 243.5 | 300.0 | 300.0 |
| | | | (88) | (231) | (119) | (72) |
| | Benowitz, Hall, et al. (1983)[c] | – | 170.0 | 259.3 | 257.6 | 373.6 |
| | | | (14) | (40) | (33) | (55) |

*Note.* Numbers in parentheses indicate number of subjects in each category.

[a]Values estimated from Figure 2, p. 443. For these data, cigarettes/day were categorized as follows: 1-10, 11-20, 21-30, >30.

[b]Values are averages for nonsmokers, light smokers who averaged 3.3 cigarettes/day, and regular smokers who averaged 22.5 cigarettes/day.

[c]Values estimated from Figure 2A, p. 141.

## Thiocyanate

Hydrogen cyanide, another compound present in high concentrations in tobacco smoke, is rapidly metabolized by the liver to SCN, which has a half-life in the body of approximately 2 weeks (Butts, Kueheman, & Widdowson, 1974). This long half-life makes SCN much less dependent than CO on the time of day when the sampling is done (Vogt et al., 1977). On the other hand, following smoking cessation, SCN levels decrease slowly, taking 3–6 weeks to reach nonsmokers' levels. Thus, unlike CO, SCN cannot be used to provide immediate feedback of changes in smoking status.

SCN levels can be measured in blood, urine, or saliva. Saliva sampling, however, is the least invasive, least expensive, and most sensitive in assessing smoking rate (Prue, Martin, & Hume, 1980). Although saliva levels are more variable than serum levels, SCN in saliva is 15–20 times higher than in serum (e.g., Pechacek, Luepker, Jacobs, Fraser, & Blackburn, 1979). SCN in urine is the least reliable, being influenced by urinary flow and other factors affecting excretion (Densen, Davidow, Bass, & Jones, 1967). Saliva samples of SCN are easily collected (using dental rolls held in the mouth for 2–3 minutes), are very stable, and store well (e.g., Pechacek, Murray, & Luepker, 1980; Prue *et al.*, 1980). Spectrophotometric procedures are used to analyze SCN, with costs being higher than those for expired-air CO (e.g., Prue *et al.*, 1980).

Although cyanides and thiocyanate are present in foods (particularly vegetables and beer), resulting in some overlap in SCN levels between smokers and nonsmokers, smokers on the average have levels two to four times higher than nonsmokers (Table 7-3). For example, Butts *et al.* (1974) demonstrated that nonsmokers averaged 44 $\mu$mol/liter of SCN, whereas cigarette smokers averaged 177 $\mu$mol/liter. Using 85 $\mu$mol/liter of SCN as a cutoff point, these investigators found 93% specificity and 98% sensitivity in classifying smokers and nonsmokers. Luepker *et al.* (1981) also found that a cutoff point of 85 $\mu$mol/liter could discriminate between adolescents smoking a few cigarettes per month and adolescents smoking less than 20 cigarettes per week, although the detection of light or infrequent adolescent smokers was more difficult. Several investigators have suggested 100 $\mu$mol/liter SCN as a cutoff point (see Table 7-3).

A number of studies have shown positive correlations between SCN and the number of self-reported cigarettes smoked per day ($r$'s = .25–.48; Cohen & Bartsch, 1980; Hill *et al.*, 1983; Rickert & Robinson, 1981; Vogt, Selvin, & Hulley, 1979; see also Table 7-2). Although these correlations

TABLE 7-3. SCN as a Biochemical Indicator of Smoking Status

| Reference | Mean | | Sensitivity | Specificity |
| --- | --- | --- | --- | --- |
| | Nonsmokers | Smokers | | |
| Vogt, Selvin, Widdowson, & Hulley (1977); Vogt, Selvin, & Hulley (1979) | 55.4 (44) | 160.1 (98) | 81 | 93 |
| Cohen & Bartsch (1980) | 73.5 (191) | 180.2 (426) | 93 | 81 |
| Fortmann *et al.* (1984) | 53.1 (970) | 163.7 (543) | 91 | 93 |

*Note.* Numbers in parentheses indicate number of nonsmokers or smokers studied. Cutoff point = 100 $\mu$mol/liter.

tend not to be as high as those found between daily smoking rate and CO, SCN has the advantage over CO of having a longer half-life; thus, SCN has been shown to be a reliable index of smoking abstinence 10–14 days after quitting (Pechacek et al., 1980; Prue et al., 1980). Moreover, the time of day when SCN sampling is done is not as critical as it is with CO.

## Nicotine and Cotinine

Nicotine in smoke is absorbed through the mucous membranes of the mouth, the bronchial tree, and the pulmonary alveoli. It is rapidly distributed throughout the body, and is primarily eliminated by metabolism to cotinine. Because nicotine metabolism can vary considerably (by as much as fourfold) among individual smokers (Benowitz, Jacob, Jones, & Rosenberg, 1982), a given level of nicotine in the body may reflect a fourfold difference in nicotine consumption. As noted by Benowitz (1983), in order "to [accurately] determine daily intake of nicotine . . . both nicotine blood concentrations and nicotine elimination rate must be measured, [a] procedure feasible for small-scale [not large-scale] studies" (p. 14). If nicotine levels are used to estimate exposure, it is probably best to measure plasma levels of nicotine late in the day, because nicotine blood concentrations reach a plateau after 6–8 hours of regular smoking (Benowitz, Kuyt, & Jacob, 1982).

Nicotine and its metabolic by-product, cotinine, are highly specific to tobacco users (cigarette, pipe and cigar smokers, users of smokeless tobaccos). However, it should be noted that persons using Nicorette® (nicotine-containing chewing gum) can have nicotine and cotinine levels indistinguishable from those of tobacco users, and that nonsmokers can have measurable amounts of nicotine and cotinine in plasma, saliva, and urine. These body levels of nicotine and cotinine in nonsmokers, however, are up to 200 times lower than those found in smokers (Jarvis, Tunstall-Pedoe, Feyerabend, Vesey, & Saloojee, 1984).

Approximately 90% of nicotine is metabolized to cotinine (Benowitz, 1983). Because cotinine has a longer half-life than nicotine (19–30 hours vs. 1–2 hours), it is often recommended over nicotine as a measure of tobacco exposure. Sampling time for cotinine is less critical than for nicotine. Regular smokers are almost always detected by urinary, blood, or salivary cotinine analyses. The average blood cotinine concentration in regular smokers is about 300 ng/ml (Langone, Van Vunakis, & Hill, 1975), whereas blood cotinine values in nonsmokers are never greater than 10 ng/ml (Benowitz, 1983). Salivary cotinine values are similar. In 94 smokers, Jarvis et al. (1984) found a mean salivary cotinine value of 310 ng/ml, compared to 1.7 ng/ml in 100 nonsmokers. Similarly, Haley, Axelrad, and Tilton

(1983) reported mean salivary cotinine levels of 361 ng/ml in 12 smokers, whereas cotinine was undetectable in the saliva of 18 nonsmokers. In addition to being able to distiguish between smokers and nonsmokers, cotinine values may be used in roughly estimating smoking rates, because positive correlations have been shown between blood cotinine concentrations and the number of cigarettes smoked per day ($r$'s = .34-.45; Rickert & Robinson, 1981; Hill *et al.*, 1983; Benowitz, *et al.*, 1983—see also Table 7-2).

Although methods are available for measuring nicotine and cotinine in urine, blood, and saliva, a number of factors recommend salivary cotinine for general screening. Urinary levels of nicotine are affected by urinary pH and flow rate, and individual variations in renal clearance of cotinine suggest that urinary levels of these compounds are not good quantitative predictors of their blood concentrations (Benowitz, 1983). Saliva samples for either nicotine or cotinine are easily obtainable, but salivary nicotine cannot be discriminated from unabsorbed nicotine deposited in the mouth. Salivary cotinine, on the other hand, is not limited in this way. The major drawback of nicotine and/or cotinine as biochemical markers of smoking is that methods for their quantification are relatively complicated and expensive. The major advantage, of course, is their specificity.

## Clinical Applications

### Screening and General Disposition

#### The Importance of Questionnaire Data

All smokers should be asked to indicate (1) the brand of cigarettes that they usually smoke, (2) the number of cigarettes usually smoked per day, (3) the number of cigarettes smoked prior to providing a breath or body fluid sample, and (4) the time at which they smoked their last cigarette. It is also important to ask smokers whether they inhale their tobacco smoke. Although asking people how *deeply* they inhale does not provide a valid quantitative estimate of actual inhalation (e.g., Stepney, 1982), those individuals who inhale minimally or not at all are usually able to report this fact accurately (Herling & Kozlowski, in press).

Noninhalers, even those smoking 10 or more cigarettes per day, and noninhaling pipe or cigar smokers can be extremely light smokers—almost "nonsmokers," from a toxicological perspective. For example, pipe and cigar smokers who do not inhale absorb little or no nicotine or CO (Turner, Sillett, & McNicol, 1977, 1981), although Wald, Idle, Boreham, Bailey, and Van Vunakis (1981) have shown that cotinine levels in pipe smokers can be as high as those found in cigarette smokers. Absence of inhalation in "primary" pipe and cigar smokers probably accounts for the lower incidence of heart and lung disease seen in these smokers (Doll & Peto, 1976). Similarly, measures of SCN and CO are generally unable to distinguish (inhaling) smokers of less than 10 cigarettes per day from nonsmokers (e.g., Petitti et al., 1981; Vogt et al., 1977, 1979). It is important to note, however, that light smokers (fewer than 10 cigarettes per day), even though not biochemically distinguishable from nonsmokers, have an increased risk of smoking-related diseases compared to nonsmokers (U.S. Public Health Service, 1979); thus smoking cessation should be a goal for light smokers as well as heavy smokers. Questionnaire information on cigarette brand, smoking rate, and style (e.g., inhalation depth), as well as other activities (exercise, diet), should be used to account for otherwise anomalous values obtained from biochemical tests (e.g., Petitti et al., 1981; Swan, Parker, Chesney, & Rosenman, 1985; Vogt et al., 1979).

In fact, Petitti et al. (1981) argue that self-reports of smoking habits in the setting of a prepaid medical care plan more accurately reflect smoking habits than do biochemical indices; moreover, they contend that the questionnaire data provide the standard against which serum SCN and expired-air CO need to be judged. These authors are especially concerned about the inability of the biochemical tests to distinguish between light smokers and nonsmokers. It may be that the detection of smoking by self-report is much better in a general screening program than in the follow-up phase of an organized smoking treatment program, where deception rates by confessed ex-smokers have been found to range up to 35% (Saloojee, Vesey, Cole, & Russell, 1982).

To determine the standard tar and nicotine yield of a client's cigarette, cigarette brand is another important piece of information that should be obtained. Smokers of low-yield (<15 mg tar) or of ultra-low-yield (<4 mg tar) cigarettes often believe that the risks to their health are minimal because they smoke low-yield cigarettes (Marsh & Matheson, 1983). However, smokers of these low-yield cigarettes can easily "compensate" for the reduced yields of these brands by smoking more cigarettes, by taking more puffs, and by inhaling more deeply (e.g., Kozlowski, 1983a). Biochemical and physical indicators (see below) can be used to raise questions in the client's mind about the "minimal risks" of low-tar cigarettes to his or her health.

Unfortunately, good normative tables do not exist for biochemical measures of smoking level. Any clinic seeing a large number of clients should develop its own norms. When a client who smokes low-yield cigarettes or just a few cigarettes per day displays high biochemical levels (e.g., above the 50th percentile), this information can be used to increase the client's motivation to try to give up smoking altogether. In Table 7-2, we have tried to approximate a "normative table" by compiling mean values for various biochemical indicators from some of the larger available data sets.

One should bear in mind, however, that individual differences in body levels of biochemical markers may be due to factors other than individual differences in the intake of cigarette smoke. For example, Benowitz, Jacob, Jones, and Rosenberg (1982) have shown that precisely calibrated intravenous injections of nicotine produce very different blood levels of nicotine in different individuals. Cotinine also appears to be affected by individual differences in pharmacokinetics (Benowitz, Kuyt, Jacob, Jones, & Osman, 1983). The presence of such individual differences means that these biochemical measures are most useful when repeated measures are made on the same individuals.

### The Problem of Hole Blocking on Ventilated-Filter Cigarettes

The most dramatic and easiest way to turn a low-yield into a high-yield cigarette is to block the ventilation holes on the filter (see Figure 7-1). The secret of the conventional 1-mg-tar cigarette is that about 80% of each puff is diluted with ambient air. Smokers of low-yield cigarettes can defeat the air dilution holes by blocking them with fingers, lips, or even tape (Kozlowski, Frecker, Khouw, & Pope, 1980). Certain brands (e.g., Barclay®) with special longitudinal ventilating channels in the filter appear to be susceptible to an unavoidable compromise (Consumers Union, 1983); furthermore, this kind of filter does not produce the stain patterns shown in Figure 7-1. The conventional ventilated-filter cigarette shows a "bull's-eye" tar stain when the ventilation holes are working properly. When the vents are blocked, the tar stain tends to spread to the outside of the filter. In cases of extreme blocking (e.g., with the lips), the tar stain forms a uniform field on the filter. Inspection of spent filters can be used, then, to indicate this misuse of low-yield cigarettes.

### Additional Considerations When Employing Biochemical Procedures

Any general screening procedure should be directed primarily toward identifying cigarette smokers, and secondarily toward identifying the heaviness of smoking. It must be remembered that not all pack-a-day smokers smoke equally. Presumably, the "heavier" pack-a-day smokers are in greater danger of developing smoking-related diseases (though, sadly, this belief has not been adequately tested). If one is concerned with the toxicology of cigarette smoking, biochemical measures of exposure to smoke toxins are of direct significance, and the self-reported cigarette intake is only an indirect measure of the risk to the smoker.

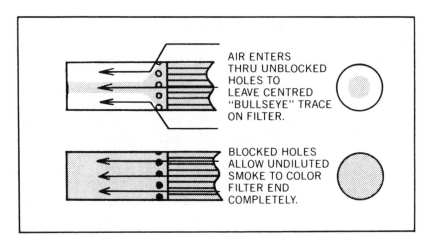

FIGURE 7-1. Stain patterns produced when ventilation holes of cigarettes are unblocked (top) or blocked (bottom). From *Tar and Nicotine Ratings May Be Hazardous to Your Health* by L. T. Kozlowski, 1982, Toronto: Alcoholism and Drug Addiction Research Foundation. Copyright 1982 by the Alcoholism and Drug Addiction Research Foundation. Reprinted by permission.

*Expired-Air CO*

If one begins using a biochemical indicator and does not have the collaboration of an analytical laboratory, we favor CO screening, using measures of expired-air CO (Horan *et al.,* 1978; Hughes, Frederiksen, & Frazier, 1978; Jarvis, Russell, & Saloojee, 1980; Jones, Ellicott, Cadigan, & Gaensler, 1958). The equipment to measure expired-air CO (e.g., Ecolyzer Model 2000, Energetics Science, Elmsford, NY 10523) is relatively inexpensive and simple to operate; it can be purchased for approximately $3,000 (U.S. dollars) and maintained for under $500 a year. An activated charcoal filter should be used to reduce the artificially high CO readings that may be obtained if a client has used alcohol (Hughes *et al.,* 1978). It is practical to have the expired-air CO analyzer set up and ready to use at any time, although the analyzer should be calibrated against a known CO concentration on a regular basis. With this type of equipment, clients (and therapists) can be given immediate feedback (e.g., Kopel, Rosen, Gajdus, & Gottlieb, 1975); one does not have to wait for a laboratory report. If samples do not need to be stored, disposable plastic bags are likely to be adequate, and it is possible to take several consecutive samples to obtain an average or median CO value.

Unlike more direct markers of tobacco intake (e.g., nicotine and its major metabolite, cotinine), CO levels can also be used to indicate toxicological problems possibly unrelated to cigarette smoking (e.g., a fault in a residential heating system; Cox & Whichelow, 1985). Clients who have high CO levels (and who deny smoking) should be evaluated for possible occupational or residential exposures to CO. This, of course, means that high CO levels may not be due to exposure to cigarette smoke, but at least the probing to discover the cause of these high levels may disclose some other toxicological problem needing correction.

It is suggested that anyone with a score of 9 ppm or above be questioned about smoking. Of course, abstinence from smoking for several hours will reduce CO levels dramatically, especially if aerobic exercise is engaged in (e.g., the elimination half-life of CO during exercise might be less than 1 hour, whereas during sleep it might be as much as eight times longer; Castleden & Cole, 1974; Wald, Howard, Smith, & Bailey, 1975). A test taken in the afternoon, assuming a "normal" morning of smoking, will be a better indicator of the heaviness of smoking than will a test taken in the morning. On the other hand, some minimum (standardized) length of time between smoking and CO sampling is often imposed, because smoking immediately prior to providing the sample will result in unusually high readings.

The sampling procedure is simple (Jones et al., 1958), although a number of slight variations on the standard procedure have been described. Basically, the client inhales fully, holds his or her breath for some specified period of time, and then exhales. Although various breath-holding times have been used, West (1984) recommends, when possible, that breath holds of 20 seconds be used. The initial portion of exhaled breath is usually discarded, and the remainder is collected in a plastic bag. Either immediately, or at some later time, the air in the bag can be measured for CO concentration using the CO analyzer.

In addition to providing the breath sample, the client should be asked a number of questions about his or her smoking and other activities on the day the sample is provided. For example, the amount and type of exercise engaged in should be noted. In addition, if the client has been exposed to unusually high CO sources other than tobacco smoke (e.g., heavy traffic areas, underground garages, open fires), this should be determined. Of course, the number of cigarettes smoked prior to providing the sample and the time since the last cigarette was smoked should be recorded.

## Cotinine

If one has ready access to an analytical laboratory (or can afford to pay for the laboratory work), we recommend salivary cotinine levels as a biochemical indicator of smoking behavior. Salivary cotinine is not necessarily better than plasma cotinine (although it is probably better than urinary cotinine), but it has the advantage over plasma cotinine in ease of collection.

Cotinine measures, in general, have the advantage over CO of having a longer half-life. Also, because cotinine is a metabolic product of nicotine, it is not as susceptible as CO to the problem of environmental sources of contamination. Finally, because of its specificity, cotinine is nearly an ideal measure for distinguishing between light smokers and nonsmokers. In addition, cotinine levels appear to be useful in estimating a nonsmoker's exposure to smoke (Jarvis *et al.*, 1984).

*Thiocyanate*

If one already has the facilities for performing SCN analyses, it is probably not worth abandoning this measure. SCN, however, because of its long half-life, is relatively insensitive to recent changes (less than a week long) in smoking habits. In addition, because of dietary confounds, SCN is not particularly useful in distinguishing between light smokers and nonsmokers. Swan *et al.* (1985) recommend that dietary questions be asked by those who employ SCN as a measure of tobacco smoke exposure; SCN levels indicative of smoking could be due to high intake of certain foods, particularly from the cabbage family (e.g., broccoli, cauliflower, spinach).

*Additional Considerations When Employing Physical Assessments*

If a client is trying to "cut down" by smoking a low-yield cigarette, the stain patterns on the filters of ventilated-filter cigarettes should be inspected. Indications of hole blocking are shown in Figure 7-1, above. Even if a smoker denies blocking the filter vents, it is possible that it is being done unintentionally (Kozlowski, Rickert, Pope, Robinson, & Frecker, 1982). Inspection of the stain patterns works best for cigarettes in the ultra-low-tar category (4 mg tar or less). Extreme cases of blocking will result in a uniform tar stain on the end of the filter.

Smokers should be given general information about the tar and nicotine yields of cigarettes and the problem of compensatory smoking. They should be told explicitly about the problem of hole blocking of ventilated-filter cigarettes. This information can be given in the form of a pamphlet or a brief lecture that describes how smoke yields are measured and how low-yield cigarettes can be turned into high-yield cigarettes (e.g., Kozlowski, 1982). Smokers should be told that if they do not miss their higher-yield cigarettes when they switch to a lower-yield cigarette, they may be compensating for the reduced yield by oversmoking in some way. It is hoped that such information about standard tar yields will increase the readiness of low-tar smokers to try to give up cigarettes completely.


## Defining the Problem

### *Biochemical Procedures*

A number of more precise and costly procedures are available for establishing a smoker's exposure to cigarette smoke constituents, but we doubt that any of them have much to add to treatment programs. Benowitz, Jacob, Jones, and Rosenberg (1982) developed an elegant procedure for estimating the actual dose of nicotine ingested by smokers. This procedure requires that a smoker be injected with a fixed dose of nicotine and have blood samples taken at regular intervals thereafter, to establish the pharmacokinetics of nicotine in that individual. With this information, plasma levels of nicotine after smoking can be used to calculate the ingested dose of nicotine (Benowitz & Jacob, 1984; cf. Feyerabend, Ings, & Russell, 1985).

Plasma nicotine, cotinine, and COHb are the mainstays of any more detailed biochemical assessments of cigarette smokers. If blood samples are being taken for other reasons, and if the analytical facilities are available, one might use these tests to resolve questions about anomalous scores obtained using simpler methods (i.e., expired-air CO, salivary cotinine, salivary SCN). Repetition or addition of one of the simpler methods, however, might be a less costly way to resolve anomalous scores.

Another use of plasma nicotine or cotinine values (salivary cotinine might be used as well) is to establish the effective levels achieved by users of nicotine-containing chewing gum (Nicorette®). Either underuse or overuse of the gum (caused either by chewing an inappropriate number of gums per day or by improper chewing technique) can be detected by such assays.


### *Physical Procedures*

Analyses of residual nicotine in cigarette butts do provide an estimate of the mouth-level exposure to nicotine (e.g., Robinson, Young, & Rickert, 1982). Although estimates of mouth-level exposure improve upon the information available from standard yields, they are not as useful as biochemical indicators of exposure (cf. Kozlowski, 1983b). As discussed above, cigarette filters should be inspected for signs of hole blocking.

## Monitoring Progress and Follow-Up Assessment

### Smoking Reduction Programs

*Biochemical Procedures*

When monitoring is used in smoking reduction programs, it is crucial to work with repeated measures on the same individuals. Any of the biochemical screening procedures discussed above are suitable. If immediate feedback is not required, cotinine and SCN have the advantage over CO and nicotine of being insensitive to recent changes in smoking behavior. A corollary of this insensitivity is that the interval between sampling (to determine if changes in smoking status or rate have taken place) should not be too short. On the other hand, with CO or nicotine as measures, a smoker could adjust his or her smoking behavior the day before a measurement session, and thus would be able to produce unrepresentative low levels.

*Physical Procedures*

If the smoker has decided to try a very-low-yield brand (or to stop blocking vent holes on a current low-yield brand), cigarette butts should be examined for evidence of hole blocking. A color-matching scale (Kozlowski, Rickert, Pope, & Robinson, 1982) can be used to give a smoker feedback about certain kinds of intensive smoking; however, this procedure is too experimental to be used without the support of information from a standard biochemical indicator.

### Smoking Cessation Programs

Unless one is willing to propose a garbology of cigarette butts (searching a client's garbage for cigarette butts), we know of no use for our physical indicators in treatments that are directed to smoking cessation. The biochemical procedures used in screening should be repeated to provide the best indication of successful abstinence.

### Case Example

R. J. reported smoking an average of 40 cigarettes per day when he presented to a brief group program for smoking cessation. At the beginning of the first of three 1-hour sessions, alveolar CO measures were taken on all clients. R. J.'s alveolar CO was 83 ppm, and he was advised that this level was very high. The scores of the other four clients in the group ranged from 20 to 45 ppm. R. J. was told that his score was higher than that found in most other cigarette smokers. As a first stage in the treatment program, clients were asked to reduce their cigarette intake as much as possible, both by switching to 1-mg-tar brands and by reducing the number of cigarettes smoked per day as much as possible.

By the second session (1 week later), R. J. was pleased to report that he had cut his intake in half (from 40 to 20 cigarettes) and had been smoking a 1-mg-tar cigarette with no difficulty for the entire week. The alveolar CO test revealed that he still had very high CO levels—75 ppm. Inspection of the stain pattern of spent cigarette butts showed that he had been blocking the filter vent holes, probably with his lips. R. J. was advised that he had been subverting the possible benefits of his reduction program by over-smoking his reduced number of cigarettes. This information was used to emphasize the necessity of his going without cigarettes entirely. After agreeing to a quit date, R. J. was given a prescription for Nicorette® as a substitute for smoking.

By the third session (after a week on Nicorette®), R. J. had stopped smoking completely and gave a CO sample of 6 ppm, fully consistent with the report of abstinence. His former scores (83 and 75 ppm) were explicitly compared with his new score, and it was indicated that this impressive reduction in CO exposure was probably very worthwhile.

Two weeks later, R. J. phoned the clinic, concerned that he might be chewing too much Nicorette® (i.e., getting too much nicotine per day). He was told that his reported consumption (30 pieces of 2-mg gum per day) was at the high end of the normal range, and he was advised to cut down as much as he comfortably could. Within a week, he reported that his use was down to 15 pieces per day, so no tests of urinary or plasma nicotine were deemed necessary to evaluate this case.

For the sake of "success" statistics kept by the clinic, R. J. agreed to provide breath samples at 3-month, 6-month, and 1-year follow-ups. He reported uninterrupted abstinence since leaving the clinic. His breath samples were consistent with not smoking—less than 6 ppm.

## Conclusion

A number of biochemical indicators of smoking are suggested for measuring the cigarette smoke consumption of individuals in smoking treatment programs. The particular measure used should be determined by the resources available and the particular needs of the smoking treatment program. Expired-air CO and salivary SCN are relatively inexpensive measures that are capable of distinguishing between regular smokers and nonsmokers, but are less useful for differentiating between light smokers and nonsmokers. Expired-air CO may be preferred if immediate feedback of smoking status or rate is required, whereas SCN may be used if relatively long intervals between samples are needed to negate short-term (e.g., 1-day) changes in smoking behavior. Nicotine and cotinine are more expensive and complicated measures, but both assays are more specific to tobacco smoke exposure than either SCN or CO, are capable of distinguishing between light smokers and nonsmokers, and have been used to measure secondhand tobacco smoke exposure in nonsmokers (Jarvis *et al.,* 1984). Moreover, both nicotine and cotinine assays can be used to measure exposure to smokeless tobaccos and Nicorette®. Because cotinine has a longer half-life, the time of day when sampling is done for cotinine is less critical than it is for nicotine. Useful, but more limited, information about smoking can be gained from the inspection of stain patterns on the filters of ventilated-filter cigarettes. Such inspection can be used in assessing the intensity of smoking among smokers of low-yield cigarettes.

## Acknowledgments

The writing of this chapter was supported in part by NSERC Canada Grant No. A1036. The opinions expressed in this chapter are our own and do not necessarily reflect those of the Addiction Research Foundation, Ontario.

## References

Benowitz, N. L. (1983). The use of biologic fluid samples in assessing tobacco smoke consumption. In J. Grabowski & C. S. Bell (Eds.), *Measurement in the analysis and treatment of smoking behavior* (NIDA Research Monograph No. 48, pp. 6–26). Washington, DC: U.S. Government Printing Office.

Benowitz, N. L., Hall, S. M., Herning, R. I., Jacob, P., III, Jones, R. T., & Osman, A.-L. (1983). Smokers of low-yield cigarettes do not consume less nicotine. *New England Journal of Medicine, 309,* 139–142.

Benowitz, N. L., & Jacob, P., III. (1984). Daily intake of nicotine during cigarette smoking. *Clinical Pharmacology and Therapeutics, 35,* 499–504.

Benowitz, N. L., Jacob, P., III, Jones, R. T., & Rosenberg, J. (1982). Interindividual variability in the metabolism and cardiovascular effects of nicotine in man. *Journal of Pharmacology and Experimental Therapeutics, 221,* 368–372.

Benowitz, N. L., Kuyt, F., & Jacob, P., III. (1982). Circadian blood nicotine concentrations during cigarette smoking. *Clinical Pharmacology and Therapeutics, 32,* 758–764.

Benowitz, N. L., Kuyt, F., Jacob, P., III, Jones, R. T., & Osman, A.-L. (1983). Cotinine disposition and effects. *Clinical Pharmacology and Therapeutics, 34,* 604–611.

Butts, W. C., Kueheman, M., & Widdowson, G. M. (1974). Automated method for determining serum thiocyanate to distinguish smokers from nonsmokers. *Clinical Chemistry, 20,* 1344–1348.

Castleden, C. M., & Cole, P. V. (1974). Variations in carboxyhaemoglobin levels in smoking. *British Medical Journal, iv,* 736–738.

Cohen, J. D., & Bartsch, G. E. (1980). A comparison between carboxyhemoglobin and serum thiocyanate determinations as indicators of cigarette smoking. *American Journal of Public Health, 70,* 284–286.

Consumers Union. (1983). The ultra-low-tar gimmick. *Consumer Reports,* pp. 26–27, 50.

Cox, B. D., & Whichelow, M. J. (1985). Carbon monoxide levels in the breath of smokers and nonsmokers: Effect of domestic heating systems. *Journal of Epidemiology and Community Health, 39,* 75–78.

Delarue, N. C. (1973). A study in smoking withdrawal. *Canadian Journal of Public Health, 64,* 5–19.

Densen, P. M., Davidow, B., Bass, H. E., & Jones, E. W. (1967). A chemical test for smoking exposure. *Archives of Environmental Health, 14,* 865–874.

Doll, R., & Peto, R. (1976). Mortality in relation to smoking: 20 years observation on male British doctors. *British Medical Journal, ii,* 1525–1536.

Feyerabend, C., Ings, R. M., & Russell, M. A. H. (1985). Nicotine pharmacokinetics and its application to intake from smoking. *British Journal of Clinical Pharmacology, 19,* 239–247.

Forbes, W. F., Robinson, J. C., Hanley, J. A., & Colburn, H. N. (1976). Studies on the nicotine exposure of individual smokers: I. Changes in mouth-level exposure to nicotine on switching to lower-nicotine cigarettes. *International Journal of the Addictions, 11,* 933–950.

Fortmann, S. P., Rogers, T., Vranizan, K., Haskell, W. L., Solomon, D. S., & Farquhar, J. W. (1984). Indirect measures of cigarette use: Expired-air Carbon monoxide versus plasma thiocyanate. *Preventive Medicine, 13,* 127–135.

Frederiksen, L. W., & Martin, J. E. (1979). Carbon monoxide and smoking behavior. *Addictive Behaviors, 4,* 21–30.

Guyatt, A. R., Holmes, M. A., & Cumming, G. (1981). Can carbon monoxide be absorbed from the upper respiratory tract in man? *European Journal of Respiratory Diseases, 62,* 383–390.

Haley, N. J., Axelrad, C. M., & Tilton, K. A. (1983). Validation of self-reported smoking behavior: Biochemical analyses of cotinine and thiocyanate. *American Journal of Public Health, 73,* 1204–1207.

Hawkins, L. (1976). Blood carbon monoxide levels as a function of daily cigarette consumption and physical activity. *British Journal of Industrial Medicine, 33,* 123–125.

Hawkins, L. H., Cole, P. V., & Harris, J. R. W. (1976). Smoking habits and carbon monoxide levels. *Environmental Research, 11,* 310–318.

Henningfield, J. E., Stitzer, M. L., & Griffiths, R. R. (1980). Expired air carbon monoxide accumulation and elimination as a function of number of cigarettes smoked. *Addictive Behaviors, 5,* 265–272.

Herling, S., & Kozlowski, L. T. (in press). The importance of direct questions about inhalation and daily intake in the evaluation of pipe and cigar smokers. *Preventive Medicine.*

Hill, P., Haley, N. J., & Wynder, E. L. (1983). Cigarette smoking: Carboxyhemoglobin, plasma nicotine, cotinine and thiocyanate versus self-reported smoking data and cardiovascular disease. *Journal of Chronic Diseases, 36,* 439–449.

Horan, J. J., Hackett, G., & Linberg, S. E. (1978). Factors to consider when using expired air carbon monoxide in smoking assessment. *Addictive Behaviors, 3,* 25–28.

Hughes, J. R., Frederiksen, L. W., & Frazier, M. (1978). Instrumentation and techniques: A carbon monoxide analyzer for measurement of smoking behavior. *Behavior Therapy, 9,* 293–296.

Jaffe, J. H., Kanzler, M., Friedman, L., Stunkard, A. J., & Verebey, K. (1981). Carbon monoxide and thiocyanate levels in low tar/nicotine smokers. *Addictive Behaviors, 6,* 337–343.

Jarvis, M. J., Russell, M. A. H., & Saloojee, Y. (1980). Expired air carbon monoxide: A simple breath test of tobacco smoke intake. *British Medical Journal, 281,* 484–485.

Jarvis, M., Tunstall-Pedoe, H., Feyerabend, C., Vesey, C., & Saloojee, Y. (1984). Biochemical markers of smoke absorption and self-reported exposure to passive smoking. *Journal of Epidemiology and Community Health, 38,* 335–339.

Jones, R. H., Ellicott, M. F., Cadigan, J. B., & Gaensler, E. A. (1958). The relationship between alveolar and blood carbon monoxide concentrations during breathholding: Simple estimation of COHb saturation. *Journal of Laboratory and Clinical Medicine, 51,* 553–564.

Kopel, S., Rosen, R., Gajdus, E., & Gottlieb, H. (1975). *Carbon monoxide monitoring: Clinical and research utility for smoking reduction.* Paper presented at the ninth annual meeting of the Association for Advancement of Behavior Therapy, San Francisco.

Kozlowski, L. T. (1981). Application of some physical indicators of cigarette smoking. *Addictive Behaviors, 6,* 213–219.

Kozlowski, L. T. (1982). *Tar and nicotine ratings may be hazardous to your health.* Toronto: Alcoholism and Drug Addiction Research Foundation.

Kozlowski, L. T. (1983a). Perceiving the risks of low-yield ventilated-filter cigarettes: The problem of hole-blocking. In V. Covello, W. G. Flamm, J. Rodericks, & R. Tardiff (Eds.), *Proceedings of the International Workshop on the Analysis of Actual versus Perceived Risks* (pp. 175–182). New York: Plenum.

Kozlowski, L. T. (1983b). Physical indicators of actual tar and nicotine yields of cigarettes. In J. Grabowski & C. S. Bell (Eds.), *Measurement in the analysis and treatment of smoking behavior* (NIDA Research Monograph No. 48, pp. 50–61). Washington, DC: U.S. Government Printing Office.

Kozlowski, L. T. (1984). Pharmacological approaches to smoking modification. In J. D. Matarazzo, S. M. Weiss, J. A. Herd, N. E. Miller, & S. M. Weiss (Eds.), *Behavioral health: A handbook of health enhancement and disease prevention* (pp. 729–754). New York: Wiley.

Kozlowski, L. T., Frecker, R. C., Khouw, V., & Pope, M. A. (1980). The misuse of "less-hazardous" cigarettes and its detection: Hole-blocking of ventilated filters. *American Journal of Public Health, 72,* 597–599.

Kozlowski, L. T., Rickert, W. S., Pope, M. A., & Robinson, J. C. (1982). A color-matching technique for monitoring tar/nicotine yields to smokers. *American Journal of Public Health, 72,* 597–599.

Kozlowski, L. T., Rickert, W, S., Pope, M. A., Robinson, J. C., & Frecker, R. C. (1982). Estimating the yield to smokers of tar, nicotine, and carbon monoxide from the "lowest-yield" ventilated filter cigarettes. *British Journal of Addiction, 77,* 159–165.

Langone, J. J., Van Vunakis, H., & Hill, P. (1975). Quantitation of cotinine in sera of smokers. *Research Communications in Chemical Pathology and Pharmacology, 10,* 21–28.

Luepker, R. V., Pechacek, T. F., Murray, D. M., Johnson, C. A., Hund, F., & Jacobs, D. R. (1981). Saliva thiocyanate: A chemical indicator of cigarette smoking in adolescents. *American Journal of Public Health, 71,* 1320–1324.

Marsh, A., & Matheson, J. (1983). *Smoking attitudes and behaviour.* London: Office of Population Censuses and Surveys.

Martin, J. E., & Frederiksen, L. W. (1980). Self-tracking of carbon monoxide levels by smokers. *Behavior Therapy, 11,* 577–587.

Moody, P. M. (1980). The relationships of quantified human smoking behavior and demographic variables. *Social Science and Medicine, 14A,* 49–54.

Ohlin, P., Lundh, B., & Westling, H. (1976). Carbon monoxide blood levels and reported cessation of smoking. *Psychopharmacology, 49,* 263–265.

Orleans, C. S., & Shipley, R. H. (1982a). Assessment in smoking cessation research: Some practical guidelines. In F. J. Keefe & J. A. Blumenthal (Eds.), *Assessment strategies in behavioral medicine* (pp. 261–294). New York: Grune & Stratton.

Orleans, C. S., & Shipley, R. H. (1982b). Worksite smoking cessation initiatives: Review and recommendations. *Addictive Behaviors, 7,* 1-16.

Pechacek, T. F., Fox, B. H., Murray, D. M., & Luepker, R. V. (1984). Review of techniques for measurement of smoking behavior. In J. D. Matarazzo, S. M. Weiss, J. A. Herd, N. E. Miller, & S. M. Weiss (Eds.), *Behavioral health: A handbook of health enhancement and disease prevention* (pp. 729-754). New York: Wiley.

Pechacek, T. F., Luepker, R., Jacobs, D., Fraser, G., & Blackburn, H. (1979). Effect of diet and smoking on serum and saliva thiocyanates. *Cardiovascular Disease Epidemiology Newsletter, 27,* 96.

Pechacek, T. F., Murray, D. M., & Luepker, R. V. (1980). *Saliva sample collection manual: Version II.* Minneapolis: University of Minnesota, School of Public Health, Health Behaviors Measurement Laboratory.

Petitti, D. B., Friedman, G. D., & Kahn, W. (1981). Accuracy of information on smoking habits provided on self-administered research questionnaires. *American Journal of Public Health, 71,* 308-311.

Pojer, R., Whitfield, J. B., Poulos, V., Eckhard, I. F., Richmond, R., & Hensley, W. J. (1984). Carboxyhemoglobin, cotinine, and thiocyanate assay compared for distinguishing smokers from non-smokers. *Clinical Chemistry, 30,* 1377-1380.

Prue, D., Martin, J., & Hume, A. (1980). A critical evaluation of thiocyanate as a biochemical index of smoking exposure. *Behavior Therapy, 11,* 368-379.

Rickert, W. S., & Robinson, J. C. (1981). Estimating the hazards of less hazardous cigarettes: II. Study of cigarette yields of nicotine, carbon monoxide, and hydrogen cyanide in relation to levels of cotinine, carboxyhemoglobin, and thiocyanate in smokers. *Journal of Toxicology and Environmental Health, 7,* 391-403.

Robinson, J. C., Young, J. C., & Rickert, W. S. (1982). A comparative study of the amount of smoke absorbed from low yield ("less hazardous") cigarettes. Part I: Non-invasive measures. *British Journal of Addiction, 77,* 383-397.

Saloojee, Y., Vesey, C. J., Cole, P. V., & Russell, M. A. H. (1982). Carboxyhaemoglobin and plasma thiocyanate: Complementary indicators of smoking behaviour? *Thorax, 37,* 521-525.

Sillett, R., Wilson, M., Malcolm, R., & Ball, K. (1978). Deception among smokers. *British Medical Journal, ii,* 1185-1186.

Stepney, R. (1982). Are smokers' self-reports of inhalation a useful measure of smoke exposure? *Journal of Epidemiology and Community Health, 36,* 109-112.

Stewart, R. D. (1975). The effect of carbon monoxide on humans. *Annual Review of Pharmacology, 15,* 409-425.

Stitzer, M. L., & Bigelow, G. E. (1983). Contingent reinforcement for reduced carbon monoxide levels in cigarette smokers. *Addictive Behaviors, 7,* 403-412.

Swan, G. E., Parker, S. D., Chesney, M. A., & Rosenman, R. H. (1985). Reducing the confounding effects of environment and diet on saliva thiocyanate values in exsmokers. *Addictive Behaviors, 10,* 187-190.

Turner, J. A. M., Sillett, R. W., & McNicol, M. W. (1977). Effect of cigar smoking on carboxyhaemoglobin and plasma nicotine concentrations in primary pipe and cigar smokers and ex-cigarette smokers. *British Medical Journal, ii,* 1387-1389.

Turner, J. A. M., Sillett, R. W., & McNicol, M. W. (1981). The inhaling habits of pipe smokers. *British Journal of Diseases of the Chest, 75,* 71-76.

U.S. Public Health Service. (1979). *Smoking and health: A report of the Surgeon General* (DHHS Publication No. 79-50066). Washington, DC: U.S. Government Printing Office.

U.S. Public Health Service. (1981). *The health consequences of smoking: The changing cigarette* (DHHS Publication No. 81-50156). Washington, DC: U.S. Government Printing Office.

Vogt, T. M., Selvin, S., & Hulley, S. B. (1979). Comparison of biochemical and questionnaire estimates of tobacco exposure. *Preventive Medicine, 8,* 23-33.

Vogt, T. M., Selvin, S., Widdowson, G., & Hulley, S. B. (1977). Expired air carbon monoxide and serum thiocyanate as objective measures of cigarette exposure. *American Journal of Public Health, 67,* 545-549.

Wald, N. J., Howard, S., Smith, P. G., & Bailey, A. (1975). Use of carboxyhaemoglobin levels to predict the development of diseases associated with cigarette smoking. *Thorax, 30,* 133-140.

Wald, N. J., Idle, M., Boreham, J., & Bailey, A. (1981). Carbon monoxide in breath in relation to smoking and carboxyhaemoglobin levels. *Thorax, 36,* 366-369.

Wald, N. J., Idle, M., Boreham, J., Bailey, A., & Van Vunakis, H. (1981). Serum cotinine levels in pipe smokers: Evidence against nicotine as a cause of coronary heart disease. *Lancet, ii,* 775-777.

West, R. J. (1984). The effect of duration of breath-holding on expired air carbon monoxide concentration in cigarette smokers. *Addictive Behaviors, 9,* 307-309.

Wilcox, R. G., Hughes, J., & Roland, J. (1979). Verification of smoking history in patients after infarction using urinary nicotine and cotinine measurements. *British Medical Journal, ii,* 1026-1028.

# IV

# EATING BEHAVIORS
# AND DISORDERS

# 8

# BEHAVIORAL AND COGNITIVE-BEHAVIORAL ASSESSMENT

**D. BALFOUR JEFFREY**
*University of Montana*

**BRENDA DAWSON**
*University of Southern Mississippi*

**GREGORY L. WILSON**
*Washington State University*

## Introduction

Over the last two decades, researchers and practitioners have witnessed rapid advances in the assessment and treatment of eating disorders. Since Stuart's (1967) initial investigation of a behavioral treatment for obesity, the popularity of such weight loss programs has grown at a phenomenal rate, with millions of individuals participating in treatment every year (Brownell, 1981; Stunkard, 1980). However, early behavioral assessment and evaluation of treatment programs were often simplistic and lacking in experimental rigor. Weight change was frequently employed as the sole dependent measure. Attention to multidimensional measures of eating disorders provides for a more sophisticated assessment, treatment, and evaluation of eating disorders.

Until recently, behavioral and cognitive assessments have represented somewhat different strategies in the evaluation of eating disorders. However, current research efforts can be characterized as a combination of behavioral and cognitive components in the assessment and treatment of eating disorders. Clearly, a combination of such strategies represents a more comprehensive approach to the assessment and subsequent treatment of obesity, anorexia nervosa, and bulimia nervosa.

In this chapter, a variety of behavioral and cognitive–behavioral strategies in the assessment of eating disorders are presented. In particular, the following four topics are covered: (1) etiologies of obesity and a behavioral perspective on the assessment of obesity; (2) assessments of adult obesity;

(3) assessments of childhood obesity; and (4) assessments of anorexia nervosa and bulimia nervosa.

## Etiologies of Obesity and a Behavioral Perspective on the Assessment of Obesity

Most theorists no longer view obesity as a unitary disorder, but regard it as a multifaceted disorder caused by several different classes of etiological factors (Brownell, 1981; Jeffrey & Knauss, 1981; Stunkard, 1978). Research indicates that obesity is multiply determined by a number of physiological and psychosocial factors. Thus, a comprehensive behavioral assessment must include multidimensional measures of obesity from a variety of etiological perspectives to insure (1) a complete analysis of the problem and (2) development of an appropriate treatment program. A brief review of some of the major etiological factors of obesity is presented here, to provide a perspective on the range of variables that need to be assessed in the development of appropriate treatment programs. (See Jeffrey & Knauss, 1981, for a more detailed review of the etiologies of obesity.)

### Physiological Etiologies

Physiological studies of obesity have focused on the organic processes responsible for the development and maintenance of body weight. Obesity is conceptualized as a malfunction or alteration in the regulatory system of body weight that leads to the excessive accumulation of adipose tissue. This tissue is composed of special body cells, or adipocytes, in which body fat in the form of esterified fatty acids is stored. Correlational investigations have demonstrated that obesity tends to occur in families (e.g., Mayer, 1957; Withers, 1964). In a large investigation, Hartz, Giefer, and Rimm (1977) collected data from approximately 10,000 individuals and reported that hereditary factors accounted for 11% of the variance of obesity, whereas the family environment accounted for 35%.

Metabolic determinants of obesity have gained increasing attention from researchers (Nisbett, 1972; Powley & Keesey, 1970; Stunkard & Mahoney, 1976). In a year's time, the average person of normal weight consumes over 1 million calories, but there is little variation in body weight because a comparable number of calories are used in bodily maintenance and activity (Jeffrey & Katz, 1977). An error in regulation of 10% in either intake or expenditure would lead to a 30-pound change in body weight within a year. It can be concluded that in normal-weight individuals, body weight is regulated with extraordinary accuracy (Stunkard & Mahoney, 1976). Moreover, research suggests that the hypothalamus is directly linked to weight regulation, containing a satiety and feeding center that maintains body weight (Kennedy, 1957; Powley & Keesey, 1970). Some studies have shown that, rather than causing obesity, metabolic and endocrinological anomalies actually result from increases in adipose tissue (Sims & Horton, 1968).

*Psychosocial Etiologies*

Before examining the impact of specific psychosocial factors in the etiology of obesity, it is necessary to distinguish among hunger, appetite, and energy balance (Kaplan & Kaplan, 1957). "Hunger" is defined as an urge to eat based upon physiological cues signaling the depletion of somatic nutrient reserves. In contrast, "appetite" refers to the urge to eat, which is determined by social learning and other psychological factors. People eat in response to both hunger and appetite cues (Jeffrey & Knauss, 1981). Appetite may stimulate an individual to eat when no hunger signals are present or to continue eating after physiological satiety has been achieved. "Energy balance" is another important concept in understanding psychosocial etiologies and assessments of obesity (Jeffrey & Katz, 1977; Stunkard, 1980). A positive energy balance is created when caloric intake is greater than calorie expenditure. Excess calories are stored as fat, and the individual gains weight. When caloric expenditure exceeds caloric consumption, a negative energy balance is created. This negative balance leads to consumption of stored fat and weight loss.

Social learning theorists have undertaken a functional analysis of behaviors that are critical to the development and maintenance of obesity. Although the etiological influence of hereditary and metabolic variables is not denied, social learning processes are seen as playing the major etiological role in most cases of obesity. A social learning theory of obesity is based on the previously discussed concept of energy balance and the assumption that our eating and physical activity habits, good or bad, are mostly acquired patterns of behavior. Thus, social learning theory specifically focuses on the acquisition and maintenance of behaviors that result from environmental factors. This conceptualization has clear implications in the assessment and subsequent treatment of an eating disorder. The first eating disorder to be discussed here is adult obesity.

## Assessments of Adult Obesity

Initially, a thorough assessment needs to be undertaken to identify the problem behaviors, their causes, and the treatment goals. In addition to the initial assessment that we conduct during the first two to three sessions, we also use this assessment information during the later treatment sessions, and conduct more detailed assessment on specific problem behaviors during the treatment stage. We thus view assessment as an ongoing process that interacts with the treatment process (Jeffrey & Katz, 1977; Knauss & Jeffrey, 1981). In this section, a number of assessment variables and procedures are presented first; a case example is then presented to illustrate the use of these assessment procedures.

## Criteria for Obesity

Broadly defined, "obesity" represents an excess of stored body fat from caloric intake that is greater than the caloric expenditure required for physical activity, somatic maintenance, and growth. Criteria of obesity employed in behavioral research typically range from 10% to 20% over ideal weight (Jeffrey & Knauss, 1981). Bray (1978) has advocated employing 30% over ideal weight as the criterion for clinical obesity. Some epidemiological research has demonstrated that there is no significant increase in medical disorders for individuals under 30% over ideal weight; however, beyond this point, there is a rapid rise in disorders related to obesity with every percentage of increase over ideal weight.

## Weight

Absolute body weight (pounds or kilograms) is a useful measure in clinical practice because it is easily understood and allows comparison with previous research reports (Brownell, 1982). However, it is not an adequate assessment of weight loss per se. For example, it is evident that a 20-pound weight loss has a very different significance for a 150-pound client than for a 300-pound client. Moreover, because muscle tissue is heavier than adipose tissue, reductions in absolute weight may not directly correspond with decreases in body fat resulting from exercise programs.

Whereas absolute weight does not account for a variety of factors, percentage over ideal weight (current weight minus ideal weight divided by ideal weight) is a better criterion for weight loss, because it takes into account both the height and weight loss goal, or ideal weight. Thus, a 20-pound weight loss represents considerable differences in percentage over ideal weight for the 150-pound client as compared with the 300-pound client. Percentage over ideal weight, however, does not represent a totally adequate measure for comparing results across studies (Jeffrey & Knauss, 1981).

Feinstein (1959) has proposed a standardized improvement criterion called the weight reduction index (RI), which is equal to the percentage of excess weight loss multiplied by relative initial obesity: $RI = (W_l/W_s)$ $(W_i/W_t) \times 100$, where $W_l$ = weight loss, $W_s$ = surplus weight, $W_i$ = initial weight, and $W_t$ = target weight. This index takes into account weight, height, amount overweight, goal, and pounds lost. Scores typically range from 0 (no weight loss) to 200 (a large weight loss).

A major difficulty in assessment strategies employing ideal weight estimates concerns the estimation of frame size in height–weight charts. Currently, there is no quantifiable method for determining frame size, and the practitioner is forced to make a subjective estimate. An alternative to using such charts in estimating ideal weight and obesity is to employ ratios of weight relative to specific powers of height. The body mass index (weight/height$^2$) has been used in epidemiological research with varied populations and has the advantage of accounting for height (Brownell, 1982). Moreover, Thomas, McKay, and Cutlip (1976) have developed a nomograph to calculate the body mass index that allows for the determination of a range of acceptable weights (see Figure 8-1). This nomograph for the body mass index provides a continuous quantitative scale of acceptable weight ranges for various heights, but it does not require an estimation of frame size to determine the acceptable range. An additional advantage of the nomograph is that, for all heights, clinical obesity is defined as the point at which the body mass index is greater than 30, and this point corresponds closely with 20% overweight (Jeffrey & Knauss, 1981).

We recommend the use of absolute weight and percentage over ideal weight for clinical purposes, because these two measures are easily obtained and understood as well as representing common measures of obesity. However, in research studies, the addition of the RI as a dependent variable permits a better cross-comparison of treatment efficacy (Knauss, Jeffrey, Knauss, & Harowski, 1983).

### Body Fat

Although amount of body fat is the criterion of obesity, gross body weight is influenced by a number of factors besides body fat, such as the amount of body water and skeletal and muscular structure. The only direct method for measuring body fat is through biopsies. However, other measurements have been developed and are more frequently used. Densitometric analysis compares regular weight to underwater weight in calculating the amount of lean body mass and body fat. Anthropometric measurements provide more practical assessments for measuring body fat. For example, body circumfer-

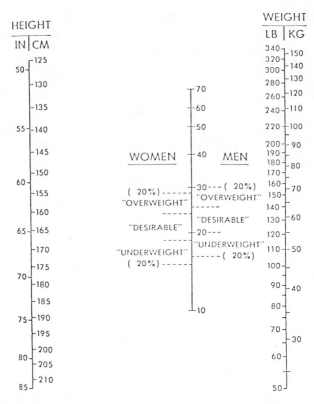

FIGURE 8-1.  Nomograph for body mass index (kg/m$^2$). From "Nomograph for Body Mass Index (kg/m$^2$)" by A. E. Thomas, D. A. McKay, and M. B. Cutlip, 1976, *American Journal of Clinical Nutrition, 29,* 302–304. Copyright 1976 by the American Society for Clinical Nutrition, Inc. Reprinted by permission.

ence and thickness of skinfold are valid methods for estimating body fat. In particular, caliper measurements of skinfolds have been advocated for use in behavioral research to provide an independent assessment of body fat. However, Bray *et al.* (1978) have concluded that "since measurement of height and weight have a smaller standard deviation than skinfolds, they would appear to be the anthropometric measurements of choice in assessing fatness rather than skinfold measurements" (p. 72). Moreover, we have found height and weight measurements convenient and practical in treatment, whereas the caliper assessments often prove less reliable across assessors. Thus, we also recommend combining the measures of weight discussed earlier with the body mass index in order to multiply assess several factors related to obesity.

*Eating Habits*

Methods employed in measuring eating behavior have included patient self-monitoring, direct observation, and paper-and-pencil assessment. Self-monitoring of eating behavior involves recording such information as the type, amount, and caloric value of food eaten, as well as the setting, time of day, and feelings associated with eating. Although limitations are evident with self-monitoring strategies (e.g., data may be biased and less reliable), such approaches represent a valuable therapeutic tool, as well as providing information that is indispensable in developing a comprehensive, individualized treatment plan. Continuous self-monitoring throughout treatment further highlights those variables that influence treatment effectiveness.

We have found in our clinical work that explicit instructions regarding self-monitored data improve reliability. During assessment periods, clients are instructed to maintain their current eating habits for 1–2 weeks and *not* to attempt to lose weight until directed to do so. Following the preliminary self-monitoring period, clients are interviewed to determine whether the assessment data represent a "typical" pattern of eating behavior. The sample eating record presented in Table 8-1 highlights data obtained from Chris during an initial self-monitoring period. Chris represents a typical obese participant in our assessment–treatment program. As can be seen, such an eating record makes it simple for the clinician to obtain important information in the assessment and subsequent treatment of eating disorders. For example, it is apparent from Chris's eating record that food was employed as a means to handle stress at work (3:00–3:45 time period).

Direct observations provide data that tend to be more reliable than self-monitored data. An early example of observational data was provided by Schachter (1971), wherein the number of crackers eaten by subjects, after various experimental manipulations, was counted. Additional observational schemes have been employed in naturalistic settings. For example, some researchers (e.g., Stunkard & Kaplan, 1977) observed subjects without their knowledge and rated such behaviors as amount of food chosen, number of chews, duration of meal, number of mouthfuls, and amount of food uneaten. Time-sampling techniques can be incorporated into observational assessments to provide specific data such as chews per minute or calories consumed per minute (Brownell, 1981). In fact, Blundell (1980) reports that calories per minute is a highly sensitive measure to assess treatment intervention effectiveness. Unfortunately, direct observations have been employed primarily in treatment outcome investigations. The potential benefits of such approaches in clinical practice are now just starting to be realized. In particular, Coates (1977) has developed the Eating Analysis and Treatment Schedule (EATS) to be used at home and completed by nonparticipant observers. The EATS is quite useful, for it assesses actual eating behavior in the natural situation in which most meals

TABLE 8-1.    Sample Eating Record

| | | | | Day: Friday Date: August 8 | | |
| | | | | Situation: home, work, restaurant | People: alone, friends | |
| Time start/stop | Quantity | Type | Calories | | | Hunger and feelings |
| --- | --- | --- | --- | --- | --- | --- |
| 7:45– 8:00 A.M. | 1 cup 2 tbs. | Coffee with sugar | 92 | Home | Spouse | Hungry, tired |
| 10:30– 10:45 A.M. | 1 2 cups 2 tbs. | Sugared doughnut Coffee with sugar | 466 92 | Office | Alone | Starving |
| 12:00– 12:45 P.M. | 1 med. 1 med. 1 glass | Hamburger Salad, no dress. Iced tea, no sugar | 350 75 1 | Office cafeteria | Friends | Moderately hungry, feeling relaxed |
| 3:30– 3:45 P.M. | 2 2 1 | Candy bars Cokes Cookie | 390 300 70 | Office | Alone | Not hungry, upset at boss |
| 6:00– 7:00 P.M. | 3 lg. pc. 1 cup 2 lg. srv. 3 med. slices 1 cup 3 cups | Bread Creamed tomato soup Mashed potatoes Ham Beets Ice cream | 180 188 180 800 60 520 | Home | Family | Not hungry, tired, upset, angry |
| 8:30– 11:00 P.M. | 3 glasses 3 med. pc. 1 cup 3 | Martinis Potato chips Peanuts Cookies | 320 325 136 140 | Cocktail party | Employees, friends | Not hungry, tired, bored |
| | | Total | 4,465 | | | |

*Note.* From *Take It Off and Keep It Off: A Behavioral Program for Weight Loss and Healthy Living* by D. B. Jeffrey and R. C. Katz, 1977, Englewood Cliffs, NJ: Prentice-Hall. Copyright 1977 by D. B. Jeffrey and R. C. Katz. Reprinted by permission.

are consumed. Although additional research appears warranted, the EATS is a promising assessment device (Brownell, 1981).

Questionnaires represent the third major strategy for measuring eating patterns. Two paper-and-pencil measures have considerable usefulness in obesity treatment and research: Wollersheim's Eating Patterns Questionnaire (EPQ) and the Revised Master Questionnaire (RMQ). The EPQ (Wollersheim, 1970) is designed to assess general patterns of eating behavior. Factor analysis (e.g., Hagen, 1974) has yielded six orthogonal factors: (1) Emotional and Uncontrolled Overeating, (2) Eating Response to Interpersonal Situations, (3) Eating in Isolation, (4) Eating as Reward, (5) Eating

Response to Evaluative Situations, and (6) Between-Meal Eating. The EPQ has considerable potential utility for both clinical practice and research. Sample items from the EPQ are presented in Table 8-2.

The RMQ (Straw, Straw, & Craighead, 1979) is a refinement of the Master Questionnaire that was developed to assess eating habits (Mahoney, Rogers, Straw, & Mahoney, 1977). The RMQ was constructed following a cluster analysis of the longer Master Questionnaire, designed to reduce the excessive length and scale overlap of the original instrument. The instrument is divided into five clusters: Hopelessness, Physical Attribution, Motivation, Stimulus Control, and Energy Balance Knowledge. These five clusters have Cronbach's alphas ranging from .65 to .85. The RMQ also demonstrates considerable usefulness in clinical and research applications (Harowski & Jeffrey, 1982). Sample items from the RMQ are also presented in Table 8-2.


*Physical Activities*

Obesity is directly related to physical inactivity and overeating (Jeffrey & Katz, 1977). Indices of levels of physical activity are critical in assessing caloric expenditure. Patient self-monitoring is a practical, cost-efficient method of obtaining data regarding physical activity levels. Self-recording of recreational activities (e.g., walking, bicycling, or tennis) as well as of routine chores (e.g., house cleaning, gardening, shopping) permits a more comprehensive behavioral assessment of physical activity.

The Physical Activity Review (Table 8-3) provides assessment information that leads to the development of an individualized exercise plan. Moreover, these data can be analyzed by calculating the number of calories expended through various activities. As can be seen in Chris's Physical Activity Review, gardening and walking around the block are common activities that can be easily incorporated into a weight loss program.

In fact, it is highly recommended that physical activities selected for treatment be based on the initial assessment. Table 8-4 illustrates Chris's Planned Physical Activities and the resulting caloric expenditure per activity. Although these activities were initiated as a starting point in Chris's treatment program, they represented an improvement over Chris's previous sedentary lifestyle. In addition, with over 2,400 calories being expended per week, Chris's weight loss from activity amounted to 0.7 pounds a week, or about 36 pounds a year.

The limitations of self-report data have resulted in a search for more reliable and objective measures of physical fitness that could be employed as dependent measures. Physical performance measures that have been used include the Harvard Step Test, which assesses the length of time clients can maintain a pace of climbing 30 steps per minute, and the sit-up

TABLE 8-2.   Factor Structure and Sample Items From the Eating Patterns Questionnaire and the Revised Master Questionnaire

---

Eating Patterns Questionnaire (EPQ)

---

Factor 1:   Emotional and Uncontrolled Eating
- Do you tend to eat when you are not busy?
- Do you go on "eating binges, i.e., sprees, when you eat a great deal?
- ...

Factor 2:   Eating Response to Interpersonal Situations
Anticipating this situation, I tend to eat (not at all . . . very much)
- The night before a big dance.
- You are entering the lecture hall for a large class.
- ...

Factor 3:   Eating in Isolation
- Do you eat while watching TV?
- Do you eat while studying?
- ...

Factor 4:   Eating as Reward
- Do you like to celebrate something important by going out to eat?
- At a party, do you eat a lot of snacks?
- ...

Factor 5:   Eating Response to Evaluative Situations
Anticipating this situation, I tend to eat (not all all . . . very much)
- You are getting up to give a speech before a large group.
- You are going into an interview for a very important job.
- ...

Factor 6:   Between-Meal Eating
- Do you snack between meals?
- Do you eat in the evening?
- ...

---

Revised Master Questionnaire (RMQ)

---

Cognitive Cluster 1: Hopelessness
   1. I have a lot of bad luck.
   2. I can't imagine what I would look like if I were thin.
   3. When it comes to will power, I am a failure. . . .
   10. I feel helpless in many aspects of my life.

Cognitive Cluster 2: Physical Attribution
   1. For me to reduce, I will probably have to eat less than 1,000 calories per day.
   2. My metabolism is probably below average. . . .
   15. I resent it when thin [people brag] about how they don't have to watch [their] weight.

Cognitive Cluster 3: Motivation
   1. I often wonder if I am not just kidding myself when I go on a new reducing program.
   2. There was a time when I think I could have stayed thin, but now it may be too late. . . .
   12. If exercise were the only way to reduce, I would be in trouble.

*(continued)*

TABLE 8-2 (Continued).

| |
|---|
| Stimulus Control Cluster |
|   1. Talking about food makes me hungry. |
|   2. If other people are eating in front of me, I will usually join in even if I'm not hungry.... |
|   9. I often use high-calorie foods as a "pick-me-up" or reward. |
| Energy Balance Knowledge Cluster |
|   1. Unless you sweat while you exercise, you are probably not burning up many calories. |
|   2. A balanced diet doesn't have to include fat.... |
|   10. Low-fat and non-fat milk products contain less protein and calcium than those made from whole milk. |

*Note.* EPQ items from Wollersheim (1970). RMQ items from Straw, Straw, and Craighead (1979).

test, which measures the number of sit-ups completed within a 1-minute period. Assessments of cardiovascular functioning have included blood pressure, resting pulse rate, and recovery rate following the Harvard Step Test.

The Eating Disorders Clinic at Stanford University is researching and developing microprocessors that measure and store the number of physical movements an individual makes. Sophisticated devices are being tested and calibrated that can be strapped to a person's leg to assess physical energy expenditure (S. Agras & B. Taylor, personal communication, 1983). This new application of computer technology has many exciting possibilities for more accurate assessment of physical activity and energy expenditure.

### Significant Others

Spouses, relatives, friends, neighbors, and coworkers represent potential allies or foes in the treatment process. Although active encouragement of failure in treatment is infrequent, subtle interventions by others may reduce

TABLE 8-3. Physical Activity Review

| Physical activity | Minutes spent per week in activity | How much you enjoy or dislike activity |
|---|---|---|
| 1. Gardening | 20 | Enjoyed a lot |
| 2. Walking around the block | 10 | Enjoyable, peaceful, calm |
| 3. Jogging | 15 | Hated this! |
| 4. Sweeping garage | 10 | Disliked moderately |

*Note.* Adapted from *Take It Off and Keep It Off: A Behavioral Program for Weight Loss and Healthy Living* by D. B. Jeffrey and R. C. Katz, 1977, Englewood Cliffs, NJ: Prentice-Hall. Copyright 1977 by D. B. Jeffrey and R. C. Katz. Adapted by permission.

TABLE 8-4.   Sample Planned Physical Activities

| Activity | Calories × expended per minute | Minutes per week doing activity | = Total calories used per activity |
|---|---|---|---|
| 1. Bicycling | 8.0 | 30 minutes | 240 |
| 2. Walking up and down stairs | 13.8 | (5 minutes per day × 7 = ) 35 minutes | 483 |
| 3. Walking around the block | 6.1 | (15 minutes per day × 7 = ) 105 minutes | 640 |
| 4. Tennis | 7.0 | 60 minutes | 420 |
| 5. Gardening | 8.6 | 60 minutes | 516 |
| 6. Making love | 5.3 | 30 minutes (actual time spent making love, not lying in bed afterward) | 159 |
| Total | | | 2,458 |

*Note.* Adapted from *Take It Off and Keep It Off: A Behavioral Program for Weight Loss and Healthy Living* by D. B. Jeffrey and R. C. Katz, 1977, Englewood Cliffs, NJ: Prentice-Hall. Copyright 1977 by D. B. Jeffrey and R. C. Katz. Adapted by permission.

treatment effectiveness. For example, "sabotaging" spouses of obese clients have acknowledged that they feared a weight loss would improve their partners' attractiveness, thus leading to extramarital affairs. In other couples where both partners were obese, husbands and wives may subtly encourage each other to overeat and not to follow the treatment procedures at home. Therefore, a comprehensive assessment plan warrants the inclusion of "significant other" data. In our clinical practice, we employ the Significant Others List (Table 8-5) to assess how others may influence successful treatment. As demonstrated in Chris's list, it was very important to understand from the start of treatment that Mary (Chris's mother) might hinder progress because of jealousy. Meanwhile, Chris's allies in attempting to lose weight included Bob (a coworker) and Jesse (Chris's spouse). With this specific assessment information, treatment strategies could then be developed to maximize those positive external factors while minimizing potentially counterproductive influences. When such external variables are understood, losing weight becomes more promising.

## Feelings and Emotions

Unpleasant affective responses and overeating commonly occur together. Negative feelings such as anger, resentment, anxiety, or loneliness, when handled by eating, lead to continued obesity and to the development and maintenance of maladaptive behavior. Thus, some individuals learn to use

TABLE 8-5.  Significant Others List

| Name | Relationship | Help | Hinder | How will this person help or hinder? |
|------|--------------|------|--------|--------------------------------------|
| 1. Mary | Mother | | × | Encourages me to eat. She's jealous. |
| 2. Bob | Coworker | × | | Encourages me to stick to my program. |
| 3. Jesse | Spouse | × | | Cares about me and my health, supports me when I'm upset. |
| 4. Lynn | Friend | × | | Understands and helps me when I'm having difficulties. |

*Note.* Adapted from *Take It Off and Keep It Off: A Behavioral Program for Weight Loss and Healthy Living* by D. B. Jeffrey and R. C. Katz, 1977, Englewood Cliffs, NJ: Prentice-Hall. Copyright 1977 by D. B. Jeffrey and R. C. Katz. Adapted by permission.

food to escape from tension or boredom or to assuage pain or depression. On the other hand, food and overeating also appear to be frequently associated with social occasions, fun, and self-gratification. Therefore, specific attention to feelings and emotions serving as antecedents or consequences to overeating gives both the clinician and client a better understanding of eating behavior.

TABLE 8-6.  Sample Feelings/Emotions Chart

| Your feelings (add specific examples) | Your typical response | Your proposed alternatives |
|---------------------------------------|-----------------------|----------------------------|
| 1. Tiredness<br>On the weekends, I'm usually burned out by midafternoon after taking care of the kids all day. | Snack on whatever's available. It seems to pick me up. | Rest quietly for 15 minutes with only a cup of coffee. |
| 2. Anger<br>My boss always gives me a ton of work before quitting time. | I usually work really slowly eat snacks until I leave. | I will discuss this situation with my boss, but in the meantime, I will attempt to complete these projects instead of "putting them off till tomorrow." |
| 3. Boredom | | |
| 4. Loneliness | | |
| 5. Anxiety | | |

*Note.* Adapted from *Take It Off and Keep It Off: A Behavioral Program for Weight Loss and Healthy Living* by D. B. Jeffrey and R. C. Katz, 1977, Englewood Cliffs, NJ: Prentice-Hall. Copyright 1977 by D. B. Jeffrey and R. C. Katz. Adapted by permission.

TABLE 8-7.   Reasons for Losing Weight

---

1. If I weighed 40 pounds less than I do now, I would look better.
2. If I lost some of this weight, I would feel better and be healthier.
3. I'd really like to impress my boss.
4. Maybe my mother would stop harassing me if I lost this weight.
5. I'll be more attractive.

---

*Note.* Adapted from *Take It Off and Keep It Off: A Behavioral Program for Weight Loss and Healthy Living* by D. B. Jeffrey and R. C. Katz, 1977, Englewood Cliffs, NJ: Prentice-Hall. Copyright 1977 by D. B. Jeffrey and R. C. Katz. Adapted by permission.

The Feelings/Emotions Chart presented in Table 8-6 outlines three primary dimensions of such an assessment: feelings, typical responses, and alternative responses. During assessment, careful attention is given to the specific feelings and to the client's typical response to those feelings. After the assessment of feelings is completed, specific noneating alternatives are discussed and implemented during the treatment phase. Thus, individualized treatment plans are the logical outgrowth of such assessments. As can be seen in Chris's Feelings/Emotions Chart (Table 8-6), Chris typically ate in response to tiredness and anger.

## Reinforcers and Commitment

The importance of assessing the client's readiness to lose weight cannot be overstated. Unless a serious desire to change long-standing eating and exercise habits exists and is maintained, failure experiences will probably be encountered. In order to avoid such incidents, reinforcers for losing weight (Table 8-7) and staying overweight (Table 8-8) must be considered. Sensitive clinical practice and careful assessment may reveal that the present is not the best time to attempt to lose weight.

In our program, we assess clients' motivations for losing weight early in treatment. As can be seen in Chris's records, a variety of reasons were associated with starting the weight loss program. In addition, Chris had a number of reasons for staying overweight. Each "reason" listed by a client needs to be discussed and understood thoroughly by the client and clinician before treatment is begun. It is often necessary to provide examples for clients to get them started. However, the time devoted to assessing commitment and motivation for treatment is always well spent.

TABLE 8-8. Reasons for Staying Overweight

| |
|---|
| 1. Eating comforts me when I'm angry or upset. |
| 2. I'm afraid to fail again. |
| 3. I don't know what I'd do if I weren't munching on snacks. |
| 4. I really enjoy rich pastries and desserts. |
| 5. It's hard to say "no" to the in-laws when they ask us over for dinner. |
| 6. If my weight were normal, I wouldn't have an excuse for not having many friends. |

*Note.* Adapted from *Take It Off and Keep It Off: A Behavioral Program for Weight Loss and Healthy Living* by D. B. Jeffrey and R. C. Katz, 1977, Englewood Cliffs, NJ: Prentice-Hall. Copyright 1977 by D. B. Jeffrey and R. C. Katz. Adapted by permission.

## Case Example

Chris represents a typical obese man or woman. Prior to initiation of individual treatment, systematic assessments were completed. Three sessions at weekly intervals were designed to evaluate Chris's eating habits (see Table 8-1), physical activity patterns (see Table 8-3), the relative influence of significant others (see Table 8-5), and Chris's "reasons" for losing weight (see Table 8-7) and/or remaining overweight (see Table 8-8). In addition to these specific assessments, clinical interviews attempted to evaluate the factors associated with Chris's initial increases in weight and the subsequent maintenance of obesity. At the conclusion of the formal evaluation period, Chris was offered a comprehensive individual treatment.

Structured treatment combined various aspects of the evaluation period (e.g., use of assessment instruments, continuous monitoring of treatment gains or losses) with specific cognitive–behavioral treatment components. For example, the assessment instruments provided a solid foundation upon which to build self-monitoring skills. The identification and modification of eating habits and physical activity patterns were initiated early in treatment and maintained throughout the program. Emphasis on setting of standards and self-reward paralleled the treatment program's goal of losing "1 pound per week."

Specific intervention strategies were developed with Chris in a collaborative manner, based on the specific data obtained from the assessment instruments. For example, Chris planned particular physical activities (see Table 8-4) from the data derived from the assessment of usual physical activities (see Table 8-3). Chris also identified and enlisted the support of significant others who provided reassurance and assisted in specific treatment plans (e.g., came along on particular activities).

Homework assignments were also developed and included such strategies as completing the Feelings/Emotions Chart (see Table 8-6), which was, in turn, used to develop specific noneating alternatives to uncomfortable feelings. For example, instead of "turning to snacks" when feeling tired, Chris developed and implemented a plan to rest for 15 minutes with a cup of coffee. The midafternoon tiredness thus became less problematic, and Chris was able to avoid snacking.

The weight loss program began with three once-weekly assessment sessions and then seven once-weekly treatment sessions. During this period, Chris's weight decreased 10 pounds, and Chris reported considerable satisfaction with the treatment gains. Because of the apparent motivation for continued weight loss, Chris contracted to begin a gradual fading of treatment sessions to maintain the gradual weight loss and increase self-control. After Chris was seen for a total of ten 1-hour weekly sessions, the therapist began a course of two sessions monthly. As Chris's weight continued to decrease, Chris was seen for 30-minute sessions once a month, then bimonthly. After 12 months in treatment, Chris had achieved a total weight loss of 54 pounds.

In summary, whereas it is increasingly evident that eating disorders are complex, multifaceted problems, assessment has in turn become more sophisticated. In recognizing that assessment and treatment are interrelated clinical activities, practitioners and researchers are better able to understand and treat eating disorders. We do not view assessment as a process completed prior to and/or after treatment; instead, assessment and treatment represent ongoing, parallel processes in clinical case management. As regards adult obesity, a wide variety of behavioral assessment strategies are available for use in individual and group treatment programs.

### Assessments of Childhood Obesity

Why children become obese and maintain obesity is not entirely clear. Differing opinions exist regarding whether obese children differ from normal-weight children in terms of amount of food eaten, amount of energy expended, or both (e.g., see Brownell & Stunkard, 1983). Clearly, more observational and demographic studies are needed to determine factors relating to the etiology and maintenance of childhood obesity.

Behavioral assessments and treatments for children follow the same basic guidelines as the assessments and treatments for adults. Specifically, treatment involves a reduction in energy intake (diet) and/or an increase in energy output (exercise). Behavioral assessment strategies have been found to be essential in developing effective weight loss treatment programs for children. Thus, this section examines (1) specific behavioral targets for assessment and intervention with children, and (2) methods of measurement designed for use with children. Practitioners must also be attentive to two important issues associated with younger clients as opposed to adults. First, because a child's cognitive abilities are in a rapid state of development, specific assessment strategies and interventions require modification appropriate to the child's cognitive level of development. Second, because the child may be dependent on adults for many basic needs, including food, assessments and interventions must consider these significant adults as well as the child.

## Targets for Assessment and Intervention with Children

### Developmental Considerations

All behavioral weight loss programs focus to varying degrees on diet, exercise, stimulus control, self-control, and reinforcement. The child's level of involvement in the weight loss program will depend, in large part, on his or her level of cognitive development. Epstein (1986) outlines four age ranges as a guideline for placing increasing responsibility for treatment adherence on the child. At ages 1-5, the program must rely on parental control. The child is generally not literate and cannot self-monitor. Motivation to lose weight is absent. At ages 5-8, the child's ability to self-monitor is still limited, although simplified, adapted assessments may be used to some extent (see "Self-Monitoring/Parent Monitoring," below). Children at this age can start learning nutritionally sound eating habits (Peterson, Jeffrey, Bridgwater, & Dawson, 1984). In addition, these children can also start learning to solicit praise and encouragement for healthy eating from significant adults (Stark, Collins, Osnes, & Stokes, 1984). Parents will still be involved significantly. At ages 8-12, the child can set goals and self-monitor. Peer pressure may provide motivation to lose weight; however, children at this age still benefit substantially from parental involvement. From age 13 on, children can use programs similar to those of adults, though they may benefit from frequent social therapeutic support for weight loss (Coates, Jeffery, Killen, & Danaher, 1982). At this stage of development, children are becoming independent of their parents, and parental guidance may not be beneficial; it may even lead to negative interactions. Parental involvement may be most beneficial in primarily supportive roles (e.g., Brownell, Kelman, & Stunkard, 1983).

### Diet

An adequate level of nutrients is essential for children's physical growth and mental development. Therefore, it is critical that a reduction in calories with children be secondary to a nutritionally sound diet. Waxman and

Stunkard (1980) report that some practitioners recommend either maintenance of weight while the child grows or moderate rates of loss (less than
0.23 kg per week). A focus on caloric reduction alone is insufficient and
not advisable (although a high caloric content will often correlate with low
nutritional value). Children as young as 5 can be taught nutritional concepts (Peterson et al., 1984).

Assessing amount eaten versus assessing habit change (e.g., eating
smaller bites) is an important issue in intervention. Brownell and Stunkard
(1983) report that, although habit change is an important aspect of weight
loss, monitoring weight loss may be more important in losing weight than
monitoring specific behaviors or calories consumed (see also Coates et al.,
1982). The maintenance of weight loss may, however, be facilitated by
focusing on habit change as opposed to weight loss per se (Brownell &
Stunkard, 1983; Kingsley & Shapiro, 1977; LeBow, 1984).

Color coding of differential calorie density per serving of foods is one
method that has been shown to be understood by children as young as 5.
Epstein, Masek, and Marshall's (1978) nutritionally balanced Traffic Light
Diet separates premeasured food portions into red, yellow, and green
categories corresponding to traffic signals. The number of red foods eaten
per week is usually targeted for change. With young children, colored stars
corresponding to foods eaten may then be exchanged for reinforcers (Epstein,
Wing, Koeske, Andrasik, & Ossip, 1981). This method of encouraging
healthy, low-calorie eating with obese children has been shown to be useful
in school as well as home settings (Epstein et al., 1978, 1981). The New
American Eating Guide, a color-coded poster similar in concept to the
Traffic Light Diet, and the Nutrition Scoreboard (Center for Science in the
Public Interest, 1977) may also be useful in weight change/eating-habit
change programs with children. The Food Exchange Diet (American Dietetic Association, 1977) is also applicable to children with help from adults
in learning the procedures. Foreyt and Parks (1975) used different-colored
tokens to represent the eight food exchanges in this diet; tokens were
transferred from one plastic box to another following consumption of food
in that group. Both Epstein et al.'s (1978) and Foreyt and Parks's (1975)
color-coded system provide effective visual analogue feedback relating to
diet for preliterate children. These premeasured portion diets also eliminate the need for rather complex caloric calculations.

Even if parents are not dieting with the child, the clinician must take
into consideration the parents' food-related behaviors that will influence
their child's eating. Parents' food-buying habits, their possible use of food
as a reinforcer, and their possible contradictory messages to the child
regarding eating all warrant assessment (see LeBow, 1984, for an attitude/
history interview form). Other factors that may influence weight change—
the child's attitude toward diet and exercise change, nutrition knowledge,
and knowledge of contingency management (e.g., Epstein et al., 1981)—

should also be assessed. In summary, it is essential to measure the child's caloric *and* nutritional intake, and it is often desirable to include an assessment of the parents' dietary patterns.

*Exercise*

Although exercise is an important component in assessing and treating childhood obesity, its role in children's weight loss during treatment has been suggested to be less important than its role in the maintenance of weight loss (Epstein, Wing, Koeske, & Valoski, 1984). These authors have also suggested that moderate levels of exercise are important, but may be less important than diet in maintaining weight loss with obese children.

Some authors recommend aerobic exercise in weight loss programs for children (e.g., Foreyt & Goodrick, 1981). Others have recommended lifestyle exercise programs for at least two reasons. First, if caloric expenditure and not aerobic fitness is the goal of the program, lifestyle exercise will accomplish that goal. More importantly, studies have found that lifestyle exercise is more likely to be adhered to, and lack of adherence is recognized as a major obstacle to effective treatment (Epstein, 1986; Epstein, Wing, Koeske, Ossip, & Beck, 1982).

*Stimulus Control Techniques*

Most behavioral weight loss programs for children teach techniques of stimulus control. Following a careful behavioral assessment of antecedents and consequences associated with problem eating or lack of exercise, a weight loss program may be individually tailored to the child's or family's needs (Wheeler & Hess, 1976). However, the child's or parents' use of stimulus control techniques is not usually assessed as closely as diet and exercise. This may be due to their relative unimportance, as well as to the simple difficulty a child or parent may have in monitoring a large number of behaviors as well as monitoring diet and exercise.

*Parental Involvement*

Parental involvement in child weight loss programs has been found to be a consistent predicator of success in initial weight loss and short-term maintenance (e.g., Kingsley & Shapiro, 1977). For example, some weight loss programs have found good success for children's initial weight loss when parents were active participants (Aragona, Cassady, & Drabman, 1975; Wheeler & Hess, 1976). Moreover, parental modeling may also be important in initial weight loss. Child weight loss programs in which obese parents are involved in losing weight have been shown to be effective as well (Epstein et al., 1981; Epstein, Wing, Koeske, & Valoski, 1984). Interestingly, the effectiveness of these parent–child treatments may be greater when the parent and child are seen separately rather than together (Epstein, in press). Thus, in the treatment of childhood obesity, it is essential to assess the parents' weight history and their motivation to become involved in the child's weight loss program.

## Parental Reinforcement

All programs for children have some sort of reinforcement or response cost component. This component varies across two basic dimensions: (1) who is the recipient of the reinforcement/response cost, and (2) what behavior is required to acquire or escape the consequence (e.g., attendance at sessions, weight loss). When these components are used in a weight loss program, they should be specified and monitored throughout treatment and follow-up.

Children younger than 8 years have generally not been the direct recipient of a response cost procedure; however, parents generally have, losing percentages of money deposited for not attending sessions (Epstein, Wing, Koeski, & Valoski, 1984), for not collecting data (Aragona et al., 1975), or for not helping their child to lose a specified amount of weight per week (Aragona et al., 1975). The effect of the response cost alone, or the differential effects of a response cost applied to the child as opposed to the parents, have not been determined.

Reinforcement of both younger and older children is a component of behavioral treatment and is usually carried out and assessed through a token system (see Epstein et al., 1978). Generally, rewards are needed more frequently with younger children (see LeBow, 1984). Also, the effectiveness of reinforcement by teachers and peers is potentially great, but further empirical evaluation is needed (Brownell & Stunkard, 1983).

For children older than 8 years, more extensive and complex reinforcement systems may be used. For example, one may monitor and reinforce both eating and activity change (see Epstein, Wing, Koeski, & Valoski, 1984). Thus, in assessing childhood obesity, it is essential to evaluate the frequency and type of reinforcement used before, during, and after treatment.

## Self-Control

For older children, there is some evidence suggesting that maintenance of weight loss is most readily achieved when they engage in self-regulation of food intake and exercise, self-reinforcement, and restrictive eating in tempting situations (Cohen, Gelfand, Dodd, Jensen, & Turner, 1980). For younger children, treatment may be enhanced by teaching self-control skills and in determining attitudes toward diet and exercise that may undermine self-control (LeBow, 1984). Indeed, as much control as parents may have over what their child eats, they cannot control what he or she eats all of the time. Shifting more responsibility to the child for weight loss should proceed systematically with age and cognitive development. Thus, the initial assessment should also include an assessment of the amount and type of self-control the child has currently developed.

*Predicting Who Will Benefit*

With the focus in childhood obesity research on devising effective treatments, relatively little attention has been given to the important area of predicting who will benefit from what treatment (LeBow, 1984). This assessment information is essential to intensive, individually tailored obesity programs. Yet most studies either do not report this information or do not emphasize it sufficiently. It is important from both a biological and a social learning perspective to know (1) whether the parents are obese, (2) which parent is obese (if both are not), (3) which parent is involved in the weight loss program, and (4) whether any siblings are obese. It is also important to determine the length of time the child has been obese and the child's and parent's pretreatment percentage of overweight. For example, Epstein, Wing, Koeske, and Valoski (1984) found that the pretreatment weight of the child and parent was the best predictor of relative weight at a 2-month follow-up. It is also important to know, for reinforcement, whether one parent is involved but the other is not or refuses to be involved. Moreover, when "family treatment" is reported, the composition of the family and weight status of the family members are often omitted. Characteristics of failures and dropouts, as well as of those who adhere to the program, should be assessed and reported.

*Methods of Measurement*

*Criteria for Childhood Obesity*

Therapists are often asked by parents how to determine whether a child is obese. There are relatively complex methods of determining obesity (e.g., relating to body fat). However, pediatricians generally obtain this information from sex–weight–height–age charts. These charts, with instructions on their use, may be found in Figure 8-2 for boys and Figure 8-3 for girls.

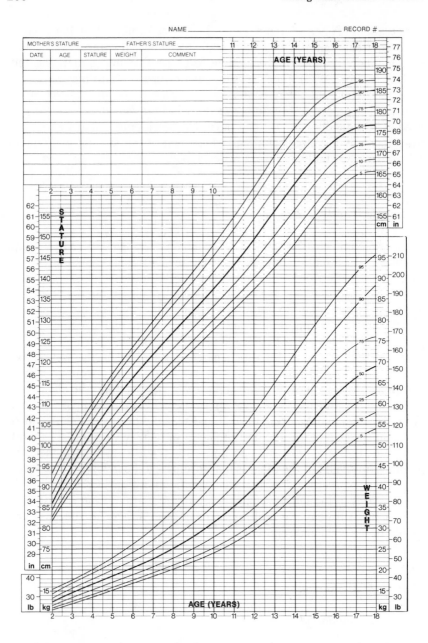

FIGURE 8-2. Growth chart for boys (height, weight, age). The weight objective may be set by first determining the percentile rank of the patient's height for age (upper curves) and then finding his weight at the same percentile rank and age (lower). Adapted from "Physical Growth: National Center for Health Statistics Percentiles" by P. V. V. Hamill, T. A. Drizd, C. L. Johnson, R. B. Reed, A. F. Roche, and W. M. Moore, 1979, *American Journal of Clinical Nutrition, 32,* 607–629. Copyright 1979 by the American Society for Clinical Nutrition, Inc. Reprinted by permission.

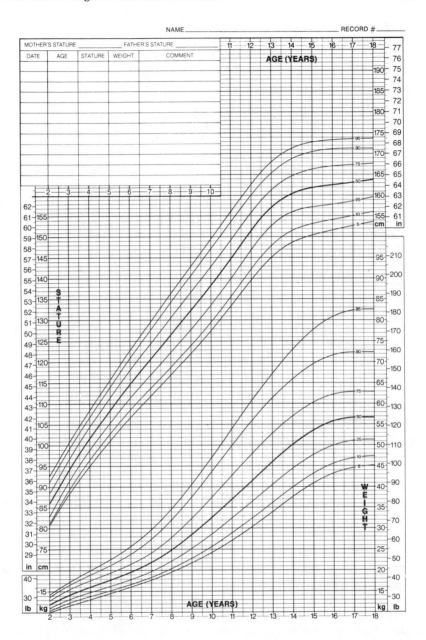

FIGURE 8-3. Growth chart for girls (height, weight, age). The weight objective may be set by first determining the percentile rank of the patient's height for age (upper curves) and then finding her weight at the same percentile rank and age (lower). Adapted from "Physical Growth: National Center for Health Statistics" by P. V. V. Hamill, T. A. Drizd, C. L. Johnson, R. B. Reed, A. F. Roche, and W. M. Moore, 1979, *American Journal of Clinical Nutrition, 32,* 607-629. Copyright 1979 by the American Society for Clinical Nutrition, Inc. Reprinted by permission.

*Self-Monitoring/Parent Monitoring*

Self-monitoring is not only a method of assesment, but also a strategy for behavior change. From age 8 on, forms for children's self-monitoring are similar to those used with adults. Usually children monitor food intake and/or exercise (e.g., Epstein *et al.,* 1981; Kingsley & Shapiro, 1977). Additional information (e.g., assessing feelings and situations which may contribute to overeating) may also be evaluated, keeping in mind that, with children as well as adults, compliance may be improved by using brief self-assessments. It is important that the self-monitoring task be pleasant in order to insure compliance. LeBow (1984) makes an interesting recommendation for a child who finds self-monitoring of exercise to be punishing. He recommends that the child monitor sedentary times instead, thus punishing the more inappropriate behavior. Examples of self-monitoring forms for food intake and exercise may be found in LeBow (1984, pp. 82–86).

Prior to age 8, parental monitoring or innovative simplifications of traditional self-monitoring forms are needed. Both Epstein *et al.*'s (1978) Traffic Light Diet and the American Dietetic Association's (1977) Food Exchange Diet lend themselves to simplification, for children may check boxes in food categories or place tokens in plastic-box analogues of food categories (Foreyt & Parks, 1975), thereby precluding literacy requirements. Parents may also be asked to monitor children younger than 8 years old (Aragona *et al.,* 1975). In this case, the therapeutic benefits of self-monitoring will not be realized unless the parent who is monitoring presents the data to the child in an understandable form.

The validity of self-assessments in predicting weight loss is difficult to determine; self-reported amounts of food eaten or energy expended do not show consistent correlations with weight loss or maintenance (Foreyt & Goodrick, 1981). One usually infers from weight loss that treatment has been adhered to. This may or may not be the case. Other unidentified factors may contribute to the results. For instance, Waxman and Stunkard (1980) found in an intensive observational study that obese boys expended as many calories as normal-weight peers when activity levels were low, but expended more calories than normal-weight peers when activity levels increased. However, they also found that the obese boys ate more and faster than normal-weight peers.

In one study that attempted to determine the reliability of parental and child monitoring of the child's dietary input and exercise (Cohen *et al.,* 1980), interobserver agreement between parent and child on caloric content was quite good at .92 for meals and .71 for snacks. Agreement between the parent and child for exercise was .64. This is encouraging, but additional assessment studies are needed to determine the validity of such measures and their clinical utility.

*Observational Measures*

Direct observation has been used occasionally in treatment studies. Epstein, Woodall, Goreczny, Wing, and Robertson (1984) used a random time-sampling procedure to determine energy expenditure of young girls in a semistructured setting of free play. Activities were rated on a 5-point scale corresponding with increasing caloric expenditure (see also Epstein, McGowan, & Woodall, 1984). Increases in activity correlated highly with increases in caloric expenditure.

Structured observation in a treatment context has also been used. For example, family dinners have been observed in order to assess eating habits and model appropriate food choices. We believe that direct observation is especially useful in tailoring treatment programs to specific individuals.

*Summary*

Behavioral assessment of childhood obesity is directly related to the assumed etiology of the disorder and subsequent targets for intervention. Those targets for assessment and intervention usually include one or more of the following: diet, exercise, parental involvement, reinforcement, response cost, stimulus control, and self-control. The child's ability to use such interventions will depend on the child's level of cognitive and emotional maturity. Parental involvement may also substantially affect the child's use of and the effectiveness of the weight loss intervention. Likewise, the child's ability to carry out a behavioral assessment will depend on his or her level of cognitive development. Generally, children as young as 5 have demonstrated an ability to become involved in limited self-monitoring if it is presented in visual analogue form, thus precluding literacy requirements. Parental monitoring of the child's treatment is generally used for children under age 8. The number and complexity of the behaviors monitored may increase with the maturity of the child. Naturalistic and structured direct observation of eating behaviors or exercise habits may also be helpful in devising and monitoring interventions. These assessments, combined with interview and questionnaire data, can provide a complete assessment on which to base a comprehensive treatment for the important health problem of childhood obesity.

## Assessments of Anorexia Nervosa and Bulimia Nervosa

Anorexia nervosa and bulimia nervosa are two eating disorders that are receiving increased attention from researchers and clinicians. Although space limitations prevent a detailed analysis of specific measurement-related issues in each disorder, a general discussion of assessment strategies applicable to both of these abnormal eating patterns is presented. As for obesity, we recommend the use of multidimensional assessments to insure a thorough understanding of the antecedents and consequences underlying each respective eating dysfunction. The specific assessments employed with anorexic and bulimic patients parallel the strategies outlined earlier in the assessment of obesity. This section highlights the following areas of assessment in anorexia and bulimia: criteria for these disorders, weight, eating habits and attitudes, physical activity, and significant others. In addition, a variety of assessment instruments specific to anorexia and bulimia are described.

### Criteria for Anorexia Nervosa and Bulimia Nervosa

Early interest in anorexia nervosa and bulimia nervosa led to controversy. Some researchers categorized anorexia and bulimia as separate syndromes, whereas others viewed the abnormal eating behaviors as facets of the same dysfunction (e.g., Ben-Tovim, Marilov, & Crisp, 1979; Beumont, George, & Smart, 1976; Casper, Eckert, Halmi, Goldberg, & Davis, 1980; Garfinkel, Moldofsky, & Garner, 1980; Hsu, 1980; Palmer, 1979; Russell, 1979). Whereas the third edition of the *Diagnostic and Statistical Manual of Mental Disorders* (DSM-III; American Psychiatric Association, 1980) recognized two separate psychopathological entities, the recent revision of the manual (DSM-III-R; American Psychiatric Association, 1987) identifies two related disorders, Anorexia Nervosa and Bulimia Nervosa, and permits the use of both diagnoses in certain instances. Under the latest revision, Anorexia Nervosa is characterized by such factors as refusal to maintain body weight, intense fear of gaining weight, disturbances in body perception, and cycles of amenorrhea. Bulimia Nervosa includes recurrent episodes of binge-eating, regular attempts to control weight by such means as strict dieting or vomiting, and a persistent overconcern with body shape and weight.

### Weight

Whereas increased body fat is the hallmark of obesity, decreased body weight is the primary factor in anorexia nervosa (Brownell, 1981). Excessive weight control and low absolute body weight is often maintained through a combination of techniques: restricted food intake, intensive exercising, self-induced vomiting, and/or laxative/diuretic abuse. Serious medical complications (e.g., bradycardia, altered hormone levels) are frequently associated with the disorder as well. Thus, in addition to careful medical assessments, absolute body weight measurement represents a critical assessment in anorexic patients. Moreover, describing absolute body weight in terms of small, gradual increments of weight gain may be most useful (Brownell, 1981).

Bulimic patients do not uniformly demonstrate any specific weight problem. Although purging behavior is typically employed as a weight control tactic, bulimia nervosa has been identified among overweight, normal-weight, and underweight individuals. In addition, most data suggest that bulimia is most closely related to difficulties with weight control, rather than to any particular psychosocial or emotional problem (Orleans & Barnett, 1984). Still, absolute body weight is a useful measure, especially in documenting weight fluctuations, which are frequently noted in bulimic patients. Like anorexic patients, bulimic patients require medical assessments, because various medical problems are associated with bulimia nervosa (e.g., dehydration, electrolyte disturbances).

### Eating Habits and Attitudes

In addition to the Eating Record (see Table 8-1) and the Feelings/Emotion Chart (see Table 8-6) described earlier, a variety of instruments are available for assessing characteristics of anorexia and bulimia. Seven scales are briefly described below. Table 8-9 gives sample items from the first five of these assessment scales.

Gormally, Black, Daston, and Rardin (1982) developed the Binge Eating Scale (BES) and the Cognitive Factors Scale (CFS) to assess binge-eating among the obese. The BES contains 16 items designed to measure the behavioral components of the binge-eating syndrome and the feelings/cognitions that serve as antecedents or consequences to the binge. The 14-item CFS can be used to assess specific dieting problems. The scale contains two factors: Strict Dieting Standards, and Self-Efficacy Expectations to Sustain a Diet. In general, cognitive factors play a crucial role in leading from an isolated slip (e.g., just one piece of pie) to a full-blown relapse or all-out binge (Marlatt & Gordon, 1980; Orleans & Barnett, 1984).

The Binge Scale (Hawkins & Clements, 1980) contains nine items designed to measure binge-eating behavior (e.g., frequency, duration, rate of eating) and attitudes associated with bulimia. The scale was also developed to parallel the diagnostic criteria described in DSM-III.

The Compulsive Eating Scale (CES), revised by Dunn and Ondercin (1981), was designed to assess emotional states related to eating and specific aspects of binge behavior. The CES includes 32 items and provides data related to degree of compulsive eating. In addition, it assesses general information about the frequency of binges, alternation of bingeing with fasting and dieting, and emotional reactions following a binge episode.

TABLE 8-9.   Sample Items from Anorexia Nervosa and Bulimia Assessment Instruments

---

### Binge Eating Scale (BES)

I don't think about food a great deal.

I have strong cravings for food but they last only for brief periods of time.

I have days when I can't seem to think about anything else but food.

Most of my days seem to be preoccupied with thoughts about food. I feel like I live to eat.

I feel capable to control my eating urges when I want to.

I feel like I have failed to control my eating more than the average person.

I feel utterly helpless when it comes to feeling in control of my eating urges.

Because I feel so helpless about controlling my eating, I have become very desperate about trying to get in control.

---

### Cognitive Factors Scale (CES)

When I start a diet, I say to myself that I will have absolutely no "forbidden foods" (Likert scale).

I don't persist very long on diets I set for myself (Likert scale).

---

### Binge Scale

How often do you binge?
  A. Seldom
  B. Once or twice a month
  C. Once a week
  D. Almost every day

Which best describes your feelings during a binge?
  A. I feel that I could control the eating if I chose.
  B. I feel that I have at least some control.
  C. I feel completely out of control.

Which most accurately describes your feelings after a binge?
  A. Not depressed at all
  B. Mildly depressed
  C. Moderately depressed
  D. Very depressed

---

### Compulsive Eating Scale (CES)

I get pleasure just thinking about food or eating (Likert scale).

I eat when I'm not hungry (Likert scale).

Eating seems to calm me down or make me feel better (Likert scale).

My weight varies and I am usually gaining or losing weight (Likert scale).

---

### Bulimia Test (Bulit)

I prefer to eat:
  A. At home alone
  B. At home with others
  C. In a public restaurant
  D. At a friend's home
  E. Doesn't matter

*(continued)*

TABLE 8-9 (Continued).

Most people I know would be amazed if they knew how much food I can consume at one sitting:
A. Without a doubt
B. Very probably
C. Probably
D. Possibly
E. No

What is the most weight you've ever lost in 1 month?
A. Over 20 pounds
B. 12–20 pounds
C. 8–11 pounds
D. 4–7 pounds
E. Less than 4 pounds

*Note.* BES and CFS items from Gormally, Black, Daston, and Rardin (1982). Binge Scale items from Hawkins and Clements (1980). CES items from Dunn and Ondercin (1981). Bulit items from Smith and Thelen (1984).

Recently, Smith and Thelen (1984) have developed and validated the Bulimia Test (Bulit). Based on the DSM–III criteria for Bulimia, the Bulit is a 32-item, multiple-choice scale designed to identify individuals with symptoms of bulimia. Cross-validation studies indicate that test scores are predictive of diagnosis (Smith & Thelen, 1984).

The Eating Disorder Inventory (EDI) is a 64-item multiscale measure that assesses psychological and behavioral components common in anorexia and bulimia. Garner, Olmstead, and Polivy (1983) designed the EDI to differentiate bulimics, extreme dieters, and particular subgroups of anorexic patients.

Finally, the Eating Attitudes Test (EAT) is a 40-item index developed by Garner and Garfinkel (1979) for the identification of anorexic patients. The EAT also assesses attitudes associated with anorexia nervosa. The authors have shown that scores of 30 or more points on the EAT discriminate anorexics from control subjects.

As discussed earlier in the chapter, data obtained from self-report measures (i.e., inventories, scales, diaries) may not accurately represent an individual's behavior, cognitions, or emotions. Of particular concern is the tendency for individuals with abnormal eating behavior (e.g., anorexic patients) to deny their maladaptive behavior (Brownell, 1981). However, some procedures can be instituted during assessment and treatment that may improve the accuracy and utility of self-report data. For example, collateral reports from appropriate individuals (e.g., roommates, friends) may provide useful checks on the patient's self-report. In addition, during the initial assessment phase, we recommend no changes in the patient's eating behavior, unless immediate intervention is required because of a serious health risk. Following this initial assessment period, the patient is interviewed to determine whether the data are representative of current functioning.

## Physical Activity

In contrast to obesity, which is often associated with physical inactivity, anorexia nervosa is frequently characterized by excessive and ritualized exercising (Brownell, 1981). Intensive, self-initiated programs of jogging, walking, or aerobic exercise may result in very high levels of caloric expenditure. Thus, indexes of physical activity levels are important in assessing anorexia nervosa. The Physical Activity Review (see Table 8-3) is a practical, cost-efficient method of obtaining data about physical activity levels. Moreover, data gathered on the Physical Activity Review can be easily incorporated into treatment plans and analyzed by calculating calories expended through various activities. In fact, we often recommend that anorexic patients reduce activity/exercise levels and caloric expenditure during treatment.

Bulimic patients vary in regard to physical activity levels. Although some individuals maintain moderate or low levels of activity/exercise, bingeing behavior is often paired with rigid and severe exercise regimens (Loro, 1984). In addition, the sporadic bursts of extreme caloric expenditure seen in some bulimics may prove harmful and are ill advised (Loro, 1984). Thus, regular assessment of physical activity with bulimics is warranted in order to measure caloric expenditure and monitor periods of physical activity and inactivity.

## Significant Others

As discussed earlier in the sections on obesity, significant others (e.g., family, friends, spouses) represent potential helpers or hinderers in the treatment of eating disorders. The assessment of social-environmental influences is important in order to examine whether (1) ongoing exposure to modeling of problematic self-control and weight management practices, (2) inadvertent reinforcement for dysfunctional eating patterns, or (3) positive role modeling and readily available support (Orleans & Barnett, 1984) are present. To identify potential allies and foes in treatment, as well as to begin investigating social-environmental influences, we employ the Significant Others List (see Table 8-5). Analysis of each individual's potential influence on the patient often proves worthwhile in understanding and treating the patient's eating disorder.

## Summary

Behavioral models of anorexia nervosa and bulimia nervosa emphasize the role of learning maladaptive eating habits, as well as the role of social learning in terms of consequences delivered by significant others (e.g., Gormally, 1984). Assessment and treatment aim to provide the patient with new or modified eating habits that are self-reinforced. In addition, unrealistic or negative thoughts about one's body and low self-esteem represent "internal targets" to address during treatment (Gormally, 1984; Loro, 1984). The measurement strategies described in this section provide a general overview of some behavioral and cognitive-behavioral approaches to assessing anorexic and bulimic patients. We believe effective treatment is dependent upon thorough assessment and individualized intervention programs. Like obesity, anorexia nervosa and bulimia nervosa are complex, multifaceted disorders. However, integrated assessment and treatment approaches have a much greater potential for providing effective interventions for these eating disorders.

## Conclusion

In conclusion, this chapter has explored a variety of behavioral strategies in the assessment of adult obesity, childhood obesity, anorexia nervosa, and bulimia nervosa. Whereas early attempts at assessment and treatment were often simplistic, rapid advancements in behavioral technology have expanded the outlook and prognosis for individuals suffering from eating disorders. We believe that a comprehensive approach to the assessment of obesity, anorexia nervosa, or bulimia nervosa provides a more solid empirical foundation from which to develop appropriate treatment strategies. Moreover, multidimensional assessments are essential in developing individually tailored treatment interventions. Although gaps remain in our ability to assess the complex, multifaceted nature of eating disorders, recent advancements in research and clinical practice continue to reveal new insights and understanding.

## Acknowledgment

The writing of this chapter was supported in part by a grant from the National Science Foundation.

# References

American Dietetic Association. (1977). *Exchange list for meal planning.* Chicago: Author.

American Psychiatric Association. (1980). *Diagnostic and statistical manual of mental disorders* (3rd ed.). Washington, DC: Author.

American Psychiatric Association. (1987). *Diagnostic and statistical manual of mental disorders* (3rd ed.—revised). Washington, DC: Author.

Aragona, J., Cassady, J., & Drabman, R. S. (1975). Treating overweight children through parental training and contingency. *Journal of Applied Behavior Analysis, 8,* 269–278.

Ben-Tovim, D. I., Marilov, V., & Crisp, A. H. (1979). Personality and mental state within anorexia nervosa. *Journal of Psychosomatic Research, 23,* 321–325.

Beumont, P. J. V., George, G. C. W., & Smart, D. E. (1976). "Dieters" and "vomiters" and "purgers" in anorexia nervosa. *Psychological Medicine, 6,* 617–622.

Blundell, J. (1980). Pharmacologic adjustment of the mechanisms underlying feeding and obesity. In A. J. Stunkard (Ed.), *Obesity* (pp. 182–207). Philadelphia: W. B. Saunders.

Bray, G. A. (1978). Definition, measurement, and classification of the syndromes of obesity. *International Journal of Obesity, 2,* 99–112.

Bray, G. A., Greenway, F. L., Molitch, M. E., Dahms, W. T., Atkins, R. L., & Hamilton, K. (1978). Use of anthropometric measures to assess weight loss. *American Journal of Clinical Nutrition, 31,* 769–773.

Brownell, K. D. (1981). Assessment of eating disorders. In D. H. Barlow (Ed.), *Behavioral assessment of adult disorders* (pp. 329–404). New York: Guilford Press.

Brownell, K. D. (1982). Obesity: Understanding and treating a serious, prevalent, and refractory disorder. *Journal of Consulting and Clinical Psychology, 50,* 820–840.

Brownell, K. D., Kelman, J. H., & Stunkard, A. J. (1983). Treatment of obese children with and without their mothers: Changes in weight and blood pressure. *Pediatrics, 71,* 515–523.

Brownell, K. D., & Stunkard, A. J. (1983). Behavioral treatment for obese children and adolescents. In P. J. McGrath & P. Firestone (Eds.), *Pediatric and adolescent behavioral medicine* (pp. 184–209). New York: Springer.

Casper, R. C., Eckert, E. D., Halmi, K. A., Goldberg, S. C., & Davis, J. M. (1980). Bulimia: Its incidence and clinical importance in patients with anorexia nervosa. *Archives of General Psychiatry, 37,* 1030–1035.

Center for Science in the Public Interest. (1977). *New American eating guide.* Washington, DC: Author.

Coates, T. J. (1977). *The efficacy of a multicomponent self-control program in modifying the eating habits and weight of three obese adolescents.* Unpublished doctoral dissertation, Stanford University.

Coates, T. J., Jeffery, R. W., Killen, J. D., & Danaher, B. G. (1982). Frequency of contact and monetary reward in weight loss, lipid change, and blood pressure reduction with adolescents. *Behavior Therapy, 13,* 175–185.

Cohen, E. A., Gelfand, D. M., Dodd, D. A., Jensen, J., & Turner, C. (1980). Self-control practices associated with weight loss maintenance in children and adolescents. *Behavior Therapy, 11,* 26–37.

Dunn, P. K., & Ondercin, P. (1981). Personality variables related to compulsive eating in college women. *Journal of Clinical Psychology, 37,* 43–49.

Epstein, L. H. (1986). Treatment of childhood obesity. In K. D. Brownell & J. P. Foreyt (Eds.), *Eating disorders* (pp. 159–176). New York: Basic Books.

Epstein, L. H., Masek, B. J., & Marshall, W. R. (1978). A nutritionally based school program for control of eating in obese children. *Behavior Therapy, 9,* 766–778.

Epstein, L. H., McGowan, C., & Woodall, K. (1984). The development and validation of a behavioral observation system for free play activity in young children. *Research Quarterly for Exercise and Sport, 55,* 180-183.

Epstein, L. H., Wing, R. R., Koeske, R., Andrasik, F., & Ossip, D. J. (1981). Child and parent weight loss in family-based behavior modification programs. *Journal of Consulting and Clinical Psychology, 49,* 674-685.

Epstein, L. H., Wing, R. R., Koeske, R., Ossip, D. J., & Beck, S. (1982). A comparison of lifestyle change and programmed aerobic exercise on weight and fitness changes in obese children. *Behavior Therapy, 13,* 651-665.

Epstein, L. H., Wing, R. R., Koeske, R., & Valoski, A. (1984). The effects of diet plus exercise on weight change in parents and children. *Journal of Consulting and Clinical Psychology, 52,* 429-437.

Epstein, L. H., Woodall, K., Goreczny, A. J., Wing, R. R., & Robertson, R. J. (1984). The modification of activity patterns and energy expenditure in obese young girls. *Behavior Therapy, 15,* 101-108.

Feinstein, A. R. (1959). The measurement of success in weight reduction: An analysis of methods and a new index. *Journal of Chronic Diseases, 10,* 439-456.

Foreyt, J. P., & Goodrick, G. K. (1981). Childhood obesity. In E. J. Mash & L. Terdal (Eds.), *Behavioral assessment of childhood disorders* (pp. 573-599). New York: Guilford Press.

Foreyt, J. P., & Parks, J. T. (1975). Behavioral controls for achieving weight loss in in the severely retarded. *Journal of Behavior Therapy and Experimental Psychiatry, 6,* 27-29.

Garfinkel, P. E., Moldofsky, H., & Garner, D. M. (1980). The heterogeneity of anorexia nervosa. *Archives of General Psychiatry, 37,* 1036-1040.

Garner, D. M., & Garfinkel, P. E. (1979). The Eating Attitudes Test: An index of the symptoms of anorexia nervosa. *Psychological Medicine, 9,* 273-279.

Garner, D. M., & Olmstead, M. P., & Polivy, J. (1983). Development and validation of a multidimensional Eating Disorder Inventory for anorexia nervosa and bulimia. *International Journal of Eating Disorders, 2,* 15-34.

Gormally, J. (1984). The obese binge eater: Diagnosis, etiology, and clinical issues. In R. C. Hawkins, W. J. Fremouw, & P. F. Clement (Eds.), *The binge-purge syndrome: Diagnosis, treatment, and research* (pp. 47-73). New York: Springer.

Gormally, J., Black, S., Daston, S., & Rardin, D. (1982). The assessment of binge eating severity among obese persons. *Addictive Behaviors, 7,* 47-55.

Hagen, R. L. (1974). Group therapy versus bibliotherapy in weight reduction. *Behavior Therapy, 5,* 222-234.

Hamill, P. V. V. , Drizd, T. A., Johnson, C. L., Reed, R. B., Roche, A. F., & Moore, W. M. (1979). Physical growth: National Center for Health Statistics percentiles. *American Journal of Clinical Nutrition, 32,* 607-629.

Harowski, K. J., & Jeffrey, D. B. (1982, November). *The role of individualized differences in weight loss and maintenance.* Paper presented at the meeting of the Association for Advancement of Behavior Therapy, Los Angeles.

Hartz, A., Giefer, E., & Rimm, A. A. (1977). Relative importance of the effect of family environment and heredity on obesity. *Annals of Human Genetics, 41,* 185-193.

Hawkins, R. C., & Clements, P. F. (1980). Development and construct validation of a self-report measure of binge eating tendencies. *Addictive Behaviors, 5,* 219-226.

Hsu, L. K. G. (1980). Outcome of anorexia nervosa: A review of the literature (1954 to 1978). *Archives of General Psychiatry, 37,* 1041-1046.

Jeffrey, D. B., & Katz, R. C. (1977). *Take it off and keep it off: A behavioral program for weight loss and healthy living.* Englewood Cliffs, NJ: Prentice-Hall.

Jeffrey, D. B., & Knauss, M. R. (1981). The etiologies, treatments, and assessments of obesity. In S. M. Haynes, & L. Gannon (Eds.), *Psychosomatic disorders: A psychophysiological approach to etiology and treatment* (pp. 269-319). New York: Praeger.

Kaplan, H. I., & Kaplan, H. S. (1957). The psychosomatic concept of obesity. *Journal of Nervous and Mental Disease, 125,* 181–201.

Kennedy, G. C. (1957). The development with age of hypothalamic restraint upon the appetite of the rat. *Journal of Endocrinology, 16,* 9–17.

Kingsley, R. G., & Shapiro, J. (1977). A comparison of three behavioral programs for the control of obesity in children. *Behavior Therapy, 8,* 30–36.

Knauss, M. R., & Jeffrey, D. B. (1981) Group behavior therapy for the treatment of obesity: Issues and suggestions. In D. Upper & S. M. Ross (Eds.), *Behavioral group therapy, 1981: An annual review* (pp. 279–307). Champaign, IL: Research Press.

Knauss, M. R., Jeffrey, D. B., Knauss, C. S. & Harowski, K. J. (1983). Therapeutic contact and individual differences in a comprehensive weight loss program. *the Behavior Therapist, 28,* 8–9.

LeBow, M. D. (1984). *Child obesity: A new frontier of behavior therapy.* New York: Springer.

Loro, A. D. (1984). Binge eating: A cognitive–behavioral treatment approach. In R. C. Hawkins, W. J. Fremouw, & P. F. Clement (Eds.), *The binge-purge syndrome: Diagnosis, treatment, and research* (pp. 183–210). New York: Springer.

Mahoney, B. K., Rogers, T., Straw, M., & Mahoney, M. J. (1977, November). *Results and implications of a problem solving treatment program for obesity.* Paper presented at the meeting of the Association for Advancement of Behavior Therapy, Atlanta.

Marlatt, A., & Gordon, J. (1980). Determinants of relapse: Implications for the maintenance of behavior change. In P. O. Davidson & S. M. Davidson (Eds.), *Behavioral medicine: Changing health lifestyles* (pp. 410–452). New York: Brunner/Mazel.

Mayer, J. (1957). Correlation between metabolism and feeding behavior and multiple etiology of obesity. *Bulletin of the New York Academy of Medicine, 22,* 744–761.

Nisbett, R. E. (1972). Hunger, obesity, and the ventromedical hypothalamus. *Psychological Review, 79,* 433–470.

Orleans, C. T., & Barnett, L. R. (1984). Bulimarexia: Guidelines for behavioral assessment and treatment. In R. C. Hawkins, W. J. Fremouw, & P. F. Clement (Eds.), *The binge-purge syndrome: Diagnosis, treatment, and research* (pp. 144–177). New York: Springer.

Palmer, R. L. (1979). The dietary chaos syndrome: A useful new term? *British Journal of Medical Psychology, 52,* 187–190.

Peterson, P. E., Jeffrey, D. B., Bridgwater, C. A., & Dawson, B. (1984). How pronutrition television programming affects children's dietary habits. *Developmental Psychology, 20,* 55–63.

Powley, T. L., & Keesey, R. (1970). Relationships of body weight to the lateral hypothalamic feeding syndrome. *Journal of Comparative and Physiological Psychology, 70,* 25–36.

Russell, G. (1979). Bulimia nervosa: An ominous variant of anorexia nervosa. *Psychological Medicine, 9,* 429–448.

Schachter, S. (1971). *Emotion, obesity, and crime.* New York: Academic Press.

Sims, E. A. H., & Horton, E. S. (1968). Endocrine and metabolic adaptation to obesity and starvation. *American Journal of Clinical Nutrition, 21,* 1455–1470.

Smith, M. C., & Thelen, M. H. (1984). Development and validation of a test for bulimia. *Journal of Consulting and Clinical Psychology, 52,* 863–872.

Stark, L. J., Collins, F. L., Osnes, P. G., & Stokes, T. F. (1984, November). *The use of nutrition training, cueing, and individual reinforcement: Procedures for modifying children's food choices at school and at home.* Paper presented at the meeting of the Society of Behavioral Medicine, Philadelphia.

Straw, R., Straw, M. K. & Craighead, L. (1979, November). *Psychometric properties of the RMQ: Cluster analysis of an obesity assessment device.* Paper presented at the annual meeting of the Association for Advancement of Behavior Therapy, San Francisco.

Stuart, R. B. (1967). Behavioural control of overeating. *Behaviour Research and Therapy, 5,* 55–62.

Stunkard, A. J. (1978). Basic mechanisms which regulate body weight: New perspectives. *Psychiatric Clinics of North America, 1,* 461–472.

Stunkard, A. J. (Ed.). (1980). *Obesity.* Philadelphia: W. B. Saunders.

Stunkard, A. J., & Kaplan, D. (1977). Eating in public places: A review of reports of the direct observation of eating behavior. *International Journal of Obesity, 1,* 89–101.

Stunkard, A. J., & Mahoney, M. J. (1976). Behavioral treatment of the eating disorders. In H. Leitenberg (Ed.), *Handbook of behavior modification* (pp. 45–73). New York: Appleton-Century-Crofts.

Thomas, A. E., McKay, D. A., & Cutlip, M. B. (1976). Nomograph for body mass index (kg/m$^2$). *American Journal of Clinical Nutrition, 29,* 302–304.

Waxman, M., & Stunkard, A. J. (1980). Calorie intake and expenditure of obese boys. *Journal of Pediatrics, 96,* 187–193.

Wheeler, M. E., & Hess, K. W. (1976). Treatment of juvenile obesity by successive approximation control of eating. *Journal of Behavior Therapy and Experimental Psychiatry, 7,* 235–241.

Withers, R. F. L. (1964). Problems in the genetics of human obesity. *Eugenics Review, 56,* 81–90.

Wollersheim, J. P. (1970). Effectiveness of group therapy based upon learning principles in the treatment of overweight women. *Journal of Abnormal Psychology, 76,* 462–474.

# 9

# COGNITIVE ASSESSMENT

JANET POLIVY
C. PETER HERMAN
DAVID M. GARNER
*University of Toronto*

## Introduction and Background

The sorts of abnormal behaviors that characterize patients with eating disorders (see Chapter 8) are accompanied and possibly mediated by a variety of cognitive aberrations. Some of these cognitive features are common to the three major syndromes—obesity, anorexia nervosa, and bulimia—whereas others are more prevalent in the latter two conditions. Although anorexia nervosa and bulimia are believed to be multiply determined (Garfinkel & Garner, 1982), and obesity also appears to be the outcome of a variety of causes or influences, the distorted cognitions, attitudes, and values present in these three disorders seem to warrant special attention as contributors to the observed psychopathologies. Regardless of etiology, treatment of eating disorders seems unlikely to be successful without attention to the underlying cognitive pathologies. Not surprisingly, then, recent treatments for eating disorders have focused increasingly on cognition (e.g., Fairburn, 1985; Garner & Bemis, 1982, 1985; Orbach, 1978).

## *Review of Cognitive Factors Observed in Eating Disorders*

The principal cognitive distortion characterizing patients with eating disorders seems to be a dysfunctional attitude toward and/or perception of weight and body shape. Attitudes range from a "relentless pursuit of thinness" (Bruch, 1973) or "morbid fear of fatness" (Russell, 1979) in anorexics[1] and bulimics, to a fear of thinness in the obese (Orbach, 1978).

1. The terms "anorexia" and "anorexics" are used occasionally throughout this chapter, without the qualifier "nervosa," in accordance with common usage. It is important to remember,

An inability to perceive their body shapes and sizes accurately has been observed in the obese and in anorexics (e.g., Bruch, 1973; Garner & Garfinkel, 1981), and this inaccuracy of perception is frequently accompanied by a general dissatisfaction with one's body. All types of eating-disordered patients report being preoccupied or even obsessed with thoughts of food or eating (or not eating) (Bruch, 1973; Orbach, 1978). Food and eating, like the body itself, are often subject to misperceptions; for instance, many patients entertain false notions about calories and their relation to weight (e.g., the belief that 1,000 calories per day is excessive and will lead to weight gain, or that a piece of cake has more than 1,000 calories in it) (e.g., Bruch, 1973; Polivy, Herman, & Kuleshnyk, 1984).

Although such weight- and food-related perceptions, attitudes, and beliefs are the most marked and obvious cognitive features observed in eating-disordered patients, they are by no means the only ones. Internal perceptions in general seem to be distorted or absent altogether in these groups (Bruch, 1973; Schachter, 1971). Less tied to the concrete realities of the body and its workings is a prevalent sense of ineffectiveness or worthlessness (Bruch, 1973; Garner & Bemis, 1982; Orbach, 1978). Other frequently noted "mental symptoms" include excessive perfectionistic desires or expectations (Bruch, 1978); a "dichotomous" thinking style (Garner, Garfinkel, & Bemis, 1982; Polivy, Herman, Olmsted, & Jazwinski, 1984); a lack of confidence in one's own thinking and decisions, or overcompliance to others (Garner & Bemis, 1982; Herman, Olmsted, & Polivy, 1983); a reluctance to form close relationships and an inability to trust others (Selvini-Palazzoli, 1978; Strober, 1980); and a fear of maturity, sexuality, or femininity (Crisp, 1980; Orbach, 1978). Although not all patients display all of these aberrant attitudes or beliefs, they are decidedly common. The presence of such distortions unrelated to food or weight indicates that eating disorders involve more than simply syndromes of disordered eating or starvation. Moreover, in many cases (at least initially), the patient will display a reluctance to give up distorted thinking even after its flawed character has been acknowledged, and sometimes even after food intake and weight have been stabilized; this may amount to a positive valuation of the disorder (e.g., Garner & Bemis, 1985; Orbach, 1978). This ego-syntonic aspect of certain attitudes or beliefs makes the disorder especially difficult to treat, because the patient may prefer the disorder to "normality."

---

however, that there are anorexias—losses of appetite—that are attributable to specific organic causes (e.g., terminal illness), and that should not be confused with anorexia nervosa. The "popularization" of anorexia nervosa in recent years has led to a contraction of the full name. This contraction may create confusion when other sorts of anorexias are being discussed; in the present chapter, however, we confine our discussion to anorexia nervosa, and safely indulge in the contraction.

## Cognitions Related to Dysfunctional Behavior

Many of the dysfunctional behavior patterns characterizing these patients are directly related to cognitions that perpetuate the eating disorder. Although the negative self-concept represented by the sense of worthlessness, overcompliance to others, lack of interpersonal trust, and excessive perfectionism does not necessarily correspond to particular behavior problems, it certainly constrains the individual and inhibits normal interactions and relationships. The flight from maturity or femininity often creates (or exacerbates) problems with sexual behavior: Patients may either avoid sex completely or act in a promiscuous but unsatisfying (and often personally distasteful) manner (Bruch, 1973; Orbach, 1978). The positive value ascribed to symptoms such as weight loss and starvation in anorexics, bingeing and purging in bulimics, and inappropriate (i.e., non-hunger-induced) eating in the obese makes it particularly difficult to substitute more acceptable behaviors.

Misperceptions about food and calories, lack of internal awareness, dichotomous thinking, obsession with food and eating, and excessive valuation of thinness all contribute to the chaotic eating behaviors of these patients. When patients cannot distinguish emotion from hunger, or cannot determine whether they are hungry or sated, it becomes more likely that they will eat in response to inappropriate (e.g., emotional) internal sensations. The desire for thinness leads to dieting, which in turn may trigger bingeing (see, e.g., Polivy & Herman, 1985a; Polivy, Herman, Olmsted, & Jazwinski, 1984). A dichotomous thinking style promotes binge-or-starve eating. Misperceptions regarding food and calories, and obsessions with food, are associated in obvious ways with disordered eating patterns.

## Comparisons among the Obesities, Anorexia Nervosa, and Bulimia

Comparisons among the eating disorders are complicated by the various types of obesity, some of which may reflect psychopathology, whereas others (possibly a majority of cases) may not. Obesity per se is not considered a psychiatric disorder in the American Psychiatric Association's (1980) *Diagnostic and Statistical Manual of Mental Disorders,* third edition (DSM-III). Several studies have shown the degree of psychopathology in the obese to be comparable to that in the general population (e.g., Crisp & McGuiness, 1976), although the well-known Midtown Manhattan Study (Goldblatt, Moore, & Stunkard, 1965) found a higher incidence (by self-report) of emotional problems in the obese. Thus it is not surprising that a comparison of 18 obese subjects with anorexic patients on "anorexic" characteristics, such as body dissatisfaction, bulimia, drive for thinness, ineffectiveness, perfectionism, and internal awareness, showed the two groups to be alike only in the dissatisfaction with their bodies (Garner, Olmsted, & Polivy, 1983a). The obese subjects scored within the normal range on all the other dimensions measured. Along with body dissatisfaction, some obese subjects resemble anorexics and bulimics in their inability to adjust their perceptions of their body size to changes in their actual body size. Specifically, all of these groups tend to see themselves as larger than they really are, even—or particularly—as they lose weight (Bruch, 1973; Garner, Garfinkel, Stancer, & Moldofsky, 1976; Glucksman & Hirsch, 1969).

Despite the apparent psychological health of the obese in general, there do appear to be some obese people who resemble anorexics and/or bulimics psychologically. In a recent investigation of obese patients (Polivy & Leiter, 1984), although the group as a whole was assessed as psychologically normal (except for the expected body dissatisfaction), some patients showed a cluster of abnormal attitudes, including a strong desire to be thin and a high degree of perfectionism or personal ineffectiveness; others showed the full spectrum of anorexic attitudes and beliefs. Also, some obese patients are bulimic (Loro & Orleans, 1981). Thus, whereas the majority of obese patients are probably quite different psychologically from anorexic and bulimic patients, there do seem to be some with similar psychopathology. As mentioned earlier, some obese "compulsive eaters" are very much like anorexic and bulimic patients in their unwillingness to give up their symptomatic behaviors; presumably they derive too much reward from them to relinquish them without a struggle.

Another consideration in the comparison of obese patients to those with anorexia or bulimia is that many obese people are not patients at all. Of course, some people suffering from anorexia nervosa and bulimia manage to escape therapeutic attention; however, in the case of many obese people, it is less obvious that such attention is warranted (Polivy & Herman, 1985b; Wooley & Wooley, 1984). It may thus be fair to conclude that obese people in treatment are not as representative of obese people in general as anorexics and bulimics in treatment are of anorexics and bulimics in general. Accordingly, comparisons of obese *patients* to anorexic or bulimic patients may overestimate the similarity of obese *people* to anorexic or bulimic people, and likewise may overestimate the degree of psychopathology in the obese population, as the aforementioned study by Crisp and McGuiness (1976) suggests. These conclusions, of course, depend for their validity on the existence of a substantial number of untreated obese people who are not in treatment, precisely because they do not suffer from the sort of debilitating psychological symptoms that would induce them to seek treatment. What proportion of the obese population exhibits this "psychologically benign" form of obesity is at present unknown.

Anorexic and bulimic patients differ primarily in their weights: Anorexics are drastically underweight, whereas bulimics may be underweight, normal-weight, or overweight. Anorexic bulimics, emaciated as they may be, tend to weight more on average than do nonbulimic (i.e., restricting) anorexic patients (Garfinkel, Moldofsky, & Garner, 1980). Although both groups differ considerably from comparable normal subjects on the kinds of cognitive characteristics detailed earlier, the bulimics tend to be even more extreme than the anorexics, particularly in their drive for thinness and body dissatisfaction (Garner & Olmsted, 1984). These differences may be "weight effects" (reflecting the bulimics' greater dissatisfaction with their weights, which are higher), or they may reflect something about the nature of bulimia itself. A more basic difference that probably *is* reflective of the nature of bulimia is the elevated impulsivity of bulimics as compared to anorexic patients. Bulimics are significantly—statistically and clinically—more likely to use street drugs or alcohol to excess, to steal, to have sexual relationships, to mutilate themselves, and to commit suicide (Garfinkel *et al.*, 1980; Strober, Salkin, Burroughs, & Morrell, 1982). The most basic difference between bulimic and nonbulimic eating, then, may be the ability to control and/or suppress impulsiveness. Whereas restricting anorexics always exert tight impulse control, bulimics are more likely to swing from one extreme to the other.

## Differentiating Eating Disorders from "Normality"

Many of the eating- and weight-related cognitive characteristics of eating-disordered patients discussed earlier seem as if they might well be prevalent in "normal" dieters in the general population. (Although we have argued that dieters are not "normal" in many respects—see Polivy & Herman, 1983, 1987—we assume for the present that, given their numerical predominance, they are not clinically disturbed. Certainly, dieting is not considered a DSM-III psychiatric disorder.) Dieters presumably diet as a "pursuit of thinness" (though the pursuit may not be "relentless") and to ameliorate dissatisfaction with their bodies. They may well have distorted views about food, calories, and their relation to weight (Polivy, Herman, & Kuleshnyk, 1984), and could well be seen as being preoccupied with food and eating (Polivy & Herman, 1985a). It has been proposed that anorexia nervosa and "normal" dieting differ mostly in degree rather than in kind. Nylander (1971) found that a majority of female high school students surveyed in Sweden had "felt fat" and that almost 10% reported at least three "anorexic" symptoms upon losing weight. Button and Whitehouse (1981) described what they called "subclinical anorexia nervosa" in a majority of female college students who had elevated scores on an objective anorexia screening scale. Similarly, Garner and Garfinkel (1980) found that populations at high risk for anorexia nervosa (e.g., ballet dancers) also yielded large proportions of subjects who displayed many symptoms of anorexia nervosa, without meeting a strict diagnostic criterion for the disorder. This would imply that the distinction between having an eating disorder and not having one is more quantitative than qualitative.

A study was conducted to test this "quantitative" hypothesis (Garner, Olmsted, Polivy, & Garfinkel, 1984). The attitudes and self-perceptions of patients with anorexia nervosa were assessed and compared to those of normal but weight-preoccupied women and normal, non-weight-preoccupied women (both normal groups consisted of college students). The two normal groups differed from each other on most measures, particularly those directly concerned with eating and body shape. They differed by definition on drive for thinness, which was used to assign the normal women to the weight-preoccupied or non-weight-preoccupied groups; however, they also differed in bulimic tendencies and body dissatisfaction. Furthermore, they differed with respect to perfectionistic striving, fear of maturity, sense of ineffectiveness, and awareness of internal sensations, with the weight-preoccupied group scoring in the "pathological" direction in each case. Only on the measure of interpersonal mistrust were the two normal groups equal, both scoring lower than the anorexic group. The weight-preoccupied group, although scoring higher than the non-weight-preoccupied group on the aforementioned measures, scored significantly lower than the anorexic group not only on mistrust, but also on sense of ineffectiveness and lack of awareness of internal sensations. Thus, whereas the weight-preoccupied subjects consistently scored higher than normal on cognitive measures associated with eating disorders, they entered the pathological range mainly on dieting-related measures, such as drive for thinness, bulimia (see Polivy & Herman, 1985a, for a discussion of the association between dieting and bulimia), and body dissatisfaction. There are both similarities and differences, then, between weight-preoccupied college students and patients with eating disorders. Moreover, when the weight-preoccupied group was submitted to cluster analysis, two subgroups emerged. One group scored consistently high (within the pathological range) on all the scales, whereas the other group scored high only on drive for thinness (by definition), body dissatisfaction, and perfectionism, scoring within the normal range on all the other measures. Clinical interviews on a subsample of these subjects confirmed the psychometric findings: Within the weight-preoccupied group, some subjects were essentially "normal" except for their concern about weight and eating, whereas others closely resembled clinical cases of anorexia nervosa and bulimia (Garner et al., 1984). This study suggests that with adequate cognitive assessment, eating disorders can—and should—be distinguished from mere (nonpathological, albeit intense) dietary and weight concerns.

## Clinical Applications

### Screening

Several instruments have been developed to assess aspects of eating disorders, or have been used in that context (although they were originally developed for other purposes). The Restraint Scale used by us and others (for reviews, see Herman & Polivy, 1980; Polivy & Herman, 1983; or Polivy, Herman, & Howard, in press) to measure "restrained eating" or chronic dieting falls basically into the latter category. It was composed originally in an attempt to assess the tendency toward "compulsive eating" in chronically dieting college coeds (Herman & Mack, 1975). Even before this initial study was completed, the concept being measured was generalized beyond eating behavior itself to encompass attitudes, behaviors, and other indices of chronic dieting. Thus, factor analyses of the Restraint Scale confirm the initial (e.g., Herman & Polivy, 1980) prediction and finding of two factors— one measuring attitudes and behaviors reflecting concern with dieting and losing weight (Diet-Related Cognitions), and the other primarily assessing the fluctuations in weight accompanying these attitudes and behaviors (Weight Fluctuations). Items from the Restraint Scale are presented in Table 9-1. A new type of Restraint Scale has been developed by Stunkard and Messick (1985); it has a third factor in addition to two similar to those in the original scale. Although this more elaborate scale has been studied psychometrically in some detail, whether it can improve on the earlier scale's success in predicting behavior has yet to be convincingly demonstrated.

TABLE 9-1.  Sample Items from the Restraint Scale

---

*Factor I.  Diet-Related Cognitions*
- How often are you dieting?
- Would a weight fluctuation of 5 pounds affect the way you live your life?
- Do you eat sensibly in front of others and splurge alone?
- Do you give too much time and thought to food?

*Factor II.  Weight Fluctuations*
- What is the maximum weight (in pounds) that you have ever lost within 1 month?
- What is your maximum weight gain within a week?
- In a typical week, how much does your weight fluctuate?

---

*Note.* From "Restrained Eating" by C. P. Herman and J. Polivy, 1980, in A. J. Stunkard (Ed.), *Obesity* (pp. 208–225), Philadelphia: W. B. Saunders. Copyright 1980 by W. B. Saunders Company. Reprinted by permission. A factor analysis of this scale is presented in Polivy, Herman, and Howard (in press).

TABLE 9-2. Sample Items from the Abbreviated Eating Attitudes Test (EAT-26)

---

*Factor I.  Dieting*
- Engage in dieting behavior
- Feel uncomfortable after eating sweets
- Aware of the calorie content of foods that I eat

*Factor II.  Bulimia and Food Preoccupation*
- Have the impulse to vomit after meals
- Have gone on eating binges where I feel that I may not be able to stop
- Give too much thought to food

*Factor III.  Oral Control*
- Take longer than others to eat meals
- Feel that others would prefer if I ate more
- Avoid eating when I am hungry

---

*Note.* From "The Eating Attitudes Test: Psychometric Features and Clinical Analysis" by D. M. Garner, M. P. Olmsted, Y. Bohr, and P. E. Garfinkel, 1982, *Psychological Medicine, 12*, 871-878. Copyright 1982 by Cambridge University Press. Reprinted by permission.

Restrained eaters have been shown to differ from unrestrained eaters in a number of respects, including greater emotionality, distractibility, and salivary responsiveness; of course, they differ as well in eating patterns (see Herman & Polivy, 1980, or Polivy & Herman, 1983, for reviews). In addition, restrained eaters seem to be more likely to be or become bulimic (Polivy & Herman, 1985a; Polivy, Herman, Olmsted, & Jazwinski, 1984; Wardle, 1980), and patients with anorexia nervosa score significantly above average on the Restraint Scale, particularly if they are also bulimic (Polivy, 1978). A high score on the Restraint Scale may thus indicate a susceptibility or tendency to bulimia, although it is by no means a certain indicant. Restraint Scale scores, then, may be useful in alerting the assessor to the presence of the characteristics detailed above—including counterregulatory or even bulimic eating—but they are not conclusive in and of themselves.

Hawkins and Clement (1980) developed a questionnaire to assess binge-eating in college student samples, but later concluded—along with other contributors to their volume on binge-eating (Hawkins, Fremouw, & Clement, 1984)—that this scale should be part of a battery of measures to assess bulimic tendencies. One recommended element of such a battery, the Eating Attitudes Test (EAT), has been widely used to assess symptoms of both bulimia and anorexia nervosa; indeed, it was developed on the basis of the clinical literature specifically to measure anorexic behaviors and attitudes. The EAT was developed by Garner and Garfinkel (1979) as a self-report measure of the symptoms of anorexia nervosa. Extensively validated both psychometrically and clinically, the EAT has recently been abbreviated on the basis of factor analysis (Garner, Olmsted, Bohr, & Garfinkel, 1982). The three subscales of the abbreviated EAT (EAT-26), as identified by factor analysis, are Dieting, Bulimia and Food Preoccupation, and Oral Control. Sample items from each subscale are found in Table 9-2.

Bulimic and restricting anorexic patients do not seem to differ in their total EAT-26 scores, but they do score differently on two of the three subscales. Normal college female control subjects scored significantly lower than the eating-disordered patients on all subscales and on total score (Garner, Olmsted, et al., 1982); the EAT-26 thus does discriminate between normal and eating-disordered groups. It also identifies eating disturbances in nonclinical samples (Button & Whitehouse, 1981; Garner & Garfinkel, 1980). However, not all individuals who score high on the EAT necessarily satisfy the criteria for either anorexia nervosa or bulimia; interviews with such nonanorexic–nonbulimic high EAT scorers indicate that their abnormal eating patterns often interfere with normal psychosocial functioning (see Garner, Olmsted, et al., 1982). Thus, high EAT scores alone indicate disturbed eating patterns, but not necessarily a clinical eating disorder with the full array of associated psychological and motivational characteristics discussed earlier. Garner, Olmsted, et al. (1982) conclude that the EAT is best used as an outcome measure for treated eating-disordered patients or as a screening instrument for nonclinical groups. However, as has been emphasized previously (Garner & Garfinkel, 1980), it is inappropriate to use the EAT or any other self-report measure as the sole means of diagnosing anorexia nervosa or bulimia. Although there is clear merit in standardized measures of the symptoms of anorexia nervosa and bulimia, diagnosis of these disorders on the basis of existing clinical criteria is sufficiently straightforward that using test results to arrive at a diagnosis is unnecessary. Moreover, it is virtually impossible to obtain satisfactory diagnostic sensitivity and specificity with a psychometric instrument when the base rate for the disorder is very low.

There are other measures of symptom clusters characterizing eating-disordered patients (Goldberg et al., 1980; Halmi, Falk, & Schwartz, 1981; Slade, 1973), but they are suitable only for inpatient administration or focus exclusively on overt symptoms of the disorder (usually eating behaviors). The Eating Disorder Inventory (EDI), by contrast, was designed specifically to assess several of the cognitive characteristics described clinically in eating-disordered patients, in addition to behavioral manifestations (Garner, Olmsted, & Polivy, 1983a, 1983b). This self-report inventory was intended to augment the EAT, which focuses primarily on dieting- and eating-related symptoms. The EDI is comprised of theoretically derived items assessing not only dieting concern or Drive for Thinness (as the EDI subscale is called) and Bulimia—two subscales that have a fair degree of similarity to two EAT subscales—but also specific cognitive, attitudinal, and behavioral qualities that may serve to distinguish individuals with true psychopathology from "normal" dieters. Thus, in addition to the two above-mentioned dieting- and eating-related subscales, there is a subscale called Body

Dissatisfaction, assessing the belief that certain body parts, especially those associated with femaleness, are too large. It has been suggested that the relentless dieting seen in anorexia nervosa is a response to such dissatisfaction with one's body, which in turn has been shown to be related to the distortions of body image often found in these patients. Other subscales are Maturity Fears, (lack of) Interoceptive Awareness, Perfectionism, Interpersonal Distrust, and Ineffectiveness. These cognitive dimensions were all derived from clinical descriptions of fundamental aspects of eating disorders (Garner et al., 1983a, 1983b). Sample items from the EDI are presented in Table 9-3.

The EDI was validated upon three subsamples of anorexia nervosa patients and three control groups of female college students. The subscales were modified on the basis of successive analyses of these subsample data until high levels of internal reliability were achieved for all subscales, maintaining an acceptable level of discriminant validity between the two types of subjects. The EDI has been used experimentally to discriminate individuals with eating disorders from nonpathological but weight-preoccupied women. Follow-up interviews confirmed that the women from the nonclinical sample whose EDI profiles were in the pathological range did seem to have true eating disorders (Garner et al., 1984). It thus seems that the EDI is well suited for assessing some of the underlying cognitive features of eating-disordered patients and for discriminating pathological from nonpathological eating behavior.

## The Clinical Interview

Anorexic and bulimic patients (and, to a lesser extent, obese patients) often enter therapy feeling that their experiences are unique and that no one—especially no one who has not also had their problem—can possibly understand what they have experienced (Bruch, 1973; Garner & Bemis, 1985). There are thus several immediate tasks that must be accomplished in the initial interviews. First, it is important to begin laying the foundation of a trusting therapeutic alliance. The therapist must communicate warmth, concern, and empathy. For many of these patients, close relationships have been consistently dangerous, fear-producing, or otherwise difficult, so establishing a therapeutic bond will require careful work (Fairburn, 1985).

The initial interview is also the time to ascertain the circumstances that have led the patient to seek treatment. Particularly in those cases where the symptoms are fulfilling some function for the patient, it is important to discover the motivations behind the decision to seek help. Regardless of whether the patient has come in response to inner distress or in response to the urgings of others, it must be established that the purpose of therapy is to alleviate the patient's underlying unhappiness. This may be

TABLE 9-3.   Sample Items from the Eating Disorder Inventory (EDI)

---

*Factor I.   Drive for Thinness*
- I feel extremely guilty after overeating.
- I am terrified of gaining weight.
- I am preoccupied with the desire to be thinner.

*Factor II.   Interoceptive Awareness*
- I get frightened when my feelings are too strong.
- I get confused as to whether or not I am hungry.
- When I am upset, I worry that I will start eating.

*Factor III.   Bulimia*
- I eat moderately in front of others and stuff myself when they're gone.
- I have the thought of trying to vomit in order to lose weight.
- I eat or drink in secrecy.

*Factor IV.   Body Dissatisfaction*
- I think that my stomach is too big.
- I think that my thighs are too large.
- I feel satisfied with the shape of my body.

*Factor V.   Ineffectiveness*
- I feel ineffective as a person.
- I feel alone in the world.
- I have a low opinion of myself.

*Factor VI.   Maturity Fears*
- I wish that I could return to the security of childhood.
- The demands of adulthood are too great.
- I feel that people are happiest when they are children.

*Factor VII.   Perfectionism*
- Only outstanding performance is good enough in my family.
- As a child, I tried very hard to avoid disappointing my parents and teachers.
- I have extremely high goals.

*Factor VIII.   Interpersonal Distrust*
- I trust others.
- I have trouble expressing my emotions to others.
- I need to keep people at a certain distance (feel uncomfortable if someone tries to get too close).

---

*Note.* From "Development and Validation of a Multidimensional Eating Disorder Inventory for Anorexia Nervosa and Bulimia" by D. M. Garner, M. P. Olmsted, and J. Polivy, 1983, *International Journal of Eating Disorders, 2,* 15-34. Copyright 1983 by John Wiley and Company. Reprinted by permission.

an opportunity to begin to explore the functions served by the disorder for the patient, and to make the patient aware of these functions. Information about the disorder, the usual manifestations, side effects, and outcome may also be provided to patients at this time, to help them acknowledge their own experiences (Fairburn, 1985; Garner & Bemis, 1985; Garner, Rockert, Olmsted, Johnson, & Coscina, 1985).

Much of the focus in the initial interviews will be on obtaining information from the patient about weight and diet history, current eating patterns, and other biographical information, with particular attention to weight, eating, self-image, and attitudes and feelings about these central issues. Symptomatic behaviors such as bingeing, purging (by means of vomiting or laxative/diuretic abuse), starving, drug use, and other weight control techniques or impulsive behaviors should be assessed. Related cognitions should likewise be explored (Bruch, 1973; Fairburn, 1985; Garner & Bemis, 1985).

## Identifying Maladaptive Cognitions

Many of the symptomatic behaviors troubling the patient are likely to be related to particular cognitions and cognitive patterns. If these cognitions are altered through therapy, then the distressing behaviors may be reduced or even eliminated. This is the general approach to the treatment of eating disorders that we advocate, along with several others in the area (e.g., Bruch, 1973, 1978; Fairburn, 1985; Garner & Bemis, 1982, 1985; Garner, Garfinkel, & Bemis, 1982; Orbach, 1978; Polivy, Herman, Olmsted, & Jazwinski, 1984). Behavioral and psychodynamic approaches, of course, also have their advocates (e.g., Goodsitt, 1985; Rosen & Leitenberg, 1985).

The cognitive patterns most likely to be causing distress to these patients include the following: their negative self-image, combined with their linking of weight to self-worth; their deficits in awareness of internal states, combined with a lack of confidence in these states as guides for behavior; their feelings of guilt or shame about their symptomatic behaviors, or, conversely, overvaluation of these symptoms and refusal to relinquish them; and their misperceptions about themselves, food, and body weight, as well as about the relations among these constructs. Direct questioning about some of these cognitions may be seen by such patients as threatening or challenging, provoking denial, further entrenchment of the maladaptive attitude, or distrust of the interviewer (Garner & Bemis, 1985). Bruch (1973) recommends adopting an "objective, fact finding attitude in which the patient and therapist are true collaborators in the search for unknown factors" (p. 338). Garner and Bemis (1985) suggest that such an emphasis on introspection and joint effort also encourages patients to begin to trust themselves and others "by legitimizing [their] experience" (p. 116). They also recommend avoiding direct confrontation of the patients' beliefs; instead, one should follow lines of inquiry that will plant seeds of doubt about those beliefs without challenging them directly. For example, to undermine the frequent anorexic premise that "thinness is a valid and dependable criterion for inferring self-worth," Garner and Bemis suggest asking, "Are you obtaining what you hoped to gain from your present state?" (p. 113). This focuses patients' attention on the presumptive benefits of the symptomatic behaviors, and by implication on the disadvantages as well.

## Cognitive Therapeutic Intervention

Once the maladaptive cognitive patterns underlying a patient's eating disorder have been identified, intervention to alter the targeted cognitions may begin. One caveat offered by Fairburn (1985) is that before such treatment is instituted on an outpatient basis, it must be established that the patient is not in any physical danger, either from suicidal inclinations (a relatively rare threat, according to Fairburn & Cooper, 1984), or, more commonly, from physical health problems stemming from the eating disorder. Such problems are often encountered in emaciated anorexia nervosa patients, who may exhibit various complications due to malnutrition, and in those bulimics who purge themselves frequently by vomiting or by laxative abuse, and who may consequently suffer from metabolic alkalosis, hypochloremia, and/or hypokalemia. Once immediate medical danger has been ruled out, however, cognitive therapy may begin.

Fairburn (1985) describes three stages of cognitive–behavioral treatment for bulimia; in our view, this framework applies well to all eating-disordered patients. In the first stage, the primary focus is on gaining control over eating; accordingly, the techniques employed are for the most part relatively behavioral in nature. With the distressing symptomatic behaviors somewhat ameliorated, the second phase may proceed. Here, the treatment emphasizes cognitive changes. It is at this point that "the identification and modification of dysfunctional thoughts, beliefs, and values" (Fairburn, 1985, p. 166) becomes the central focus of therapy. Finally, the last stage attempts to ensure the maintenance of the gains achieved in therapy. Fairburn (1985) thus endorses an approach that actually combines cognitive and behavioral targets and interventions, rather than exclsuively focusing on either one.

The approaches that we have advocated for treating eating disorders are characterized by a cognitive–behavioral synthesis similar to Fairburn's (1985) (e.g., Garner & Bemis, 1982, 1985; Garner, Garfinkel, & Bemis, 1982; Polivy & Herman, 1983). For example, we (Polivy & Herman, 1983) suggest the use of a variety of behavioral techniques for helping patients to gain control of their eating behavior while the presumably more difficult but far-reaching cognitive changes are being effected. Regular eating habits (i.e., consistent meals at consistent times) are encouraged, to enable the "dieters" (of whatever weight and diagnosis) to once again—or perhaps for the first time—identify internal signals of hunger and satiety; such identification, in turn, will help promote controlled eating. The intended cognitive changes focus on eliminating all-or-none, dichotomous thoughts about "good" (diet) and "bad" (binge) foods, and corresponding all-or-none eating habits. At the same time, the therapist must attempt to foster a new acceptance by patients of their bodies and themselves.

Garner and Bemis (1985) describe their cognitive–behavioral approach to the treatment of eating disorders as "distinguished by its *explicit* concern with beliefs, values, and assumptions" (p. 115) and as being adapted from a variety of more general cognitive therapies. As they see it, the basic assumption of cognitive–behavioral treatment is "that maladaptive feelings and behaviors are mediated by distorted or maladaptive thinking and that the primary aim of clinical intervention is to alter these cognitive processes" (p. 116). They modify these interventions, however, to take into account specific facets of the psychological makeup of eating-disordered patients (as outlined earlier). Thus, the treatment of eating disorders may require a longer duration of therapy to allow for the development of a trusting therapeutic relationship. Garner and Bemis, like Fairburn, also advocate paying particular attention to potential physical complications of these disorders, and educating patients to these dangers. Similarly, they note that the patients need to regain accurate perception of internal events and to develop trust in these signals as behavioral guides. Finally, identifying and remedying the basic self-concept deficiencies characteristic of these patients are critical aspects of therapy. The normalization of weight and eating is thus seen as a behavioral accompaniment to the cognitive treatment outlined earlier.

One example of the sort of specific cognitive pattern that Garner and Bemis (1985) suggest targeting for intervention is the pervasive style of dichotomous or absolutist thinking observed in eating-disordered patients; such thinking often extends beyond the domains of food and eating into every aspect of the patients' lives, including interactions with other people. Garner and Bemis (1985) suggest that patients be made aware of such cognitive styles and their implications in a gradual way. Arguing and even prolonged questioning of the patients are to be avoided, because they often as not exacerbate the patients' negative self-concept and feeling of inadequacy, not to mention distrust of the therapist. The patients' gradual recognition of their dichotomous thinking allows them to acknowledge it as a distortion and to develop a better sense of an appropriate middle ground.

In one case, a bulimic patient was able over a period of months in therapy to perceive and accept the connection between her need to "be in complete control" and eat nothing at all, on the one hand, and subsequent binges when she felt totally out of control, on the other. After she recognized that her starving actually precipitated her bingeing, and that her dichotomous view of herself as having to be entirely in or out of control left her no feasible alternative to starving or bingeing, she was able to adjust her eating to avoid both extremes, although she still swung from "dieting" to "overeating" to a lesser extent during times of stress. Only after many more months of therapy was she able to make the more general connection between her dichotomous thinking and her mood swings from elation to depression. Months of gradual cognitive restructuring allowed her to recognize that she had been dichotomizing her moods in much the same way as her eating, striving to achieve the "perfection" of an elated state. Because she could not possibly maintain such a state, her "failure" would send her crashing into a severe depression, where her dichotomous logic forced her to remain until she could summon the energy to reach an elated state once again. The recognition that neither extreme was comfortable for her, and that one inexorably led to the other, allowed her to work on developing a realistic middle emotional ground. The experience of recognizing the effect of her cognitions on her eating behavior, and then changing that behavior, set the stage for identifying the more pervasive effects of her cognitions and for attempting to change her emotional responses to them (Polivy, 1984).

### Monitoring Progress: Patients' Reports of Cognitive and Behavioral Changes

The patient just described illustrates the interrelation of cognitive and behavioral changes. A change in her dichotomous thinking about eating and starving appeared to lead to a parallel change in those eating behaviors; as her cognitive pattern became less extreme and dichotomous, she reported a corresponding change in her eating pattern. This behavioral change was then followed by a further cognitive shift, which will, it is hoped, permit more sweeping behavioral changes as therapy progresses. Such a positive feedback cycle, ideally, will bring more cognitive, emotional, and self-esteem improvements.

It is not necessary to argue that either cognitive or behavioral improvements are primary, just as the etiology of the disorder need not be either cognitive or behavioral in order for such interventions to relieve it. As social psychologists have long theorized (e.g., Bem, 1972), one's perception of one's own personality is strongly influenced by one's perception of one's own behavior. If individuals see themselves binge-eating less often, for example, they begin to think of themselves as less "disturbed." Conversely, attitudes and beliefs about oneself influence one's behavior. If individuals believe that they are likely to binge in a particular situation, such a belief may become a self-fulfilling prophecy. Changing either pathological cognitions or pathological behaviors should thus initiate a cycle of mutual alterations affecting both cognitions and behaviors, particularly if both are under examination in therapy.

### Progress as Observed by the Therapist

The most obvious indicant of altered eating behavior is a change in the patient's weight. Unfortunately, this measure is often the one given the most attention by the patient, therapist, and others involved with the patient, perhaps because it is so obvious. Although weight changes do reflect behavioral changes, they do not necessarily indicate a corresponding change in the patient's self-image. Weight gain in an anorexic, or weight loss in an overweight patient, will often elicit compliments from others, but it will not necessarily reflect or precipitate an improvement in self-esteem. Many patients become more anxious when their eating and weight "improve." At the very least, they may worry that they will be unable to persist in the new behaviors or maintain the new weight. And even alterations in behavior that lead to desired alterations in weight need not reflect a true change in attitude or self-perception; they may simply be a temporary response to a therapeutic ploy or external event (such as a job change). Therefore it is incumbent upon the clinician to monitor patients' attitudes and feelings about themselves closely, rather than emphasizing weight changes. Besides, improvements in behavior and self-image may well have little effect on weight (especially in the case of bulimics who are abnormally maintaining a normal weight), but such improvements are the ultimate goal of therapy.

In some cases, the therapist may be well advised to ignore weight changes, for excessive attention to the patient's weight may reinforce the prevailing opinion that the patient's problem is a "weight problem." Many overweight and underweight patients are afraid to change their weight because their "weight problem" is the only obvious excuse they have—in the eyes of their family, friends, and even themselves—to seek help or be less than perfect. One overweight patient remarked that she did not dare lose her excess weight, because if she were at a normal weight, there would not be "room for any mistakes"; she would then have to be perfect (Polivy, 1984). Anorexic patients voice similar fears, observing that as soon as they gain some weight they are deemed "cured" by their friends and relatives and are treated accordingly. It is thus up to the therapist to emphasize the importance of cognitive and emotional changes, in addition to the behavioral and weight changes upon which everyone else is focusing so intently.

During the course of therapy, changes in the patient's attitudes, beliefs, and feelings are likely to become apparent to the therapist. Progress may also be monitored by readministering standardized psychometric instruments and comparing current scores to pretreatment scores and to nonpathological norms. The method of observation is not crucial, as long as these attitudes toward the self, which are crucial, are monitored so that the therapist is not misled by visible weight changes.

## Follow-Up Assessment

Ideally, patients should be followed after therapy has ended, both to assess continuing changes in cognitions and behaviors and to evaluate the maintenance of therapy-induced improvement. Follow-up interviews will be maximally informative if they include further measurements with previously used instruments, as well as patients' self-report regarding both improvement and lingering problems or backsliding. The impact of such gains and deficits on the patients' general functioning and on other areas of their lives should be assessed. It is to be hoped that the progress made will expand to cover other areas of the patients' lives, with a corresponding expansion of self-esteem.

Finally, it is important to determine the degree to which changes achieved during therapy persist afterward. Are therapeutic gains maintained in the face of renewed life stresses? Do improvements in weight help anorexic and obese patients to recover further? As might be expected, therapy progresses better in anorexic patients whose weight has risen to the point where they are no longer suffering from direct starvation effects (Garfinkel & Garner, 1982), but do these improvements continue after therapy ends, or does backsliding occur? Weight gain alone can sometimes be counterproductive (Bruch, 1978; Garfinkel & Garner, 1982); however, more research is needed even to demonstrate the lasting effectiveness of less superficial therapeutic changes in these patients.

Obese patients are notoriously unsuccessful at maintaining therapeutically induced weight losses (Stunkard & Penick, 1979). A recent study of the effectiveness of psychotherapy for obesity, however, found not only encouraging degrees of weight loss, but excellent maintenance of these losses (Stunkard, 1980). Stunkard speculates that the unexpectedly successful results that he found may have been attributable to a general improvement of personal functioning for the patients involved. He acknowledges, however, that further research is needed to support such an inference (Stunkard, 1980). Similarly, Fairburn (1985) concludes his presentation of cognitive therapy for bulimia with the observation that controlled outcome studies are needed "before any treatment for bulimia can be wholeheartedly advocated" (p. 189). He recommends the use of "reputable standardized measures"; assessment of "each facet of the condition, including patients' eating habits, mood, and (most important) their attitudes toward their shape and weight" (p. 189); and a follow-up period of 2 years at the absolute minimum. These recommendations seem valid for assessing treatments for all eating disorders.

## A Clinical Case Example

This chapter has described an ideal for cognitive assessment and treatment of eating disorders. How might such an ideal be attained, and how would such a therapeutic intervention be experienced by a patient? A case example may help to illustrate the process.

A 21-year-old female presented with a 5-year history of severe bulimia (up to five episodes per day of binge-eating followed by vomiting), preceded by a 2-year history of weight loss and amenorrhea indicative of anorexia nervosa. The patient had been training to be a gymnast when the anorexia nervosa began; she continued this training for 3 years. Her father was intensely involved in this activity, driving the patient and her younger sister to their classes and attending all of their competitions. When the patient finally decided to quit gymnastics, her father was extremely disappointed. The patient was very concerned with pleasing both of her parents, who held high expectations for their three children (the patient also had an older brother). The patient described herself as having been a "well-behaved" child until she began binge-eating every day and quit the gymnastics program. She then traveled in Europe for a year, working at odd jobs. When she returned home, she and two friends moved into a house owned by her parents near the local university. The patient began working as a waitress to pay her living expenses and the nominal rent her parents accepted for the house. Her relationship with her parents and siblings deteriorated when they learned of her bulimia, and she began to avoid them because she felt that they were always watching what she ate. She had several close friends of both sexes and a steady boyfriend at the time of presentation. She continued to work as a waitress, despite the increased bingeing that she associated with this work; it seemed that she could not commit herself to any other work that she might not do "perfectly."

The patient completed the EDI after her initial interview. Her scores were extremely high on the Bulimia, Perfectionism, (lack of) Interoceptive Awareness, and Drive for Thinness subscales. All her other subscale scores were above the norms for females of her age and consistent with norms for patients with anorexia and bulimia. Thus, the clinical picture of a severely bulimic person—out of touch with her body, wanting to be thin and "perfect," yet feeling ineffective and afraid of the responsibilities of adulthood— was confirmed by the questionnaire.

The patient was treated in group therapy (see Polivy, 1981, or Polivy & Garfinkel, 1984, for a detailed description of this type of therapy group) for 12 weeks, and then the EDI was readministered. In the group sessions, she had learned to recognize the feelings that precipitated her eating binges, and had begun to have several bingeless days a week. She had cut down on her waitressing and entered a technical training program at a community college, in which she was excelling. Her mother was extremely supportive, and the patient felt that she had a new respect and understanding for her mother. The EDI scores at the second administration reflected these changes. The patient's Bulimia score had dropped to within the normal range, as had her Ineffectiveness, (lack of) Interoceptive Awareness, Maturity Fears, and Body Dissatisfaction scores. Perfectionism was the only subscale still elevated.

After a further 10 months of group therapy, the patient was hardly ever bingeing, was working at her new career, had left waitressing completely, and was feeling good about herself in general. Therapy was terminated at this point, and the EDI again reflected her improved status, with scores of 0 or 1 for Bulimia, Maturity Fears, (lack of) Interoceptive Awareness, and Ineffectiveness, and extremely low scores (2) for Body Dissatisfaction and Interpersonal Distrust. Her Drive for Thinness score was within the normal range, and only Perfectionism remained high. Because this subscale is often elevated in nonpathological college students (Garner *et al.,* 1984), it was not deemed grounds for concern. At a 1-year follow-up, the patient reported rarely bingeing—less than once a month—and never being concerned about it. She was being promoted very quickly at work, getting along better with her parents and brother (but not with her sister), and feeling happy with herself and her life. Again, her EDI scores remained stable and normal (Polivy, 1984).

Obviously, not all cases are so successful; however, in our experience, questionnaire scores tend to correspond to the clinical picture described by patients' self-report and perceived by the therapist. Cognitive and behavioral changes are closely intertwined, and if anything, potentiate each other if focused on together. We thus conclude that assessment and treatment of eating disorders are well served by an emphasis on cognitive as well as behavioral features.

## References

American Psychiatric Association. (1980). *Diagnostic and statistical manual of mental disorders* (3rd ed.). Washington, DC: Author.

Bem, D. J. (1972). Self-perception theory. In L. Berkowitz (Ed.), *Advances in experimental social psychology* (Vol. 6, pp. 34–66). New York: Academic Press.

Bruch, H. (1973). *Eating disorders: Obesity, anorexia nervosa and the person within.* New York: Basic Books.

Bruch, H. (1978). *The golden cage.* Cambridge, MA: Harvard University Press.

Button, E. J., & Whitehouse, A. (1981). Subclinical anorexia nervosa. *Psychological Medicine, 11,* 509–516.

Crisp, A. H. (1980). *Anorexia nervosa: Let me be.* New York: Grune & Stratton.

Crisp, A. H., & McGuiness, B. (1976). Jolly fat: Relation between obesity and psychoneurosis in the general population. *British Medical Journal, i,* 7–9.

Fairburn, C. G. (1985). Cognitive-behavioral treatment for bulimia. In D. M. Garner & P. E. Garfinkel (Eds.), *Handbook of psychotherapy for anorexia nervosa and bulimia* (pp. 160–192). New York: Guilford Press.

Fairburn, C. G., & Cooper, P. J. (1984). The clinical features of bulimia nervosa. *British Journal of Psychiatry, 284,* 1153–1155.

Garfinkel, P. E., & Garner, D. M. (1982). *Anorexia nervosa: A multidimensional perspective.* New York: Brunner/Mazel.

Garfinkel, P. E., Moldofsky, H., & Garner, D. M. (1980). The heterogeneity of anorexia nervosa: Bulimia as a distinct subgroup. *Archives of General Psychiatry, 37,* 1036-1040.

Garner, D. M., & Bemis, K. M. (1982). A cognitive-behavioral approach to anorexia nervosa. *Cognitive Therapy and Research, 6,* 123-150.

Garner, D. M., & Bemis, K. M. (1985). Cognitive therapy for anorexia nervosa. In D. M. Garner & P. E. Garfinkel (Eds.), *Handbook of psychotherapy for anorexia nervosa and bulimia* (pp. 107-146). New York: Guilford Press.

Garner, D. M., & Garfinkel, P. E. (1979). The Eating Attitudes Test: An index of the symptoms of anorexia nervosa. *Psychological Medicine, 9,* 273-279.

Garner, D. M., & Garfinkel, P. E. (1980). Socio-cultural factors in the development of anorexia nervosa. *Psychological Medicine, 10,* 647-656.

Garner, D. M., & Garfinkel, P. E. (1981). Body image in anorexia nervosa: Measurement, theory, and clinical implications. *International Journal of Psychiatry in Medicine, 11,* 263-284.

Garner, D. M., Garfinkel, P. E., & Bemis, K. M. (1982). A multidimensional psychotherapy for anorexia nervosa. *International Journal of Eating Disorders, 1,* 3-64.

Garner, D. M., Garfinkel, P. E., Stancer, H., & Moldofsky, H. (1976). Body image disturbances in anorexia nervosa and obesity. *Psychosomatic Medicine, 38,* 227-236.

Garner, D. M., & Olmsted, M. P. (1984). *The Eating Disorder Inventory Manual.* Odessa, FL: Psychological Assessment Resources.

Garner, D. M., Olmsted, M. P., Bohr, Y., & Garfinkel, P. E. (1982). The Eating Attitudes Test: Psychometric features and clinical correlates. *Psychological Medicine, 12,* 871-878.

Garner, D. M., Olmsted, M. P., & Polivy, J. (1983a). Development and validation of a multidimensional Eating Disorder Inventory for anorexia nervosa and bulimia. *International Journal of Eating Disorders, 2,* 15-34.

Garner, D. M., Olmsted, M. P., & Polivy, J. (1983b). The Eating Disorder Inventory: A measure of the cognitive/behavioral dimensions of anorexia nervosa and bulimia. In P. L. Darby, P. E. Garfinkel, D. M. Garner, & D. V. Coscina (Eds.), *Anorexia nervosa: Recent developments* (pp. 173-184). New York: Alan R. Liss.

Garner, D. M., Olmsted, M. P., Polivy, J., & Garfinkel, P. E. (1984). Comparison between weight-preoccupied women and anorexia nervosa. *Psychosomatic Medicine, 46,* 255-266.

Garner, D. M., Rockert, W., Olmsted, M. P., Johnson, C., & Coscina, D. V. (1985). Psychoeducational principles in the treatment of bulimia and anorexia nervosa. In D. M. Garner & P. E. Garfinkel (Eds.), *Handbook of psychotherapy for anorexia nervosa and bulimia* (pp. 513-572). New York: Guilford Press.

Glucksman, M. L., & Hirsch, J. (1969). The response of obese patients to weight reduction. *Psychosomatic Medicine, 31,* 1-7.

Goldberg, S. C., Halmi, K. A., Eckert, E. D., Casper, R. C., Davis, J. M., & Roper, M. (1980). Attitudinal dimensions in anorexia nervosa. *Journal of Psychiatric Research, 15,* 239-251.

Goldblatt, P. B., Moore, M. E., & Stunkard, A. J. (1965). Social factors in obesity. *Journal of the American Medical Association, 192,* 1039-1042.

Goodsitt, A. (1985). Self psychology and the treatment of anorexia nervosa. In D. M. Garner & P. E. Garfinkel (Eds.), *Handbook of psychotherapy for anorexia nervosa and bulimia* (pp. 55-82). New York: Guilford Press.

Halmi, K. A., Falk, J. R., & Schwartz, E. (1981). Binge-eating and vomiting: A survey of a college population. *Psychological Medicine, 11,* 697-706.

Hawkins, R. C., & Clement, P. F. (1980). Development and construct validation of a self-report measure of binge-eating tendencies. *Addictive Behaviors, 5,* 219-226.

Hawkins, R. C., Fremouw, W. J., & Clement, P. F. (Eds.). (1984). *The binge-purge syndrome: Diagnosis, treatment, and research.* New York: Springer.

Herman, C. P., & Mack, D. (1975) Restrained and unrestrained eating. *Journal of Personality, 43,* 647–660.

Herman, C. P., Olmsted, M. P., & Polivy, J. (1983). Obesity, externality, and susceptibility to social influence: An integrated analysis. *Journal of Personality and Social Psychology, 45,* 926–934.

Herman, C. P., & Polivy, J. (1980). Restrained eating. In A. J. Stunkard (Ed.), *Obesity* (pp. 208–225). Philadelphia: W. B. Saunders.

Loro, A., & Orleans, C. S. (1981). Binge eating in obesity: Preliminary findings and guidelines for behavioral analysis and treatment. *Addictive Behaviors, 6,* 155–166.

Nylander, I. (1971). The feeling of being fat and dieting in a school population: Epidemiologic interview investigation. *Acta Sociomedica Scandinavica, 3,* 17–26.

Orbach, S. (1978). *Fat is a feminist issue.* London: Paddington Press.

Polivy, J. (1978, September). *Anorexics as overly restrained eaters.* Paper presented at the annual convention of the American Psychological Association, Toronto.

Polivy, J. (1981). Group therapy as an adjunctive treatment for anorexia nervosa. *Journal of Psychiatric Treatment and Evaluation, 3,* 279–283.

Polivy, J. (1984). [Clinical case notes].

Polivy, J., & Garfinkel, P. E. (1984). Anorexia nervosa. In H. Roback (Ed.), *Group intervention with medical-surgical patients and their families* (pp. 60–78). San Francisco: Jossey-Bass.

Polivy, J., & Herman, C. P. (1983). *Breaking the diet habit.* New York: Basic Books.

Polivy, J., & Herman, C. P. (1985a). Dieting and binging: A causal analysis. *American Psychologist, 40,* 193–201.

Polivy, J., & Herman, C. P. (1985b). Dieting as a problem in behavioral medicine. In E. S. Katkin & S. B. Manuck (Eds.), *Advances in behavioral medicine* (Vol. 1, pp. 1–38). New York: SAI.

Polivy, J., & Herman, C. P. (1987). The diagnosis and treatment of normal eating. *Journal of Consulting and Clinical Psychology, 55,* 635–644.

Polivy, J., Herman, C. P., & Howard, K. I. (in press). The Restraint Scale: Assessment of dieting. In M. Hersen & A. S. Bellack (Eds.), *Dictionary of behavioral assessment techniques.* New York: Pergamon Press.

Polivy, J., Herman, C. P., & Kuleshnyk, I. (1984). *More on the effects of perceived preload calories on dieters and nondieters: Salad as a "magical" food.* Unpublished manuscript, University of Toronto.

Polivy, J., Herman, C. P., Olmsted, M. P., & Jazwinski, C. (1984). Restraint and binge eating. In R. C. Hawkins, W. J. Fremouw, & P. F. Clement (Eds.), *The binge-purge syndrome: Diagnosis, treatment, and research* (pp. 104–122). New York: Springer.

Polivy, J., & Leiter, L. (1984). [Preliminary data].

Rosen, J. C., & Leitenberg, H. (1985). Exposure plus response prevention treatment of bulimia. In D. M. Garner & P. E. Garfinkel (Eds.), *Handbook of psychotherapy for anorexia nervosa and bulimia* (pp. 193–212). New York: Guilford Press.

Russell, G. F. M. (1979). Bulimia nervosa: An ominous variant of anorexia nervosa. *Psychological Medicine, 9,* 429–448.

Schachter, S. (1971). Some extraordinary facts about obese humans and rats. *American Psychologist, 26,* 129–144.

Selvini-Palazzoli, M. (1978). *Self-starvation: From individual to family therapy in the treatment of anorexia nervosa.* New York: Jason Aronson.

Slade, P. D. (1973). A short anorexic behavior scale. *British Journal of Psychiatry, 122,* 83–85.

Strober, M. (1980). Personality and symptomatological features in young, non-chronic anorexia nervosa patients. *Journal of Psychosomatic Research, 24,* 353–359.

Strober, M., Salkin, B., Burroughs, J., & Morrell, W. (1982). Validity of the bulimia-restricter distinction in anorexia nervosa. *Journal of Nervous and Mental Disease, 170,* 345–351.

Stunkard, A. J. (1980). Psychoanalysis and psychotherapy. In A. J. Stunkard (Ed.), *Obesity* (pp. 355–368). Philadelphia: W. B. Saunders.

Stunkard, A. J., & Messick, S. (1985). The three-factor eating questionnaire to measure dietary restraint and hunger. *Journal of Psychosomatic Research, 29,* 71–83.

Stunkard, A. J., & Penick, S. B. (1979). Behavior modification in the treatment of obesity: The problem of maintaining weight loss. *Archives of General Psychiatry, 36,* 801–806.

Wardle, J. (1980). Dietary restraint and binge eating. *Behavior Analysis and Modification, 4,* 201–209.

Wooley, S. C., & Wooley, O. W. (1984). Should obesity be treated at all? In A. J. Stunkard & E. Stellar (Eds.), *Eating and its disorders* (pp. 185–192). New York: Raven Press.

# 10

# PHYSIOLOGICAL FACTORS

STEPHEN C. WOODS
DEBORAH J. BRIEF
*University of Washington*

## Introduction

The purpose of this chapter is, first, to discuss some aspects of the normal physiological control of food intake in humans and how this control appears to be altered in three eating disorders: obesity, anorexia nervosa, and bulimia. We then attempt to relate certain aspects of eating behavior in humans to addictive behaviors, by drawing on recent evidence for a role of conditioning factors in the development and maintenance of tolerance to alcohol and opiate drugs.

## Control of Food Intake

As depicted in Figure 10-1, the influences over food intake can be partitioned into three major categories. One of these, discussed at length in this chapter, relates to the current level of adiposity, which appears to be rigorously regulated by humans and animals. We have reviewed this phenomenon elsewhere (Woods & Porte, 1978; Woods *et al.*, 1985) and point out here that a person who is below his or her regulated weight tends to eat larger meals until weight achieves the regulated level (Bray, 1976; Keesey, 1980). Conversely, if a person is above his or her regulated weight, meals will be smaller (or temporarily absent) until weight is lost (Sims *et al.*, 1968). Thus, changes in the amount of food eaten represent the most common way to achieve weight regulation in normal people and animals. Changes of exercise (energy output) and/or altered metabolic efficiency can and do occur when one is overweight or underweight, but these normally are of little importance unless food intake is prevented from changing.

The second set of factors affecting the amount of food eaten during a meal relates to the food itself and how it interacts with the digestive system. A popular contemporary theory states that many of the hormones

**296**

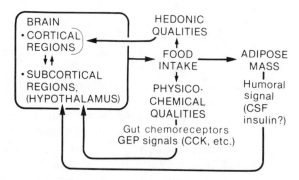

FIGURE 10-1. Schematic depiction of the controls over food intake. GEP, gastro-entero-pancreatic; CCK, cholecystokinin; CSF, cerebrospinal fluid.

secreted by the gut that help control the progress of digestion also provide information to the brain concerning the progress of the meal and ultimately create the sensation of feeling full (Gibbs & Smith, 1984; Woods *et al.*, 1981). In animals that are general omnivores, such as humans (i.e., we eat almost anything!), the digestive system must be prepared for a potentially wide array of foodstuffs. In concert with this, the particular digestive hormones secreted when we eat customize the digestive process (e.g., the choice of which particular digestive enzymes to be secreted, the rate at which various foodstuffs pass through the system, etc.) to the meal being consumed; some of these hormones, as they accumulate in the blood, inform the brain when sufficient or too much food has been eaten (Gibbs & Smith, 1984). The evidence that these compounds (collectively termed "satiety hormones") create a natural feeling of fullness, rather than reducing meal size by creating malaise or through some other nonspecific action, is as follows:

- The administration of these hormones just prior to the presentation of food results in a dose-dependent reduction of meal size in experimental animals and in humans.
- The sequence of behaviors that occurs after receiving these hormones appears identical to the sequence of behaviors that occurs when animals normally stop eating.
- The occurrence of other behaviors (e.g., water intake) is not reduced by these hormones
- Doses of these hormones that reduce meal size do not cause animals to form taste aversions, a sign of malaise.
- Humans given these hormones prior to eating eat less food and do not feel sick or uncomfortable.

A number of digestive hormones have been purported to be satiety hormones, and the best-known of these is cholecystokinin (CCK) (see Gibbs & Smith, 1984; Woods *et al.*, 1981). CCK reduces meal size in every species tested, including humans (Kissileff, Pi-Sunyer, Thornton, & Smith, 1981), when administered just before a meal is presented. The greater the dose of exogenous CCK, the greater the reduction of meal size. In support of the hypothesis that CCK normally acts during spontaneous meals to limit meal size, foods that are especially potent at eliciting endogenous CCK secretion also cause premature satiety, relative to equicaloric foods that do not (Anika, Houpt, & Houpt, 1977; Gibbs, Falasco, & McHugh, 1976).

As is seen in Figure 10-1, meal size is also influenced by what we refer to as "hedonic" aspects of the situation. These include the palatability of the food, the social setting, habits and past experiences, stress levels, and so on. All of these are important determinants of food intake, especially by humans (e.g., Rodin, 1980; Sclafani, 1980).


## Obesity

Obesity is an excess of body fat relative to control individuals of the same age, gender, and level of physical activity (Bray, 1976). Standards or norms for body weight have often been derived from actuarial tables and/or from studies of entire communities, and it is generally accepted that mild obesity exists when a person is up to 10% over the average weight for his or her control population. Frank obesity exists between 10% and 20% above normal weight, and morbid obesity exists beyond 20%. Most instances of human obesity are characterized by consumption of an excess of food at some time in the person's life; hence obesity is appropriately included in a discussion of eating disorders. Excellent reviews of many aspects of obesity can be found in Bray (1976), Salans (1986), and Stunkard (1980).

Estimates of the prevalence of obesity range up to 50%–60% or more, with some isolated populations (e.g., certain tribes of American Indians) having an even higher incidence. There are many schemas for categorizing the obese population. For example, obesity can be characterized by an excess number of fat cells (hyperplastic obesity) and/or enlarged fat cells (hypertrophic obesity). In general, when obesity exists early in life it is characterized by increased numbers of fat cells, whereas adult-onset obesity is characterized by enlarged cells. However, there is a maximum size that fat cells can reach, such that extreme obesity of either type is associated with both larger and more adipocytes. Obesity can also be classed according to the presence or absence of other disorders often associated with being overweight, such as diabetes mellitus, hypertension, hyperlipidemia (excess fat particles in the blood), or gall bladder disease. Obesity greatly increases the risk of having one or more of these problems, and the existence of other complications greatly increases the risk potential (e.g., morbidity or mortality) of obesity. Finally, obesity can fall into a number of categories based upon the presence of specific genetic abnormalities. However, even though genetic factors are perhaps the most important determinants of adult body weight, the incidence of specific genetic abnormalities is rare.

Although numerous theories as to the causes of obesity have been proposed over the years, none has gained universal acceptance. One thing that *is* clear is that the amount of fat in the body appears to be precisely regulated and maintained (e.g., Bray, 1976; Keesey, 1980; Woods, Decke, & Vasselli, 1974). This means that it is relatively difficult to change one's amount of fat; if a change does occur, physiological reflexes will act to restore fat levels to normal (Woods et al., 1985). The most obvious demonstration of this is the experience of dieting to lose weight. One can, with effort, eat less food for (sometimes) prolonged periods of time, and the result is generally loss of weight. The longer the dieting is maintained, the more weight will be lost, and the greater the proportion of lost fat (as opposed to lost water or other compounds) will be. However, as weight is lost, there is a tendency for appetite to increase, and underweight people tend to become more and more uncomfortable over time. The result too often experienced is that after a period of enthusiasm for dieting wanes, slight overeating occurs and weight is restored. This is the most common experience of people wanting to lose weight. In addition, because weight loss is rarely permanent, there may be an additional problem associated with repeated episodes of dieting over one's lifetime. There are some indications that this "yo-yo" effect may make it more difficult to lose weight in the long run, as the body may become more resistant (Simpoulous & Van Itallie, 1984).

The weight system is symmetrical. Extra weight is just as difficult to put on as it is to lose; if weight gain is achieved, it is associated with feelings of discomfort and reduced appetite, and it tends to be short-lived (Bernstein, Lotter, Kulkosky, Porte, & Woods, 1975; Sims et al., 1968). These phenomena have led to the concept of a "set point" for body weight, suggesting that the brain tries to maintain a fixed or constant amount of fat, and that one means of control over the amount of fat is the amount of food eaten (e.g., Keesey, 1980). There are many compelling data supporting this concept. Besides the tendency to restore weight to normal after dieting (or overeating), if fat tissue is surgically removed (an operation called "lipectomy"), there is increased food intake following the surgery until weight is restored (Faust, Johnson, & Hirsch, 1977). When the diet is adequate, the exact amount of weight lost will be regained. In animal experiments, when animals are caused to be underweight and prevented from overeating, they adopt other strategies to regain their weight. Some exercise less, and others reduce their overall metabolic rate. In both instances, less energy is expended. Thus the amount of fat in the body tends to be maintained by robust physiological and behavioral reflexes (see Mrosovsky & Powley, 1977).

Obesity is not an example of a failure to regulate weight. Obese individuals regulate their weight perfectly well; hence their difficulty with losing weight. Rather, obese people seem to have an elevated set point or weight that their brains try to maintain (Keesey & Corbett, 1984). It is unclear what factors determine the set point or defended weight that one has, but genetic factors and perhaps nutritional factors early in one's life are the most important (Salans, 1986). It is also known that certain areas in the hypothalamus of the brain can influence the level of defended weight, with some areas acting to increase it and others to decrease it.

The fact that adiposity is regulated suggests that the brain has a way of knowing how much fat exists at any time, in order to best adjust food intake and metabolic processes. Considerable research has focused on what signal the brain uses, with the hope that once the signal is known, it can be used therapeutically to help people lose weight. If taking a drug could provide a false signal to the brain that the body is overweight (i.e., heavier than it actually is), the brain should respond by reducing appetite and causing weight loss. To date, the best candidate for the elusive fat signal is the hormone insulin. Insulin levels in the blood are directly correlated with adiposity; the insulin in the blood gains access to areas of the brain important in the regulation of appetite and adiposity; and the experimental administration of small amounts of insulin directly into the brains of animals reduces their food intake and body weight (see Woods *et al.,* 1985, for a review).

## Behavioral Characteristics of Bulimia and Anorexia Nervosa

### Bulimia

Diagnostic criteria for Bulimia and Anorexia Nervosa are outlined in the *Diagnostic and Statistical Manual of Mental Disorders,* third edition (DSM-III; American Psychiatric Association, 1980). A diagnosis of Bulimia is warranted when the following occur: (1) recurrent episodes of binge eating, defined as rapid consumption of a large amount of food in a discrete period of time; (2) an awareness of the abnormality of eating patterns, but a fear of not being able to stop voluntarily; and (3) a depressed mood and self-deprecating thoughts following the binge. Three of the following symptoms must also be present for a diagnosis of Bulimia: (1) consumption of high-calorie food during a binge; (2) inconspicuous eating during a binge; (3) termination of eating episodes by abdominal pain, sleep, social interruption, or self-induced vomiting; (4) repeated attempts to lose weight by severely restrictive diets, self-induced vomiting, or use of cathartics or diuretics; or (5) frequent weight fluctuations greater than 10 pounds due to alternating binges and fasts.

Most bulimics are within the normal weight range for their height at the time of the onset of the disorder (Boskind-Lodahl & White, 1978; Fairburn & Cooper, 1983; C. L. Johnson & Berndt, 1983; Mitchell, Hatsukami, Eckert, & Pyle, 1985; Pyle, Mitchell, & Eckert, 1981; Stangler & Printz, 1980; Weiss & Ebert, 1983), although the syndrome of bulimia has been described in underweight (Casper, Eckert, Halmi, Goldberg, & Davis, 1980), overweight (Pyle *et al.,* 1981), and obese (Stunkard, 1959) populations. However, many bulimics have a history of having been overweight (Abraham & Beumont, 1982; Beumont, George, & Smart, 1976; Fairburn & Cooper, 1982, 1983; Halmi, Falk, & Schwartz, 1981; Stunkard, 1959), and a smaller percentage have a history of having been underweight or anorexic (Abraham & Beumont, 1982; Fairburn & Cooper, 1982, 1983, 1984; Pyle *et al.,* 1981; Russell, 1979).

Bulimia is far more prevalent among females than males (Fairburn & Cooper, 1983; Halmi, Goldberg, Eckert, Caspar, & Davis, 1977; Striegel-Moore, Silbertstein, & Rodin, 1986) and has an average age of onset between 18 and 21 years (Fairburn & Cooper, 1982, 1983; C. L. Johnson & Berndt, 1983). The prevalence of bulimia within the general population has been estimated at 1%–4%, although various studies have reported an incidence of 6%–13% within different samples (Halmi *et al.,* 1981; Pope & Hudson, 1984; Pyle *et al.,* 1983; Stangler & Printz, 1980).

*Anorexia Nervosa*

A DSM–III diagnosis of Anorexia Nervosa requires the following essential features: (1) an intense fear of becoming obese, which does not diminish as weight loss progresses; (2) a disturbance of body image (i.e., feeling fat in an emaciated state); (3) weight loss of at least 25% of original body weight; (4) a refusal to maintain body weight over a minimal normal weight for age and height; and (5) no known physical illness that would account for weight loss. Unusual food-related practices that have been described include the following: hoarding food, preparing elaborate meals for others despite refusing to eat, and consuming only low-calorie foods. The course of anorexia nervosa is often severe—from requiring hospitalization to prevent starvation, to being fatal in 15%–21% of the cases (American Psychiatric Association, 1980).

Anorexia nervosa also occurs predominantly in females (Crisp, Kalucy, Lacey, & Harding, 1977), with an average age of onset of 17 years of age (Crisp *et al.,* 1977; Halmi *et al.,* 1977). It has been estimated that 1 in 250 females between the ages of 12 and 18 may develop this disorder (Crisp, Palmer, & Kalucy, 1976; Nylander, 1971). A family history of eating disorders in patients with anorexia has also been documented (Crisp, Hall, & Holland, 1985; Garfinkel & Garner, 1982; Gershon et al., 1983; Strober, Morrell, Burroughts, Salkin, & Jacobs, 1985).

Patients with anorexia nervosa have been further subdivided into "restricters" and "bulimics" (Garfinkel, Moldofsky, & Garner, 1980; Garfinkel & Garner, 1982). Restricter anorexics generally avoid food. Vomiting occurs in some restricter anorexics, but only after they have consumed small quantities of food. Unlike restricter anorexics, anorexics with bulimic symptoms alternate between bingeing–vomiting and starvation diets (Casper et al., 1980; Crisp, 1981; Halmi et al., 1977, 1981; Johnson & Larson, 1982; Pyle et al., 1981; Russell, 1979; Stangler & Printz, 1980; Wardle & Beinart, 1981), use vomiting and purgatives with greater frequency to control weight, and follow faddish food practices more regularly (Garfinkel et al., 1980; Garfinkel & Garner, 1982). Bulimic anorexics have also been reported to have more labile moods, to make more suicide attempts, and to use alcohol and other drugs more frequently than restricter anorexics (Garfinkel et al., 1980; Garfinkel & Garner, 1982).

## Physiological Characteristics of Bulimia and Anorexia Nervosa

### Physical Complications of Vomiting, Diuretic Abuse, and Laxative Abuse

Physiological complications of chronic self-induced vomiting, diuretic abuse, and laxative abuse in bulimics and bulimic anorexics have been well documented (Crisp, 1981; Pope & Hudson, 1984; Pyle et al., 1981; Russell, 1979; Weiss & Ebert, 1983). Some of the more frequent clinical symptoms of these behaviors are as follows (see Copeland, 1985; Dwyer, 1985; Spack, 1985, for thorough reviews of these complications):

- Amenorrhea
- Constipation
- Abdominal pain
- Delayed gastric emptying
- Intolerance to cold
- Hypotension (especially postural hypotension)
- Hypothermia (95°F or less)
- Dry skin
- Lanugo hair (downy pelage)
- Cardiac arrhythmia
- Bradycardia (resting pulse of 60 or less)

- Diuresis
- Edema

Whereas differences in the physical appearance of individuals with anorexia nervosa and bulimia may reflect obvious nutritional differences, physiological complications related to vomiting, diuretic abuse, and laxative abuse are generally not reflected in physical appearance and may be well guarded by normal-weight and overweight bulimics. Laxative and diuretic abuse are uncommon among restricter anorexics, but frequently occur in bulimic anorexics and bulimics (Dwyer, 1985).

Many of the complications associated with vomiting are direct results of the regurgitation of acid from the stomach. Electrolyte imbalance can result from either reduced intake and/or vomiting, laxative, and diuretic abuse, as is indicated in Table 10-1. The loss of potassium, which is associated with both vomiting and diuretic abuse, produces extremely dangerous symptoms of cardiac abnormalities, decreased muscle contractility (skeletal, smooth, and cardiac), skeletal muscle weakness, and fluid abnormalities (e.g., defects in renal and urine-concentrating abilities) (Copeland, 1985; Spack, 1985). Diabetes insipidus has been reported in approximately 25% of patients with anorexia nervosa (Vigersky & Loriaux, 1977).

## Symptoms Associated with Anorexia Nervosa and Starvation

Many of the psychological and physiological symptoms associated with anorexia nervosa have also been found with weight loss induced by involun-

TABLE 10-1. Physical Complications Resulting from Self-Induced Vomiting and from Laxative and Diuretic Abuse

| Vomiting | Laxative abuse | Diuretic abuse |
|---|---|---|
| Dental erosion | Electrolyte imbalance | Electrolyte imbalance |
| Irritation of the esophagus | (especially | (especially hypokalemia) |
| Sore throat | hypophosphatemia) | Intestinal abnormalities |
| Swelling of the | Loss of normal intestinal | Cardiac electrical |
| parotid gland | muscle action | conduction abnormalities |
| Hiatus hernia | Intestinal inflammation | Skeletal muscle weakness |
| Dehydration | Urinary problems | |
| Electrolyte imbalance | Kidney failure | |
| (especially hypokalemia | | |
| and hypochloremia) | | |
| Loss of control over the | | |
| vomiting reflex | | |
| Acute gastric dilatation | | |
| and rupture | | |

tary starvation (Warren & VandeWiele, 1973). Psychological symptoms that are shared by starvation and anorexia nervosa include the following: difficulty with concentration, obsession with food, loss of emotional responsivity, depression, irritability, and sleep disturbance. These symptoms do not always subside immediately following refeeding in anorexia or starvation.

Table 10-1 summarizes some of the major clinical symptoms that are frequently reported in anorexia nervosa (Spack, 1985) and that have been used for diagnostic purposes in anorexia (Halmi *et al.*, 1977). It can be seen that this list includes symptoms of endocrine, gastrointestinal, cardiovascular, nutritional, and fluid and electrolyte abnormalities. These symptoms have also been reported following starvation (Keys, Brozek, Henschel, Mickelson, & Taylor, 1950; Warren & VandeWiele, 1973) and can result from the combined effects of a dramatic decrease in caloric intake and subsequent weight loss. In addition to the symptoms listed, there is some evidence for delayed gastric emptying in anorexics who report early satiety and postprandial pain (Dubois, Gross, Ebert, & Castell, 1979; Saleh & Lebwohl, 1980).

Whereas weight loss of greater than 25% from normal body weight places a patient at high risk from a nutritional standpoint, weight loss of 40%–50% is usually incompatible with survival without tube feeding or total parenteral nutrition (Dwyer, 1985). Dwyer (1985) has suggested the importance of assessing both the total amount of weight loss and the rate of weight loss at a given time to determine the seriousness of the problem. During the earliest stages of starvation, weight loss is fairly slow, because fat is the predominant tissue being lost. However, the onset of rapid weight loss is considered a dangerous sign, because it suggests that lean tissue is now being lost. Complications of lean tissue loss include impaired respiratory functioning, cardiac muscle wasting, and cardiac abnormalities. The major causes of death in anorexia nervosa include physiological complications of emaciation (i.e., electrolyte imbalance and/or cardiovascular abnormalities), suicide, and cardiac events (Hsu, 1980; Schwartz & Thompson, 1981). Although cardiac function returns to normal with nutritional reconstitution of the starved patient, the stress of rapid refeeding may threaten the cardiac system, leading to sudden death after weight gain (Spack, 1985).

When weight loss decreases body fat to less than 20% of total body weight, menses generally cease for all females, regardless of whether other symptoms of anorexia are present (Eisenberg, 1981). However, the onset of amenorrhea prior to weight loss has been reported in a subgroup of anorexics and in many cases persists, even after weight recovery (Warren & VandeWiele, 1973). Thus, it has been suggested that amenorrhea is a response to psychic stress or indicative of an underlying hypothalamic disorder. Endocrine changes in males have been associated with hypogonadism, impotence, and decreased libido, which are reversed by weight gain.

TABLE 10-2.   Endocrine Changes in Anorexia Nervosa

| *Reproductive hormones* | *AVP* |
|---|---|
| Decreased estrogen | Decreased plasma AVP |
| Decreased LH | Increased CSF AVP |
| Decreased FSH | |
| Immature LH secretory pattern | *Adrenocortical hormones* |
| Decreased testosterone (both males and | Increased cortisol |
| females) | Loss of diurnal variation in cortisol |
| | sensitivity to glucocorticoid inhibition |
| *Thyroid hormones* | (positive dexamethasone suppression test) |
| Decreased TH | Decreased androgen secretion |
| Delayed TSH response to TRH | |
| | *Pancreas* |
| *Growth hormone* | Decreased insulin |
| Increased GH | |
| Increased GH response to TRH | *Liver* |
| | Hypoglycemia |
| | Increased liver enzymes (mild–moderate) |

The underlying endocrine changes that occur in anorexia nervosa are listed in Table 10-2 (Copeland, 1985; Spack, 1985) and affect the following: (1) the pancreatic hormone, insulin; (2) reproductive hormones (luteinizing hormone [LH], follicle-stimulating hormone [FSH], estrogen, and testosterone); (3) thyroid hormone (TH); (4) growth hormone (GH); (5) adrenocortical hormones; and (6) vasopressin (AVP) (see Copeland, 1985, and Spack, 1985, for reviews of this literature). Changes in temperature regulation (Copeland, 1985) and carbohydrate metabolism (Leibowitz, 1984) have also been noted. No abnormalities of CCK or bombesin—peptides that produce satiety—have been found in patients with anorexia nervosa or bulimia.

These changes are thought to represent a combination of the effects of starvation and psychoneuroendocrine abnormalities that are specific to anorexia nervosa (Copeland, 1985). In the chronic starvation state, the body attempts to conserve lean body mass and use its energy reserves as slowly as possible (Dwyer, 1985). Thus endocrine changes are initiated to decrease metabolic rate, protect against accelerated protein breakdown, and shift use to ketone bodies rather than glucose. These changes are associated with a number of clinical symptoms. For example, symptoms associated with a decrease in thyroid functioning include decreased metabolic rate, as well as hypothermia, bradycardia, dry skin, and constipation. However, anorexics are not considered true cases of hypothyroidism, and are therefore not considered appropriate for thyroid supplement treatment.

In general, endocrine and neurotransmitter changes have been shown to be reversed by increased caloric intake and weight gain to approximately 85% of normal body weight. However, an immature LH secretory pattern and increased cerebrospinal (CSF) AVP levels have been reported to persist beyond weight recovery. It is interesting to note that the observed increase in cortisol is opposite to the effect seen with malnutrition alone (Doerr, Fichter, Pirke, & Lund, 1980), suggesting that this may be linked to anorexia nervosa per se, rather than simply decreased caloric intake or weight loss. Whereas refeeding leads to a decrease in cortisol levels to normal in anorexics, cortisol levels have been found to increase to a normal level following refeeding in malnutrition.

Several of the neuroendocrine changes seen in anorexia nervosa have also been seen in normal-weight bulimics, including a blunted thyroid-stimulating hormone (TSH) response to thyrotropin-releasing hormone (TRH) (Gwirtsman, Roy-Byrne, Yager, & Gerner, 1983; Wartofsky & Burman, 1982), a positive dexamethasone suppression test (i.e., an early release of cortisol) (Hudson et al., 1983), and an increase in the GH response to TRH (Mitchell & Bantle, 1983). It is interesting to note that the positive dexamethasone suppression test is also found in individuals with endogenous depression. Amenorrhea has also been observed in bulimia and is thought to be related to a past history of weight loss, excessive exercise, or stress (Copeland, 1985).

### Neurogenic Binge-Eaters

Rau and Green (1984) have suggested that there is a subgroup of patients with a neurological cause for binge-eating. These patients are described as generally in good physical health and underweight, normal-weight, or overweight. However, unlike other binge-eaters, they experience (1) an aura prior to binge-eating, (2) a postictal phenomenon following the binge, and (3) perceptual disturbances (i.e., feelings of depersonalization during the binge). Neurological "soft signs" in these patients include rage attacks and/or temper tantrums, headaches, dizziness, stomachaches or nausea, and paresthesia (i.e., numbness and/or tingling in the upper or lower extremities). Rau and Green (1984) have also found that these patients have an abnormal electroencephalogram (EEG) pattern (i.e., the 14 + 6 positive spike pattern). Although they report a positive treatment outcome for patients with neurological signs and a weight deviation of greater or less than 25% from normal body weight, other studies have reported less promising results with anticonvulsants (see W. Johnson & Brief, 1983, for a review of this; see also Wermuth, Davis, Hollister, & Stunkard, 1977).

According to Rau and Green (1984), an assessment of neurological abnormalities would include determination of the following:

1. Occurrence of an aura prior to binge (e.g., flashes of light, unusual smells, increased tension or fear until engaging in the behavior).

2. Feelings of depersonalization during the binge.
3. Absence of a psychological pattern to the bingeing.
4. Occurrence of a postictal phenomenon (e.g., extended sleep, loss of consciousness, confusion, memory loss, loss of bladder control).
5. The presence of neurological "soft signs."
6. The presence of the 14 + 6 positive spike pattern (usually seen while drowsy or asleep).

## Major Affective Disorder Theory of Eating Disorders

Pope and Hudson (1984) have suggested that both anorexia and bulimia are variants of a major affective disorder. Evidence for this includes (1) reports of depression in anorexia and bulimia before the onset of symptoms of the eating disorder; (2) persistence of depressive symptoms in anorexia nervosa beyond weight recovery; (3) a positive family history of a major affective disorder in anorexic and bulimic patients; (4) positive biological indicators of depression in anorexia and bulimia (i.e., positive dexamethasone suppression and TRH stimulation tests); and (5) positive treatment outcomes for patients on antidepressant medications (see Pope & Hudson, 1984, for a review). However, not all patients with eating disorders respond to antidepressants, and many recover without the use of antidepressant medication (Wilson, 1985). It may be necessary to determine whether there is a subpopulation of patients with eating disorders who also have a major affective disorder, and to treat this accordingly. Both a clinical interview and biological tests for depression could be performed as confirmation. However, current research does not support the notion that all patients with eating disorders are suffering from a major affective disorder, or that antidepressants should be prescribed in all cases.

## Summary of Areas for Physiological Assessment of the Patient with Eating Disorders

Below is listed a summary of areas that might be assessed for patients who present symptoms of eating disorders. The combined results of these tests would enable one to develop an individualized treatment program that is specific to the needs of each patient.

1. Dietary and weight history records provide information on energy intake and allow for the calculation of energy needs to maintain or increase weight. However, this must be adjusted in the case of individuals who are either vomiting or using laxatives and/or diuretics, or who are exercising excessively. These records can also be used to obtain information on the temporal relationship between important environmental factors and bingeing,

in order to determine whether these events elicit metabolic changes that are related to stimulation of food intake.

2. Questions on history of laxative abuse, use of diuretics, and vomiting provide information on possible physiological complications associated with these behaviors.

3. Biochemical tests confirm low intake, self-induced vomiting, and laxative and/or diuretic abuse.

4. Electrocardiograms (EKGs) provide information on electrolyte imbalances and the wasting of cardiac muscle.

5. EEGs and questions about neurological signs will provide information on the possibility of a neurogenic disorder.

6. A dexamethasone suppression test could be used to confirm the coexistence of a major affective disorder.

## Relationship between Eating Disorders and Addictive Behaviors

Because of the habitual nature of the attitudes and behaviors associated with both bulimia and anorexia nervosa, these eating disorders can be compared to other compulsive or habitual behaviors, such as drug addiction. In this section, we review one of the major correlates of drug addiction — drug tolerance — and try to make the case that recent developments concerning the causes of tolerance are also pertinent to eating and perhaps can account for some of the symptoms of eating disorders as well.

### Drug Tolerance

Drug tolerance develops when a drug is repeatedly administered to a person or an animal, and the person's or animal's response to it lessens over time. For example, the analgesic effects of heroin, the motor discoordination caused by alcohol, and the appetite-suppressing quality of amphetamine-type drugs all diminish with repeated drug usage, such that more of a drug must be taken each time to achieve the same level of effect. Explanations of tolerance have traditionally been based upon physical changes that occur in specific organs or tissue as a result of being exposed to the drug (Jaffe, 1985; Kalant, LeBlanc, & Gibbins, 1971; Tabakoff & Rothstein, 1983).

If the body develops the capacity to degrade a drug at a faster rate in the liver, or to excrete it more efficiently into the urine at the kidney, or to metabolize it faster, the change is called "dispositional tolerance." It means that the body is more easily able to dispose of the drug when it is taken, and that less of the drug is therefore available to affect critical tissue such as the brain. It is true that the body does develop more efficient ways to dispose of drugs that have repeatedly been inflicted upon it, but the magnitude of the effect is small; it is unlikely that this dispositional tolerance accounts for much of the tolerance seen at the behavioral level (Kalant et al., 1971; Tabakoff & Rothstein, 1983).

A second explanation for tolerance usually falls under the heading of "functional tolerance," which refers to a reduced sensitivity of critical target tissues. For example, if centers in the brain that control motor coordination become less responsive to alcohol over time, such that a constant amount of alcohol creates a smaller and smaller disruption of motor performance each time it is taken, this is an example of functional tolerance. Such tolerance may be due to altered properties of the membranes of critical cells, or to altered numbers of receptors, or to recruitment of alternate neuronal systems that are otherwise labile. All of these have formed the basis of one or another theory of functional tolerance, and there is evidence supporting each (Kalant et al., 1971; Tabakoff & Rothstein, 1983). As we note below, however, these changes cannot be the most likely explanation for most instances of tolerance, and they may represent merely cellular or tissue adaptations as opposed to whole-body tolerance.

It should be noted that until recently these two explanations of drug tolerance were considered to be exhaustive (although not mutually exclusive). A smaller drug response (i.e., drug tolerance) was thought to occur either because less of the drug reaches critical target tissue (dispositional tolerance) or because the target tissue is less responsive to the drug (functional tolerance).

*Behavioral Tolerance*

In the past few years, a third explanation of tolerance has been forwarded. "Behavioral tolerance," as it is called, occurs when the animal or person receiving a drug learns or is conditioned to make a response that counters the drug effect. For example, if a particular drug causes body temperature to decrease, the lowered temperature itself may serve as a stimulus to trigger compensatory temperature-elevating responses. Every time the drug is taken, these same reflexes are elicited, such that temperature is never allowed to decrease to the point it would reach if the drug acted in the absence of the compensatory reflexes. To the extent that the presence of a drug in the body can be reliably predicted, the person or animal ought to be able to anticipate receiving the drug and make the appropriate compensatory responses before the drug is actually administered. Such an anticipatory response, which counters a specific drug effect, would lessen the impact of the drug and may account for tolerance. Behavioral tolerance, in this schema, is caused by the development of a learned response acquired through Pavlovian conditioning (Hinson & Siegel, 1982; Siegel, 1983).

Siegel, who has been a leader in elucidating the phenomenon of behavioral tolerance, initially found that tolerance to morphine in rats follows many properties of classical conditioning (1975); a considerable literature now exists documenting behavioral tolerance for many drugs (see reviews in Hinson & Siegel, 1982; Siegel, 1983). The important point is that tolerance can be explained by the elicitation of conditioned reflex responses that create changes in the body opposite to those caused by a drug. When an animal can reliably anticipate receiving a drug that causes decreased pain sensitivity (e.g., morphine or heroin), it adjusts its pain sensitivity upward (Siegel, 1975, 1977, 1978); if a drug causes lowered body temperature (e.g., alcohol), the animal elevates its temperature in anticipation (Mansfield, Benedict, & Woods, 1983; Mansfield & Cunningham, 1980).

One interesting prediction of such a model is that if an animal is placed in a situation in which it anticipates receiving a drug, but does not in fact get the drug, it should make the learned reflex response and create a change in some bodily parameter opposite to what the drug would cause. Anticipating but not receiving morphine is associated with an increased sensitivity to pain (Siegel, 1975, 1977); anticipating but not receiving alcohol is associated with an increase of body temperature (Mansfield & Cunningham, 1980); and so on. In these instances, actually taking the drug lessens the impact of the learned compensatory response.

This has important implications for the phenomenon of drug withdrawal. Drug withdrawal occurs when a person or animal who has been receiving a drug regularly no longer has the drug available. Symptoms of drug withdrawal are always opposite in nature to symptoms caused by the drug itself (see Jaffe, 1985). Withdrawal from depressants (e.g., alcohol) is associated with hyperactivity, tremors and shakes, heightened temperature, and so on; withdrawal from stimulants (e.g., amphetamine) is associated with depression and lethargy; and withdrawal from analgesics (e.g., heroin) is associated with increased pain sensitivity (and actual pain). The severity of the symptoms of withdrawal is often attributed to the tendency to continue taking a drug once tolerance and addiction are achieved (Jaffe, 1985; Tabakoff & Rothstein, 1983).

Another interesting prediction of the learning model is that tolerance ought to occur only when those stimuli normally associated with drug taking are present. Mansfield and Cunningham (1980) made rats tolerant to alcohol by repeatedly giving them the drug in the presence of particular stimuli. That is, the first time they received alcohol their body temperature decreased, but over a period of several weeks of alcohol administration they became tolerant, and body temperature did not change when they were given the drug. When Mansfield and Cunningham later presented these alcohol-associated stimuli in the absence of alcohol, the rats made the learned compensatory response (i.e., they elevated their body temperatures). Importantly, when the rats were given alcohol in a different setting without the normal predictive cues, they did not appear tolerant, and their temperatures were reduced to the same extent as in drug-naive animals. The tolerance was therefore situation-specific and could not simply be due to altered properties of "marinated" membranes.

*Tolerance to Food*

In some ways, eating a meal can be likened to taking a drug. In both instances, a particular behavior is made, and changes of a number of regulated parameters occur. During and after a meal, these changes include (among many others) increases of nutrients such as glucose in the blood. Blood glucose is a very tightly regulated parameter (Porte & Halter, 1981; Porte & Woods, 1983), with many neural and endocrine reflexes that can quickly raise or lower blood glucose as needs in the body vary. There are pressures to keep glucose levels high (e.g., the brain requires considerable glucose from the blood at all times, lest its functioning should decline and the individual should go into a coma), as well as to keep them low (elevated glucose levels are the major symptom of diabetes mellitus and are associated with numerous physical ailments). The result is that glucose levels normally do not deviate from normal for large periods of time. Even when a person is exercising for long periods and there is increased demand for glucose by the muscles, blood levels are relatively normal (Porte & Halter, 1981; Porte & Woods, 1983). Similar mechanisms exist for controlling the levels of fats in the blood.

Eating disrupts this homeostatically controlled system by creating a flood of glucose and fats into the blood from the gut. Eating is obviously a very necessary behavior, but the actual amount of fuels flowing from the digestive system into storage depots throughout the body creates an imbalance in the levels of fuels in the blood and may pose a potential threat to normal functioning.

When one takes a drug regularly, he or she can anticipate what effects are likely to occur and make appropriate compensatory responses. Likewise, one can correctly anticipate when food will be ingested. And if some of the consequences of eating really do pose a problem of sorts to the body, the body ought to respond as it does when it anticipates receiving a drug; that is, it ought to make responses that will counter the (undesirable) changes associated with the meal itself. In effect, the body ought to make responses that will lower, or at least provide a tighter control over, fuels in the blood when one expects to eat.

*Cephalic Insulin*

People and animals secrete the hormone insulin during meals in response to the elevated levels of fuels at that time, because the major action of insulin in the blood is to lower blood levels of both glucose and fats. This response occurs directly at the level of the B-cells in the pancreas, which synthesize and secrete insulin. However, the brain can also cause the pancreas to secrete insulin (Woods & Porte, 1974), and one time it does this is at the beginning of meals. Such insulin is termed "cephalic insulin" because the brain rather than the pancreas initiates the response (see Powley, 1977). Cephalic insulin enables the body to remove more quickly the fuels that enter the blood during a meal, for when cephalic insulin secretion is prevented, fuels linger in the blood, and the person or animal appears diabetic (Louis-Sylvestre, 1978; Trimble, Siegel, Berthoud, & Renold, 1980).

What has become apparent in recent years is that cephalic insulin secretion occurs in anticipation of meals. When people or animals are presented with stimuli that reliably predict that food is inevitable, even if no fuels actually enter the blood (e.g., when individuals smell or taste food, eat food that does not reach the stomach, or consume noncaloric foods), they still secrete insulin (see reviews in Berthoud, Bereiter, Trimble, Siegel, & Jeanrenaud, 1981; Powley, 1977; Woods, 1983). Hypnotizing people and telling them they are eating is also associated with apparent insulin secretion, because the levels of fuels in their blood decrease at that time (Goldfine, Abraira, Gruenwald, & Goldstein, 1970).

Cephalic insulin secretion can be brought under stimulus control through classical conditioning. When rats received food in strict association with arbitrary stimuli (time of day and/or a specific odor), they learned to secrete insulin in the presence of those stimuli (Woods, 1977; Woods *et al.,* 1977); this paradigm has long been associated with a conditioned decrease of blood glucose (see Woods, 1983; Woods & Kulkosky, 1976).

In short, animals and people anticipate meals and the meal-associated disruption (elevation) of fuel levels in the blood. And just as in drug withdrawal, when the anticipation occurs in the absence of the event, the learned compensatory response can create an imbalance of its own.

*Reactive Hypoglycemia*

Reactive hypoglycemia is a hard-to-diagnose syndrome characterized by a decrease (rather than the normal increase) of blood glucose associated with meals (Permutt, 1976). Reactive hypoglycemia is known to be caused by an oversecretion of insulin during meals (Permutt, 1976), and it is reasonable to postulate that the excess insulin is mainly cephalic in origin; cutting the nerve between the brain and the pancreas (Boulet, Vidal, Joyeux, & Mirouze, 1954), or else blocking those neural signals pharmacologically (Veverbrants, Olsen, & Arky, 1969), eliminates the response. It may well be that individuals with reactive hypoglycemia have an eating history that is especially conducive to learning to secrete cephalic insulin, and we have made this argument elsewhere (Woods, 1983; Woods & Kulkosky, 1976). The point is that eating shares an important component with drug taking. Both can become habitual and predictable in some situations and therefore can become associated with learned anticipatory responses. And whereas both drug and meal tolerance are normally adaptive, both can also become associated with undesirable end results (withdrawal; perhaps reactive hypoglycemia). It is also possible that the addicting nature of certain habits or modes of eating may predispose individuals to certain eating disorders.

## Other Similarities of Eating Disorders to Addictive Behaviors

There appears to be a significant overlap between the behavioral symptoms of Substance Abuse and Bulimia as these diagnoses are described in DSM-III (American Psychiatric Association, 1980). The symptoms that overlap include (1) repeated episodes of excessive use of a substance (in this case, food); (2) repeated, unsuccessful efforts to stop excessive use of the substance voluntarily; (3) a distortion of lifestyle to provide time and money for the behavior; (4) an increase in the severity of symptoms over time (Wilson, 1985); (5) decreased social adjustment due to the symptoms of the disorder (Norman & Herzog, 1984); (6) high relapse rates following treatment (Wilson, 1985); and (7) an increased urge to binge after consuming small amounts of the substance (in this case, forbidden foods) (Wilson, 1985).

It also appears that there is an overlap between the symptoms of Bulimia and of Substance Dependence, which, by DSM-III criteria, is considered a more severe form of Substance Abuse. According to DSM-III (American Psychiatric Association, 1980) criteria, the occurrence of both tolerance and dependence is symptomatic of Substance Dependence. We have already discussed similarities between the conditioning of tolerance to drug effects and the conditioning of cephalic insulin release in response to a meal. In both instances, an adaptive physiological response occurs when the ingestion of a substance (e.g., a drug or food) that upsets homeostasis can be predicted by the organism. Thus, whereas conditioned hyperthermia prevents alcohol-induced hypothermia, conditioned insulin release may reduce the risks associated with meal-induced hyperglycemia.

Withdrawal-like symptoms may also occur when either a drug or food is expected but not ingested. These symptoms are opposite in direction to those induced by the ingestion of the substance. For example, when alcohol is expected but not consumed, hyperthermia occurs. In relation to eating, this response may be a conditioned hypoglycemic response. We have already suggested that the amount of cephalic insulin released may depend on an individual's prior learning history (e.g., pattern of meal consumption). Thus, it is possible that learning to expect a large meal may increase the size of insulin release to insure a sufficient removal of excess fuels. If a meal is not then consumed, as may be the case with chronic dieters, reactive hypoglycemia may result. This hypothesis is supported by the finding that dieters have elevated cephalic insulin responses (Sjostrom, Garellick, Krotkievsky, & Luyck, 1980). The important point is that certainly tolerance and perhaps dependence (indicated by the occurrence of reactive hypoglycemia) may occur with both drug use and eating.

Similarities between the pathophysiology of anorexia nervosa and opiate addiction have been reviewed by Marrazzi and Luby (1986) in an autoaddiction model of anorexia. According to their model, anorexia involves a progression through three stages. During the first two stages, the factors that motivate the person to develop a fear of eating and weight gain and to develop ritualistic behaviors in regard to dieting and exercising are primarily psychological. However, anorexics who successfully starve themselves below prepubertal weight may enter the third stage, during which an increase in opiate levels may serve to perpetuate the disorder. Whereas an increase in opiate levels is seen as an adaptive physiological response to starvation, which serves to stimulate food intake (Morley & Levine, 1981) and downregulate metabolism (Margules, 1979), it may also make the weight loss process highly reinforcing.

### Conclusions

We have shown that the behavioral symptoms of eating disorders and addictions overlap. We are suggesting two important points. One is that a similar process of conditioning toward food and eating, on the one hand, and drug taking, on the other, may occur. The other is that the way in which these processes interact with an individual's social situation and genetic background provides a common link between eating and addictions. Whether the similar histories of conditioning produce a common physiological change, as the autoaddiction model (Marrazzi & Luby, 1986) suggests, or whether different physiological changes occur within each regulatory system to produce similarities in behavior remains unclear.

There are interesting and potentially important implications (in a therapeutic sense) of the apparent commonalities between addictive behaviors and certain eating disorders. It may be, for example, that certain individuals have a predisposition to develop compensatory responses to homeostatic challenges. Such individuals may be especially susceptible to acquiring drug dependencies (e.g., on caffeine, nicotine, or drugs with more serious effects). Likewise, such individuals may, for a variety of reasons (e.g., fear of exposure or strong commitment against the use of drugs), turn this tendency toward food or meals instead of drugs. Such persons would be expected to have exaggerated cephalic responses to meals. If these persons also develop an obsession with weight and appearance, this could lead to dieting, weight loss, and a further exaggeration of the tendency to overrespond cephalically to food-related cues. The exaggerated cephalic response may cause sufficient metabolic perturbations (e.g., lowered blood glucose or some other critical parameter) to create extreme craving for food, leading to bingeing. The fact that these responses are easily conditioned to environmental events provides for a high degree of influence of selected factors in one's life upon important metabolic events. The following case history provides an example of this.

## Case Study of Bulimia

The following is a simulated case study that is designed to highlight several possible areas of assessment for patients with bulimia. We focus our discussion of this case on possible physiological parameters that might be assessed, rather than on cognitive or behavioral parameters, which are discussed in other chapters.

Janice was a 25-year-old female whose body weight was within the normal range. An initial interview revealed symptoms consistent with a DSM–III diagnosis of Bulimia (American Psychiatric Association, 1980), including (1) a 6-year history of binge-eating; (2) a 5-year history of self-induced vomiting with occasional excessive laxative use following consumption of large amounts of high-carbohydrate foods; (3) a 7-year history of repeated attempts to lose weight by severely restrictive diets; (4) frequent weight fluctuations greater than 10 pounds, presumably due to alternating bingeing and fasting; (5) depressed mood and self-deprecating thoughts following binges; and (6) an awareness of the abnormality of her eating patterns, but an inability to stop the binge–purge cycle voluntarily. At the time Janice initially started dieting, she was approximately 10% overweight, but was able to reduce her weight to within the normal range. However, Janice's symptoms of bulimia developed after she reached her goal weight, and they became progressively worse over the next 4 years.

Once information was obtained during the initial interview on Janice's history of self-induced vomiting and laxative abuse, more specific questions about the frequency of these behaviors and occurrence of related symptoms were included in a second interview. It was discovered that

Janice occasionally took large doses of laxatives following a binge, but not more than once a month. Her primary method of coping with the consumption of large amounts of food was to induce vomiting. For the past 3 years, she had been bingeing at least once a day and vomiting after each episode. The interview also revealed that Janice experienced symptoms of muscle weakness, cramping, and fatigue following vomiting.

Given the frequency of vomiting and associated symptoms, Janice was referred for a medical and dental evaluation. The medical evaluation included blood analyses, an EKG, and neuroendocrine tests. The second interview also involved an assessment of possible neurological signs, as recommended by Rau and Green (1984). An EEG was not performed, in the absence of symptoms suggested by Rau and Green to be indicators of a neurological disorder.

The findings of the medical and dental tests were consistent with Janice's self-reported history of frequent vomiting. They included (1) an electrolyte imbalance (low potassium levels); (2) muscle weakness; (3) dehydration; (4) episodes of tachycardia; (5) loss of control over the vomiting reflex; and (6) dental erosion. There was no evidence of physical complications associated with either laxative or diuretic abuse. Neuroendocrine tests, which included the TSH response to TRH, the GH response to TRH, and the CCK response to a meal, were within normal limits. Although Janice reported depressive symptomatology, the dexamethasone suppression test was also negative. However, the patient was amenorrheic.

A dietary history, obtained during the first interview, indicated that the patient's diet, excluding food eaten during binge episodes, was nutritionally deficient. However, as a result of her bingeing and vomiting, it was difficult to assess her actual level of daily caloric intake. Detailed questions about her dieting history also revealed that the patient had a tendency to alternate between a very-low-calorie diet and bingeing on large amounts of high-calorie food. A detailed weight history, taken at the same time, indicated that Janice had recently been able to maintain her weight at a fairly constant level within the normal range, despite a history of weight fluctuations.

To clarify (1) the actual level of Janice's intake; (2) the relationship between her energy intake, energy expenditure, and weight regulation; and (3) the relationship between environmental events and binge episodes, Janice was asked to keep dietary records for 1 week prior to her second assessment interview. This history revealed that Janice was maintaining her weight at a normal level on a very low level of intake at meals and with limited exercise. Although caloric intake during the binges varied between 500 and 1,500 calories, it was not possible to determine how many of these calories were eliminated by vomiting. It was also determined that most of Janice's episodes of bingeing occurred soon after stressful telephone conversations with family members. The possibility that these calls might trigger a metabolic response that could enhance appetite was noted.

Following the 2-week assessment period, Janice was started on a 12-week cognitive–behavioral treatment program similar to Fairburn's program (Fairburn, 1985). The decision not to treat the patient with antidepressant medications, despite symptoms of depression, was supported by the negative dexamethasone suppression test findings and an absence of a family history of affective disorder. The program included (1) self-monitoring of meals, bingeing, vomiting, and exercise habits; (2) education about physical complications of bulimia; (3) information on techniques for normalizing eating patterns; (4) examination of situational and intrapersonal factors related to bingeing and vomiting, with a special emphasis on Janice's relationship and reaction to family members' attitudes toward her weight and appearance; (5) modification of dysfunctional thoughts and values related to eating and weight; and (6) techniques for preventing relapse (e.g., coping more effectively with family members' comments about her appearance).

During the first month, treatment focused on the normalization of eating habits and identification of factors related to bingeing. Janice continued to keep records of (1) daily food intake, including meals and binges; (2) episodes of vomiting or laxative abuse; and (3) situational factors related to bingeing. These records included information on the types and amounts of foods eaten, the frequency of vomiting following a binge, and the temporal relationship between bingeing and important environmental events (e.g., contact with the family). A weekly assessment of symptoms related to the vomiting, such as fatigue, dizziness, and muscle weakness, was also completed.

Janice was able to meet her goal of eating three meals a day by the end of 1 month and to reduce the frequency of bingeing and vomiting to once a week. Other than a high-calorie snack approximately every 3 days, her meals tended to be low-calorie, but nutritionally adequate. She did not experience weight gain during this period relative to the assessment period, despite the increase in caloric intake during meals. Janice was also able to learn to change the nature of her contacts with family members and to experience less emotional distress as a result of their intrusiveness, criticisms, and comments about her appearance.

The normalization of eating habits and the self-reported reduction in vomiting frequency were corroborated by the results of a second medical evaluation at the end of 1 month. Findings at this time included (1) electrolytes within normal limits; (2) an EKG within normal limits; (3) no evidence of dehydration; (4) a decrease in the number of subjective physical symptoms associated with vomiting; (5) no additional dental erosion; and (6) control over the vomiting reflex. The patient was still amenorrheic at this time, although neuroendocrine test findings were still within normal limits.

These tests were repeated throughout treatment and at follow-up to provide collaborative evidence for self-reported changes in behavior and to insure improvements in the physical condition of the patient as behavioral and cognitive changes occurred. For example, although Janice was still amenorrheic at 1 month, she had begun to menstruate again by the end of the 12-week treatment.

## Acknowledgment

The writing of this chapter was supported in part by National Institutes of Health Grant Nos. AM 17844 and AA 07455.

## References

Abraham, S., & Beumont, P. J. (1982). How patients describe bulimia or binge eating. *Psychological Medicine, 12,* 625–635.

American Psychiatric Association. (1980). *Diagnostic and statistical manual of mental disorders* (3rd ed.). Washington, DC: Author.

Anika, S. M., Houpt, T. R., & Houpt, K. A. (1977). Satiety elicited by cholecystokinin in intact and vagotomized rats. *Physiology and Behavior, 19,* 761–766.

Bernstein, I. L., Lotter, E. C., Kulkosky, P. J., Porte, D. Jr., & Woods, S. C. (1975). Effect of force-feeding upon basal insulin levels of rats. *Proceedings of the Society for Experimental Biology and Medicine, 150,* 546–548.

Berthoud, H. R., Bereiter, D. A., Trimble, E. R., Siegel, E. G., & Jeanrenaud, B. (1981). Cephalic phase, reflex insulin secretion: Neuroanatomical and physiological characterization. *Diabetologia, 20,* 393–400.

Beumont, P. J., George, G. C., & Smart, D. E. (1976). "Dieters" and "vomiters and purgers" in anorexia nervosa. *Psychological Medicine, 6,* 617–622.

Boskind-Lodahl, M., & White, W. C. (1978). The definition and treatment of bulimarexia in college women—a pilot study. *Journal of the American College Health Association, 27,* 84–97.

Boulet, P., Vidal, J., Joyeux, R., & Mirouze, J. (1954). Hypoglycemie spontanée: Guérison après vagotomie. *Montpellier Medicine, 46,* 40–45.

Bray, G. A. (1976). *The obese patient.* Philadelphia: W. B. Saunders.

Casper, R. C., Eckert, E. D., Halmi, K. A., Goldberg, S. C., & Davis, J. M. (1980). Bulimia: Its incidence and clinical importance in patients with anorexia nervosa. *Archives of General Psychiatry, 37,* 1030–1035.

Copeland, P. M. (1985). Neuroendocrine aspects of eating disorders. In S. W. Emmett (Ed.), *Theory and treatment of anorexia nervosa and bulimia: Biomedical, sociocultural and psychological perspectives* (pp. 51–72). New York: Brunner/Mazel.

Crisp, A. H. (1981). Anorexia nervosa at normal body weight: The abnormal normal weight control syndrome. *International Journal of Psychiatric Medicine, 11,* 203–233.

Crisp, A. H., Hall, A., & Holland, A. J. (1985). Nature and nurture in anorexia nervosa: A study of 34 pairs of twins, one pair of triplets, and an adoptive family. *International Journal of Eating Disorders, 4,* 5–27.

Crisp, A. H., Kalucy, R. S., Lacey, J. H., & Harding, B. (1977). The long-term prognosis in anorexia nervosa: Some factors predictive of outcome. In R. Vigersky (Ed.), *Anorexia nervosa* (pp. 55–67). New York: Raven Press.

Crisp, A. H., Palmer, R. L., & Kalucy, R. S. (1976). How common is anorexia nervosa: A prevalence study. *British Journal of Psychiatry, 128,* 549–554.

Doerr, P., Fichter, M., Pirke, K., & Lund, R. (1980). Relationship between weight gain and hypothalamic–pituitary–adrenal function in patients with anorexia nervosa. *Journal of Steroid Biochemistry, 13,* 529–537.

Dubois, A., Gross, H., Ebert, M., & Castell, D. (1979). Altered gastric emptying and secretion in primary anorexia nervosa. *Gastroenterology, 77,* 319–323.

Dwyer, J. (1985). Nutritional aspects of anorexia nervosa and bulimia. In S. Emmett (Ed.), *Theory and treatment of anorexia nervosa and bulimia: Biomedical, sociocultural and psychological perspectives* (pp. 20–50). New York: Brunner/Mazel.

Eisenberg, E. (1981). Toward an understanding of reproductive function in anorexia nervosa. *Fertility and Sterility, 36,* 543–550.

Fairburn, C. G. (1985). Cognitive-behavioral treatment for bulimia. In D. Garner & P. Garfinkel (Eds.), *Handbook of psychotherapy for anorexia nervosa and bulimia* (pp. 160–192). New York: Guilford Press.

Fairburn, C. G., & Cooper, P. J. (1982). Self-induced vomiting and bulimia nervosa: An undetected problem. *British Medical Journal, 284,* 1153–1155.

Fairburn, C. G., & Cooper, P. J. (1983). The epidemiology of bulimia nervosa. *International Journal of Eating Disorders, 2,* 61–67.

Fairburn, C. G., & Cooper, P. J. (1984). The clinical features of bulimia nervosa. *British Journal of Psychiatry, 144,* 238–246.

Faust, I. M., Johnson, P. R., & Hirsch, J. (1977). Surgical removal of adipose tissue alters feeding behaviors and the development of obesity in rats. *Science, 197,* 393–396.

Garfinkel, P. E., & Garner, D. (1982). *Anorexia nervosa: A multidimensional perspective.* New York: Brunner/Mazel.

Garfinkel, P. E., Moldofsky, H., & Garner, D. M. (1980). The heterogeneity of anorexia nervosa. *Archives of General Psychiatry, 37,* 1036–1040.

Gershon, E. S., Hamovit, J. R., Schreiber, J. L., Dibble, E. D., Kaye, W., Nurnberger, J. I., Andersen, A., & Ebert, M. (1983). Anorexia nervosa and major affective disorders associated in families: A preliminary report. In S. Guze, F. Earls, & J. Barrett (Eds.), *Childhood psychopathology and development* (pp. 279–284). New York: Raven Press.

Gibbs, J., Falasco, J. D., & McHugh, P. R. (1976). Cholecystokinin-decreased food intake in rhesus monkeys. *American Journal of Physiology, 230,* 15–18.

Gibbs, J., & Smith, G. P. (1984). The neuroendocrinology of postprandial satiety. *Frontiers in Neuroendocrinology, 8,* 223–245.

Goldfine, I. D., Abraira, C., Gruenwald, D., & Goldstein, M. S. (1970). Plasma insulin levels during imaginary food ingestion under hypnosis. *Proceedings of the Society for Experimental Biology and Medicine, 133,* 274–276.

Gwirtsman, H. E., Roy-Byrne, P., Yager, J., & Gerner, R. H. (1983). Neuroendocrine abnormalities in bulimia. *American Journal of Psychiatry, 140,* 559–563.

Halmi, K. A., Falk, J. R., & Schwartz, E. (1981). Binge-eating and vomiting: A survey of a college population. *Psychological Medicine, 11,* 697–706.

Halmi, K. A., Goldberg, S., Eckert, E., Casper, R., & Davis, J. M. (1977). Pretreatment evaluation in anorexia nervosa. In R. A. Vigersky (Ed.), *Anorexia nervosa* (pp. 43–54). New York: Raven Press.

Hinson, R. E., & Siegel, S. (1982). Nonpharmacological bases of drug tolerance and dependence. *Journal of Psychosomatic Research, 26,* 495–503.

Hsu, L. (1980). Outcome of anorexia nervosa: A review of the literature (1954 to 1978). *Archives of General Psychiatry, 37,* 1041–1043.

Hudson, J. I., Pope, H. G., Jonas, J. M., Laffer, P. S., Hudson, M., & Melby, J. (1983). Hypothalamic–pituitary–adrenal axis hyperactivity in bulimia. *Psychiatry Research, 8,* 111–117.

Jaffe, J. H. (1985). Drug addiction and drug abuse. In A. Gilman, L. Goodman, & A. Gilman (Eds.), *The pharmacological basis of therapeutics* (pp. 532–581). New York: Macmillan.

Johnson, C. L., & Berndt, D. J. (1983). Preliminary investigation of bulimia and life adjustment. *American Journal of Psychiatry, 140,* 774–777.

Johnson, C. L., & Larson, R. (1982). Bulimia: An analysis of moods and behavior. *Psychosomatic Medicine, 44,* 341–353.

Johnson, W., & Brief, D. (1983). Bulimia. *Behavioral Medicine Update, 4,* 16–21.

Kalant, H., LeBlanc, A. E., & Gibbins, R. J. (1971). Tolerance to, and dependence on, some non-opiate psychotropic drugs. *Pharmacological Reviews, 23,* 135–191.

Keesey, R. E. (1980). A set-point analysis of the regulation of body weight. In A. J. Stunkard (Ed.), *Obesity* (pp. 144–165). Philadelphia: W. B. Saunders.

Keesey, R. E., & Corbett, W. W. (1984). Metabolic defense of the body weight set-point. In A. J. Stunkard & E. Stellar (Eds.). *Eating and its disorders* (pp. 87–96). New York: Raven Press.

Keys, A., Brozek, J., Henschel, A., Mickelson, O., & Taylor, H. L. (1950). *The biology of human starvation.* Minneapolis: University of Minnesota Press.

Kissileff, H. R., Pi-Sunyer, F. X., Thornton, J., & Smith, G. P. (1981). C-terminal octapeptide of cholecystokinin decreases food intake in man. *American Journal of Clinical Nutrition, 34,* 154–160.

Leibowitz, S. (1984). Noradrenergic function in the medial hypothalamus: Potential relation to anorexia nervosa and bulimia. In K. Pirke & D. Ploog (Eds.), *Anorexia nervosa* (pp. 35–45). Berlin: Springer-Verlag.

Louis-Sylvestre, J. (1978). Relationship between two stages of prandial insulin release in rats. *American Journal of Physiology, 235,* E103–E111.

Mansfield, J. G., Benedict, R. S., & Woods, S. C. (1983). Response specificity of "behaviorally augmented tolerance" to ethanol supports a learning interpretation. *Psychopharmacology, 79,* 94–98.

Mansfield, J. G., & Cunningham, C. L. (1980). Conditioning and extinction of tolerance to the hypothermic effect of ethanol in rats. *Journal of Comparative and Physiological Psychology, 94,* 962–969.

Margules, D. L. (1979). Beta-endorphin and endoloxone: Hormones of the autonomic nervous system for the conservation or expenditure of bodily resources and energy in an anticipation of famine or feast. *Neuroscience and Biobehavioral Reviews, 3,* 155–162.

Marrazzi, M. A., & Luby, E. D. (1986). An auto-addiction opioid model of chronic anorexia nervosa. *International Journal of Eating Disorders, 5,* 191–208.

Mitchell, J. E., Hatsukami, D., Eckert, E. D., & Pyle, R. L. (1985). Characteristics of 275 patients with bulimia. *American Journal of Psychiatry, 142,* 482–485.

Mitchell, J. E., & Bantle, J. P. (1983). Metabolic and endocrine investigations in women of normal weight with the bulimia syndrome. *Biological Psychiatry, 18,* 355–365.

Morley, J. E., & Levine, A. S. (1981). Dynorphin (1–13) induces spontaneous feeding in rats. *Life Sciences, 29,* 1901–1903.

Mrosovsky, N., & Powley, T. L. (1977). Set-points for body weight and fat. *Behavioral Biology, 20,* 205–223.

Norman, D. K., & Herzog, D. B. (1984). Persistent social maladjustment in bulimia: A 1-year follow-up. *American Journal of Psychiatry, 141,* 444–446.

Nylander, J. (1971). The feeling of being fat and dieting in a school population: Epidemiologic interview investigation. *Acta Sociomedica Scandinavica, 3,* 17–26.

Permutt, M. A. (1976). Postprandial hypoglycemia. *Diabetes, 25,* 719–733.

Pope, H., & Hudson, J. (1984). *New hope for binge eaters.* New York: Harper & Row.

Porte, D., Jr., & Halter, J. B. (1981). The endocrine pancreas and diabetes mellitus. In R. Williams (Ed.), *Textbook of endocrinology* (6th ed., pp. 716–843). Philadelphia: W. B. Saunders.

Porte, D., Jr., & Woods, S. C. (1983). Neural regulation of islet hormones and its role in energy balance and stress hyperglycemia. In M. Ellenberg & H. Rifkin (Eds.), *Diabetes mellitus: Theory and practice* (3rd ed., pp. 267-294). New York: Medical Examination.

Powley, T. L. (1977). The ventromedial hypothalamic syndrome, satiety, and a cephalic phase hypothesis. *Psychological Review, 84,* 89-126.

Pyle, R. L., Mitchell, J. E., & Eckert, E. D. (1981). Bulimia: A report of 34 cases. *Journal of Clinical Psychiatry, 42,* 60-64.

Pyle, R. L., Mitchell, J. E., Eckert, E. D., Halvorson, P. A., Neuman, P. A., & Goff, G. M. (1983). The incidence of bulimia in freshmen college students. *International Journal of Eating Disorders, 2,* 75-85.

Rau, J., & Green, R. (1984). Neurological factors affecting binge eating: Body over mind. In R. Hawkins, W. Fremouw, & P. Clement (Eds.), *The binge-purge syndrome: Diagnosis, treatment, & research* (pp. 123-142). New York: Springer.

Rodin, J. (1980). The externality theory today. In A. J. Stunkard (Ed.), *Obesity* (pp. 226-239). Philadelphia: W. B. Saunders.

Russell, G. (1979). Bulimia nervosa: An ominous variant of anorexia nervosa. *Psychological Medicine, 9,* 429-448.

Saleh, J., & Lebwohl, P. (1980). Metoclopramide-induced gastric emptying in patients with anorexia nervosa. *American Journal of Gastroenterology, 74,* 127-132.

Salans, L. B. (1986). The human obesities. *Clinical Diabetes, 4,* 104-113.

Schwartz, D. M., & Thompson, M. D. (1981). Do anorectics get well? Current research and future needs. *American Journal of Psychiatry, 138,* 319-323.

Sclafani, A. (1980). Dietary obesity. In A. J. Stunkard (Ed.), *Obesity* (pp. 166-181). Philadelphia: W. B. Saunders.

Siegel, S. (1975). Evidence from rats that morphine tolerance is a learning response. *Journal of Comparative and Physiological Psychology, 89,* 498-506.

Siegel, S. (1977). Morphine tolerance acquisition as an associative process. *Journal of Experimental Psychology: Animal Behavior Processes, 3,* 1-13.

Siegel, S. (1978). Tolerance to the hyperthermic effect of morpine in the rat is a learned response. *Journal of Comparative and Physiological Psychology, 92,* 1137-1149.

Siegel, S. (1983). Classical conditioning, drug tolerance, and drug dependence. *Recent Advances in Alcohol and Drug Problems, 7,* 207-246.

Simpoulos, A., & Van Itallie, T. (1984). Body weight, health, and longevity. *Annals of Internal Medicine,* 285-294.

Sims, E. A. H., Goldman, R. F., Gluck, C. M., Horton, E. S., Keleher, D. C., & Rowe, D. W. (1968). Experimental obesity in man. *Transactions of the Association of American Physicians, 81,* 153-170.

Sjostrom, L., Garellick, G., Krotkievsky, M., & Luyck, A. (1980). Peripheral insulin in response to the sight and smell of food. *Metabolism, 29,* 901-909.

Spack, N. (1985). Medical complications of anorexia nervosa and bulimia. In S. W. Emmett (Ed.), *Theory and treatment of anorexia nervosa and bulimia: Biomedical, sociocultural and psychological perspectives* (pp. 5-19). New York: Brunner/Mazel.

Stangler, R. S., & Printz, A. M. (1980). DSM-III: Psychiatric diagnosis in a university population. *American Journal of Psychiatry, 137,* 937-940.

Striegel-Moore, R. H., Silberstein, L., & Rodin, J. (1986). Toward an understanding of risk factors for bulimia. *American Psychologist, 41,* 246-263.

Strober, M., Morrell, W., Burroughs, J., Salkin, B., & Jacobs, C. (1985). A controlled family study of anorexia nervosa. *Journal of Psychiatric Research, 19,* 239-246.

Stunkard, A. J. (1959). Eating patterns of obese persons. *Psychiatric Quarterly, 33,* 284-292.

Stunkard, A. J. (Ed.). (1980). *Obesity.* Philadelphia: W. B. Saunders.

Tabakoff, B., & Rothstein, J. D. (1983). Biology of tolerance and dependence. In B. Tabakoff,

P. B. Sutker, & C. L. Randall (Eds.), *Medical and social aspects of alcohol abuse* (pp. 187–220). New York: Plenum.

Trimble, E. R., Siegel, E. G., Berthoud, H. R., & Renold, A. E. (1980). Intraportal islet transplantation: Functional assessment in conscious unrestrained rats. *Endocrinology, 106,* 791–797.

Veverbrants, E., Olsen, W., & Arky, R. A. (1969). Role of gastro-intestinal factors in reactive hypoglycemia. *Metabolism, 18,* 6–12.

Vigersky, R., & Loriaux, D. (1977). The effect of cyproheptadine in anorexia nervosa: A double-blind trial. In R. Vigersky (Ed.), *Anorexia nervosa* (pp. 349–356). New York: Raven Press.

Wardle, J., & Beinart, H. (1981). Binge eating: A theoretical review. *British Journal of Clinical Psychology, 20,* 97–109.

Warren, M. P., & VandeWiele, R. L. (1973). Clinical and metabolic features of anorexia nervosa. *American Journal of Obstetrics and Gynecology, 117,* 435–449.

Wartofsky, L., & Burman, K. (1982). Alteration in thyroid function in patients with systemic illness: The "euthyroid sick syndrome." *Endocrine Reviews, 3,* 164–217.

Weiss, S. R., & Ebert, M. H. (1983). Psychological and behavioral characteristics of normal-weight bulimics and normal-weight controls. *Psychosomatic Medicine, 45,* 293–303.

Wermuth, B. M., Davis, K., Hollister, L., & Stunkard, A. J. (1977). Phenytoin treatment of the binge-eating syndrome. *American Journal of Psychiatry, 134,* 1249–1253.

Wilson, G. T. (1985, August). *The treatment of bulimia nervosa: A cognitive behavioral perspective.* Paper presented at the annual convention of the American Psychological Association, Los Angeles.

Woods, S. C. (1977). Conditioned insulin secretion. In Y. Katsuki, M. Sato, S. Takagi, & Y. Oomura (Eds.), *Food intake and the chemical senses* (pp. 357–365). Tokyo: University of Tokyo Press.

Woods, S. C. (1983). Conditioned hypoglycemia and conditioned insulin secretion. *Advances in Metabolic Disorders, 10,* 485–495.

Woods, S. C., Decke, E., & Vasselli, J. R. (1974). Metabolic hormones and regulation of body weight. *Psychological Review, 81,* 26–43.

Woods, S. C., & Kulkosky, P. J. (1976). Classically conditioned changes of blood glucose levels. *Psychosomatic Medicine, 38,* 201–219.

Woods, S. C., & Porte, D., Jr. (1974). Autonomic control of the endocrine pancreas. *Physiological Reviews, 54,* 596–619.

Woods, S. C., & Porte, D., Jr. (1978). The central nervous system, pancreatic hormones, feeding and obesity. *Advances in Metabolic Disorders, 9,* 283–312.

Woods, S. C., Porte, D., Jr., Bobbioni, E., Ionescu, E., Sauter, J., Rohner-Jeanrenaud, F., & Jeanrenaud, B. (1985). Insulin: Its relationship to the central nervous system and to the control of food intake and body weight. *American Journal of Clinical Nutrition, 42,* 1063–1071.

Woods, S. C., Vasselli, J. R., Kaestner, E., Szakmary, G. A., Milburn, P., & Vitiello, M. V. (1977). Conditioned insulin secretion and meal-feeding in rats. *Journal of Comparative and Physiological Psychology, 91,* 1164–1168.

Woods, S. C., West, D. B., Stein, L. J., McKay, L. D., Kenney, N. J., Porte, S. G., Lotter, E. C., & Porte, D., Jr. (1981). Peptides and the control of meal size. *Diabetologia, 20,* 305–313.

# V

# OTHER DRUGS OF ABUSE

# 11

# CANNABIS ABUSE

**ROGER A. ROFFMAN**
*University of Washington*

**WILLIAM H. GEORGE**
*State University of New York at Buffalo*

## Introduction

Relatively little attention has been devoted to assessment and treatment of the chronic marijuana user. Published work in this area has focused primarily on delineating the adverse effects of acute and chronic marijuana consumption or on estimating rates of use in the general population. Recently, much attention and concern have been directed toward the prevention and treatment of marijuana consumption among children and adolescents. For the adult user, there has been little systematic effort to assess and understand problematic marijuana use. The tacit assumption seems to be that, because marijuana does not evince the physical dependence and lethal dosage properties of other recreational drugs such as alcohol, extensive use by adults is by definition less problematic.

The aim of this chapter is to identify and discuss the physiological and psychological factors associated with assessment of chronic marijuana use by adults. With an emphasis on individualized evaluation and treatment planning, we examine the range of issues and procedures that pertain to assessment of marijuana use–abuse. Our presentation has been organized according to the tripartite-systems approach to assessment: behavioral, cognitive, and physiological dimensions.

Many of the practical techniques we discuss derive from our experience in clinical practice with marijuana abusers. Our clinical work has been largely influenced by cognitive–behavioral conceptualizations and strategies, particularly Marlatt's relapse prevention model (Marlatt, 1982; Marlatt & George, 1984; Marlatt & Gordon, 1985). Consequently, we construe assessment as a continuous endeavor that is woven into the treatment process rather than as a discrete diagnostic exercise. Many of the assessment strategies that are described here have direct utility as intervention exercises.

325

## Background Issues

Assessment of marijuana abuse does not have the extensive history of systematic conceptualization and scrutiny enjoyed by other, more pervasive substance abuse disorders. Consequently, there is not as rich a tradition of assessment strategies that can be reacted to or built upon. Nevertheless, there are significant background developments and issues that warrant discussion.

### Overconcern with Adverse Consequences

Perusal of the published literature on marijuana use reveals a striking overemphasis on assessment of marijuana's pharmacokinetic properties and its adverse consequences. Certainly, this was an appropriate path of inquiry for a recreational drug that was becoming increasingly popular and was relatively unknown to the Western world's research enterprise. However, our early research efforts may have been affected by the prevailing political tempest associated with marijuana use during the 1960s and early 1970s. As Weil and Rosen (1983) suggest, in some cases scientific objectivity may have become confounded by "efforts to prove preconceived ideas" (p. 115) commensurate with marijuana's status as an illicit substance. Not surprisingly, the literature on adverse effects is filled with contradictory empirical trends that seem to bear a suspicious correspondence to undulating political *Zeitgeists*. In sum, the literature on adverse effects is extensive, convoluted, and greatly beyond the scope of the current presentation. The interested reader is referred to recent presentations by Blum (1984), Glantz (1984), and Petersen (1980).

Nevertheless, a few robust trends have emerged from this literature, and they merit our attention. We are highly selective in our treatment of adverse consequences, limiting our comments to those effects pertaining to the educational and clinical needs of the marijuana-abusing client who is seeking assessment and treatment.

### Estimating Rates of Excessive Use

Efforts to determine the consumption patterns of cannabis users and the risks associated with those patterns are plagued with many of the same definitional and data base problems that are found in the drug dependence field in general. Nonetheless, some light has been shed on this subject by two national surveys sponsored by the National Institute on Drug Abuse (NIDA) and a longitudinal study of a sample of regular cannabis users.

The 1982 NIDA national survey on drug abuse (Miller *et al.,* 1983), the seventh in a series that began in 1971, included the population aged 12 and older living in households in the contiguous United States. In contrast to the trend from 1971 through 1979, the 1982 data indicated modest reductions in lifetime prevalence as well as current user rates for youths (aged 12-17) and young adults (aged 18-25), while demonstrating continued increases in these variables for older adults (aged 26+). It was estimated that approximately 20 million people (2.7 million youths, 9.1 million young adults, and 8.3 million adults) had used marijuana at least once in the month prior to the 1982 survey, and thus were classified as current users.

In 1982, most individuals across all age groups who had at one point in their lives been daily or near-daily users for at least a month currently were not using at that level. The 1982 study indicated that 1.4 million youths (21.7% of those youths who had ever used marijuana), 7 million young adults (33.1%), and 5.3 million older adults (18.3%) were *at some point* daily or near-daily users. Nearly one in four marijuana consumers (somewhat more than 13.5 million people) at some point used the drug quite steadily, based on this criterion. Overall, 4.2 million people (or 7.4% of the 56 million people who had ever used the drug) indicated that they were *currently* daily or near-daily users for the month just prior to being surveyed.

An NIDA-sponsored national survey of high school seniors has been conducted annually since 1975 by the University of Michigan Institute for Social Research (e.g., Johnston, Bachman, & O'Malley, 1982; Johnston, O'Malley, & Bachman, 1986). The decline in rates of current daily or near-daily use (10.7% in 1978; 5.0% in 1984) corresponds with the trend findings reported by Miller *et al.* (1983).

Another approach to estimating the risk of marijuana use's becoming abuse is based on prospective research with regular users. Weller and Halikas (1980) devised a set of criteria for marijuana abuse that focused on consequences that reflect interference in multiple life areas. Using these criteria in a 5- to 6-year follow-up of 97 regular users who had first been interviewed in 1969–1970, they found that 9.3% met the abuse criteria (see the Appendix).

Data on treatment admissions in federally funded agencies provide yet another imperfect indicator of the use–abuse relationship. Somewhat more than 35,000 individuals (less than 1% of the approximately 30 million people who had used marijuana that year) were admitted to treatment in 1981, reporting that their primary drug of use was cannabis. The 1978 figure for this population was approximately 23,000, indicating an increase of about 50% in 3 years. These data are difficult to interpret, because the increases could reflect expanded treatment resources over the 3-year period, the use of drug treatment resources for general mental health service (with a consequent mislabeling of marijuana problems as a means of obtaining eligibility), and/or other factors not related to the actual occurrence of marijuana-associated problems. Despite an apparent decline in the number of marijuana users, the overall indication is that a substantial number of adults use marijuana on a regular and perhaps excessive basis.

## Public Attitudes, Social Policy, and Assessment

The very substantial changes in marijuana use patterns over the past 15 years have been accompanied by rather dramatic shifts in public attitudes and social policy. An era of punitive criminal laws in the 1950s and 1960s gave way to a liberalization movement that saw penalties for marijuana possession lowered throughout the nation. The decriminalization concept advocated by the National Commission on Marihuana and Drug Abuse (1973) was endorsed by numerous professional and civic organizations, including the American Medical and Bar Associations.

The liberalization movement in the early and mid-1970s was reinforced by civil liberties arguments concerning individual rights, as well as by President Carter's (1977) declaration that the penalties for a behavior (e.g., possession of marijuana) ought not to be more detrimental for the individual than the natural consequences of engaging in that behavior. The focus of public attention changed, however, in the later years of that decade as younger people began using the drug, outlets for the sale of drug paraphernalia proliferated, and the potency of marijuana increased considerably. Rather than defining the marijuana control debate as a matter of adult civil liberties, the attention of the American public shifted to an emphasis on the protection of children (Roffman, 1977). A national movement of concerned parents grew rapidly in strength of numbers and in influence over social policy.

It is likely that these events have had considerable influence on the clinical assessment process. Individuals whose marijuana use has resulted in disturbance in one or more domains of life functioning may find support for their denial of a problem in the rhetoric of those arguing for legalization. In our experience of treating compulsive marijuana smokers, it has been common for clients to ascribe their prior hesitancy to seek help to a belief that the drug is not associated with adverse behavioral effects, including dependence. Many are surprised that clinical services for chronic marijuana users are available to and used by consumers of the drug. Some specialists in the field believe that many users interpret endorsement of decriminalization to mean that marijuana use is without risk (R. DuPont, cited in Anderson, 1981).

Another influence on the assessment process pertains specifically to those in late adolescence. One of the strongly advocated positions of the parents' movement was a rejection of the dichotomy of responsible versus irresponsible use for children and youths. Finding that drug treatment specialists often encouraged consideration of this distinction in the process of determining whether intervention was warranted, the leaders in this movement argued that *any* level of use by youths represents a problem by definition and must be prevented or stopped (Schuchard, 1981). As a consequence, the therapist conducting an assessment of an older adolescent must be particularly sensitive to potential intrafamilial value conflicts, perhaps of greater intensity than is often witnessed regarding alcohol use by young people.

Finally, the assessment of clients who are marijuana users is likely to necessitate client education concerning basic facts pertaining to the drug. The heated controversies of recent years have often found expression in widely disseminated drug education films, documentaries, pamphlets, books, and newspaper articles, with distortion of research findings. Clients and members of their families are likely to seek expert interpretation of the research literature from a therapist, having found that sensationalism in the public media is an obstacle to accurate determination of the facts (Trebach, 1984).

## Assessment of Component Systems

With more pervasive addictive disorders (e.g., alcoholism), the literature reveals that the assessment process is frequently construed from a behavioral, cognitive, or physiological perspective or some combination thereof. Accordingly, the literature on these disorders is replete with an ever-growing array of assessment instruments and procedures expressly designed to address one or more of the three dimensions. Given this history, any discussion of these addictions and their assessment or treatment can be readily adapted to the tripartite-systems framework. However, in the literature on marijuana use–abuse, there is no history of applying the tripartite-systems approach for conceptualizing the assessment process and for organizing assessment procedures. In our efforts to apply the tripartite framework to the problem of assessing marijuana use–abuse phenomena, we have attempted in the following sections of this chapter to sort the available instruments into the tripartite dimensions and to break down our own assessment strategies accordingly. Though in some cases these divisions seem somewhat artibrary to us, our hope is that this organizational scheme will aid readers in comparing these assessment processes with those used in other addictive disorders. Ideally, such comparisons will generate some cross-fertilization of ideas and lead to development of a fuller range of procedures for assessing marijuana use–abuse. At present, the assessment of marijuana use–abuse is very much a fledgling enterprise, with plenty of room for growth.

## Behavioral Assessment: Issues and Procedures

The chief objective in this section is to describe the behaviors and environmental conditions that characterize the individual's pattern of marijuana consumption. The expectation is that an adequate description will lead to a more refined analysis of the determinants of consumption, and thereby will dictate the nature of the intervention.

The diagnostic protocol provided by the *Diagnostic and Statistical Manual of Mental Disorders,* third edition (DSM–III; American Psychiatric Association, 1980), offers a scheme for assessing and classifying four clinical syndromes associated with marijuana use. Weller and Halikas (1980) and Carroll (1981) have also sought to conceptualize marijuana abuse. Summaries of each of the latter two diagnostic outlines are included in the Appendix.

In our work with marijuana abusers, we have not incorporated diagnosis as part of our assessment exercises. It has been our experience that formal diagnosis of the marijuana abuser is valuable primarily for the fulfillment of three administrative functions. One, of course, is communication with other professionals about a particular client, especially if the client comes in contact with a mental health treatment facility where an official diagnosis is required. A second function served by diagnosis is in the completion of insurance forms, provided that the insurance carrier provides reimbursement for treatment of cannabis abuse or dependence. It should be noted that clients who are in treatment for marijuana abuse tend to be very wary about any official documentation of their marijuana involvement. They often express the fear that insurance forms will eventually be seen by their employers. Although marijuana use has attained wider public acceptance in recent years, it is still an illicit activity and is still considered a symbol of social deviance in many circles. Whereas in many contexts it has become almost fashionable to undergo treatment for alcoholism, marijuana abusers who pursue treatment are not accorded the same measure of respect, admiration, support, or encouragement. Finally, diagnosis has important research utility. In this regard, the DSM–III diagnostic criteria emphasize nomothetic guidelines that enable researchers to ascertain the comparability of different subject samples.

Aside from these primarily administrative considerations, diagnosis has not been a focus in our assessment efforts. We have instead concentrated on more individually tailored description, analysis, and treatment planning. From a behavioral perspective, the key assessment targets are adverse consequences, past and present use patterns, influences in the social environment, and social skills.

## Assessing Adverse Behavioral Consequences

### Questionnaire Measurement

Self-administered questionnaires can be used to identify the manner in which the client has experienced adverse consequences. An NIDA monograph (Rittenhouse, 1979) presents a pool of questionnaire items developed to tap users' perceptions concerning the effects of marijuana use on their lives. This publication is particularly valuable for those seeking standardized instruments for research purposes. Another NIDA monograph (Huba, Bentler, & Newcomb, 1981) provides several examples of questionnaire items for assessing both positive and negative marijuana consequences; these are presented in Table 11-1.

### Problem List

Some therapists may prefer to gather data concerning adverse consequences in other ways than a self-administered questionnaire. In our clinical experience, it has been useful to assign clients the task of compiling a written inventory of the problems brought about or worsened by marijuana use. The client is instructed to generate as extensive a list as possible by considering how marijuana use has affected every aspect of his or her life. The therapist gives examples of the domains in which such problems might have occurred (e.g., feelings about oneself, thinking abilities, emotional balance, relationships with others, performance on the job or at school, problems with health, difficulties with the law, etc.), and requests that the client bring a written list of the adverse consequences that he or she has experienced to the next session. Because these instructions encourage the client to review cognitive and physiological domains as well as behavioral concerns, this technique assesses adverse consequences for each of the tripartite dimensions.

Importantly, the consequent process of reviewing, paraphrasing, and refining this client-generated problem list seems to enhance motivation to work toward change. This is an especially valuable side benefit, because the client's motivation to change typically wavers during the treatment process. The problem list can serve as a potent reminder of how problematic life was during the pretreatment consumption pattern. The compilation of this list can also facilitate goal setting concerning future marijuana use. Although we recommend that each of our clients initially undergo a 30-day period of abstinence from marijuana use, we are open to longer-term goals of either abstinence or moderate use. We do not attempt to dissuade the client who believes from the start that abstinence is a necessity. However, for those clients who are hoping to return eventually to using

TABLE 11-1.   Items for Client Self-Report of Positive and Negative Impact of Marijuana Use

Sometimes the effects you experience when you take drugs are the ones you want; sometimes they are not. Sometimes drugs improve things for you; sometimes they make matters worse. This section asks about the *short-term effects* you get just after you take marijuana. (Check one answer for each question.)

The short-term or immediate effect of marijuana on your:

|  | Usually made better | Usually made worse | Sometimes better; sometimes worse | Usually no effect |
|---|---|---|---|---|
| Ability to think clearly | — | — | — | — |
| Excitement and enthusiasm for life | — | — | — | — |
| Enjoyment of sex | — | — | — | — |
| Ability to avoid angry feelings | — | — | — | — |

Using marijuana sometimes leads to changes in people's lives. For each question listed below, check whether you think marijuana has *improved, impaired,* or had *no effect* on your life. What we are asking about here are *long-term effects,* not the effects you experience just after taking the drug.

The long-term effect of marijuana on your:

|  | Improved | Impaired | No effect |
|---|---|---|---|
| Ability to cope and solve life's problems | — | — | — |
| Physical health | — | — | — |
| General self-confidence | — | — | — |
| Ability to concentrate on complex tasks | — | — | — |
| Work performance (including school and housework) | — | — | — |
| Relations with employers or teachers | — | — | — |
| Memory | — | — | — |
| General level of energy | — | — | — |

*Note.* Adapted from *Assessing Marijuana Consequences: Selected Questionnaire Items* (DHHS Publication No. ADM 81-1150) by G. J. Huba, P. M. Bentler, and M. D. Newcomb, 1981, Washington, DC. U.S. Government Printing Office.

marijuana, the problem list can be a useful resource: If old problems re-emerge, they signal the need to reformulate the moderate-use guidelines adopted earlier.

*Assessing the Amotivational Syndrome*

The term "amotivational syndrome" was coined some years ago (Smith, 1968) to describe what was considered a group of subtle yet reliable behavioral sequelae to regular marijuana use. The symptoms have been described as including apathy; passivity; lethargy; loss of effectiveness; and inability or unwillingness to concentrate, follow routines, and engage in meaningful goal-directed behavior. Presumably, both acute intoxication and chronic use may generate amotivational symptoms in otherwise goal-directed individuals. Whereas the evidence for this claim is limited and inconclusive, the growing indication is that any correlation between marijuana consumption and reduced motivation is mediated by personality characteristics of the user, by social expectations, or by the cultural milieu (Babor, Mendelson, & Kuehnle, 1976; Comitas, 1976; Creason & Goldman, 1981; Mellinger, Somers, Davidson, & Manheimer, 1976). Very little attention has been given by researchers to the relationship between marijuana use and work performance in the United States, although the published studies of heavy users in other countries have not documented evidence of amotivation (Rubin & Comitas, 1975).

Aside from the lack of definitive research evidence and the need for further inquiry, it is important to note that clients who voluntarily seek treatment for marijuana abuse typically complain of amotivational effects. Frequently, these individuals perceive that their activity level and vigor have generally correlated negatively with their marijuana consumption. No matter how productive or unproductive the individual is, he or she invariably feels that his or her effectiveness would be greatly improved without marijuana. Often, further behavioral assessment will reveal episodes of marijuana smoking that routinely initiate prolonged periods of inactivity and passive entertainment. Because of obvious and extensive overlap in symptomatology, clinicians should be aware that amotivation complaints attributed to marijuana consumption may in fact represent clinical levels of depression and social withdrawal.

## Past and Present Use Patterns

### Questionnaire Measurement

Self-report concerning the client's past and current usage patterns can be measured in part via a standardized series of questions. Table 11-2 presents a questionnaire adapted from a review of available research instruments published by NIDA (Huba et al., 1981). In addition to some of the more general deficiencies in self-reported quantitative-use data (e.g., purposeful falsification or faulty memory, resulting in under- or overestimation), the reporting of these data can be confounded by a number of other important factors. How potent is the marijuana? Does the individual smoke to a point of profound alteration in consciousness or to a much less extreme level? How have these factors changed (or not changed) over the client's marijuana-smoking career? The clinician will need to ask about potency, degree of intoxication typically attained, and patterns over time, but at present does not have the benefit of a well-tested instrument that incorporates each of the mentioned elements. In contrast with the available dose–response curves and ethanol-proof data in alcohol use measurement, the quantification of historical marijuana use patterns is far less amenable to standardization.

A standardized list of questions can also be useful in posttreatment assessment. We have found it useful to seek data routinely from clients following termination. This helps us to know in very general terms the degree to which our intervention has helped, despite the many ways in which these data may be biased. It gives the client an opportunity to review progress as well, perhaps stimulating a decision to work again toward change if the treatment outcome was not positive. Table 11-3 presents the follow-up questionnaire.

### Behavioral Interviewing

Considerable information about the behavioral characteristics of a person's marijuana consumption can be acquired through skillful face-to-face interviews. Because a greater sense of trust and confidentiality can be established in interview interactions, clients may feel more at ease when discussing and describing their pattern of use than when responding to a questionnaire. An initial aim of the behavioral interview is to describe fully the client's present marijuana-smoking routine and its historical development. In interviewing about both past and present use, the questioning should move gradually from a broad perusal of all facets of their use into a finer-grained analysis of key environmental and historical determinants. As in all idiographic assessment procedures, the move is from comprehensive data collection to selective hypothesis testing. A few introductory comments at the start of the interview are valuable in preparing the client for such a detailed account of what he or she experiences as an automatic habit characterized by an indivisible sequence of behaviors.

*Past Use.* An examination of the history of use can yield important information about the client's relationship with marijuana. This historical mapping of the use–abuse pattern is crucial to the assessment process.

In collecting this material, it is useful to construe the client's relationship with marijuana as a time line punctuated by a series of critical events or mileposts. Some of these mileposts are common to all or most marijuana users—for example, the initial use or the first attempt at abstinence or reduction. Other mileposts will be specific to the particular client, and identification of these experiences is an obvious objective of the interview. The assessment of these mileposts is important for two reasons. First, it will highlight environmental, interpersonal, and intrapersonal factors that have

TABLE 11-2. Brief Self-Report History of Marijuana Use

---

1. How old were you when you first tried marijuana or hashish?
   (indicate age) _____ years old

2. About how many times altogether (if any) have you ever used marijuana or hashish?
   1. 1–9 times
   2. 10–39 times
   3. 40–59 times
   4. 60–99 times
   5. 100–999 times
   6. 1,000 times or more

3. When was the most recent time you used marijuana or hashish?
   1. Today
   2. Yesterday
   3. Two to seven days ago
   4. Eight days to four weeks ago
   5. One to 12 months ago
   6. More than 12 months ago (skip to question 7)

4. How often did you use marijuana or hashish *during the past 12 months?*
   1. None
   2. Once or twice during the year
   3. Three to 11 times during the year
   4. Once a month, or a total of 12 times
   5. Two or three times a month, or a total of 13 to 36 times
   6. Once a week, or a total of 37 to 52 times
   7. Two or three times a week, or a total of 53 to 150 times
   8. Four to six times a week, or a total of 151 to 300 times
   9. Every day

5. How often (if at all) have you used marijuana or hashish *during the last 30 days?*
   1. None
   2. Once a month
   3. Two or three times a month
   4. Once a week
   5. Two or three days a week
   6. Four to six days a week
   7. Every day

6. *During the last 30 days,* about how many marijuana cigarettes (joints, reefers) or the equivalent, did you smoke a day, on the average? If you shared them with other people, count only the amount *you* smoked.
   1. None
   2. Less than one a day
   3. One a day
   4. Two to three a day
   5. Four to six a day
   6. Seven or more a day

7. Has there been a period in your life when you used marijuana or hashish on a daily, or almost daily, basis for at least a month? Circle one answer.
   1. Yes
   2. No (skip the remaining questions)

*(continued)*

TABLE 11-2 (Continued).

---

8. How old were you when you first smoked marijuana or hashish that frequently, that is, used it daily or almost daily for at least a month?
   (indicate age) ____ years old

9. Do you still use marijuana or hashish on a daily or near-daily basis?
   1. Yes (skip to question 11)
   2. No

10. If you answered "no" to the question above, how old were you when you last used marijuana or hashish that frequently?
    (indicate age) ____ years old

11. Altogether, adding up the different months when you used DAILY, for about how much of your life would you estimate that you have used marijuana and/or hashish daily or almost daily?
    1. Less than 3 months
    2. About 3 to 9 months
    3. About 1 year
    4. About 1½ years
    5. About 2 years
    6. About 3 to 5 years
    7. About 6 to 9 years
    8. About 10 or more years

---

*Note.* Adapted from *Assessing Marijuana Consequences: Selected Questionnaire Items* (DHHS Publication No. ADM 81-1150) by G. J. Huba, P. M. Bentler, and M. D. Newcomb, 1981, Washington, DC: U.S. Government Printing Office.

helped to promote and maintain the client's involvement with marijuana. Frequently, factors that were influential early in the user's history will still be operating or will provide clues to inconspicuous present-day determinants. Second, to the extent that each milepost captures the quantitative features of the individual's consumption at that time, it contributes a data point to a mental graph of the client's lifetime use pattern. This mental graph helps provide a context for understanding the severity of present use.

Certain types of information will need to be assessed for each milepost. In the next subsection, a guide for questioning the client about *present* use is provided. Many of these same questions should be employed to collect information about historical mileposts. In addition, certain mileposts will evoke particular questions. Some common mileposts are listed below, along with some specific questions. It will be noted that in some instances the questions being raised extend beyond purely behavioral–environmental phenomena to elicit perceptions, beliefs, and feelings. In these instances, we have opted for a bit more procedural fidelity at the expense of the chapter's organizational imperatives. Common mileposts include the following:

1. *Initial knowledge.* When did the client first learn about marijuana and its use? Who imparted this information and how was it described?

TABLE 11-3.   Follow-Up Questionnaire

---

_____

Code number

The date of our last session was _____. That was __ weeks ago (as of _____).

1. Since our last session, have you smoked marijuana on at least one occasion?
   Yes __   No __ (If "no," go on to question 9)

2. Since our final session, have there been any weeks in which you smoked marijuana on *at least four days?*
   Yes __   No __ (If "no," go on to question 4)

3. About how many weeks have there been since our final session in which you smoked on at least four days?
   _____ weeks

4. Since our last session, have there been any weeks in which you smoked marijuana on *one, two, or three days?*
   Yes __   No __ (If "no," go on to question 6)

5. About how many weeks have there been since our final session in which you smoked on one, two, or three days?
   _____ weeks

6. Since our final session, have there been any weeks in which you felt dissatisfied with the amount of marijuana you had used (in other words, you felt that you had exceeded your own standards for yourself)?
   Yes __   No __ (If "no," go on to question 8)

7. About how many weeks have there been since our last session in which you were dissatisfied with your marijuana use because of the amount you used?
   _____ weeks

8. Since our final session, have you received counseling from another counselor (or been in a self-help group such as AA or NA) for help with marijuana use?
   Yes __   No __

9. Since our final session, have there been any periods of time when you felt that you were having a problem with your use of alcohol?
   Yes __   No __

10. Since our final session, have there been any periods of time when you felt that you were having a problem with use of drugs other than marijuana or alcohol?
    Yes __   No __

THANKS for completing this questionnaire!
Please mail it back to me *as soon as possible.*

---

2. *Initial use.* The client should be asked to describe his or her first use of marijuana, including age at the time, location, circumstances, who was present, amount consumed, reactions to the experience, and so on. Frequently, clients have vivid memories about these early experiences and talk freely, perhaps even wistfully, about them.

3. *Initial intoxication.* Many clients, particularly those who began their use prior to the recent influx of higher-potency cannabis, distinguish

between their initial use and their first "high." If this is the case, the same information should be obtained about the first "high" experience as about the first use. How many smoking experiences intervened between the initial use and the initial intoxication?

4. *First experience with daily or near-daily use.* Typically, clients can recount a time when they began regular and frequent consumption. The circumstances of this shift should be explored. Generally, such a shift reflects a sudden increase in access to marijuana, which could result from any number of factors: increased income, new relationship with a heavy user and/or dealer, personal involvement with drug trafficking, harvest of one's first homegrown crop, and so forth.

5. *Frustration with unavailability.* Some clients have distinct memories of early experiences of being unable to get marijuana when they wanted it. The client's feelings and reactions to those encounters should be explored. These experiences are often very important because they may have led the client to adopt a policy designed to insure availability (e.g., "I always keep a secret stash"). This information will certainly come in handy for planning the intervention.

6. *First concern about use.* When was the first time that the client considered that marijuana use could be problematic?

7. *Attempts at voluntary abstinence.* The client should be asked to recount all previous attempts to abstain from marijuana consumption, including his or her reasons, techniques, and relapse experiences.

8. *Involvement with alcohol or other drugs.* How did the client's consumption of alcohol and other drugs fluctuate with marijuana consumption? Many clients will report that they became more or less involved with other substances as a function of their marijuana use.

To identify other mileposts, the client should be asked to describe any other events or experiences that led to major changes in his or her marijuana use.

*Present Use.* In gathering information about present use, the clinician may want to begin by asking the client to describe a representative marijuana-smoking episode. Guidelines for soliciting this type of information are provided below. Again, these same guidelines can be applied to the collection of information about past use.

1. *Particular cannabis preparation(s) being consumed.* Typically, this will be marijuana, hashish, or hashish oil.

2. *Methods of consumption.* Is the client smoking or eating it? Because smoking creates a substantially more rapid bloodstream delivery of tetrahydrocannabinol (THC) and generally produces a higher peak intoxication level, it is much more amenable to an abusive use pattern. Even so, clients will often report significant past experiences associated with edible preparations of marijuana. The client may see such experiences as significant

because of a subjective impression of a qualitatively different intoxication, or because he or she made the common mistake of eating too much and overshooting the desired intoxication level and duration. Common edible preparations include brownies, cakes, cookies, and candies. Some individuals have been known to simply sauté marijuana in butter and eat it with a fork! Overall, smoking is the normative consumption method. Hereafter, our discussions of marijuana consumption assume that the client is smoking it.

3. *Methods of smoking.* Are cigarettes (joints) or a pipe being used? Though users generally smoke cannabis using whatever method is available, many individuals report a decided preference for either smoking joints or smoking from a pipe. Such preferences do not appear to be related to severity of use.

4. *Items of paraphernalia being used.* For many marijuana users, paraphernalia items (e.g., bongs, waterpipes, stashpipes, roach clips) are not merely implements of use. Instead, these are perceived as important elements of the consumption rituals. Frequently, clients report feeling quite attached to a particular piece of paraphernalia and give any number of reasons for the attachment (e.g., special gift from lover, handcrafted item, imported piece, etc.). This is important to assess, because the client may erroneously view an attachment to a particular piece of roach clip jewelry, for instance, as unrelated to his or her commitment to quit marijuana.

5. *Perceived potency of the cannabis.* The client should be asked to estimate potency level of the marijuana that he or she is currently smoking.

6. *Times and locations of smoking.* Is it at home, at school, in the car, only at parties, or any place where the risk of detection is low?

7. *Social functions of smoking, if any* (i.e., does he or she smoke alone or with regular smoking buddies?).

8. *Whether the client is a grower and/or a dealer.*


*Self-Monitoring*

*Record Keeping.* Upon interview, many marijuana users will supply few detailed responses to the queries above. Primarily, this reflects the fact that they are unaccustomed to thinking about their smoking behavior in objective terms. For this and other reasons, it is important to augment the interview information through the use of self-monitoring procedures, whereby the client is asked to keep an ongoing log of current use. The instructions for the recording of these data are to indicate the following information for each occasion of use:

1. *Date and time of day.*
2. *Location.*
3. *People present.*

4. *Circumstances* (e.g., lunch party, going to movie, or preparing dinner).

5. *Amount smoked.* Based on his or her method of consumption, the client should select a standard unit for determining the amount consumed. Examples have included joints (or fractions thereof), pipe bowlfuls, and number of "tokes" or "hits."

6. *Urges to smoke.* Commonly, clients who decide to seek treatment for marijuana will have voluntarily quit or reduced their consumption when the assessment process begins. Obviously, much can be learned about their previous use patterns through behavioral interviewing. In addition, prospective data can be gained by instructing the individual to monitor his or her urges to smoke and the correlates of these urge occurrences. Urges are typically precipitated by the same events that are regularly associated with the marijuana consumption.

7. *Other substances being used at that time* (e.g., alcohol and tobacco).

8. *Level of intoxication.* The client can be asked to use a subjective rating scale. This information is especially relevant for clients who are interested in embarking on a controlled-use program, because it enables them to appreciate that the degree of satisfaction derived from a particular smoking episode varies according to such factors as setting, amount, and frequency of use.

9. *Mood.* To get at less obvious internal correlates, clients can also be asked to describe and numerically rate mood states that precede or follow consumption.

This list of self-monitoring targets is not exhaustive, nor should any one client necessarily be expected to keep track of all of these factors. Consistent with an idiographic assessment orientation, the self-monitoring targets and procedures should be tailored to the particular individual.

*Troubleshooting and Reviewing.* After assignment of self-monitoring, the clinician and client should periodically troubleshoot the procedures and review the data. Troubleshooting is oriented toward maximizing compliance and the usefulness of the data. This may involve efforts to make record keeping more convenient, less conspicuous, more streamlined, and less disruptive. Troubleshooting may also involve working with the client to overcome resistance to self-monitoring. Common sources of resistance include (1) feelings of guilt about how much is being consumed; (2) embarrassment about sharing this information with another person; (3) fear of demystification (some clients report that record keeping diminishes reinforcing feelings of secrecy and specialness associated with their smoking); and (4) association with schoolwork (for many clients, this association activates a host of feelings that inhibit record keeping). Typically, these sources of resistance can be minimized through open discussion oriented toward ventilation, clarification, and reassurance.

The clinician should periodically review the data with the client. This helps maintain the client's motivation for accurate and conscientious record keeping. In reviewing the data, clients often describe a reactivity effect, noting that record keeping seems either to facilitate or to attenuate their consumption. Acknowledging that this is a normal reaction, but one that inevitably compromises data accuracy, the therapist should encourage the client to resist this tendency. From a methodological standpoint, it must be noted that self-monitoring data are vulnerable to the same sources of inaccuracy that affect other self-report data: unreliable record keeping, faulty recall, biased reporting, demand characteristics, reactivity effects, and so on. Some of these influences can be reduced through effective troubleshooting; others are inherent in the procedure.

When reviewing the self-monitoring data, the client should be encouraged to look for patterns in the data that highlight environmental and intrapersonal correlates. Pattern recognition goes a long way toward identification of "controlling variables" that maintain the consumption rate. Obviously, these controlling variables should later dictate the focus of treatment and follow-up interventions.

*Graphs.* Preparing graphs that summarize the self-monitoring data helps clients to identify important variables. Graphs may be used in various ways. The simplest use is to have the client prepare a graph showing the amount smoked each day. This type of graph is helpful in identifying temporal patterns that suggest obvious correlates; for example, the graph may show that most smoking takes place on paydays or on weekends. Another option is for the client to prepare a bar graph indicating how much is smoked in particular high-risk situations. Such a graph may show that most smoking occurs at parties, after marital spats, or following work. During treatment, the client can be instructed to graph the amount smoked as a function of the use or nonuse of various coping strategies. The visual representation provided by graphs facilitates the delineation of important correlates and controlling variables.

## Social Environment and Coping Skills

As is common with heavy users of any other mood-changing, nonmedical substance, there is a likelihood that the heavy marijuana user will have selectively altered his or her friendships to have become immersed in a peer group of other marijuana-using individuals. Among the exceptions to this, in our experience, have been some professionals (e.g., physicians, lawyers, brokers, etc.) who have succeeded in keeping their marijuana use hidden from colleagues as well as from most significant others.

Assessment of the social environment begins with self-monitoring data that reveal regularity in the client's smoking acquaintances. Social contacts are often critical variables in maintaining marijuana usage. The clinician will want to alert clients who seek treatment for marijuana abuse to the importance of being prepared for the various kinds of influence that might be exerted by friends and family members. We have found it useful in the assessment process to request clients to develop three lists of their familial and social contacts: (1) those individuals from whom the clients anticipate receiving support for their efforts to achieve change, and to whom the clients would be able to turn for understanding, encouragement, or companionship if they feel unhappy or distressed; (2) those individuals who are likely to "test" the clients' resolve and perseverance by doing such things as offering them excuses to "take a break" from their control efforts; and 3) those individuals who are so clearly a risk to the clients' control efforts that they must choose to avoid being with them, either temporarily or permanently.

Once such a set of lists has been compiled, the therapist can engage the client in a discussion of each person identified. What approach will the client take in dealing with that person: self-disclosure of trying to change use patterns, the use of a prepared justification for not smoking marijuana, or another approach? Which individuals, if any, are potential sources of sabotage? How skillful is the client in implementing his or her coping strategies? This process of assessing the social network may lead to the need for social skills training (e.g., assertiveness) as a component of the therapy.

Skills assessment extends beyond social abilities to include more general coping skills. A working assumption generated by the relapse prevention model (Marlatt, 1982) is that the excessive user has come to rely maladaptively on marijuana consumption as a way of coping with stress. In effect, smoking marijuana has become the habitual counterpunch to and refuge from life's hassles. As this process unfolds, the user's repertoire of adaptive coping skills gradually narrows. Consequently, evaluating the range and effectiveness of the user's coping abilities (e.g., relaxation or exercise routines) is an important assessment task.

**Cognitive Assessment: Issues and Procedures**

Historically, cognitive assessment of the marijuana user has emphasized the effects of acute and chronic consumption on intellectual capabilities. This literature is considerable and is beyond the scope of the current chapter; nonetheless, it is a necessary departure point. Cognitive assessment also focuses on client cognitions that facilitate marijuana consumption.

Finally, cognitive assessment should determine whether the client can design a set of coping strategies.

## Assessing Adverse Cognitive Effects

Research investigators examining the effects of marijuana on cognition distinguish between acute and chronic effects. "Acute effects" refer to cognitive consequences of marijuana intoxication; "chronic effects" refer to the long-term cognitive deficits induced by regular marijuana consumption.

### Acute Effects

The question being addressed in research on acute marijuana effects is simply this: How does marijuana affect an individual's performance of cognitive tasks? In the typical paradigm, a cannabis or placebo preparation is administered to subjects; the subjects then perform a series of exercises that entail cognitive abilities.

Overall, the findings from these studies have been less than clear-cut (see review by Ferraro, 1980). The extent to which a deficit is demonstrated depends on a host of variables, including cannabis dosage, method of consumption, a subject's prior use history (tolerance), task difficulty and complexity, set and setting factors, and motivation to perform (e.g., financial incentives). Under some conditions, acute marijuana intoxication impairs performance on cognitive tasks. Under other conditions, marijuana has no effect or may even improve performance on certain tasks. In addition to all of these sources of experimental variability, many of these studies have employed inadequate methodological controls, thus making it difficult to draw definitive conclusions.

One position on acute marijuana effects is that memory functions are central to any cognitive impairment. Accordingly, a great deal of the research on acute marijuana effects has employed various memory paradigms. The effort has been to pinpoint in exactly what way marijuana disrupts memory processes. Though the evidence from these efforts is still equivocal, some reliable trends seem to be emerging. Marijuana-induced memory impairment is most apparent on tasks that require storage in long-term memory. Marijuana seems to have no effect on retrieval from long-term memory. At high dosages, marijuana disrupts short-term memory.

In the clinical assessment process, there is little interest in the acute effects of marijuana on cognition and memory. One exception, of course, is determining whether a person is presently intoxicated on marijuana. Conversational evidence of memory disturbance may provide indications of present intoxication.

*Chronic Effects*

The long-standing and predominant question on marijuana and cognitive effects has been this: Does regular marijuana consumption lead to premature deterioration in intellectual and memory functions? Findings from early studies suggesting chronic detrimental effects were flawed by problematic methodology. More recent, better-controlled investigations (e.g., Schaeffer, Andrysiak, & Ungerleider, 1981) have generally failed to reveal chronic cognitive deficits. Though the research on this question is far from conclusive, the strong indication is that heavy marijuana consumption does not cause long-term cognitive deterioration. Evidently, the cognitive and memory deficits attributed to marijuana are only short-term.

However, much remains to be known about chronic cognitive effects. In particular, very little is known about the long-term effects of heavy consumption of high-potency marijuana on individuals who began using the drug in childhood or early adolescence. The research evidence for acute marijuana effects on short-term memory suggests that such usage would certainly interfere with the opportunity to take optimal advantage of classroom education.

*Client Concerns*

Individuals who seek treatment for marijuana abuse often express concern about deterioration in cognitive abilities that they fear have been induced by heavy marijuana consumption. Typical complaints take the form of "I'm just not as mentally sharp as I used to be," or "I'm always forgetting things," or "Things seem fuzzy most of the time." A client may be so concerned as to request some type of formal evaluation that will rule out marijuana-induced cognitive deficits.

For individuals who request cognitive testing, the clinician should explain the limited utility of such evaluation. Several considerations apply. First, to determine the nature of any real deficit, the testing procedures would have to sample a wide range of abilities. This could not be accomplished merely with intelligence or memory tests, but would instead necessitate the comprehensiveness afforded by a neuropsychological test battery, such as the Halstead–Reitan or Luria–Nebraska batteries. The Halstead–Reitan battery, for example, samples verbal and nonverbal intellect, short- and long-term memory, sensory–perceptual functions, abstract problem solving, expressive and receptive language abilities, psychomotor functions, and personality (see, e.g., Boll, 1981; B. P. Jones & Butters, 1983). Such a wide sampling of abilities permits more sophisticated clinical inferences based on level of performance, patterning of performance, specific deficits or pathognomic signs, and interhemispheric comparisons.

Second, whatever cognitive deficit that the client is experiencing may be partially due to the acute effects of marijuana. Because THC is a fat-soluble substance, it metabolizes very slowly and accumulates in the body. Consequently, the regular smoker always has some measure of THC in his or her system. Therefore, if the client is currently consuming cannabis every day, then he or she may be undergoing continual intoxication effects. Because of tolerance development, the individual may experience very little subjective sense of intoxication between smoking episodes, while still experiencing acute cognitive and memory deficits induced by marijuana. In light of this possibility, clients who seek referral for cognitive testing should be asked to abstain from marijuana for 4–6 weeks to eliminate any effects due to acute intoxication or residual THC. To be more certain, the individual could forego cognitive evaluation until he or she produces urine samples that are no longer positive for THC. In our clinical experience, after 4 weeks of abstinence most clients report sharpened sensory, memory, and intellectual functioning.

Third, because scientific efforts have failed so far to establish a link between marijuana use and chronic cognitive deficits, it is unlikely that any single evaluation of an individual could demonstrate such a causal tie. Any apparent deficit revealed by such an individual evaluation could not clearly be attributed to marijuana consumption. In fact, it could be convincingly argued that an individual's involvement in marijuana consumption has developed secondarily to poor cognitive skill and educational performance.

Any interpretation of testing results on the question of chronic marijuana effects would be severely limited and highly suspect. On the one hand, there are no normative data. For chronic marijuana users, unlike alcoholics, there is no body of data that characterizes performance on psychological test batteries. Consequently, there are no normative grounds to justify attribution of the client's test results to marijuana usage. On the other hand, it is unlikely that clients would have ready access to test results from their premarijuana days that could provide a meaningful comparison for current test performance. Even if the client could furnish comparative test results that predate marijuana use, any demonstrable decline in cognitive function could not be solely attributed to marijuana use. It would be too difficult to distinguish the influence of marijuana from the influence of other sources of cognitive deficit that are known (e.g., alcohol and other drug use) and unknown (e.g., mild closed head injuries or transient ischemic attacks) to the client.

Personality features are still another consideration. It is entirely possible that the client's insistence on being formally tested is symptomatic of a more pervasive psychiatric disturbance. This possibility should not be summarily dismissed, especially if the client fails to comprehend or appreciate the limitations described above. More general psychiatric and/or psychotherapeutic referral and intervention may be warranted.

Of course, the client may decide to pursue formal evaluation in full appreciation of the aforementioned interpretive limitations and in recognition of the requisite time and financial expenditures. The client indeed may be experiencing real cognitive deficits that are unrelated to marijuana but are instead due to some undetected neuropathological processes. Results that fall in the normal range will no doubt alleviate the client's worries. Abnormal results may lead to early detection of a problematic neuropsychological condition.

It is important to point out that neuropsychological testing is time-consuming and relatively expensive—a consideration to be weighed against the client's insistence on testing. In the Seattle area, for instance, the cost for administration and interpretation of a full Halstead–Reitan battery runs approximately $450 in a medical center setting and $550 or more in the private sector. Administration of the procedures takes about 7–8 hours and is preferably done in 1 day. Clients who want to pursue these procedures should be referred to the nearest university-affiliated medical center to inquire about the availability of neuropsychological testing services. These procedures are not to be confused with or substituted for neurological exams or embellished intelligence testing that incorporates the Bender–Gestalt as an indicator of presumed organicity.

### Assessing Cognitions That Facilitate Cannabis Use

As in many behavioral and addictive disorders, cognitive activity plays an important role in mediating the use of marijuana. Though unavailable for direct observation, these cognitive processes are often instrumental in the initiation, facilitation, and maintenance of the individual's consumption pattern. In any adequate assessment of the individual or effective plan for treatment interventions, cognitive processes must be investigated.

### "Great Expectations"

Users often hold inflated positive expectations about the effects of consuming marijuana. From an assessment standpoint, it is important to identify these expectations, because they are integral to the sequence of events that precipitates various smoking episodes. Early in the marijuana-smoking career, these expectations are acquired through social channels. Later, the individual evolves a set of expectations that is based largely on his or her own experiences with marijuana. For the heavy user, these expectations overshadow perceptions of the delayed negative consequences of consumption.

The behavioral interview and the self-monitoring procedures described earlier may be used to assess client expectations. On interview, the client can simply be asked to describe what he or she generally expects to experience when consuming marijuana. Similarly, with self-monitoring, the client can be instructed to record the specific expectations associated with each smoking episode. Typical expectations include "It relaxes me," "It's the only way that I can tune out the outside world and just focus on myself," or "It just makes whatever I'm doing seem more interesting and enjoyable." In treatment planning, such expectations are of obvious import in forecasting high-risk situations and in designing substitute indulgences that are more constructive.

### Identification and Self-Image

A more robust set of cognitions is generated by the extent to which the client adopts a self-image as a "pot smoker." For many clients, seeing oneself as a marijuana user becomes an important source of identity. Often, this self-identification process results from having cultivated a social network that includes other marijuana consumers. For some clients, this group becomes the primary reference group, and they may tend to spend the majority of their social time with other marijuana users; at the same time, they may tend to withdraw from nonsmoking social contacts, viewing them as outgroup members. Marijuana consumption may come to be seen as symbolic of the group's sense of cohesion and unity. For an individual involved in such a group, images of cameraderie and a sense of belonging provide strong cognitive support for continued usage.

Aside from group identification, for many users marijuana becomes an important symbol of one's own internalized sense of nonconformity, "coolness," and quiet disobedience. This feature of marijuana consumption can become especially important for individuals who attain high-level or professional job roles. Having cultivated a pejorative image of nonusers as boring, "straights," "squares," or "do-gooders," continued marijuana consumption enables the individual to retain his or her sense of nonconformity despite outer trappings of conventionality. Some clients describe this as living a "double life" and derive some satisfaction from the mild deception and intrigue. Clients professing a desire to quit marijuana experience considerable conflict when they encounter the resistance created by their self-image as a "pot smoker." Not uncommonly, these individuals will express concern about becoming straight and losing their specialness.

Of course, individuals who see themselves as experts or connoisseurs in cannabis cultivation and usage undergo a more potent self-identification process. Like the wine connoisseur, these individuals are hobbyists; they derive considerable satisfaction from their involvement with marijuana, aside from its psychoactive properties. For individuals who become engaged in trafficking, their involvement expands to become a source of livelihood.

On balance, most marijuana users develop some degree of self-identification with the substance. The important point here, of course, is that these cognitive processes facilitate continued consumption. From an assessment standpoint, we have found the autobiographical sketch a very valuable procedure for tapping into powerful yet sometimes subtle self-image/identification processes. The client is instructed to prepare two autobiographies: one as a marijuana user and one as a nonuser. Comparison of the two sketches enables both the client and the clinician to explicate important cognitive mediators of the use pattern.

### Cognitive Coping Strategies

A final concern in cognitive assessment is to determine whether the client can design a set of change-facilitating strategies that have intuitive validity at the time of initiating change, as well as later, when the task is maintaining control.

We have experienced some benefit from asking clients to tell us whether they have some hunches about things that they can do by themselves, with the therapist, or with others that will facilitate the accomplishment of their goals. These ideas might include behaviors such as carrying some written mottos to refer to, attending meetings of Alcoholics Anonymous or Narcotics Anonymous, or writing and periodically rereading an autobiographical statement that portrays the individual as having succeeded in achieving control for 5 years. These hunches can also include examples of self-talk (e.g., "When I feel deprived and discouraged, I'll remind myself that I'm going through a temporary state of changing that is supposed to be stressful but will only last for a short while. The payoff will be worth it!").

As the therapist reinforces the identifying of these constructive coping strategies, he or she may also suggest that at later points in the process of achieving control, one or more alternative behaviors/cognitions may become relevant and helpful. The client may also be able to identify hunches concerning ways in which he or she can envision a personal act of sabotage of the attainment of change objectives. Perhaps recalling the experience of having failed in the past will generate ideas. It is common for a client to anticipate a rationalization such as the following: "I can picture myself saying that it would be O.K. to get high after a few weeks of being abstinent. It would be a kind of reward." Or, "I can imagine myself slipping after having a drink or two on a Saturday night, particularly if I'm with Nancy." Although there may not be much of an empirical relationship between a fantasized relapse episode and the actual incidence of slipping, the effort to identify facilitating and impeding self-talk can be an effective component of learning in general to be a systematic monitor of one's self-control repertoire.

## Physiological Assessment: Issues and Procedures

### Adverse Physiological Consequences

*Respiratory System*

The research data currently available concerning respiratory system effects are limited and, in several respects, inconclusive. No large-scale epidemiological studies have been conducted so far.

Heavy use of hashish by American soldiers stationed in Germany was found to be associated with inflammation of the bronchial tubes (bronchitis), sore throat, and inflammation of the lining membrane (rhinitis) or sinuses (sinusitis) of the nose (Tennant, Preble, Prendergast, & Ventry, 1971). Difficulty in breathing, sputum-producing coughs, and wheezing were also commonly found.

Studies of heavy marijuana smokers in other cultures have produced mixed results. Hall (1975) found a frequent occurrence of chronic bronchitis among heavy marijuana smokers in Jamaica. Most users, however, were also tobacco smokers, which confounds the interpretation of the results. Contrary evidence was found in a second Jamaican study (Rubin & Comitas, 1975) and one in Costa Rica (Hernandez-Bolanos, Swenson, & Coggins, 1976), both of which failed to document differences in terms of chronic respiratory disease rates between smokers and nonsmokers of marijuana.

Tashkin, Calvarese, Simmons, and Shapiro (1980) reported that habitual marijuana smoking produces a mild increase in resistance to airflow in the large airways. Henderson, Tennant, and Guerry (1972) found abnormal pulmonary function in high-dose hashish smokers. It appears from these and other studies that a mild, reversible airway obstruction affecting both the large and small airways is likely to occur following 6–8 weeks of heavy daily marijuana smoking (National Research Council Institute of Medicine, 1982).

Analyses of the gaseous and particulate components of marijuana smoke, some of which have been found to be carcinogenic in animal studies, have resulted in an expectation that marijuana should cause at least as much respiratory irritation as does tobacco and possibly more (Tashkin & Cohen, 1981). Although there are no data from human studies concerning the risk of lung cancer from marijuana smoking, the possibility that heavy users may be predisposed to the development of this disease is based on two factors: (1) the presence of known carcinogens in marijuana smoke, and (2) the finding in the central airways of heavy hashish users of microscopic abnormalities that have been correlated with the subsequent development of lung cancer in long-term tobacco smokers (Tennant, Guerry, & Henderson, 1980).

Clients who express concern that their cannabis use may have contributed to lung disease may wish to seek medical evaluation and to read pertinent literature. A useful publication that describes the structure and function of the respiratory system and also summarizes current knowledge concerning the smoking of tobacco and cannabis is *Marijuana Smoking and Its Effects on the Lungs* (Tashkin & Cohen, 1981).

Spirometry permits the measurement of vital capacity (total volume of gas exhaled after a maximal inspiratory effort) and forced expiratory volume (that fraction of the vital capacity exhaled in 1 second). This test of lung function is probably the most logical and inexpensive ($37–$60) procedure to perform on someone who has been inhaling toxic material. If there is substantial concern about possible damage from smoking paraquat-contaminated marijuana, tests of lung volumes and diffusing capacity to detect disease processes causing pulmonary scarring may be warranted. Such medical procedures are likely to cost approximately $200.

*Reproductive System*

Studies of both animals and humans indicate that cannabis has a reversible suppressive effect on male testicular functioning. Lowered testosterone levels have been found in males who are heavy marijuana users (Cohen, 1976; Kolodny, Masters, Kolodner, & Toro, 1974), although other researchers have failed to confirm this phenomenon (Coggins, Swenson, & Dawson, 1976; Hembree, Nahas, Zeidenberg, & Huang, 1979; Mendelson, Kuehnle, Ellingboe, & Babor, 1974). Other hormonal changes pertinent to the growth of the testes, a reduction in sperm count, a decrease in sperm motility, and an increase in abnormal forms of sperm have been reported (Cohen, 1976; Hembree et al., 1979; Issidorides, 1979; Kolodny et al., 1974). At present, the clinical implications of these findings remain inconclusive.

Very little has been published concerning the effects of marijuana on female reproductive functioning. Bauman (1980) studied the hormonal profiles and menstrual patterns of female chronic users, finding no differences with control subjects in terms of pertinent plasma hormonal levels. Differences were found, however, which the author suggested might be associated with subfertility. Nevertheless, the need is clear for additional research concerning women who use marijuana.

Because cannabis constituents cross the placenta, there is the potential for teratogenicity. Human studies, however, have not produced evidence of embryonic damage that can be attributed to cannabis use. Several researchers (Finnegan, 1980; Fried, 1980) have reported that subtle developmental effects in offspring may occur, including nervous system abnormalities and reductions in birth weight and height. Further study is needed.

Data concerning genetic hazards in humans are also very limited. Abnormalities in cell division, as well as changes in chromosome structure and deoxyribonucleic acid (DNA) synthesis, have been found in some animal studies; however, other standard tests for mutagenesis have failed to detect a mutagenic effect (Glatt, Ohlsson, Agurell, & Oesch, 1979). The weight of evidence is that marijuana does not cause chromosome breaks (National Research Council Institute of Medicine, 1982).

Women who are concerned about the potential effects of their marijuana use on ovulation can seek evaluation from a gynecologist. The physician may choose to take a history of the woman's menstrual cycles and associated midcycle pain, to chart basal body temperature, or to take a biopsy of the lining in the uterus. Because ovulatory variation is common in some fertile women, and because the carrying out of extensive procedures may excessively raise the patient's fears (with an adverse impact on ovulation), the physician is likely to suggest waiting for as long as a year and a demonstration of continued infertility before proceeding with extensive testing. He or she is also very likely to emphasize the fact that abnormalities in the patient's reproductive functioning are likely to be associated with causes unrelated to marijuana use, based on current knowledge.

Testosterone and other hormonal levels in males can be measured through blood testing. Seminal fluid analysis is a standard test and is used to measure the structure of the sperm (i.e., sperm count, motility, and abnormal forms). Male fertility can also be studied using a sperm penetration assay—a laboratory test that examines the capacity of human sperm to penetrate hamster eggs. Although these procedures are useful in predicting infertility, they can be in error. Before this assay is conducted, a 3-month period of abstinence from marijuana use is necessary.

*Brain*

A determination of whether chronic marijuana use causes irreversible changes in the structure or function of the brain is an elusive task. Methodological difficulties are common in the published studies, with a consequent need for caution in the interpretation of results, as well as for more and better research.

Early in the 1970s, a British investigation suggested a possible relationship between heavy marijuana smoking and brain atrophy (Campbell, Evans, Thompson, & Williams, 1971). Two subsequent studies that were better controlled found no such evidence (Co, Goodwin, Gado, Mikhael, & Hill, 1977; Kuehnle, Mendelson, Davis, & New, 1977).

Evidence of brain changes detectable by electron microscopy has been reported by investigators studying rhesus monkeys exposed to marijuana smoke or intravenous THC (Heath, Fitzjarrell, Garey, & Myers, 1979). Because of the limited number of animals studied, the absence of replication, and uncertainty as to the significance of the brain changes that were found, interpretation of these findings is difficult. Moreover, it is possible that deficits in mental function may occur as a consequence of marijuana use even without accompanying structural change in the brain.

Electroencephalographic (EEG) measures of brain electrophysiology have not indicated the persistence of EEG changes in the absence of marijuana use (Fink, 1976; Rodin, Domino, & Porzak, 1970). Here too, however, methodological limitations in the literature preclude definitive conclusions.

There is evidence that marijuana causes some chemical changes in the brain, specifically in the neurotransmitter acetylcholine (Domino, 1981). At high doses, marijuana affects nucleoprotein synthesis (Luthra, Rosenkrantz, & Braude, 1976). The clinical significance of these effects in humans is unknown.

*Other Systems*

Researchers have examined the long-term impact of chronic marijuana use on several other systems. Because marijuana increases the heart rate, and in some people also increases blood pressure, individuals with hypertension, cerebrovascular disease, and coronary atherosclerosis may be at risk. However, there is no evidence that those with normal cardiovascular systems are vulnerable to permanent adverse consequences as a result of marijuana use.

Although there is clear evidence of the acute effects of marijuana on coordination, tracking performance, perceptual tasks, vigilance, the operating of motor vehicles and flying simulators, and short-term memory, as well as evidence that acute dosages can cause the occurrence of an acute brain syndrome, transient panic reactions, and flashbacks (National Research Council Institute of Medicine, 1982), very little is known about long-term effects in relation to these and other cognitive and behavioral functions. To date, there is no conclusive evidence of permanent adverse effects in these areas.

Studies concerning the effects of marijuana on the human immune system are contradictory. No epidemiological studies have indicated a causal relationship between heavy use and a greater prevalence of infections or other diseases.

*Who Is at Risk?*

Despite all of the remaining uncertainty concerning long-term effects, the therapist can give a prudent response to the concerned client who seeks a "judgment call" based on what is currently known. The following persons may be taking a risk if they use marijuana:

1. People with chronic diseases of the heart, lungs, or liver.
2. People with epilepsy.
3. People taking medications, particularly in the treatment of diabetes or epilepsy.
4. People with high levels of anxiety or depression.
5. Individuals with psychotic illness.
6. Pregnant or nursing women.
7. Individuals with marginal fertility.
8. People intending to drive, fly, or operate dangerous equipment.
9. People who need to be concerned about their vulnerability to drug habituation.
10. Children and adolescents, whose psychological development may be impaired by frequent intoxication with any mood-altering substance.

*Tolerance*

The research literature on both animals and humans gives clear evidence of tolerance to most THC effects (R. T. Jones, 1983). Two general mechanisms may contribute to this loss of sensitivity to the effects of a drug: "dispositional tolerance," or a reduced concentration of the drug at its sites of action due to increased rates of metabolism and/or excretion; and "functional tolerance," or a decreased sensitivity of the target cells (Kalant, LeBlanc, & Gibbons, 1971). R. T. Jones (1982) suggests that the mechanism is more functional than dispositional.

There does not appear to be a biological basis for the so-called "reverse tolerance" (i.e., increased sensitivity to the same dose following repeated administration). If this phenomenon occurs at all, it probably is facilitated by a learned association between familiar environmental cues and the subjective experience of being "high," which then produces a set of expectations in the user.

Physical dependence is usually defined by tolerance development and signs of withdrawal symptoms when drug use is discontinued. Despite the popular contention that marijuana does not promote physical dependence, heavy users commonly exhibit tolerance and withdrawal indicators that would suggest a physically addicting process. Empirically, R. T. Jones,

Benowitz, and Bachman (1976) reported that heavy consumption in an inpatient ward setting led to tolerance and mild withdrawal symptoms in regular users. Among the withdrawal symptoms observed were mood changes, sleep disturbance, decreased appetite, restlessness, feverishness, and tremulousness. In our clinical practice, some clients do report withdrawal symptomatology in varying degrees, whereas others do not. In assessing the marijuana abuser, the clinician should inquire about past and present experiences with abstinence, in order to probe for possible withdrawal symptoms.

### Cannabinoid Detection Procedures

The past decade has seen considerable effort being devoted to the development of biological fluid assays of cannabinoids (Hawks, 1982). Among the potential applications for this technology are the roadside assessment of marijuana-associated impairment in drivers and the screening of individuals in high-risk positions (e.g., airline pilots, locomotive engineers, and bus drivers). The Defense Department also has a great deal of interest in perfecting the capacity to detect recent marijuana intoxication, because of growing concern about marijuana use among members of the armed services.

The technological difficulties are substantial. Less than 1% of the THC in the plant material is excreted by the body. Two-thirds of the THC is eliminated in the feces; only one-third is eliminated in the urine. The quantity measured in the urine is reported as nanograms (a nanogram is a billionth of a gram) per milliliter. The high lipid solubility of the drug contributes to its uneven rate of elimination. Evidence may appear in the urine after an initial period of several days, with no detectable amounts following the last incident of marijuana use.

Blood tests are not very helpful, because of the rapid disappearance of THC metabolites from the blood stream. After about 20 minutes, long before the "high" state has ended, there are no remaining detectable metabolites in the blood.

The two principal urine assay tests are an enzyme multiple-immunoassay test (EMIT) developed by the Syva Corporation, and a radioimmunoassay (RIA) developed by Roche Diagnostics. Gas-liquid chromatography (GLC) and gas chromatography–mass spectrometry (GC–MS) are additional detection methods.

In order to reduce the possibility of false-positive results, a 100 ng/ml cutoff point is recommended (Cohen, 1983). At that level, a positive urine assay might be expected from 1 to 72 hours after smoking a single marijuana joint. The highest urinary concentration occurs at 5 hours. Detectable levels of THC metabolites may be found several weeks after cessation of marijuana use in the person who has been a daily user.

Currently available tests do not permit a dose–response curve that can indicate a presumed level of impairment. A positive finding may occur in a heavy user who stopped several weeks ago or a person who has smoked as recently as the past few hours.

Tests using saliva and the breath are under development; both of these are likely to indicate recent usage for approximately a 4- to 5-hour period. As is the case with other biological tests, however, these measures will not correlate with the degree of intoxication.


## Case History

Marilyn was 28 years old, married, 4 months pregnant with her first child, and not employed when she sought treatment. Concern for the health of her child was a primary motivating factor in prompting this self-referral.

Marilyn's alcohol and drug history included fairly heavy periods of use, as well as intervals of time in which she reattained control. In her last year of high school, she used marijuana three or four times a week for several months. Her alcohol use was occasional (less than weekly) at that time, rarely resulting in intoxication. Her school grades were better than average, and she believed that she functioned well at home, in school, and with her peers.

She attended a university for 4 years, living in a dorm at first and being pleased both with having lost 50 pounds (she had been overweight as a teenager) and with acquiring numerous friends. Alcohol use during her college years was generally limited to the weekends. Episodes of drunkenness were rare, although she frequently consumed one or another substance along with alcohol. Marijuana use occurred three to six times each week. She first experimented with "speed" (amphetamine) early in her college years. In the last 2 years of college, she used "speed" two to three times per week for weight control and as a study aid. Marilyn used LSD twice a month during her first 2 years in college; as a junior and senior, she used LSD twice per year.

As she looked back on those years, Marilyn wished that she had given greater priority to her studies and less to drug use. She recalled gradually feeling more and more dependent on marijuana, and purposely limited her use of "speed," in part because of the advice given her by concerned friends that her use was becoming excessive.

For 2 years following completion of her college degree, Marilyn worked as an office assistant. Her marijuana use was daily or near-daily, and she drank three to five drinks 1 or 2 days each week. She experimented briefly with cocaine.

For a 4-year period (when she was aged 23–26), Marilyn worked as a bartender. Her regular marijuana use continued; she had one drink most days and drank heavily 1 or 2 days each week. For 3 months she used cocaine at increasing rates until she chose to stop, fearing the onset of dependence. A year of unemployment followed, during which time Marilyn escalated her alcohol intake, drinking heavily 3 or 4 days each week. Once re-employed as a bartender, she returned to her previous pattern of nightly moderate alcohol intake and heavier drinking 1 or 2 days each week. That year she was 27 years old, had met and was living with the man whom she would later marry, and was using LSD with him approximately twice per month. She returned to using cocaine, reaching a level of two or three times per week. Her marijuana use stayed as it had been for nearly 10 years.

Marilyn became pregnant at the age of 28. On her own, she succeeded in stopping cocaine and LSD use and reduced her alcohol intake to one glass of wine three times per week. She had been unable to reduce her marijuana use, however.

Neither Marilyn's parents (divorced when she was aged 18) nor her siblings had been excessive users of alcohol or other drugs. Her husband, however, was a moderate marijuana user who supplemented his income as a small-business owner by dealing marijuana. The present marriage was his third; his first wife had been an alcoholic.

In the month prior to her initial interview, Marilyn had been feeling depressed and had consulted with her gynecologist to discuss her mood. Her physician reinforced her inclination to work toward abstaining from marijuana use and to seek the assistance of a therapist to deal with her depression.

Marilyn requested information concerning the possible risk to the fetus from maternal marijuana ingestion. The therapist gave her copies of a few pertinent publications and discussed the conclusions that might be drawn. He also introduced her to a learning-based perspective on drug dependence and gave her an overview of the approach he would employ.

Marilyn kept a daily log, as requested by the therapist. The data reflected multiple daily marijuana usage, generally beginning in late morning and continuing throughout the day and evening at about 2- to 3-hour intervals. During the day she smoked by herself while at home; in the evening she was often joined by her husband. It also was evident that some of the people with whom she and her husband socialized were not marijuana smokers.

Marilyn prepared a list of the problems and concerns brought about by her marijuana use:

1. Pregnancy: not knowing the effects on the fetus.
2. Weight control: minimal control when stoned.
3. Effects on self-esteem/personal control: smoking at inappropriate

    times, unrealistic to be stoned all of the time, do not like myself
    then.
4. Lack of motivation.
5. Lack of career direction: mismanagement of time and responsi-
    bilities.
6. Depression and moodiness accentuated by marijuana use.
7. Disapproval and distance from my sister, whose time and opinion
    I value.
8. I put off time I could spend with my stepdaughter and nieces.
9. Impairs my ability to discuss emotionally charged issues with my
    husband, whom I feel I am letting down.
10. Masks part of my being that I would like to set free.

    In selecting short- and long-term goals, Marilyn decided to work
initially toward a 1-month period of abstinence from marijuana use. She
hoped to be able to resume using the drug at the end of that period, but on
a greatly reduced level. However, she postponed making decisions until the
initial abstinence period had ended.

    In addition to teaching Marilyn a series of general cognitive and
behavioral strategies that would be useful in attaining and maintaining
abstinence, the therapist identified three specific topics that warranted
attention: (1) Marilyn's anger at her husband, (2) her low self-esteem, and
(3) the lack of lifestyle balance between her obligations and personal
rewards.

    One reason why Marilyn became angry with her husband was that he
frequently canceled plans with her at the last minute, nearly always claiming
that his business required his attention. The therapist and client discussed
alternatives that she could consider in dealing with this problem, including
her willingness to set limits with her husband concerning his authority to
determine each of their schedules. As Marilyn began to plan for herself
more often, and also to have backup plans for those occasions when her
husband canceled an occasion that they were to have spent together,
Marilyn found herself becoming less depressed and needing marijuana less.
She was creative in finding new social contacts, as well as activities that she
could engage in by herself.

    The matter of her low self-esteem was dealt with in several ways. She
agreed to the therapist's suggestion that she give herself daily written
positive affirmations for working at resolving her drug dependency. She
also was willing to experiment with shaping her husband's feedback by
positively reinforcing his encouraging remarks and giving no reinforcement
to his negative or critical comments. Taking notes on these behaviors, she
was happy when a change in the desired direction began to occur.

    Finally, Marilyn agreed to modify her daytime schedule to reduce the
monotony that had accompanied being a full-time housekeeper. Her sister

was instrumental in assisting Marilyn in getting out more often, visiting others, hosting visits, touring galleries, and so forth.

Marilyn kept notes concerning craving incidents as well as her use of a specific series of coping strategies. The therapist demonstrated a way of graphically illustrating these data to indicate trends over time. A figure was designed that showed daily rates of the following: (1) craving incidents, (2) thought-stopping behaviors, and (3) events that enhanced lifestyle balance.

After the fourth session, Marilyn began a 1-month period of abstinence. She slipped once and temporarily felt dejected, but quickly placed that incident in a useful perspective. At the end of the month, she decided to continue abstaining from marijuana through the end of her pregnancy and the cessation of breast feeding.

At 10 weeks after the termination of treatment, Marilyn responded to the follow-up questionnaire and indicated that she had had one slip. Three months later, the therapist received a birth announcement, along with the following note: "He is perfect, healthy, and beautiful! I am stoned on him and this miracle."

As noted earlier, the clinician's selection of specific assessment tools will depend on factors unique to each case. In working with Marilyn, the therapist used the following assessment strategies: (1) a chronological history of her drug and alcohol use (including data on specific substances and their amount and frequency of use, Marilyn's perceptions of the impact of use over time on her functioning, and the manner in which people in her social network reacted to her drug and/or alcohol involvement); (2) a general social history (with emphasis on the possible association between periods of particularly positive or negative impact and changes in Marilyn's drug–alcohol consumption patterns); (3) the identification of current problematic consequences associated with her use (with emphasis on the specific difficulties or concerns that led her to seek treatment); (4) a log of Marilyn's daily use patterns and a process of analyzing the contents of this written record that reinforced in her the ability to identify situations that placed her at high risk; (5) an inventory of her coping repertoire in relation to each of the risk factors that emerged in history taking and analysis of the log; (6) the use of a log of craving incidents and the employment of coping strategies (a graphic illustration was produced from these data); and (7) a follow-up questionnaire.

## Concluding Comments

The assessment procedures described in this chapter are responsive to two general objectives in the clinical setting: (1) helping the client to acquire accurate information concerning the nature and degree of adverse behavioral, cognitive, and physiological consequences resulting from his or her chronic marijuana use; and (2) identifying pertinent aspects of the client's patterns of use, social network influences, coping skills repertoire, and overall lifestyle balance that suggest foci for therapeutic work. In emphasizing the recording of risk situations and use of coping skills in the log as a means of assessment throughout treatment, the therapist can model and reinforce a self-monitoring and self-learning pattern that will support the posttreatment maintenance of control.

## Appendix. Diagnostic Criteria

### Analogies to Alcoholism Diagnostic Criteria

Weller and Halikas (1980) have developed a set of diagnostic criteria for marijuana abuse, based on the life interference foci used in diagnosing alcoholism:

1. Adverse physiological and psychological drug effects
   Includes toxic delirium or anxiety reaction, physical health problems, blackouts, or subjectively defined addiction or dependence.
2. Control problems
   Includes unsuccessful attempts to stop, an inability to limit use, early-morning marijuana use, or a history of going on binges (e.g., 48 hours or more of nearly continuous marijuana use with default of normal obligations).
3. Social and interpersonal problems
   Includes arrests due to behaviors when "high," traffic violations, job problems, fighting, or the loss of friends.
4. Adverse opinions
   Includes a self-perception of use being excessive, objections raised by family members or others, or guilt feelings related to the effects of use on the individual's life.

Weller and Halikas (1980) followed a group of regular marijuana users for a 5-year period and found that 9% fulfilled the criteria as either definite (interference in all four life areas) or probable (interference in three of the four areas) marijuana abusers.

### Other Diagnostic Criteria

Carroll (1981) also uses a life interference perspective, but includes a quantitative measure as one of his five criteria for diagnosing marijuana abuse.

1. *The person.* The risk of negative consequences is greater for those persons

who are less emotionally stable, in poor physical health, and/or younger and less mature.

2. *The pattern of use.* Potentially more harmful than the occasional use of moderate amounts of marijuana is multiple drug use involving marijuana and more potent psychoactive substances.

3. *Motivation for use.* Risk is greater when marijuana is being used as a near-exclusive means of coping with stress or uncomfortable emotions.

4. *Frequency, amount, and duration.* Greater potential for harm occurs with daily or near-daily use of three or more joints for at least 1 month or binges of use.

5. *Evidence of negative psychobiosocial consequences.* The risk increases when marijuana use leads to impairment in physical or mental health, job or school performance, or family and social relationships.

# References

American Psychiatric Association. (1980). *Diagnostic and statistical manual of mental disorders* (3rd ed.). Washington, DC: Author.

Anderson, P. (1981). *High in America.* New York: Viking Press.

Babor, T. F., Mendelson, J. H., & Kuehnle, J. (1976). Marihuana and human physical activity. *Psychopharmacology, 50,* 11-19.

Bauman, J. (1980, January 16-17). *Marijuana and the female reproductive system.* Testimony before the Subcommittee on Criminal Justice of the Committee on the Judiciary, U.S. Senate, "Health Consequences of Marijuana Use" (pp. 85-88). Washington, DC: U.S. Government Printing Office.

Blum, K. (1984). *Handbook of abusable drugs.* New York: Gardner Press.

Boll, T. J. (1981). Assessment of neuropsychological disorders. In D. H. Barlow (Ed.), *Behavioral assessment of adult disorders* (pp. 45-86). New York: Guilford Press.

Campbell, A. M. G., Evans, M., Thompson, J. L. G., & Williams, M. R. (1971). Cerebral atrophy in young cannabis smokers. *Lancet, ii,* 1219-1225.

Carroll, J. F. X. (1981). Perspectives on marijuana use and abuse and recommendations for preventing abuse. *American Journal of Drug and Alcohol Abuse, 8,* 259-282.

Carter, J. E. (1977, August 2). U.S. President, Message to the Congress: Drug abuse. *Weekly Compilation of Presidential Documents, 13,* 1154-1160.

Co, B. T., Goodwin, D. W., Gado, M., Mikhael, M., & Hill, S. Y. (1977). Absence of cerebral atrophy in chronic cannabis users. *Journal of the American Medical Association, 237,* 1229-1230.

Coggins, W. J., Swenson, E. W., & Dawson, W. W. (1976). Health status of chronic heavy cannabis users. *Annals of the New York Academy of Sciences, 282,* 148-161.

Cohen, S. (1976). The 94-day cannabis study. *Annals of the New York Academy of Sciences, 282,* 211-220.

Cohen, S. (1983). Marijuana use detection: The state of the art. *Drug Abuse and Alcoholism Newsletter, 12*(No. 3).

Comitas, L. (1976). Cannabis and work in Jamaica: A refutation of the amotivational syndrome. *Annals of the New York Academy of Sciences, 282,* 24-32.

Creason, C. R., & Goldman, M. (1981). Varying levels of marijuana use by adolescents and the amotivational syndrome. *Psychological Reports, 48,* 447-454.

Domino, E. F. (1981). Cannabinoids and the cholinergic system. *Journal of Clinical Pharmacology, 21* (Suppl.), 249S–255S.

Ferraro, D. P. (1980). Acute effects of marijuana on human memory and cognition. In R. C. Petersen (Ed.), *Marijuana research findings: 1980* (NIDA Research Monograph No. 31, DHHS Publication No. ADM 80-1001, pp. 98–119) Washington, DC: U.S. Government Printing Office.

Fink, M. (1976). Effects of acute and chronic inhalation of hashish, marijuana, and delta-9-tetrahydrocannabinol on brain electrical activity in man: Evidence for tissue tolerance. *Annals of the New York Academy of Sciences, 282,* 387–398.

Finnegan, L. P. (1980). Pulmonary problems encountered by the infant of the drug-dependent mother. *Clinics in Chest Medicine, 1,* 311–325.

Fried, P. A. (1980). Marihuana use by pregnant women: Neurobehavioral effects on neonates. *Drug and Alcohol Dependence, 6,* 415–424.

Glantz, M. D. (Ed.). (1984). *Correlates and consequences of marijuana use* (DHHS Publication No. ADM 84-1276). Washington, DC: U.S. Government Printing Office.

Glatt, H., Ohlsson, A., Agurell, S., & Oesch, F. (1979). Delta-1-tetrahydrocannabinol and 1-alpha, 2-alpha-epoxyhexahydrocannabinol: Mutagenicity investigation in the Ames Test. *Mutation Research, 66,* 329–335.

Hall, J. A. S. (1975). *Testimony in marihuana–hashish epidemic hearing of the Committee of the Judiciary, U.S. Senate.* Washington, DC: U.S. Government Printing Office.

Hawks, R. L. (Ed.). (1982). *The analysis of cannabinoids in biological fluids* (NIDA Research Monograph No. 42, DHHS Publication No. ADM 82-1212). Washington, DC: U.S. Government Printing Office.

Heath, R. G., Fitzjarrell, A. T., Garey, R. E., & Myers, W. A. (1979). Chronic marihuana smoking: Its effect on function and structure of the primate brain. In G. G. Nahas & W. D. M. Paton (Eds.), *Marihuana: Biological effects. Analysis, metabolism, cellular responses, reproduction and brain* (pp. 713–730). Oxford: Pergamon Press.

Hembree, W. C., Nahas, G. G., Zeidenberg, P., & Huang, H. F. S. (1979). Changes in human spermatozoa associated with high dose marihuana smoking. In G. G. Nahas & W. D. M. Paton (Eds.), *Marihuana: Biological effects. Analysis, metabolism, cellular responses, reproduction and brain* (pp. 429–439). Oxford: Pergamon Press.

Henderson, R. L., Tennant, F. S., & Guerry, R. (1972). Respiratory manifestations of hashish smoking. *Archives of Otolaryngology, 95,* 248–251.

Hernandez-Bolanos, J., Swenson, E. W., & Coggins, W. J. (1976). Preservation of pulmonary function in regular, heavy, long-term marijuana smokers. *American Review of Respiratory Diseases, 113* (Suppl.), 100.

Huba, G. J., Bentler, P. M., & Newcomb, M. D. (1981). *Assessing marijuana consequences: Selected questionnaire items* (Research Issues No. 28, DHHS Publication No. ADM 81-1150). Washington, DC: U.S. Government Printing Office.

Issidorides, M. R. (1979). Observations in chronic hashish users: Nuclear aberrations in blood and sperm and abnormal acrosomes in spermatozoa. In G. G. Nahas & W. D. M. Paton (Eds.), *Marihuana: Biological effects. Analysis, metabolism, cellular responses, reproduction and brain* (pp. 377–388). Oxford: Pergamon Press.

Johnston, L. D., Bachman, J. G., & O'Malley, P. M. (1982). *Student drug use, attitudes, and beliefs: National trends 1975–1982* (DHHS Publication No. ADM 83-1260). Washington, DC: U.S. Government Printing Office.

Johnston, L. D., O'Malley, P. M., & Bachman, J. G. (1986). *Drug use among American high school students, college students, and other young adults: National trends through 1985* (DHHS Publication No. ADM 86-1450). Washington, DC: U.S. Government Printing Office.

Jones, B. P., & Butters, N. (1983). Neuropsychological assessment. In M. Hersen, A. E.

Kazdin, & A. S. Bellack (Eds.), *The clinical psychology handbook*. New York: Pergamon Press.

Jones, R. T. (1983). Cannabis tolerance and dependence. In K. O. Fehr & H. Kalant (Eds.), *Cannabis and health hazards: Proceedings of an ARF/WHO scientific meeting on adverse health and behavioral consequences of cannabis use, Toronto, Canada (30 March–3 April, 1981)* (pp. 617–689). Toronto: Addiction Research Foundation.

Jones, R. T., Benowitz, N., & Bachman, J. (1976). Clinical studies of cannabis tolerance and dependence. *Annals of the New York Academy of Sciences, 282,* 221–239.

Kalant, H., LeBlanc, A. E., & Gibbons, R. J. (1971). Tolerance to, and dependence on, some non-opiate psychotropic drugs. *Pharmacology Review, 23,* 135–191.

Kolodny, R. C., Masters, W. H., Kolodner, R. M., & Toro, G. (1974). Depression of plasma testosterone levels after chronic intensive marijuana use. *New England Journal of Medicine, 290,* 872–874.

Kuehnle, J., Mendelson, J. H., Davis, D. R., & New, P. F. J. (1977). Computed tomographic examination of heavy marijuana smokers. *Journal of the American Medical Association, 237,* 1231–1232.

Luthra, Y. K., Rosenkrantz, H., & Braude, M. C. (1976). Cerebral and cerebellar neurochemical changes and behavioral manifestations in rats chronically exposed to marijuana smoke. *Toxicology and Applied Pharmacology, 35,* 455–465.

Marlatt, G. A. (1982). Relapse prevention: A self-control program for treatment of addictive behaviors. In R. B. Stuart (Ed.), *Adherence, compliance, and generalization in behavioral medicine* (pp. 329–378). New York: Brunner/Mazel.

Marlatt, G. A., & George, W. H. (1984). Relapse prevention: Introduction and overview of the model. *British Journal of Addiction, 79,* 261–273.

Marlatt, G. A., & Gordon, J. R. (Eds.). (1985). *Relapse prevention: Maintenance strategies in addictive behavior change*. New York: Guilford Press.

Mellinger, G. D., Somers, R. H., Davidson, S. T., & Manheimer, D. I. (1976). The amotivational syndrome and the college student. *Annals of the New York Academy of Sciences, 282,* 37–55.

Mendelson, J. H., Kuehnle, J., Ellingboe, J., & Babor, T. F. (1974). Plasma testosterone levels before, during and after chronic marihuana smoking. *New England Journal of Medicine, 291,* 1051–1055.

Miller, J. D., Cisin, I. H., Gardner-Keaton, H., Harrell, A. V., Wirtz, P. W., Abelson, H. I., & Fishburne, P. M. (1983). *National survey on drug abuse: Main findings 1982* (DHHS Publication No. ADM 83-1263). Washington, DC: U.S. Government Printing Office.

National Commission on Marihuana and Drug Abuse. (1973). *Drug use in America: Problem in perspective* (Stock No. 5266-0003). Washington, DC: U.S. Government Printing Office.

National Research Council Institute of Medicine. (1982). *Marijuana and health: Report of a study by a Committee of the Institute of Medicine, Division of Health Sciences Policy*. Washington, DC: National Academy Press.

Petersen, R. C. (Ed.). (1980). *Marijuana research findings: 1980* (NIDA Research Monograph No. 31, DHHS Publication No. ADM 80-1001). Washington, DC: U.S. Government Printing Office.

Rittenhouse, J. D. (1979). *Consequences of alcohol and marijuana use: Survey items for perceived assessment* (DHEW Publication No. ADM 80-920). Washington, DC: U.S. Government Printing Office.

Rodin, E. A., Domino, E. F., & Porzak, J. P. (1970). The marihuana-induced "social high": Neurological and electroencephalographic concomitants. *Journal of the American Medical Association, 213,* 1300–1302.

Roffman, R. A. (1977). Marijuana and its control in the late 1970's. *Contemporary Drug Problems, 6,* 533–551.

Rubin, V., & Comitas, L. (1975). *Ganja in Jamaica: A medical anthropological study of chronic marijuana use.* The Hague: Mouton.

Schaeffer, J., Andrysiak, T., & Ungerleider, J. T. (1981). Cognition and long term use of ganja (cannabis). *Science, 213,* 465-466.

Schuchard, K. (1981). Parent power and parent limits: A dilemma for private and professional judgment. In R. de Silva, R. L. DuPont, & G. K. Russell (Eds.), *Treating the marijuana-dependent person* (pp. 19-22). New York: The American Council on Marijuana and Other Psychoactive Drugs.

Smith, D. (1968). Acute and chronic toxicity of marijuana. *Journal of Psychedelic Drugs, 2,* 37-47.

Tashkin, D. P., Calvarese, B. M., Simmons, B. S., & Shapiro, B. J. (1980). Respiratory status of seventy-four habitual marijuana smokers. *Chest, 78,* 699-706.

Tashkin, D. P., & Cohen, S. (1981). *Marijuana smoking and its effects on the lungs.* New York: The American Council on Marijuana and Other Psychoactive Drugs.

Tennant, F. S., Guerry, R. L., & Henderson, R. L. (1980). Histopathologic and clinical abnormalities of the respiratory system in chronic hashish smokers. *Substance and Alcohol Misuse, 1,* 93-100.

Tennant, F. S., Preble, M., Prendergast, T. J., & Ventry, P. (1971). Medical manifestations associated with hashish. *Journal of the American Medical Association, 216,* 1965-1969.

Trebach, A. (1984). Heroin, marijuana and the need for truth in government. In J. Gampel (Ed.), *Drug use in society: Proceedings of Marijuana and Health Conference—November, 1983.* Washington, DC: Council on Marijuana and Health.

Weil, A., & Rosen, W. (1983). *Chocolate to morphine: Understanding mind-active drugs.* Boston: Houghton Mifflin.

Weller, R. A., & Halikas, J. A. (1980). Objective criteria for the diagnosis of marijuana abuse. *Journal of Nervous and Mental Disease, 168,* 98-103.

# 12

## COCAINE ABUSE

**ARNOLD M. WASHTON**
*The Washton Institute, New York City*

**NANNETTE S. STONE**
*Creative Solutions and Associates, New York City*

**EDWARD C. HENDRICKSON**
*Addiction Recovery Center, Yorktown Heights, New York*

## Introduction and Background

### The Cocaine Epidemic

Cocaine use in the United States has reached epidemic levels in recent years. Nationwide surveys estimate that over 22 million Americans have already tried cocaine at least once in their lifetimes and that as many as 2–3 million may be currently dependent on the drug (Adams & Kozel, 1985). Callers to a national drug hotline have supplied dramatic evidence of the human suffering associated with cocaine abuse (Washton & Gold, 1987; Washton, Gold, & Pottash, 1983, 1984).

At the outset of this epidemic, it appeared that cocaine use was especially pervasive among America's middle class (Stone, Fromme, & Kagan, 1984); however, with lower prices, increased supplies, and more widespread acceptance, cocaine has spread to virtually all socioeconomic groups and to all geographic areas of the country (Washton, 1985; Washton & Gold, 1987).

The willingness of many people to at least try cocaine probably stems in part from the drug's long-standing popular image as a chic, nonaddictive, and harmless intoxicant. Most who try it believe that they will have no difficulty in controlling their use and will suffer no adverse effects. Contrary to these popular beliefs, recent observations suggest that the potent reinforcing properties of cocaine can rapidly take control of the user's behavior, such that even "occasional" use may pose significant risks. Observations from at least several different sources, such as hotline callers (Washton & Gold, 1987), treatment applicants (Washton, 1985), and animal experiments (Johanson, 1984), have revealed the addictive properties of cocaine. Apart from initial exposure to the drug and continued access to supplies, it is impossible to predict exactly who among the total pool of "occasional" users will become addicted to the drug. From a clinical standpoint, one especially striking feature of the current cocaine epidemic is that so many reasonably mature, well-integrated people with good jobs, a history of good functioning, no previous drug addiction, and no serious psychiatric illness seem to have become full-blown cocaine addicts (Stone et al., 1984).

Because cocaine use in the United States has become more prevalent, the full range of medical, psychological, and social consequences associated with its use has been revealed. Some of the statistical indicators of this trend include a more than threefold increase in cocaine-related emergency room visits over the first few years of this decade, and a more than sixfold increase in requests for treatment of cocaine dependence in government-sponsored programs (Adams & Kozel, 1985). Many cocaine abusers who seek help prefer private rather than public treatment settings, and so it is not surprising that private clinicians (psychologists, psychiatrists, and family physicians) and private treatment facilities in many different areas of the United States have seen an increasing number of cocaine abusers requesting assistance. The rapid emergence of a nationwide cocaine addiction problem has forced treatment personnel, both public and private, to acquire skills in the proper assessment and treatment of the problem.

## Cocaine: The Drug and Its Effects

Cocaine is a potent central nervous system (CNS) stimulant (Jones, 1987) derived from the *Erythloxylon coca* plant, which is grown primarily in the mountainous regions of Central and South America. Cocaine is extracted from the leaves of the coca plant and processed into a white powder (cocaine hydrochloride), which sells on average for $75–$150/g on the street.

Cocaine is most commonly self-administered by one of three different methods:

1. *Intranasal use.* The white powder is inhaled ("snorted" or "sniffed") into the nostrils, usually through a straw, from a small "coke spoon," or through a rolled-up dollar bill.

2. *Freebase smoking.* The white powder can be transformed into cocaine freebase, using baking soda or ether as the reagent, and then smoked in a glass pipe. The purpose of transforming the powder into freebase is to yield a form of the drug with a vaporization point low enough to be smoked. Smoking cocaine, as compared to snorting it, produces a much more rapid and intense euphoria, similar to intravenous injection. A recent development in the illegal marketing of cocaine has been the direct sale of cocaine freebase in the form of ready-to-smoke tiny pellets or

"rocks," known on the street as "crack" (Washton, 1986). The availability of "crack" has led to a dramatic rise in the incidence of cocaine freebasing problems.

3. *Intravenous (i.v.) injection.* Cocaine hydrochloride powder is readily soluble in water, and thus a solution of the drug can be drawn up into a syringe and injected directly into a vein. Most i.v. cocaine users have previous or current involvement with heroin and sometimes mix the two drugs simultaneously in the same injection, known as a "speedball."

The pleasurable, mood-altering effects of cocaine include feelings of euphoria, exhilaration, energy, self-confidence, and mental alertness. Many users report instantaneous mood elevation, sexual arousal, and decreased inhibitions. The "high" is extremely short-lived, lasting no more than 10–20 minutes after each dose; it is often followed by an equally unpleasant rebound reaction, the "crash," characterized by feelings of depression, irritability, restlessness, and craving for more cocaine. The intensity of the crash tends to increase with the dosage and chronicity of cocaine use, and also tends to be more severe with freebase smoking and i.v. use. The "high–crash" process is one of the pharmacological characteristics of cocaine that actively promotes a pattern of escalating and compulsive use. The user is driven to recreate the short-lived "high" and escape the unpleasant "crash." This phenomenon is exaggerated with smoking or i.v. administration, in which the intense euphoria may last only 5–10 minutes and the rebound dysphoria is more exaggerated.

Many of the physiological effects of cocaine include those typical of other stimulant drugs, such as amphetamines (Jones, 1987). Cocaine increases the user's heart rate and blood pressure, and dilates the pupils. Unlike other stimulants, cocaine is also a local anesthetic and a vasoconstrictor. It blocks afferent nerve conduction in sensory pathways, causing a numbing or "freezing" of mucous membranes to which it is applied. It also constricts surrounding blood vessels in the applied area, thereby prolonging the drug's anesthetic action. When cocaine is "snorted" it temporarily numbs the user's nasal and throat passages—a side effect anticipated by all experienced users. Dealers often adulterate cocaine with cheaper local anesthetics, such as procaine, lidocaine, or tetracaine, to reduce the purity of street cocaine while retaining the drug's anticipated effects. Other adulterants or "cuts" include various types of white powders (e.g., lactose, mannitol) and stimulants such as methamphetamine.

### Consequences of Chronic Use

Perhaps the most obvious evidence indicating that a tolerance to cocaine develops with chronic usage is that many users escalate to dose levels that would have been lethal at the early stages of use. Moreover, chronic users find that the euphoria and other pleasurable effects diminish rapidly with increasing doses and frequency of use. Chronic users often find themselves caught in a futile, obsessive chase to recapture the original cocaine "high," but as dosages and frequency increase, so does the user's tolerance to the euphoric effects.

When cocaine use continues well beyond the point of tolerance to the euphoria, there will usually be a complete reversal of the drug's effects. For example, mood elevation and euphoria are replaced by depression, anxiety, and irritability. Increased alertness and spontaneity are replaced by distractibility, poor concentration, and mental confusion. Increased drive and energy are replaced by apathy and fatigue. Increased sociability, talkativeness, and sexuality are replaced by social withdrawal, nonresponsiveness, and a total loss of sexual desire. Severe high-dose abuse can lead to extreme agitation, explosiveness, neglect of personal care, and in some cases to a severe paranoid psychosis with elaborate delusions and hallucinations (Post, 1975).

The exact consequences of cocaine use cannot be predicted with certainty for any single user (Washton & Stone, 1984). They will vary according to many different factors, including the amount used; the chronicity and frequency of use; the route of administration; the expectations, mood, and personality of the user; the setting and circumstances under which the drug is taken; and the concomitant use of other drugs. The mood-altering effects of cocaine can range from mildly pleasant to profoundly euphoric, or from slightly unpleasant to terrifying. Medical evidence shows quite clearly that cocaine can indeed be fatal (Wetli, 1987), even in an "occasional" user; the most popular method of using cocaine, intranasal administration or "snorting," offers no inherent protection against either developing an addiction to it or suffering serious medical and psychological consequences (Washton & Gold, 1984; Washton *et al.,* 1983).

## Definitions of "Abuse" and "Addiction"

Because this chapter deals with assessing the cocaine "abuser" or "addict," it is important to define these terms. As with alcohol and other mood-altering drugs, there are no sharp dividing lines with cocaine between patterns of use, abuse, or dependency/addiction. In a strictly legal sense, any use whatsoever of cocaine (or any other illegal drug) is considered "abuse."

For clinical purposes, it can be said that "abuse" is present whenever the person's use of a drug results in adverse effects to self or others, even though the user may be unwilling or unable to acknowledge that such adverse effects are occurring. It is quite common for the cocaine abuser, like the alcoholic, to claim that his or her drug use is nonproblematic and merely a "social" or "recreational" phenomenon. The user's tendency to deny the existence of drug-related problems, despite clear-cut evidence to the contrary, may itself be indicative of abuse.

As distinguished from "abuse," the terms "addiction" and "dependency" (which can be used interchangeably) usually connote a more serious problem. In addition to experiencing drug-related consequences to health and functioning, the cocaine-dependent or cocaine-addicted person also suffers from an irresistible craving and compulsion to use the drug that may go beyond his or her volitional control; cocaine use is no longer a choice. Cocaine dependency or addiction is characterized by the following: (1) inability to control amount and frequency of use; (2) irresistible cravings and urges; (3) continued use despite adverse effects; (4) denial of indisputable negative consequences; and (5) tendency to abuse other mood-altering drugs (or alcohol), either concomitantly or in the absence of cocaine.

Unlike heroin, alcohol, or sedative–hypnotic drugs, cocaine does not produce a dramatic physical withdrawal syndrome. However, recent evidence suggests that the physical addiction to cocaine may emerge in the form of a biologically based craving for the drug; this results from cocaine-induced stimulation of neural pathways in the brain's basic "reward" centers (Gold, Washton, & Dackis, 1985; Wise, 1984). Cocaine-induced neurochemical changes in these brain areas may give rise to intense cravings and urges, thus providing a physical substrate that propels the addictive behavior. Such findings cast doubt on the validity of the long-standing distinction between "physical" versus "psychological" addiction; it appears that both may be intimately linked through a common physiological process. In addition, because it now seems entirely possible that cocaine dependence can be chemically induced by repeated self-administration of the drug, traditional notions that addiction develops only in those with pre-existing psychopathology, an "addictive personality," or other dysphoric psychological states may not be valid in many cases. Among the ranks of cocaine abusers who seek treatment are many who are reasonably mature, well integrated, and highly functional persons, with no history of previous addiction or significant psychiatric illness (Stone *et al.,* 1984).

The factors that contribute to the initiation and maintenance of cocaine use may change over the course of one's involvement with the drug. Early use, in most cases, tends to be motivated primarily by such factors as curiosity, social encouragement, the presumed harmlessness of the drug, and the desire to repeat a pleasurable experience that is thought to be largely devoid of significant health risks. In the middle stages, when the pattern of use is still intermittent or sporadic, continued use is often perpetuated by the powerfully rewarding effects of the drug (e.g., euphoria, energy, and enhanced sexuality) and the absence of any significant negative consequences directly attributable to the drug use. In the later stages, compulsive drug-taking behavior develops as a result of biological (craving) and behavioral (conditioning) factors, and usually continues despite tolerance to the euphoria and the emergence of an increasing number of negative effects.

In this chapter, we do not dwell on the semantic distinctions between "abuse," "dependency," "addiction," and other terms. For the most part, these terms are used interchangeably. For clinical assessment purposes, the most important questions are these: What are the clinical indications for treatment? What type of treatment is best suited to each patient's needs?

In general, treatment is needed by anyone who is unable and/or unwilling to stop using cocaine, despite the presence of significant drug-related problems. This would apply irrespective of the exact amount and frequency of drug use. Many "weekend-only" snorters of cocaine and other sporadic or "binge" users develop irresistible cravings for the drug and a habitual pattern of intermittent use that may be very difficult to break without outside help. The exact amount or frequency of cocaine use that will cause problems for any given individual is impossible to predict in advance.

No single treatment approach is best for all cocaine abusers. Although the basic elements of effective treatment programs may be similar for many different types of patients (Washton, 1987), certain aspects of the treatment must be individualized according to each patient's needs. Cocaine abusers seeking treatment represent an extremely heterogeneous group in their medical, psychiatric, and socioeconomic status. Formulating a treatment plan for the cocaine abuser requires a comprehensive and thorough clinical assessment to provide an initial data base from which rational treatment decisions can be made.

## Assessment Procedures

The clinical assessment of a treatment applicant must be an ongoing process, extending over the first few weeks of treatment or beyond. Information gathered in the initial interview should be continually modified and updated as the patient progresses through treatment and as new information becomes available. The initial assessment should cover a wide range of relevant issues, including dosage, patterns, chronicity, and method of use; drug-related medical, social, and psychological problems; and the patient's motivation, attitude, and expectations of treatment.

The interpretation of assessment data is inevitably influenced by the clinician's theoretical orientation and philosophy of treatment. The material presented in this chapter is based on our view of cocaine dependency as a form of chemical dependency and an addictive disease. Within this model, cocaine dependency is dealt with as a primary disorder and not merely as a symptom of underlying psychopathology, even if such psychopathology coexists with the cocaine dependency. The major goal of treatment is defined as complete and total abstinence from all mood-altering chemicals, including alcohol and marijuana. Returning to "occasional" or "controlled" use of cocaine or any other mood-altering drug is not seen as an acceptable treatment goal. Consistent with this model, our treatment approach combines the recovery-based principles derived from the Twelve Steps of Alcoholics Anonymous (AA) with professional treatment interventions using cognitive, behavioral, supportive, and insight-oriented techniques as described elsewhere (Washton, 1987).

The assessment procedures described in this chapter are geared primarily toward treatment of the cocaine abuser on an outpatient basis. The discussion of assessment procedures to be presented here follows the organizational format of other chapters in this section of the volume: The procedures are divided into behavioral, cognitive, and physiological components. For each component, the relevant assessment issues are linked to progressive phases of a structured treatment approach (Washton, 1987) as outlined below.

### Treatment Program

Treatment is conducted on an outpatient basis and lasts approximately 6–12 months. The program is structured, problem-oriented, and primarily concerned with patients' present drug abuse problems and life circumstances, rather than their past. It is an active process, with emphasis on cognitive-behavioral techniques, family involvement, and directive/educational counseling, especially at the beginning of treatment. The responsibility for change rests primarily on the patient, who is encouraged to participate actively in the planning and execution of all therapeutic interventions, with the therapist/counselor providing information, advice, support, and encouragement. The program is divided into four stages.

### Stage 1

The initial abstinence phase of the program, comprising the first 30–60 days, focuses primarily on stopping all drug and alcohol use and preventing early treatment dropout. Treatment interventions include the following: frequent counseling visits to support early abstinence; drug education lectures for patients and family members; and a family support group to promote the involvement and assistance of family members in the treatment.

*Stage 2*

The intermediate phase of the program lasts approximately 6 months and focuses primarily on developing a drug-free lifestyle and preventing relapse. Patients attend a twice-weekly relapse prevention recovery group, supplemented by individual sessions at least once every other week.

*Stage 3*

This phase of the program, lasting another 6 months or more, focuses on long-term abstinence issues and the resolution of personal problems related to drug use. Patients attend a weekly "advanced" recovery group and/or individual psychotherapy sessions at least once a week.

*Stage 4*

After a patient completes the program, follow-up visits are scheduled with decreasing frequency from once every month to once every 3–6 months, according to progress. "Booster" sessions are scheduled on an as-needed basis as unexpected problems arise. Throughout the entire program, urine testing for all drugs is conducted at least twice weekly in order to help patients control their drug urges and to verify abstinence.

### Behavioral Assessment Procedures

The behavioral component of the assessment process focuses primarily on the patient's pattern of drug-taking behavior and its resulting consequences on his or her health and functioning. If the clinician is to gather this information accurately, the patient must be cooperative and neither intoxicated nor "crashing" from any mood-altering substance. The absence of any drug and alcohol use for at least 12 hours is an absolute minimum for conducting a reasonably valid assessment interview.

Most of the information is obtained through the patient's self-report. Family members and significant others should also be interviewed to provide supplemental information and, if possible, to verify the accuracy of the patient's report. A combination of denial, clouded memory, and mistrust may contribute to distortions in the patient's self-report. Although a urine test should be administered to identify which drugs the patient has used within the past several days, it should be noted that such tests provide little or no information about the specific pattern, frequency, and amount of drug use. In a voluntary program, in which patients know from the outset that no adverse consequences will result from initially reported levels of drug use and that frequent urine testing is mandatory and will immediately uncover any unreported use, we have found that most patients give a reasonably accurate reporting of their drug use at the initial interview. Nonetheless, during the first few weeks of treatment as confidence and trust develop, patients may volunteer additional, hitherto unreported information about their earlier drug use.

To facilitate the patient's reporting of complete, detailed information about his or her drug use, one of us (Washton) has developed an assessment questionnaire, the Cocaine Abuse Assessment Profile (CAAP)—an extensive self-report intake form completed by the treatment applicant immediately prior to the initial assessment interview. In addition to describing current drug use, the CAAP elicits information about previous use of alcohol and drugs; the nature and extent of drug-related consequences to health and functioning; history of psychiatric/psychological problems; treatment history for drug and alcohol abuse; and family history of drug and/or alcohol abuse and psychiatric problems.

A 38-item rating questionnaire (Table 12-1) is included in the CAAP to assess the severity of the patient's cocaine abuse problem. The total number of questionnaire items scored "yes" by the patient provides a rough index of cocaine abuse severity. Few if any treatment applicants who are genuinely in need of treatment will have a score of less than 10 on this questionnaire. Those who score above 30 seem to require more intensive efforts in the early stage of outpatient treatment to achieve initial abstinence.

Sample items from the CAAP are presented at several points in this chapter. The CAAP has been administered to more than 750 treatment applicants at our facilities, and it has been found to be an extremely useful assessment tool. In addition to providing a wealth of clinical data useful in the assessment process, the CAAP has also yielded direct therapeutic benefit to patients by addressing the problem of denial. The extensive, detailed questions in the CAAP about drug use and drug-related consequences have often helped to facilitate the patients' awareness of the severity of their drug problem and the unavoidable need for treatment. Many of our patients have stated that prior to completing the CAAP they had never before been forced to evaluate the extent to which cocaine and other drug or alcohol use was adversely affecting their lives.

The subsections that follow address several key issues in the behavioral assessment of cocaine abusers seeking treatment.

*Patterns of Use*

The patient's preferred method or route of cocaine administration is an important issue to be addressed in evaluating the severity of abuse and in

TABLE 12-1.    Sample Items from the Cocaine Abuse Assessment Profile: Addiction/
Dependency Self-Test

---

Please answer yes or no to each question below. Do not leave any questions unanswered.

|  |  | YES | NO |
|---|---|---|---|
| 1. | Do you have trouble turning down cocaine when it is offered to you? | — | — |
| 2. | Do you tend to use up whatever supplies of cocaine you have on hand, even though you try to save some for another time? | — | — |
| 3. | Have you been trying to stop using cocaine but find that somehow you always go back to it? | — | — |
| 4. | Do you go on cocaine binges for 24 hours or longer? | — | — |
| 5. | Do you need to be high on cocaine in order to have a good time? | — | — |
| 6. | Are you afraid that you will be bored or unhappy without cocaine? | — | — |
| 7. | Are you afraid that you will be less able to function without cocaine? | — | — |
| 8. | Does the sight, thought, or mention of cocaine trigger urges and cravings for the drug? | — | — |
| 9. | Are you sometimes preoccupied with thoughts about cocaine? | — | — |
| 10. | Do you sometimes feel an irresistable compulsion to use cocaine? | — | — |
| 11. | Do you feel psychologically addicted to cocaine? | — | — |
| 12. | Do you feel guilty and ashamed of using cocaine and like yourself less for doing it? | — | — |
| 13. | Have you been spending less time with "straight" people since you've been using more cocaine? | — | — |
| 14. | Are you frightened by the strength of your cocaine habit? | — | — |
| 15. | Do you tend to spend time with certain people or go to certain places because you know that cocaine will be available? | — | — |
| 16. | Do you use cocaine at work? | — | — |
| 17. | Do people tell you that your behavior or personality has changed, even though they might not know it's due to drugs? | — | — |
| 18. | Has cocaine led you to abuse alcohol or other drugs? | — | — |
| 19. | Do you ever drive a car while high on cocaine, alcohol, or other drugs? | — | — |
| 20. | Have you ever neglected any significant responsibilities at home or at work due to cocaine use? | — | — |
| 21. | Have your values and priorities been distorted by cocaine use? | — | — |
| 22. | Do you deal cocaine in order to support your own use? | — | — |
| 23. | Would you be using even more cocaine if you had more money to spend on it or otherwise had greater access to the drug? | — | — |
| 24. | Do you hide your cocaine use from "straight" friends or family because you're afraid of their reactions? | — | — |
| 25. | Have you become less interested in health-promoting activities (e.g., exercise, sports, diet, etc.) due to cocaine use? | — | — |

*(continued)*

TABLE 12-1 (Continued).

| | YES | NO |
|---|---|---|
| 26. Have you become less involved in your job or career due to cocaine use? | — | — |
| 27. Do you find yourself lying and making excuses because of cocaine use? | — | — |
| 28. Do you tend to deny and downplay the severity of your cocaine problem? | — | — |
| 29. Have you been unable to stop using cocaine even though you know that it is having negative effects on your life? | — | — |
| 30. Has cocaine use jeopardized your job or career? | — | — |
| 31. Do you worry whether you are capable of living a normal and satisfying life without cocaine? | — | — |
| 32. Are you having financial problems due to cocaine use? | — | — |
| 33. Are you having problems with your spouse or mate due to cocaine use? | — | — |
| 34. Has cocaine use had negative effects on your physical health? | — | — |
| 35. Is cocaine having a negative effect on your mood or mental state? | — | — |
| 36. Has your sexual functioning been disrupted by cocaine use? | — | — |
| 37. Have you become less sociable due to cocaine use? | — | — |
| 38. Have you missed days of work due to cocaine use? | — | — |
| TOTALS | — | — |

formulating an initial treatment plan. In general, the majority of intranasal users can be treated successfully as outpatients, without hospitalization, whereas freebase and i.v. users are more likely to need an initial period of hospitalization to separate them from the drug and to facilitate recuperation from drug-induced psychiatric symptoms, medical problems, and psychosocial dysfunction.

Severity of abuse and the need for initial hospitalization is not merely determined by route of administration alone. Although freebase and i.v. users tend to suffer more severe impairment from their drug use, many intranasal users develop a severe dependency on the drug and experience a wide range of drug-related problems. Contrary to long-standing beliefs, intranasal use per se offers no protection against addiction or serious medical and psychosocial consequences (Washton *et al.,* 1983, 1984).

In addition to route of administration, the specific pattern of cocaine use must be assessed in detail. It is important to evaluate both the amount and frequency of use, as shown by items from the CAAP listed in Table 12-2. Levels of cocaine use may span a very wide range among treatment applicants: from use of several grams a month to several grams a day; from sporadic "binges" of intensive use, separated by days or weeks of temporary abstinence, to continuous daily use for at least several hours every day. Other descriptive aspects of usage patterns include the following: the amount of money spent on drugs in recent weeks; the settings and circumstances of use, such as the most common time of day or week cocaine is used (e.g., some patients may use cocaine only in the evening or weekend,

TABLE 12-2. Sample Items from the Cocaine Abuse Assessment Profile: History and Patterns of Cocaine Use

---

1. How long ago did you first try cocaine? _____

2. How did you use it the first time?
   __ Snort   __ Freebase   __i.v.

3. How long did you use cocaine on an "occasional" basis before your use became regular and intensified? _____

4. Have you ever freebased? __ Yes   __ No

5. Have you ever injected cocaine? __ Yes   __ No

6. Currently, what is your usual method of use?
   __ Snort   __ Freebase   __ i.v.

7. On average, how many grams of cocaine do you use per week? ____ grams

8. How much money do you spend on cocaine per week? $____ per week

9. On average, how many days per week do you use cocaine? ____ days

10. Do you tend to go on "binges"? __ Yes   __ No
    If yes, how long does the binge usually last? ____ days
    How many grams do you use during at typical binge? ____ grams

11. In what types of situations do you usually use cocaine? (Check all that apply.)

    __ Alone                        __ At home
    __ With friends                 __ At parties
    __ With spouse/mate             __ At work
    __ With other sexual partner

12. During what portion of the day do you usually use cocaine? (Check all that apply.)
    __ Morning   __Afternoon   __ Evening   __ Late night

13. Since you first started using cocaine on a regular basis, what is the longest time you've been able to stop completely? _____

---

whereas others may be most likely to use it at work); how and where drug supplies are obtained; whether the drug use occurs mainly alone, in social situations, or at work; and whether it occurs in the company of certain friends, acquaintances, or family members. This information will help to identify many of the environmental "triggers" and "high-risk" situations that can be expected both to elicit cravings for cocaine and to increase the potential for relapse, especially during the early phase of treatment.

*Withdrawal Symptoms*

Unlike heroin or alcohol, cocaine does not produce a severe physical withdrawal syndrome when discontinued, but there is often a cluster of postuse symptoms that can last for several days after chronic or high-dose cocaine use is stopped abruptly. These symptoms typically include mood disturbances such as depression, anxiety, and irritability, as well as somatic symptoms such as insomnia, reduced appetite, and nausea. Apart from the immediate "crash" or "hangover" following intensive cocaine use, which usually lasts no more than 12–24 hours, most patients report no lingering postcocaine "withdrawal" symptoms. In fact, quite the opposite is usually found: Patients often report a marked improvement in mood and mental state within the first week of drug abstinence.

The absence of a clear-cut withdrawal syndrome and serious medical risk following abrupt cessation of the drug use obviates the need either for switching the cocaine-dependent patient to a substitute drug or for having to "detoxify" the patient by means of a gradual withdrawal procedure, as is routinely done in the treatment of heroin addicts and severe alcoholics. The absence of a withdrawal syndrome requiring rigorous medical management eliminates one of the major indications for hospitalization in the majority of cocaine abusers who seek treatment. However, before deciding against hospitalization, the clinician must carefully ascertain that the applicant is not physically addicted to other drugs or alcohol, which *do* require medical withdrawal.

## Other Drug Use

Polydrug abuse is a common feature of cocaine dependence, and thus a thorough and detailed assessment of the patient's use of *all* mood-altering drugs is an essential part of the initial evaluation process (see Table 12-3). Drugs such as alcohol, sedative–hypnotics, marijuana, or opiates may have been taken in substantial amounts and with sufficient regularity by the cocaine abuser to cause additional dependencies. Because these drugs are usually taken to alleviate cocaine side effects and not necessarily for their own euphoric effects, the cocaine abuser is often unaware of having acquired a multiple dependency.

Two critical treatment issues related to the assessment of multiple-drug use include (1) the importance of insisting upon total abstinence and (2) deciding whether the cocaine abuser requires initial hospitalization because of physical dependency on other drugs. Any cocaine abuser who has abused other drugs, either in combination with cocaine or prior to cocaine involvement, is at risk for returning to these substances for substitute "highs" during attempted cocaine abstinence. The drugs that should raise the most concern about the need for a medically supervised inpatient detoxification are opiates, barbiturates, benzodiazepines, and alcohol. If discontinued too abruptly after chronic use, each of these drugs can lead to severe withdrawal reactions and potentially serious medical consequences. Assessment of the need for medical detoxification must be conducted by a

TABLE 12-3. Sample Items from the Cocaine Abuse Assessment Profile: Other Drug Use

---

1. Have you *ever* used any of the following substances?

| | |
|---|---|
| Marijuana | __ Yes __ No |
| Amphetamines | __ Yes __ No |
| LSD or other psychedelics | __ Yes __ No |
| Heroin | __ Yes __ No |
| Quaaludes | __ Yes __ No |
| Barbiturates (sleeping pills) | __ Yes __ No |
| Cigarettes/nicotine | __ Yes __ No |
| Alcohol | __ Yes __ No |
| Valium or other tranquilizers | __ Yes __ No |

2. Check below any substances you are currently using (within past 30 days) and indicate how much and how often you use each one?

| | How much | How often |
|---|---|---|
| __ Marijuana | | |
| __ Amphetamines | | |
| __ LSD/other psychedelics | | |
| __ Tranquilizers (Valium, etc.) | | |
| __ Sleeping pills (barbiturates) | | |
| __ Quaaludes | | |
| __ Heroin | | |
| __ Other opiates | | |
| __ Alcohol | | |
| __ Cigarettes/nicotine | | |

3. Do you currently feel dependent on any of these substances?
__ Yes __ No. If yes, please explain: _____

4. Have you ever had a problem with any of these substances in the past? __ Yes __ No. If yes, please describe: _____

5. Have you ever used any of these substances on a regular basis for one month or longer? __ Yes __ No. If yes, please describe: _____

6. Are you currently taking any prescription medication? __ Yes __ No. If yes, please describe and give physician's name and reason for use: _____

---

clinician thoroughly familiar with the relevant pharmacological and medical issues pertaining to the drug(s) in question.

## Cocaine-Related Consequences

Cocaine abusers who seek treatment are usually suffering from at least several drug-related problems that must be addressed in the treatment plan. It is thus important that the scope and severity of all such drug-related problems be assessed upon treatment entry. The checklists in Table 12-4, taken from the CAAP, can facilitate this assessment and may also help the treatment applicant to better realize the full scope of his or her own drug-related problems. As mentioned earlier, this can help to break through the patient's denial.

*Psychiatric Illness*

All treatment applicants should be assessed for the presence of major psychiatric illness. If such illness is present and is left untreated or otherwise ignored, the prognosis for successful recovery from cocaine dependency will be markedly diminished. Some patients may require psychotropic medication, which should not be unreasonably withheld on the extremist grounds that no drugs whatsoever should be used in the treatment of chemically dependent individuals. Although addicts should not be given euphorigenic dependence-producing drugs (e.g., benzodiazepines, barbiturates, or amphetamines), there are indeed cases where psychotropic medication (e.g., antidepressants, lithium, etc.) may be clinically indicated.

A major problem in the psychiatric evaluation of drug abusers is the potential confounding of chronic drug effects with true psychiatric symptomatology. Cocaine abuse can itself lead to chemically induced symptoms of depression, mania, paranoid psychosis, or some other affective illness, the full dissipation of which may require at least several days (or, for depressive symptoms, perhaps several weeks) of drug abstinence. Such symptoms are usually not responsive to psychotropic medication, and the premature introduction of such medication may severely cloud the diagnostic picture. (Noteworthy exceptions include suicidal, violent, or otherwise unmanageable patients, who may require immediate pharmacotherapy.)

To avoid misdiagnosis, the psychiatric assessment of the cocaine abuser should be clearly isolated from recent drug use episodes; ideally, it should be based not on a single diagnostic interview, but rather on a longitudinal series of evaluations extending over the first few weeks of treatment.

*The Need for Hospitalization*

Determining whether a cocaine abuser needs initial hospitalization or can be treated entirely as an outpatient is one of the most important tasks in the initial assessment process (Washton, 1987). In addition to the presence of physical dependency on other drugs, the indications for inpatient treat-

TABLE 12-4. Sample Items from the Cocaine Abuse Assessment Profile: Cocaine-Related Consequences

---

1. Check below any physical problems caused by your cocaine use:

   __ Low energy
   __ Sleep problems
   __ Hands tremble
   __ Runny nose
   __ Nasal sores, bleeding
   __ Sinus congestion
   __ Headaches
   __ Cough, sore throat
   __Other (describe) _____

   __ Chest congestion
   __ Hepatitis
   __ Other infections
   __ Heart "flutters"
   __ Nausea
   __ Chills
   __ Seizures with loss of consciousness
   __ Excessive weight loss

2. Check below any negative effects of cocaine on your mood or mental state:

   __ Irritable
   __ Short-tempered
   __ Depression
   __ Memory problems
   __ Difficulty concentrating
   __ Loss of sex drive
   __ Other (please describe) _____

   __ Paranoia
   __ Anxiety/nervousness
   __ Panic attacks
   __ Suicidal impulses
   __ Violent impulses

3. Check any negative effects of cocaine on your relationships with other people:

   __ Causes arguments with spouse/mate
   __ Spouse/mate has threatened to leave
   __ Caused relationship to break up
   __ Became socially isolated and withdrawn
   __ Harmed social life, felt less sociable
   __ Harmed sexual relationship
   __ Harmed ability to talk openly and honestly with others

4. Check any negative effects of cocaine use on your work or studies:

   __ Came late to work/school
   __ Missed days of work/school
   __ Reduced productivity at work/school
   __ Other (please describe) _____

   __ Spent too much time on breaks
   __ Harmed relationship with boss
   __ Got fired from a job

5. Check any negative effects of cocaine use on your financial situation:

   __ Used up all money in bank
   __ Gotten in debt
   __ Other (please describe) _____

   __ Unable to keep up with bills
   __ No extra money

6. Check any legal consequences of your cocaine use:

   __ Arrested for possession or sale of cocaine
   __ Arrested for other crime(s) related to cocaine sale/use

   Has your cocaine use caused you to:

   __ Have a car accident
   __ Have a physical fight with someone
   __ Have an unwanted sexual encounter

   __ Physically hurt someone
   __ Attempt suicide
   __ Deal drugs
   __ Steal from work, family, or friends

ment of the cocaine abuser include (1) serious medical or psychiatric problems, such as systemic infections, neurological symptoms, paranoid psychosis, and suicidal or violent impulses; (2) poor motivation and/or heavy involvement in drug dealing; (3) failure in outpatient treatment; (4) severe psychosocial dysfunction; and (5) the inability of the patient to immediately discontinue all drug use as an outpatient.

### Cognitive Assessment Procedures

It is essential to assess the patient's desire to stop using drugs and his or her expectations of the treatment program. Cognitive and motivational factors often play a significant, if not a dominant, role in determining the outcome of treatment. Successful recovery from chemical dependency is not just a matter of blindly complying with a suggested regimen of drug abstinence; it requires major shifts in attitudes, beliefs, and cognitive orientation toward drug use. Motivation for change and receptivity to treatment are the essential catalysts for successful recovery. An accurate assessment of these factors is needed to formulate an initial treatment plan and to make subsequent adjustments in the treatment. Some of the key issues in cognitive assessment are discussed below.

#### Motivation for Change

The specific reasons why the patient has decided to seek treatment should be carefully assessed. Many cocaine abusers seek help when they become distressed by drug-related problems and their inability to control the drug use on their own. The clinician should try to determine whether applicants are seeking treatment solely for the purpose of getting others "off their backs." Those who have little or no desire to change may secretly plan to attend the program only for a few weeks, in a perfunctory manner, simply to satisfy the request of a family member or employer and/or to alleviate an immediate crisis situation. Patients whose motivation for change appears highly questionable should not be accepted directly into a group-oriented treatment program, because they usually have a negative, demoralizing impact on other patients who may be working hard to remain abstinent. In some cases, preparatory work with an initially unmotivated patient can be extremely helpful in facilitating changes in motivation and attitude that may render the patient more receptive to treatment. In other cases, the patient may be so resistant to being helped that no intervention is possible at that point and treatment must be denied.

*Acceptance of Treatment Goals and Strategies*

Many treatment applicants strongly resist the idea of total abstinence. They usually accept the need for complete rather than partial cessation of cocaine use, but have difficulty with the notion of giving up marijuana and alcohol, because these are often not perceived as being "problems." If this difficulty persists despite education about the rationale for total abstinence, the patient should be asked nonetheless to comply with this requirement for at least the duration of treatment, in the hope that a change in attitude will occur through participation in the program.

Many applicants also reject the program's request to involve family members, as well as the idea of being in a recovery group or self-help group with other patients. Several weeks of preparatory work by the therapist may be needed to help the patient understand the potential benefits of these activities and to counteract exaggerated or unrealistic fears. The therapist must assess how and when to ease the patient into family and group activities so as to maximize their acceptability. The therapist must also assess whether family or group involvement may be distinctly contra-indicated in certain cases. For example, family members who have maintained a long-standing destructive, uncaring, and unempathetic posture toward the patient may do more harm than good if involved in the treatment. In such cases, the therapist should assist the patient in separating from family members, rather than fostering more destructive involvement. Assessing the patient's appropriateness for entering a recovery group should be based, in part, on how well he or she may fit in with current group members in terms of psychiatric, socioeconomic, and motivational factors. The therapist should seek to maximize the patient's chances of identifying with other group members and of having the members readily accept the new patient into their peer group. Self-help groups such as AA or Cocaine Anonymous (CA) are usually sufficiently large and heterogeneous that almost any newcomer can find someone to identify with. Also, the extremely nonjudgmental and caring attitudes typically displayed in these self-help meetings often foster greater acceptance by newcomers.

*Relapse Potential*

Throughout the entire course of treatment, patients should be continually assessed for certain cognitive factors that may increase their potential for relapse:

1. *"Romanticizing" the cocaine high.* This is a problem of selective memory for the "good" effects of cocaine. When the "bad" effects have faded into memory and are no longer immediately obvious and pressing,

the user's thoughts and associations to cocaine once again become positive, focusing on the euphoria and enjoyable experiences he or she has had while on the drug. To the extent that the user has this selective "euphoric recall" of cocaine, the drug continues to be seen as attractive and desirable, and the potential for relapse is elevated. The therapist must counteract this "romanticizing" of cocaine by educating patients about this phenomenon and by constantly reminding patients of the many problems resulting from cocaine use.

2. *Testing control.* After a period of successful abstinence, many patients start thinking about trying cocaine or other drugs again to see whether they have acquired enough strength to handle "controlled" usage. This will almost always precipitate a relapse and thus must be actively exposed and challenged by the therapist.

3. *The "abstinence violation effect" (AVE).* The AVE (Marlatt, 1982) pertains to the powerful defeatist reaction that may be precipitated by a "slip" (i.e., any violation of total abstinence). In such instances, no matter how minor or short-lived the violation may be, the patient tends to feel that all progress up to that point has been nullified by the single act of transgression and that it is a reflection of personal weakness, helplessness, and lack of willpower. These negative cognitions sap the patient's motivation to regain abstinence and often fuel a rapid escalation of the "slip" into a full-blown relapse. Patients must be educated about the AVE and how to counteract its potentially destructive consequences.

### Physiological Assessment Procedures

### Physical Health Problems

Among cocaine abusers seeking treatment, the incidence of severe or life-threatening medical problems tends to be surprisingly low. The most common physical complaints include insomnia, weight loss, anergia, headaches, and sexual dysfunction. Other symptoms vary with the route of administration. Snorters typically complain of nasal sores, nasal bleeding, and congested sinuses. Freebase smokers report chest congestion, wheezing, chronic cough, black phlegm, sore throat, and hoarseness. Intravenous users may show abscesses at injection sites, elevated liver enzymes, and systemic infections such as hepatitis and endocarditis. The rapid-dosing methods of freebase and i.v. use can cause cocaine-induced brain seizures with loss of consciousness.

A preliminary assessment of cocaine-related physical problems can be obtained using the self-report checklist in the CAAP (Table 12-4). When there is evidence of significant medical problems, the patient should be given a thorough physical examination and clinical laboratory tests, and/or referred to an appropriate medical specialist for further evaluation and treatment.

*Urine Testing for Drugs*

Urine screening for all drugs of abuse is an absolutely essential part of both assessment and treatment. Urine testing provides the only objective, biological measure of the patient's drug use. In the initial assessment, urine testing can objectively confirm the patient's reported drug use, as well as uncover unreported use. The major therapeutic uses of urine testing are as follows: (1) to provide an objective indicator of treatment progress for patient, clinician, and significant others, often eliminating unnecessary suspiciousness, fear, and accusations; and (2) to facilitate the patient's ability to resist urges and cravings for drugs by establishing accountability for drug use and preventing denial.

Specific laboratory methods of urine drug testing are described elsewhere (Verebey, 1987). The most practical and sensitive types of urine tests for routine clinical use are procedures such as the enzyme multiple-immunoassay technique (EMIT), which can reliably detect the presence of most drugs in the urine for up to 72 hours after last use. Less sensitive, cheaper tests, such as thin-layer chromatography (TLC), are too susceptible to false-negative results (i.e., failure to detect the presence of a drug that is actually present in the urine) to be clinically useful, especially when critical treatment planning decisions depend to a significant extent on the results. On the other hand, the most sensitive testing method, gas chromatography combined with mass spectroscopy (GC–MS), is usually too expensive for routine clinical use (a single test for one drug may cost over $75).

With EMIT testing, a urine sample should be taken from the patient every 48–72 hours (i.e., every 2–3 days) throughout the entire course of treatment to maintain accurate surveillance of drug use. The voiding of every sample should be supervised to insure that it is valid. In addition to testing for cocaine, samples should be routinely tested for amphetamine, barbiturates, benzodiazepines, opiates, marijuana, and PCP.

## Case Examples

Two case vignettes are presented below to help illustrate some of the major assessment issues already discussed in this chapter.

*Case 1: Linda*

Linda was a 33-year-old sales representative for a publishing firm. Immediately before entering treatment, she was smoking cocaine freebase (6–10 g/week at an average of $800/week). Her pattern of use consisted mainly of marathon binges lasting an entire weekend, from Friday evening to Monday morning. Occasionally, she used cocaine on weekday evenings after work, but on these occasions she limited her use to 1–2 g so she could still function at work the next morning.

To alleviate the postcocaine "jitters" and insomnia, Linda would drink vodka and/or take 20–50 mg of Valium. Her drug use occurred almost always in the company of her steady boyfriend, himself a cocaine dealer and heavy freebase smoker.

The onset of Linda's cocaine problem had been rapid and severe, dating back about 9 months before she entered treatment, when the divorce from her former husband became final and she started living with her current boyfriend. This boyfriend had introduced Linda to freebase smoking and readily gave her large quantities of high-purity cocaine. She had no previous history of drug addiction, although as a teenager and college student she had periodically used marijuana and hallucinogens, and reported getting drunk at parties on quite a few occasions.

Within the past year, she had snorted cocaine at least several times, finding the experience "mildly pleasant" before "falling in love" with freebasing. The night before her initial evaluation interview, Linda stayed up almost all night smoking freebase in an attempt to have her "last fling" before quitting for good. At the time of the interview the next day (3 P.M.), she was not actively intoxicated, but complained of being extremely fatigued and frightened by the previous night's experience. She felt somewhat relieved, however, that she kept her appointment despite her strong ambivalence about giving up cocaine and her realization that doing so would not be an easy task.

Her responses on the CAAP revealed that the adverse consequences of her drug use were fairly extensive, as reflected by an addiction self-test score of 35 out of a maximum of 38. Her major complaints included insomnia, memory/concentration problems, chronic fatigue, chest congestion, extreme irritability, and a complete loss of sexual desire. Most striking was the profound and intolerable depression she felt for at least several days after each freebasing binge. She reported having thoughts of suicide and contemplated taking an overdose of sleeping pills or jumping out of her ninth-floor apartment window, although she was quick to add that she really didn't think she would ever do either. She showed no signs of major psychiatric illness and reported no history of such problems. Her current severe depression was thought to be largely drug-induced, but she had not been abstinent long enough in recent months to permit an assessment of whether there was an underlying depression independent of the drug use.

Linda sought treatment because of her increasingly severe and debilitating depression and her fear of the powerful drug addiction that had taken control of her life. She was missing days of work because she was hung over from cocaine, and with increasing frequency she was calling in sick or coming in late with numerous vague excuses. She had canceled several important business trips because she was afraid of either transporting cocaine or being without it. Because she had a fairly high-level executive position in the firm, Linda was not held tightly accountable for her time and had not yet encountered serious difficulties with her immediate superior. However, coworkers with whom she had previously snorted cocaine at several office parties and who had often heard her extol the pleasures of freebasing were expressing increasing concern to her about changes in her personality and behavior at work, which they strongly suspected were drug-related.

For several weeks before entering treatment, Linda had tried to stop cocaine on her own but had been unsuccessful. Intense drug cravings and constant re-exposure to the drug by her live-in boyfriend had made it impossible for her to stay away from cocaine for more than 5 or 6 days at a time. She had used cocaine every weekend without exception for the past 6 months.

At the initial interview, she expressed a preference for outpatient treatment, fearing the confinement and stigma of hospitalization. She readily acknowledged the need for total abstinence from cocaine, but did not want to give up alcohol; it was an integral part of her interaction with business clients, and she feared feeling overly self-conscious if she were unable to drink at all.

After the initial interview, the therapist recommended inpatient treatment, based on the following considerations: (1) Linda felt unable to resist her drug cravings; (2) she had continuous, unlimited access to the drug via her boyfriend; (3) she reported suicidal ideation and extreme depression; and (4) she did not feel capable of extricating herself from the relationship with her boyfriend or asking him to live elsewhere. There was initially some question about whether she was physically dependent on Valium, but her pattern of intermittent usage on weekends routinely followed by at least several days of abstinence from the drug indicated that an inpatient withdrawal procedure was not necessary.

Linda completed a 30-day inpatient treatment program, followed by an additional 12 months in outpatient aftercare treatment. Her depressive symptoms lifted almost completely within the first 2 weeks of hospitalization, without psychotropic medication. With the assistance of friends, Linda decided to end the relationship with her drug-involved boyfriend, forced him to move out of her apartment, and had all drug supplies and paraphernalia removed before she returned home.

While participating in outpatient aftercare treatment (consisting of twice-weekly recovery group meetings, once weekly individual counseling, and thrice-weekly urine tests), Linda initially remained abstinent from all drugs, but on a couple of occasions she drank "socially" at business meetings. The alcohol stimulated powerful cravings for cocaine, and on one occasion alcohol led her to "slip" into freebasing immediately following several drinks at a business meeting. As a result of this experience, Linda became convinced of the need for total abstinence. During outpatient treatment, she made substantial changes in her lifestyle and attitudes toward drugs. Much of the time she formerly devoted to using and recuperating from drugs she now spent on life-enhancing activities such as sports, exercise, and social relationships with people who did not use drugs. In addition to group and individual treatment, at approximately 6 months into recovery Linda finally decided to attend CA meetings and found them extremely helpful. Linda completed 12 months of outpatient treatment, continued attending CA meetings, and at the time of this writing has remained drug-free for over 3 years.

### Case 2: Mike

Mike was a 28-year-old married businessman who had been snorting cocaine sporadically for 5 years before seeking treatment. His use had escalated dramatically in the last 2 years to a level of 5–6 g/week. He was using cocaine almost every night at home after his wife fell asleep. He would stay awake for several hours on the drug, watching television or losing himself in sexual fantasies.

Mike said he had stopped using cocaine for 3 weeks before the treatment interview, but was experiencing powerful urges and cravings that made him feel on the verge of relapse. He reported several previous attempts to stop using cocaine over the past 2 years, each of which had been successful for no more than 3 or 4 weeks. Now he was feeling extremely "run down" from cocaine and was having arguments with his wife, who threatened to dissolve the marriage if he did not do something about his drug problem. The couple's finances were suffering; Mike's attendance at work was becoming unreliable; and his wife was anxiously putting off getting pregnant until he stopped using drugs. Mike felt "hung over" almost ever morning after cocaine. He reported an absence of sexual desire or sexual contact with his wife for at least the past 6 months. On occasions when she had approached him sexually, Mike had rejected her with anger.

At the initial interview Mike maintained that he had no problems with drugs other than cocaine, but upon completing the CAAP he realized that his beer consumption in fact was quite high and that he was using sleeping tablets in far greater doses than prescribed by his family physician. The CAAP also revealed that his cocaine use was causing severe headaches, sinus congestion, nasal sores, and constant "sniffling" that he would routinely excuse to others as symptoms of a "cold" or "allergies." He also reported being in serious debt because of his cocaine habit and avoiding family and friends as his drug use escalated.

Although Mike's initial purpose in coming for the interview was to satisfy his wife and save their marriage, by the end of the session he seemed to acquire a slightly better appreciation of the severity of his problem and the possible need for treatment. He was reluctant to accept total abstinence, thinking that beer was not really alcohol and that the sleeping pills were justifiable because the medication was legitimately prescribed by a physician.

The assessment indicated that Mike was suitable for outpatient treatment without hospitalization. He had already stopped using cocaine for the past 3 weeks (his urine test was negative for all drugs at the interview); he was not physically dependent on other drugs or alcohol; he showed no signs of past or present psychiatric illness; and he said he felt capable of continuing to remain abstinent on an outpatient basis if he received help in fighting off the urges and cravings for cocaine. He was willing to try total abstinence from all drugs and alcohol, although he was not entirely convinced of the need to do so.

During the first 3 months of outpatient treatment, Mike had two "slips," each of which triggered off intense feelings of failure, guilt, and nullification of progress symptomatic of the AVE. These feelings were exacerbated by his wife and parents, who had hoped unrealistically that after he joined the program Mike would never use drugs again. Mike participated in a twice-weekly recovery group for 9 months in conjunction with individual, couples, and family counseling. He eventually stopped "romanticizing" cocaine after re-establishing a good relationship with his wife and realizing that he had nearly lost the relationship to cocaine. His wife and parents attended a family education and support group that helped them to a better understanding of Mike's chemical dependency problem and what they could do to help. At the time of this writing, Mike has been abstinent for approximately 26 months. He has completed formal treatment, but now regularly attends CA meetings to facilitate continued recovery.

### Final Comment

Doing an accurate assessment of a cocaine abuser requires specific knowledge of a broad range of clinical and pharmacological issues. Some of these issues are specific to cocaine, but others are common to all forms of chemical dependency.

Some of the clinically relevant differences between cocaine and alcohol include the following:

1. Unlike alcohol, which is a CNS depressant that impairs the user's

performance, cocaine is a powerful stimulant often taken for its initial performance-enhancing effects.

2. Dependence on cocaine can occur very rapidly, sometimes within only a few weeks or months, rather than over the course of several years.

3. Because there is no withdrawal syndrome from cocaine and no lingering aftereffects, there can be more denial about the existence of a problem and the need for treatment. Many patients tend to feel instantly "cured" after stopping cocaine for a week.

4. Cocaine is often self-administered by more intensive routes of administration (i.e., freebase smoking and i.v. use), which grossly magnify and complicate drug-related problems and thus require special consideration in the treatment process.

5. Because cocaine is illegal, patients are often initially more guarded and suspicious toward the treatment staff and extremely concerned about confidentiality. Fears about public exposure may cause a heightened resistance toward participating in group sessions and self-help meetings. In addition, the use of illegal drugs may also engender deceptive, manipulative, and devious behavior, which the clinician must be prepared to handle without being judgmental or personally offended.

6. Many cocaine abusers are upwardly mobile "baby boomers" who may have a somewhat elitist attitude about their problem, considering themselves "a cut above" alcoholics or other drug addicts. Emphasis on the generic nature of cocaine dependence as a form of chemical dependency and addictive disease is therefore extremely important, although essential differences should not be overlooked.

7. The educational component of treatment for cocaine abusers should focus on cocaine first and other drugs second, instead of vice versa. Also, wherever possible, cocaine abusers should be placed into recovery groups that contain at least several other cocaine abusers. Like alcoholics or those with other chemical dependency problems, the cocaine abuser can benefit greatly from identification with recovering peers who share the same problem. It is a mistake to treat the cocaine abuser as an alcoholic who has simply chosen a different drug.

The clinical assessment of a cocaine abuser is not a static listing of observations, but rather an ongoing dynamic process that is an essential prerequisite to good treatment planning. It includes a wide range of subjective and objective data that should be constantly revised as the assessment and treatment process unfolds.

No single treatment modality is best for all cocaine abusers. Treatment must be tailored, within limits, to each patient's individual needs and circumstances. A thorough and sensitive clinical assessment of the cocaine abuser is the starting point of good treatment.

# References

Adams, E. H., & Kozel, N. J. (1985). Cocaine use in America. In N. J. Kozel and E. H. Adams (Eds.), *Cocaine use in America: Epidemiologic and clinical perspectives* (NIDA Research Monograph No. 61, DHHS Publication No. ADM 85-1414, pp. 1-7). Washington, DC: U.S. Government Printing Office.

Gold, M. S., Washton, A. M., & Dackis, C. A. (1985). Cocaine abuse: Neurochemistry, phenomenology, and treatment. In N. J. Kozel and E. H. Adams (Eds.), *Cocaine use in America: Epidemiologic and clinical perspectives* (NIDA Research Monograph No. 61, DHHS Publication No. ADM 85-1414, pp. 130-150). Washington, DC: U.S. Government Printing Office.

Johanson, C. (1984). Assessment of the dependence potential of cocaine in animals. In J. Grabowski (Ed.), *Cocaine: Pharmacology, effects, and treatment* (NIDA Research Monograph No. 50, DHHS Publication No. ADM 84-1326, pp. 54-71). Washington, DC: U.S. Government Printing Office.

Jones, R. T. (1987). Psychopharmacology of cocaine. In A. M. Washton & M. S. Gold (Eds.), *Cocaine: A clinician's handbook* (pp. 55-72). New York: Guilford Press.

Marlatt, G. A. (1982). Relapse prevention: A self-control program for the treatment of addictive behaviors. In R. B. Stuart (Ed.), *Adherence, compliance and generalization in behavioral medicine.* New York: Brunner/Mazel.

Post, R. M. (1975). Cocaine psychosis: A continuum model. *American Journal of Psychiatry, 132,* 225-231.

Stone, N. S., Fromme, M., & Kagan, D. (1984). *Cocaine: Seduction and solution.* New York: Clarkson N. Potter.

Verebey, K. (1987). Cocaine abuse detection by laboratory methods. In A. M. Washton & M. S. Gold (Eds.), *Cocaine: A clinician's handbook* (pp. 214-228). New York: Guilford Press.

Washton, A. M. (1985, July 16). *The cocaine abuse problem in the U.S.* Testimony presented before the Select Committee on Narcotics Abuse and Control, U.S. House of Representatives, Washington, DC.

Washton, A. M. (1986, September). "Crack": The newest lethal addiction. *Medical Aspects of Human Sexuality,* pp. 49-52.

Washton, A. M. (1987). Outpatient treatment of cocaine abuse. In A. M. Washton & M. S. Gold (Eds.), *Cocaine: A clinician's handbook* (pp. 106-117). New York: Guilford Press.

Washton, A. M., & Gold, M. S. (1984). Chronic cocaine abuse: Evidence for adverse effects on health and functioning. *Psychiatric Annals, 14,* 733-743.

Washton, A. M., & Gold, M. S. (1987). Recent trends in cocaine abuse as seen from the "800-COCAINE" hotline. In A. M. Washton & M. S. Gold (Eds.), *Cocaine: A clinician's handbook* (pp. 10-22). New York: Guilford Press.

Washton, A. M., Gold, M. S., & Pottash, A. C. (1983). Intranasal cocaine addiction. *Lancet, ii,* 1378.

Washton, A. M., Gold, M. S., & Pottash, A. C. (1984). Survey of 500 callers to a national cocaine helpline. *Psychosomatics, 25,* 771-775.

Washton, A. M., & Stone, N. S. (1984). The human cost of chronic cocaine use. *Medical Aspects of Human Sexuality, 18,* 122-130.

Wetli, C. V. (1987). Fatal reactions to cocaine. In A. M. Washton & M. S. Gold (Eds.), *Cocaine: A clinician's handbook* (pp. 33-54). New York: Guilford Press.

Wise, R. A. (1984). Neural mechanisms of the reinforcing action of cocaine. In J. Grabowski (Ed.), *Cocaine: Pharmacology, effects, and treatment* (NIDA Research Monograph No. 50, DHHS Publication No. ADM 84-1326, pp. 15-33). Washington, DC: U.S. Government Printing Office.

# 13

# HEROIN ADDICTION

**EDWARD J. CALLAHAN**
*University of California at Davis Medical Center*

**ELLA H. PECSOK**
*West Virginia University*

## Introduction and Background

During the past 25 years there has been a substantial increase in the sophistication of the assessment of human behavior. This period has witnessed a shift away from assessment for the presence or absence of disease states and toward measurement of frequency and intensity of critical behaviors. One area in which progress has lagged has been the assessment of the use of and addiction to narcotics. Even today, most assessment of narcotic addiction is based on a model in which observations are used to determine the presence or absence of narcotic addiction as a disease. Despite that problem, there is a growing body of literature providing more accurate description of behaviors associated with the use of narcotics. The purpose of this chapter is to review the assessment of narcotic addiction across a variety of assessment methodologies, including self-report, direct observation, laboratory analysis of bodily fluids, and physiological assessment. Before we begin our exploration of the assessment of narcotic addiction, we briefly review the way narcotic addiction has been seen in the United States, in order to develop a perspective on the parallel evolution of the assessment of narcotic addiction.

The past 100 years have seen a substantial change in the way in which the narcotic addict is seen in the United States. Historically, opiates have been seen as powerful and useful; in fact, the abbreviation of GOM, for "God's Own Medicine," was a common term in Great Britain as early as the 1700s (Brecher, *et al.*, 1972). Morphine addiction first appeared as a serious problem in the United States during the Civil War. Three phenomena during this period contributed to this development. First, the Civil War saw the introduction of the hypodermic syringe, which provided a more potent route for ingestion of morphine. Second, many people were injured in the war, creating a whole population with chronic pain problems. Finally, at the same time, local healers were selling opiates in patent medicines to predominantly middle-aged and older women, who used these mixtures to deal with postmenopausal complaints. Because no labeling of ingredients was required, people were unaware that they were taking opiates. Thus, postmenopausal women made up the bulk of the opiate addicts in the United States in the late 1800s, while their addiction went unnoticed.

Serious attempts to control opiates began only when a new population of opiate users moved to the western United States. Many of the Chinese laborers who were recruited to build the railroads in the late 1800s brought the custom of smoking opium with them. Local laws were passed against the use of opiates, first in San Francisco and then more widely across the nation in response to a perceived cultural threat. Thus, the initial laws against opiate use in the United States were aimed at controlling a racial minority whom the general population feared, the Chinese laborers (Platt & Labate, 1976). Annexation of the Philippines after the Spanish-American War added another element to the problem: Opium smoking was a common practice among Chinese laborers there also. When the United States imposed legislation against opiate use and banned government employment of addicts, the Chinese government considered this act as another racist attack, because the bulk of opium smokers in the Philippines were Chinese.

At roughly the same time, the United States became involved in attempts to open trade routes to China, which sought modernization and increased trade. To accomplish this, strained U.S.-Chinese relations had to be repaired. To improve relations with China, the United States offered help in controlling China's opium problem. In the process, the United States became the leader in the worldwide movement to control opiate sales and use. Yet, going into the Shanghai Conference in 1909, the United States faced the potentially embarrassing situation of proposing tough international laws against opiate sales without having any such laws on its own books. To remedy that, federal laws against the sale and use of opiates were passed in the United States. These laws were relatively weakly enforced until 1914 when the Harrison Act was passed, strengthening the penalty against the use of opiates. A later series of U.S. Supreme Court decisions in 1919–1920 put further force into these laws by stripping away the physician's right to prescribe opiates except in the process of detoxification.

With Supreme Court rulings making it illegal for most physicians to prescribe opiates, there was a further evolution in the identity of the opiate addict—from the elderly grandmother who used opiates to deal with her postmenopausal symptoms to the criminal. This criminal was usually (or at least was perceived to be) a member of an ethnic minority who became involved in the underworld in the 1920s when legal sources of opiates dried up. Because legal sources of opiates were no longer available, sale and distribution of the drug became economically attractive to organized crime.

This further centralized the sale and use of opiates in ethnic-minority communities, because those were areas that had least police control.

Concurrent with these changes in the identity of the opiate addict in the United States, psychological material began to emerge that described the opiate user as a disordered personality. Such a description made sense in light of the fact that the user, by definition, had become a criminal.

## Personality Assessment

Given the mid-1900s view of the addict as a criminal, personality tests were used to try to identify the opiate addict. Over time, however, personality tests have come under increasing fire for their lack of utility in predicting who uses opiates. Repeated studies have found psychopathy and depression in addicts on personality profiles. The vast literature that has been generated appears to have at least one crucial confound: The scores that have been obtained when the profiles have been given without special instructions look extremely pathological. Markedly different Minnesota Multiphasic Personality Inventory (MMPI) scores have been obtained from addicts instructed *not* to use experience while on a narcotic as a basis for answering items (Glazer, 1978); under these specific instructions, the addicts appear fairly normal.

Most of the work done on the assessment of the narcotic addict has emphasized the trait concept of addiction; that is, the heroin user is labeled an addict on the basis of the evidence that any narcotic is in his or her system. This overstatement is most clearly encapsulated in the contention that opiate use alters the user's metabolism. Dole and Nyswander (1965) argued that even a single use of a narcotic alters the person's metabolism permanently, making the person normal only when on the narcotic. Such an argument suggests that all those who use a narcotic once ought to become addicted in an attempt to be normal. There has been little effort to study those who use narcotics and do not become addicted to them, but their numbers appear large. Notable exceptions to the absence of research on controlled use of narcotics ("chipping") are studies by Powell (1973) and Robbins, Davis, and Nurco (1974). The exact size of the "chipping" population is not clear, although there is evidence that some people use narcotics throughout their lives while maintaining vocational, social, and physical functioning. These individuals may never be recognized by legal authorities or treatment facilities. Further descriptions and analyses of this nonaddicted population are needed.

The recognition of a population that uses narcotics without addiction leads to a focal question: What are the functional effects of heroin use? This question is critical, because an adequate assessment of a narcotic user must consider areas of adjustment that may be influenced, such as personal, work, family, and social areas. These concerns suggest that narcotic treatment programs, which typically are evaluated solely according to the number of clients who are helped to become opiate-free in the short term, also need to evaluate their effectiveness in building job preparedness and social adjustment in their clientele; these are critical factors in determining whether an addict will relapse (Haertzen, Kocher, & Miyasato, 1983; McCaul, Stitzer, Bigelow, & Liebson, 1982; Rounsaville, Tierney, Crit-Cristoph, Weissman, & Kleber, 1982; Sackstein, 1983). Thus, multiple levels of assessment are needed to provide a complete picture of the individual addict or the narcotic clinic population. In looking at the assessment of narcotic addiction, we first review the few studies that describe the immediate effects of heroin, because these reports have implications for how to assess clients in treatment programs.

## Direct Observation after the Use of Heroin

Literature describing the immediate effects of heroin is sparse (see Callahan & Rawson, 1980) compared to that describing alcohol use (see Bridell & Nathan, 1976; Mello & Mendelson, 1965; Nathan & O'Brien, 1971; Schaefer, Sobell, & Mills, 1971; Sobell & Sobell, 1978). Few studies have been conducted observing individuals in a controlled setting after the use of heroin. The first direct observation of the effects of heroin was published by Wikler (1952), in a report on the experimental readdiction of a 33-year-old client at the Federal Narcotics Treatment Center in Lexington, Kentucky. Unfortunately, the observations were not straightforward descriptions of behavior changes, but frequently involved description through a psychoanalytic perspective. In addition, readdiction within a treatment facility is not the same as readdiction in the natural environment. Despite these drawbacks, this study was clearly innovative and deserves careful attention.

Perhaps the most important observation from Wikler's study was that, as the patient began to use heroin, he began to withdraw socially from his peers and the staff. At one point, the patient was told that he would have to stop using the drug soon. At first his reaction was to voluntarily decrease his intake; however, he quickly reversed that pattern and took all heroin made available. Once he had fully withdrawn from the heroin, he refused Wikler's offer of psychotherapy. In each of these behaviors, it appears that he engaged in patterns similar to those found in the natural environment.

Many years passed before further direct observation studies appeared. In the first of these, Griffith, Fann, and Tapp (cited in Mirin, Meyer, & McNamee, 1976) allowed inpatient addicts to earn morphine by pressing a response lever. Despite ready access to morphine, complaints of withdrawal symptoms, anger, and despondence increased over time, independently of the dosage of morphine made available. These mood changes occurred quickly after readdiction was under way. The initial euphoria reported by subjects was soon replaced by an increase in negative affect, which was then avoided by increasing the amount of narcotic consumed. The cycle appeared to occur more rapidly over time.

The same basic pattern of affective changes was reported by Haertzen and Hooks (1969). They found that self-report of euphoria following each shot of morphine decreased over 3 months of self-injection, and that somatic complaints and irritability increased. Martin, Jasinski, and Mansky (1973) further replicated this pattern with observations in their methadone clinic: Initial euphoria was replaced by negative mood over time with repeated use. Thus, increased irritability and missed appointments may be critical for treatment programs to track, because they may signal the beginning of readdiction.

One of the flaws in each of the previously cited studies was that the observers were not blind to opiate use, leaving room for observer bias. Further research might minimize this confound by using observers blind to the subjects' condition and by introducing coding systems that look at simple behaviors rather than at global states such as despondency or euphoria. The increased interobserver agreement accomplished with recording discrete behaviors works against observer bias.

A key series of studies using direct observation was conducted by Roger Meyer and his colleagues. In these studies, subjects underwent experimental re-exposure to narcotics in an inpatient setting, sometimes with and sometimes without a narcotic antagonist. "Narcotic antagonists" are drugs (e.g., naltrexone) that block the euphoric effects of narcotics, presumably by effectively competing for available receptor sites. Although they are powerful enough to induce immediate withdrawal if taken while an individual has a narcotic in his or her system, they merely block the effect of drugs taken later by an individual who takes the antagonist with no narcotic in his or her system. Meyer and his colleagues (Babor, Meyer, Mirin, McNamee, & Davies, 1976; McNamee, Mirin, Kuehnie, & Meyer, 1976; Meyer, Mirin, Altman, & McNamee, 1976; Mirin et al., 1976) took clinical ratings of psychopathology, behavioral ratings, and plasma levels of heroin. Measures were taken across successive phases in which patients were, first, functioning drug-free; second, using heroin; third, detoxifying from heroin; fourth, beginning to use the narcotic antagonist; and finally, using heroin while blocked with the narcotic antagonist.

The first phase of the research provided the baseline for later changes in mood and behavior. Immediately after the clients began to use heroin, self-reported feelings of positive affect increased. However, fairly quickly, subjects began to report increasing anger between the times that they were injecting heroin. These self-reports were corroborated by clinical ratings given by the staff, who observed increasing belligerence and negativity.

These mood changes were probably pharmacologically induced, but may not have reflected changes in the natural environment with full accuracy.

Initial use of heroin resulted in decreases in somatic complaints and depression as measured on the Current and Past Psychopathology Scale (CAPPS). Longer use, over 8–10 days, produced increases in somatic complaints, anxiety, depression, and social isolation. Thus the initial effects of the drug reversed quickly. The same symptoms that heroin initially alleviated were soon induced as aftereffects of taking the drug. These changes are consistent with Solomon's (1980) opponent-process theory of addiction, which is discussed below. Meyer's group's observations may provide valuable clues for clinicians operating in mental health centers and heroin programs, by suggesting ways of recognizing that a person may be starting readdiction. Clearly, social withdrawal, irritability, physical symptoms, and the missing of appointments at the clinic are early indicators of relapses.

Across each of the studies reviewed, changes that occur with the gradual readdiction to narcotics suggest the value of Solomon's (1980) opponent-process theory in understanding heroin addiction. In Solomon's model, the immediate effects of a drug are counteracted by the body with opposing effects. The body "strives towards homeostasis" by producing effects directly opposing the pharmacological effect of the drug. These compensatory changes are conditioned over time to the cues associated with administration of the drug, thus lessening the body's immediate response to the drug. In this way, Solomon's model explains the phenomenon of tolerance. Over time these compensatory reactions gradually become stronger than the effects of the drug itself. Thus Solomon unravels the seeming paradox that heroin ultimately produces those symptoms that it masks initially. Although heroin produces clear changes across users, each individual who uses heroin will have idiosyncratic symptomatic changes with its use and will develop his or her own unique set of stimuli that lead to increased probability of using heroin. Therefore, the most effective means of monitoring a person's response to treatment will be to develop an idiosyncratic assessment methodology for that individual. In the next section, we discuss some of the ways in which these idiosyncratic behavior changes have been used to monitor clinical processes.

## Self-Observation

### Research Projects

Henry Boudin, founder of the Drug Project in Gainesville, Florida, introduced several critical concepts to self-observation for narcotic addiction. Boudin and his colleagues trained their clients to define and record a variety of behaviors or "pinpoints." These pinpoints were particular behaviors that were thought to be possible predictors of increasing probability of narcotic usage for a given client. These measures tapped behaviors, affective states, cognitions, and environmental events that were seen as possible links in the behavior chain leading to opiate use. For example, after interviewing to determine recent chains of events leading to drug use, a client might be asked to record ounces of alcohol consumed, anxiety level, self-deprecating statements, and where he or she had dinner if these events appeared to be part of the chain leading to heroin use. For each individual, an attempt was made to determine the best combination of predictive variables. Requiring clients to phone in measures several times a day made close monitoring of behavioral chains, urges, and their antecedents possible (Boudin, 1972; Boudin, Valentine, Ruiz, & Regan, 1980).

Similar procedures were applied in a research effort in a racially mixed community (predominantly Chicano) by Callahan and his colleagues (Callahan, Price, & Dahlkoetter, 1980; Callahan, Rawson, Glazer, McCleave, & Arias, 1976; Callahan, Rawson, et al., 1980; Rawson et al., 1979). Using self-monitoring proved more difficult for clients in this program than it appeared to be for the better-educated and predominantly white clientele seen by Boudin et al. (1980). The Chicano clients may have been less willing or less able to make accurate self-observations. However, with considerable training, the technique was used successfully as a process measure with most clients. A case example is now presented from this experience to illustrate self-monitoring as a tool in functional analysis of heroin use.

### Case Example

Tomas was a 23-year-old Chicano client seen at the Heroin Antagonist and Learning Theory (HALT) project. To gain entry as a full client of the HALT project, Tomas was required to fulfill a contract requiring several behaviors: (1) successfully completing a 14-day detoxification program; (2) providing one drug-free urine sample each day for the first week and three drug-free urine samples for the second week of program membership; and (3) providing contracted information during each of four phone calls made to the project daily. These phone calls were scheduled for 8:30 A.M., 11:30 A.M., 4:00 P.M., and 7:00 P.M. Each time that he called the project, Tomas was required to report the location he was calling from, the phone number, the persons he was with (if any), his activities since the last phone call, and his plans for the next time period. Through this self-monitoring and the discussion of his previous experiences in relapsing to heroin use, particular pinpoints were chosen for continued monitoring as Tomas became a full member of the HALT project. These pinpoints included the following:

urges to use heroin, anxiety rating, number of cigarettes smoked, amount of marijuana smoked, and ounces of alcohol consumed. In addition, particular locations were flagged as potential problems. These included being at the house of his friend, Richard, and spending time at one particular hamburger stand in the barrio. The phone number at Richard's house was noted on the telephone recording sheet as a high-risk situation requiring notification of Tomas's counselor or the staff person on call.

For the first 2 weeks of full involvement in the HALT project, Tomas had drug-free urine samples and fairly low levels of each of these pinpoints. In the third week, however, there was a drastic increase in the amount of marijuana smoked and in frequency of urges to use heroin as reported to the volunteer who was recording phone data. On one of these phone calls, he reported that he felt he was likely to use heroin. The staff member on call was notified; the staff member called him back and arranged to meet with him at a coffee shop. During the meeting, Tomas reported that he had had an argument with his girlfriend that day and had been strongly tempted to go to Richard's house to score and use heroin. The counselor then worked with him on ways of dealing with the issues that had arisen between him and his girlfriend, and suggested that if the two of them wanted to come in to talk out the issue further, they could. At this point, arguments with the girlfriend were added as a monitored pinpoint.

With the completion of 1 month of heroin-free urine samples, Tomas became eligible for the work development program, in which he was initially trained in how to interact in an application process for the vocational rehabilitation program. This training was videotaped, and he was provided with direct feedback on his social skills in the interview process. This training in interviewing skills continued for 1 month. With his continuing success in staying drug-free, Tomas was gradually reduced to one phone call per day. At the end of this time, with continued drug-free urine samples, he was sent to the vocational rehabilitational program and was successfully enrolled. The agency agreed to keep him in the program as long as he was an active member of the HALT project. Later in the program, Tomas missed two appointments, made one phone call giving Richard's number but another location, and provided a urine sample giving evidence of drug use when a staff member went to his home to obtain it. Counseling, urine tests, and self-monitoring through phone calls were all intensified at this point, and Tomas was put on probation by the project. Another missed appointment or positive urine sample would have resulted in his suspension from the program; furthermore, the employment training program would be notified. These events did not occur: Tomas graduated from the program at 1 year and provided a drug-free urine at the 1-year follow-up. He reported that changing his place of residence, making friends with nonusers, and feeling busy and productive with work all helped him remain off drugs. These efforts at a functional analysis were successful and appeared therapeutically valuable, but assessment of drug abuse is usually much less direct (Bassett, 1980).

## Physiological and Biochemical Measures of Heroin Use

Existing indirect measures of narcotics use vary according to content and objectivity. Because actual drug use is nearly impossible to assess, correlates of drug use comprise the content of most measures. The efforts described above were rare exceptions in establishing discreet measures of potential drug use by each client on an individual basis; however, each of these programs relied heavily on biochemical measures to validate the self-observation measures employed. This review of assessment now turns to a discussion of physiological and laboratory tests, highlighting strengths and weaknesses for each procedure. Suggestions to enhance effective use of these procedures are offered as well.

### Clinical Lab Tests

Clinical laboratories can provide excellent assessment of the use of narcotics (Stewart, 1982). Assessment in the clinical laboratory can guide emergency treatment of substance abuse patients, provide a collateral measure of drug use, and offer feedback on treatment effects (Green, 1982). Perhaps most importantly, urine results are a constant validity check on verbal report. Missed appointments to submit urine samples are also important, as they may signal the hiding of a positive sample. Because clinical laboratories vary in procedures and reliability, each health care provider needs to investigate all available services (Stewart, 1982) and understand what information he or she is receiving from the laboratory. If a laboratory has a high rate of false positives (readings that find narcotics present when none are in the sample), confronting a client with positive results will be very difficult. Even a 5% false-positive rate makes confrontation quite uncomfortable. Steiner (1971) warns against two potential therapist role traps: the therapist as "patsy" and the therapist as "persecutor." Accurate information on laboratory tests and self-observations can be critical in avoiding these roles.

All clinical laboratory tests analyze biofluids such as urine, blood, saliva, gastric contents, and secretions. The most readily available and commonly analyzed fluid is urine. It is important that fluids be sent quickly for analysis, because all biofluids degrade over time (S. Cohen, 1981). Some procedures yield qualitative results (i.e., identification of drug substances in the biofluid specimen), whereas others also allow quantification of the drug. Quantitative data are necessary for management of emergency treatment (Kaye, 1980), but management of the client requires only qualitative assessment of drug levels (S. Cohen, 1981).

*Urinalysis*

The most widely used screening test is urinalysis (Green, 1982). Although this procedure offers only qualitative information, the identification of the presence of heroin and a variety of drugs is important in the treatment of heroin addiction. Awareness that a client has used heroin is critical to any effort to identify antecedents of use. Abuse of other drugs and alcohol can be unwanted sequelae of withdrawal from heroin. Paying attention to the smell of a client's breath is important for this reason, as is monitoring for drugs other than heroin. Urinalysis is a valuable way to assess use, for several reasons. First, urine is easily obtained. Second, testing urine for other drugs requires little time, money, or effort. The procedure can identify a variety of drugs, including amphetamines, antidepressants, antihistamines, carbamazepine, ephedrine, phencyclidine, ethylclorovynol, flurazepam, meprobamate, methaqualone, phenothiazine, codeine, morphine, heroin, methadone, meperidine, propoxyphene, benzodiazepines, ethanol, phencyclidine, phenytoin, and salicylates (Green, 1982). The urine sample needs to be collected under direct observation to insure its validity. The urine of many an addict's beloved grandmother has been analyzed by careless treatment programs.

Urinalysis is particularly useful to detect recent heroin intake. However, these tests are less accurate when dosage levels are low, when the time between abuse and analysis increases, and when the drug has been chronically abused. Chronic abusers tend to demonstrate low drug levels because of increased metabolic efficiency in clearing the drug (Stewart, 1982). In addition, most addicts know that drinking large amounts of beer (or even water) can flush their systems and produce drug-free urine specimens within 24 hours. This suggests that clinics might want to monitor the specific gravity of urine samples also, because low specific gravity of the urine may indicate flushing.

Programs can facilitate accuracy and turnaround time by promptly submitting sample specimens and monitoring the amounts submitted (Dito, 1981). Clients who claim they cannot urinate can be given coffee, tea, or another diuretic and be required to wait until they produce an adequate sample, because "inability" to urinate is often associated with recent drug use. Urine samples are preferred to blood samples because they are painless and less invasive. However, blood samples can provide useful information when they are used. The next section provides detailed information for those who might use these measures in their work. Casual readers may prefer to resume their reading at the section dealing with the physiological parameters of addiction (p. 403).

*Serum Analyses*

Unlike urine samples, the concentration of blood serum samples remains constant. As a result, serum samples allow quantitative analyses. There are problems with these analyses, however: increased cost and longer turnaround time (Pribor, Morrel, & Schen, 1981). Each of these factors makes serum analysis less useful for client therapy and program evaluation, even though more accurate quantification is sometimes desirable.

Even serum analysis can be faulty because of problems that fall into three categories: the patient, the degree of abuse, and the abused drug. Factors such as age, sex, degree of adiposity, presence of concomitant disease, drug tolerance, and inherited metabolic differences influence drug response (Pribor *et al.,* 1981). Their influence is not critical in most clinic applications. Disease states, such as renal disease (a common by-product of long-term heroin use) and uremia, allow drug toxicity to increase by impairing metabolic processes. In addition, the rate of these metabolic processes is lowered as the body mass of the user decreases. Because of this, the same dose will have greater effects on women than men (Pribor *et al.,* 1981).

The history of abuse is another factor that affects drug serum levels (Pribor *et al.,* 1981; Stewart, 1982). As the history of use lengthens, serum levels tend to decrease. The mechanism involved is unknown; however, it is possible that biotransformation of the drug becomes more efficient as the body's experience with the drug increases. Therefore, plasma drug levels, relative to observable clinical signs, tend to be suppressed among chronic opiate users (Kalman & Clark, 1979).

Drug-related factors, including dose size, route of administration, and routes of elimination, also influence serum levels. Because heroin is a basic drug, it is not absorbed well in the acidic environment of the stomach, but is absorbed well in the alkaline environment of the small intestine. Serum levels will not provide an accurate assessment if taken during the absorption process (soon after ingestion).

*Drug Assays*

Drug assays measure the total amount of heroin present in the body (Kalman & Clark, 1979), both protein-bound and free. Heroin is active only in the free (unbound) state, however. Therefore, as the amount of protein-bound heroin increases, the pharmacological effects decrease.

Assays that reveal only the total levels of the parent drug and do not detect pharmacologically active metabolites can be misleading (Kalman & Clark, 1979; Stewart, 1982). The active heroin metabolite is 4-hydroxyglutethimide. This metabolite is considered fairly potent, because it persists longer than heroin and produces similar pharmacological effects. The health care provider should consider metabolite activity when discrepancies between clinical observations and laboratory assays occur (Stewart, 1982).

To benefit fully from available clinical laboratory resources, each clinician should be familiar with procedures available locally. Laboratories differ from locale to locale, as do substance abuse practices (Stewart, 1982). Usually the local substance abuse pattern dictates what procedures are available; in addition, laboratories will be willing to add new tests if such tests will be used frequently. In general, qualitative procedures are cheaper and can assess a number of substances. Accuracy typically decreases as the assessment category broadens, however. Therefore, accurate interpretation of lab results requires consideration of local protocols and procedures. Ideally, the clinician needs to know whether the assay measures metabolites. Perhaps the most crucial bits of information, however, are the false-positive and false-negative rates and which substances contribute to each (Kalman & Clark, 1979).

*Toxicological Analyses*

The primary toxicological analyses include chromatographic, spectrophotometric, and immunological procedures (Kaye, 1980). Chromatography uses the physical and chemical properties of a substance to separate the substance's mobile carrying phase from its stationary phase. Every substance has a characteristic distance (Rf) between the mobile and stationary phases. When the unknown Rf is compared to known standards, the substance may be identified. There are three chromatographic procedures: thin-layer chromatography (TLC), gas–liquid chromatography (GLC), and high-pressure liquid chromatography (HPLC) (Gough & Baker, 1983; Stewart, 1982). Each procedure is reviewed in turn.

*Thin-Layer Chromatography.* TLC represents the initial qualitative screening procedure for urine. In this procedure, a silica gel coats a glass slide (chromatographic plate) to form a stationary phase. Through capillary action, the mobile phase ascends the plate and stops at a certain point. Application of a reagent allows the mobile phase spot to become visible. Measurement of the distance between the stationary phase (place of application of the unknown substance) and the mobile phase yields the Rf value. The place of specimen application marks the stationary phase, whereas the spot made visible by the reagent indicates the mobile phase.

TLC is economical in time, money, and effort. In addition, it produces qualitative results, identifying parent and metabolite compounds while leaving the specimen intact for further analyses. Its greatest disadvantage is its inaccuracy relative to other procedures. Frequently, the Rf values match several standards. To identify the substance correctly, confirmation by other procedures is required. GLC is used commonly to perform this function.

*Gas-Liquid Chromatography.* GLC involves the separation of the substance's liquid phase from its gas phase. First, a gas carries the volatile form of the unknown substance through a column packed with oil-coated inert material. Then the volatile phase of the substance is introduced. The gas that fills the column then carries the substance through the column. Because the unknown's physical properties determine the rate at which it travels, a strip chart at the opposite end of the column measures the rate in the form of peaks.

GLC produces both qualitative and quantitative results. Qualitative identification is obtained by measuring the length of time between introduction of the substance into the tube to the first peak formed, while the area underneath each peak quantifies the amount of the substance (Gough & Baker, 1983). GLC is also quick and relatively simple (Kalman & Clark, 1979).

Two primary limitations may exclude GLC as the procedure of choice. First, GLC is limited to substances that can be volatilized. For example, quantitative results regarding heroin may be obtained only by combining GLC with mass spectrography. Second, GLC analyses of some substances are expensive. The frequency of urinalyses in heroin programs precludes using GLC procedures for screening. However, it is often used as a follow-up procedure with samples found positive on TLC.

*High-Pressure Liquid Chromatography.* The last form of chromatography is HPLC, in which mobile solvent travels through a column packed with nonpolar beads while measurement occurs at the opposite end. The substance is detected by spectrophotometer or fluorometer. The primary advantage of HPLC over GLC and TLC is its ability to simultaneously separate multiple substances. However, the increased cost and complexity of procedure make it less useful (Gough & Baker, 1983).

*Enzyme-Linked and Fluorescent Immunoassays.* Other techniques that clinicians may wish to consider include immunoassays (Kalman & Clark, 1979) and radioimmunoassays (Khupulsup, Petchclai, & Chiewsilp, 1981), although these are not commonly used. More common techniques are enzyme-linked and fluorescent immunoassays (ELISA). Unlike the procedures previously described, ELISA procedures are easily conducted (Green,

1982). An enzyme-linked procedure, the enzyme multiple-immunoassay technique (EMIT), is available as a commercial kit. The ELISA procedures produce a sensitivity equal to other immunological procedures, a simple protocol, and quick results (Stewart, 1982). However, these results are only quasi-quantitative, and only one drug can be analyzed at a time. This prohibits assessment of polydrug usage and makes the results less useful for the clinician dealing with the user in the 1980s. Metabolites of parent drugs remain undetected, and the procedures are expensive. Therefore, accuracy, simultaneous detection of metabolites and other substances, and economy are sacrificed to increased usability (Pribor *et al.*, 1981; Stewart, 1982).

*Summary*

In summary, the appropriate use of clinical laboratory resources requires a working knowledge of available services. To place the interpretation of laboratory results in context demands consideration of the client's current and past physical, psychological, and social functioning. Assessment of body biochemistry has a crucial place in the assessment of opiate addiction. Much less value has been demonstrated in the assessment of physiological response to heroin and associated stimuli, and in several unusual biochemical measures associated with heroin use.

*Physiological Parameters of Addiction*

In addition to clinical laboratory tests, physiological responses may be used for assessment (Blachly, 1973; Wang, Kochar, Hasegawa, & Roh, 1982). For example, providing naloxone (a narcotic antagonist of which naltrexone is a long-acting variant) can be a test for use, because it will produce measurable withdrawal symptoms.

*Naloxone and Methadone Measures*

Naloxone-induced withdrawal is sometimes used to estimate the degree of opiate dependence (Wang *et al.*, 1982). The procedure involves careful observation of physical withdrawal signs after an 0.8-mg intramuscular injection of naloxone. Observation requires the tracking of three features of eight withdrawal signs. The features include the sign's presence or absence, severity rating, and time of onset. Each feature of a physical sign is given a rating, and these are combined to yield a value for each sign. The sum of values across all physical signs yields an overall withdrawal score. The physical signs include gooseflesh, vomiting, tremor, profuse sweating, restlessness, lacrimation, nasal congestion, and yawning. Calculation of the overall withdrawal score is done at the end of each of three successive 10-minute intervals following the injection of naloxone (Wang *et al.,* 1982). When the changes in physical withdrawal signs are observed over time, estimates of the severity of the addiction may be obtained.

Methadone can be used in a similar manner to estimate physical dependence (Aylett, 1982; McCaul *et al.,* 1982). After a 12- to 24-hour drug fast, physiological correlates associated with drug use are observed upon each dose of methadone. The initial dose is usually 10 mg given orally. If no physical signs appear within 1 minute, 10-mg oral allotments are given over successive 10-minute intervals.

Those addicted to heroin demonstrate a high cross-tolerance to methadone (Aylett, 1982). The dose of one of these drugs required to produce the physical signs associated with use, such as flushing, tachycardia, lowered systolic blood pressure, and sedation, will be related to the individual's experience with the other. Addicts usually show physical signs after the first dose whereas former addicts do not, unless the doses exceed the therapeutic levels (Aylett, 1982).

*Beta-Endorphin Measures*

Compared to nonaddicts, heroin users show elevated beta-endorphin levels (Goldstein, 1983). Endorphin assessment is impractical now, because of high costs, methodological flaws, and limited understanding of the endorphin system. One major problem is that endorphins are measured in peripheral circulation; it is unknown how these measures correlate with central endorphins. Because physical addiction intimately involves the endorphin system (Christie & Chesher, 1982), improving the assessment of endorphins holds considerable promise. As the understanding of physiological mechanisms of addiction increases, more accurate and objective measures may be developed (Goldstein, 1983). Although the future promise of endorphin assessment is obvious, it is less clear how assessment of another correlated physiological event, the T-lymphocyte, will proceed.

*T-Lymphocyte Measures*

A primary constituent of the immune system is the T-lymphocyte. Production and release of these cells are important in the defense against disease. These cells are released upon stimulation by a foreign substance, an antigen. When the immune system is compromised, lymphocyte production decreases. The degree of T-lymphocyte depression may develop into an important health assessment procedure in the future. Compared to nonabusers, heroin addicts require higher levels of antigens to stimulate lymphocyte production (Lazzarin *et al.,* 1984). However, the lymphocyte levels of heroin addicts progressing well on methadone therapy approach normal levels, as assessed by erythrocyte-rosette assays. Thus an inverse relationship exists between lymphocyte levels and heroin use. As use increases, lymphocyte function declines and improves when abuse subsides. The relationship of T-lymphocyte suppression to the spread of acquired immune deficiency syndrome (AIDS) in intravenous-drug-using populations is unknown at the time of this writing. Exploration of such issues should provide interesting information for both the assessment of addiction and the understanding of biochemical mechanisms in the maintenance of health. Although these developments are fascinating, they fail to shed much light on current means of treatment outcome monitoring.

## Treatment Outcome

Methods that have been used to attempt to predict treatment outcome fall into one of three general categories: clinical ratings, self-report procedures, and client variables. Most predictive efforts are based on client variables; sociodemographic, environmental, behavioral, cognitive, and affective parameters are often examined to determine which provide predictor variables. No one group of variables has proven to be a reliable predictor of drug use, relapse, or treatment outcome to date. Instead, numerous variables with questionable utility have been identified as correlates of use. Let us briefly examine some of these variables, while keeping in mind the necessary limitations of this broad-band generic assessment.

### Clinical Ratings

*Degree of Client Psychopathology*

Recently, a 10-point global rating of the degree of psychological adjustment upon admission was demonstrated to be the best single predictor of outcome for alcohol and drug abuse samples (McLellan, Woody, Luborsky, O'Brien, & Druley, 1982). In this study, individuals were rated as having low, moderate, or high levels of psychopathology. Those who were rated as having few psychiatric problems and who reported a history free of psychiatric problems were assigned to the low-psychopathology group. Individuals who demonstrated anxiety, depression, or confusion, and who reported having adjustment problems in the past, were assigned to the moderate-psychopathology group. The last group of individuals, the high-psychopathology group, demonstrated pronounced psychopathology (e.g., suicidal ideation, paranoia, or a history of recurring psychopathology).

In addition to the clinical ratings, subjects were assigned to programs designed to treat low, moderate, or high levels of psychopathology. "Treatment matching" was defined as assignment to treatment according to the client's level of diagnosis. For example, a client who demonstrated some anxiety and had a history of adjustment problems would be assigned to the moderate-psychopathology treatment group. "Treatment mismatching" involved placement of a client in a group addressing a level of psychopathology different from that with which he or she was diagnosed. The fit between the client's presenting problems and treatment condition was examined as a prognostic factor.

McLellan *et al.* (1982) demonstrated that subjects who were matched to treatment by degree of psychopathology were better adjusted during treatment and at a 6-month follow-up than subjects who were mismatched to treatment. Thus, treatment effectiveness was improved by matching clients to the most appropriate program, based on their psychiatric rating. It should be noted that treatment matching had an insignificant effect on the low-psychopathology group; individuals in this group responded well to treatment, regardless of the treatment assignment. By contrast, matching to treatment was particularly important for the moderate-psychopathology group: Individuals in this group who were matched to treatment demonstrated treatment progress and 6-month adjustment approaching the levels achieved by the low-psychopathology group, whereas those who were mismatched to treatment approached the adjustment parameters of the high-psychopathology group. Individuals assigned to the high-psychopathology group demonstrated the highest recidivism. Rehospitalization was twice as frequent among this population as in the low-psychopathology group. Among individuals in the high-psychopathology group, those assigned to extended inpatient programs had the most favorable outcome, whereas those in outpatient treatment showed the worst outcome. Thus, assessing degree of psychopathology as a continuum orthogonal to heroin addiction has shown great utility. It further underlines the fact that heroin addiction is not a unitary phenomenon.

*Treatment Variables*

Other studies have emphasized variables related to treatment per se as determinants of outcome. Craig and Rogalski (1982) found four variables that differentiated opiate detoxification program graduates from dropouts. The variables that were significantly higher among treatment dropouts were (1) staff absenteeism during treatment, (2) number of admissions during treatment, (3) prescription of methadone, and (4) primary therapist absenteeism. A discriminant functional analysis demonstrated the validity of these four variables when 88% of the sample were correctly classified as either treatment dropouts or graduates. Furthermore, 75% of an independent sample consisting of 25 treatment graduates and 25 dropouts were correctly identified using these four variables. Treatment graduates were three times more likely to remain drug-free than dropouts. Ironically, although this is an intriguing study on defining response to treatment, staff behavior provided two of the four key predictors of treatment success. Assessment and reporting of staff behavior is rare; perhaps it deserves more attention.

## Self-Report Measures

Another area that probably deserves more attention is self-report measurement. In general, health care providers and the legal system consider self-reports from heroin users invalid. Frequently, the likelihood of severe consequences for heroin use (i.e., being jailed or thrown out of a program) has precluded the possibility of accurate self-report, and the consequences for lying have been positive (i.e., complaining of nonexistent pain can produce a prescription for a narcotic). For this reason, procedures using collateral indices have been developed. Because self-report procedures represent the most direct way to assess self-administration of drugs, further development of reliable self-report, as in the work of Boudin et al. (1980) and Callahan, Price, and Dahlkoetter (1980), seems worthwhile. Relapse prevention cannot be developed as a therapeutic strategy without substantial involvement of self-monitoring, which, in turn, requires that severe punishers for accurate reports be kept to a minimum.

Alcohol assessment shares a similar legacy. During the early stages of assessment development, self-reports from alcoholics were considered biased. However, with improved procedures, self-reports of drinking problems have been demonstrated to be valid (Maisto, Sobell, & Sobell, 1979; Sobell & Sobell, 1978). Although these self-reports concern drinking history more than current drinking, the results are encouraging. Several factors increase the accuracy of self-reports among alcoholics: delivery of information in a structured interview; inclusion of items that specify frequency and drinking situations; use of collateral reports; and the addition of objective measures of blood alcohol content. Under these conditions, the accuracy of self-report increases, particularly when reports concern abstinence (Polich, 1982).

Assessment of narcotic use may be improved by incorporating similar features. Current research is beginning to address these issues in existing assessment procedures. A recent study examined the validity of self-reports from drug abusers (Maisto, Sobell, & Sobell, 1982–1983). Self-reports of recent drug- and alcohol-related arrests and hospital admissions occurring 1 year before and 1 year following admission to a drug treatment program were validated by general records. The other information sources included number of local arrests, hospital admissions, and driver's-license suspensions related and unrelated to drug–alcohol use. A high correlation was found between self-reports and the general records. The agreement between the two sources of information provides some proof of the validity of the self-report measures, but does not mean that truthful self-report can be expected when punishment for reporting of use is severe (e.g., probation violation program, expulsion, etc.).

One scale has been based on self-report when no punishment for truthfulness is involved: the Drug Abuse Screening Test (DAST; Skinner, 1982). This 28-item self-report measure is used for clinical screening and treatment evaluation. The items concern consequences of drug abuse and collectively produce a quantified index. Validation procedures have been conducted with objective criteria such as urinalysis, and internal consistency has been established (split-half reliability). The DAST appears to be a unidimensional scale that does not correlate well with measures of psychopathology, drug use during the past year, or background variables related to drug use. To date, the clinical utility of the scale has not been demonstrated.

### Client Variables

#### Sociodemographic Variables

Considerable effort has been invested in using sociodemographic variables as predictors of relapse, drug use, and treatment outcome. Recently, the application of these variables has been questioned (Whitman, Croughan, Miller, & McKay, 1982). Whitman and his associates (1982) suggest that it is necessary to restrict use of sociodemographic variables to the identification of high-risk populations. However, many investigators continue to use sociodemographic data to predict treatment outcome (Judson & Goldstein, 1982; McCaul et al., 1982).

In a prospective study, Judson and Goldstein (1982) examined which client variables predicted the outcome of methadone treatment at a 5-year follow-up. Treatment success was defined as being abstinent since treatment and having no drug-related arrests. To qualify for inclusion, subjects completed 6 months of a methadone treatment program. Only 17 of the 140 subjects were classified as successful abstainers. These 17 tended to be older married white males who had more years of work experience and education, and tended to be married to or living with a nonaddict (Judson & Goldstein, 1982). Lower levels of posttreatment use were associated with being employed and having an intact home in a later study as well (Haertzen *et al.,* 1983). Designing treatment programs to focus on just these high-potential clients would clearly be unethical; however, these data suggest some areas to target for strength building (e.g., employment, interpersonal skills, etc.).

Findings regarding education are conflicting. Several investigators (Judson & Goldstein, 1982; McCaul *et al.,* 1982) cite education as a variable that correlates negatively with use. However, in the Haertzen *et al.* (1983) study, addicted and heavy users were *more* likely to have completed high school.

A number of investigators (Haertzen *et al.,* 1983; McCaul *et al.,* 1982; Rounsaville *et al.,* 1982; Sackstein, 1983) emphasize employment as a primary predictor of treatment outcome. When program retention, psychological symptoms, illicit drug use, illegal activities, and occupational functioning are tested as predictors of treatment outcome, occupational functioning is the most informative predictor. Occupational status of the client also correlates with social functioning, psychological symptoms, illicit drug use, and criminal activity in those who continue to use heroin. Lower levels of use are associated with being employed (Haertzen *et al.,* 1983).

In general, employed individuals demonstrate better social adjustment, present fewer psychological symptoms, and are less likely to abuse opiates. Not surprisingly, employment after treatment is strongly associated with a history of employment. In fact, the more recent the history of employment prior to treatment, the more likely an individual is to be employed upon release. Therefore, vocational training, placement, and follow-up represent important treatment considerations. Employment is probably a "behavioral trap"; that is, the initial set of responses (committing oneself to the job) has considerable potential for determining where a person spends time, with whom, and what activities are available. Failure to address poor job attainment and employment maintenance skills probably contributes to the high recidivism of heroin abusers (Rounsaville *et al.,* 1982). Assessment of existing job skills and performance in a job-training program would appear to be important components of effective treatment programs.

*Reinforcement History*

The addict's learning history with the drug is probably important. Crawford, Washington, and Senay (1983) made an early attempt to explore learning history empirically by asking users and addicts what route of drug ingestion they used and the consequences of their continued use of drugs. Heavy users and addicts reported injecting heroin during their first experience, whereas moderate and light users tended to report snorting first. Addicts were more likely to have become high and to have enjoyed the experience during their first use, and were less likely to have experienced unpleasant side effects. On the other hand, light users preferred the relaxed social feelings and tended to dislike the "nod" (falling asleep after injecting). Compared to the light and moderate users, the heavy and addicted users were more likely to have tried heroin again within 1 month of the first experience. Reinforcement from the first experience was identified in another study as a reliable predictor across a wide variety of drug substances. The greater the reinforcement from the first experience with heroin, the more likely it was that use would continue (Haertzen *et al.,* 1983). However, because these ratings of liking were retrospective, some caution is needed in their interpretation.

*Behavioral Variables*

Illegal activities (Haertzen *et al.,* 1983; Judson & Goldstein, 1982); use of two or more illicit drugs, such as barbiturates, amphetamines, or LSD (Haertzen *et al.,* 1983); pattern of opiate use; and use of alcohol before and/or during treatment (Judson & Goldstein, 1982) have all been identified as predictors of opiate use and response to treatment. High criminal involvement before treatment correlates highly with poor treatment outcome. Use of illicit drugs (Haertzen *et al.,* 1983) or alcohol (Judson & Goldstein, 1982) during periods of abstinence and/or concomitantly with heroin is strongly associated with a poor prognosis.

One of the more unusual methods of inferring degree of drug use has employed conditioned verbal behavior (Haertzen & Ross, 1980a, 1980b). Subjects were required to identify words that had the highest association with being high. Three classes of words—"clean," "drug-relevant," and "names of opiates"—were presented to occasional, beginning, and heavy heroin users. Results indicated that differential conditioning had occurred across the three subject groups. Among beginners and those terminating use, clean words were most strongly associated with being high. Names of opiates produced the strongest response among occasional users, whereas drug-relevant words elicited strongest responses from those in the advanced stages of addiction. Although this finding probably has few applied implications, it is of theoretical interest because it relates physiological and cognitive variables by means of learning history.

*Cognitive Evaluations of Drugs*

Addicts and heavy, moderate, and light users all reported different private statements related to drug use in one study (Crawford *et al.,* 1983). First, the light users preferred other drugs over heroin. Many did not enjoy the high from heroin, whereas others feared addiction, overdose, or other negative consequences. Of the light-user sample, 92% reported that they were not likely to use heroin again. Crawford *et al.* (1983) distinguished heavy users from addicts on several cognitive variables. Heavy users intentionally limited use to avoid addiction and to give their bodies a break. Addicts (82.4%) were more likely to identify heroin as their preferred drug, as compared to heavy users (61.4%) and moderate users (11.8%); moderate users tended to identify alcohol or marijuana as their preferred drug. Moderate users also cited fear of addiction and negative physical consequences as primary deterrents of future use. Thus, degree of heroin use influences the cognitive behavior of users in ways that may have some assessment value for clinicians and researchers.

*Affective Variables*

Affective variables may also yield interesting information. Depression is commonly cited as a reason for using heroin (Dackis & Gold, 1983; McLellan *et al.,* 1982; McLellan, Woody, & O'Brien, 1979), yet some researchers (Rounsaville *et al.,* 1982; Uhde, Redmond, & Kleber, 1982) disagree. Simply put, the depression theory states that opiate addiction results from attempts to self-medicate endogenous depression (Dackis & Gold, 1983). The high prevalence of depression among addicts when they are opiate-free is cited as support. If depression underlies narcotic addiction, then assessment and treatment of depression should constitute a major thrust in intervention. On the other hand, major depression in addicts may be a product of the addiction process. Rounsaville *et al.* (1982) point out that pre-existing depressive illness would be an unlikely prompt for self-medication, because depression is a passive state incompatible with the work required to find and buy opiates. Still other investigators (McLellan *et al.,* 1979; McLellan *et al.,* 1982) attribute use of opiates to depression in conjunction with environmental factors. In these theories, the major determinants of substance abuse are thought to be concurrent environment and interpersonal problems that contribute to depressive symptoms. Environmental and interpersonal factors interact to produce effects that would not result from either alone (McLellan *et al.,* 1979).

Assessment of depression may be more informative in predicting relapse. Individuals having a history of psychiatric problems tend to respond poorly to treatment (Croughan, Miller, Mator, & Whitman, 1982). In addition, use of heroin increased among subjects without psychiatric histories when stressful events (e.g., a recent loss or separation, interpersonal difficulties) occurred (Judson & Goldstein, 1982; Krueger, 1981). In fact, the sources of stress appeared to be less important than the subjective experience of stress, suggesting that continued heroin use may be a conditioned response to a stressful environment (Hinson & Siegal, 1982; Judson & Goldstein, 1982). Such a conceptualization clearly fits with the treatment efforts of Boudin et al. (1980) and Callahan, Price, and Dahlkoetter (1980), as well as with Marlatt and Gordon's (1980) relapse prevention model.

Using similar reasoning, one group has proposed to measure addiction by symptoms. The Addiction Severity Index (McLellan, Luborsky, & O'Brien, 1980) is used to assess seven areas commonly affected by addiction. In a structured interview format, clients answer objective questions concerning the extent of various symptoms during the past 30 days and during their lifetime. Answers are quantified according to either frequency, duration, or intensity; thus clients' self-reports indicate the severity and importance of their problems (McLellan, Luborsky, & Erdlen, 1980; McLellan, Luborsky, & O'Brien, 1980). This scale would appear to have good potential for assessing heroin users in the future, although ongoing self-monitoring may provide more valuable information. Retrospective recall is not always as accurate in such efforts as ongoing self-monitoring.

## Discussion and Conclusion

There is clearly a need to identify potentially productive directions for further development of the assessment of heroin addiction. To date, personality assessment has dominated other approaches, but has failed to produce a clear picture of the addict or a useful strategy for effective treatment (Craig, 1982). Over the years, elaborate schemes for personality assessment have evolved into specific classification systems, but even these systems have not demonstrated their usefulness (G. H. Cohen, Griffin, & Wiltz, 1982). Meanwhile, much research still assumes that addictive behaviors develop from pathological personality. Seeing addiction as a disease that develops from an individual's inherent weakness leads to placing clients in a submissive and dependent role in treatment (Sackstein, 1983). Such treatment strategies reinforce feelings of helplessness by disregarding the development of skills that can enhance the reintegration of the addict into society.

In attempts to define the common personality factors of heroin addicts, extensive research has been conducted using the MMPI. These research efforts continue, despite the fact that the MMPI has consistently failed to discriminate heroin from polydrug users, or even to control for confounding variables that seriously cloud assessment in this area (Craig, 1979, 1982). Perhaps the greatest confounding variable in prior MMPI research has been ethnic background. Craig (1982) emphasizes the point that previously reported personality profiles are the product of race rather than actual drug habits. In addition, as noted earlier in this chapter, psychopathology demonstrated by MMPI decreases substantially when the test taker is instructed to respond to questions using only "straight" experience and to ignore experiences that occurred while under the influence of heroin (Glazer, 1976). Although these problems do not prove that the MMPI can never be useful in the assessment of heroin addiction, they underline the fruitlessness of such efforts to date. Given the ease of administering the MMPI, research in this area is likely to flourish, regardless of the problems demonstrated; however, more useful developments in assessment are likely to be generated by more intensive assessment practices.

Perhaps the most exciting developments in the assessment of heroin addiction have been provided by a behavior-analytic approach. Boudin's pioneering efforts (Boudin, 1972; Boudin *et al.,* 1980) focused on intensively training addicts to self-monitor events leading to increased probability of drug use. While this technology is probably easier to teach to a predominantly white, well-educated population, such as that worked with by Boudin, the technology has been used successfully with hard-core addicts with less education from minority communities (Callahan *et al.,* 1976; Callahan, Rawson, *et al.,* 1980; Rawson *et al.,* 1979). Self-monitoring of behavior chains provides the groundwork essential for treatment using Marlatt's relapse prevention model as well (Cummings, Gordon, & Marlatt, 1980; Marlatt & Gordon, 1980). Further development of applied and conceptual aspects of self-monitoring training promises to be productive, both for assessment and for treatment.

Self-monitoring training for assessment regards addiction as a product of idiosyncratic learning history. There is no presumption that all addicts share a collection of predisposing qualities. By assessing existing strengths and weaknesses, programs can focus on development of skills that individuals need to adjust to life in the "straight" community (e.g., communication, employment, and education), without needing to deal with the argument of how to define "narcotics addiction."

Trying to define "narcotics addiction" has proven a consistently thorny issue (Goldstein, 1983; Hinson & Siegal, 1982; Newman, 1983). There is no consensus on an acceptable operational definition of "addiction," although most definitions emphasize physiological withdrawal (Newman, 1983). Even this approach has serious problems, because numerous factors influence physiological indices of drug levels (Stewart, 1982). In fact, physiological indices of addiction are sometimes found in "nonaddicted" individuals, but not in "addicted" individuals (Newman, 1983). Some of these variations stem from biological differences between people, whereas others are the result of classically conditioned compensatory responses to drugs. These classically conditioned responses play a major role in the development of tolerance and posttreatment relapse (Hinson & Siegal, 1982). Use and addiction probably differ in terms of how much classical conditioning has occurred, and thus how strong the classically conditioned responses to drug-related stimuli are. In fact, there is strong evidence that "use" and "addiction" are separate and distinct phenomena in which environmental factors may be important. In a sample of 943 returning Vietnam veterans, Robbins *et al.* (1974) found that 50% had become addicted while in Vietnam, but that only 10% had continued their addiction in the United States. Thus, a radical change in environment appeared to help these men overcome heroin addiction. This finding underlines a need to study those who have used heroin but either have avoided addiction or have broken their addiction on their own.

Those who use heroin, yet have the skills to control their use, are rarely identified (Newman, 1983). To learn more about heroin addiction, it may be helpful to clearly discriminate controlled from uncontrolled users by studying interactions among the subjects, their environments, and self-administration. It may be fruitful to investigate the effects of membership within social groups that provide rituals and sanctions for use—a salient feature of "chippers" (Crawford *et al.,* 1983; Powell, 1973). Because social variables appear to have a great influence on the degree of use, idiosyncratic assessment of the individual "chipper'"s lifestyle seems most likely to be powerful. Conceptualizations of addiction are likely to become more useful if they are changed from simple physiological responses to an integration of many adaptive processes occurring from the cellular to the complex operant levels, especially noting Solomon's (1980) opponent-process theory. "Dependence," the product of addictive behavior, might also be a more useful term if it were to embrace the variety of factors from which uncontrolled use develops (Goldstein, 1983).

Addiction may most usefully be seen as the compulsive ingestion of a substance that occurs in the presence of both common and unusual environmental stimuli and that produces toxic effects on the user's biological or interpersonal functioning (in employment, family, education, or friendships). The addictive behavior is reinforced by immediate and complex biochemical changes. These biochemical changes are reinforcing not only because of their immediate positive effects (i.e., pleasure), but also because they overcome competing negative biochemical responses triggered in the body by cues associated with previous use. Each addict can be seen as an individual for whom certain stimuli, alone or in combination, result in virtually certain ingestion of that substance. Whereas forced abstinence from a substance sets the stage early in the process of becoming "clean" for extinction of the urges to use that are provoked by many common stimuli, the less common, complex stimuli found in stressful situations are likely to produce relapse. Over time, despite the fact that the former addict feels more confident, sudden "spontaneous remission" of the strong urges will recur in the presence of either weak or strong stimuli. The successful assessment of treatment for addiction will monitor the development of skills and factors that insulate the addict from high-risk environments (a "straight" job, "straight" friends, etc.) and the development of the ability to recognize high-risk stimulus patterns (stressors or reliable antecedents of use). With powerful assessment, powerful treatment can be close at hand.

## References

Aylett, P. (1982). Methadone dose assessment in heroin addiction. *International Journal of the Addictions, 17,* 1329-1336.

Babor, T. F., Meyer, R. E., Mirin, S. M., McNamee, H. B., & Davies, M. (1976). Behavioral and social effects of heroin self-administration and withdrawal. *Archives of General Psychiatry, 33,* 363-367.

Bassett, R. (1980). *Analytic procedures for therapeutic drug monitoring and emergency toxicology.* New York: Biomedical.

Blachly, P. H. (1973). Naloxone for the diagnosis in methadone. *Journal of the American Medical Association, 224,* 334-335.

Boudin, H. M. (1972). Contingency contracting as a therapeutic tool in the deceleration of amphetamine use. *Behavior Therapy, 3,* 604-605.

Boudin, H. M., Valentine, V. E., Ingraham, R. D., Brantley, J. M., Ruiz, M. R., Smith, G. G., Catlin, R. P., & Regan, E. J. (1977). Contingency contracting with drug abusers in the natural environment. *International Journal of the Addictions, 12,* 1-16.

Boudin, H. M., Valentine, V. E., Ruiz, M. R., & Regan, E. J. (1980). Contingency contracting for drug addiction: An outcome evaluation. In L. Sobell, M. C. Sobell, & E. Ward (Eds.), *Evaluating alcohol and drug abuse treatment effectiveness* (pp. 109-128). New York: Pergamon Press.

Brecher, E. M., *et al.* (1972). (Ed.). *Licit and illicit drugs.* Boston: Little, Brown.

Bridell, D. W., & Nathan, P. E. (1976). Behavioral assessment and modification with alcoholics: Current status and future trends. In M. Hersen, P. Miller, & R. Eisler (Eds.), *Progress in behavior modification* (Vol. 2, pp. 2-51). New York: Academic Press.

Callahan, E. J., Price, K. A., & Dahlkoetter, J. (1980). Behavioral treatment of drug abuse. In R. Daitzman (Ed.), *Clinical behavior therapy and behavior modification* (pp. 175-248). New York: Garland Press.

Callahan, E. J., & Rawson, R. A. (1980). Behavioral assessment of narcotic addiction and treatment outcome. In L. C. Sobell & M. B. Sobell (Eds.), *Treatment outcome evaluation in alcohol and drug abuse* (pp. 77-92). New York: Plenum Press.

Callahan, E. J., Rawson, R. A., Glazer, M., McCleave, B. A., & Arias, R. (1976). Comparison of two naltrexone treatment programs: Naltrexone alone versus naltrexone plus behavior therapy. In D. Julius & P. Renault (Eds.), *Narcotic antagonists: Naltrexone* (NIDA Research Monograph No. 9, pp. 150-157). Washington, DC: U. S. Government Printing Office.

Callahan, E. J., Rawson, R. A., McCleave, B. A., Arias, R. J., Glazer, M. A., & Liberman, R. P. (1980). Treatment of heroin addiction: Naltrexone alone and with behavior therapy. *International Journal of the Addictions, 15,* 795-807.

Christie, M. J., & Chesher, G. B. (1982). Physical dependence on physiologically released endogenous opiates. *Life Sciences, 36,* 1173-1178.

Cohen, G. H., Griffin, P. T., & Wiltz, G. M. (1982). Stereotyping as a negative factor in substance abuse treatment. *International Journal of the Addictions, 17,* 371-376.

Cohen, S. (1981). *The substance abuse problem.* New York: Hawthorne Press.

Craig, R. J. (1979). Personality characteristics of heroin addicts: A review of the empirical literature with critique—Part II. *International Journal of the Addictions, 14,* 607-626.

Craig, R. J. (1982). Personality characteristics of heroin addicts: A review of empirical research 1976-1979. *International Journal of the Addictions, 17,* 227-248.

Craig, R. J., & Rogalski, C. (1982). Predicting treatment dropouts from a drug abuse rehabilitation program. *International Journal of the Addictions, 17,* 641-653.

Crawford, G. A., Washington, M. C., & Senay, E. C. (1983). Careers with heroin. *International Journal of the Addictions, 18,* 701-715.

Croughan, J. L., Miller, J. P., Mator, A., & Whitman, B. Y. (1982). Psychiatric diagnosis and prediction of drug and alcohol dependence. *Journal of Clinical Psychiatry, 43,* 353-356.

Cummings, C., Gordon, J. R., & Marlatt, G. A. (1980). Relapse: Prevention and prediction. In W. R. Miller (Ed.), *The addictive behaviors* (pp. 291-321). Oxford: Pergamon Press.

Dackis, C. A., & Gold, M. S. (1983). Opiate addiction and depression—cause or effect? *Drug and Alcohol Dependence, 11,* 105-109.

Dito, W. R. (1981). Instrumentation and techniques for therapeutic drug monitoring. *Clinical Laboratory Medicine, 1,* 451-466.

Dole, V. P., & Nyswander, M. A. (1965). Medical treatment for diacetyl morphine (heroin) addiction. *Journal of the American Medical Association, 193,* 645-656.

Glazer, M. (1978). *The use of a modified instruction set with the MMPI with heroin addicts.* Unpublished doctoral dissertation, University of New Mexico.

Goldstein, A. (1983). Some thoughts about endogenous opioids and addiction. *Drug and Alcohol Dependence, 11,* 11-14.

Gough, T. A., & Baker, P. B. (1983). Identification of major drugs of abuse using chromatography: An update. *Chromatography, 21,* 145-53.

Green, S. (1982). Use of the toxicology laboratory. *Critical Care Quarterly, 2,* 19-23.

Haertzen, C. A., & Hooks, N. T. (1969). Changes in personality and subjective experience associated with the chronic administration and withdrawal of opiates. *Journal of Nervous and Mental Disease, 148,* 606-613.

Haertzen, C. A., Kocher, T. R., & Miyasata, K. (1983). Reinforcements from the first drug experience can predict later drug habits and/or addiction: Results with coffee, cigarettes, alcohol, barbiturates, minor and major tranquilizers, stimulants, marijuana, hallucinogens, heroin, opiates, and cocaine. *Drug and Alcohol Dependence, 11,* 147-165.

Haertzen, C. A., & Ross, F. E. (1980a). Degree of suppression of associations to the stages of addiction by the response of "high." *Journal of Psychology, 105,* 111-121.

Haertzen, C. A., & Ross, F. E. (1980b). Measurement of strong and weak drug habits and associations to stages of addiction, steps in drug-taking and drug effects in response to opiate names and nonopiate names. *American Journal of Drug and Alcohol Abuse, 7,* 175-191.

Hinson, R. E., & Siegal, S. (1982). Nonpharmacological bases of drug tolerance and dependence. *Journal of Psychosomatic Research, 26,* 495-503.

Judson, B. A., & Goldstein, A. (1982). Prediction of long-term outcome for heroin addicts admitted to a methadone maintenance program. *Drug and Alcohol Dependence, 10,* 383-391.

Kalman, S., & Clark, D. (1979). *Drug assay: The strategy of therapeutic drug monitoring.* New York: Masson.

Kaye, S. (1980). *Handbook of emergency toxicology* (4th ed.). Springfield, IL: Charles C Thomas.

Khupulsup, K., Petchclai, B., & Chiewsilp, D. (1981). Comparison of hemagglutination inhibition test and radioimmunoassay for morphine in urine. *Journal of the Medical Association in Thailand, 64,* 72-75.

Krueger, D. W. (1981). Correlates of relapse of clients in a methadone maintenance program. *Journal of Human Stress, 7,* 3-8.

Krueger, R. A. (1981). A method for time domain filtering using computerized fluroscopy. *Medical Physics, 8,* 466-470.

Lazzarin, A., Mella, L., Trombini, M., Uberti-Foppa, C., Franzetti, F., Mazzoni, G., & Galli, M. (1984). Immunological status in heroin addicts: Effects of methadone maintenance treatment. *Drug and Alcohol Dependence, 13,* 117-123.

Maisto, S. A., Sobell, L. C., & Sobell, M. B. (1982-1983). Corroboration of drug abusers' self-reports through the use of multiple data sources. *American Journal of Drug and Alcohol Abuse, 9,* 301-308.

Maisto, S. A., Sobell, L. C., & Sobell, M. B. (1979). Comparison of alcoholics' self reports of drinking behavior with reports of collateral informants. *Journal of Consulting and Clinical Psychology, 47,* 106-112.

Marlatt, G. A., & Gordon, J. R. (1980). Determinants of relapse: Implications for the maintenance of behavioral change. In P. Davidson & S. Davidson (Eds.), *Behavioral medicine: Changing health lifestyles* (pp. 410-452). New York: Brunner/Mazel.

Martin, W. R., Jasinski, D. R., & Mansky, P. A. (1973). Naltrexone, an antagonist for the treatment of heroin dependence. *Archives of General Psychiatry, 28,* 784-791.

McCaul, M. E., Stitzer, M. L., Bigelow, G. E., & Liebson, I. A. (1982). Initial opiate use and treatment outcome in methadone detoxification patients. In L. S. Harris (Ed.) *Problems of drug dependence, 1982* (NIDA Research Monograph No. 43, DHHS Publication No. ADM 83-1264, pp. 280-286). Washington, DC: U. S. Government Printing Office.

McLellan, A. T., Luborsky, L., & Erdlen, F. (1980). The addiction severity index. In E. Goltheil, A. T. McLellan, & K. A. Druley (Eds.). *Substance abuse and psychiatric illness* (pp. 178-194). New York: Pergamon Press.

McLellan, A. T., Luborsky, L., & O'Brien, C. P. (1980). Improved evaluation instrument for substance abuse patients. *Journal of Nervous and Mental Disease, 168,* 26-33.

McLellan, A. T., Woody, G. E., Luborsky, L., O'Brien, C. P., & Druley, K. A. (1982). Increased effectiveness of drug abuse treatment from patient-program matching. In L. S. Harris (Ed.), *Problems of drug dependence, 1982* (NIDA Research Monograph No. 43, DHHS Publication No. ADM 83-1264, pp. 335-342). Washington, DC: U. S. Government Printing Office.

McLellan, A. T., Woody, G. E., & O'Brien, C. P. (1979). Development of psychiatric illness in drug abusers. *New England Journal of Medicine, 301,* 1310-1314.

NcNamee, H. B., Mirin, S. M., Kuehnie, J. C. & Meyer, R. E. (1976). Affective changes in chronic opiate use. *British Journal of Addiction, 3,* 275-280.

Mello, N. K., & Mendelson, J. H. (1965). Operant analysis of drinking patterns in chronic alcoholics. *Nature, 206,* 43-46.

Meyer, R. E., Mirin, S. M., Altman, J. L., & McNamee, B. (1976). A behavioral paradigm for the evaluation of narcotic antagonists. *Archives of General Psychiatry, 3,* 371-377.

Mirin, S. M., Meyer, R. E., & McNamee, B. (1976). Psychopathology and mood during heroin use: Acute versus chronic effects. *Archives of General Psychiatry, 33,* 1503-1508.

Nathan, P. E., & O'Brien, J. S. (1971). An experimental analysis of the behavior of alcoholics and normal drinkers during prolonged experimental drinking: A necessary precursor to behavior therapy? *Behavior Therapy, 2,* 495-476.

Newman, R. G. (1983). The need to redefine addiction. *The New England Journal of Medicine, 308,* 1096-1098.

Platt, J. J., & Labate, C. (1976). *Heroin addiction: Theory, research and treatment.* New York: Wiley.

Polich, M. (1982). The validity of self-reports in alcoholism. *Addictive Behaviors, 7,* 123-132.

Powell, D. H. (1973). A pilot study of occasional heroin users. *Archives of General Psychiatry, 28,* 586-594.

Pribor, H., Morrel, G., & Schen, G. (1981). *Drug monitoring and pharmacokinetic data.* Park Forest, IL: Pathotox.

Rawson, R. A., Glazer, M. A., McCleave, B. A., Arias, R. D., Flores, W., McCann, M. J., Liberman, R. P., & Callahan, E. J. (1979). Naltrexone and behavior therapy for heroin addiction. In N. Krasnegor (Ed.), *Behavioral analysis and treatment of substance abuse* (NIDA Research Monograph No. 25, pp. 26–43). Washington, DC: U. S. Government Printing Office.

Robbins, L. N., Davis, D. H., & Nurco, D. N. (1974). How permanent was Vietnam drug addiction? *American Journal of Public Health, 64* (Suppl.), 38–43.

Rounsaville, B. J., Tierney, T., Crit-Cristoph, K., Weissman, M. W., & Kleber, H. D. (1982). Predictors of outcome in treatment of opiate addicts: Evidence for the multidimensional nature of addicts' problems. *Comprehensive Psychiatry, 23,* 462–478.

Sackstein, E. (1983). Rehabilitation of drug dependent persons: Where are we going wrong? *Drug and Alcohol Dependence, 11,* 77–81.

Schaefer, H. H., Sobell, M. B., & Mills, K. C. (1971). Baseline drinking behaviours in alcoholics and social drinkers: Kinds of sips and sip magnitude. *Behaviour Research and Therapy, 9,* 23–27.

Skinner, H. A. (1982). The Drug Abuse Screening Test. *Addictive Behaviors, 7,* 363–371.

Sobell, M. B., & Sobell, L. C. (1978). *Behavioral treatment of alcohol problems.* New York: Plenum.

Solomon, R. L. (1980). The opponent process theory of acquired motivation: The costs of pleasure and benefits of pain. *American Psychologist, 35,* 691–712.

Steiner, C. (1971). *Games alcoholics play.* New York: Ballantine.

Stewart, D. C. (1982). The use of the clinical laboratory in the diagnosis and treatment of substance abuse. *Pediatric Annals, 11,* 669–682.

Uhde, T. W., Redmond, D. E., & Kleber, H. D. (1982). Psychosis in the opioid addicted patient: Assessment and treatment. *Journal of Clinical Psychiatry, 43,* 240–247.

Wang, R. I., Kochar, C., Hasegawa, A. T., & Roh, B. L. (1982). Initial methadone dose in treating opiate addiction. *International Journal of the Addictions, 17,* 357–363.

Whitman, B. Y., Croughan, J. P., Miller, J. P., & McKay, J. (1982). Nonpsychiatric prediction of narcotic dependence: A prospective study with a five year follow up. *International Journal of the Addictions, 17,* 473–491.

Wikler, A. (1952). A psychodynamic study of a patient during experimental self-regulated readdiction to morphine. *Psychiatric Quarterly, 26,* 270–293.

# VI

## ASSESSMENT IN THE EVALUATION OF TREATMENT PROCESS AND OUTCOME

# 14

# ASSESSMENT OF
# TREATMENT OUTCOME

STEPHEN A. MAISTO

*Brown University Medical School*
*Butler Hospital*

GERARD J. CONNORS

*Research Institute on Alcoholism, Buffalo, New York*

## Introduction

Since publication of the esteemed "Boulder model" of clinical psychology (Raimy, 1950), many people have considered treatment evaluation research to be among the unique contributions that psychologists have to make to the advancement of mental health services. (The idea that clinicians should be scientists too has also been adopted by other mental health disciplines, such as psychiatry and social work.) This idea has been put into practice in the conduct of research on the psychological treatment of a variety of disorders, and the addictive behaviors have been no exception. Indeed, in the last 20 years there have been numerous published evaluations of treatment for the addictions, and many of these are of high scientific merit. Unfortunately, poorly designed and conducted studies still appear in journals, and it can only be assumed that the unpublished research is of even lesser quality. Furthermore, much of the scholarly work on the effectiveness of treatment for the addictive and other disorders is not written with a slant toward the practitioner. As a result, even if what was preached were uniformly good, it would rarely get practiced.

The purpose of this chapter, therefore, is to articulate the basic assumptions and methods of treatment outcome research in the addictive behaviors. Although the conceptual and practical points that are discussed here are of importance to anyone with an interest in treatment research on the addictions, practitioners are the primary audience for this chapter. The following section concerns the definition and scope of treatment outcome, assumptions about the utility of treatment research for clinical practice, and practical considerations in the conduct of treatment research in different clinical settings. It is important to note that the points made apply to the evaluation of treatment of any psychological (i.e., behavioral, emotional, cognitive) disorder, and not just the addictions. The next section focuses on models of the addictive behaviors and their implications for treatment outcome research on these behaviors. In the last conceptual section, there are descriptions of two general paradigms for evaluating psychological treatments, as well as a critique of them. This section is followed by a switch to methodology, with a discussion of major methodological points in the conduct of treatment outcome research on the addictions. Where relevant, the points are illustrated by describing published studies on addictive behaviors.

## Treatment Outcome Evaluation

The evaluation of treatment outcome is concerned with the measurement of treatment effectiveness (Kazdin, 1983). This translates in practice to assessing an individual's functioning on some level (physiological, psychological, or behavioral) at some time after the beginning of treatment, usually after formal treatment has been terminated. The objective, of course, is to establish as clearly as possible the connections between changes in functioning and the treatment(s) under evaluation.

It is assumed in many respected circles that systematic measurement of treatment outcome results in healthy clinical practice. For example, Bloom and Fischer (1982) have argued, "The essence of successful clinical practice is ability to demonstrate that what we have done (our intervention) has worked (is effective). Probably the most productive way of assessing whether or not our practice is successful, then, is through use of systematized, objective methods of research that are capable of being repeated (replicated) by others" (p. 16). In a similar vein, Barlow, Hayes, and Nelson (1984) have described three "primary" and related activities of practitioners. These are (1) the consumption of clinical research from the large research centers and application of that newfound knowledge; (2) the use of systematic, empirical methods to evaluate the effectiveness of the interventions that are used clinically in order to increase accountability; and (3) the initiation of research in the clinical setting and the publication of the resulting data to the scientific community. Through these activities, according to Barlow *et al.,* the practitioner becomes accountable for the results of the intervention that he or she has applied. Such accountability is the product of knowledge of what treatment techniques have empirical support for their effectiveness. This knowledge is acquired by using objective methods of measuring behavioral change. It is unmistakable from these comments that the research-oriented clinical practice is a highly valued enterprise because of its assumed benefits to enhanced psychological and behavioral functioning for patients.

Although few practitioners and mental health professionals in general would disagree that there is value in clinical research of all kinds, the absence of essentially full-time practitioners among those who generate clinical research data is conspicuous. Many wonder aloud why, even while the answer is obvious: With all the demands on the time of many practitioners, who has time for research? Although this reason is intuitively acceptable, the discrepancy between beliefs about and the practice of clinical research can be analyzed more specifically and productively. There have been some recent excellent attempts at such an analysis. For example, Barlow *et al.* (1984) have discussed some possible reasons why practitioners tend not to use or initiate clinical research. The authors suggest that the relevance of the published clinical research for the practitioner is greatly diminished by traditional methods in design and assessment, which have stressed the statistical (not clinical) significance of differences among group means (not individual performance). Of course, when working with any one patient, the practitioner is not concerned with the functioning of the "average" individual from a group of individuals who may or may not seem to have characteristics similar to the patient in question. Rather, the practitioner is concerned with what to do with *that patient.* As a result, many of the publications on treatment outcome may appear, at least in the short run, not to be pertinent to what the practitioner has to know.[1]

Barlow *et al.* (1984) have also proposed several reasons why practitioners do not seem to conduct much of their own clinical research. As alluded to above, one reason is that traditional research methodology simply is impractical for the majority of service settings, as the accumulation of large groups of subjects is beyond their resources (see also Bloom & Fischer, 1982). Also related to traditional methodology is the requirement of administering "fixed" treatment interventions to each patient, regardless of his or her individual characteristics. The practitioner, on the other hand, gears interventions to the individual patient. Therefore, according to these two ideas, practitioners do not do clinical research for the same reasons that they do not use the research that is done. Another reason cited by Barlow *et al.* is the need to use evermore sophisticated measurement instrumentation, at least for investigating some clinical disorders, if it is assumed to be essential to keep up with the latest developments in measurement technology.

The last proposed reason for practitioners' low rate of participation in

1. An important trend in recent work published by clinical researchers is their addressing the question of group means and individual performance. For example, Jacobson and his colleagues (Jacobson, Follette, & Revenstorf, 1984; Jacobson, Follette, Revenstorf, Baucom, *et al.,* 1984) have made significant contributions to understanding individuals' outcomes in group studies of behavioral marital therapy. Similarly, Foy, Nunn, and Rychtarik (1984) and M. B. Sobell and Sobell (1976) provided individual patients' drinking outcome profiles in their group studies of treatments for alcoholism.

clinical research is ethical concerns (Kazdin, 1980). Although, in the extreme, the researcher is concerned first with obtaining the best data from a scientific viewpoint, the practitioner's first concern is the welfare of his or her patient. For example, practitioners may feel very strongly about applying treatments of unestablished efficacy or about withholding treatment of any kind, at least for some time—either of which is often required in conducting treatment outcome measurements.

In summary, this section sets the stage for our saying that we hold strongly the value that good clinical research makes good clinical practice, but that we also recognize the obstacles to research and the use of clinical research data that many practitioners may face. These problems apply to mental health professionals in general; those who specialize in treating the addictive behaviors are no exception. Part of the task in this chapter's last major section, which concerns methodology, is to discuss research options that may be implemented in a range of service settings where the addictive behaviors are treated.

### Models of the Addictive Behaviors and Implications for Treatment Outcome Evaluation

The existence of numerous and often conflicting models and theories of the disorders that are treated has been a long-standing and continuing problem in the mental health professions. Furthermore, decisions to choose among different models or theories can rarely be made on an empirical basis. It would appear that some conceptual framework to organize models would help clinicians and researchers in their efforts to improve their level of understanding about psychological and behavioral problems and the efficacy of their treatment. Brickman and his colleagues (1982) have provided a conceptual framework to organize models of helping and coping that can be applied to models of the addictive behaviors.

Brickman *et al.* (1982) have created a four-category classification, based on responsibility for development of a problem and responsibility for its solution. In this connection, the four categories of models emerge from all combinations of whether people are responsible for a problem's development and whether they are responsible for its solution. Furthermore, it is argued (p. 369) that the models are internally coherent and that each model is in some way not compatible with the other three. Brickman *et al.* call the four models the "moral model," the "compensatory model," the "medical model," and the "enlightenment model."

According to the moral model, people are viewed as responsible for both the development and the solution of their problems. Therefore, external agents see neither an obligation nor an ability to help afflicted individuals with their problems. Rather, it is up to the person with the problem to exert willpower to get back on track. Historically, the moral model has been prominent in accounting for and determining policy for treatment of alcohol and other drug abuse and obesity (Maisto & Caddy, 1981).

The compensatory model asserts that people are not blamed for the development of problems, but are seen as responsible for their solution. Accordingly, people have to compensate for handicaps or obstacles resulting from untoward circumstances and events by making extra or special efforts, alone or with the help of others. Responsibility for using any of the resources made available by others is seen to lie with the individual.

In the medical model, people are not responsible for the development or the solution of their problems. The most obvious application of the medical model is in the theory and practice of treating physical illnesses. However, the model more generally applies to any problem that is seen as the result of uncontrolled (and uncontrollable) forces. People who are seen as ill are expected to try to get well (if possible), and the proper way to do this is through following the advice of experts (e.g., doctors) in solving the problem.

In the enlightenment model, people are blamed for the development of problems but are not responsible for their solution. The model's name is based on the perceived need to educate (enlighten) people about the nature of their problems, and then to do whatever is necessary to solve them. Because problem solutions are not seen as the responsibility of individuals, they may require submission to strict social controls.

As can be surmised, each of the four models of coping and helping has advantages and disadvantages in application. These are reviewed in detail by Brickman et al. (1982). For the purpose of this chapter, however, the question is how the framework helps to clarify models of the addictions. Such clarification should help to guide the design and conduct of treatment outcome assessment. This assertion may be illustrated by comparing models of addiction with regard to their definitions of the problem, proposed etiologies, treatments, and treatment goals (see Siegler & Osmond, 1974).

Maisto and Caddy (1981) have shown that a wide range of models has been proposed for each of several addictions—alcohol and other drug abuse, cigarette smoking, and obesity—and that these models are similar across addictions. As a consequence, an illustration that compares medical and compensatory models of alcoholism will serve well in thinking about all these addictive behaviors, because of the popularity of these models and the contrast they afford. Table 14-1 presents such a comparison; it shows the Alcoholics Anonymous (AA) model as most closely resembling Brickman et al.'s (1982) medical model, and the behavioral/social learning model as most closely resembling their compensatory model.

There are several major points in measuring treatment outcome that

TABLE 14-1.    Illustrative Comparisons of Selected Models of Alcoholism

| Model of alcoholism | Dimension | | | |
|---|---|---|---|---|
| | Definition | Etiology | Goal | Treatment |
| The Alcoholics Anonymous (AA) model | Alcoholism is an incurable disease that manifests itself as an inability to drink normally; an alcoholic is one whose life has become intolerable because of alcohol. | Alcoholics are emotionally impaired and drink to compensate for this. Later their lives become intolerable because of alcohol. | Permanent abstinence from alcohol. | Permanent involvement in AA. |
| The behavioral/ social learning model | Alcohol use is a voluntary, learned behavior that exists on a continuum from light, nonproblem drinking to heavy, maladaptive use of alcohol, called alcohol abuse. | Alcohol abuse is determined by the interaction of biological, psychological, social, and environmental factors over time. All users of alcohol can potentially become alcohol abusers. | A range of nonproblem drinking goals, from abstinence to moderate drinking, is possible. What goal is chosen depends on an individual's history and current conditions. | Multivariate in approach, treatment is determined individually according to the causal and maintaining factors in abusive drinking. |

*Note.* The comparison dimensions are largely adapted from Siegler, Osmond, and Newell (1968).

may be deduced from Table 14-1. Two of these concern *what* is measured and *how* it is measured. The models of alcoholism, consistent with their assumptions about the individual's responsibility in etiology and treatment, are in stark contrast on these questions. A look across the board at AA suggests that, for strong adherents of this model, alcohol consumption is the most important question about a patient's behavior, with little competition from other behaviors for that position. Therefore, though it may be useful to gather information about other aspects of the individual's functioning, the *sine qua non* of outcome is drinking behavior. Accordingly, outcome evaluations must include some measure of drinking behavior to give any information about treatment effectiveness. More importantly, this strong AA position suggests that it is not critical to know how much a patient has been drinking, but whether he or she has been drinking at all. It follows that measures may be designed as nominal scales, and a review of the alcoholism treatment outcome literature shows that traditionally this is what outcome researchers have done (Maisto & McCollam, 1980). A typical measure of drinking behavior has been to code the patient's drinking in reference to some period of time as "abstinent," "improved" (drinking, but some quantity less than at pretreatment), or "not improved." As can be seen, these are categorical, mutually exclusive codings. Whereas the vast majority of measures of drinking behavior that have been published have been based on patients' self-reports, more recently used physiological measures would also be useful to the researcher adhering to the AA position, especially as supplements to self-reports. For example, measures of liver functioning, such as serum glutamic–oxaloacetic transaminase (SGOT) and gamma-glutamyl transpeptidase (GGT), provide evidence about whether the patient has engaged in recent heavy drinking (Ersner-Hershfield, Sobell, & Sobell, 1980).[2]

In the behavioral approach, the measurement of drinking is required for outcome assessment, but measures of other areas of functioning are also seen as part of good outcome evaluation. This follows from the view that an understanding of the causes and effective treatments of alcohol abuse requires looking at alcohol use in the context of the individual's internal and external environment. Therefore, drinking behavior is not a sole focus, but one of a series of variables requiring measurement. In addition, drinking behavior and other variables are best measured with continuous scales, because information on the extent and consequences of alcohol use—not merely whether the individual has consumed any alcohol at all—is required for assessment of drinking outcomes.

Applying the Brickman et al. (1982) framework to two models of alcohol abuse shows how two contrasting models of coping and help have different implications for the ways in which outcome is evaluated. Of course, researchers and clinicians can apply the Brickman et al. scheme to other models of the addictive behaviors to clarify their assumptions about such behavior. In this connection, although explicit articulation of beliefs about behavior is preferable in the planning of outcome studies, the influences of beliefs about behavior on outcome studies are often implicit. From the viewpoints of science and practice, it would be an advance if all outcome researchers in the addictions (and other specialty areas) clearly presented their theoretical beliefs about the behavior(s) they are treating before presenting data. It would make their data far more interpretable for all.

---

2. It is often overlooked that, at least according to hypotheses about etiology, personality appraisal could also be justified as an important outcome factor by AA adherents (see Table 14-1). This has not emerged in the literature, probably because of what the AA model calls an "alcoholic," what motivates his or her drinking once physical dependence has been incurred, and what point the alcoholic typically has to hit ("bottom" and often physical dependence) before he or she is ready to benefit from treatment. Another possibility is the strong emphasis in AA on personal anonymity.

## A Note on Multivariate Models of the Addictive Behaviors

Many of the models of the addictive behaviors that have been proposed through the years are examples of what Schwartz (1982) has called "formistic" and "mechanistic" models. According to Schwartz, such beliefs about behavior "represent concrete, relatively binary, single-category, single-cause approaches to viewing health and illness" (1982, pp. 1042–1043). However, there has recently been a trend among some prominent researchers and clinicians away from single-cause explanations and toward "contextual" and "organistic" models of health and illness. Such explanations are based on the idea that events emerge from the interaction over time of multiple causes. Another way of viewing this is that wholes (e.g., the patterns that we label the addictive behaviors) emerge from the dynamic interaction between the individual (and his or her "subsystems") and the environment. As this model is applied to the addictive behaviors, it is essential to look at how an individual with a unique biological, psychological, and behavioral makeup has interacted with specific environmental stressors, if researchers and clinicians are to understand the phenomena that are called addictive behaviors. The recent trend in some circles toward consideration of multivariate models is not just of academic interest for this chapter. As Maisto and Caddy (1981) and H. J. Shaffer and Neuhaus (1984) have shown, recent models of the addictions have emphasized the multivariate approach. Table 14-1, for example, shows that the current behavioral model of alcohol abuse (and other addictive behaviors) takes a multivariate perspective.

Taking a multivariate perspective has definite consequences for measuring treatment outcome: It requires the assessment and interpretation of variables representing multiple levels (biological, psychological, environmental) in interaction over time. In practice, this suggests that assessments for treatment planning and evaluation must cover biological, psychological, and social factors. Another critical point for measuring outcome is the assumption that treatment is *only one* environmental event that interacts with the person and other elements of his or her environment.

One of the best-articulated cases for a multivariate perspective in the addictive behaviors is Pattison, Sobell, and Sobell's (1977) discussion of alcohol dependence. According to this perspective, alcohol dependence is a health problem that arises from different drinking patterns and their adverse physical, psychological, and/or social consequences. As such, alcohol problems are often associated with other life problems. Furthermore, diverse populations of individuals who drink can potentially experience alcohol problems. Finally, the development and maintenance of alcohol problems follow variable patterns over time (Pattison *et al.,* 1977, p. 4). These major points serve to contrast the multivariant perspective with traditional models of alcoholism and make clear the need for assessment to cover multiple areas of functioning, not just drinking behavior.

## Models of Treatment Outcome and Its Assessment

The measurement of treatment outcome is influenced not only by the model of behavior that the evaluator holds, but also by the model of treatment outcome that is followed. (See Lambert, 1983, for an excellent discussion of this point that centers on the psychotherapy research area.) By far the most prevalent model of treatment outcome used in designing evaluations is based on procedures associated with the evaluation of drugs or vaccines (i.e., with the evaluation of medical treatments). Examples in the addictions would be evaluations of the effectiveness of such drugs as disulfiram (Antabuse) or methadone in eliminating target substance use. Cronbach (1982) and others (Moos & Finney, 1983) have called this the "summative" model of treatment outcome evaluation, and it has provided the guidelines for evaluations of psychological and behavioral interventions since the earliest days of psychotherapy research (Wilkins, 1984).

As Cronbach (1982) notes, the summative model is suited to the evaluation of "fixed" treatments. If some medical intervention, such as a new drug, is tried and proved successful, the intervention is adopted. On the other hand, if the intervention fails, then the investigator typically returns to the laboratory to attempt new chemical syntheses that may work. These decision rules seem simple because, relatively speaking, they are. Their straightforwardness is possible because whatever data are gathered in the evaluation are not likely to be powerfully affected by social setting or institutional factors. In fact, the only qualifier on the data is likely to be normal variability in the biological response of individuals to the intervention. If research is well designed, such interactions can be assessed and described.

The summative model has probably been adapted and maintained among social and behavioral scientists because it is the apparent underpinning of placing a high scientific value on treatment outcome data. This is achieved through an emphasis in the summative model on establishing relationships between cause (i.e., the treatment intervention) and effect (i.e., outcome). In this view, therefore, other variables that may be correlated with treatment effects are nuisance variables, which preferably are "controlled out" through randomization. Such a view is apparent in many publications on clinical research in the addictions. For example, in a widely cited article, Nathan and Lansky (1978) have suggested that *a useful treatment* of the addictions should be powerful enough to induce an extreme difference (in outcomes) between treated and untreated groups. Ogborne (1980) has noted that drug and alcohol abusers make extensive use of treatment resources, and that events outside of treatment (e.g., change in marital status, loss of job, illness, or death of friends) are likely to affect prognosis; such events are viewed as "confounding" the interpretation of the effects of treatment.

A model of treatment outcome that is in the minority but becoming increasingly popular is called the "systems model" (Moos & Finney, 1983). It is important to note that the systems model of outcome closely parallels the multivariate models of illness and health that have been described earlier. According to the systems model, an understanding of outcome requires an appraisal of the individual's total life (biological, psychological, and environmental) context. This differs from the traditional view because treatment is seen as not an entity unto itself that "causes" outcome. Rather, it is but one event in the context of many that interact over time. Therefore, treatment's "effects" may be established only in view of the other variables that may also influence behavior.

The systems perspective of outcome is important because, as Cronbach (1982) has noted, social and behavioral interventions are not "fixed" like their medical counterparts and are not independent of setting in which they are presented. Accordingly, "a treatment effect results from the interaction of population, treatment, and setting; therefore, the quest for an effect 'free and clear' of other effects is unrealistic" (Cronbach, 1982, p. 32). This point is currently being recognized and discussed as it pertains to the addictive behaviors. For example, Colvin and Crist (1983) have criticized behavioral researchers' tendency to accept the assumption that maintenance of weight loss following treatment of obesity is only a function of treatment. The problem with this assumption is that, taken alone, a relatively short-term (e.g., 3-month) treatment program for obesity is a small force, compared to biological and social factors that affect eating. Another notable area in which the influence of factors other than treatment on outcome is being recognized is research on relapse and spontaneous remission of the addictive behaviors (e.g., Cummings, Gordon, & Marlatt, 1980; Donovan & Chaney, 1985; Krueger, 1981; Shiffman, 1982; Tuchfeld, 1981). These and other studies have suggested strongly that intrapersonal and social-environmental variables combine with treatment to influence outcome.

Finally, there is the "stage approach," another strategy for conceptualizing behavior change processes and treatment outcomes. This approach focuses on the varied processes that underlie the modification (or non-modification) of addictive behavior patterns (e.g., Marlatt, 1985; Prochaska & DiClemente, 1984). An example of this approach is the creative and sophisticated work of Prochaska and DiClemente (1983, 1984). These researchers have identified four central stages of change. The first stage, "precontemplation," is defined as the period in which the patient is either unaware of the problem or, if aware, is not seriously considering changing his or her behavior. The stage of "contemplation" is characterized by an awareness of the problem. Patients in this stage typically are more distressed and concerned than those in the precontemplation stage. The third stage, "labeled action," includes the occurrence of behavioral change. The fourth stage includes maintenance of gains occurring during the action phase and the avoidance of relapse (which represents a fifth stage for those who return to a pattern of problem behavior). It is worth noting that Prochaska and DiClemente (1984) view these stages as invariant. Also, these stages can account for behavior change that occurs with or without clinical intervention.

Another component of the Prochaska and DiClemente (1984) model includes the processes by which change is thought to occur. Prochaska and DiClemente have identified 10 processes of behavior change: "consciousness raising," "self-liberation," "social liberation," "self-reevaluation," "environmental reevaluation," "counterconditioning," "stimulus control," "reinforcement management," "dramatic relief," and "helping relations." Importantly, these processes can be applied to different degrees during each of the stages noted above. For example, Prochaska and DiClemente (1983) found that smokers in the precontemplation stage were significantly lower than smokers in the other stages on 8 of the 10 process variables. Prochaska and DiClemente (1984) have also noted that the consciousness-raising process is pronounced during the contemplation phase and that self-reevaluation is a core element in moving from the contemplation to action stages.

A number of implications for design and measurement of treatment outcome follow from Prochaska and DiClemente's (1984) model. One example, among others, is that the model suggests that processes of change are at least as important as their products. Therefore, a major emphasis in evaluation design should be on capturing the individual's *experience* (a cognitive variable) of changes in addictive behaviors over time. Accordingly, it is important to obtain continuous measures of behavior when possible, and assessments should be completed relatively frequently.

In summary, each of the models of behavior and behavior change discussed in this section has implications for the evaluation of treatment and posttreatment functioning. Taking any particular approach has consequences for the design and assessment of treatment outcome, some of which have been cited earlier. These ramifications are elaborated below in parts of the discussion on methodological points in measuring treatment outcome in the addictive behaviors.


## Methodological Points in Conducting Treatment Outcome Evaluation

A variety of methodological points should be considered in measuring treatment outcome. These points cannot be overemphasized, because diligence in addressing them helps to determine the degree of our understanding of the relationship between clinical interventions and a person's general level of functioning. This section consists of an overview of major factors and their relative importance in comprehensive treatment outcome evaluations in the addictive behaviors. Ways to avoid methodological pit-falls are also described.

### Experimental Design

The type of information derived from treatment outcome studies depends in part on the experimental design used to evaluate interventions. The two basic alternatives available to researchers are between-subjects and within-subject designs. Although a detailed discussion of these two basic designs is beyond the scope of this chapter, a brief overview is warranted.

### Between-Subjects Designs and the Use of Comparison Groups

When a between-subjects design is used, the influence of a treatment intervention on a group of subjects is studied in comparison to a group receiving no treatment or a different treatment. Perhaps the most essential and critical expectation inherent in the use of between-subjects designs is the random assignment of subjects across a wide range within a given population (e.g., obese individuals, alcohol abusers) to different treatments. As described by Chassan (1979), random assignment, when properly conducted, "eliminates the element of personal bias in the decision as to which patients are to receive which treatment, regardless of whether such bias be deliberate, unconscious, or unwitting" (p. 107). Random assignment increases the likelihood that the groups studied will not differ significantly on pretreatment variables that can affect outcome (assuming that the subjects have been drawn from an identifiable population).

The number of groups to be studied in any given investigation can vary considerably. The minimum number of groups, of course, is two. One of these is the experimental group; the second typically serves as the comparison group. Formerly, the standard comparison group consisted of subjects who received no treatment; however, as noted earlier, the use of such groups over recent years has been less frequent for ethical reasons.

There have been attempts in some studies to develop a waiting-list no-treatment group that receives treatment after the experimental subjects have completed their treatment. Unfortunately, whereas the waiting-list subjects serve as a control group for the duration of the experimental treatment, they do not remain for comparison purposes as viable long-term posttreatment follow-up subjects if they also receive the same treatment. One selection bias that may result is the exclusion of the most seriously disturbed patients, who tend to require immediate professional attention. Furthermore, Wilson (1978) has argued that even if a no-treatment group is included, other controls are needed. He suggests that a group of subjects be exposed to nonspecific therapy techniques. In addition, some investigators include an attention-placebo group (in which subjects have contact with clinical services but receive no specific treatment) or a minimal-treatment/advice group. Such groups can help control for unidentified treatment factors (e.g., simply being exposed to a therapist) that may account for behavioral change, as opposed to identified components of the experimental treatment that may be responsible for any such change. An excellent recent paper on "placebo" factors and treatment outcome evaluation is that by Critelli and Neumann (1984).

It is important to note that there are other options in generating comparison groups. For example, an experimental treatment program for smokers could be compared to a treatment center's standard regimen for treating smoking or to the best available treatment protocol. Although these approaches do not control for such factors as therapist contact or the passage of time, they do permit the differential evaluation of the two programs being assessed. Another strategy, and one that could be used with the one just described, is to compare treatment outcome rates to actuarial data. For example, a smoking cessation researcher may wish to compare his or her treatment outcome data to rates of self-initiated change for smokers (i.e., changes in smoking rates among smokers who do not seek clinical services). Another application of actuarial data could involve driver's-license records of persons arrested for driving under the influence of alcohol. When a no-treatment group is not available, it may be possible to assess general recidivism rates on the basis of these records.

Another good strategy for developing comparison groups would be to create a core treatment protocol, and then compare it to variations of that program that differ in whether certain components are included. For example, many multimodal treatment programs for obese patients include relaxation training. If a researcher wished to assess whether this procedure contributes significantly to the variance in treatment outcome, he or she could compare a group of subjects receiving the standard treatment (including relaxation training) to a group receiving the standard treatment with the relaxation procedure deleted from the protocol. Importantly, this strategy can provide information on the relative cost-effectiveness of the different treatment combinations.

A final point concerns settings where random assignment of patients to different treatment conditions is not possible or practical. Certainly many clinicians are faced with this problem. Fortunately, during the last 20 years, a sophisticated methodology has been developed to allow the collection of valuable research data in such circumstances. The interested reader should refer to Cook and Campbell (1979) for a detailed discussion of the use of "quasi-experimental" designs when random assignment is not a feasible strategy.

## Within-Subject Designs

In comparison to between-subjects designs, within-subject designs entail assessment of treatment interventions applied to the same individual (or series of individuals) over time. It should be noted that within-subject designs may be used on a group level or in a single-subject design. Judgments about the effects of the treatment condition(s) are based on a visual inspection of the data or on more formal statistical procedures (see Kazdin, 1976). Within-subject designs, which have received less recognition than is warranted, are richly described by Hersen and Barlow (1976) and Kazdin (1982).

Perhaps the most important point to be made in assessing between-subjects and within-subject designs is that neither is necessarily superior to the other. Rather, each has specific advantages and strengths, and the selection of either should vary according to the amount of knowledge about an intervention, the specific research questions being addressed, and the pragmatic considerations of conducting research in a given setting. For example, Nathan and Lansky (1978) noted that it is easier to generalize from between-subjects than from within-subject designs, but that the latter can offer more specific information on behavioral changes occurring over time. Within-subject designs can also yield pertinent treatment intervention data that are masked when treatment outcome data are summarized across a group of subjects. This consideration may be particularly critical in evaluating treatments for obesity, because of the wide interindividual variations often found within this population (Wilson, 1978). A strength of between-subjects designs is that investigators will be able to study the interaction between patients and treatments. In this regard, it might be possible to determine which patients benefit from which treatments and to what degree. Finally, a combination of the two design strategies can be implemented. As an example, within-subject designs could be used to identify possible hypotheses regarding behavior change—hypotheses that could then be tested in a between-subjects design. Alternatively, a between-subjects design might yield information on the effectiveness of a particular treatment package, and within-subject studies could be conducted to determine which treatment package components are more powerful than others. Other advantages and disadvantages of between-subjects and within-subject designs are provided elsewhere (Hersen, 1982; Hersen & Barlow, 1976; Kazdin, 1982).

Because single-subject designs have been used relatively infrequently to evaluate treatments for the addictions, it is useful to provide an illustration of such application. Turner, Daniels, and Hollandsworth (1985) used a multiple-baseline, single-subject design to assess the effectiveness of a smoking cessation program (consisting of brand fading and stimulus control) with four chronic obstructive pulmonary disease (COPD) patients. The participants, ranging in age from 43 to 63 years, were smoking at least one pack of cigarettes per day prior to treatment. Subjects first recorded the number of cigarettes smoked daily for baseline periods ranging from 7 to 16 days. (Multiple-baseline designs entail the implementation of a treatment at different points in time following intake so that effects can be attributed to the treatment and not to extraneous factors.) The treatment protocol included weekly decreases in nicotine levels through brand fading and the use of stimulus control procedures to gradually reduce smoking in particular situations. Baseline, treatment, and 6-month follow-up smoking and nicotine intake rates for the four subjects are shown in Figure 14-1. Inspection of the data suggested positive treatment outcomes overall. Although only one subject quit smoking, all showed decreases in nicotine intake. Further, except for subject 4, the number of cigarettes smoked daily also decreased.

In summary, an overall understanding of treatment effectiveness will be derived through the judicious use of both between-subjects and within-subject designs. The superiority of either depends not on the type of design chosen per se, but rather on the match between the design chosen and the questions being investigated. The ultimate test of any treatment, of course, is whether the intervention is replicable, regardless of what type of design originally was used.

### Reliability and Validity of Measures

"Reliability" refers to the consistency of data collection in similar circumstances, and provides what Chassen (1979) has described as "a property of dependability." "Validity" refers to the extent to which the measures used accurately reflect the phenomenon under investigation. Determination of these two properties is essential to the use of any type of measure; however, at least in addictions research and treatment, questions of reliability and validity have been raised most frequently about self-report measures. This is critical, because researchers in the addictive behaviors have traditionally relied on the self-reports of their subjects in reporting treatment outcome data.

As discussed by Maisto and Cooper (1980), reliance on self-report data has been viewed as tenuous for several reasons. For example, following treatment, subjects may deny or minimize negative events such as drinking, use of drugs, exceeding of caloric intake guidelines, or smoking. The reason that some subjects deny or minimize negative outcomes will probably vary among patients and the research projects in which they are participating. One plausible explanation for patients' inaccurate reporting is the embarrassment that they may feel over "failing" in their efforts, or over the stigma in being labeled with a diagnosis such as "alcoholism." In

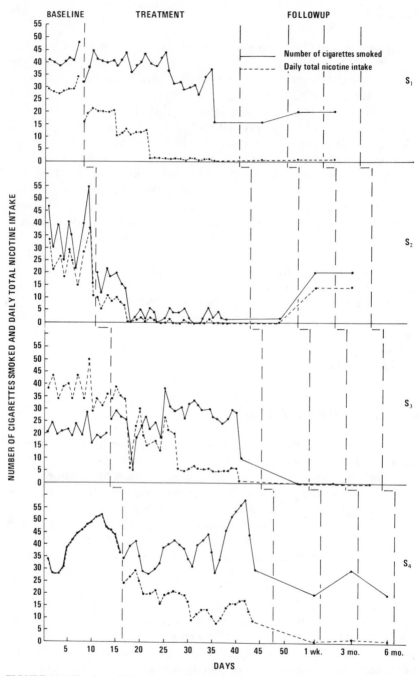

FIGURE 14-1. Number of cigarettes smoked and daily total nicotine intake of subjects during baseline, during treatment, at 1-week posttreatment, and at 3- and 6-month follow-ups. From "The Effects of a Multicomponent Smoking Cessation Program with Chronic Obstructive Pulmonary Disease Outpatients" by S. A. Turner, J. L. Daniels, and J. G. Hollandsworth, 1985, *Addictive Behaviors, 10,* 87–90. Copyright 1985 by Pergamon Press, Ltd. Reprinted by permission.

**436**

this regard, patients may view any occurrence of the behavior itself, and not its frequency or magnitude, as the most critical factor in self-appraisal of their functioning. For example, some subjects may considerably reduce their rate of smoking and still feel like treatment failures because they continue to smoke at all. Such all-or-none evaluative thinking has been described by Marlatt and Gordon (1980) as an "abstinence violation effect": Anything other than total abstinence is seen as a failure. Researchers more recently have tried to prevent or attenuate the biasing effects of patients' abstinence violation on the accuracy of their self-reports by being empathetic and understanding rather than evaluative in collecting treatment outcome data (see L. C. Sobell, 1978).

Another reason why subjects may present themselves in a favorable light is to please the researchers. Most subjects know what will be evaluated as a positive versus a negative outcome, and may wish to fulfill the researchers' expectations by minimizing any difficulties in functioning. As noted above, one of the best strategies for dealing with this would be to inform subjects before the follow-up that experience has shown that a range of positive and negative outcomes is within expectations.

For many years, the assumption of the unreliability and invalidity of self-reports of substance use went untested. Fortunately, more recently there have been studies of this question; these suggest that alcohol and drug abusers' self-reports of substance use and related consequences are reliable and valid, at least when collected in a treatment setting in which confidentiality is assured and subjects are not intoxicated (e.g., Maisto, Sobell, & Sobell, 1982–1983; L. C. Sobell, Sobell, Maisto, & Fain, 1983; L. C. Sobell, Sobell, & Ward, 1980). Similarly, smokers' self-reports of their use of cigarettes have been shown to be reliable and valid (Condiotte & Lichtenstein, 1981; McMahon, Richards, & Strong, 1976), especially when subjects are told that an objective measure of smoking will be obtained (Evans, Hansen, & Mittelmark, 1977).

Reliability of measurement is generally easier to determine than is validity. In the majority of cases, a test–retest correlation coefficient is calculated to determine the constancy of the measure used to assess the same phenomenon. For example, a researcher may ask a smoker to indicate how many cigarettes were smoked during the first 2 weeks following the completion of treatment. The degree of agreement in response to this same question asked a week later should be substantially determined by the constancy (reliability) of the reporting of this behavior. As is probably clear, a measure that does not consistently yield comparable information for a given behavior at some point in time is virtually impossible to interpret, and thus an insensitive outcome index.

It helps to think about the reliability and validity of any given measure in tandem. A reliable measure cannot be efficiently used if it is not also valid. Assessing validity, however, is accomplished with varying degrees of difficulty. The validity of a patient's self-report of a 10-pound weight loss can be assessed rather easily by asking him or her to come to the clinic for a weighing. On the other hand, assessing the validity of a self-report of daily caloric intake of 1,600 calories will be quite difficult if the researcher is not in a position to observe the subject's daily food intake. Similarly, some alcohol abusers may report that they have not been drinking and may show no blood test elevations on enzymes sensitive to alcohol consumption. However, this does not *demonstrate* that some alcohol consumption has not occurred (whether it be moderate or immoderate). Clinicians facing this dilemma have responded in two ways. The first has been to collect in-field breath or urine samples during unannounced "spot checks" with patients, to assess their current drinking, smoking, or drug use. A second technique has been the collection of corroborating data that reflect a patient's functioning. This has typically taken the form of official records (e.g., police arrest files, driver's-license records) or reports provided by collaterals, who are often "significant others" in the patient's environment (e.g., spouse, friends, coworkers). The gathering of such data can be used to estimate "convergent validity" (L. C. Sobell & Sobell, 1980) of measures of a patient's functioning during and following a treatment intervention.

### Measurement of Subject Characteristics

One of the central goals of treatment outcome evaluation is to determine whether a treatment produces some desired effect(s) with a given population. Following this, researchers attempt to determine the extent to which a treatment can be similarly used with another, comparable group. To determine the generalizability of the effective application of a treatment, it is critical that the researcher provide a description of the characteristics of the patients in his or her study. In this regard, it is important that a detailed and comprehensive picture of each patient's life-functioning be gathered.

A shortcoming of many reports of studies that include persons with addictive behaviors is that they include information about patients' diagnosis or history of, for example, alcoholism or cocaine abuse, but provide few other relevant data besides demographics (e.g., sex, age, race, education). As a result, less is known of other pertinent information, such as duration of problems with the substance, negative consequences of these problems, how patients were referred to the treatment, variability in the problem behavior prior to seeking treatment, evidence of dependence (especially in the case of alcohol and drug abuse), and so on.

Fortunately, researchers are providing these data more frequently on subjects included in their studies. One example is a recent report by Sanchez-Craig, Annis, Bornet, and MacDonald (1984). These investigators were studying the effects of a cognitive–behavioral treatment program for alcohol abusers. Seventy problem drinkers were randomly assigned to either an abstinence-oriented treatment or a controlled-drinking treatment. Relevant to the present discussion is the fact that Sanchez-Craig *et al.* provided a detailed and broad-based description of the subjects in each of these two groups. Assessments were made in five general domains: social and demographic data (including employment); cognitive functioning; alcohol use; consequences of alcohol use; and use of other drugs. A variety of quantifiable data were presented within each category. Thus a clinician wishing to use the treatment procedures described by Sanchez-Craig *et al.* would be able to determine fairly easily with which population these procedures were tested. Importantly, Sanchez-Craig *et al.* also described in detail how patients were referred to their program.

It should be noted that researchers studying obese individuals, smokers, or drug abusers are also providing more information on subject characteristics. In addition, greater efforts are being made to identify the contribution to outcome that other individual variables make, such as motivation, past attempts to terminate or reduce substance use on one's own, past treatment experiences, personal treatment goals, and social supports.

A discussion of the importance of assessing patient characteristics in treatment outcome research would not be complete without mention of recent interest in discovering patient × treatment interactions. As we have noted earlier, interest in such interactions is one outgrowth of newer models of treatment outcome that emphasize the evaluation of a treatment in the context of the person who is exposed to it and the setting where the treatment is applied. One common research strategy that has evolved from the interest in patient characteristics is to discover "typologies" of patients within a diagnostic category. Patient "types" are generally based on combinations or clusters of variables typically pertaining to psychological functioning and history of the target problem (e.g., patterns of drug or alcohol use, number of years of cigarette smoking). Of course, variables from any domain can be used to construct patient types. An example of a recent attempt to establish a typology of narcotic addicts was provided by J. W. Shaffer, Wegner, Kinlock, and Nurco (1983), who developed their typology based on a concept of the addict's "lifestyle." Therefore, the array of variable domains measured for creating the typology was broad and included alcohol and drug use, interpersonal functioning, crime and illicit income, productive activities, other activities, and daily life. From these factors, eight patient types were derived. Of course, much of the potential value of this or any other patient-typing scheme is whether typing a patient (much like assigning a diagnosis) can be a path to choosing more effective and efficient treatment.

Another common approach taken to the discovery of patient × treatment interactions is to measure patients on some individual dimension(s) and to correlate such measurements with outcome following some treatment intervention. When predictive power of multiple variables is being assessed, regression analysis is a good statistical technique to use. Another way of investigating this same question is to compare on different factors clients who are "successes" with those who are not at a given time, according to some outcome criterion. Discriminant analysis is one formal statistical technique that can be used if this approach is taken.

One of the more sophisticated designs is to use patient assessments to predict differential outcomes following different treatments. The most productive research strategy to take is to relate conceptually the patient characteristics measured to the "what" and "how" of treatment. This general approach to discovering patient × treatment interactions is illustrated in a study by Walker, Donovan, Kivlahan, and O'Leary (1983), who measured patients' neuropsychological functioning in order to discover whether it helped to differentiate outcomes following one of two alcohol treatment programs requiring different lengths of hospitalization.

## Collection of Pretreatment Data

To assess treatment outcome among substance abusers, it is important to have completed a comprehensive assessment of pretreatment functioning. A failure to collect such information makes it difficult to interpret post-treatment outcome data, because the pretreatment level of functioning provides a baseline or "comparison point." Therefore, it is not possible to assess the extent and range of change from pretreatment to posttreatment and to follow-up assessments (L. C. Sobell, 1978).

If comprehensive data on pretreatment functioning are absent, an outcome study was most probably not preplanned. In such cases, there is typically more information available on posttreatment functioning. However, the lack of pretreatment data precludes a strong evaluation of posttreatment functioning, because change from pretreatment to posttreatment may have varied dramatically across patients. Perhaps not too surprisingly, most studies that are not preplanned are "retrospective" and do not involve random assignment of subjects to treatments (Maisto & Cooper, 1980). In the typical retrospective design, the effectiveness of a treatment is assessed by evaluating the outcomes of patients who already have been through specific treatment experiences. In such cases, it is often impossible to collect *any* data (retrospective or otherwise) directly from patients. Rather, outcome data are typically limited to what is available in patient charts or records. Other problems inherent in retrospective designs have been noted earlier.

It is important here to distinguish between retrospective designs and the failure to collect baseline data, and the collection of baseline data through patients' retrospective self-reports. A major advantage in using retrospective self-reports as baseline data is often overlooked: It is possible to measure past substance use over considerable periods of time. This is especially important in the addictive behaviors, because assessment of behavior up to 1 year before treatment is often desirable. Another important advantage of retrospective reports is that assessment is possible when measuring current behavior, as assessment during baseline (see the discussion of self-monitoring, below) is not. For example, if a patient's problem behavior is life-threatening or otherwise harmful to self or to others, it may be essential to begin a treatment intervention immediately.

As discussed above, "retrospective" self-report is a common method of measurement in treatment research, even in designs that involve random assignment and include longitudinal data collection. It should be noted that subjects' self-reports can also concern current events in longitudinal designs if self-monitoring procedures are used. In this method, subjects are instructed to keep track of (monitor) certain events such as alcohol and drug use according to some format. Self-monitoring has been used most commonly in single-subject research, but there is no necessary restriction to its use in group designs. The major advantage of self-monitoring over retrospective self-reports is that failings of memory are far less likely to distort the data. However, one disadvantage of self-monitoring, in addition to the demand characteristics that can also influence retrospective self-reports, is the impracticality of collecting data for any great length of time, especially during baseline. Another problem, called "reactivity," is that the act of self-monitoring a behavior can itself affect the frequency of the behavior's occurrence.

Another important point related to the collection of pretreatment data is the length of the pretreatment interval assessed. Although there is no generally accepted "best" pretreatment interval, comprehensive data collection covering a period of 6–12 months will generally provide a good reflection of pretreatment functioning and the constancy of the behaviors of interest. Such information may be particularly valuable in those cases in which substance abuse is at its peak just prior to entry to treatment (e.g., Cooper, Sobell, Maisto, & Sobell, 1980). For example, two alcohol or drug abusers could have similar patterns of substance abuse during the 30–45 days prior to treatment (a commonly used pretreatment interval), but different patterns of abuse for the 4 preceding months. As a result, one patient over an extended period may show a consistently high degree of substance abuse, and the other a more sporadic or gradually increasing pattern. A short pretreatment interval would not reveal any such differences in the patients' substance abuse patterns beyond the more acute 30–45 days preceding treatment. These longer-term differences in substance use patterns may well be important in understanding the context of substance use for each patient and in predicting differential responses to treatment.

The implications of this discussion are clear: Treatment studies should be preplanned; should incorporate the assessment of the dependent measures at pre- and posttreatment as well as at follow-up; and should include a pretreatment baseline assessment that is representative of the subject's general life functioning.

## Specification of Treatment

A distinguishing characteristic of the scientific method is that research findings must be replicated under comparable conditions and then further studied to assess the extent to which they generalize to other populations and settings. A prerequisite to this process in the conduct of clinical treatment intervention is the specification of what the treatment entails and how it is administered. Along these lines, several critical areas need to be specified.

One of the most crucial requirements is to detail the content of the treatment procedures. It is not adequate, for example, to state that "a cognitive–behavioral intervention was used," because the meaning of this remark is not consistent across clinicians and researchers. Thus, a clear delineation of treatment components and their order of presentation is necessary. Equally important is the specification of how often treatment sessions are held and the period of time involved in the treatment application. It is plausible, for instance, that a 10-session, 10-week treatment for obesity will have an influence on outcome different from that of a 10-session, 5-week treatment. Also pertinent is a description of the treatment setting and an indication of how many patients are involved in the group sessions.

The question of therapists' training and therapists' characteristics should also be considered. For example, researchers have demonstrated that treatments for obesity provided by professionally trained therapists and by more experienced therapists are associated with better outcomes (Jeffrey, Wing, & Stunkard, 1978; Levitz & Stunkard, 1974). Therefore, researchers should describe therapists' characteristics and, in group studies, should statistically control for any therapist effects that occur independently of or in interaction with the actual treatment. It follows that clinicians should be aware that their decisions about the use of a given treatment should include consideration of the contribution that a given "type" of therapist makes to treatment effects.

## Treatment Outcome Goals

Assessing functioning following a given intervention per se does not necessarily answer questions regarding the effectiveness of a treatment. The extent to which any given pattern of treatment outcome is "acceptable" will vary according to the investigator's interpretation of the data, which is largely determined by personal perspectives on the etiology and functional aspects of the addictive behavior (see earlier sections on models of the addictive behaviors).

There are three questions relevant to evaluating the extent to which a treatment is "successful." The first is how "success" is defined; issues related to this question have been raised earlier, in the discussion of operationalizing outcome measures as continuous versus ordinal variables. One frequently used method, for example, is to describe the posttreatment functioning of drug abusers as "abstinent" or "nonabstinent" for any given follow-up period. Thus, patients who have reduced their drug use by half and have substantially reduced the extent to which this use impairs life functioning have been classified in many cases as treatment "failures." Accordingly, such individuals have been grouped with those persons who perhaps have made no changes in their drug use behavior. Abstinent individuals have similarly tended to be grouped together without much attention to the extent of overall effective life functioning, despite the finding that abstinence, at least in the case of alcohol abuse, is not necessarily correlated with improved life functioning (Pattison, 1966). Thus, a researcher's perspectives on what represents "success" or "improvement" constitute an important determinant of treatment outcome evaluations.

A second point regarding outcome goals is the timing of the evaluation of outcome. It is clear that information on the immediate posttreatment effects of a treatment is important, but the more telling factors are the long-term effects of treatment. Therefore, "success" at one point in time following treatment is often not associated with "success" at a later time.

A third question pertinent to the assessment of outcome goals is the patient's own evaluation of his or her outcome. The obese individual who loses some but not a lot of weight may be pleased with this outcome because of his or her sense of accomplishment. The patient's own evaluation of posttreatment functioning thus becomes a variable that warrants attention, particularly because there is likely to be a wide range of perceptions regarding any treatment outcome.

## Types of Outcome Measures

Treatment outcome measures can generally be classified into three broad categories: behavioral, cognitive, and physiological. Taken together, these categories of evaluation have been referred to as the "triple-response model" because they tap several domains of a particular response complex (e.g., smoking, drug use). It is a positive step that researchers have increasingly been emphasizing the collection of quantifiable data on posttreatment behaviors from these domains. More than a few past studies have classified subjects' posttreatment outcomes as either improved, unchanged, or worse. Probably because of increasing acceptance of more complex models of the addictive behaviors and of the use of parametric statistical techniques, researchers in recent years have been collecting and reporting more detailed information on their subjects. One of the more important changes has been the collection of detailed quantity *and* frequency data on the respective addictive behaviors. The variety of behavioral, cognitive, and physiological measures that can be used in assessing the varied addictive behaviors is addressed directly in other chapters of this volume; however, it may be helpful to identify some examples of measures within each of these response classes.

Behavioral measures generally assess objective and verifiable indicators of the addictive behavior. For example, an obesity researcher might have subjects return to the clinic 6 months after treatment to be weighed. An alcohol abuse investigator might gather state arrest records to determine whether subjects have been arrested for driving under the influence of alcohol. Another behavioral measure would be a client's logbook of drug use or possibly a collateral's report of drug use. In each case, an indication of the subject's behavioral pattern is gathered. It should be noted, of course, that behavioral measures, like all other classes of measures, need to be evaluated for their reliability and validity.

Cognitive measures, by virtue of the constructs assessed, are much more subjective than behavioral measures. Cognitive variables frequently studied include expectations regarding the use of different substances and attributions regarding responsibility and causality in one's environment. A related variable, self-efficacy (Bandura, 1977), has attracted increasing interest over the past decade. Clinicians have also been studying more clients' attitudes toward their addictive behavior and their attitudes toward treatment. Overall, awareness and respect for the role of cognitive and process-oriented variables in the assessment and treatment of addictive behavior have been growing.

The third type of measurement is physiological. Included in this category primarily are biochemical indicators related to addictive behaviors. For example, in their outcome evaluations, alcohol treatment researchers may include breath analyses to assess blood alcohol levels, or blood tests to assess liver enzymes such as GGT (which, when elevated, are suggestive of recent alcohol usage). Comparable measures are available in evaluating other addictive behaviors. Carbon monoxide readings can be used in the posttreatment evaluation of smokers, and urine samples are widely used to determine ingestion of various substances. Importantly, physiological measures are often easier to relate to physical illness or disease processes and are less subjective than some of the measures previously described.

The gathering of behavioral, cognitive, and physiological data, taken together, has been an important advancement in our posttreatment evaluation of persons treated for addictive disorders. Reliance on one response mode can be misleading, because measures of the three response domains are not necessarily highly correlated.

## *Multiple Measures of Outcome*

One of the implicit assumptions of more traditional models of treatment outcome discussed earlier in this chapter is that the target of treatment is a particular disorder or illness per se (e.g., obesity, drinking or smoking behavior, drug use). As a result, the focus of assessment, treatment, and evaluation of posttreatment functioning has been strictly on the behaviors most representative of the presumed disorder (drinking, eating behavior or weight, smoking, drug usage). As Maisto and McCollam (1980) have noted, a corollary of such an assumption is that other domains of overall life functioning are unlikely to be positively influenced by treatment without absolute resolution of substance use.

More recent research, especially in the treatment of alcohol abuse, has shown that such assumptions may not be accurate. Reviews of alcoholism treatment outcome studies (see Maisto & McCollam, 1980, and Pattison, 1966) have shown that, although drinking outcomes may be positively correlated with outcomes in other domains of life functioning, studies have revealed that desired drinking outcomes in some cases are associated with decrements in more general life functioning (Gerard, Saenger, & Wile, 1962; Pattison, 1966, 1976). Thus, functioning in varied areas of life, whether assessed before or after treatment, may not necessarily follow the same course as substance use.

It is not difficult to imagine clinical scenarios in which changes in addictive behaviors may not be related to enhancement of general life functioning. Consider, for example, the following: A young drug abuser terminates his use of drugs, but finds that doing so alienates him from his drug-using friends. At the same time, the patient perceives himself as insufficiently skilled socially when he is with persons who have not been drug abusers or when he is not under the influence of drugs. This absence of meaningful social ties causes him to feel lonely and depressed. As a result of these decrements in social and emotional functioning, the recovering drug abuser's efforts to improve himself vocationally are impaired. Another plausible scenario is that of an obese woman who, following significant weight loss, has difficulties with the altered relationships she now has with men and other women. Men may find her more attractive, and she fears the social and sexual implications of this attention. Therefore, although she is not now obese and her physical functioning has improved, her contacts with her environment (social, occupational) are stressful and unrewarding.

It should be noted that many treatment programs for addictive behaviors are multidimensional and are designed to help patients acquire skills for dealing with problems in different domains of functioning. Unfortunately, these other domains are often not assessed in any systematic way. It is our impression that the failure to assess multiple areas of outcome is more common in the evaluation of treatments for obesity and cigarette smoking. However, assessment of multiple areas of functioning is no less important for these two addictions. A prospective study of relapse to cigarette smoking by Manley and Boland (1983) is consistent with this argument. These authors found that one correlate of "successful" outcome (abstinence from cigarette smoking) was a significantly higher weight gain among patients with this outcome than in patients who relapsed following treatment. It would seem essential for clinicians to be aware of such correlates of change in target behavior(s) if they are to develop treatments that benefit patients' functioning as fully as possible.

*Extratreatment Factors*

The increasing popularity among addiction researchers of the "systems model" of treatment outcome (Moos & Finney, 1983) has been a major stimulant of interest in discovering what effects the events outside of treatment have on patients' functioning. The empirical investigations of extratreatment variables that have been published suggest that such factors have important connections to posttreatment functioning among individuals who have been treated for addiction problems. For example, in a review based in part on their extensive research program concerning the role of extratreatment variables in recovery from alcoholism, Moos and Finney (1983) (see also Billings & Moos, 1981) suggested that extratreatment factors accounted independently for 7%–27% of differences in outcome, compared to the 4%–20% accounted for by patient characteristics and treatment combined. Included among the extratreatment factors were negative life events such as economic or legal problems, as well as stressful work and family environments. Interestingly, whether such extratreatment factors were associated with a relapse (to drinking) was dependent on patients' coping response styles.

Extratreatment factors also seem important in the outcome of treatment of the other addictive behaviors, although the evidence has not been collected as systematically as in Moos and his colleagues' studies of recovery from alcoholism. For example, Gunn (1983) found that men experiencing higher current levels of life stress were more likely to continue smoking and to drop out of a stop-smoking clinic. "Life stress" was defined in terms of major life changes (e.g., marriage and divorce; job changes; changes in living arrangements; illness or death of a close friend or relative; legal and financial concerns; and failure to achieve major life goals). Similarly, Rhoads's (1983) longitudinal study of heroin addicts released from detoxication suggested that life changes and social supports covaried with a resumption of drug use, especially among women.

It appears that any study of the outcome of treatment for the addictive behaviors must include measurement of extratreatment factors. Such research not only would increase the level of understanding about the disorder, but would also provide a more sensitive, complete evaluation of treatments.

## Times of Assessment and Length of Follow-Up Interval

Researchers in the addictive behaviors do not agree on what is an "appropriate" period of time for following patients after treatment. It has been argued that using relatively short follow-up periods (e.g., 3 or 6 months) is not adequate for determining durable changes in behavior. Whereas most relapses tend to occur within the first few months after treatment (Hunt, Barnett, & Branch, 1971), a significant number of subjects engage in a longer period of stabilized behavior before relapsing (i.e., returning to problematic use of alcohol or drugs, smoking, or gaining weight). One of the challenges, of course, is to follow the course of posttreatment functioning and determine what factors predict not only relapse but the nature and duration of relapse episodes.

The question of the follow-up period is particularly important in assessing alcohol abuse treatment because of the highly variable nature of drinking behavior in general over time (Clark & Cahalan, 1976). Past research has also shown that short-term outcomes following treatment for alcoholism do not necessarily predict long-term outcomes. Polich, Armor, and Braiker (1981) have reported that abstinence at a 6-month follow-up is not a strong predictor of abstinence at later follow-up points. Thus it appears that longer follow-up periods are essential to evaluating treatment interventions, especially because of the wide variability and fluctuations in the course of posttreatment functioning. It has been recommended that a minimum follow-up period for alcohol and drug abusers is 18–24 months (Nathan & Lansky, 1978; L. C. Sobell, 1978). However, some interventions may warrant longer follow-up periods. For example, Maisto, Sobell, Zelhart, Connors, and Cooper (1979) reported that the average period of time between first and second arrests for driving under the influence of alcohol (DUI), based on state driver's-license records, was 23.5 months. Thus, assessing DUI recidivism among first offenders as early as 6 or 12 months following treatment can yield overly optimistic results. In this regard, Maisto et al. (1979) suggested that the appropriate follow-up period is at least 3 years if DUI recidivism is to be used as an outcome criterion in the evaluation of a treatment program.

Another important concern is when and how often the follow-up assessments occur. It is not uncommon in evaluating programs for the addictive behaviors to conduct a one-shot follow-up contact 12 months after treatment. Although such contacts yield global information on patients' life functioning, they probably will not yield the more detailed information that is more desirable in evaluating treatment. Patients' recall of significant posttreatment events over an extended period of time may be incomplete, or patients may reinterpret events over time. These possibilities become less likely with more frequent follow-up periods (although the influence of frequent contacts serving as extended therapeutic care must be recognized; see L. C. Sobell & Sobell, 1980). It appears that fairly frequent follow-up contacts (e.g., every 1, 2, or 3 months) have the greatest likelihood of yielding sensitive, continuous data on addictive behavior processes, the recovery process, and overall life functioning in general.

It is important to note that obtaining such data permits the assessment of direction of changes in substance use over time, which, as noted above, is often characterized by fluctuation rather than stable patterns. Such "process-oriented" assessment contrasts with the "dipstick" assessment that represents traditional one-shot follow-up evaluations (Marlatt, 1983). In this respect, statistical analyses that summarize groups' or individuals' behavior over time would be an excellent approach to use on continuous data on drinking or other substance use (e.g., Maisto, Sobell, Sobell, Lei, & Sykora, in press).

### Attrition Rates during Follow-Up

One of the most serious problems facing researchers who investigate treatment outcome in the addictive behaviors is patient attrition. "Attrition" refers to the loss of contact with a patient, and thus the loss of data pertaining to his or her functioning. How the researcher handles this loss can significantly affect the reported results. At least for alcohol and drug abuse, it has been shown that patients who are difficult to find or who are lost to follow-up are likely to be faring less well than those who are contacted (Moos & Bliss, 1978; M. B. Sobell & Sobell, 1976). As a result, it sometimes happens that lost patients are classified as treatment failures and evaluated as such. More typically, unfortunately, reported results are based on data collected from available patients, thereby creating a positive bias that can make a treatment look better than it may actually be.

Because researchers are concerned with evaluating the effects of a treatment on a set of individuals, there has been a stronger emphasis on reducing patient attrition rates. Specific techniques and guidelines have been proposed to enhance the likelihood of maintaining contacts with patients treated for various addictive behaviors (e.g., Hagen, Foreyt, & Durham, 1976; L. C. Sobell, 1978). Some major techniques are as follows:

1. *Informed consent.* It is important to make patients aware that follow-up is part of their treatment, and it is suggested that patients' informed consent be obtained before the study begins. This helps researchers to track difficult-to-find patients and to insure the collection of data about them.

2. *Informing collaterals.* It is important that a patient's significant others be informed about what will be requested of them during the follow-up study. This procedure substantially increases cooperation in obtaining data about patients' functioning when the follow-up contacts are initiated.

3. *Obtaining locator information.* The researcher has an invaluable aid in finding patients after they leave treatment if he or she obtains and verifies pertinent locator information (phone numbers, addresses, driver's-license number, Social Security number).

4. *Interview style.* It is suggested that follow-up interviews with patients be personable and nonevaluative, in order to elicit the greatest degree of cooperation. Furthermore, the interviewer should be as helpful as possible to the patient, without, of course, conducting "therapy."

5. *Frequency of contact.* The data suggest that more frequent follow-up contacts result in better rates of sample maintenance. A caveat in following this rule is not to ask so much of patients that they may refuse to agree to, or later refuse to comply with, the follow-up assessment requests.

The use of these procedures will assist researchers in collecting outcome data from the greatest number of patients possible.

## General Summary and Conclusions

The purpose of this chapter is to provide clinicians and researchers with an overview of what we consider to be the more important conceptual and methodological points in measuring treatment outcome in the addictive behaviors. To this end, the chapter has included discussion of the definition of treatment outcome, as well as of practical and ethical considerations in conducting outcome research in clinical settings. The major conceptual questions of models of the addictive behaviors and their implications for outcome assessment have been examined. Implications for outcome measurement of models of treatment outcome have also been reviewed. These topics provide a foundation in theory for a survey of the major methodological points that must be addressed in designing outcome evaluations.

Although there is a long history of conducting research on outcome of treatments for the addictive behaviors, much of the empirical work is of fairly low quality. Furthermore, little clinical research has been published by people who identify themselves primarily as clinicians. Fortunately, in the last 15 years the quality of research on addictions treatment has increased considerably, largely through the development and publication of methodological advancements. This has resulted in substantial progress in the field. The next development that would push addictions research progress further would be a far greater involvement of clinicians in the generation and use of treatment research than is true now. This chapter, if it has met its objectives, is a step in that direction.

## References

Bandura, A. (1977). Self-efficacy: Toward a unifying theory of behavior change. *Psychological Review, 84,* 191–215.

Barlow, D. H., Hayes, S. C., & Nelson, R. O. (1984). *The scientist practitioner.* New York: Pergamon Press.

Billings, A. G., & Moos, R. H. (1981). Psychological processed of recovery among alcoholics and their families: Implications for clinicians and program evaluators. *Addictive Behaviors, 8,* 205–218.

Bloom, M., & Fischer, J. (1982). *Evaluating practice: Guidelines for the accountable professional.* Englewood Clifs, NJ: Prentice-Hall.

Brickman, P. Rabinowitz, V. C., Karuza, Jr., J., Coates, D., Colin, E., & Kidder, L. (1982). Model of helping and coping. *American Psychologist, 37,* 368–384.

Chassan, J. B. (1979). *Research design in clinical psychology and psychiatry* (2nd ed.). New York: Wiley.

Clark, W. B., & Calahan, D. (1976). Changes in problem drinking over a four-year span. *Addictive Behaviors, 1,* 251–259.

Colvin, R. H., & Crist, K. (1983). The futility of follow-up in current behavioral studies of obesity. *The Behavior Therapist, 6,* 152–158.

Condiotte, M. M., & Lichtenstein, E. (1981). Self-efficacy and relapse in smoking cessation programs. *Journal of Consulting and Clinical Psychology, 49,* 648–658.

Cook, T. D., & Campbell, D. T. (1979). *Quasi-experimentation: Design and analysis issues for field settings.* Chicago: Rand McNally.

Cooper, A. M., Sobell, M. B., Maisto, S. A., & Sobell, L. C. (1980). Criterion intervals for pretreatment drinking measures in treatment evaluation. *Journal of Studies on Alcohol, 41,* 1186–1195.

Critelli, J. W., & Neumann, K. F. (1984). The placebo: Conceptual analysis of a construct in transition. *American Psychologist, 39,* 32–39.

Cronbach, L. J. (1982). *Designing evaluations of educational and social programs.* San Francisco: Jossey-Bass.

Cummings, C., Gordon, J. R., & Marlatt, G. A. (1980). Relapse: Prevention and prediction. In W. R. Miller (Ed.), *The addictive behaviors* (pp. 291–321). New York: Pergamon Press.

Donovan, D. M., & Chaney, E. F. (1985). Alcoholic relapse prevention and intervention: Models and methods. In G. A. Marlatt & J. R. Gordon (Eds.), *Relapse prevention: Maintenance strategies in the treatment of addictive behaviors* (pp. 351–416). New York: Guilford Press.

Ersner-Hershfield, S., Sobell, M. B., & Sobell, L. C. (1980). Interviewing and identifying persons with alcohol problems. In M. Juspe, J. E. Nieberding, & B. D. Cohen (Eds.),

*Handbook of psychological factors in health care: A practitioner's text in health care psychology* Lexington, MA: Lexington Books.

Evans, R. I., Hansen, W. B., & Mittelmark, M. B. (1977). Increasing the validity of self-reports of smoking behavior in children. *Journal of Applied Psychology, 62,* 521–523.

Foy, D. W., Nunn, B., & Rychtarik, R. G. (1984). Broad-spectrum behavioral treatment for chronic alcoholics: Effects of training controlled drinking skills. *Journal of Consulting and Clinical Psychology, 52,* 218–230.

Gerard, D. L., Saenger, G., & Wile, R. (1962). The abstinent alcoholic. *Archives of General Psychiatry, 6,* 83–95.

Gunn, R. C. (1983). Smoking clinic failures and recent life events. *Addictive Behaviors, 8,* 83–87.

Hagen, R. L., Foreyt, J. P., & Durham, T. W. (1976). The dropout problem: Reducing attrition in obesity research. *Behavior Therapy, 7,* 463–471.

Hersen, M. (1982). Single-case experimental designs. In A. S. Bellack, M. Hersen, & A. E. Kazdin (Eds.), *International handbook of behavior modification and therapy* (pp. 167–203). New York: Plenum.

Hersen, M., & Barlow, D. H. (Eds.). (1976). *Single-case experimental designs: Strategies for studying behavior change.* New York: Pergamon Press.

Hunt, W. A., Barnett, W., & Branch, L. G. (1971). Relapse rates in addiction programs. *Journal of Clinical Psychology, 27,* 455–456.

Jacobson, N. S., Follette, W. C., & Revenstorf, D. (1984). Psychotherapy outcome research: Methods for reporting variability and evaluating clinical significance. *Behavior Therapy, 15,* 336–352.

Jacobson, N. S., Follette, W. C., Revenstorf, D., Baucom, D. H., Hahlweg, K., & Margolin, G. (1984). Variability in outcome and clinical significance in behavioral marital therapy: A reanalysis of outcome data. *Journal of Consulting and Clinical Psychology, 52,* 497–504.

Jeffrey, R. W., Wing, R. R., & Stunkard, A. J. (1978). Behavioral treatment of obesity: The state of the art. *Behavior Therapy, 9,* 189–199.

Kazdin, A. E. (1976). Statistical analyses for single-case experimental designs. In M. Hersen & D. H. Barlow (Eds.), *Single-case experimental designs: Strategies for studying behavior change* (pp. 265–316). New York: Pergamon Press.

Kazdin, A. E. (1980). *Research design in clinical psychology.* New York: Harper & Row.

Kazdin, A. E. (1982). *Single-case research designs.* New York: Oxford University Press.

Kazdin, A. E. (1983). Treatment research: The investigation and evaluation of psychotherapy. In M. Hersen, A. E. Kazdin, & A. S. Bellack (Eds.), *The clinical psychology handbook* (pp. 265–284). New York: Pergamon Press.

Krueger, D. W. (1981). Stressful life events and return to heroin use. *Journal of Human Stress, 7,* 3–8.

Lambert, M. J. (1983). Introduction to assessment of psychotherapy outcome: Historical perspective and current issues. In M. J. Lambert, E. R. Christensen, & S. S. DeJulio (Eds.), *The assessment of psychotherapy outcome* (pp. 3–32). New York: Wiley.

Levitz, L. S., & Stunkard, A. J. (1974). A therapeutic coalition for obesity: Behavior modification and patient self-help. *American Journal of Psychiatry, 131,* 423–427.

Maisto, S. A., & Caddy, G. R. (1981). Self-control and addictive behavior: Present status and prospects. *International Journal of the Addictions, 16,* 109–133.

Maisto, S. A., & Cooper, A. M. (1980). A historical perspective on alcohol and drug treatment outcome research. In L. C. Sobell, M. B. Sobell, & E. Ward (Eds.), *Evaluating alcohol and drug abuse treatment effectiveness: Recent advances* (pp. 1–14). New York: Pergamon Press.

Maisto, S. A., & McCollam, J. B. (1980). The use of multiple measures of life health to assess alcohol treatment outcome: A review and critique. In L. C. Sobell, M. B. Sobell, & E.

Ward (Eds.), *Evaluating alcohol and drug abuse treatment effectiveness: Recent advances* (pp. 15–76). New York: Pergamon Press.

Maisto, S. A., Sobell, L. C., Sobell, M. B., Lei, H., & Sykora, K. (in press). Profiles of drinking patterns before and after outpatient treatment for alcohol abuse. In D. Cannon & T. Baker (Eds.), *Recent advances in the treatment of the addictive behaviors.* New York: Praeger.

Maisto, S. A., Sobell, L. C., Zelhart, P. F., Connors, G. J., & Cooper, T. (1979). Driving records of persons convicted of driving under the influence of alcohol. *Journal of Studies on Alcohol, 40,* 70–77.

Maisto, S. A., Sobell, M. B., & Sobell, L. C. (1982–1983). Reliability of self-reports of low ethanol consumption by problem drinkers over 18 months of follow-up. *Drug and Alcohol Dependence, 9,* 273–278.

Manley, R. S., & Boland, F. J. (1983). Side-effects and weight gain following a smoking cessation program. *Addictive Behaviors, 8,* 375–380.

Marlatt, G. A. (1983). The controlled drinking controversy: A commentary. *American Psychologist, 38,* 1097–1110.

Marlatt, G. A. (1985). Relapse prevention: Theoretical rationale and overview of the model. In G. A. Marlatt & J. R. Gordon (Eds.), *Relapse prevention: Maintenance strategies in the treatment of addictive behaviors* (pp. 3–70). New York: Guilford Press.

Marlatt, G. A., & Gordon, J. R. (1980). Determinants of relapse: Implications for the maintenance of behavior change. In P. O. Davidson & S. M. Davidson (Eds.), *Behavioral medicine: Changing health lifestyles.* (pp. 410–452). New York: Brunner/Mazel.

McMahon, C. A., Richards, M. L., & Strong, J. B. (1976). Self-reported data. *Atherosclerosis, 23,* 477–488.

Moos, R. H., & Bliss, F. (1978). Difficulty of follow-up and outcome of alcoholism treatment. *Journal of Studies on Alcohol, 39,* 473–490.

Moos, R. H., & Finney, J. W. (1983). The expanding scope of alcoholism treatment evaluation. *American Psychologist, 38,* 1036–1044.

Nathan, P. E., & Lansky, D. (1978). Common methodological problems in research on the addictions. *Journal of Consulting and Clinical Psychology, 46,* 713–726.

Ogborne, A. C. (1980). Controlled evaluative studies of treatment for alcohol and drug abuse. *Acta Psychiatrica Scandinavica, 62*(Suppl. 284), 66–76.

Pattison, E. M. (1966). A critique of alcoholism treatment concepts with special reference to abstinence. *Quarterly Journal of Studies on Alcohol, 27,* 49–71.

Pattison, E. M. (1976). A conceptual approach to alcoholism treatment goals. *Addictive Behaviors, 1,* 177–192.

Pattison, E. M., Sobell, M. B., & Sobell, L. C. (1977). *Emerging concepts of alcohol dependence.* New York: Springer.

Polich, J. M., Armor, D. J., & Braiker, H. B. (1981). *The course of alcoholism: Four years after treatment.* New York: Wiley.

Prochaska, J. O., & DiClemente, C. C. (1983). Stages and processes of self-change of smoking: Toward an integrative model of change. *Journal of Consulting and Clinical Psychology, 51,* 390–395.

Prochaska, J. O., & DiClemente, C. C. (1984). *The transtheoretical approach: Crossing traditional boundaries of therapy.* Homewood, IL: Dorsey Press.

Raimy, V. C. (Ed.). (1950). *Training in clinical psychology (The Boulder Conference).* Englewood Cliffs, NJ: Prentice-Hall.

Rhoads, D. L. (1983). A longitudinal study of life stress and social support among drug abusers. *International Journal of the Addictions, 18,* 195–222.

Sanchez-Craig, M., Annis, H. M., Bornet, A. R., & MacDonald, K. R. (1984). Random assignment to abstinence and controlled drinking: Evaluation of a cognitive–behavioral program for problem drinkers. *Journal of Consulting and Clinical Psychology, 52,* 390–403.

Schwartz, G. E. (1982). Testing the biopsychosocial model: The ultimate challenge facing behavioral medicine. *Journal of Consulting and Clinical Psychology, 50,* 1040–1053.

Shaffer, H. J., & Neuhaus, C., Jr. (1984). Testing hypotheses: An approach for the assessment of addictive behaviors. In H. B. Milkman & H. J. Shaffer (Eds.), *Addictions: Multidisciplinary perspectives and treatments* (pp. 87–103). Lexington, MA: Lexington Books.

Shaffer, J. W., Wegner, N., Kinlock, T. W., & Nurco, D. H. (1983). An empirical typology of narcotic addicts. *International Journal of the Addictions, 18,* 183–194.

Shiffman, S. (1982). Relapse following smoking cessation: A situational analysis. *Journal of Consulting and Clinical Psychology, 50,* 71–86.

Siegler, M., & Osmond, H. (1974). *Models of madness, models of medicine.* New York: Macmillan.

Siegler, M., Osmond, H., & Newell, S. (1968). Models of alcoholism. *Quarterly Journal of Studies on Alcohol, 29,* 571–591.

Sobell, L. C. (1978). Critique of alcoholism treatment evaluation. In G. A. Marlatt & P. E. Nathan (Eds.), *Behavioral approaches to alcoholism* (pp. 166–182). New Brunswick, NJ: Rutgers University Center of Alcohol Studies.

Sobell, L. C., & Sobell, M. B. (1980). Convergent validity: An approach in increasing confidence in treatment outcome conclusions with alcohol and drug abusers. In L. C. Sobell, M. B. Sobell, & E. Ward (Eds.), *Evaluating alcohol and drug abuse treatment effectiveness: Recent advances* (pp. 177–183). New York: Pergamon Press.

Sobell, L. C., Sobell, M. B., Maisto, S. A. & Fain, W. (1983). Alcohol and drug abusers while incarcerated. *Addictive Behaviors, 8,* 88–92.

Sobell, L. C., Sobell, M. B., & Ward, E. (Eds.). (1980). *Evaluating alcohol and drug abuse treatment effectiveness: Recent advances.* New York: Pergamon Press.

Sobell, M. B., & Sobell, L. C. (1976). Second year treatment outcome of alcoholics treated by individualized behaviour therapy: Results. *Behaviour Research and Therapy, 14,* 195–215.

Tuchfeld, B. S. (1981). Spontaneous remission in alcoholic: Empirical observations and theoretical implications. *Journal of Studies on Alcohol, 42,* 626–641.

Turner, S. A., Daniels, J. L., & Hollandsworth, J. G. (1985). The effects of a multicomponent smoking cessation program with chronic obstructive pulmonary disease outpatients. *Addictive Behaviors, 10,* 87–90.

Walker, R. D., Donovan, D. M., Kivlahan, D. R., & O'Leary, M. R. (1983). Length of stay, neuropsychological performance, and aftercare: Influences on alcohol treatment outcome. *Journal of Consulting and Clinical Psychology, 51,* 900–911.

Wilkins, W. (1984). Psychotherapy: The powerful placebo. *Journal of Consulting and Clinical Psychology, 52,* 570–573.

Wilson, G. T. (1978). Methodological considerations in treatment outcome research in obesity. *Journal of Consulting and Clinical Psychology, 46,* 687–703.

# 15

## SURVIVAL ANALYSIS
## AND ASSESSMENT
## OF RELAPSE RATES

**SUSAN CURRY**
*Group Health Cooperative of Puget Sound*
*Center for Health Studies, Seattle, Washington*

**G. ALAN MARLATT**
*University of Washington*

**ARTHUR V. PETERSON, JR.**
*Fred Hutchinson Cancer Research Center, Seattle, Washington*

**JON LUTTON**
*University of Washington*

### Introduction

#### Traditional Approaches to the Assessment of Relapse

Assessment of relapse in the change of addictive behaviors is important from two perspectives: (1) description and evaluation of treatment *outcome;* and (2) exploration of the *processes* involved in relapse and abstinence over time. Outcome questions focus on the status of individuals regarding their use or nonuse of a target substance (e.g., alcohol, cigarettes) at one or more follow-up times. Process questions focus on patterns of change in status over time and on correlates of different outcomes. The material in this chapter concentrates primarily on questions of outcome. However, because assessment of relapse rates provides a foundation upon which process questions can be addressed, some discussion of techniques relevant to the assessment of the relapse process is also included.

A key focus for outcome assessment is treatment evaluation. A general consensus among professionals in the area of addictive behaviors is that most treatment approaches are capable of producing significant quit rates in target behaviors (e.g., alcohol consumption, cigarette smoking, opiate use). Unfortunately, relapse rates following treatment for addictive behaviors have remained quite high. Estimates from aggregate analyses of relapse rates across different addictive behaviors indicate that as many as 80% of program participants engage in the target behavior at least once during the first year after treatment (Hunt, Barnett, & Branch, 1971). Evaluations of treatment methods must, therefore, include careful assessment of long-term relapse rates. If a treatment is to be proven effective, it is insufficient to demonstrate that large proportions of treatment participants success-fully change their target behavior by the conclusion of treatment; it must also demonstrate that these changes endure over time.

The vast majority of treatment outcome studies do report cross-sectional relapse rates over time. Often, however, such assessments do not provide as much information about relapse rates as one might like. Several reviews provide excellent critiques of relapse assessment and suggestions for improvement (Litman, Eiser, & Taylor, 1979; Marlatt & Gordon, 1985; Miller & Hester, 1980; Sobell & Sobell, 1978). The following two common factors contribute to limitations in relapse assessment: (1) Follow-ups often include only participants who have completed treatment (eliminating par-ticipants who begin but do not complete treatment results in inflated claims of success); and (2) follow-up periods are often too short. Recent recommendations for treatment outcome research stress the importance of a minimum 6-month follow-up duration; a 12-month duration is most desirable. Studies that end their follow-up 30 days after treatment provide no information about long-term relapse rates.

Other important issues that are often not addressed when developing a relapse protocol are (1) how to define relapse, and (2) how to summarize relapse data in a way that allows for the exploration of the relapse process as well as for description of outcome. Concerning the first point, many investigators fail to make a distinction between a "lapse" and a "relapse." A "lapse" refers to any instance of return to the target behavior, regardless of subsequent use. A "relapse" refers to resumption of regular, baseline behavior. Thus, the most conservative description of treatment outcome would classify any individual who has lapsed as a "relapser." In this instance, reported relapse rates indicate the proportion of treatment participants who have any occurrence of the target behavior. Alternatively, "relapse" could be defined as a return to greater than some fraction of baseline behavior, with baseline behavior being defined in terms of frequency or amount.

Many follow-ups that include longitudinal assessments report their findings as cross-sectional or "dipstick" assessments. Such assessments involve reporting the percentage of participants who can be classified as "relapsed" at one or more discrete posttreatment intervals. Thus, at each follow-up, the investigator drops his or her "measuring stick" into the pool of subjects and reports how many relapsers cling to the stick. A limitation of the dipstick assessment is that it fails to take into account a participant's status at the preceding follow-up.

Often, the proportion of subjects who are abstinent at each follow-up time is plotted as a cross-sectional relapse curve. For example, Hunt *et al.* (1971) presented relapse curves, using aggregate data from treatment outcome studies with smoking, drinking, and heroin use. Their data indicated a high rate of relapse during the first 3 posttreatment months. One might infer from these data that the rate of relapse stabilizes over time, with fewer and fewer relapses occurring beyond 3 months after treatment.

Sutton (1979) points out that a cross-sectional relapse curve is not designed to present information on the relative risk of relapse during different intervals following treatment. Sutton proposes the use of a relapse rate curve as an alternative method for summarizing relapse data. The distinguishing feature of this curve is that the relapse rate at each interval is expressed as a proportion of the number of individuals who were eligible for relapse at the start of the interval, rather than as a proportion of the total number of individuals in the study.

Consider the following hypothetical example: 100 participants in a treatment outcome study are followed up at the end of treatment and at 3 and 6 months after treatment. At the end of treatment, all 100 participants are abstinent; at 3 months, 50 participants are abstinent; and at 6 months, 50 participants are abstinent. However, between the 3- and 6-month follow-ups, 10 individuals who were relapsers at 3 months have attained abstinence, whereas another 10 individuals who were abstinent at 3 months have resumed smoking. Because the proportion of the total sample who have relapsed has not changed from 3 to 6 months, the cross-sectional relapse curve shows identical relapse rates at those two follow-up points. From these data, one might assume that no relapses have occurred between 3 and 6 months, and, therefore, that the risk of relapsing during that interval is zero.

The relapse rate curve tells a different story. The curve does not reflect the fact that 10 relapsers have "recovered" (a limitation we return to later). However, the curve does reflect a relative risk of relapsing equal to 10 (number of relapsers) out of 50 (number of participants eligible for relapse during that interval), or 20%, during the interval from 3 to 6 months.

## Survival Analysis as an Alternative Assessment Approach

A relapse rate curve is a way of presenting longitudinal data that is part of the statistical methodology of "survival analysis" (one form of which is called "life table analysis")—the analysis of time-to-event data. Survival analysis has enjoyed widespread application in the biomedical area, and has recently begun to be applied in psychological research with affective disorders (Keller, Shapiro, Lavori, & Wolpe, 1982; Lavori, Keller, & Klerman,

1984) and addictive behaviors (Cottraux *et al.,* 1983; Poikolainen, 1983). The relapse rates expressed with survival analysis are noncumulative; once an individual is no longer at risk for relapse (i.e., he or she has already relapsed), he or she is no longer included in the relapse rate calculations.

The purpose of this chapter is to describe how survival analysis methodology can be usefully applied in addictive behaviors. As noted above, survival analysis concerns the analysis of time-to-event data. The event must be a *single, well-defined* event. (Extension of survival analysis to multiple events—e.g., multiple relapses—is a topic beyond the scope of this chapter.) For example, if the first relapse is used as the event, then subsequent abstinence and relapse are not considered in the analysis. Once individuals have met the criteria for relapse, they cannot be "resurrected" in subsequent intervals. There is evidence from outcome research with alcoholics and smokers (Armour, Polich, & Stambul, 1978; Curry, Marlatt, & Gordon, 1985) that the relapse process may be similar to the hypothetical example given above, in which individuals move in and out of relapse in a more dynamic process. However, we believe that survival analysis can be applied in ways that offer a rich body of information about both relapse rates and the relapse process.

Our goals in this chapter are these: (1) to describe the fundamental concepts of survival analysis to professionals in the area of addictive behaviors, in order to encourage its application to treatment outcome data (in addition, description of the fundamentals will enable practitioners to interpret findings reported from such analysis); (2) to discuss the relevant assessment questions to which survival analysis can be applied; and (3) to illustrate the application of survival analysis with data from two recent investigations in the area of smoking cessation.

## Fundamentals of Survival Analysis

### Survival Functions

Time-to-event data (one datum per individual) can be summarized descriptively by any one of a number of curves as a function of follow-up time. Two commonly used functions are discussed below. We limit this discussion to examples in which time-to-event data are collected only at specified follow-up intervals (e.g., 1, 3, 6, and 12 months), so that the actual dates of relapse may not be known.

The "cumulative survival function" describes the proportion of all individuals who have survived (i.e., have not met the criteria for relapse) as a function of follow-up time. Subtracting this function from 1 yields the cumulative relapse rate, or the proportion of all individuals who have relapsed as a function of follow-up time.

The "hazard function" describes the instantaneous probability that an individual who is still abstinent at the start of an interval will relapse before the end of that interval. For example, 12 intervals may be determined by grouping 365 days into intervals of 30 days. In this instance, the hazard rate for each interval provides an estimate of the risk of relapsing at any time during a given 30-day period.

Obviously, with life table analysis the estimates of these functions will vary, depending on the specified size of the intervals. The cumulative survival distribution can also be estimated using a product-limit estimate (Kaplan & Meier, 1958). This estimate provides results independent of the choice of intervals. For a lucid exposition of the motivation for and calculation of Kaplan–Meier curves and the log-rank test statistic, see Peto *et al.* (1977).

### Statistical Packages and Their Data Requirements

Two commonly available statistical packages, BMDP and SPSS, provide a convenient way to use a variety of survival analysis methods. The BMDP package includes both life table and product-limit estimate analyses. SPSS calculates life table analysis only. Both packages have similar data requirements, which are described below.

Two data points are required for each subject: (1) start date (e.g., date of completing treatment or date of initial abstinence), and (2) termination date. The termination date is defined by the event of interest (e.g., date of resuming the addictive behavior). If the event of interest does not occur, then the termination date is the end of the observation period. The investigator has some flexibility in defining the event that determines a termination date caused by resumption of the addictive behavior. As we have discussed above, one's definition of relapse may focus on *absolute use* (e.g., the date of first use of a substance) or on *relative use* (e.g., date of first return to greater than 10% of baseline use). The primary requirement for defining the termination event is that it is allowed to occur only once: Once an individual has been "terminated," he or she may not re-enter the survival analysis.

Individuals who have not relapsed by the conclusion of the observation period and individuals who have been lost to follow-up are considered "censored" because their exact survival time is unknown. As is indicated above, individuals who are followed up and have not relapsed are assigned termination dates corresponding to the end of the observation period. A recommended method for assigning termination dates to lost subjects is to treat them as "relapsed" and to assign the end of the last observation period in which they have provided data as their termination date.

In addition to specifying survival times, individuals must be assigned a code that indicates their status at their termination date. For example, three codes could be used to reflect the following: (1) relapsed at termination date; (2) lost to follow-up at termination date; and (3) still abstinent at termination date.

The time intervals reported in life table analysis can be determined by the investigator during the application of packaged computer software. Note, for example, that data need not be collected monthly for the survival functions to be expressed in monthly intervals. The primary requirement would be to have an accurate record of the specific date that a "terminal event" has occurred. Obviously, more frequent data collection intervals can provide greater accuracy and greater flexibility in defining a terminal event (i.e., relapse). At a minimum, the investigator will want to know during what interval (e.g., what week or month) the terminal event has occurred.

Excerpts from a life table output by the BMDP survival analysis program are shown in Table 15-1. The table summarizes survival data from participants in a smoking cessation study. Survival times were computed for the first posttreatment year, using start and termination dates as described above. The maximum survival time was 371 days; the minimum survival time was 1 day.[1] Survival times were grouped into 30-day intervals.

## Assessment Applications

### Description and Evaluation of Treatment Outcome

As we have discussed above, the cumulative survival function describes treatment outcome in terms of the proportion of participants who have never relapsed at each follow-up time. One might characterize a graph of this function as a "time-lapse photo" of the relapse process. Graphs of the relapse process for a treatment program provide a summary of treatment outcome. Several graphs, one for each of several treatment groups, provide a visual comparison of treatment outcomes between treatment groups.

Visual comparisons of survival functions are supplemented with formal statistical tests and estimates of the differences between treatment programs. Straightforward nonparametric tests derived specifically for time

---

1. BMDP does not include any cases with survival times of zero in the analysis. Therefore, if the investigator wants to include participants who have never quit smoking as relapsers during the first interval, such cases must be assigned a minimum survival time of 1 day. SPSS does include cases with survival times of zero.

TABLE 15-1.   Selected Output from BMDP Survival Analysis

| Interval | Entered | Withdrawn | Lost | Dead | Exposed | Proportion surviving | Cumulative proportion surviving at beginning of interval | Hazard (SEM) |
|---|---|---|---|---|---|---|---|---|
| 0.00- 30.92 | 145 | 47 | 0 | 40 | 122 | .6721 | 1.0000 | .0127 |
|  |  |  |  |  |  |  | 0.0000 | .0020 |
| 30.92- 61.83 | 58 | 0 | 0 | 10 | 58 | .8275 | .6721 | .0061 |
|  |  |  |  |  |  |  | .0425 | .0019 |
| 61.83- 92.75 | 48 | 0 | 0 | 5 | 48 | .8958 | .5562 | .0036 |
|  |  |  |  |  |  |  | .0485 | .0016 |
| 92.75-123.67 | 43 | 0 | 0 | 4 | 43 | .9070 | .4963 | .0032 |
|  |  |  |  |  |  |  | .0499 | .0016 |
| 123.67-154.58 | 39 | 0 | 0 | 2 | 39 | .9487 | .4520 | .0017 |
|  |  |  |  |  |  |  | .0503 | .0012 |
| 154.58-185.50 | 37 | 0 | 0 | 2 | 37 | .9459 | .4288 | .0018 |
|  |  |  |  |  |  |  | .0503 | .0013 |
| 185.50-216.42 | 35 | 0 | 0 | 1 | 35 | .9714 | .4056 | .0009 |
|  |  |  |  |  |  |  | .6502 | .0009 |
| 216.42-247.33 | 34 | 0 | 0 | 0 | 34 | 1.0000 | .3940 | .0000 |
|  |  |  |  |  |  |  | .0501 | .0000 |
| 247.33-278.25 | 34 | 0 | 0 | 2 | 34 | .9412 | .3940 | .0020 |
|  |  |  |  |  |  |  | .0501 | .0014 |
| 278.25-309.17 | 32 | 0 | 0 | 0 | 32 | 1.0000 | .8708 | .0000 |
|  |  |  |  |  |  |  | .0498 | .0000 |
| 309.17-340.08 | 32 | 0 | 0 | 0 | 32 | 1.0000 | .3708 | .0000 |
|  |  |  |  |  |  |  | .0498 | .0000 |
| 340.08-371.00 | 32 | 32 | 0 | 0 | 16 | 1.0000 | .3708 | .0000 |
|  |  |  |  |  |  |  | .0498 | .0000 |

data can be applied to relapse data outcomes from different treatment programs to assess their relative effectiveness. BMDP uses two widely accepted test statistics—the Mantel-Haenszel (Mantel, 1966) and Breslow's version of the generalized Wilcoxon statistic (Breslow, 1970). SPSS uses the Lee-Desu statistic (Lee & Desu, 1972). The Mantel-Haenszel is the most commonly reported statistic.

### Identification of Critical Periods for Intervention

As we have mentioned earlier, a closer look at the relapse experience within certain periods is provided by the hazard function estimates. Thus, the hazard function can be used to visually pinpoint those posttreatment intervals when intervention could reduce the risk of relapse. Times specified *a priori,* such as holiday seasons, summer vacations, and the like, may present constant "high-risk times" that may become apparent if the hazard functions shift with treatments that end at different times during the year.

For example, let us assume that Thanksgiving weekend is a stable and usual high-risk time for relapses (with relapse defined in terms of relative daily caloric intake) for individuals with eating-behavior problems. The hazard rate for any treatment program would be expected to increase for the particular posttreatment interval during which the Thanksgiving holiday occurs. Thus, a program that ends 6 months prior to the holiday will show an increased hazard rate 6 months after treatment; a program ending 4 months prior to Thanksgiving will show an increased hazard rate 4 months after treatment. However, rather than concluding that the programs themselves result in different patterns of relapse, the investigator who notes the actual dates of these high-risk periods will conclude that the holiday weekend itself is a high-risk time.

Hazard functions can also be used to identify subgroups of individuals who relapse during different high-risk intervals. These groups can be compared to see whether there are individual difference factors (e.g., demographics, substance use history, motivational or attitudinal variables) associated with propensity to relapse at different times. This information can then be used to tailor relapse prevention procedures to the particular needs of the subgroups.

## Sample Applications: Smoking Cessation

### Data Bases

Outcome data from two investigations of relapse following smoking cessation are used here to illustrate the applications of survival analysis described above. The first investigation (Study A) was a longitudinal, natural history study of a sample of individuals attempting to quit smoking without participating in a formal treatment program. The second investigation (Study B) was a prospective treatment outcome study in which two programs for smoking cessation were compared: (1) a cognitive–behavioral program, which emphasized skill training for identifying and coping with situations involving high risk for relapse; and (2) a traditional absolute-abstinence behavior modification program, with an emphasis on contingency management and aversive conditioning for controlling urges to smoke. Each program was offered in both group and self-help (correspondence) formats, resulting in a 2 × 2 factorial design.

Both investigations were carried out by G. Alan Marlatt, Susan Curry, and Judith Gordon at the Addictive Behaviors Research Center in the

Department of Psychology at the University of Washington. Brief descriptions of the samples and methodologies for each study follow.

*Study A*

Smokers who planned to quit smoking on or before January 1, 1981 were recruited from the general public via public service newspaper and radio ads. A total of 153 smokers were enrolled in the study. The sample was composed of adult smokers (56% female) with a long history of heavy smoking. Their average age was 38 years. They had been smoking an average of 27 cigarettes per day for 19 years. Participants reported an average of three prior attempts to quit smoking.

No treatment program was offered to this sample. Participants were only interviewed regarding their experiences relevant to attempting to quit smoking. Follow-up data were obtained 1 month, 4 months, 1 year, and 2 years after participants' quit dates. Specific relapse dates (i.e., dates of first smoking occasions that followed a minimum of 48 hours of abstinence) were obtained at the 1- and 4-month follow-ups. Discussions of relapse and survival functions focus on the 4-month outcome in this sample.

*Study B*

Smokers who wished to participate in a treatment program for smoking cessation were recruited via public service radio announcements and paid newspaper ads. A total of 145 individuals were enrolled in this study. The sample was similar to those who participated in Study A. Again, the sample was composed of adult smokers (51% female) with a long history of heavy smoking. Their average age was 40 years. They had been smoking an average of 28 cigarettes per day for 22 years. Participants reported an average of four prior attempts to quit smoking.

Of the 145 initial enrollees, the 139 who remained active were randomly assigned to one of the four treatment conditions: (1) relapse prevention (RP), group format; (2) RP, self-help format; (3) absolute-abstinence program (AA), group format; and (4) AA, self-help format. The number of participants who actually began treatment was 96, and 64 participants completed treatment. Smoking data were obtained monthly for 1 year after treatment. Participants reported the average number of cigarettes smoked per day and/or the total number of cigarettes smoked for each week of the target month. Self-reported abstinence was verified using both saliva thiocyanate samples and collateral information from two verifiers. Termination dates were determined by the ending date of the week in which a participant either reported a first smoking occassion after at least 48 hours of abstinence, or had missing smoking data.

## Application 1: Description and Evaluation of Treatment Outcome

### Comparison of the Four Treatment Groups in Study B

Data from all subjects who began treatment ($n = 96$) are included in these analyses. Survival curves for the four treatment groups in Study B are illustrated in Figure 15-1. Several comparisons are suggested by these curves:

1. For the RP program, the proportion of subjects surviving at the end of each interval was the same for the group and self-help formats. For the AA program, larger proportions of subjects receiving AA in a group format "survived" at every follow-up time than those of subjects receiving AA as a self-help program.

2. During the first several months after treatment, although more participants in the AA/group condition were surviving, the proportions surviving to the end of each interval were the same for three of the four groups by the last three intervals.

3. Beginning with the third time interval, the AA/self-help condition had noticeably lower survivor proportions.

4. The "shape" of the survival function curves was quite similar for all four groups: There was a large drop in the proportion surviving for the first few time intervals (e.g., the first 3 months after treatment); there were smaller declines in survivor proportions during the next few intervals (e.g., 4–7 months after treatment); and there was no drop in survivor proportions during the last few intervals (e.g., 8–12 months after treatment).

A comparison of the survival experiences of the four treatment groups using the generalized Wilcoxon statistic (Breslow, 1970) indicated that the four functions came from the same survival distribution, $W$ ($n = 96, 3$) = 2.86, $p = .41$. Despite the above-mentioned differences in the proportions surviving to the end of each time interval, these outcomes were not statistically significant.

### Comparisons of Study A and Study B Outcomes

When different treatment programs do not differ significantly in their outcomes, an important question is whether treatment as a whole makes a difference. Are larger proportions of treatment participants "survivors" at each follow-up than would be if they had not received treatment? As we have stated above, one experimental design would include a concurrent group of no-treatment control subjects. In many instances, however, investigators do not wish to withhold treatment from individuals with addictive behavior problems, for two main reasons: (1) It is ethically difficult to deny treatment; and (2) individuals who are denied treatment are likely to seek it

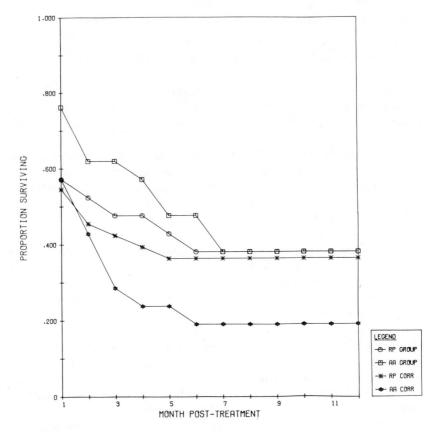

FIGURE 15-1. Twelve-month survival rate curves for four smoking cessation treatment groups. CORR, self-help (correspondence) format.

elsewhere. There may be additional motivational differences between self-quitters and those who seek treatment. Self-quitters may be unlikely to volunteer for a treatment study. Similarly, individuals seeking treatment may be less motivated to make a self-initiated attempt to change their behavior. An alternative approach, then, is to compare the treatment outcome data with an existing data base from unaided quitters.

Four-month outcome data from all subjects who began treatment in Study B were compared with four-month outcome data from Study A. The cumulative survival rate curves for these two groups of subjects are illustrated in Figure 15-2. Comparison of the two functions using the generalized Wilcoxon statistic indicated that it was highly probable that the functions were derived from different survival distributions, $W$ ($n = 249, 1$)

= 12.85, $p$ = . 0003. The similarity between the shapes of the functions was apparent; however, it appeared that more treatment participants than unaided quitters survived to the end of each interval.

These data suggest that treatment participation does have a positive impact on survival or relapse prevention. Relapse—resumption of regular, baseline behavior—was less common in the sample of individuals who participated in treatment than in the sample of unaided quitters. The cumulative percentage surviving at the end of 4 months in Study A was 19%, compared to 44% in Study B.

A skeptic, however, might ask this: What about all of the participants in the treatment outcome study who did not begin treatment? And, if these

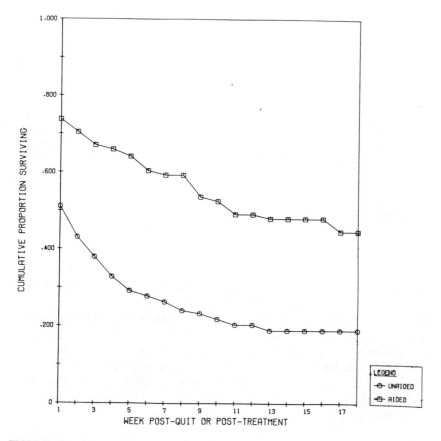

FIGURE 15-2. Four-month survival rate curves for two samples of smokers: treatment participants and unaided quitters.

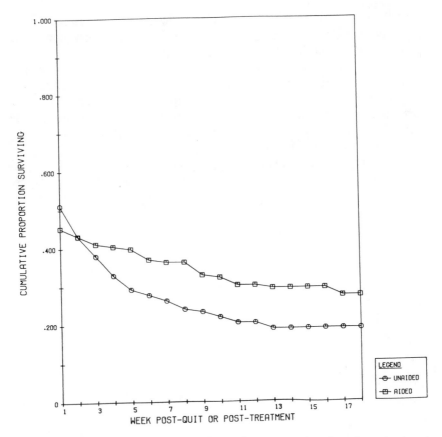

FIGURE 15-3. Four-month survival rate curves for two samples of smokers: treatment enrollees and unaided quitters.

individuals were included in the survival analysis, would the survival functions still be significantly different? To find out, we calculated an alternative comparison between the two samples that included all study participants. In the treatment outcome sample, participants who did not begin program participation were assigned survival times of zero, just as participants in the unaided quitter study who never quit smoking were assigned survival times of zero.[2] The cumulative survival function curves with this adjustment (including program nonparticipants with survival times of zero) are illustrated in Figure 15-3.

2. In BMDP, it is necessary to use survival times of some small number greater than zero to force these cases into the calculations.

Including participants who failed to begin treatment in the survival analysis as immediate relapsers resulted in reduced proportions of survivors at every time interval for Study B. Although the survival proportions were more similar, statistical comparisons of the functions for the two studies still indicated marginally significant differences between them, $W$ $(n = 299, 1) = 4.18, p = .074$. When participants who did not begin treatment were included, 27% of the sample in Study B were survivors at the end of 4 months, again compared to 19% in Study A. These findings lend support to the conclusion that treatment can have a significant effect on preventing relapse.

### Application 2: Identification of Critical Periods for Intervention

Although our findings thus far suggest that treatment can have a significant effect on preventing relapse, only 33% of treatment participants were relapse-free at 1 year after treatment. One approach to improving upon this survival rate would be to identify critical periods for further intervention. The hazard function can be used to identify intervals when individuals are at particularly high risk for relapse. The hazard function expresses the probability that any individual still abstinent at the start of an interval will relapse before the end of the interval. Using Study B as an example, the hazard function that we calculated for the third time interval expressed the probability that an individual who was still abstinent at the start of the third posttreatment month would relapse during that month.

The hazard function for outcome data from Study B is illustrated in Figure 15-4. Data from the four treatment groups were collapsed because we found no statistically significant difference between their survival functions. Months 1 and 2 after treatment were the intervals during which individuals were at the greatest risk for relapse. There was also a slight peak at month 7. In this instance, however, this peak represented only 2 relapses out of 34 individuals who were abstinent at the start of that month. Because of the small number of individuals in our sample, and the large drop in the hazard rate between months 1 and 2, we might dichotomize the relapse risk period into 0 to 1 month versus 2 to 12 months after treatment.

Once high-risk intervals have been identified, a question arises that has both theoretical and practical importance: Why does relapse occur more often in some intervals? From a theoretical perspective, the pattern of relapse risk evidenced in our data (a high risk for relapse immediately after treatment that declined sharply and then leveled off) suggests that two possible mechanisms may have been at work in the relapse process—learning and selection. Improvement in the probability of surviving with increased time from the end of treatment could have indicated that participants were becoming more and more proficient at the skills necessary for them to

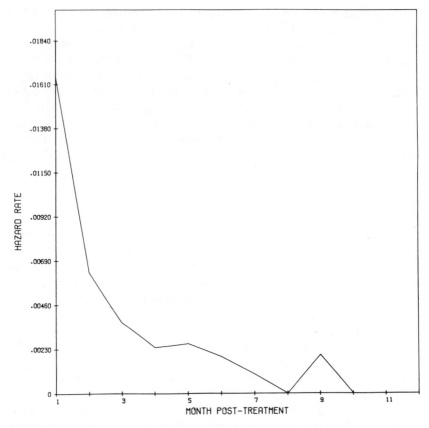

FIGURE 15-4. Twelve-month hazard function for four smoking cessation treatment groups combined.

remain nonsmokers. On the other hand, high rates of relapse immediately following treatment could have indicated that the poorest candidates for becoming nonsmokers were immediately "selected out."

The issue of selection and/or learning mechanisms as determinants of relapse risk has practical implications for the development of interventions that are targeted at high-risk intervals. Selection factors (e.g., smoking history, age, or sex) that contribute to poor prognosis immediately following treatment may necessitate the development of entirely different treatment approaches for certain subgroups of individuals. Learning factors (e.g., decline in coping skill ability or lessening of vigilance for high-risk situations) may necessitate the development of skill assessment techniques and booster training sessions for individuals with underdeveloped abilities.

One way of addressing both the practical and theoretical issues just raised is to divide relapsers into subgroups according to whether they relapse during high- or low-risk periods. These groups can then be compared on a number of characteristics that were assessed prior to treatment participation. Similarities and differences between the subgroups can then be used to determine what types of interventions might be most effective during these relative risk periods.

We divided relapsers in Study B into two subgroups according to whether they relapsed during a high-risk interval (0–1 month posttreatment) or a low-risk interval (2–12 months posttreatment). These subgroups were compared on a number of variables measured prior to treatment assignment and participation. Earlier and later relapsers did not differ in several general categories of variables, including demographics, smoking history, general outcome expectances, and lifestyle factors. The demographic variables on which they were similar included age, sex, income, employment status, and marital status. Similar variables of smoking history included age of onset of smoking, number of years of regular smoking, baseline smoking rate, degree of physical dependence on cigarettes, number of prior quit attempts, and participation in prior treatment for quitting. Earlier and later relapsers had similar expectations for how difficult it would be to quit smoking, how ready they were to quit, and how confident they were in their ability to quit smoking. Finally, earlier and later relapsers did not differ on whether they had any hobbies, engaged in regular exercise, or used a relaxation technique regularly.

Several interesting differences did emerge. A lower percentage of the earlier relapsers had postcollege education (4% vs. 19%, respectively), $\chi^2$ ($n = 54$, $df = 2$) $= 6.23$, $p = .044$. Earlier relapsers had significantly higher severity ratings on the Daily Hassles Scale (DeLongis, Coyne, Dakof, Folkman, & Lazarus, 1982). This scale measures the frequency (number of hassles checked) and severity (1- to 3-point rating) of over 100 daily hassles. Thus, whereas earlier and later relapsers did not differ in the overall number of hassles reported, earlier relapsers rated their hassles as more severe ($M$'s $= 79.96$ and $54.08$, respectively), $t$ (52) $= 2.02$, $p = .048$.

Participants indicated how much social support they expected to receive by listing up to 10 potential supports and rating (on a 1- to 5-point scale) how supportive they expected these people to be. On the average, earlier relapsers expected more support from others than did later relapsers ($M$'s $= 4.23$ and $3.80$, respectively), $t$ (52) $= 2.48$, $p = .017$.

The final factor on which earlier and later relapsers differed relates to the concept of self-efficacy. "Self-efficacy," in this context, refers to a person's confidence in his or her ability to cope with a specific high-risk situation without smoking (Bandura, 1977). In our investigation, we assessed self-efficacy on three dimensions. Participants were presented with a list of 22 high-risk situations for smoking and were asked to rate them (on 1- to

7-point scales) in terms of (1) how often they encountered each situation; (2) how tempted they were to smoke in each situation; and (3) how confident they were that they could get through each situation without smoking. Earlier relapsers indicated that they encountered the situations significantly more often ($M$'s = 4.59 and 4.21, respectively), $t$ (51) = 2.17, $p$ = .034, and that they were significantly more tempted to smoke in the situations ($M$'s = 5.17 and 4.58, respectively), $t$ (47) = 2.41, $p$ = .02. These two groups did not differ in their confidence for refraining from smoking in each situation ($M$'s = 4.52 and 4.63, respectively), $t$ (47) = −0.31, $p$ = .759.

Among the approaches to improving long-term survival following treatment that these findings suggest are the following:

1. Screening program participants on perceived daily stress and frequency of exposure to tempting high-risk situations.
2. extra emphasis on daily stress management during the treatment phase for participants with high daily stress.
3. stress management booster sessions for high-stress participants, scheduled biweekly, then monthly, and gradually tapering off.
4. A longer treatment program, in which more time is devoted to training for anticipating high-risk situations and to practicing various ways of coping with these situations.
5. Review of written treatment materials to insure that they are at a reading and comprehension level appropriate for non-college-educated participants.

Clearly, many possibilities emerge from this use of survival analysis data to identify and compare subgroups of relapsers.

## Summary and Conclusions

Relapse assessment is a critical component of evaluating the effectiveness of treatment programs for addictive behaviors. Both practitioners and clinical investigators have an interest in obtaining useful information about the long-term success of individuals they have treated. For the strongest possible analyses of outcome and process, we have recommended the following procedures in this chapter:

1. Include in the follow-up all participants who began treatment, regardless of whether they completed treatment.
2. Follow participants for *at least* 6 months after treatment concludes.
3. During the follow-up, interview participants 1 month after treatment as well as at the conclusion of the follow-up.

4. Instruct participants to keep a follow-up calendar on which they note the date of any use of the target substance. In addition, participants should note dates when and if they subsequently return to abstinence.
5. Obtain retrospective information on amounts of the target substance used on a weekly or even daily basis throughout the follow-up.
6. Have some way of objectively verifying reported abstinence (e.g., collateral verification or an appropriate laboratory test for the presence of the target substance).
7. Conservatively treat all missing data as relapsed or 100% of baseline substance use.

In addition to these minimum recommendations, assessment protocols could include these procedures:

1. Collect follow-up data on a regular monthly, biweekly, or even weekly basis. One approach is to give participants postpaid postcards that they can complete and mail in at the end of each month. On the postcards they can record daily and/or weekly substance use. Nonresponders can be phoned for information.
2. Extend the follow-up period to 12, 18, or 24 months, or beyond. Long-term follow-up data will provide more insights into the duration of treatment effects.
3. Include individuals who do not begin treatment in the follow-up. It is interesting to see whether these people make significant changes on their own or through other programs.

Our purpose has been to discuss and illustrate the applicability of survival analysis techniques to data that meet these minimum recommendations. Survival analysis, including cumulative survival functions and hazard functions, enable one to do the following: (1) graphically illustrate relapse rates over time; (2) compare treatment approaches on their relapse rates over time; (3) compare relapse rates following treatment with relapse rates following self-initiated change; (4) identify posttreatment intervals with particularly high relapse rates; and (5) group individuals who relapse during high- versus low-risk intervals, to identify factors associated with the propensity to relapse during high-risk periods.

Our hope is that this discussion of the application of survival analysis to relapse data will be a springboard for other approaches to relapse assessment and program evaluation and development. We have acknowledged earlier that survival analysis does not automatically provide data on the stability of outcome over time. However, one can approach the issue by applying survival analysis to "time-to-recovery" data; the date of relapse can be considered the start date, and the date of return to abstinence will be the termination date. From this perspective, the cumulative survival function illustrates the proportion of individuals who remain relapsers during each time interval. Hazard functions indicate time intervals following relapse during which recovery or return to abstinence is most likely.

Mark Twain has provided an oft-quoted description of the relapse process and smoking: "Quitting smoking is easy; I've done it hundreds of times." Careful assessment of such experiences and the application of analytic techniques, such as survival analysis, may help make Twain's experience less common.

# References

Armour, D. J., Polich, J. M., & Stambul, H. B. (1978). *Alcoholism and treatment.* New York: Wiley.

Bandura, A. (1977). Self-efficacy: Toward a unifying theory of behavioral change. *Psychological Review, 84,* 191-215.

Breslow, N. (1970). A generalized Kruskal-Wallis test for comparing $k$ samples subject to unequal patterns of censorship. *Biometrika, 57,* 579-594.

Cottraux, J. A., Hart, R., Boissel, J. P., Schbath, J., Boward, M., & Gillet, J. (1983). Smoking cessation with behaviour therapy or acupuncture—a controlled study. *Behaviour Research and Therapy, 21,* 417-424.

Curry, S., Marlatt, G. A., & Gordon, J. R. (1985, August). *Unaided smoking cessation: What makes a difference?* Paper presented at the 93rd annual convention of the American Psychological Association, Los Angeles.

DeLongis, A., Coyne, J. C., Dakof, G., Folkman, S., & Lazarus, R. S. (1982). Relationship of daily hassles, uplifts, and major life events to health status. *Health Psychology, 1,* 119-136.

Hunt, W. A., Barnett, L. W., & Branch, L. G. (1971). Relapse rates in addiction programs. *Journal of Consulting and Clinical Psychology, 27,* 455-456.

Kaplan, E. L., & Meier, P. (1958). Nonparametric estimation for incomplete observations. *Journal of the American Statistical Association, 53,* 457.

Keller, M. B., Shapiro, R. W., Lavori, P. W., & Wolpe, N. (1982). Recovery in major depressive disorders: Analysis with the life table and regression models. *Archives of General Psychiatry, 39,* 905-910.

Lavori, P. W., Keller, M. B., & Klerman, G. L. (1984). Relapse in affective disorders: A reanalysis of the literature using life table methods. *Journal of Psychiatric Research, 18,* 13-25.

Lee, E., & Desu, M. (1972). A computer program for comparing $k$ samples with right censored data. *Computer Programs in Biomedicine, 2,* 315-321.

Litman, G. K., Eiser, J. R., & Taylor, C. (1979). Dependence, relapse and extinction: A theoretical critique and behavioral examination. *Journal of Clinical Psychology, 35,* 192-199.

Mantel, N. (1966). Evaluation of survival data and two new rank order statistics arising in its consideration. *Cancer Chemotherapy Reports, 50,* 163.

Marlatt, G. A., & Gordon, J. R. (Eds.). (1985). *Relapse prevention: Maintenance strategies in the treatment of addictive behaviors.* New York: Guilford Press.

Miller, W. R., & Hester, R. K. (1980). Treating the problem drinker: Modern approaches. In W. R. Miller (Ed.), *The addictive behaviors* (pp. 11-141). New York: Pergamon Press.

Peto, R., Pike, M. C., Armitage, R., Breslow, N. E., Cox, D. R., Howard, S. V., Mantel, N.,

McPherson, K., Peto, J., & Smith, P. G. (1977). Design and analysis of randomized clinical trials requiring prolonged observation of each patient: II. Analysis and examples. *British Journal of Cancer, 35,* 1-38.

Poikolainen, K. (1983). Survival methods in the evaluation of the outcome of alcoholism treatment. *British Journal of Addiction, 78,* 403-407.

Sobell, M. B., & Sobell, L. C. (1978). *Behavioral treatment of alcohol problems.* New York: Plenum.

Sutton, S. R. (1979). Interpreting relapse curves. *Journal of Consulting and Clinical Psychology, 47,* 96-98.

# 16

# MATCHING CLIENTS TO TREATMENT
## Treatment Models and Stages of Change

### G. ALAN MARLATT
*University of Washington*

## Introduction

It is difficult to speak in general terms about type of treatment as a treatment matching variable. Type of treatment matched with what? Most studies of treatment effectiveness seek a "main effect" for treatment, *averaged across* individual differences in the client population. Treatment matching studies, on the other hand, are concerned with "interaction effects," in which treatment type is assumed to have a selective or interactive effect with specified client variables (e.g., demographic factors, personality, level of severity of presenting problems, etc.). Because client variables have been reviewed in other chapters of this book, they are not covered in the present chapter except for illustrative purposes. It is important, nonetheless, to keep the interaction hypothesis in mind as types of treatment are discussed.

In some cases, client variables and type of treatment will interact in such a way as to obscure any main effects due to treatment type. As an illustration, consider a comparative treatment outcome study in which Treatments A and B are evaluated on effectiveness. Let us assume in addition that a particular client variable (e.g., level of education) interacts with treatment type. Suppose it is found in one study that Treatment B has a better outcome than Treatment A for clients with a *low* educational level. In a second study, the opposite findings are obtained: Treatment A works better for clients with a *high* level of education. In a third study, no differences are found between Treatments A and B for clients in the midrange of educational level. If all educational levels were averaged, no main effect for treatment type would appear, leading to the erroneous conclusion that the treatments are equivalent. In fact, however, there is an underlying significant interaction between educational level and treatment type: for certain clients, there is a substantial difference in effectiveness between Treatments A and B (Miller & Hester, 1986).

The treatment-matching hypothesis also assumes that specific types of treatment will be "more effective" than others for specific client characteristics. Yet how is treatment effectiveness assessed? Matching may be more or less effective, depending on the outcome variables chosen for evaluation. In addition to the general criteria used to evaluate overall treatment outcome (e.g., long-term abstinence, social adjustment, job performance, etc.), other outcome criteria may show differential findings. For example, matching may enhance motivation for treatment and/or compliance and adherence to the treatment program, regardless of eventual outcome. Matching may also enhance client–therapist ratings of satisfaction with the type of treatment received. On yet another level, matching may enhance treatment efficiency or cost-effectiveness—criteria that have important economic implications for health care delivery. With these general considerations in mind, let us turn to the topic of treatment type as a matching variable for the treatment of addiction problems.

## Treatment Models in Addiction

There are many approaches to treatment for addiction problems, ranging from chemical aversion to spiritual conversion. To complicate matters further, there is a wide range of addiction problems—including (but not necessarily limited to) alcoholism, various forms of substance abuse, smoking, compulsive gambling, certain eating disorders, and perhaps other forms of "compulsive–impulsive" behaviors (e.g., sexual addiction, addictive relationship problems, etc.). Various conflicting theoretical positions have been put forth to explain the etiology of addiction, along with corresponding recommendations for treatment. Some approaches favor a disease model of etiology, whereas others focus more upon acquired psychosocial factors. There is a growing acceptance of a multivariate model of etiology, in which addiction is defined as a "biopsychosocial" disorder.

A one-to-one correspondence between models of etiology and the effectiveness of various treatment modalities may not exist in the arena of addiction treatment. For some other diseases (e.g., tuberculosis), there is a clearly defined linkage between the etiological "cause" of the disorder (e.g., the tubercle bacillus) and its corresponding treatment (e.g., pharmacotherapy); by contrast, there is no consensus of opinion or convergence of evidence concerning the underlying "cause" of addiction. Treatment may be effective, however, even when the causative factors are unknown or are thought to be unrelated to treatment outcome. Traditional views of alcoholism reflect this anomaly: Alcoholism, defined as an inherited biochemical disease, is thought to be best treated by a self-help spiritual fellowship, Alcoholics Anonymous (AA). Strange bedfellows! A disease of the body is "treated" by surrender to a higher power.

How are we to make sense of the relationship between these apparently contradictory models of etiology and treatment? Is it possible to match treatment modality with specific etiological factors, or are etiology and response to treatment independent factors? One attempt to clarify this issue was proposed by Brickman and his colleagues at the University of Michigan (Brickman *et al.*, 1982). These authors drew an important distinction between the initial *development* (etiology) of an addiction problem and factors associated with *changing* or treating these addictive behaviors. In an attributional analysis of this issue, Brickman *et al.* have asked the following two questions: (1) To what extent is the individual with an addiction problem considered personally responsible for the *development* of the problem? (2) To what extent is the person held responsible for *changing* the problem? Based on responses to these two questions, Brickman *et al.* derive four general models or approaches: the "moral," "compensatory," "medical," and "enlightenment" models.

> In the first (called the moral model because of past usage of this term) actors are held responsible for both problems and solutions and are believed to need only proper motivation. In the compensatory model, people are seen as not responsible for problems but responsible for solutions, and are believed to need power. In the medical model, individuals are seen as responsible for neither problems nor solutions and are believed to need treatment. In the enlightenment model, actors are seen as responsible for problems but as unable or unwilling to provide solutions, and are believed to need discipline. (Brickman *et al.*, 1982, p. 368)

Although Brickman *et al.* describe these four models with reference to all forms of human "problems" and "solutions," the analysis seems to have particular relevance for understanding diverse approaches to how we conceptualize and handle addiction problems. Each of the four models has its proponents and critics within the addiction field.

The moral model has little support within contemporary professional approaches to addiction treatment, although this was the predominant approach prior to the rise of the disease model. The temperance movement defined addiction as a moral weakness in character; individuals with this moral weakness were expected to change their behavior through personal effort or enhanced motivation, frequently by the exercise of "willpower." "Under the moral model, for example, drinking is seen as a sign of weak character, requiring drinkers to exercise willpower and get control of themselves in order to return to sobriety and respectability" (Brickman *et al.*, 1982, p. 370). It may be the case that many people who attempt to change an addictive behavior on their own, without treatment, conceptualize what they are doing in terms of the moral model. Many smokers who quit successfully on their own (estimated to be the vast majority of ex-smokers) appear to adopt an implicit moral model: "I take responsibility for the fact that I'm a smoker, and I'll take responsibility for quitting on my own." The chief limitation to the moral model is that people who *fail* to change are made to feel guilty and to blame, as if their failure were due primarily to a lack of willpower or moral fiber. Fundamentalist religions often capitalize on these feelings of guilt and self-blame (addiction is a "sin" in their eyes) in an attempt to attract new recruits in need of salvation. The "born-again" Christian who swears off alcohol and drugs as part of a religious conversion experience is an example of the moral model of change.

The opposite of the moral model is the medical or disease model of addiction. In a strict medical model, neither the disease nor the treatment is the patient's responsibility. The alcoholic is not to blame for the development of his or her drinking problem—it is a disease caused by uncontrollable biological/genetic factors. Treatment is administered by experts in the medical profession who apply external biomedical treatments geared toward the alleviation or arrest of the underlying condition (e.g., medication, dietary change, genetic engineering, etc.). The main advantage of the medical model is that it allows people to claim and accept help without being blamed for their weakness. Because experts disagree, however, concerning the etiological factors, there is yet no consensus as to the most effective biomedical treatment or "magic bullet" cure for alcoholism or any other addiction.

In the enlightenment model, so called because the central emphasis is placed on "enlightening" people as to the true nature of their addiction problem, individuals are considered responsible for the origin of the problem (which they otherwise might deny), but are not considered capable of changing their behavior on their own (by willpower or self-control strategies). Instead, change is possible only by relinquishing personal control to a "higher power" or collective group entity. Brickman places the various self-help anonymous groups (AA, Narcotics Anonymous, Overeaters Anonymous, etc.) in this category, along with therapeutic communities:

> Therapeutic communities, like Synanon, Daytop Village, Overeaters Anonymous, and Alcoholics Anonymous, appear to embody the assumptions of the enlightenment model. . . . Clients bring a problem, such as drug addiction, for which they feel responsible and yet without resources to cure. The discipline of the therapeutic community allows them to see the prospects for change as having a hopeful, external source that has apparently been successful with people even more down and out than they. (Brickman *et al.*, 1982, p. 379)

The final model is the compensatory model, in which people are not considered responsible for the development of the addiction problem (etiology of the problem may involve biological and learning factors that are beyond individual control), but are able to "compensate" for the problem by assuming personal responsibility for changing their behavior.

Brickman *et al.* place treatment approaches such as cognitive-behavior therapy in this group: Clients are taught self-management skills and related techniques to bring about a change in the addiction problem. Our own work on relapse prevention at the University of Washington is an example of the compensatory model, for clients are encouraged to accept personal responsibility for preventing or coping with relapse in the recovery process.

To date, no research has attempted to match clients to the four models of change outlined by Brickman *et al.* (1982). To do so would require a careful assessment of each individual's own attributional model of the addiction problem and of his or her beliefs about the perceived efficacy of the four models of change. Perhaps clients with a more external locus of control would benefit more from either the disease or the enlightenment approaches, whereas those with an internal locus of control would respond better to a compensatory approach. Assessment of the client's willingness to abdicate personal control to a higher power or group authority may also be necessary to get a good "fit" with a particular treatment model.

Selection of one of the four models outlined by Brickman will also dictate the type of therapist or "change agent" who will work with the addicted individual. Professional therapists are more likely to be associated with both the medical model (e.g., physicians, nurses, and allied medical staff) and the compensatory model (e.g., psychologists and other psychotherapists), whereas paraprofessionals, recovered addicts, and peers are associated more with the enlightenment model. With the moral model, one is more likely to work with a religious group (e.g., the Salvation Army) or a pastoral counselor. Others in this approach will attempt to change on their own or with minimal outside help.

In our own laboratory, my colleagues and I have found that personal beliefs about the nature of the addiction problem and associated approaches to treatment are important determinants of treatment compliance. In one study (Marlatt, Curry, & Gordon, 1986), smokers were asked to give their own opinions as to whether they thought smoking was primarily a physiological addiction to nicotine (minimum personal responsibility for the development of the addiction) or an acquired "bad habit" that they had learned (maximum personal responsibility). After this assessment of prior beliefs, subjects were randomly assigned to one of two treatment programs that differed in whether smoking was treated as a physical addiction or as a learned maladaptive habit. In assessing initial dropouts from treatment, it was found that subjects who were *mismatched* in treatment assignment (based on their underlying beliefs about the etiology of the problem) were significantly more likely to discontinue treatment than subjects who received a treatment program that was matched with their personal belief system. Further research is clearly needed to determine whether this type of matching has similar results with other types of addiction problems.

## Stages of Change: Implications for Matching

A recent conceptual advance in the field of addictions treatment is the notion of "stages of change." Originally developed with reference to the stages that people appear to go through in smoking cessation (Prochaska & DiClemente, 1983), this approach has merit for understanding the stages of change associated with a variety of addiction problems, including both self-initiated and treatment-aided change (Brownell, Marlatt, Lichtenstein, & Wilson, 1986).

The basic idea is that individuals proceed through a series of relatively discrete stages in the change process. First is the "precontemplation" stage, which characterizes the ongoing addiction pattern *prior to* any active consideration of change (this period may last for several months or years before the addict recognizes a need for change or is forced to consider change based on external pressure or events). Next comes the "contemplation" stage (also called the "motivation and commitment" stage), in which the individual considers doing something about the problem. Some people remain in the contemplation stage indefinitely (the "I'll quit tomorrow" syndrome), presumably reflecting the motivational conflict and ambivalence about change that characterize this stage. The next stage is called the "action" stage, in which the individual makes an active attempt to change, either on his or her own or by seeking outside help. Most addiction treatment programs are geared toward the action stage, and represent attempts to inculcate abstinence (e.g., to stop all drug use) or moderation (e.g., as in some eating disorders). The final stage, often neglected because of our usual focus on the action stage, is the "maintenance" stage. Whether or not the results of the action stage will be maintained over time (stable recovery vs. relapse) depends largely on what happens during the critical maintenance stage. As has been noted in recent research by Moos and his colleague (Finney, Moos, & Newborn, 1980), most of the "variance" in treatment outcome in the addictions field can be accounted for by events that transpire *after* the completion of a formal treatment program.

The "stages of change" model is applicable to addiction treatment, *regardless* of the type of interventions employed during the action phase (e.g., whether treatment is medical, psychosocial, spiritual, or community-based). Matching strategies can be employed with each stage in the change process. Adherence or compliance with a particular treatment regimen may reflect problems associated with the contemplation or motivation stage, rather than with the type of treatment employed. Clients may be more willing to stick with treatment, regardless of format, if they are given assistance or guidance to help them overcome their motivational conflicts and uncertainties. In this regard, a number of motivation-enhancing strategies can be matched to the individual's particular deficit, once a detailed assessment has been made. For some, education and information about the positive health consequences of quitting may be essential, whereas for others, resolving an underlying conflict may be the key. Still others may benefit from rallying social support.

In addition to matching clients to particular treatment programs in the action stage (discussed in the foregoing section), matching is particularly appropriate in the maintenance stage. How are we to handle clients who have "failed" to change in the action stage or who experience setbacks and relapses in the posttreatment phase? Analysis of various determinants of relapse may provide clinicians and clients with a guide to changes that may be necessary. Relapse may be a response to a host of variables, including but not restricted to such factors as environmental and personal stress, lack of adequate coping skills, insufficient social support, motivational deficits, and so on. A detailed assessment of such factors may lead to the development of a relapse prevention plan (Marlatt & Gordon, 1985) that can be employed regardless of the type of intervention used in the action stage. Research on the assessment of relapse risk is a promising trend in recent years (Shiffman & Wills, 1985). Variables predictive of relapse include ratings of self-efficacy, or perceived ability to cope with specific high-risk situations; degree of social support; and occurrence of stressful life events and/or "daily hassles."

## Treatment Matching: A Graded-Intensity Approach

The addiction treatment field continues to be permeated with "uniformity myth" problems, stemming from the traditional idea that each addiction is a unique and uniform disorder (e.g., alcoholism vs. heroin addiction vs. smoking, etc.). Corollaries of this myth include the notion that addictions such as alcoholism represent unidimensional diseases that follow a specific course (usually downward, as in the progressive disease model). From this perspective, treatment itself is considered a uniform "entity" and is recommended for everyone who exhibits signs of the particular addiction problem. The ubiquitous 30-day inpatient treatment program favored by many experts in the United States for a variety of addiction problems (e.g., alcoholism, cocaine dependence, bulimia, etc.) is a manifestation of this uniformity assumption, as is the recommendation that inpatient treatment be followed by lifelong participation in one of the many "anonymous" self-help groups. All too often, however, the data on recovery and relapse do not support the effectiveness of the uniformity approach to treatment.

One alternative to the uniformity concept is the notion that treatment for addiction problems should be graded in intensity, relevant to the magnitude of the presenting problem. A good example of this approach comes from the field of hypertension treatment research. Hypertension, like addiction, is a multidetermined problem (it has both biopsychosocial and genetic determinants), with serious associated health risks (e.g., cardio-vascular disease). Treatment for this problem, unlike present treatments for the addictions, is geared toward the severity of the problem. For borderline hypertension cases, for example, the treating physician may begin by asking the patient to make specified changes in his or her lifestyle (e.g., to cut down on salt, exercise regularly, avoid excessive use of alcohol, learn a relaxation technique, etc.). If the problem does not improve after a monitored period, the physician may recommend that the patient take a relatively mild medication (usually a diuretic) for several weeks or months, again under continued monitoring to see how the blood pressure responds. Finally, if these combined interventions fail to make an impact, more intensive medication may be required (e.g., beta-blockers). And so on: Each intervention is tested for efficacy before the next more intensive procedure is introduced and evaluated (M. B. Sobell & L. C. Sobell, personal communication, 1985).

A similar graded series of interventions would seem appropriate for many addiction problems. Because many people give up addictive habits on their own, without costly and lengthy professional assistance, why not begin by asking the client first to attempt to change on his or her own or with the help of a minimal intervention procedure, such as reading a self-help manual and/or attending a self-help group? If a positive change is made on this basis, it may not be necessary to proceed to the next, more intensive step. If progress is not made, however, a more intensive form of treatment (e.g., outpatient professional treatment coupled with a self-help group) can be tried. Finally, if all else fails, the use of long-term inpatient treatment programs can be implemented as a last resort. Careful assessment of the nature and severity of the addictive behavior pattern will be necessary at each stage of the graded intervention process to monitor progress and select a matched treatment strategy. Choice of treatment goal (abstinence vs. moderation) can also be made on this basis. For less dependent clients (e.g., problem drinkers), moderation may be the most appropriate goal to begin with. If a client does not respond well to this approach, it may be necessary to recommend total abstinence (a goal that may be accepted more readily by some clients *after* they have been unsuccessful with a moderation approach).

Traditional treatment programs provide little if anything in the way of detailed assessment for treatment matching for addiction problems. Many inpatient programs rely on poorly trained personnel to administer some kind of "Twenty Questions" screening test to determine the presence or absence of alcoholism or other addictive disease. Individual differences in age, gender, ethnic status, personality, cognitive functioning, socioeco-nomic status, social support, coping skills, and belief systems are too often overlooked or blended together under a single disease entity, or attributed largely to genetic predisposition or the unifying influence of physical dependency. The assessment procedures outlined in this book, on the other hand, are tailored to the development of unique, client-oriented methods of intervention. Rather than reducing all individual differences to one common denominator (e.g., "alcoholism"), the approach outlined here favors individual assessment across multiple response systems (behavioral, physiological, and self-report) in diverse stimulus settings. As assessment of the development and maintenance of the addictive behavior in an individual client continues over time, providing a more comprehensive picture of the problem, the therapist will find an appropriate intervention strategy emerging from the assessment data. Similarly, continued assessment and self-monitoring is an essential part of follow-up. Without careful assessment, treatment matching is a meaningless undertaking. For a more detailed discussion of treatment matching issues, readers are referred to articles by Ewing (1977), Finney and Moos (1986), Glaser (1980), McLellan, Woody, Luborsky, O'Brien, and Druley (1980, 1983), Miller and Hester (1986), and Skinner (1982).

## Acknowledgment

Portions of this chapter were presented at a Technical Review Meeting on Matching Clients to Treatment, National Institute on Drug Abuse, Washington, DC, October 1986.

## References

Brickman, P., Rabinowitz, V., Karuza, J., Coates, D., Cohn, E., & Kidder, L. (1982). Models of helping and coping. *American Psychologist, 37,* 368–384.

Brownell, K. D., Marlatt, G. A., Lichtenstein, E., & Wilson, G. T. (1986). Understanding and preventing relapse. *American Psychologist, 41,* 765–782.

Ewing, J. A. (1977). Matching therapy and patients: The cafeteria plan. *British Journal of Addiction, 72,* 13–18.

Finney, J. W., & Moos, R. H. (1986). Matching patients with treatment: Conceptual and methodological issues. *Journal of Studies on Alcohol, 47,* 122–134.

Finney, J. W., Moos, R. H., & Newborn, C. R. (1980). Posttreatment experiences and treatment outcome of alcoholic patients six months and two years after hospitalization. *Journal of Consulting and Clinical Psychology, 48,* 17–29.

Glaser, F. B. (1980). Anybody got a match? Treatment research and the matching hypothesis. In G. Edwards & M. Grant (Eds.), *Alcoholism treatment in transition* (pp. 178–196). Baltimore: University Park Press.

Marlatt, G. A., Curry, S., & Gordon, J. R. (1986). *A comparison of treatment approaches in smoking cessation.* Unpublished manuscript, University of Washington.

Marlatt, G. A., & Gordon, J. R. (Eds.). (1985). *Relapse prevention: Maintenance strategies in the treatment of addictive behaviors.* New York: Guilford Press.

McLellan, A. T., Woody, G. E., Luborsky, L., O'Brien, C. P., & Druley, K. A. (1980). Increased effectiveness of substance abuse treatment: A prospective study of patient treatment and matching. *Drug and Alcohol Dependence, 5,* 189–195.

McLellan, A. T., Woody, G. E., Luborsky, L., O'Brien, C. P., & Druley, K. A. (1983). Increased effectiveness of substance abuse treatment: A prospective study of patient treatment and matching. *Journal of Nervous and Mental Disease, 17,* 597–605.

Miller, W. R., & Hester, R. K. (1986). Matching problem drinkers with optimal treatments. In W. R. Miller & N. Heather (Eds.), *Treating addictive behaviors: Processes of change* (pp. 175–203). New York: Plenum.

Prochaska, J. O., & DiClemente, C. C. (1983). Stages and processes of self-change of smoking: Towards a more integrative model of change. *Journal of Consulting and Clinical Psychology, 51,* 390–395.

Shiffman, S., & Wills, T. A. (Eds.). (1985). *Coping and substance use.* New York: Academic Press.

Skinner, H. (1982). Different strokes for different folks: An examination of patient treatment matching. *British Journal of Addiction, 13,* 1246–1251.

# INDEX

Italic numerals denote figures or tables.